Emerson, Romanticism, and Intuitive Reason

Emerson, Romanticism, and Intuitive Reason

THE TRANSATLANTIC "LIGHT OF ALL OUR DAY"

Patrick J. Keane

University of Missouri Press
Columbia and London

University of Missouri Press, Columbia, Missouri 65201
Printed and bound in the United States of America

5 4 3 2 1 09 08 07 06 05

Library of Congress Cataloging-in-Publication Data

Keane, Patrick J.
Emerson, romanticism, and intuitive reason : the transatlantic "light of all our day" / Patrick J. Keane.
p. cm.
Summary: "Comparative study in transatlantic Romanticism that traces the links between German idealism, British Romanticism (Wordsworth, Coleridge, Carlyle), and American Transcendentalism. Focuses on Emerson's development and use of the concept of intuitive Reason, which became the intellectual and emotional foundation of American Transcendentalism"—Provided by publisher.
Includes bibliographical references and index.
ISBN-13: 978-0-8262-1602-1 (alk. paper)
ISBN-10: 0-8262-1602-1 (alk. paper)
1. Emerson, Ralph Waldo, 1803–1882—Criticism and interpretation. 2. Emerson, Ralph Waldo, 1803–1882—Knowledge—Literature. 3. American literature—English influences. 4. American literature—German influences. 5. Transcendentalism (New England) 6. Romanticism—United States. 7. Intuition in literature. 8. Reason in literature. I. Title.
PS1638.K36 2005
814'.3—dc22

2005015124

∞™ This paper meets the requirements of the American National Standard for Permanence of Paper for Printed Library Materials, Z39.48, 1984.

Designer: Stephanie Foley
Typesetter: Phoenix Type, Inc.
Printer and Binder: The Maple-Vail Book Manufacturing Group
Typeface: Plantin

The University of Missouri Press gratefully acknowledges the support of John Smarrelli, academic vice president of LeMoyne College; Linda LeMura, dean of Arts and Science of LeMoyne College; Julie Grossman; and David Lloyd.

For Margaret, Kelly, Samantha, and Rebecca Margaret

Contents

PART IV. THE ART OF LOSING

Acknowledgments

The original stimulus for this project was provided by Ann Ryan, my colleague in the Le Moyne College English Department. She asked me to say something to her class about the relationship between Emerson's Transcendentalism, particularly as reflected in his 1836 book *Nature,* and British Romanticism, specifically in terms of Wordsworth and Coleridge. The book that eventually resulted, though it has gone well beyond Emerson's *Nature,* nevertheless adheres in many ways to her original assignment. In that sense, as the book's "onlie begetter," she has only herself to blame. For help as I went along, I owe much to the conversation of Roger Lund and to the enthusiasm and support of Pernille Aegidius Dake. Other friends who offered needed encouragement include Jonathan Schonsheck, Dan Orne, Annie Smith, Bruce Shefrin, and Dan Grinnals. I owe a special debt of gratitude to these LeMoyne colleagues: John Smarrelli, academic vice president; Linda LeMura, dean of Arts and Sciences; Julie Grossman; and David Lloyd. My thanks, too, to Annette Wenda for her meticulous copyediting, to Nancy K. Humphreys for preparing a difficult index, and, especially, to Jane Lago, for her skill, good humor, and infinite patience. Richard Gravil gave the first version of this study a reading as richly informed and sharply critical as one might expect of the author of *Romantic Dialogues: Anglo-American Continuities, 1776–1862,* though one that exceeded any reasonable expectations in its thoroughness, appreciation, and generosity.

Other public friends and aids to reflection include, for obvious reasons, Harold Bloom and *his* mentor, M. H. Abrams—among many other accomplishments, our indispensable guide to the radiating Miltonic complexities of Wordsworth's "Prospectus" to *The Recluse,* one of Emerson's favorite poems. A half-dozen other mentors have been, at different times over the years, what Wordsworth and Emerson called "benefactors": Elizabeth Sewell, author of *The Orphic Voice,* and the first teacher to see something in me; Robert Boyers, editor of *Salmagundi,* my colleague at Skidmore, and a supporter in every way; Denis Donoghue, who has himself written briefly but brilliantly on *Nature;* David Erdman, who taught me how to fuse history and literature without abusing either; the late M. L. Rosenthal, who provided an example of how to lovingly repossess poems; and Helen Vendler, who did the same, and of whose essay on my abiding text, Wordsworth's Intimations Ode, I have been a "thankful receiver" from the day she first sent me a draft copy many years ago. I only hope, to complete and alter Blake's axiom, that I bear in the book that follows—if for no other reason than to properly honor my own shaping influences and benefactors—some semblance of a "plentiful harvest."

There is a more general debt, shared in common with all students of Coleridge, Wordsworth, and Emerson. Some might provisionally mock what Emerson condemned in "The American Scholar" as the bookworms, the "emendators, the bibliomaniacs of all degrees," what Yeats, playing off this passage in his poem "The Scholars," called the "old, learned, respectable bald heads," who "Edit and annotate" literature written by impassioned young men. But legions of devoted scholars and bibliographers, editing and annotating published and unpublished texts alike, have made these four authors perhaps the most impressively accessible writers in the entire Anglo-American canon. More immediately, I am in the debt of those who have helped me to read Emerson in a Romantic context. When I began this book I was an amateur reader of Emerson and a complete novice in terms of Emerson scholarship, rapidly becoming an industry as we approached the bicentennial of Emerson's birth. The past few years alone have seen the publication of Barbara Packer's long and illuminating survey "The Transcendentalists" (1995); *The Cambridge Companion to Ralph Waldo Emerson* (1999), containing an important essay by Robert Weisbuch building on his pioneering study, *Atlantic Double-Cross: American Literature and British Influence in the Age of Emerson* (1984); *A Historical Guide to Ralph Waldo Emerson* (2000); and, all in 2001, *The Later Lectures of Ralph Waldo Emerson,* an ample Norton Critical Edition of the *Prose and Poetry of Ralph Waldo Emerson,* and Richard Gravil's succinct *Romantic Dialogues: Anglo-American Continuities, 1776–1862.*

The bicentennial year saw the appearance of two significant studies: *Understanding Emerson,* Kenneth S. Sacks's exploration of the context of "The American Scholar" address, and Lawrence Buell's *Emerson,* which places this most iconic of American writers in his full transatlantic, indeed global, context. There were also two new gatherings, often of little-known material: the interviews and reminiscences collected by Ronald A. Bosco and Joel Myerson in *Emerson in His Own Time* (2003) and the political and reformist writings brought together by David M. Robinson in *The Political Emerson* (2004). All of these texts affected what I had to say, especially the transatlantic studies by Weisbuch and Gravil and Buell's magisterial overview, all of which, in print and sometimes in emphasis, anticipated me in ways at first dismaying and, finally, liberating. (Joel Pace's *Transatlantic Transcendentalist: Wordsworth and American Romanticism* appeared too late for me to take advantage of it.) Other benefactors include Carlos Baker,

Gordon Boudreau, Lee Rust Brown, Stanley Cavell, Leon Chai, Julie Ellison, Armida Gilbert, and Frank T. Thompson. Separately, and precisely because they insist on Emerson's irreducible and affiliated yet unaffiliated originality, I am grateful to Stephen Whicher, Robert D. Richardson Jr., Thomas McFarland, and the most adamant champion of Emersonian originality, here as always in a category all his own, Harold Bloom.

My last (and my first) acknowledgment is to my mother, to whose memory this book is dedicated. In the midst of the almost constant pain of her final years, she never ceased to encourage me. She had a particular interest in the outcome of the final chapter. I called her late one night to tell her I had decided to end it by citing the final line of Wordsworth's "Elegiac Stanzas": "Not without hope we suffer and we mourn." I also read her a journal entry in which Emerson—having had a troubling dream, a premonition of the death of his little boy—spent a restless night filled with premonitions of his own death. As he awoke, he wondered, "Where shall I be then? I lifted my head and beheld the spotless orange light of the morning beaming up from the dark hills into the wide universe." Emerson's son Edward, many years later, chose this passage to read at his father's funeral, presumably finding it—as I did—a luminous, tentatively affirmative, characteristically "Emersonian" intimation of immortality.

I wondered what my mother thought about "all this." "Oh," she said, "I believe that there's a life after death, a heaven, and that I'm going to it." She had earned that consolation. I told her I shared her confidence, said I would call her the next day, and we hung up. For her, there was no next day, and these turned out to be our last words together. I lack the firm faith of my friend Gordon Boudreau, whose wife, Grace, suffering from Alzheimer's, was close to death as he finished his splendid book on Thoreau, a book that owed much to her encouragement and her "discerning and demanding intelligence" as a reader. "She will not, when it is finally published, be able to understand a word of it," Gordon wrote in the final paragraph of his preface. "Her reading must come hereafter, in a revised edition." Less certain of that hereafter, I can at least imagine a bright reversion in the sky and hope—for it *is* "not without hope we suffer and we mourn"—that my mother's spirit, like Wordsworth's "Song" in the great "Prospectus,"

> With star-like virtue in its place may shine
> Shedding benignant influence.

Abbreviations

The following abbreviations, which appear parenthetically throughout the book, indicate frequently cited texts.

EMERSON

The Belknap Press *Collected Works,* in progress since 1971, is not yet complete, and few readers are likely to have either it or the twelve-volume Centenary Edition at hand. Thus, I vary from scholarly practice by quoting Emerson, when possible, from the *most accessible* accurate editions: either the Library of America *Essays and Lectures* or the recent Norton Critical Edition, abbreviated, respectively, as:

E&L *Emerson: Essays and Lectures.* Edited by Joel Porte. New York: Library of America, 1983.

EPP *Emerson's Prose and Poetry.* Edited by Joel Porte and Saundra Morris. New York and London: W. W. Norton, 2001.

In cases where the texts do not appear in either of these books, I cite from the following:

CPT *Emerson: Collected Poems and Translations.* Edited by Harold Bloom and Paul Kane. New York: Library of America, 1994.

CS *The Complete Sermons of Ralph Waldo Emerson.* Edited by Albert J. von Frank et al. 4 vols. Columbia: University of Missouri Press, 1989–1992.

EL *The Early Lectures of Ralph Waldo Emerson.* Edited by Stephen E. Whicher, Robert E. Spiller, and Wallace E. Williams. 3 vols. Cambridge: Harvard University Press, 1964, 1972.

L *The Letters of Ralph Waldo Emerson.* Edited by Ralph L. Rusk (vols. 1–6, 1939) and Eleanor M. Tilton (vols. 7–10). 10 vols. New York: Columbia University Press, 1939–1995.

LL *The Later Lectures of Ralph Waldo Emerson, 1843–1871.* Edited by Ronald A. Bosco and Joel Myerson. 2 vols. Athens: University of Georgia Press, 2001.

TN *The Topical Notebooks of Ralph Waldo Emerson.* Edited by Ralph H. Orth, Susan Sutton Smith, Ronald A. Bosco, and Glen M. Johnston. 3 vols. Columbia: University of Missouri Press, 1990–1994.

W *The Complete Works of Ralph Waldo Emerson.* Centenary Edition. Edited by Edward Waldo Emerson. 12 vols. Boston and New York: Houghton Mifflin, 1903–1904.

Though there is a selection from Emerson's journals in *EPP,* almost all my citations refer to:

JMN *The Journals and Miscellaneous Notebooks of Ralph Waldo Emerson.* Edited by William H. Gilman, Ralph H. Orth, et al. 16 vols. Cambridge: Harvard University Press, Belknap Press, 1960–1982.

COLERIDGE

Individual volumes of Coleridge are quoted from the following:

CC *The Collected Works of Samuel Taylor Coleridge.* Edited by Kathleen Coburn and Bart Winer. 16 vols. London: Routledge and Kegan Paul; Princeton: Princeton University Press, 1969–2001.

The most frequently cited are abbreviated as follows:

AR *Aids to Reflection.* Edited by John Beer. Beer's edition includes James Marsh's influential "Preliminary Essay" introducing his 1829 edition (vol. 9 of *CC,* 1993).

BL *Biographia Literaria.* Edited by James Engell and Walter Jackson Bate. 2 vols (vol. 7 of *CC,* 1983).

F *The Friend.* Edited by Barbara Rooke. 2 vols (vol. 4 of *CC,* 1969).

LS *Lay Sermons.* Edited by R. J. White. It includes *The Statesman's Manual* (vol. 6 of *CC,* 1972).

Coleridge's letters and notes are cited from, respectively:

CL *Collected Letters of Samuel Taylor Coleridge.* Edited by E. L. Griggs. 6 vols. Oxford: Clarendon Press, 1956–1971.

CN *The Notebooks of Samuel Taylor Coleridge.* Edited by Kathleen Coburn. 5 vols. Princeton: Princeton University Press, 1957– .

Though now replaced by the three-volume edition edited by J. C. C. Mays (vol. 16 in *CC*), my citations of Coleridge's poetry and plays are to this work:

CPW *The Complete Poetical Works of Samuel Taylor Coleridge.* Edited by Ernest Hartley Coleridge. 2 vols. Oxford: Clarendon Press, 1912.

WORDSWORTH

E *The Excursion.* Vol. 2 of *Wordsworth: The Poems,* edited by John O. Hayden. New Haven: Yale University Press, 1981.

P *The Prelude, 1799, 1805, 1850.* Edited by Jonathan Wordsworth, M. H. Abrams, and Stephen Gill. New York and London: W. W. Norton, 1979. Except where indicated, I quote the 1850 version, the one known to Emerson.

WP *Wordsworth: The Poems.* Edited by John O. Hayden. 2 vols. New Haven: Yale University Press, 1981. All of Wordsworth's poems, other than *The Prelude,* are cited from this edition, as are my references to the notes to Isabella Fenwick and Wordsworth's preface to the second edition of *Lyrical Ballads* and the "Essay, Supplementary to the Preface" to the 1815 *Poems.*

The Convention of Cintra is cited from the first volume of *The Prose Works of William Wordsworth.* Edited by W. J. B. Owen and J. W. Smyser. 3 vols. Oxford: Clarendon Press, 1974.

MILTON

PL *Paradise Lost.* Edited by Alastair Fowler. Longman Annotated Poets. London: Longman, 1968.

Emerson, Romanticism, and Intuitive Reason

Prologue

"Every author," William Wordsworth observes in the "Essay, Supplementary to the Preface" to *Poems* (1815), as far as he is "great and at the same time *original,* has had the task of *creating* the taste by which he is to be enjoyed." He was concurring with a remark made to him by his "philosophical friend," Samuel Taylor Coleridge, whose word *Genius* he takes up next. "The predecessors of an original Genius of a high order will have smoothed the way for all that he has in common with them;—and much he will have in common; but, for what is peculiarly his own," he will, like Hannibal in the Alps, "be called upon to clear and often to shape his own road." Where does the "real difficulty" lie "of creating that taste by which a truly original Poet is to be relished?" Does it consist, Wordsworth asks rhetorically, "in divesting the Reader of the pride that induces him to dwell upon those points wherein Men differ from each other, to the exclusion of those in which all Men are alike, or the same . . . ?" Does it lie, above all, in establishing "that dominion over the spirits of Readers by which they are to be humbled and humanized, in order that they may be purified and exalted?"

If these ends are to be attained "by the mere communication of *knowledge,*" the difficulty "does *not* lie" in "Taste," a "metaphor, taken from a *passive* sense of the human body, and transferred to things which are in their essence *not* passive,—to intellectual *acts* and *operations*" associated with "IMAGINATION," our "noblest" faculty. But authorial imagination still requires an "auxiliar impulse": the "exertion of a co-operating *power* in the mind of the Reader." Of course, that correspondent power can be evoked only by the power of the poet, a power requiring "Genius," which Wordsworth, again borrowing from Coleridge, defines as "the introduction of a new element into the intellectual universe," or, at least, "the application of powers . . . to produce effects hitherto unknown." And what, he asks, again rhetorically, is all this "but an advance, or a conquest, made by the soul of the Poet?" Is it to be supposed that, passively, "the Reader can make progress of this kind . . . ? No, he is invigorated and inspirited by his Leader, in order that he may exert himself, for he cannot proceed in quiescence, he cannot be carried like a dead weight. Therefore to create taste is to call forth and bestow power, of which knowledge is the effect; and *there* lies the true difficulty."

Anxious not to be misunderstood as disrespecting "the judgment of the people," Wordsworth makes a pivotal distinction. The voice that issues from the "great Spirit of human knowledge" is that "Vox populi which the Deity inspires." Only a fool would "mistake for this a local acclamation, or transitory outcry," which, "under the name of the PUBLIC, passes itself, upon the unthinking, for the PEOPLE." And to the People, and to the "embodied spirit of their knowledge, so far as it exists and moves, at the present, faithfully supported by its two wings, the past and the future," his respect and reverence are due. He offers them "willingly and readily," and, this done, Wordsworth "takes leave of his Readers, by assuring them" that he would not bother to save his poems from "immediate destruction" were he not persuaded that they "evinced something of the 'Vision and the Faculty divine'; and that, both in words and things, they will operate in their degree, to extend the domain of sensibility for the delight, the honour, and the benefit of human nature."[1]

The book that follows attempts to flesh out much of what Wordsworth says in this peroration—about "an original Genius" who (as Coleridge said) creates the taste by which he is enjoyed, absorbing his "predecessors" (in Wordsworth's case, John Milton above all), yet departing from them to clear his own "new" road; about the "passive" and "active" faculties; about a writer calling forth *and* bestowing "power," requiring a "co-operating power" in the minds of readers, even as he establishes imaginative dominion over them, humbling and humanizing them so that "they may be purified and exalted"; about being a benefactor, one whose work, stressing commonality rather than differences, aims to "extend the domain of sensibility" for the delight and "benefit of human nature"; and, finally, about "the Vision and the Faculty Divine": Wordsworth's own phrase (*E* 1:79), a line repeatedly cited by Coleridge to define the all-important *intuitive Reason,* variously referred to as Reason or Intuition or Imagination or Spirit.

A primary feature of this comparative, intertextual study is the exploration in depth of a number of Ralph Waldo Emerson's apparently casual but almost always illuminating allusions, either overt or covert, to *his* "predecessors." I am engaged primarily with Emerson's part in the transatlantic dialogue between British Romanticism (itself the conduit to German idealism) and American Transcendentalism: a dialogue in which, in turn, a central role is played by a poet in whom all three of my major figures (Coleridge, Wordsworth, and Emerson) were saturated: John Milton, "foremost of all men," according to Emerson, "in the power *to inspire*" (*EL* 1:148–49). As I worked through these connections, Milton's Raphael, the archangel

1. Wordsworth, "Essay, Supplementary," in *WP* 2:944–47, 949–50.

sent to Adam and Eve in Eden, became something of a necessary angel both in Coleridgean-Wordsworthian Romanticism and in that other dawn risen on midnoon, Emersonian Transcendentalism.

Thematically, the book is based on several premises, all of them conducive to the generation, preservation, and enhancement of *power.* The first two constitute the foundation of Emerson's thought and work, both deriving essentially from his rather uncritical absorption, but nevertheless seminal and finally liberating application, of Coleridge's creative—and Miltonic—revision of Kantian and post-Kantian thought. The first premise, then, is the talismanic distinction between understanding and Reason, by which Coleridgean Emerson means not the discursive reason but *intuitive Reason.* Whether the source of illumination is conceived of as within or above or both, intuitive Reason is, in the Wordsworth image that provides my subtitle, the "fountain light of all our day," "a master light" (or, in Emerson's telling revision, "*the* master light") of all our seeing. That "light," to which Coleridge and Emerson endlessly allude, radiates out to illuminate Emerson's indebtedness to, and creative liberation from, his precursors and "benefactors."

The identification of this Romantic and Transcendentalist concept of intuitive Reason—by Coleridge, and Emerson after him—with the Intimations Ode's "master light" depends not only on Coleridge's revisionary reading of Kant but also on the distinctions drawn by Milton's archangel between understanding and Reason and between the lower ("discursive") and higher ("intuitive") Reason. Miltonic and Kantian thought, once "filtered" through that transatlantic pipeline, Coleridge, and conveyed (by himself and through Wordsworth) to New England, came out as American Transcendentalism. Milton and Wordsworth might call that *my* "high argument," even though I myself remain torn between attraction to that light and skeptical of the grandiose, perhaps obscurantist, even delusional, claims made on its behalf.

The second feature of Emerson's thought was intrinsic to his temperament and characteristic of the age, though, intellectually, he was again learning principally from Coleridge, and from Goethe. I mean the dominant, even obsessive, emphasis on natural and mental polarity, the dynamic at the heart of existence as well as a dialectical method of individual perception and development. As with all polar thinkers, Emerson sees distinctions, what the discursive reason and mere understanding perceive as "contradictions," as the prerequisite to progression, with the interpenetrating opposites reconciled and raised to a higher unity. Polarity is implicit in my project as a whole in the tension between quotation and originality, tradition and the individual talent, the Over-Soul and the Self.

Two additional points follow from the first two. What has been understandably but inadequately described—reflecting that legendary Emersonian "optimism" impervious to evidence of evil—as a refusal or inability to mourn actually takes the form, under the auspices of the inward or higher "light," of a reconciliation of such polar antagonisms as fate and freedom, defeat and victory, issuing in the conviction, even in the face of repeated personal and familial tragedy, that it is, in Wordworth's elegiac phrase, "not without hope we suffer and we mourn." That is the subject of the final section of this study, an attempt to get beyond the partially understandable caricature of Emerson as a cheery optimist oblivious to the darker aspects of life, a man lacking, in W. B. Yeats's charge, "the Vision of Evil." Demonstrating that the impact of Coleridge and Wordsworth is not only critical and literary but personal as well, I focus there on the curious interweaving of Emerson's recollection of passages in Coleridge and, far more significantly, in Wordsworth, with the terrible sequence of deaths in his family between 1831 and 1842.[2]

My second point, and my argument throughout, is that, among Emerson's many influences in his own language, the least dispensable (even given the considerable impact of Carlyle) are Coleridge and Wordsworth. I refer specifically to those writing in English, for there is, of course, the pervasive intellectual influence, upon Emerson as upon the age in general, of Goethe, the "recent genius" whose "effect upon mankind" was unequalled and whose "tonic books" Emerson treasured (*JMN* 5:314, 10: 167). He did so with that anxiety-free "gratitude" he rightly said characterized Goethe's own interactions with his "great contemporaries" (*EL* 2: 125–26; *EPP* 329). The relationship with those writing in his own language was more complicated. For all Emerson's self-reliance and authentic originality, and despite his attempts, in the early and middle work especially, to displace and erase, deny and decry, Coleridge and Wordsworth emerge as perhaps his principal "benefactors," the twin pillars upon which his most characteristic thinking and writing are based. Even more immediately than Goethe and Carlyle, Coleridge is his major thinker, critic, and aid to reflection, both in his own right and (along with Carlyle and Victor Cousin)

2. Both Emerson and Whitman seemed to Yeats by 1922 to have become "superficial precisely because they lack the Vision of Evil" (*Autobiographies,* 246). In *A Vision* (144), even his admired Shelley is included in the charge. In finding Wordsworth's poetry a consolation in distress, Emerson was participating in a pattern that embraces, among many others, John Stuart Mill and William James. Like James, Emerson found much consolation in the speeches of the Wanderer in *The Excursion.* In the final chapter, I trace the effect of the Intimations Ode on "Threnody," the elegy for Waldo, a poem that may be read as an Emersonian version of Wordsworth's elegiac and affirmative ode.

as a conduit to the distinctions and dialectics of Germano-Romantic idealism. Though Emerson, for the most part, retains his originality, I concur with the following characterizations of the Coleridge-Emerson connection. The first is from Henry Hedge; the second, echoing Hedge, from Barbara Packer; the third from Alexander Kern.

Frederic Henry Hedge, the original proposer of a Transcendentalist "symposium," the group Emerson often referred to as "Hedge's Club," was the author of a seminal article on Coleridge and German idealist thought. Trained in Germany, Hedge was fluent in the language and had read, in the original, Kant, Schelling, Fichte, and Jacobi. That knowledge of Kant and the post-Kantian tradition enabled him, almost uniquely in the United States, to present a judiciously balanced assessment of Coleridge. He did so in "Coleridge's Literary Character," an 1833 essay second in influence only to James Marsh's essay introducing his 1829 U.S. edition of Coleridge's *Aids to Reflection.* Hedge admired Coleridge's poetry and criticism, and, though acknowledging his crucial importance as a transmitter of German thought to America, was aware, as Emerson and others were not, of the creative liberties Coleridge had taken with Kant, especially when it came to the distinction of paramount importance to the Transcendentalists in general and to Emerson above all; only toward the end of his essay, and then in passing, does Hedge mention Coleridge's un-Kantian Reason-understanding distinction. Those final pages also expose what Hedge considered Coleridge's blurry theology. Nevertheless, he ends his essay by quoting with approval Coleridge's defense of his own career in the final pages of chapter 10 of the *Biographia:* "Would that the criterion of the scholar's utility were the number and moral value of the truths which he has been the means of throwing into the general circulation, or the number and value of the minds whom by his conversation or letters he has excited into activity, and supplied with the germs of their aftergrowth!" (*BL* 1:220).[3]

Barbara Packer ends the second section of her superb 1995 survey, "The Transcendentalists," by quoting this conclusion of Hedge, who, as she says, "welcomed Coleridge's unconscious heterodoxy" and saw him as "a valuable importer and disseminator of ideas that are quite easily separable from the husk of Anglican piety in which they are contained." Judged by "the standards" Coleridge himself lays out in the passage quoted by Hedge, she concludes: "Coleridge's contribution to American intellectual life had been as great as he could have wished." As Coleridge himself said to Arthur Hallam and Richard Monckton Milnes during their visit to Highgate in

3. Hedge, "Coleridge's Literary Character," 129.

the early 1830s, "Go to America if you have the opportunity. I am a poor poet in England, but I am a great philosopher in America." That judgment, validated by Frank Thompson (whose work is discussed in the chapter that follows), is also to be found in Alexander Kern's 1981 essay on Coleridge's influence on American Romanticism. Just as Coleridge "solved his own religious, philosophical, and critical problems, so he was able a generation later" to answer American needs. "A group of New England Unitarians who were also dissatisfied with the cold rationalism and mechanical psychology of the Enlightenment were able to use his version of German philosophy to create American Transcendentalism." And Kern concludes no less unequivocally: "It is clear that Coleridge, more than Wordsworth, Carlyle, or any German writer, precipitated American Transcendentalism. His identification of Reason with Spirit became the catalyst which broke the Lockean and Associationist bond of mechanical necessity. The emphasis on insight, intuition, and imagination permitted a contact with nature which has dominated subsequent American literature and thought."[4]

Still, only the right reader is prepared to receive the light. Although there is not the slightest doubt of the electrifying effect on Emerson and his circle of Coleridge's distinction between Reason and understanding, and the privileging of intuitive Reason, we have to remember that Emerson, steeped in Plato and Plotinus, had been saying related things about Reason as early as the autumn of 1822. We are, he recorded in his journal for September 8, endowed with "an intelligence which reveals to man another condition of existence and a nearer approach to the Supreme Being. This intelligence is Reason," and, he added on November 2, the divine "law is a moral one, addressed to men's reason, and not their sense." He had also named intuitive Reason's empiricist enemies: "The highest species of reasoning upon divine subjects is rather the fruit of a sort of moral imagination, than of the 'Reasoning Machines' such as Locke and . . . David Hume" (*JMN* 2:14, 38). In short, he was ripe for Coleridge.

Despite this initial barrage of testimony to the indispensable importance of Coleridge to the American Transcendentalists, I am even more concerned with the impact of Wordsworth on Emerson. Wordsworth is the flawed but great poet who made the Coleridgean word flesh, who pioneered a paradoxically unmediated yet thoughtful interaction with nature, and who also served, poetically if not always politically, as a champion of

4. Packer, "The Transcendentalists," 2:361ff; Kern, "Coleridge and American Romanticism: The Transcendentalists and Poe," 113, 133. Coleridge's remark to Hallam and Milnes, quoted in Thomas Reid's biography of Milnes, is repeated by John J. Duffy in his introduction to *Coleridge's American Disciples: The Selected Correspondence of James Marsh,* 1.

the common, the low, the humble. In addition, he became the provider, for Emerson as for so many others, of much needed consolation in distress. What were for Emerson the primary benefactions of Coleridge and Wordsworth were later summed up in brief comments made by Matthew Arnold shortly after Emerson's death. When Arnold described Emerson as "the friend and aider of those who would live in the spirit," he was quietly but aptly reminding us of Coleridge and of the specific works of that Inquiring Spirit—*The Friend* and *Aids to Reflection*—that had first and profoundly influenced Emerson. Three years later, Arnold concluded his essay on Wordsworth, an essay that had repeatedly stressed his "power," by quoting the poet himself (from an 1807 letter to Lady Beaumont) on the moral effect of his poems: "They will co-operate with the benign tendencies in human nature and society, and will, in their degree, be efficacious in making men wiser, better, and happier." Emerson would have concurred with that ending; he thought Wordsworth's shedding of benignant influence his chief value and had himself quoted from that same 1807 letter, the thrust of which was repeated in the conclusion of the "Essay, Supplementary to the Preface" to the 1815 *Poems.*[5]

In unfolding the latent processes of Emerson's dialectical thought, then, I am particularly interested in the ways in which his work testifies to the influence upon him of intellectual Coleridge and consolatory and power-exemplifying Wordsworth. To a degree that I should have anticipated, Milton—venerated by Coleridge, Wordsworth, and Emerson alike—became central to my project, conceptually and as part of what increasingly became a web of allusion. In particular, Milton's archangel Raphael emerged as a foundational figure. His explanation to Adam, in book 5 of *Paradise Lost,* of the Great Chain of Being, perhaps the fullest exposition in English literature of that medieval and Renaissance idea, is indispensable to understanding the principal Coleridgean distinction inherited by Wordsworth, De Quincey, Carlyle, and Emerson. In addition, the ramifications of Raphael's teaching, in tandem with Milton's own 1644 *Tractate on Education,* help to illuminate the tuition-intuition distinction stressed by Wordsworth

5. Arnold, "Wordsworth," 385. Emerson would have been in accord with Arnold's emphasis on Wordsworth's "power," his praise of the Intimations Ode and "Laodamia" (Emerson's two favorite Wordsworth poems), and his singling out of the "Prospectus" to *The Recluse,* which (despite his notorious emphasis on the shorter lyrics at the expense of the longer works) Arnold cites four times in the essay (377, 379, 381, 382). Comparing Wordsworth and Emerson in *Discourses in America,* Arnold states: "As Wordsworth's poetry is, in my judgment, the most important work done in verse, in our language, during the present century, so Emerson's *Essays* are, I think, the most important work done in prose" (196). Emerson was, he thought, a great man if not quite a "legitimate" poet (160).

in his 1833 interview with Emerson: a primary theme in the "Polarities" section.

I am also interested in Emerson's own influence—specifically upon his best reader and most enthusiastic European disciple, Nietzsche. Just as the narrow focus of many Americanists on our indigenous literary culture caused them to lose sight of the formative influence of Coleridge on Emerson, so too a mixture of European snobbery and American provincialism enabled scholars to dismiss, downplay, or deny—at least until quite recently—an equally obvious fact: that Nietzsche was an unapologetic and ardent disciple of Emerson, a thinker whose influence deeply affected both his life and his work. In addition, I have found it hard not to think of—and to bring into the discussion at various points—the two paramount modern poets in the Romantic tradition, W. B. Yeats and Wallace Stevens. But I anticipate. Let me lay out the premises and the general shape of what follows.

I am engaged, above all, in exploring the tension between tradition and innovation, the "filterings" and "vampings" that define a genuine writer's relationship to his or her precursors. As Coleridge, himself saturated in Milton, knew better than anyone else, Wordsworth was immensely indebted to Milton, yet he could rightly say that, whereas in "imaginative power" Wordsworth of all modern writers stood nearest to Shakespeare and Milton, it was "yet in a kind perfectly unborrowed and his own" (*BL* 2:151). The case for Emersonian originality seems to me less compelling. Still, for all his indebtedness to Milton and Goethe, Coleridge and Wordsworth, Emerson felt comfortable enough to quote, and to implicitly apply to his own situation, the case Coleridge made for Wordsworth, and Goethe made for himself. Goethe frankly acknowledged his enormous debts to his precursors and contemporaries yet—in Emerson's paraphrase in "Quotation and Originality"—could declare, "My work is an aggregation of beings taken from the whole of Nature; it bears the name of Goethe" (*EPP* 329). As Shakespeare's Edgar insists, "Ripeness is all." Nietzsche, the self-acknowledged and deeply indebted heir of both Goethe and Emerson, and as prodigious a reader as they, warned, precisely as Emerson does, not against reading, but against the danger of books in the hands of an unripened reader, one not yet prepared to be both a thankful and a creative recipient. It is no accident that, of all modern writers, Goethe and Nietzsche, Coleridge and Emerson, provide the richest examples of what Thomas McFarland has called "the paradox of originality": profound indebtedness, sometimes to the point of what the vulgar call "plagiarism," accompanied by the triumphant assertion that the creative receiver takes only what tallies with his own thoughts, enabling him, providing he possesses genius, to retain and even enhance his own originality.[6]

But it may be less an instance of "paradox" than of the reciprocity epitomized in Coleridge's Each and All, that polarity Emerson seized on in reading the eleventh of the essays on method in *The Friend.* Having cited the Intimations Ode to demonstrate that everything *Without* is, for the contemplative man, "a modification of *his own being,*" Coleridge went on to discuss the relationship of the "individual" to "inter-communion" with others: "It is the idea of the common centre, of the universal law, by which all power manifests itself in opposite yet interdependent forces . . . [that], enlightening inquiry, multiplying experiments, and at once inspiring humility and perseverance will lead him to comprehend gradually and progressively the relation of each to the other, of each to all, and of all to each" (*F* 1:511). A similar fusion of singularity and universality occurs at a pivotal moment of *The Prelude.* "O Friend," Wordsworth exclaims, speaking directly to Coleridge:

> Of genius, power,
> Creation and divinity itself
> I have been speaking, for my theme has been
> What passed *within me.*

He continues: "Points have we *all* of us within our souls / Where *all* stand *single,*" with "*each*" of us "a memory to himself." For "there's not a man / That lives who hath not known his godlike hours" (*P* 3:189–95; italics added). We are, each and all of us, individuals, equally capable of remembering divine hours, though only the poet of genius, standing "single," possesses the creative power required to transcribe godlike experiences shared by all.

Once we accept the role of Coleridge as a catalyst in Emerson's thinking, it becomes difficult to put too much weight on the ramifications of this Each-and-All passage. Two poems of Emerson may help to make the point. During his lifetime, all editions of his verse began with "The Sphinx," a perplexing dragon placed at the very threshold. "Who'll tell me my secret?" she asks in the opening stanza, before elaborating on Nature's many opposites in eternal "alternation," and suggesting that "To vision profounder / Man's spirit must dive," before concluding, enigmatically, "Who telleth *one* of my meanings / Is master of *all* I am." In 1859, eighteen years after he wrote the poem, Emerson himself told the secret: "I have often been asked the meaning of 'The Sphinx.' It is this,—*The perception of identity*

6. See McFarland, *Coleridge and the Pantheist Tradition,* 43–46; and *Originality and Imagination,* 4–5, 14–17.

unites all things and explains one by another. . . . [I]f the mind live *only in particulars*, and see *only differences* (wanting *the power to see the whole—all in each*), then the world addresses to this mind a question it cannot answer, and each new fact tears it to pieces, and it is *vanquished by the distracting variety*" (*W* 9:212; italics added).

The Each-and-All doctrine applies to Nature and to "History," the "whole" of which, in the essay of that title, is "to be explained from individual experience." Recalling his own recently written poem, Emerson notes, "The Sphinx must solve her own riddle." That riddle is indistinguishable from the mind that "must read it," since, in the essay's opening each-and-all sentence, "There is *one* mind common to *all individual men*" (*E&L* 237). As Emerson put it in a poem anticipating the theme of "The Sphinx," this one actually titled "Each and All," one does not know

> what argument
> Thy life to thy neighbor's creed has lent.
> *All* are needed by *each one;*
> Nothing is fair or good alone.
> (*EPP* 432; italics added)

The doctrine applies as well to *literary* interactions. The relation between the Romantic zeitgeist and the individual talent was well synopsized by Percy Bysshe Shelley in his preface to *Prometheus Unbound:* "It is impossible that anyone who inhabits the same age with such writers as those who stand in the foremost ranks of our own, can conscientiously assure himself, that his language and tone of thought may not have been modified by the study of the productions of those extraordinary intellects."[7]

Individual thinkers, part of "one mind" or not, necessarily participate in the spirit of the age. Writing in 1840 on Emerson's works as part of "American philosophy," Richard Monckton Milnes observed that they were also part of "European philosophy." Though we find in Emerson the "same" emphases we find in Carlyle, "this voice has come to us over the broad Atlantic," and all is "sufficiently modified by circumstances of personality and place to show that the plant is assimilated to the climate and the soil, though the seed may have been brought from elsewhere." The organic image echoes not Carlyle, but the claim of *Coleridge* (who had, a few years earlier, assured Milnes in person of the impact in the United States of Coleridgean philosophy) to have "excited into activity" many minds and supplied them "with the germs of their aftergrowth" (*BL* 1:220). With "no disrespect to Mr. Emerson," Milnes continues, "there is little in such of his works as have reached us" (and he had read *Nature,* "The American

7. Shelley, *Shelley's Poetry and Prose,* 134.

Scholar," and the Divinity School Address, among other Emersonian writings) "which would be new to the competent student of European philosophy." Yet the "general English reader," encountering much that is extravagantly, even "absurdly," original, must be gratified "at reading thoughts already familiar to him, arrayed in language so freshly vigorous, so eloquently true." Some of the language as well as the thoughts would be familiar to readers of Wordsworth, too, since Emerson's "Idealistic Pantheism" asserts—in Milnes's synopsis of, mostly, passages from *Nature*—

> the identity of man with nature, the primary duty of a "wise passiveness" to the superincumbent spirit, the "occult relation between man and the vegetable," the creed "I am nothing—I see all—the currents of the Universal Being circulate through me—I am part and particle of God," [all of which] have been uttered often before . . . ; but here they are all-in-all, and they are propounded as if they lay [unproblematically] on the surface of truth, and within the grasp of all men.[8]

In the polarity between Each and All, the individual talent, no matter how fiercely "original," is necessarily part of a greater whole, a democracy of the spirit, a republic of letters. The author of "Tradition and the Individual Talent" himself insisted that the "most individual parts" of a genuine poet's work "may be those in which the dead poets, his ancestors, assert their immortality most vigorously" and that the struggle between Each and All is less a competition over "originality" than an assertion of individual power and a making new of what has been received. In a passage germane not only to his immediate subject in "A Complex Dialogue: Coleridge's Doctrine of Polarity and Its European Contexts" but also to the dialogue I am engaged in throughout this study, Thomas McFarland asserts: "Texts are possible only in contexts. . . . There are no Robinson Crusoes of the intellect. Indeed, in a cultural ambiance dominated by the vision of the reconciliation of polar opposites," the dominant example may be "the polarity of the individual talent and the tradition in which it functions."[9]

Five of Emerson's statements on the subject may serve to illustrate this paradox and polarity. Demonstrating in action what Goethe called "elective affinity," these passages, by allying individualism with universality, reveal how one can be immensely indebted yet claim to function creatively—as Coleridge said of Wordsworth—"in a kind perfectly unborrowed and his own." The first, from "Self-Reliance," is well known: "A man should learn

8. Milnes, "American Philosophy—Emerson's Works" (1840), reprinted in *The Recognition of Ralph Waldo Emerson,* edited by Milton Konvitz, 16–17.

9. McFarland, "Complex Dialogue," 79. As T. S. Eliot put it in pt. 5 of "East Coker," "there is no competition," only the struggle to "recover what has been lost / And found and lost again and again" (*The Complete Poems and Plays, 1909–1950,* 128).

to detect and watch that gleam of light which flashes across his mind from within, more than the lustre of the firmament of bards and sages. Yet he dismisses without notice his thought, because it is his. In every work of genius we recognize our own rejected thoughts: they come back to us with a certain alienated majesty" (*E&L* 259). In "Spiritual Laws," discussing a "man's genius, the quality that differences him from every other," his "susceptibility to one class of influences, the selection of what is fit for him, the rejection of what is unfit," Emerson describes such a man as, in another key Coleridgean term, a "method,"

> a progressive arrangement; a selecting principle, gathering his like to him, wherever he goes. He takes only his own, out of the multiplicity that sweeps and circles around him. . . . No man can learn what he has not preparation for learning, however near to his eyes is the object. . . . God screens us evermore from premature ideas. Our eyes are holden that we cannot see [Luke 24:13–16] things that stare us in the face, until the hour arrives when the mind is ripened; then we behold them, and the time when we saw them not, is like a dream. (*EPP* 154, 155)

The third illustrative passage occurs in a note of October 1841. "I am not such a fool," says Emerson, "but that I taste the joy" that comes from reading "a new and prodigious" writer. Even if "the basis of this joy is at last the *instinct* that I am only let into *my own estate,* that the poet and his book and his story are only fictions and semblances in which *my thought* is pleased to *dress itself,* I do not the less *yield myself to the keen delight of difference and newness*" (italics added). That delight derives from a kindred spirit, a writer who, however new and different, is in turn part of a universal, and impersonal, whole that subsumes others, including the self who recognizes in the genius of those others one's own thoughts returning with a certain alienated majesty. The "insight" of a heightened perspective allying us with "the Universe" does not "overvalue particular truths," Emerson declares in the great essay "Fate." This, our fourth illustration, recalls the impersonal, elevated perspective of the transparent eyeball:

> We eagerly hear every thought and word quoted from an intellectual man. But, in his presence, *our own mind is roused to activity,* and we forget very fast what *he* says, much more interested in *the new play of our own thought,* than in any thought of his. 'Tis the majesty into which we have suddenly mounted, the impersonality, the scorn of egotisms, the sphere of laws, that engage us. Once we were stepping a little this way, and a little that way; now we are as men in a balloon, and do not think so much of the point we have left, or the point we would make, as of the liberty and glory of the way. (*E&L* 955–56; italics added)

In the fifth and final passage, from "Quotation and Originality," Emerson again insists on both individuality and universality. There "remains the indefeasible persistency of the individual to be himself." Every mind "is different; and the more it is unfolded, the more pronounced is that difference." A man "must draw the elements into him," but, "however received," if genius and originality are present, "these elements pass into the substance of his constitution, will be assimilated, and tend always to form, not a partisan, but a possessor of truth." Taking up Coleridge's word, Emerson claims that against "the preponderance of the Past, the single word *Genius* is a sufficient reply." The "divine," which

> resides in the new... never quotes, but is, and creates. The profound apprehension of the Present is Genius, which makes the Past forgotten. Genius believes its faintest presentiment against the testimony of all history; for it knows that... a state of mind is the ancestor of everything. And what is Originality? It is being, being one's self, and reporting accurately what we see and are. Genius is in the first instance, sensibility, the capacity of receiving just impressions from the external world, and the power of coordinating these after the laws of thought. (*EPP* 329)

Embracing the Kantian-Coleridgean coordinating power of the mind and rejecting the limited way in which self-reliance tends to be interpreted, Emerson goes on to again endorse egotism-scorning universality rather than the private ownership of ideas. If a "thinker feels that the thought most strictly his own is not his own, and recognizes the perpetual suggestion of the Supreme Intellect, the oldest thoughts become new and fertile while he speaks them." Thus, the ancient Greeks claimed "that the bard spoke not his own, but the words of some god. True poets have always ascended to this lofty platform, and met this expectation. Shakspeare, Milton, Wordsworth, were very conscious of their responsibilities. When a man thinks happily, he finds no foot-track in the field he traverses" (*EPP* 329–30). It is as well to know from the outset that we are dealing with a paradoxical thinker who—having resolved the tensions, even bridging apparent contradictions, between originality and quotation, the individual genius and tradition, self-reliance and participation in an impersonal Universe—is able, in a spirit of keen delight, to derive almost the whole of his philosophy from European Romanticism (above all, from Coleridge and Wordsworth, Carlyle and Goethe) while simultaneously claiming to find "no foot-track in the field he traverses."

The first section of the book that follows, titled "Preliminaries," consists of four chapters. In the Introduction (Chapter 1), I synopsize, and amplify, modern critical responses to Emerson's own account of his relationship to European and especially to British Romanticism. I also discuss the origins of Transcendentalism as described by three key participants in the movement: Hedge; Theodore Parker, the Transcendentalist pastor and abolitionist who first took fire from Emerson's Divinity School Address; and Emerson himself, who, in a late lecture, attributes the movement, informal as it was, to certain individuals reading with excitement Coleridge, Wordsworth, Goethe, and Carlyle. In this lecture, he also falls back on the Coleridgean distinction between intuitive Reason and mere understanding, which, forty-five years earlier, he had employed in, at first reluctantly, agreeing with the idea, advanced by his Coleridgean friend Hedge, of forming a "symposium" or club. In depicting Transcendentalism as largely, though of course not exclusively, shaped by Coleridge, the principal disseminator of European Romanticism to the United States, I am (like others before me) taking into account the impact in New England of *The Friend, Biographia Literaria,* and, above all, at least at first, Marsh's edition of *Aids to Reflection.* That impact and influence include the German idealism "filtered" through Coleridge, to use a term he himself employed in his 1833 meeting with Emerson, and which was taken up, consciously or unconsciously, by Emerson's biographer and the editor of his letters, Ralph L. Rusk, in designating Coleridge the "filter" through which Emerson read the bulk of his German philosophy (*L* 1:lvii).[10]

Chapter 2 begins by focusing on the passage in book 5 of *Paradise Lost* in which the archangel Raphael distinguishes Reason from understanding and discursive from intuitive Reason. Coleridge's alteration of Kant in the light of the Miltonic passage defines much of the intellectual and visionary foundation of American Transcendentalism: a lineage clearly understood by Hedge and at least partially grasped by Emerson, who refers to "Milton Coleridge & the Germans" in explaining the distinction between intuitive Reason and mere understanding in a seminal 1834 letter to his brother Edward. I also deal with Marsh's influential "Preliminary Essay" to his edition of Coleridge's *Aids to Reflection,* concluding with Marsh's—and Emerson's and Coleridge's—revealing citation of the pivotal ninth

10. Having praised an "extract" Coleridge had "quoted" in the opening essay of volume 3 of *The Friend,* Emerson, during his 1833 interview, expressed an interest in seeing the entire work. Coleridge replied that the extract—it is from William Sedgwick's *Justice upon the Armie Remonstrance*... (1648)—was indeed "excellent" but that "the passage would no doubt strike you more in the quotation than in the original, for I have filtered it" (*E&L* 772). See *F* 1:411–14, and notes for the full text and Coleridge's filtering, which involved adding to, omitting, altering, and rearranging Sedgwick's text. In that form, the extract became a favorite recital piece on Emersonian platforms (see *TN* 3:319).

stanza of the Intimations Ode, specifically the lines that supply my subtitle and organizing theme.

Chapters 3 and 4 share a main title, "Emerson's Discipleship." In the course of engaging contemporary critical response to the transatlantic dialogue, I trace, in Chapter 3, specific echoings of Coleridge and Wordsworth in the most celebrated passage in Emerson. But I begin by discussing Emerson's visits to his precursors in the summer of 1833. Those visits, with the exception of that to the vigorous Carlyle, disappointed him, though the semicomical anticlimaxes were—as Weisbuch, Ellis, and Gravil have noted—largely predetermined by a youthful and unaccomplished Emerson's Adamic refusal to be overawed by the phenomenon of a venerable but superannuated Europe, especially as embodied in the aged and now conservative Coleridge and Wordsworth. In this chapter, focusing on Emerson's public resistance, his aggressive defensiveness against the influence of his Romantic precursors, I note several instances of "effacement" in *Nature*. For example, Coleridge is cited without either attribution or quotation marks, and erased from notes that otherwise made it into *Nature* in the case of a passage that haunted Emerson: the crucial concept of the sensible world as "Symbolical, one mighty alphabet" to be read by the human mind. Chapter 4 involves a more confident Emerson and thus a more generous acknowledgment of his indebtedness. After tracking Emerson's history of response, public and private, to both Coleridge and Wordsworth, this first section ends by unpacking the recurrent image of the "shedding" of light as both spiritual illumination and a metaphor for influence.

The next three chapters, clustered under the title "Polarities," offer variations on a theme, illustrations of a mode of thinking pervasive in both Coleridge and Emerson. Indeed, nothing is more central to the Romantic zeitgeist—which embraces German idealism, British Romanticism, and Emersonian Transcendentalism—than the principle of polarity. In these chapters, attempting to interrelate, in terms of Coleridgean-Emersonian polarities, such antagonisms as quotation and originality, tuition and intuition, passivity and activity, Nature and Mind, I contrast discursive knowledge and immediately experienced "life," in which Nature is alternately a quasi mother and our best teacher—before becoming, though infused with spirit, a servant to the sovereign mind. According to volume 3 of Schelling's *System of Transcendental Idealism,* the polarity of subject and object, conscious intelligence and unconscious nature, could be resolved by the imagination. Adapting Schelling, Coleridge goes on to identify imagination with the intuitive Reason. Thus, the analytic, "lower" faculty, the understanding, clears the way for the reunion of the all in one under the higher auspices of the eternal Reason: that reconciliation and inclusion of contradictions Coleridge called "multeity in unity" (*F* 1:522).[11]

One of the most obvious "contradictions" in Emerson, though derived from Wordsworth rather than Coleridge, is that between praise and condemnation of "books," denigrated in favor of originality and full-blooded life. It is in this vitalistic context of an original apprehension of life that we encounter—stemming from Wordsworth, picked up by Emerson, and passed on to Nietzsche—a provisional denigration of "history" and of "books," both useful, until the point at which study of the past and "reading" threaten to fetishize what preceded us, and so fail in their primary purpose in the present: less to instruct than to confirm and, even more crucially, to provoke, thus quickening new creation. Uncreative, we become like the "dwarf child" produced by the tyrannical (indeed Satanic) systems of education condemned by Wordsworth in book 5 of *The Prelude,* or like that "pigmy" six year old who so appalls him in the Intimations Ode, acting "As if his whole vocation / Were endless imitation," a state Emerson compared (in "Self-Reliance") to "suicide." Because repose is half of the fundamental polarity between Rest and Motion, considerable emphasis falls, particularly in Chapter 7, on wise passiveness, even apparent indolence, as an indispensable element in creativity, as well as on a point stressed in both chapters: the value of instinctual life, "being" rather than mere "knowing."

In the next three-chapter section, "Divinities," I explore some of the ambiguous ramifications of the concept of Divinity Within, particularly in terms of the doctrine of self-reliance, the crucial relation between the merely private, biographical self and the "enlarged," universal or spiritual, Self, as well as between that Self and God, whether considered as immanent or transcendent. While "divinity within" has a hubristic and lethal context in *Paradise Lost,* the Romantics and Emerson do not forget that the archangel Michael promises Adam, in the final book of Milton's epic, a compensating "paradise *within thee,* happier far" than the Eden Adam and Eve lost by sinning and *falsely* feeling "divinity within" (*PL* 9:1010, 12:587). Coleridge's Latin axiom, "*Quantum sumus, scimus,*" became, with the help of Coleridge's own gloss in *Aids to Reflection,* a momentous source for Emerson's finding "within ourselves," a self that is paradoxically "more than ourselves," the ground and substance of the moral life and "all other knowledge." This sanction for self-reliance leads into a discussion of the polar tension between Solitude and Society, the Coleridgean Each and All, the pull between withdrawal into the realm of one's own creative labor and the need to engage

11. The concept of converting multitude to unity recurs frequently, especially in *BL,* but the actual phrase—"The most general definition of beauty, therefore, is . . . Multeity in Unity"—occurs in "On the Principles of Genial Criticism," available only in John Shawcross's edition of *Biographia Literaria* (2:219–52; quote on 232).

politically, which Emerson presents (employing Coleridge's term *Genius*) as a tension between his "individual genius" and the "universal genius." In this context, I explore, in Chapter 8, the concept of "power" in Emerson, as well as his reluctant but not insubstantial sociopolitical activism in the great issues of the day, particularly the crisis brought about by the resuscitation of the old fugitive-slave legislation. His slowly gathering but finally passionate commitment to the abolition of slavery was the cause of his uncharacteristically savage denunciation of Webster, a leader he once admired, and of his nation-stunning comparison of the "gallows" of John Brown to the "cross" of Christ.

In Chapter 9, the Divinity School Address and the public outcry that greeted it are discussed as both a watershed between engagement in public issues and a decisive if temporary withdrawal as well as a dramatic example of the Emersonian emphasis on Man (whose moral constitution makes him a potential Temple of Deity) rather than on the Jesus of historical Christianity, who was, according to Emerson, merely the first to realize that God was incarnate in man. Intriguingly—and curiously, given their later religious conservatism—Coleridge and Wordsworth figure in the Divinity School Address: Coleridge as an aspect of Uriel, the titular angel in the poem in which Emerson took on his critics, Wordsworth by way of quotation. In discussing Emerson's more than rhetorical preference of an animated paganism to corpse-cold apathy, I supplement Emerson's own Wordsworthian quotation in the address (he would rather be "a Pagan, suckled in a creed outworn" than defrauded of his own intuitive insights and his bond with nature by an alienating "historical Christianity") with similar thoughts to be found in that most religiously orthodox of Wordsworthian pantheists, the Wanderer in Emerson's favorite book of *The Excursion.* Though the tenth chapter, also focusing on the concept of "divinity within," again engages the Wanderer of book 4 of *The Excursion,* it goes well beyond any form of orthodoxy. Moving from the extreme subjectivism of Coleridge's "Dejection: An Ode" through Wordsworth's psychological dislocation of Miltonic theology in the "Prospectus" to *The Recluse,* the chapter examines the similarly humanized and "Orphic" revelations in the introduction to and peroration of Emerson's *Nature,* and concludes by completing the Wordsworthian and Emersonian texts with their rather obvious twentieth-century parallel: "Sunday Morning" by Wallace Stevens, whose ninth canto of *Notes toward a Supreme Fiction,* discussed at the end of Chapter 9, also exemplifies Divinity Within.

The final section, "The Art of Losing," consists, like the opening section, of four chapters. As suggested by its title (borrowed from Elizabeth Bishop's marvelous villanelle), it engages Emerson's various responses, frequently filtered through Wordsworth, to the terrible series of early deaths of those he most loved. By way of preamble, the celebrated, or notorious, issue of Emerson's so-called optimism is addressed in Chapter 11. The chapter that follows tracks his responses to the deaths of his first wife, Ellen, who died when she was only nineteen, and of his brother Edward, only twenty-nine when he succumbed to a complication of mania and tuberculosis. The final chapters address Emerson's struggle with the death of Charles, the brother with whom he was most intimate (Chapter 13), and finally, in Chapter 14, Emerson's mourning, or supposed inability to grieve, in the case of his first son, Waldo, dead of scarlet fever before the age of six. In both cases, Emerson's reading of Wordsworth supplied much needed consolation; the sense, first, that even the most precious material losses were "Fallings from us, vanishings," and, second, that it is "Not without hope we suffer and we mourn." The Appendix offers brief analyses of the two Wordsworth poems that Emerson consistently ranked second only to the Intimations Ode, "Laodamia" and "Dion."

Readers are entitled to some initial clarification of my political and critical "positions." In engaging Emerson, I obviously place him in a Romantic context. But to focus on the central epistemological and imaginative issues of the Romantic period is not to completely depoliticize Emerson. After all, Coleridge and Wordsworth began as ardent supporters of the French Revolution and, even in their conservatism, remained engaged by sociopolitical issues; indeed, both claimed that they gave more thought to society and politics than to poetics. Still, my central texts remain the standard ones: *Nature* (1836) and the enduring works Emerson produced between 1837 and 1844 ("The American Scholar," the Divinity School Address, "Self-Reliance," "Circles," "The Transcendentalist," "Experience," and "The Poet"). But I also emphasize "Uses of Great Men" from *Representative Men,* passages on Emerson's visits to England in *English Traits,* the essays "Fate" and "Power" in that great volume *The Conduct of Life,* the even later essay "Character," and, along with other Wordsworthian poems by Emerson, the elegy for Waldo, "Threnody." And, of course, the *Journals.*

As I am primarily engaged by the central Romantic-Transcendentalist polarities—the relationship between mind and nature, subject and object, ideal and real, self and society, and the problematics of the divinity within—I do not here participate in the anticanonical "New Americanist" critique of the American Renaissance typified by such multicultural activists as Donald Pease and John Carlos Rowe. For example, Rowe, author of *At Emerson's Tomb* (1997), has even more recently edited a collection pairing Emerson and Margaret Fuller, in which he candidly informs us that he is "rehistoricizing both authors as representatives of the political and social conflicts," not only of their period but of ours as well. Though I too "re-historicize," sociopolitical issues are essential only to my long eighth chapter. Still, I am hardly dismissive of Rowe's claim that "the Emerson who has the most to teach us in our late modernity and postmodernity is the idealist who struggled with political and social urgencies that are still very much with us: racism, sexism, class distinctions, xenophobia, and nationalism without rationalism." Indeed, David M. Robinson concludes his introduction to *The Political Emerson: Essential Writings on Politics and Social Reform* (2004) by noting that although, until recently, Emerson's role as a "cultural critic and public intellectual," including "his intervention in the political life of the United States," has been "overlooked or denigrated," his political writings are "of a piece with his earlier spiritual and ethical writings," in that both are "expressions and enactments of the moral responsibility incumbent upon every man and woman."[12]

A similar emphasis is to be found in the work of Stanley Cavell, most explicitly in his *Cities of Words: Pedagogical Letters on a Register of the Moral Life,* also published in 2004. Positioning Emerson as the initiator of American philosophy, Cavell identifies his aim not with "ultimate perfection," but with what Emerson himself called the "unattained but attainable": to reform or change the world, remolding it nearer to the heart's desire. Whether this view or calling—which Cavell has named "moral perfectionism"—is "essentially elitist, or on the contrary whether its imagining of justice is essential to the aspiration of a democratic society, is a guiding question" in his book. Noting that "a principal object of Emerson's thinking is to urge a reconsideration" of the relation, and the relative "priority," of soul (or self) and society, Cavell implies an association made explicit in a forthcoming study by Jennifer Gurley, who reads Emerson's *Nature* through the prism of Plato's Allegory of the Cave, emphasizing the enlightened individual's communal responsibility to enlighten others—a task later assumed by Nietzsche's Zarathustra. Cavell alludes to an Emersonian and contemporary "continuity"—as political as it is epistemological—with "the ancient wish of philosophy to lead the soul, imprisoned and distorted by darkness and confusion, into the freedom of the day."[13] It is an aspiration and an image I associate with Wordsworth's variation on Plato and Plotinus

12. Rowe, *Ralph Waldo Emerson and Margaret Fuller,* 4, 10; Robinson, *The Political Emerson,* 21–22. See also T. Gregory Garvey, ed., *The Emerson Dilemma: Essays on Emerson and Social Reform.* As Garvey says, the essays on Emerson and social reform in this collection show "how Emerson's reform activism emerges out of his transcendentalism and how" his early Transcendentalism "shaped his involvement in reform movements during later periods" (xi).

13. Cavell, *Cities of Words,* 2, 3, 4, 14; Gurley, "Emerson's Platonic Dialogue," forthcoming. Denis Donoghue, writing in 2005, is having none of this. Rejecting the depiction of Emersonian individualism as a "social value," even "the flowering of democracy" (a thesis nuanced in Cavell, "strenuous" in George Kateb), Donoghue presents an "arch-radical" with "no interest in providing professors of politics with a theory of

in the Intimations Ode, culminating in that "light of all our day" to which Emerson repeatedly refers.

Finally, taken as a whole, what follows is less an "influence study" than an exploration of elective affinities, family resemblances, and analogies binding together in a visionary company a number of highly individual writers exhibiting "original Genius of a high order"—especially, though not exclusively, Milton, Coleridge, Wordsworth, and Emerson, with more peripheral attention to Carlyle, Hazlitt, Keats, Thoreau, Whitman, Nietzsche, Yeats, and Stevens. As a study in what McFarland has called "the paradox of originality," the book should have some appeal for those interested in the Anglo-American Romantic tradition and the innovations of the individual talent, especially in the capacity of a man of genius such as Emerson not only (to revert to the language of the Wordsworth essay with which we began) to absorb his "predecessors" but also, using them as a stimulus to his own creative power, to "shape his own road." In two notebook poems of the early 1830s, Emerson announces, "I dare attempt to lay out my own road," only to concede that no one is really "separate / But all are cisterns of one central sea / All are mouthpieces of the Eternal Word" (*JMN* 4:47, 65). That these Romantic cisterns and mouthpieces, the particular figures and particular themes focused on, are also bound together in the mind of the present writer may be less a matter of arbitrariness than a final illustration of the mind's quest to find what Coleridge called multeity in unity. Last and hardly least, the present exploration has offered an opportunity to express gratitude to my own benefactors and to experience again the pleasure of merely circulating among them—a pleasure conveyed, I hope, to those who read these pages.

society." Emerson was "really an anarchist; necessarily so, since he cultivated the thrill of glorifying his own mind and refused to let any other consideration thwart him" (*The American Classics: A Personal Essay* [New Haven and London: Yale University Press, 2005], 42–43).

Part I

PRELIMINARIES

Chapter 1

Introduction

THE CRITICS AND THE PARTICIPANTS

I distrust the received scholarship that sees Emerson as the American disciple of Wordsworth, Coleridge, and Carlyle, and thus indirectly a weak descendent of German High Transcendentalism.

—HAROLD BLOOM, *Agon: Towards a Theory of Revisionism*

Coleridge meant more to Emerson than a mere transmitter of Kantian metaphysics. Coleridge felt that he had a system of philosophy of his own to present, and we are almost led to think that Emerson discovered it. Besides . . . only Coleridge was prepared to present to Emerson the Wordsworth that everyone now accepts, the greatest figure of the Romantic movement. I like to think of Coleridge coming to Emerson as he came to Wordsworth and opening the springs of his intellectual being.

—FRANK T. THOMPSON, "Emerson's Indebtedness to Coleridge"

In fact, it is impossible to imagine Emerson without Wordsworth's relocation of Milton's heaven of heavens within the human mind or Coleridge on imagination.

—ROBERT WEISBUCH, "Post-colonial Emerson and the Erasure of Europe"

The thankful receiver bears a plentiful harvest.

—WILLIAM BLAKE, *The Marriage of Heaven and Hell*

Readers of this book are rather less likely to be familiar with Frank Thompson, writing more than three-quarters of a century ago, than with that formidable presence, and self-confessed "fierce Emersonian," Harold Bloom. Bloom is, of course, fully aware of Emerson's affiliation with the British High Romantics, whom he readily concedes were Emerson's immediate precursors. Indeed, he registers, in *The Western Canon: The Books and School of the Ages,* the telling point that "Emerson had the same relation to Wordsworth's poetry that Johnson had to Pope's, and like Johnson, Emerson chose the other harmony of prose"—an observation applicable as well to James Joyce, who, in the shadow of Yeats, made a similarly wise choice. But Bloom, for once unengaged by "influence," prefers to dwell on the poetic progeny rather than the progenitors of his gnostic and shamanic Emerson, a man free of any received doctrine. He is also, supposedly, free of the attendant anxiety. In *The Anxiety of Influence: A Theory of Poetry,* Bloom, at first ambivalent about Emerson's denial of influence, eventually allies him with Nietzsche and discovers that his own theory "owes more" to them than to those who, like Johnson and Coleridge, acknowledge the burden of the past. I quote the passage since it brings together many of those who figure centrally in the present book—though, while rightly stressing Nietzsche as "heir to Goethe," Bloom oddly neglects to mention his direct indebtedness to Emerson:

> Nietzsche, like Emerson, is one of the great deniers of anxiety-as-influence. . . . Nietzsche, as he always insisted, was the heir of Goethe in his strangely optimistic refusal to regard the poetical past as primarily an obstacle to fresh creation. Goethe, like Milton, absorbed precursors with a gusto evidently precluding anxiety. Nietzsche owed as much to Goethe and to Schopenhauer as Emerson did to Wordsworth and Coleridge, but Nietzsche, like Emerson, did not feel the chill of being darkened by a precursor's shadow. "Influence," to Nietzsche, meant vitalization.[1]

That is certainly what it meant as well to both of Nietzsche's precursors, Goethe *and* Emerson. If I have chosen to dwell in detail on what Emerson actually "owed to . . . Wordsworth and Coleridge," it is not meant to be completely at the expense of the power of the recipient, a reader whose mental activity and self-reliance enabled him, for the most part, to engage his precursors as a stimulus rather than an obstacle to his own creativity.

Bloom's sweeping dismissal, in *Agon,* of any and all traditions that would diminish Emerson's American, Adamic, and Orphic originality, was anticipated by Lewis Mumford and Stephen Whicher. "With most of the

1. Bloom, *Western Canon,* 194; *Anxiety of Influence,* 31, 50.

resources of the past at his command, Emerson achieved nakedness," said Mumford in the same year that Thompson's essay was published. "The past for Emerson was neither a prescription nor a burden: it was rather an aesthetic experience." For Whicher, author of what for most of the half century since it was published was the single most influential study, Emerson, "borrowing hints and phrases from all around him," and "from Coleridge more than anyone else," nevertheless retains his "independence, . . . freedom and mastery," a power "overflowing all the authority of the past."[2] This anticipates the formulation of biographer Robert D. Richardson Jr., whose superb *Emerson: The Mind on Fire,* reveals an omnivorous reader whose mental fire was fueled from many sources, many "benefactors," each becoming, however, merely a "premonition of Emerson." Morton M. Sealts Jr. concludes the introduction to *Emerson on the Scholar,* his harvesting of a lifetime of study, by emphasizing that his "primary focus" is on the course of Emerson's "own thinking over the years, not on his literary sources. Though Emerson read widely, his goal as a writer and speaker was original creation." And Sealts quotes Emerson's famous strictures, from "The American Scholar," on the peripheral importance of the work of others ("Books are for the scholar's idle times"), in order to justifiably claim that his focus is in the Emersonian spirit and honors "these characteristic pronouncements." In an "influence" study combining tact and erudition, Gustaaf Van Cromphout, whose subject is Goethe as Emerson's exemplar in the exploration of self-definition and modernity, balances Emerson's indebtedness with his creative receptivity:

> Emerson put into practice his (and Goethe's) theory of influence; his relationship to Goethe's works took the form not of passive acceptance but of constructive engagement. Therefore, he interpreted, extended, transformed, and absorbed Goethean concepts and insights, and thus integrated them into his own thinking. My aim is to identify Goethe's contributions before their complete integration into Emerson's thought, that is, before Emerson's creativity made them completely Emersonian.

2. Mumford, *The Golden Day: A Study in American Literature and Culture,* 16; Whicher, *Freedom and Fate: An Inner Life of Ralph Waldo Emerson,* 56. Here is Bloom's grand dismissal of any traditional alignment that would undermine Emerson's uniqueness: "The native strain in Emerson rejected any received religion. I am unable to accept a distinguished tradition in scholarship that goes from Perry Miller to Sacvan Bercovitch, and that finds Emerson to have been the heir, however involuntary, of the line that goes from Mathers to Jonathan Edwards." Following his "distrust" of the Romantic alignment, he concludes: "And to fill out my litany of rejections, I cannot find Emerson to be another Perennial Philosophy Neoplatonist, mixing some Swedenborgianism into the froth of [the Cambridge Platonist Ralph] Cudworth and Thomas Taylor" (*Agon,* 162–63).

More recently, and perhaps most memorably, Joel Porte, after referring to the wide reading of Emerson, a man "as well versed in world culture of anyone in his time," his head filled with the writings of, among others, Plato and Shakespeare, Milton and Goethe, Wordsworth and Carlyle, concludes: "Like some immense Moby-Dick of the mind, he strained all this intellectual plankton through himself and it became Emerson."[3]

It seems petty to disagree, and, at least for the most part, I *don't.* Besides, I like what Emerson, who characterized his own and Goethe's cases in much the same way, would have called the "valor" of such statements. Still, these accounts of the assimilation process suggest a serenity and ease that seem—well, "Emersonian" in something of the caricatural sense. Bloom's insistence that Emerson was *utterly* free of that "anxiety of influence" Bloom himself made famous, though an excessive claim, is clarified by a statement of Emerson quoted by Bloom in the introduction to his recent survey, *Genius.* That title gestures toward Emerson and Emerson's mentor Coleridge (the book is strewn with innumerable contrasts of genius and talent); its subtitle, *A Mosaic of One Hundred Exemplary Creative Minds,* hints at such precursor texts as Emerson's *Representative Men,* Carlyle's *On Heroes and Hero-Worship,* and Nietzsche's *Untimely Meditations,* celebrating the "highest" and most "valuable exemplars." Transposing his former combative imagery from Oedipal psychodrama between poetic fathers and sons to psychomachia (what matters now is the "*agon* with the self," and the fear that one's own powers are inadequate), Bloom embraces Goethean-Emersonian "gratitude," epitomized in Blake's axiom that the bearer of "a plentiful harvest" must be a "thankful receiver." He bases his book, asserts Bloom, on his "belief that appreciation is a better mode for the understanding of achievement than are all the analytical kinds of accounting for the emergence of exceptional individuals. Appreciation may judge, but always with gratitude, and frequently with awe and wonder." And he goes on in his introduction to *Genius* to quote Emerson from "Uses of Great

3. Sealts, *Emerson on the Scholar,* 7; Van Cromphout, *Emerson's Modernity and the Example of Goethe,* 10; Porte, "Introduction: Representing America—the Emerson Legacy," 12. Discussing *Nature,* Richardson insists on Emerson's originality, even as he enumerates some of his sources. "*Nature* is a modern Stoic handbook, Marcus Aurelius in New England. It is also a modern version of Plato, an American version of Kant." Yet "Emerson is at last neither derivative nor eclectic. His insistence on grounding thought, action, ethics, religion, and art in individual experience is his center. He makes a modern case for the idea that the mind common to the universe is disclosed to each individual through his or her nature. In this respect, Plato is a Greek premonition of Emerson, Marcus Aurelius a Roman one, and Kant a German one." Though fully aware of the crucial influence of Coleridge and (to a lesser extent) of Wordsworth, Richardson omits those "British premonitions" of Emerson (*Mind on Fire,* 233, 234). Sealts also engages in some erasure of Coleridge and Wordsworth.

Men," the introduction to *Representative Men:* "We need not fear excessive influence. A more generous trust is permitted. Serve the great" (*E&L* 629).[4]

Such generosity almost makes the question of plagiarism, let alone simple influence, irrelevant. Confronted by Thomas De Quincey's evidence, first broached in *Tait's Edinburgh Magazine,* of the recently deceased Coleridge's plagiarism of Schelling, Emerson wondered in his journal, "Why could not he have said generously like Goethe I owe all" (*JMN* 5:59).[5] Emerson would have known that Coleridge states, in *Biographia Literaria,* that it was in Schelling's *System of Transcendental Idealism* (1800) and in his *Naturphilosophie* (1806) that "I first found a genial coincidence with much that I had toiled out for myself, and a powerful assistance in what I still had to do" (*BL* 1:160). No doubt, though that does not explain the *verbal* as well as conceptual similarities between, say, the opening sections of the *Naturphilosophie* and the important twelfth chapter of the *Biographia.* In a private note recorded between the publication of Schelling's two texts, Coleridge had himself raised, and made an attempt to answer, Emerson's more than rhetorical question. To the future readers of his projected "Metaphys[ical] Works," Coleridge remarks that in his preface he "should say—Once & [for] all read [Johann] Tetens, Kant, Fichte, &c—& there you will trace or if you are on the hunt, track me." And Schelling? Trackers may find him notable by his absence, or reduction to "&c," in this list of German precursors. Coleridge next poses and responds to Emerson's, and our, question about scrupulously "acknowledging" his obligations. He could not, he says, "without a lie," because in "a multitude of glaring resemblances," the thought

> had been mine, formed & fully formed in my own mind, before I had ever heard of these Writers, because to have fixed on the partic[ular] instances in which I have really been indebted to these Writers would have [been] very hard if possible, to me who read for truth & self-satisfaction, not to make a book, & who always rejoiced & was jubilant when I found my own ideas well expressed already by others . . . & lastly, let me say, because (I am proud perhaps but) I seem to know, that much of the matter remains my own, and that the Soul is *mine.* (*CN* 2:2375)

Whatever self-justification and defensive track covering may be going on here, this private note is not to be reduced to a pilferer's rationalizations; there is too much vestigial truth in the statement for it to be dismissed—

4. Bloom, *Genius,* 9.
5. See De Quincey, *The Collected Writings of Thomas De Quincey,* 1:152–53.

as there is in the remarks of Emerson (quoted in my own Preface) about a man of genius, when he "thinks happily" and finds "keen delight" in the thoughts of others that seem the garments "in which my own thought is pleased to dress itself," finding "liberty and glory" and "no foot-track in the field he traverses." What Bloom calls receptive "gratitude," even "awe and wonder," and Emerson "a more generous trust," surely *is* permitted, especially when the thoughts to which we are indebted turn out to be our own, or part of a more inclusive whole.

Perhaps ripeness *is* all, but although one is moved, in the case of both Emerson and Bloom, by this late, generous, and anxiety-free appreciation of greatness, it supersedes without completely erasing the earlier Oedipal struggle between an ephebe and his exemplar-precursors. Indeed, even in this very text, Emerson had, just three paragraphs before the words Bloom cites, recalled the admonition in "Self-Reliance" that imitation is "suicide," as well as crucial passages in the "American Scholar" address: both its proto-Nietzschean admiration of great exemplars *and* the old warning about being "warped" by the attraction of books "out of my own orbit, and made a satellite instead of a system" (*E&L* 57). "What indemnification is one great man for populations of pigmies!" exclaims Emerson in "Uses of Great Men," yet "a new danger appears in the excess of influence of the great man. His attractions warp us from our place. We have become underlings and intellectual suicides" (*E&L* 627). But this is to undercut the *primary* point being made by Emerson in this introduction, which ends on the generous note that "great men exist that there may be greater men," so that "the germs of love and benefit may be multiplied" (*E&L* 632). Significantly, Emerson here echoes his own benefactors, "the poet Wordsworth," who, faced with exceptional men, "asked, 'What one is, why may not millions be?' Why not? Knowledge exists to be imparted" ("Progress of Culture," *W* 8:226, quoting *P* 13:87–89), and Coleridge, who wished to be judged by "the number and value of the minds" he had "excited into activity, and supplied with the germs of their after-growth!" (*BL* 1:220).

So Bloom is quite right to emphasize Emerson's advocacy of a more generous trust and service to the great. But to catch the flavor of this compendium, the idiosyncratic brilliance of Bloom, his now famously hyperbolic contempt for the state of his own often untrusting and ungenerous profession ("the school of *ressentiment*") and for contemporary culture in general, as well as the centrality of Emerson to the entire enterprise, one other passage should be quoted. A brief synopsis titled "Genius: A Personal Definition," it is also worth quoting because Bloom replicates Emerson's own polarity—the assertion of a fierce originality even amid the visionary company of his Romantic precursors—and focuses on the importance of the God within. Pondering his "mosaic of one hundred exemplary creative minds," he arrives, says Bloom,

> at a tentative and personal definition of literary genius. The question of genius was a perpetual concern of Ralph Waldo Emerson, who is the mind of America. . . . For Emerson, genius was the God within, the self of "Self-Reliance." That self, in Emerson, therefore is not constituted by history, by society, by languages. It is aboriginal. I entirely agree. . . . Fierce originality is one crucial component of literary genius, but this originality itself is always canonical, in that it recognizes and comes to terms with precursors. . . . If genius is the God within, I need to seek it there, in the abyss of the aboriginal self, an entity unknown to nearly all our current Explainers, in the intellectually forlorn universities and in the media's dark Satanic mills.[6]

Although a little of this goes a long way, it strikes a chord with me. Because "originality" is, along with "power," still the Bloomian sine qua non in determining genius, Bloom's Emerson, though recognizing and coming to terms with his precursors, retains his vital originality. I want to quote Bloom, and say, "I *entirely* agree," but I cannot repress my own, "Yes, but . . ." It is hard to quibble when faced with an authority having eidetic command of the very tradition to which he refuses to relegate Emerson. Nevertheless, I consider the present book a kind of vindication of Frank Thompson. Since his work in the 1920s, Emerson's indebtedness, as we have seen, has been not only acknowledged but also, often without much demonstration, taken for granted, and, again, absorbed into that capacious maw of Emersonian originality. Most recently, a fine balance between indebtedness and American originality has been achieved in Richard Gravil's *Romantic Dialogues,* a study that among other things demonstrates the rightness of Robert Weisbuch's groundbreaking *Atlantic Double-Cross.* My own debt to Weisbuch and Gravil takes two forms: appreciation of their

6. Bloom, *Genius,* 5, 11. For all Emerson's centrality, in Bloom's thinking and in this book, the chapter on him is essentially devoted to Emerson on Shakespeare. This has its own Bloomian logic since Bloom has become the Bardolater-in-chief, but it is typical of his maddening organization. The many and brilliant things he has to say about Emerson are scattered throughout the book; needless to say, there is neither index nor footnotes. Bloom wears his hostile notices in the *New York Times Book Review* as badges of honor, and he received another badge with *Genius.* But even this hostile reviewer, Judith Shulevitz, concludes: "What Bloom loves he loves with a largeness of heart that he transforms into a fundamental critical principle, and at a time when critics vie with one another to see who can manifest the greatest degree of suspicion, such generosity is nothing to laugh at" (11).

richly informed discussions of the transatlantic dialogue and gratitude that, as a non-Americanist, I read their work *after* I had worked through my own connections between Emerson and his British Romantic precursors.

Frank Thompson was not the first, though he was perhaps the most lucid and precise, to trace the links between German idealism, British Romanticism (Wordsworth, Coleridge, Carlyle), and American Transcendentalism. Coleridge's role, both as an original thinker and as a transmitter of German thought, was understood early on by Henry Hedge and later by, for example, G. W. Cooke, whose biographical and intellectual background study, *Ralph Waldo Emerson: His Life, Writings, and Philosophy* (1880), was published the year before Emerson's death and four years before the first book-length biography, by Oliver Wendell Holmes. In a single decade early in the twentieth century, four scholars—H. C. Goddard (*Studies in New England Transcendentalism* [1908]), F. B. Wahr (*Emerson and Goethe* [1915]), H. G. Gray (*Emerson: A Statement of New England Transcendentalism as Expressed in the Philosophy of Its Chief Exponent* [1917]), and Paul Elmer More (in his contribution to the 1918 edition of the *Cambridge History of American Literature*)—all stressed the importance of Coleridge to the Transcendentalists, in his own right, and as the principal conduit to German idealism, particularly to Kant and Schelling. Nevertheless, Thompson, writing in the midtwenties, focused impressively on Coleridge, who, as a philosopher, "influenced both Carlyle and Wordsworth" and so shaped Emerson's reading of both. Thus, until "we have considered in more detail . . . what Emerson owed to Carlyle and Wordsworth, we cannot pass final judgment upon what he gained from Coleridge." Pending that final judgment, Thompson's modest but affirmative conclusion (quoted fully in my epigraph) is that Coleridge, no mere transmitter of Kantian metaphysics, presented Emerson not only with "the Wordsworth that everyone now accepts" but also with a body of critical thought and crucial distinctions that, just as they had for Wordsworth, "opened the springs of [Emerson's] intellectual being."[7]

7. Thompson, "Emerson's Indebtedness to Coleridge," 55, 57, 58, 64, 76. This and two other articles stem from Thompson's dissertation (University of North Carolina, 1925). In the second of these articles, "Emerson and Carlyle" (1927), Thompson discusses that well-known relationship. In the third, "Emerson's Theory and Practice of Poetry," he makes the unsurprising distinction Emerson made between Coleridge, a methodical philosopher and brilliant literary critic, and Wordsworth, who became for Emerson—after he read Coleridge *on* Wordsworth—the greatest and sanest poet of the age and superior to all but Milton and Shakespeare. As Thompson had noted in the first of these articles, Emerson returned to Wordsworth, after his earlier desultory encounters, "with the praise of Coleridge ringing in his ears" (58).

Thompson's study of the Coleridge-Emerson connection has been succeeded, but not quite superseded, by the work of such critics as J. O McCormick, Alexander Kern, Mark Ledbetter, Richard E. Brantley, Barbara Packer, and, in several places, Anthony John Harding, along with Weisbuch and Gravil.[8] But my original debt is still to Thompson, that early laborer in the vineyard—specifically to the perceptive and persuasive but often neglected essay cited, "Emerson's Indebtedness to Coleridge," and to a lesser article published two years later, "Emerson's Theory and Practice of Poetry," in which Thompson identified the "Ode: Intimations of Immortality from Recollections of Early Childhood" as the Transcendentalists' "supreme" poem and "the medium by which we can measure what Emerson gained from Wordsworth."[9]

Even Bloom agrees that the Great Ode is "the single poem that haunts all of the Transcendentalists," a poem (as my former Le Moyne colleague Gordon Boudreau graphically put it in his fine book on Thoreau) that came "readily to the lips" of reading Americans at this period and, indeed, "gnawed at the psychic vitals of virtually every New England Transcendentalist." Emerson himself, aware of flaws—some "torpid places in his mind," some "egotistic puerilities"—in Wordsworth's poetry, had no reservations whatever when it came to *this* poem, for him a triumph of intellect and imagination, and a genuine voyage of exploration. The ode was "the high-water-mark which the intellect has reached in this age. New means were employed, and new realms added to the empire of the muse, by his courage" (*E&L* 928). In a subsequent journal entry, he declares that in writing the ode, a way was "made through the void by this finer Columbus" (*JMN* 14:98), a phrase he liked enough to repeat frequently.[10] Yet, as has been observed by Eric Carlson, editor of and commentator on a compendium

8. The essays by Kern and Packer have already been noted in the prologue. The other references are to Ledbetter, "Changing Sensibilities: The Puritan Mind and the Romantic Revolution in Early American Religious Thought," in *The Interpretation of Belief: Coleridge, Schleirmacher and Romanticism*, ed. David Jasper, 176–84; Brantley, *Coordinates of Anglo-American Romanticism: Wesley, Edwards, Carlyle and Emerson*, 129–33; and Harding, "Coleridge and Transcendentalism," "James Marsh as Editor," and, in greatest depth, *Coleridge and the Inspired Word.*

9. F. T. Thompson, "Theory and Practice," 1183, 1184. I later apply the ninth stanza of the ode (which, as Thompson realizes, becomes, after 1831, the most important in the poem for Emerson) to the autobiographical crisis of 1842: the death of Waldo, followed by the elegy for the boy, "Threnody."

10. As Armida Jennings Gilbert has pointed out in her dissertation, Emerson "was to repeat this *bon mot* frequently in the coming years: to William Makepeace Thackeray at a dinner party in December 1855, to Charles Woodbury in their conversations around 1865, and finally in an interview [reprinted in the *Chicago Tribune,* January 10, 1874] for *Frank Leslie's Illustrated Newspaper,* when he added, 'Wordsworth is the great English poet, in spite of Peter Bell'" ("Emerson and the English Romantic Poets," 180–81, 189nn8–10).

of Emerson's literary criticism, "despite the fifty-year history of the influence of this ode on Emerson, one finds no extended criticism of it by him." Though Emerson seldom engages in practical criticism or close reading, *this* does seem a lacuna worth noting. What is lacking in explicitness and quantity of comment is made up for in a network of allusion (almost exclusively to the ode's crucial ninth stanza) notable for its passionate intensity, both philosophic and personal.[11]

A second, no less significant, lacuna in Emerson's work is the absence of a full-scale lecture or essay on the criticism and thinking of Samuel Taylor Coleridge. Given the subject hinted at in the subtitle of this book (an allusion to the passage in the Intimations Ode that most haunted Emerson), these may seem like convenient gaps indeed: less lacunae than simple omissions, and omissions of more concern to me than to Emerson. I may be suspected of starting with a preemptive response—No!—to three questions likely to be raised by readers: Are we in for a tendentious and finally unpersuasive argument in which the author makes too much of "influences" that Emerson noted but seldom publicly commented on in a sustained way? Are we being set up for yet another postmodern argument that what is absent (or peripheral) is more significant than what is present (or central)? Are we to be subjected to a tedious and mean-spirited attempt to diminish the very emphases we (general readers as well as Emerson's major commentators) preeminently associate with Emerson—self-reliant individualism, an original relation to the universe, the championship of creativity over suicidal imitation? While I hope the answer *is* no, especially when it comes to mean-spiritedness, it is, of course, up to the individual reader to determine whether I have avoided these pitfalls in exposing the extent of Emerson's indebtedness to Coleridge and Wordsworth.

Mingling direct influence and analogy, family resemblance and creative swerve, I will be tracing lines of affinity and affiliation connecting Emerson, Coleridge, and Wordsworth—along with their common precursor, Milton. Because, in many ways, Emerson really *is* as original as he claims, I *do* risk undermining that originality, a sordid enterprise at best and perhaps no more productive than obsessing, as many commentators have, on Coleridgean plagiarism. Not so incidentally, *this* accusation, a charge that has long bedeviled the study of Coleridge, was addressed by Emerson, who—although he wondered why Coleridge could not have said, "generously like Goethe," that he owed all—refused the temptation to wag a chas-

11. Bloom, "Bacchus and Merlin: The Dialectic of Romantic Poetry," 295; Boudreau, *The Roots of Walden and the Tree of Life,* 6, 152; Carlson, *Emerson's Literary Criticism,* 198.

tising finger.[12] Responding to an essay on Coleridge sent to him by the author (James Hutchinson Stirling) in draft form, Emerson said he found the criticisms of character and "unacknowledged borrowings . . . painful, yet I fear irrefutable." Yet—humane, perceptive, and fully aware of *his own* debt to Coleridge—he instantly went on to insist on "merits understated" by Stirling and to reaffirm Coleridge's role as the crucial "benefactor to that generation of which he had the teaching." Recognizing that "original power in men is usually accompanied with assimilating power," Emerson observed in a journal entry later incorporated into "Quotation and Originality," "I value in Coleridge his excellent knowledge & quotations, perhaps as much, possibly more, than his original suggestions." And in another journal entry not used in that essay, he proclaims that "the quoter's selection honors & celebrates the author. The quoter gives more fame than he receives aid. Thus Coleridge." It takes one to know one. As his own great aid to reflection, Coleridge is a thinker Emerson himself often quotes and paraphrases in stimulating his own originality (*JMN* 16: 67, 82; cf. 8:59).[13]

The potential diminution of Emerson's uniqueness is at the heart of Bloom's dismissal of any traditional alignments, which would fail to account for his hero's "American difference." Of course, the *Romantic* "scholarly tradition" is the one tradition Bloom "distrusts" rather than rejects outright. In fact, there is an irony in the fact that the most strenuous insistence on Emersonian originality should come from Bloom, for, as Lee Rust Brown has observed, Emerson's project was essentially "shaped" by the European Romantic principles he imported from Coleridge, and the "chief figure" in the "critical movement that discovered powerful and surprising things to say about" European Romanticism, Harold Bloom, "has also been largely responsible for reestablishing Emerson, for American

12. Here is the passage of Goethe Emerson has in mind, both here and in "Quotation and Originality": "People are always talking about originality; but what do they mean? As soon as we are born, the world begins to work upon us, and this goes on to the end. And, after all, what can we call our own except energy, strength, and will? If I could give an account of all that I owe to great predecessors and contemporaries, there would not be much left over" (*Gesprache,* 3:204, no. 2331, quoted in McFarland, *Pantheist Tradition,* 45).

13. The manuscript to which Emerson was responding in the first comment quoted was Stirling's "De Quincey and Coleridge upon Kant" (to which Emerson referred simply as "Coleridge"); it was later included in Stirling's *Jerrold, Tennyson and Macauley with Other Critical Essays* (1868). One wonders: in finding Coleridge's "merits understated" by Stirling, was Emerson aware that his mentor had not only revised but also *reversed* Kant on the elevation of Intuition over Understanding? And had Emerson read De Quincey not only on Coleridge's plagiarisms but also on the crucial distinction between "the literature of *knowledge*" and "the literature of *power*"?

critics, as a writer who stands capably, even centrally, in the high ground occupied by the men he visited in Britain," with Emerson indebted to "Coleridge, especially." For Brown, writing between Weisbuch and Gravil,

> The transatlantic pathways opened up (though not necessarily explored) by recent criticism make it more readily possible to find, at least in outline, most of Emerson's mature stances of self-reliance and orphic originality already prescribed in the work of his romantic forebears. All this makes the issue of Emerson's foundational role in American literary life a more complex one, as the boundaries between what Emerson founded and what he imported become harder to see.[14]

Is Emerson, then, all a matter of filtration? It would be not only paradoxical but a supreme irony as well, if American Transcendentalism—whose chief spokesman exalted self-reliance, individual insight, instinct, originality, and an intuitive divinity within and repudiated outworn institutions and established authority—were to be reduced to an *un*original movement, with *all* of its ideas having their antecedents in earlier religious, philosophic, and literary traditions.[15] Of all the rhapsodic celebrators of originality and liberation from the dead weight of the past, Emerson seems the most oracular, the least equivocal. And so, at times, he is—as in the insistence, in "Self-Reliance," that to be a man one "must be a nonconformist," since "nothing is at last sacred but the integrity of your own mind." "What have I to do," he asks rhetorically, "with the sacredness of traditions, if I live wholly from within?" (*E&L* 261, 262). "Insist on yourself, never imitate," never rely on "the adopted talents of another":

> It is only as a man puts off all foreign support, and stands alone, that I see him to be strong and to prevail. He is weaker by every recruit to his banner. Is not a man better than a town? . . . He who knows that power is inborn, that he is weak because he has looked for good out of himself and elsewhere, and so perceiving, throws himself unhesitatingly on his thought, instantly rights himself, stands in the erect position, commands his limbs, works miracles. (*E&L* 278, 281–82)

14. Brown, *The Emerson Museum: Practical Romanticism and the Pursuit of the Whole,* 89–90. See also Perry Miller, "New England's Transcendentalism: Native or Imported?" first published in 1964 and now available in *EPP.*

15. Of Emersonian Transcendentalism's obvious "sources," whether indigenous (New England Puritanism), perennial (Platonism, ancient and Cambridge Neoplatonism, Swedenborgianism), or "Oriental" (India's sacred texts, the Persian poetry of Saadi and Hafīz), the *most* crucial is Romanticism, both British and German, with Goethe in a class by himself and with Coleridge and Carlyle Emerson's principal guides to the idealist philosophers, Kant, Schelling, Fichte, and Jacobi.

Even earlier, in a journal entry of November 15, 1834, Emerson vowed: "Henceforth I design not to utter any speech, poem, or book that is not entirely & peculiarly my own work." But even *that* entry had begun: "Hail to the quiet fields of my fathers!" (*JMN* 4:335). For Emerson is alternately a radical individualist and a no less impassioned venerator of tradition, a grateful acknowledger of the debt every thinker and writer owes to the past. "The truth," he says in an 1835 lecture, "The Age of Fable," is that

> all works of literature are Janus-faced and look to the future and to the past. Shakespear, Pope, and Dryden borrow from Chaucer and shine by his borrowed light. . . . There never was an original writer. Each is a link in an endless chain. To receive and to impart are the talents of the poet and he ought to possess both in equal degrees. . . . Every great man, as Homer, Milton, Bacon, and Aristotle, necessarily takes up into himself all the wisdom that is current in his time. (*EL* 1:284–85)

Indeed, our debt is "so massive" that one might say, as he does in that splendid late lecture "Quotation and Originality," "there is no pure originality. All minds quote."[16]

In the text just cited, Emerson has a related but more graphic image than the Coleridgean "filter." As an example of the sort of "borrowing" that is "often brave enough, and comes of magnanimity and stoutness," Emerson quotes from one of his favorite Wordsworth poems, "Character of the Happy Warrior": "Wordsworth's hero acting 'on the plan which pleased his boyish thought,' is Schiller's 'Tell him to reverence the dreams of his youth,' and earlier, Bacon's *'Consilia juventutis plus divinitatis habent'* [The urgings of one's youthful spirit have more of divinity in them]. In Romantic literature examples of this vamping abound" (*EPP* 323). This "vamping," or literary vampirism, had been prefigured from the lecture's opening image, of "flies, aphides, gnats and innumerable parasites, and even infant . . . mammals," all remarkable for the "extreme content they take in suction." In a library, we see "the same function on a higher plane, performed with like ardor" (*EPP* 319). But although "by necessity, by proclivity, and by delight, we all quote," there is, of course, a danger; later in "Quotation and Originality," Emerson tells us—anticipating the negative aspect of Yeats's positive image of "Italy sucking at the dugs of Greece"—that those for whom this suction is the whole of their relationship to books and to the past are "invalided," becoming inferior mimics with "nothing of their own."

16. This 1859 lecture, first published in 1868, may be found in *W,* vol. 8. Omitted from *E&P,* it is reprinted in its entirety in *EPP* 319–33. For convenience I quote from this text, here, p. 320.

> In every kind of parasite, when Nature has finished an aphis, a teredo or a vampire bat,—an excellent sucking-pipe to tap another animal, or a mistletoe or dodder among plants,—the self-supplying organs wither and dwindle, as being superfluous. In common prudence there is an early limit to this leaning on an original. In literature, quotation is good only when the writer whom I follow goes my way, and, being better mounted than I, gives me a cast, as we say; but if I like the gay equipage so well as to go out of my road, I had better have gone afoot. (*EPP* 324)[17]

That "I had better" echoes a more famous Emersonian saying, from "The American Scholar": "Books . . . are for nothing but to inspire. I had better never see a book, than to be warped by its attraction clean out of my own orbit, and made a satellite instead of a system" (*E&L* 57). Still, in "Quotation and Originality," as in the "American Scholar" address, Emerson characteristically alternates—in this case between deploring a debilitating dependence on books and celebrating their potential as a source of inspiration, a stimulus to one's own creative power. "In the highest civilization the book is still the highest delight. . . . We expect a great man to be a good reader; or in proportion to the spontaneous power should be the assimilating power" (*EPP* 320). He expands on this point later in "Quotation and Originality," in a passage that combines Coleridge (including his invaluable "distinctions") with the seminal 1833 essay *upon* Coleridge by Emerson's friend Hedge—from whom Emerson borrowed the sentence, "Next to the writer of a good book, he most deserves our gratitude, who," by quoting and so drawing our attention to that book, "helps to increase its circulation."[18] For good measure, Emerson also incorporates the revivifying power of Shakespeare (quoting, in the process, Walter Savage Landor's *Imaginary Conversations*) and an anecdote (presumably passed on to him during his actual conversation in 1847 with Thomas De Quincey) highlighting the creative assimilation and assertiveness of Wordsworth:

> Original power is usually accompanied with assimilating power, and we value in Coleridge his excellent knowledge and quotations perhaps as much, possibly more, than his original suggestions. If an author give us just distinc-

17. With *The Waste Land,* Conrad Aiken observes, Eliot had created what Pound referred to as "a literature of literature," a poem admittedly "brilliant" and "important" but so riddled with quotations and allusions that it amounted to "a kind of parasitic growth on literature, a sort of mistletoe." I suspect Emerson, whatever he would have made of the poem's tone, would have applauded Eliot's use of quotations and have seen in *The Waste Land* what Pound saw: the European tradition, whether assimilated or regurgitated, "made new." See Aiken, "An Anatomy of Melancholy," 54–55.

18. Compare that brilliant quoter and subversive bête noir of orthodox Calvinism, Pierre Bayle, who said, in a sentence that epitomizes his own work: "There is not less wit nor less invention in applying rightly a thought one finds in a book, than in being the first author of that thought" (*Dictionnaire historique et critique* [1697–1702]).

tions, inspiring lessons, or imaginative poetry, it is not so important to us whose they are. If we are fired and guided by these, we know him as a benefactor. . . . We respect ourselves the more that we know them.

Next to the originator of a good sentence is the first quoter of it. . . . Genius borrows nobly. When Shakespeare is charged with debts to his authors, Landor replies: "Yet he was more original than his originals. He breathed upon dead bodies and brought them into life." . . . Wordsworth, as soon as he heard a good thing, caught it up, meditated upon it, and very soon reproduced it in his conversation and writing. If De Quincey said, "That is what I told you," he replied, "No: that is mine,—mine, and not yours." On the whole, we like the valor of it. (*EPP* 325, 326)

Emerson liked the "valor" of it because, for all the "originality" (supposed *and* authentic) of his own movement, he was fully aware that it stood in precisely the sort of relationship to Wordsworth, Coleridge, and Carlyle (and the German idealist tradition filtered to him through the latter two) that required him, at least in the early and middle work, to say with Wordsworth, "No, that is mine,—mine, and not yours," or, with Coleridge, even when he *was* profoundly indebted, "that much of the matter remains my own, and that the Soul is *mine*" (*CN* 2:2375). Whatever the truth in such claims, the claimants often protest too much.

I have already referred to that pioneering essay by Henry Hedge, which concludes splendidly by referring us to Coleridge's own implicit claim to the "minds" he had "excited into activity, and supplied with the germs of their after-growth!" (*BL* 1:220). A half century later, recalling for James Elliot Cabot the origins of what he casually refers to as "the 'Transcendental' business," Hedge reports that he, Emerson, George Ripley, and an unnamed fourth (George Putnam) chanced to confer together on the "unsatisfactory" state of current opinion "in theology & philosophy," particularly "the reigning sensuous philosophy dating from Locke," on which their Unitarian theology was based. "The writings of Coleridge recently edited by Marsh & some of Carlyle's earlier essays" (he specifies "Characteristics" and "Signs of the Times") had "created a ferment in the minds of some of the young clergy of that day." Though there was, even after they were joined by others, "no club, properly speaking," there *was* "a promise in the air of a new era of intellectual life."[19]

Supporting testimony comes, less belatedly but no less definitively, from other key Transcendentalist players. The year 1859, the year Emerson gave

19. Hedge to Cabot, December 8, 1883, in Ronald A. Bosco and Joel Myerson, eds., *Emerson in His Own Time*, 100–101.

his lecture on "Quotation and Originality," was also the year in which, just before his premature death at the age of fifty, Theodore Parker—who had attended the first organized meeting of "Hedge's Club"—offered an account of the movement's origins, a summary most notable for its moving tribute to Emerson and its singling out of Transcendentalism's primary precursors. "The brilliant genius of Emerson," he said—playing upon the Wordsworthian "star-like virtue . . . / Shedding benignant influence," in the "Prospectus"—"rose in the winter nights, and hung over Boston, drawing the eyes of ingenuous young people to look up to that star . . . as it led them forward along new paths, and towards new hope. America had seen no such light before; it is not less a blessed wonder now." With the "weakening" of the "power of the old supernaturalism," men were set—says Parker, echoing Emerson's "moral constitution of man" and his celebration of a human spirit that "builds itself a house" (*E&L* 48)—to study "the moral constitution of man more wisely than before, . . . laying the foundation of which many a beneficent structure was soon to rise. The writings of Wordsworth were becoming familiar to the thoughtful lovers of nature and man, drawing men to natural piety." What is—to quote the final line of the epigraph to the Intimations Ode, the line Parker is remembering—"Bound each to each by natural piety" is not only "nature and man" but also British Romanticism and American Transcendentalism.

Parker goes on immediately to refer to Carlyle, his imagery suggesting particular emphasis, as in Hedge and Emerson himself, on Carlyle's great early essay "Characteristics" (1831) and *Sartor Resartus,* introduced to the United States through the efforts of Emerson.

> Carlyle's works got reprinted in Boston, diffusing a strong, and then also, a healthy influence on old and young. The writings of Coleridge were reprinted in America, all of them "aids to reflection," and brilliant with the scattered sparks of genius;[20] they incited many to think, more especially young Trinitarian ministers; and, spite of the lack of both historic and philosophic accuracy, and the utter absence of all proportion in his writings; spite of his haste, his vanity, prejudice, sophistry, confusion, and opium—he yet did great service in New England, helping to emancipate enthralled minds.[21]

20. Parker's "all" embraces *Biographia Literaria* as well as, of course, Marsh's two editions of Coleridge, *Aids to Reflection,* in 1829, accompanied by the important "Preliminary Essay," and *The Friend,* in 1831, the latter the immediate stimulus for Hedge's essay, though Emerson was reading the English edition before that.

21. This 1859 letter, published by Parker's church as *Theodore Parker's Experience as a Minister,* is quoted in Perry Miller, ed., *The Transcendentalists: An Anthology,* 487. Parker also pays tribute to the French works of Victor Cousin, "more systematic and more profound as a whole." They also "became familiar to the Americans," at least secondhand—"reviews and translations going where the eloquent original was not

His own superb mind evidently enthralled to the (understandable) caricature of Coleridge as a political apostate, opium eater, and disorganized genius, Parker could only partly see that the new paths illuminated by the brilliant genius of his friend were the very paths lit for Emerson by Coleridge *and* by the Wordsworth revealed to him *by* Coleridge.

The most significant retrospective is from Emerson himself, in the form of his one hundredth and final lecture at the Concord Lyceum, on February 4, 1880, though much of the material dated back to lectures given in 1867.[22] Emerson had been present at the very origin—his meeting with Hedge, Ripley, and Putnam—of what would become the "Club." It took place on September 8, 1836, auspiciously enough the day before the publication of *Nature.* By the second meeting a week and a half later, the group of four had grown to ten (it never exceeded two dozen), including Parker, Bronson Alcott (that idealist who, said Emerson, put "Coleridge . . . in the zenith"), Orestes Brownson, and Margaret Fuller's friend James Freeman Clarke. Leery at first, and preferring the stimulating one-on-one of his recent and challenging three weeks of discussions with the "very accomplished & very intelligent" Fuller, Emerson came to enjoy the gatherings, and it was he who arranged for women to join the group, starting with Elizabeth Hoar and the formidable Fuller, who, "with her radiant genius & fiery heart, was perhaps the chief centre that drew so many & so various individuals to a seeming union" (*JMN* 16:21–22).[23]

Emerson went on to tell his audience, in terms that proved to have legs, that "there are always two parties, the party of the Past and the party of the Future, the Establishment and the Movement." At times the resistance between the two "is reanimated, the schism runs under the world and appears in Literature, Philosophy, Church, State, and social customs." The schism reanimated by Transcendentalism seemed "a war" of sorts, "a crack in Nature, which split every church" and divided politics—with the "new conscience" addressing such issues as slavery. (Though the great antislavery activist in the group was Parker, "our Savanarola," as Emerson called him, Thoreau and, eventually, Emerson himself became ardent abolitionists.)

---

heard." As with Coleridge, the effect was emancipatory, helping to "free the young mind from the gross sensationalism of the academic philosophy on the one side, and the grosser supernaturalism of the ecclesiastic theology on the other." Cousin's influence upon Emerson himself was intense but short-lived.

22. Emerson, "Historic Notes of Life and Letters in New England," first published in the *Atlantic Monthly* in 1883. Most of the lecture has been printed in Miller, *The Transcendentalists: An Anthology,* 494–502, and, more recently in *EPP* 415–27.

23. This praise, however, was confined to the journal from which his notes derived; in the lecture as delivered in 1880, we hear only of "some noble papers" Fuller published in the short-lived but important Transcendentalist organ the *Dial* (1840–1844), which for a time she edited.

"The key to the period appeared to be that mind had become aware of itself," men growing "reflective and intellectual." Though this can be overstressed, the effect seemed more solitary than social. Sacrifice of the individual to the state was reversed; the "modern mind," said Emerson, "believed that the nation existed for the individual." Margaret Fuller had said long before, "Man is not made for society, but society is made for man," but she was echoing Emerson's old emphasis, in "Self-Reliance," on the nonconformist, self-trusting individual, who takes his way *from* communal man, not *to* man, since "society everywhere is in conspiracy against the manhood of every one of its members" (*E&L* 261). In fact, Emerson's next statement in the 1880 lecture will recall for us that movement of Wordsworth and Coleridge away from radical politics, particularly activist in Coleridge's case: the transmutation of anticipated political revolution into a revolution that was cognitive, imaginative, immanent: "This idea [of the individual], roughly written in revolutions and national movements, in the mind of the philosopher had more precision; the individual is the world."

Wordsworth and Coleridge, those early rebels, had earned their move to quietism in consequence of a genuine revulsion (also motivated, at first and in part, by fear of domestic repression) from the bloody course of the French Revolution and its Napoleonic aftermath. Confronted with no such earthshaking crisis, some of the young American Transcendentalists, Emerson prominent among them, had nevertheless participated in a form of the complex Romantic *ricorso* from activist engagement to "quietist" withdrawal, a preference for solitary contemplation over social commitment that would soon be complicated by the need to publicly address the increasingly momentous issue of slavery. Having registered that initial inward movement, Emerson turns to literature, Goethe's *Faust,* "the most remarkable literary work of the age," having "for its hero and subject precisely this introversion"—the "look inwards" he associated, in "England," with "Wordsworth" (*JMN* 3:71). Germany also supplied the pivotal philosophers: Hegel and, first and foremost, Kant, who had made "the best catalogue of the human faculties and the best analysis of the mind."

In an 1866 note that was a main source for his later lecture, Emerson said of "the name of Transcendentalism" that "nobody knows who gave [it], or when it was first applied" (*EPP* 529), though a quarter century earlier, he had implied, in his January 1842 lecture titled "The Transcendentalist," that the name derived from Kant. Although "there is no such thing as a Transcendentalist *party*" and "no pure Transcendentalist," Emerson told those in his audience at the Masonic Temple in Boston something he supposed was "well known to most" of them:

> The Idealism of the present day acquired the name of Transcendental, from the use of that term by Immanuel Kant, of Konigsberg, who replied to the skeptical philosophy of Locke, which insisted that there was nothing in the intellect which was not previously in the experience of the senses, by showing that there was a very important class of ideas, or imperative forms, which did not come by experience, but through which experience is acquired; that these were intuitions of the mind itself; and he denominated them *Transcendental* forms. The extraordinary profoundness and precision of that man's thinking have given vogue to his nomenclature, in Europe and America, to the extent that whatever belongs to the class of intuitive thought is popularly called at the present day *Transcendental.* (*E&L* 198–99)[24]

But, as we shall see, what for Emerson was "very important," even "imperative," as indicated by his climactic emphasis on "*intuitions* of the mind" and "the class of the *intuitive,*" was *not* at all the paramount emphasis of Kant, but of the thinker through whom Emerson received his Kant: Samuel Taylor Coleridge.

Emerson's denial, in the 1842 talk, of the existence of an American Transcendentalist "party" was reaffirmed in the late lecture. Did the beneficiaries of all this ferment he has been describing constitute a movement? In retrospect, Emerson even more blandly reports that even at the time he and his friends were "surprised at this rumor" of a school, a sect. Of course, *at the time*—and to both themselves and their enemies—they certainly gave the *appearance* of participating in a vanguard movement determined to overcome America's cultural dependence on Europe, as well as to launch a revolt against Lockean epistemology, spiritless rationalism and mechanism, crass materialism, and what they took to be the cruder forms of historical Christianity. In the movement's heyday, and in the privacy of his journals, Emerson was considerably more expansive on the subject, claiming, for example (in an entry for October 23, 1841), that "Society" ought to see

> that this movement called the Transcendental . . . has an interest very near & dear to them. That it has a necessary place in history is a Fact not to be overlooked, not possibly to be prevented, and however discredited to the heedless & to the moderate & conservative persons by the foibles or inadequacies

24. The reference to Kant's "precision" suggests a less than intimate familiarity with either the original or the revised version of Kant's *Critique of Pure Reason,* both notorious for their difficulty, their sometimes almost impenetrable obscurity. Though praised by Emerson for his "extraordinary . . . precision," Kant himself winningly and accurately acknowledged in his own clarification and condensation of the main ideas in the first and revised editions of the *Critique* that he had been "dry, obscure, . . . and moreover long-winded."

> of those who partake the movement[,] yet it is the pledge & the herald of all that is dear to the human heart, grand & inspiring to human faith. I think the genius of this age more philosophical than any other has been, righter in its aims, truer, with less fear, less fable, less mixture of any sort. (*EPP* 506)

In short, Transcendentalism, however much a "party of the Future" arrayed against "the party of the Past," had its roots in "the *genius of this age.*" Emerson's conclusion on this particular point, a reworking of a July 1866 journal entry, at once downplays the notion of a "movement" and reveals Transcendentalism's essentially British transatlantic roots. It may be that "there prevailed at that time a general belief in Boston that there was some concert of *doctrinaires* to establish certain opinions and inaugurate some movement in literature, philosophy, and religion." If so, it was a "design" of which "the supposed conspirators were quite innocent; for there was no concert, and only here and there two or three men or women who read and wrote, each alone, with unusual vivacity. Perhaps they only agreed on having fallen upon Coleridge and Wordsworth and Goethe, and then on Carlyle, with pleasure and sympathy" (*EPP* 421).

The indispensable figures, then, aside from Goethe, were part of the British Romantic movement—the immediate antecedent movement to American Transcendentalism, with no language barrier, whether German or (in the case of Cousin) French. Appropriately, the first of the lecture's two epigraphs (the other is from Emerson himself) is a quatrain that clarifies and supports Emerson's own distinction between the old and new, the parties of the past and of the future. It also casually epitomizes the project of regeneration announced by Wordsworth and Coleridge in the more elevated formulations of their own visionary, transformative movement:

> Of old things all are over old,
> Of good things none are good enough;—
> We'll show that we can help to frame
> A world of other stuff.
>
> (*EPP* 415)

The lines, later echoed by Tennyson's Ulysses, are from a favorite poem of Emerson's, "Rob Roy's Grave," by Wordsworth.[25] And the figure *Wordsworth* had, in Emerson's phrase, "fallen upon" to help him frame another

25. Wordsworth, "Rob Roy's Grave," lines 85–88; *WP* 1:654. The poem was written in 1805–1806, during the apogee of Napoléon's power. Wordsworth actually envisaged "our brave Rob Roy," who loved "The *liberty* of Man," as arisen from that grave and joining the struggle against France's "present Boast." Had it been your lot, he tells the dead hero, to be now living, "Thou wouldst have nobly stirred thyself, / And battled for the Right" (95, 103–8).

and better world during a "time / Of dereliction and dismay" was Coleridge: to whose guiding and goading letter of September 1799 Wordsworth is directly responding in the passage of *The Prelude* to which I have just alluded. Together Wordsworth and Coleridge, "joint-labourers in the work," would, as "Prophets of Nature," speak to men of "their deliverance," providing (in the final lines of *The Prelude*):

> A lasting inspiration, sanctified
> By reason, blest by faith: what we have loved,
> Others will love, and we will teach them how;
> Instruct them how the mind of man becomes
> A thousand times more beautiful than the earth
> On which he dwells, above this frame of things
> (Which, 'mid all the revolutions in the hopes
> And fears of men, doth still remain unchanged)
> In beauty exalted, as it is itself
> Of quality and fabric more divine.
> (*P* 14:443–54)[26]

Wordsworth's insistence that the mind of man was far superior to nature was the primary contribution of his joint laborer, Coleridge, Romanticism's chief exponent of the dominance of Reason—man's divine mind, his genius and imagination. It was this dominion of the human mind that Emerson synopsized—paradoxically, in his book titled *Nature*—as "the kingdom of man over nature" (*E&L* 49). In addition, Coleridge was the thinker who had given Emerson and the other Transcendentalists the distinctions they needed to clarify their own philosophy: above all, that between intuitive Reason and mere understanding. This distinction, applied to those with whom we actually engage, was at the heart of Emerson's belated endorsement of Hedge's proposal to establish what became the "Club." Thus, Coleridgean thinking was a demonstrable part of the motive and origin of the American movement we know as Transcendentalism. Hedge might have been troubled by the intellectual pedigree of Coleridge's un-Kantian distinction; Emerson was delighted to be armed with it, ready to be used as part of his "magazine of power."

26. "Faith," in line 444, was a late addition; for years the phrase had read, "By reason and by truth . . ." The previous passage ("this time / Of dereliction and dismay") is from 2:440–41. In the full passage (2:432–41), Wordsworth is responding to a September 1799 letter in which Coleridge implored his friend to write a blank-verse poem "addressed to those who, in consequence of the complete failure of the French Revolution, have thrown up all hopes of the amelioration of mankind" and are sinking into a "selfishness" disguised as "domestic attachment, and contempt for visionary *philosophes*. It would do great good, and might form a part of 'The Recluse'" (*CL* 1:527).

Having apologized for his delay in responding to Hedge's "project of the symposium," Emerson reveals in a letter of July 20, 1836, his reasons for hesitation. In the process, he also reveals the characteristic working of his mind, a mixture of seemingly indolent rumination and insight, working speculatively, serpentinely, and quietly to cover a whole trajectory. It was, in short, the undulatory *via illuminativa* of the intuitive Reason rather than the materialist way of the men of the world and of mere understanding, practical types seeking mathematical proof, *quod erat demonstrandum.*

> The men of strong understanding exercise an influence even baleful upon my power of conversation which is only sufficient to convey my meaning in calm times & quiet places when it is permitted to stretch out its sloven length & by many fragments of thought to dot out the whole curve. The men of strong understanding are a menacing trenchant race—they cut me short—they drive me into a corner—I must not suggest, I must define—& they hold me responsible for a demonstration of every sentiment I endorse. (*L* 2:29)

Having anticipated Yeats's favorite among the sayings of Nietzsche's Zarathustra, "Am I a barrel of memories that I can give you my reasons?"[27] Emerson continues by anticipating his own essay "Friendship," with its definition of true communion: "Two may talk and one may hear, but three cannot take part in a conversation of the most sincere and searching sort" (*E&L* 349). That was especially true if the group included men of understanding, practical types demanding demonstrative proofs.

> Whilst therefore I cannot sufficiently give thanks for the existence of this class, without whom there could not be either porridge or politics I do, for my particular, thoroughly avoid & defy them. But it happens that some individuals of the Reasonable class are endowed with Understanding; then again I am struck dumb & can scarcely give an intelligible sign of sympathy & respect. For this reason I have never found that uplifting & enlargement from the conversation of many which I find in the society of one faithful person. (*L* 2:29–30)

If Hedge, reading this letter, had not at this point given up hope for his projected symposium, it would be because, knowing Emerson, he could anticipate a volte-face. And he would have been right. After elaborating on his reluctance to collaborate in such a symposium, reasons that illuminate his resistance to communal projects in general, Emerson commits himself, confessing that "the experiment you propose has never been fairly tried by us." He calls for a preliminary meeting, urging that membership,

27. Yeats, *The Letters of W. B. Yeats,* 650.

initially limited by Hedge to ministers, be expanded so "you . . . admit Mr. [Bronson] Alcott over the professional limits, for he is a God-made priest," an idealist who sets "Coleridge . . . in the Zenith" (*L* 2:30). In fact, Alcott, whose *Orphic Sayings* make him a prime candidate for the original of Emerson's "Orphic Poet" in the finale of *Nature,* is for Emerson a Wordsworthian as well as a Coleridgean figure. It was to Alcott, he would say late in life, that "Wordsworth should have come . . . for the origin of the Pedlar," that is, the Wanderer, the central figure in *The Excursion,* and the Wordsworthian speaker most frequently cited by Emerson.[28]

Emerson also refers to Alcott in this letter as a man "forever occupied with one problem—how spirit makes matter or how Be becomes Seem" (*L* 2:30). That problem, which has engaged all idealists and students of the Great Chain of Being, certainly occupied Coleridge—nowhere more specifically than in his various analyses of the seminal Chain-of-Being passage in *Paradise Lost.* Since those lines (5:469–90) are also at the heart of Emerson's legacy from Coleridge, I will end this Introduction, which I have already "permitted to stretch out its sloven length" beyond decent limits, and reserve to Chapter 2 a full discussion of the Milton passage, and its ramifications.

28. Charles J. Woodbury, *Talks with Ralph Waldo Emerson,* 99.

Chapter 2

Intuitive Reason

THE LIGHT OF ALL OUR DAY

Fancy and understanding, whence the soul
Reason receives, and reason is her being,
Discursive or intuitive. . . .

—John Milton's RAPHAEL, in *Paradise Lost*

Do you draw the distinction of Milton Coleridge & the Germans between Reason & Understanding[?] I think it a philosophy itself.

—RALPH WALDO EMERSON, in a letter to his brother Edward

High instincts . . . ;
Those shadowy recollections,
Which, be they what they may,
Are yet the fountain light of all our day . . .
. . . truths that wake,
To perish never. . . .

—WILLIAM WORDSWORTH, Intimations Ode

The passage from book 5 of *Paradise Lost* is foregrounded by Coleridge, by his American editor, and, in turn, by Emerson. My orienting text is the well-known letter of May 3, 1834, to his brother Edward, in which Emerson attributed the distinction between "Understanding" and the "eternal Reason" to the triumvirate "Milton Coleridge & the Germans." Like good Unitarians we can distill this trinity to one: Samuel Taylor Coleridge, the mediator between Emerson and Milton's archangel Raphael. That "winged

Seraph" arrives in Paradise in all his glory—"another morn / Risen on mid-noon" (*PL* 5:310–11). There he engages in sustained discussion with Adam, including, since Raphael had affably accepted an invitation to join in the midday meal, a disquisition on angelic digestion. That "ridiculous" topic, actually a dignifying of natural function related to his higher theme, soon yields to the sublime.

Raphael's more elevated theme is the Great Chain of Being—what the Jesuit Robert Bellarmine called (in his 1615 book of that title) the "Ascent of the Mind to God by a Ladder of Created Things," or, as Milton himself describes it later in book 5, the "Scale of Nature" (509). The process is Plotinian as well: a cyclical emanation of all created things from, and—providing they are not alienated by choosing evil—epistrophic return to, God. "There is nothing else but God," and wherever "I look / All things hasten back to him." So wrote Emerson in a poem whose Delphic title, "Know Thyself," he derived from Coleridge, who retained the Greek in titling his own poem (*JMN* 3:294; *W* 9:289–90). This hastening back to the divine is that famous Plotinian "flight of the alone to the Alone," cited by Emerson in a later journal entry (*JMN* 7:430) and in his essay on Swedenborg (*E&L* 663). To synopsize Milton's Scale of Nature: The primal matter from which arises all created being, whether called soul or body, emanates directly from God, infinite and incorruptible Spirit; the varieties of the efflux from the Deity, though radically one, are differentiated into an ascending series, from the lowest *inorganic* form up to the *vegetable,* thence to the *animal,* thence to the *human,* and so to the *angelic,* the first created and the nearest in nature to the divine original. The famous passage from *Paradise Lost* takes the form of a response. Asked to compare the "lowly" human and the "high" angelic, the "winged Hierarch" replies:

> O *Adam,* one Almighty is, from whom
> All things proceed, and up to him return,
> If not depraved from good: created all
> Such to perfection, one first matter all,
> Indued with various forms, various degrees
> Of substance, and in things that live, of life;
> But more refined, more spiritous, and pure,
> As nearer to him placed or nearer tending
> Each in their several active spheres assigned,
> Till body up to spirit work, in bounds
> Proportioned to each kind. So from the root
> Springs lighter the green stalk, from thence the leaves
> More airy, last the bright consummate flower
> Spirit odorous breathes; flowers and their fruit
> Man's nourishment, by gradual scale sublimed

> To vital spirits aspire, to animal,
> To intellectual, give both life and sense,
> Fancy and understanding, whence the soul
> Reason receives, and reason is her being,
> Discursive or intuitive; discourse
> Is oftest yours, the latter most is ours,
> Differing but in degree, of kind the same.
>
> (*PL* 5:469–90)

The lines present a traditional yet (given the up-and-down movement between spirit and matter and the natural and spiritual elaboration of the figure of the plant) dynamically revitalized poetic vision, one with momentous nineteenth-century consequences in both Old and New England. According to Raphael, "understanding," along with fancy, proceeds from "animal" to "intellectual." Higher up the aspiring *scala naturae,* or cosmic ladder, is Reason; this the "soul" receives, and Reason becomes "her being," soul's distinguishing characteristic. But just as there is both continuity and differentiation between "understanding" and "reason," so there is a significant overlap and subdistinction within reason itself, between "discursive" and "intuitive." Angels, hierarchically superior to human beings, usually reason *intuitively* (*intueri:* to look into), seeing things with immediacy and quickness, unlimited by ratiocinative processes of piecemeal, logical intellection. Yet Milton makes Raphael a monist. Rejecting traditional assumptions, he asserts that *both* angels and men possess "intuitive" *and* "discursive" reason, rational faculties that differ, not absolutely but only relatively—"in *degree.*" Thus, there is continuity rather than utter cleavage, as in Pauline and Augustinian dualism, between pure spirit and the human admixture of matter and spirit. "Discourse"—by which Milton meant, as Coleridge pointed out, discursive reason—is "oftest" human, "intuitive" reason "most" angelic. So angels are, at times at least, discursive, human beings intuitive—presumably when they most closely approximate the angelic.

In the final dozen lines—those Emerson has primarily in mind in the letter to his brother—Milton (through Raphael) is taking up concepts and distinctions with a long history, looking before and after: from Plato (*Republic* 533ff), through Saint Paul, Plotinus, Cornelius Agrippa, Aquinas, Dante (*Purgatorio* 18), Hooker's *Laws of Ecclesiastical Polity* (2:7), the Cambridge Platonists, Milton himself in *Comus* (459ff) and *De Doctrina Christiana* (1:7), and, of course, ahead to, for example, Pope (*Essay on Man,* 1: 233–46), Samuel Taylor Coleridge, and Ralph Waldo Emerson. According to Milton's angel, "by gradual scale sublimed," the natural is raised, the body refined to spirit. Milton's original text here may be 1 Corinthians 15, a Pauline passage Emerson himself alluded to in describing a fact, through contemplation, being "raised, transfigured; the corruptible has put on incorruption" (*E&L* 60–61). The transfiguring power is intuitive Reason.

In the letter to his brother Edward, Emerson next mentions "Coleridge," and for a very good reason. Emerson knew how important these lines of Milton were to Coleridge from his reading of *Aids to Reflection* (including the "Preliminary Essay" with which Marsh introduced his 1829 edition of that volume) and of *Biographia Literaria,* in the tenth chapter of which Coleridge quoted lines 485–90 of the Miltonic passage, subjecting them to close analysis and commentary (*BL* 1:172–74).[1] Unless Emerson ("in whose mind," as James Russell Lowell joshed, "all creation is duly respected / As parts of himself—just a little projected") could have projected himself into the future, to visit the Victoria and Albert Museum and leaf through Coleridge's annotations in his thirteen-volume set of Anderson's *Works of British Poets, with Prefaces, Biographical and Critical,* he would have no way of knowing that Coleridge had subjected these Miltonic lines to even more rigorous philosophic and spiritual scrutiny. The result was in accord with his consistent emphasis on Reason as a higher faculty than understanding. The annotator concluded that "matter can neither be *ground* or distilled into spirit," the "Spirit" being "an Island harbourless, and every way inaccessible," so that matter can exist only "as a mode of Spirit, and derivatively." What puzzled Bronson Alcott, as Emerson told Hedge, was just "how spirit makes matter or Be becomes Seem" (*L* 2:29–30). For Coleridge (the idealist whom Alcott set "in the Zenith"), the "most doubtful position in Milton's ascending series" in Raphael's speech was "the Derivation of Reason from the Understanding—without a medium."[2]

1. Coleridge led up to his citation by acknowledging that he was following Hooker, Milton, and others in designating "the *immediateness* of any act or object of knowledge by the word *intuition,* used sometimes objectively, even as we use the word, thought; now as *the* thought, or act of thinking, and now as *a* thought, or the object of our reflection." When he says that he is "re-introducing" the terms *objective* and *subjective,* Coleridge reveals his essentially Kantian reversal of Duns Scotus's *subjectivum* (the actual object of thought) and *objectivum* ("the thing as constituted though the perceiving mind"). In the new distinction, "I think" has, in his editors' apt synopsis, "transcendental significance and is the *a priori* condition of all knowledge" (*BL* 1:172–73n). "Lastly," Coleridge notes, "I have cautiously discriminated the terms, the REASON, and the UNDERSTANDING, encouraged and confirmed by the authority of our genuine divines, and philosophers, before the revolution." At this point, as though to clinch his argument (as he so often does by quoting Wordsworth's poetry), Coleridge quotes Milton's Raphael (*PL* 5:485–90), capitalizing the key terms.

2. Lowell, *A Fable for Critics,* 35–36. Coleridge's thirteen-volume set of *British Poets* (1794–1795) is in fact in the Victoria and Albert Museum, though my knowledge of the annotation comes from Roberta Florence Brinkley, ed., *Coleridge on the Seventeenth Century,* 589–90. His denigration of matter may explain his one error in transcribing the Miltonic passage as an epigraph to chapter 13 of *Biographia Literaria,* where Milton's "one first *matter* all" (line 472) becomes "one first *nature* all" (*BL* 1:295).

At a stroke, Coleridge in effect here seems to reverse the most significant of the two profound antimedieval concepts that "constitute the basis of [Milton's] thought: the metaphysical idea that matter is real and that there is no sharp distinction between spirit and matter, the one passing insensibly into the other."[3]

Though Emerson would not have known of this Coleridgean insistence on a gap in Milton's ascending series, he was familiar with Coleridge's innumerable oppositions of understanding and Reason and was aware of Coleridge's gloss on Milton's further distinction. "Milton opposes the discursive to the intuitive as the lower to the higher," says Coleridge in appendix C of *The Statesman's Manual.* The characteristic of the "discursive" understanding, he continues in this famous appendix, is "Clearness without Depth," producing "a knowledge of superficies without substance," so much so that it "entangles itself in contradictions." The "completing power," which "unites clearness with depth," is "the IMAGINATION, impregnated with which the understanding itself becomes intuitive, and a living power." Coleridge equates this Imagination with "REASON," by which he does not mean "abstract" or "scientific" reason, but Reason as the "integrated Spirit of the regenerated man, reason substantial and vital." *This* Reason, without being either the sense, the understanding, or the imagination, "contains all three within itself"; and Coleridge repairs to a pastiche of phrases from the Apocryphal Wisdom of Solomon to describe this power: "One only, yet manifold, overseeing all, and going through all understanding; the breath of God, and a pure influence from the glory of the Almighty; which remaining in itself regenerateth all other powers, and in all ages entering into holy souls maketh them friends of God and prophets." Viewed from a modern, skeptical perspective, a little of this seems too much, a matter less of philosophy than of assertive faith. As Coleridge remarked in 1829, "It is wonderful, how closely Reason and Imagination are connected and Religion the union of the two" (*LS* 69).[4]

Coleridge repeatedly makes this distinction between the "material" faculty, understanding, and the potentially "spiritual" faculty, Reason. Though, like the Transcendentalists he influenced, Coleridge focuses on the higher, "intuitive" Reason, he is also, for the most part, insistent in distinguishing understanding, a faculty shared by brutes and humans, from the lower or "discursive" reason—one explanation for his frequent citation of Hamlet's depiction of his mother, driven by lust to her o'erhasty remarriage, as worse than "a beast that wants [lacks] *discourse* of reason" (for example, see *AR*

3. James Holly Hanford, *A Milton Handbook,* 205.

4. Coleridge's 1829 remark was recorded on the flyleaf of a copy of vol. 2 of *The Friend* (1:203n).

218n, 219; and *LS* 69). It is not too much to say that Coleridge maintained a lifelong obsession with the lines Milton placed in the breathless mouth of his archangel.

And the import of those lines was communicated, via Coleridge, across the Atlantic. In the 1834 letter to his brother, Emerson makes precisely the idealist distinction between Reason and understanding Coleridge had made in the course of his amplification and alteration of the speech of Milton's angel. "Philosophy," Emerson tells Edward, "affirms that the outward world is only phenomenal," the everyday activities that become our "whole concern" and "whereof men make such account." This merely phenomenal world, what he calls in the finale to *Nature* "an accident and an effect," is, really, "a quite relative & temporary one—an intricate dream—the exhalation of the present state of the Soul—wherein the understanding works incessantly as if it were real but the eternal Reason[,] when now & then he is allowed to speak[,] declares it is an accident[,] a smoke nowise related to his permanent attributes." The "necessary" truths, said Emerson after encountering Coleridge's paramount distinction, *are* accessible, "scanned & approved by the Reason far above the Understanding" (*JMN* 3:236). As he would later say in the Divinity School Address, "There is no doctrine of the Reason which will bear to be taught by the Understanding" (*E&L* 80). It will not bear it because that higher Reason intuits indispensable truth, truth Coleridge set far above and different in kind from the inferential, logical, propositional, sense-based data derived from mere understanding.

After asking Edward if he joins him in drawing "the distinction of Milton Coleridge & the Germans between Reason & Understanding," Emerson describes that distinction as "a philosophy itself & like all truth very practical." He suggests that Edward put the letter temporarily aside and later

> take up the following dissertation: . . . Reason is the highest faculty of the soul—what we mean often by the soul itself; it never *reasons,* never proves, it simply perceives; it is vision. The Understanding toils all the time, compares, contrives, adds, argues, [it is] near sighted but strong-sighted, dwelling in the present[,] the expedient[,] the customary. Beasts have some understanding but no Reason. Reason is potentially perfect in every man—Understanding[,] in very different degrees of strength. (*L* 1:312)

Here, as later in *Nature* and in fact throughout his work, Emerson adheres precisely to Coleridge. Having connected—via the *Biographia*—Raphael's speech in book 5 with Kant's terms, though not Kant's distinction, Emerson goes on in the letter to further denigrate understanding at the expense of Reason, associated with our first spontaneous, visionary apprehensions of what is right and true:

> The thoughts of youth, & "first thought," are the revelations of Reason[,] the love of the beautiful & of Goodness as the highest beauty[,] the belief in the absolute & universal superiority of the Right & the True[.] But Understanding[,] that wrinkled calculator[,] the steward of our house to whom is committed the support of our animal life[,] contradicts evermore these affirmations of Reason & points at Custom & Interest & persuades one man that the declarations of Reason are false & another that they are at least impracticable. (*L* 1:312–13)

Yet we come to see later in life that "our Master," Reason, "was the Truth," that "our first & third thoughts usually coincide," revealing to us "the real[,] the absolute," even if we cannot logically demonstrate it; indeed, whatever the "Understanding sticks to it are chimeras he can prove it." As he will later put it in describing intuitive Reason in the essay "Intellect," we are to "trust instinct to the end though you can render no reason" (*E&L* 419). Here as so often, Emerson seems to be recalling Wordsworth's unprovable ("be they what they may. . .") but indisputable and undeniable intimations, the Great Ode's "master light of all our seeing." Unprovable by the machinations of mere understanding, Reason is the light that illuminates everything. Emerson concludes: "The manifold applications of the distinction to Literature[,] to the Church[,] to Life[,] will show how good a key it is. So hallelujah to the Reason forevermore" (*L* 1:313).[5]

❧ Hallelujah, indeed. But classifications and distinctions are one thing, imaginatively creative application another. That creativity, already evident in the "little allegory" Emerson presents to Edward,[6] would come to fru-

5. This crucial distinction has been discussed by several critics. Whicher has an admirably succinct note on Reason and understanding in his edited volume *Selections from Ralph Waldo Emerson: An Organic Anthology* (407n), though he misleadingly limits its constant use by Emerson to the 1830s. See also Joel Porte, *Emerson and Thoreau: Transcendentalists in Conflict,* 84–89; and Sherman Paul, *Emerson's Angle of Vision,* 38–39. Elsewhere, discussing Hart Crane's "Bridge of Estador," and fusing the Emersonian angle of vision and vision of the All with a Coleridge-derived Reason-understanding distinction, Paul says: "Like Emerson," Crane in this poem advises us "not to follow the Understanding in pursuit of particulars, but to follow the Reason (Imagination): 'Do not think too deeply, and you'll find/ A soul, an element in it all.' The spiritual element matters, the *all* of it" (*Hart's Bridge,* 55).

6. Barbara Packer—who earlier, in *Emerson's Fall: A New Interpretation of the Major Essays,* theorized his invention of "fables" to explain the fallenness of the world—depicts Emerson's explication in this letter of the Reason-understanding distinction as "a little allegory," in which the understanding, at first "merely the myopic servant of the visionary," turns, as "the allegory darkens," into "a voice of worldly prudence, and the individual who listens to its promptings instead of to the Reason's is, like Peter in Gethsemane, denying the true Christ he will someday acknowledge again in tears and repentance" ("The Transcendentalists," 356).

ition in the work Emerson would produce in the next astonishing decade, beginning with the seminal text *Nature,* half of its chapters organized on the basis of that Miltonic-Kantian hybrid: Coleridge's distinction between the Lockean and the spiritual-imaginative; between understanding and discursive reason on the one hand and, on the other, the intuitive Reason, which reconciles what mere understanding perceives as "contradictions" and allies us with the angels. In the wake of Marsh's edition of *Aids to Reflection,* all the Transcendentalists scurried about applying this distinction, seizing on a rock against which empiricism and doubt could not prevail: the conception of a divine Reason that was transcendent yet interior, here, now, and within the individual. There is no calculating the many personal benefactions, the spiritual, intellectual, and emotional solace that crossed the ocean in the form of Coleridge's crucial distinction.[7] But few of us today read, say, James Freeman Clarke or, for that matter, *Aids to Reflection;* we *do* read Emerson.

In addition to *Aids to Reflection,* Emerson found in *Biographia Literaria* another primary Coleridgean source to draw on in linking "Milton Coleridge & the Germans." As he knew, Coleridge had quoted almost the whole of the Miltonic passage (all but the last two and a half lines) as an epigraph to the famous thirteenth chapter, "On the Imagination, or Esemplastic Power." The suspicion that Milton along with the third in Emerson's list, "the Germans," came together because of that tertium quid, "Coleridge," is reinforced by the discussion of the crucial terms in Emerson's letter, a discussion that follows precisely Coleridge's modification, transformation, and distortion of the teaching on this subject by the "venerable Sage of Koenisberg" (*BL* 1:297), Kant—to give a local habitation

7. One example: When a senior, John Bates, wrote to university president James Marsh in February 1840 perplexed as to how election "can be made a *reasonable* doctrine," Marsh addressed "the two cardinal doctrines of a divine government and the free agency and accountability of man" as "*incomprehensible,*" an "apparent contradiction" to "our finite understandings." Yet "both doctrines are true." The "philosophical view," he said, is "best stated" in *Aids to Reflection* in a passage holding that "each individual is concerned with the doctrine only as it is *practical and of immediate reference to his own character and condition.*" If the young man ascribed his conversion not to his own "foresight or wisdom" but to "the grace of God," then "do you not practically believe in the doctrine of election?" The difficulty, Marsh noted, is aggravated by some "hard sayings of Calvin and his more zealous followers," urging unduly the points of doctrine in apparent conflict, instead of "suggesting the true ground of solution," which demanded "an explicit belief or assent of the understanding to doctrines which *for the understanding are* contradictory and irreconcilable. Whereas it is only by a consciousness more or less distinct that the truth transcends our understandings and in this consciousness, yielding to the authority of reason and our moral convictions, that we can receive these articles of faith in singleness of heart" (Duffy, *Coleridge's American Disciples,* 226–28; italics in original). Perplexities resolved, Bates later entered the ministry.

and a name to the primary figure who stands for "the Germans" in Emerson's letter.

In keeping with his Miltonic and occasionally more than Miltonic distinction between Reason and mere understanding, Coleridge wants to make his earlier authorities accord with the new philosophic thought from Germany. He wants, in short, to accommodate anti-Lockean Kantian idealism to all that he had learned from Plato and his followers—from the Neoplatonists to "our genuine divines, and philosophers, before the revolution" (*BL* 1:174), that is, the native Cambridge Platonists and other English writers prior to the Glorious Revolution of 1688. This tradition, and Scholasticism as well, are explicitly *spiritual* in orientation and emphasis. Coleridge's commitment to this Christianized perennial philosophy culminated in his own insistence, in *Aids to Reflection,* on Reason as an indwelling Platonic light: reflection as the "*seeing* light, the *enlightening* eye" (*AR* 15) that penetrates to ultimate truths.

It was of course precisely *this*—the idea that human reason can arrive at such ultimate truths—that Kant rejected in *The Critique of Pure Reason,* a rejection meant to be constructive, since he hoped to salvage a new non-traditional metaphysics by limiting its range. Kant's project may be said to take the form of a response to his two principal protagonists. Famously roused from his "dogmatic slumber" by Hume's skeptical challenge to rationalism, yet unwilling to accept Leibniz's assertion that thought can reveal the whole universe of possible entities, Kant tried to salvage whatever of rationalism could survive the wrecking ball of Hume's empiricist assault.

That assault had been felt across the ocean as well. From his early twenties on, Emerson resisted, yet remained fascinated by, Hume's potentially nihilistic challenge. Indeed, it was to a great extent Hume's skeptical denial that truth can ever be attained that Emerson, and Transcendentalism in general, set out to refute, a refutation armed principally with Coleridge's version of Kant. Extrapolating from his denial of a rational basis for the principle of causality, Hume had concluded that reason provides no standard to which objective reality must conform. The claim that "every event has a cause" is *not* "necessarily" but only "contingently" true; the necessity we impute to the maxim is the result of our mental processing of sensory impressions received when we regularly observe conjoined events (such as flames and heat) and out of that experience develop a habit of mind that gives us our idea of cause and effect. Thus, "causality" is reduced to subjective effects and merely practical purposes. Thought is naturalistic, instrumental, limited to the experiential; we can never, whatever our delusive aspirations, know the nature of ultimate reality.

Registering the impact of Hume's "irrefutable" critique, Kant agreed that human knowledge was limited to things as they appear to us because of our mode of experiencing them; ultimate reality, "things-in-themselves," we can never know. Speculative reason reveals to us the *idea* of the Infinite, the Unlimited. But although we can, to take a crucial example, form the idea of an omniscient, omnipotent Deity, we can have no rational guarantee of the objective truth of such a Being. We cannot "know" God as we know sensuous objects. But how is objective knowledge, even of the experiential world, possible? In the first *Critique,* Kant presents a "two-world" vision: a *noumenal* realm, forever beyond the reach of "pure reason," and a knowable world of *phenomena,* at first passively received but then actively ordered by forms, such as Space and Time, which are "in the mind," a priori, that is, independent of sensory experience. This emphasis on an active, orchestrating mind resembles Leibniz's concept of pure reason, self-legislating and possessed of creative power. But Kant, agreeing with Hume rather than Leibniz, denies that reason, out of its own inherent resources, can apprehend the immense realm of possibility. In the following passage, from section 2 ("On the Origin of Ideas") of *Enquiry Concerning Human Understanding,* Hume presents, and simultaneously rejects as a false belief, precisely what had seemed to Leibniz a wonderful truth, and which would later strike Coleridge and Wordsworth as—to quote the Intimations Ode—a "vision splendid" exemplifying "truths that wake, to perish never": an intuitive, imaginative power enabling us, "in an instant," to "travel" to the very shores of eternity. "Nothing, at first view," notes Hume,

> may seem more unbounded than the thought of man, which not only escapes all human power and authority, but is not even restrained within the limits of nature and reality. To . . . join incongruous shapes . . . costs the imagination no more trouble than to conceive the most natural and familiar objects. And while the *body is confined* to one planet, along which it creeps with pain and difficulty; the *thought can in an instant transport us into the most distant regions of the universe; or even beyond the universe, into the unbounded*. . . . What never was seen, or heard of, may yet be conceived; nor is any thing beyond the power of thought, except what implies an absolute contradiction.

Having anticipated, even as he rejects it, the principal Romantic power, Hume immediately limits Imagination to what Coleridge would later call the Fancy, and Reason to Coleridge's understanding: the lower terms, in each case, reduced by Coleridge to simple, uncreative arrangers of sensory materials. And Hume concludes—and this is my final reason for quoting the passage at length—by unintentionally prefiguring the Romantic divinity within: the godlike self, in which "God" becomes, when they are at their most creatively audacious, just another name for Wordsworth or Emerson or Wallace Stevens. Though our thought "seems," says Hume, "to possess" the "unbounded liberty" he has just noted, we find, on closer examination, "that it is really confined within very narrow limits, and that all this creative power of the mind amounts to no more than the faculty of compounding, transposing, augmenting, or diminishing the materials afforded to us by the senses and experience." When, for example, we think of a "golden mountain," or a "virtuous horse," we merely join two formerly known ideas, *gold* and *mountain, virtue* and *horse.* Indeed, when we analyze our ideas, even the most sublime, we invariably find that they "resolve themselves into such simple ideas as were copied from a precedent feeling or sentiment. Even those ideas, which, at first, seem the most wide of this origin, are found, upon a nearer scrutiny, to be derived from it. The idea of God, as meaning an infinitely intelligent, wise, and good Being, arises from *reflecting on the operations of our own mind,* and augmenting, without limit, those qualities of goodness and wisdom."[8]

The Humean critique of miracles and prophecy, assent to which are matters of a man's being "moved by faith" (an assent that "subverts all the principles of his understanding"), as well as this strictly empiricist derivation of the "idea of God," will remind us that the Kant roused by Hume was out to save more than philosophy. Kant did not want to sacrifice religion on the altar of what many saw as the irresolvable skepticism of the equally plausible contradictions inherent in his own "three antinomies." He was, of course, aware of the consternation he had caused by denying the possibility of any theoretical knowledge of Free Will, Immortality, and, above all, God. Reversing Hume's priorities, Kant pointedly observed in the preface to the 1787 edition of the first *Critique* that he could not "assume *God, freedom and immortality,*" ideas that transcend a reason that, he conceded to Hume, can "reach only to objects of possible experience.... Thus I had to deny *knowledge* in order to make room for *faith.*"[9]

But, as Emerson would later say, "nothing is got for nothing" (*E&L* 971). Whether one is resisting an overreaching Leibniz, one immediate object of Kant's refutation, or, later, the hubristic system of Hegel, whom Nietzsche accused of "Gothic heaven-storming," the cost is high: abdication of the belief that human reason, pure and unaided, can ever attain ultimate knowledge of things-in-themselves—truths about entities that by their very nature can never be objects of experience. Although God, Free Will, and

8. Hume, *Enquiry,* 13; italics added.

9. Ibid., 108; Kant, *Critique of Pure Reason,* Bxxx (117); B refers to the second edition, A to the first.

Immortality were beyond the reach of reason in the first *Critique,* Kant's emphasis on spontaneity and human freedom prepared the ground for their recuperation in the *Groundwork of the Metaphysics of Morals* (1785) and in its expansion, *The Critique of Practical Reason* (1788). But the denial of metaphysical knowledge, even if it was a provisional preclusion in the effort to save philosophy, was intolerable to Coleridge. Kant would have to be subjected to creative misprision by a reader who seems to have been aware of what he was doing.

Thus (and, unlike Hedge, Emerson was almost certainly unaware of this), Coleridge's Reason-understanding distinction starts from, but goes on to stretch, Kant's occasionally impenetrable but nevertheless wholly *cognitive* distinction between *Vernunft* (Reason) and *Verstand* (understanding). Kantian understanding integrates, builds upon, and forms "concepts" based on the sensory impressions apprehended by "Intuition" (*Anschauung*), whereas Reason transcends the senses and unifies our mental processes. Kant finds it necessary to distinguish between "sensory intuition" and "pure intuition," since no merely sensory intuition could supply a "representation" (*Vorstellung*) of such "ideal" infinities as Time and Space. But even pure intuitions can play no cognitive role until they are "synthesized" by a priori concepts of understanding; in fact, in order for a judgment to be possible, intuition had to be brought under, and apparently subordinated to, this combining power.

Coleridge, indeed every English translator, has rendered *Anschauung* as "intuition," since Kant's German word signified precisely what he had meant in his earlier work by the Latin word *intuitus.* But what he meant in both instances—immediate representations offered by the senses—catches only the notion of cognitive *immediacy* most of us, including Coleridge (*BL* 1:172), associate with "intuition," a word whose connotations in English have nothing to do with the Kantian limitation of the term to sensory apprehension. Thus, whereas Kant insists that "only from the unification" of understanding and intuition "can cognition arise," Coleridge saw not mutual dependence but apparent demotion, and preferred Milton's *privileging* of Intuition.[10]

Accordingly, when he takes up the German's distinction between Reason and understanding, Coleridge makes the former "transcendent" in a way specifically ruled out in *The Critique of Pure Reason;* in addition, he transforms Intuition (bracketed with but seemingly subservient to the understanding in Kant) into a virtual synonym (in keeping with Plotinus, Hooker, and Milton) for the highest Reason, that intuitive Reason of paramount importance to Coleridge and, through him, to Wordsworth as well

10. Kant, *Critique of Pure Reason,* B76/A52 (194; see also 709n39).

as, at a third remove, to Emerson. At his most Coleridgean, Wordsworth, in *The Prelude,* identifies this Miltonic "right reason" or "highest reason in a soul sublime" with intuitive Reason or the Imagination: a power of "clearest insight, amplitude of mind," or "reason in her most exalted mood" (*P* 12:26, 5:40, 13:169–70). In the final book, Wordsworth speaks of the "power" of "higher minds" (14:86, 90)—minds that "are truly from the Deity," for they are "powers" filled with blissful self-awareness,

> the consciousness
> Of Whom they are, habitually infused
> Through every image, and through every thought
> And all affections, by communion raised
> From earth to heaven, from human to divine;
> Hence endless occupation for the Soul,
> Whether discursive or intuitive.
>
> (*P* 14:112–20)

Predictably, Wordsworth, like Coleridge, places climactic emphasis on the intuitive Reason of Milton's archangel, the most heavenly and divine power to which humanity may aspire. Unlike Kant's *Vernunft,* cut off from any knowledge of the *noumenal* world, this higher or intuitive Reason of Coleridge, Wordsworth, and Emerson *is* capable of creative insight into things-in-themselves, ultimate reality: the divine life within us and abroad. For them, knowledge need not be "subverted" (as in Hume) or provisionally "denied" (as in Kant) to make room for faith; it is coterminous with faith, or at least with a visionary faculty in *some* sense "divine."

Indeed, for Coleridge Reason is the luminous source of our spiritual "intimations of immortality." In a letter of October 13, 1806, to Thomas Clarkson, Coleridge, asked to explain "the difference" between "Vernunft und Verstand," identifies "Understanding" as "that Faculty of the Soul which apprehends and retains the mere notices of Experience"—figure, magnitude, color of objects, "all the mere [phenomena] of our nature." Reason, on the other hand, is not dependent on experience; indeed, "Experience itself would be inconceivable without" this faculty:

> Reason is therefore most eminently the Revelation of an immortal soul, and its best Synonime—it is the forma formans, which contains in itself the soul of its own conceptions. Nay it is highly probable, that the contemplation of essential Form as remaining the same thro' all varieties of color and magnitude and development, as in the acorn even as in the Oak, first gave to the mind the ideas, by which it explained to itself those notices of its Immortality revealed to it by its conscience. (*CL* 2:1198–99)

Thus, knowledge of the *noumenal* world, prescinded from in the first *Critique,* becomes the main region of Coleridge's spiritualized Reason. The valorization of *intuition* in his further crucial distinction between "discursive" and "intuitive" Reason, deriving essentially from Plotinus and from Raphael's speech in book 5 of *Paradise Lost,* has no support in Kant, for whom sensory intuition is merely the "sensible," object-apprehending faculty, whereas, as just noted, even pure intuition, without which concepts are merely empty formal rules, requires *combination with* concepts. In fact, and famously, in the second paragraph of the "Transcendental Logic" section, we are told, "Without sensibility no object would be given to us, and without understanding no object would be thought. Thoughts without content are empty, intuitions without concepts [formed by that very "understanding" denigrated by Coleridge and his followers] are blind."[11] Paradoxically, then, what for Kant (intuition without understanding) was "blind" (even though *Anschauung* is German for "viewing") became, for the British Romantics and American Transcendentalists, precisely Coleridge's "seeing light," Wordsworth's "master light of all [their] seeing": the faculty divine that in effect usurped what Kant meant by pure Reason.

Following Coleridge, Emerson too wanted to stress continuity rather than differences between Milton and Coleridge on the one hand, Kant and the post-Kantian German idealists on the other. He links—without commas, almost as if they were indivisible—"Milton Coleridge & the Germans." He continues in the letter to tell his brother that "Reason" is not only "the highest faculty of the soul" but, in fact, "the soul itself," a faculty that, in the discursive sense, "never reasons" and *is* "vision." "Let me guide your eye"—Emerson would later invite the Harvard Divinity School seniors and faculty—to what he considered the crucial point: "The intuition of the moral sentiment is an insight of the perfection of the laws of the soul"; while "the doors of the Temple stand open, night and day, before every man, and the oracles of this truth cease never, it is guarded by one stern condition; this, namely; it is an intuition" (*E&L* 76, 79).

It was precisely such visionary intuition that Coleridge identified with Plotinian "highest and intuitive knowledge as distinguished from the discursive, or in the language of Wordsworth, 'the vision and the faculty divine'" (*BL* 1:241, quoting *E* 1:79). We can be reasonably sure that Emerson is remembering *this* passage of the *Biographia* as well, not only because of the similarity of his language in this 1834 letter and four years later in the Divinity School Address but also because, as we will see, he too quotes

11. Ibid., B75/A51 (193–94).

prominently, and in several places, the very Ennead of Plotinus that Coleridge is here glossing with the help of Wordsworth.[12]

In the letter to Edward, Emerson, like Coleridge but decidedly unlike Kant, reduces understanding to an incessantly toiling but "near-sighted" and "wrinkled calculator," capable only of "adding and arguing." This degenerate version of understanding, repeated in *Nature,* dwells in the chimeras of "the present, the expedient, the customary," a mere "steward" of the temporary "house" of our "animal life." Intuitive Reason, on the other hand, is our "Master," source of the "truth" associated with "Religion Poetry Honor," the "real, the absolute." When, in the "Idealism" chapter of *Nature,* he refers to this power as the "eye of Reason" (*E&L* 33), Emerson is probably recalling a crucial and influential passage from *Aids to Reflection,* identifying Reason (Reflection) as the higher, and distinctively human, "gift." In addition to the "Life" breathed into man and animal alike,

> God transfused into man a higher gift, and specially inbreathed:—even a living (that is, self-subsisting) soul, a soul having its life in itself. "And man became a living soul" [Gen. 2:7]. He did not merely *possess* it, he *became* it. It was his proper *being,* his truest *self,* the man *in* the man. None then, not one of human kind, so poor and destitute, but there is provided for him, even in his present state, *a house not built with hands* [2 Cor. 5:1]. Aye, and spite of the philosophy (falsely so called) which mistakes the causes, the conditions, and the occasions of our becoming *conscious* of certain truths and realities for the truths and realities themselves—a house gloriously furnished. Nothing is wanted but the eye, which is the light of this house, the light which is the eye of this soul. This *seeing* light, this *enlightening* eye, is Reflection. It is more, indeed, than is ordinarily meant by that word; but it is what a *Christian* ought to mean by it, and to know too, whence it first came, and still continues to come—of what light even this light is *but* a reflection. This, too, is THOUGHT; and all thought is but unthinking that does not flow out of this, or tend towards it. (*AR* 15–16)

Coleridge surely aligns his first biblical quotation—"And man becomes a living soul"—with the Wordsworthian moment when, laid asleep in body, we "become a living soul." Thus empowered, we are—in Wordsworth's visual image—able to "*see* into the life of things" with "an *eye* made quiet by the power / Of harmony and the deep power of joy" ("Tintern Abbey,"

12. This particular case is, as I try to show, rather clear. Elsewhere, Emerson was, of course, not dependent on Coleridge for references to Plotinus, whom he often preferred even to Plato. Emerson knew (mostly in Thomas Taylor's translations) Plato, Plotinus, Proclus, and others in the "perennial" tradition, writers who made him feel while he was reading them that (as he said in 1841) he was "present at the sowing of the seed of the world" (*JMN* 7:413).

lines 46–49). Similarly, Coleridge's references to the "enlightening eye," what Emerson would later call the "eye of Reason" (*E&L* 33), and to that light of which even the light of Reason is but a reflection, hint at a Coleridgean Wordsworth. In "To William Wordsworth," a poem we know Emerson read (*JMN* 5:74), Coleridge—referring to the fair seed time of the Wordsworthian soul as described in book 1 of *The Prelude,* with its joint ministry of beauty and of fear—names that sublime pair the "first-born . . . twin birth" of "Reason." As "twin" suggests, Coleridge is again recalling Milton: the passage in which Michael tells fallen Adam that "Since thy original lapse," true or "Rational liberty" is "lost, which always with right reason dwells / Twinned" (*PL* 12:81–85). Coleridgean Reason, always intuitive rather than discursive, is a transcendental progenitor occupying an obviously higher status than the sense-limited understanding. Such a higher faculty enables interfusion at moments "When," as Coleridge says of Wordsworth, "power streamed from thee, and thy soul received / The light reflected as a light bestowed" ("To William Wordsworth," 12, 18–19). Making the same distinction in the same imagery, Emerson insists in the final chapter of *Nature* that when man acts "upon nature" from understanding alone, he applies "but half his force." In an act altogether inadequate to his sovereign potential, such a man sacrifices his openness to influxes of light to a mean gradualism in darkness: "This is such a resumption of power, as if a banished king should buy his territories inch by inch, instead of vaulting at once into his throne. Meantime in the thick darkness, there are not wanting gleams of a better light,—occasional examples of the action of man upon nature with his entire force—with reason as well as understanding" (*E&L* 46).

These "gleams," reflecting the "visionary gleam" of the Intimations Ode and Coleridge's intuitive Reason, earlier appeared in Emerson's notes on the mind. Of the "original laws of the mind" (which constitute his "First Philosophy"), Emerson says: "These laws are Ideas of the Reason, and so are obeyed easier than expressed. They astonish the Understanding and seem to it gleams of a world in which we do not live" (*JMN* 5:270). Later, in "Self-Reliance," we will be told that "a man should learn to detect and watch that gleam of light which flashes across his mind, more than the lustre of the firmament of bards or sages" (*E&L* 259). In the finale of *Nature,* following his list of luminous and illuminating examples (ranging from "the history of Jesus Christ" through "the abolition of the Slave trade" to "the wisdom of children"), Emerson transcends the Kantian categories of Time and Space to affirm those gleams, the reciprocal "power" Coleridge says "streamed" from Wordsworth when he received light: "These are examples of Reason's momentary grasp of the sceptre; the exertion of a power which exists not in time or space, but an instantaneous in-streaming causing power" (*E&L* 46–47): in short, Wordsworth's "Knowledge not purchased with the loss of power" (*P* 5:424–25).

Like his climactic example, "the wisdom of children," this "better light," instreaming and empowering, also suggests that Emerson is recalling, as he had in the 1834 letter I began with, the Intimations Ode. If "Master"—the word Emerson there used to describe this "absolute" Reason—suggests to me Wordsworth's "fountain light of all our day," the "*master* light of all our seeing," it is because Emerson, no less than Coleridge, seems obsessed by these lines from the Intimations Ode, lines he repeatedly cites or alludes to and that closely resemble the Wordsworthian "vision and faculty divine" Coleridge himself cited in praising the elevated guidance of what Emerson called those immortal "hints" that are "the light of all our day" (*L* 4:14).

Emerson, who often used Coleridge as his guide to Milton and Wordsworth, and occasionally to Plotinus, had at least two prominent conduits to Coleridge himself: James Marsh, editor of Coleridge's *Aids to Reflection,* and his own aunt Mary. By the end of 1829, Emerson was absorbing *Biographia Literaria* and, even prior to Marsh's 1831 edition, all three volumes of *The Friend.* He told Mary in December 1829 that he was "reading Coleridge's *Friend,*" a work to be spoken of with "respect." Coleridge has "a tone a little lower than greatness—but what a living soul, what a universal knowledge!" A second letter, three days later, praises without reservation: "I say a man so learned and a man so bold, has a right to be heard, and I will take off my hat the while and not make an impertinent noise. At least I became acquainted with one new mind I never saw before." His final comment reveals a multiperspectival openness that allowed Emerson to transcend what would have been his obvious objections to Coleridge's trinitarianism: "His theological speculations are, at least, *God viewed from one position;* and no wise man would neglect that one element in concentrating the rays of human thought to a true and comprehensive conclusion. Then I love him that he is no utilitarian, nor necessarian nor scoffer, nor *hoc genus omne,* tucked away in the corner of a sentence of Plato" (*L* 7:189). In pronouncing Coleridge no "scoffer," Emerson was probably recalling his favorite passage of Coleridge's poetry—here, the lines (27–35) from *The Destiny of Nations* in which materialistic "free" thinkers are said to "Chain down the winged thought, *scoffing* ascent, / Proud in their meanness," scoffers "Untenanting creation of its God."

Emerson was preaching to the converted. Aunt Mary, who had read *The Friend,* was also reading Marsh's edition of *Aids to Reflection,* where Coleridge's adherence to Christian doctrine was even more explicit. Four months before this letter from her nephew, Mary (in passages of her "Almanack" Emerson had transcribed that very summer) was discussing Kant and Fichte—but, without fully realizing it, through a Coleridgean filter. In an entry made on August 19, 1829, she says: "We consider the grand characteristic of Kant to be the distinction between understanding & reason," the latter a higher faculty able to discern a "region where logic & argument does not reach," where poetry and virtue abide in a "sea of light at once the fountain & the termination of all true knowledge." But this is not Kant. It is Coleridge (directly or via Marsh), and Mary adapts not only his alteration of Kant's *Vernunft* but also his employment of Wordsworthian imagery to express the ineffable: here, a fusion of the "mighty waters" of eternity and that famous "fountain light," both from the ninth stanza of the Intimations Ode, a poem she had read and praised as early as 1815.

Mary goes on in this entry to worry about the "Divine idea" of Fichte, which she feared was a Germanic projection of an intuitive Reason threatening to disconnect human and divine, the inner self—the Fichtean *Ich,* the "I" or Ego—from a now superfluous, untenanted deity. "How wonderful," she exclaims sarcastically, "is the mechanism of that hypothesis [that] in recognizing a divine idea—a God within—banishes the only God who self-exists—in whom we live and move." In effect, she was joining those who, in the *Atheismusstreit,* the rancorous academic controversy of 1799, had accused Fichte of atheism, bringing to an end his meteoric career at the University of Jena. And here, too, almost a decade before the controversy over Emerson's Divinity School Address, is the seed of the disagreement with her nephew that would lead Mary to essentially side with Andrews Norton in the attack on the "infidelity" of a man who, his self-reliance almost as all-determining as the Fichtean *Ich,* is one of those who "announces his own convictions," Norton complained, "as if from their having that character, they were necessarily indisputable."[13]

It was in reading Coleridge, as she confirms in "Almanack" entries over the next several months, that Mary saw the way to sustain her affirmation of the inward, intuitive, instinctual Reason without blasphemously banishing God. Like Marsh himself, whose knowledge of Kant came largely through Coleridge, she was still confusing what Kant had said with what Coleridge made of Kantian reason.[14] But she was of course right to see in

13. Norton's response (August 27, 1838) is cited from Konvitz, *Recognition of Emerson,* 7; Mary's "Almanack" (which is in the Houghton Library, Harvard University) is quoted in Phyllis Cole, *Mary Moody Emerson and the Origins of Transcendentalism: A Family History,* 208–9.

14. In a letter to Coleridge of March 23, 1829, Marsh admits that although he has "read a part of the works of Kant it was under many disadvantages, so that I am

Coleridge, a Bible-oriented man of faith rather than a scoffer, a force for reconciliation, a Christian thinker who depicted intuitive Reason as an "agency" of, rather than a false substitute for, God. "Nothing that God has made is more intelligible than the emotions—instincts, or rather to use Cole[ridge's] phrase[,] reason itself may be the power which perceives—communes with the divine omnipresence. . . . I feel that where the agency—power—contrivance of God is, there he is." Though she attributes this resurgence in confidence to the "Kantian deffinition" of "reason," it was actually Coleridge's *re*definition that "reposes me on the omnipresence in the fullest sense."[15]

While Mary was busy reading Coleridge, so was her nephew. Asked in 1830 by his brothers William and Edward, "What books I read?" Emerson responded: "Coleridge's 'Friend' with great interest; Coleridge's 'Aids to Reflection' with yet deeper [interest]" (*L* 1:291).[16] The latter was, initially, the most influential of all these immensely influential works. The extraordinary impact of Coleridge's *Aids* was enhanced, in the 1829 U.S. edition, by the long and cogent "Preliminary Essay" by Marsh, minister and president of the University of Vermont. As time passed, Calvinists would enjoy twitting moderate Unitarians for having opened the Pandora's box of Transcendentalism. But in this case, and at its intellectual origins, a moderate Calvinist himself opened just that box. Marsh had discovered in *Aids to Reflection* what an early-twentieth-century commentator astutely described, in a Coleridgean organic metaphor, as "the enflowered and perfect statements of truths which had been struggling for expression in his own mind."[17] But there were, in 1829, other receptive minds on the horizon, with their own assimilative and creative flowerings, however un-

---

indebted to your own writings for the ability to understand what I have read of his works" (Duffy, *Coleridge's American Disciples,* 80).

15. M. M. Emerson, "Almanack," quoted in Cole, *Mary Moody Emerson,* 208. Though Cole seems right in claiming that Mary anticipated Emerson by emphasizing the reason-understanding distinction "often cited as a turning point in the development of Transcendentalist views" (346n50), and is certainly accurate in saying that "Mary saw with an explicitness never matched in [Emerson's] reflections on Kantian reason the erosive skepticism at the heart of the new philosophy" (208), she follows Mary (and Emerson himself) in confusing Kant's reason with Coleridge's Miltonic alteration.

16. Such comments refute the assertion by J. Lasley Dameron, in "Emerson and *Fraser's* on Coleridge's *Aids to Reflection,*" that Emerson was dependent for his knowledge of the book on John Abraham Heraud's review of it in *Fraser's* in June 1832. Still, Emerson was a regular reader of *Fraser's;* indeed, on October 11, 1833, he was anxious to reacquire the July 1833 issue, containing "a capital print of Coleridge which I should regret losing" (*L* 1:379).

17. John Wright Buckham, "James Marsh and Coleridge," 308.

expected and uncongenial those efflorescences might prove to an open-minded intellectual, but still trinitarian minister, such as Marsh.

Emerson and his fellow subversives, reading Marsh, disregarded what they found uncongenial (the more conservative aspects of his preface), absorbed his clarifications of Coleridge, and went on to radicalize Coleridgean theology. Thus, as Perry Miller astutely synopsizes the ironic turn of events, Marsh "put into the hands of Emerson, Parker, Alcott, and their group the book that was of the greatest single importance in the formation of their minds. This was entirely beside Marsh's intention, but it happened." Similarly, Robert Richardson Jr. recognizes "the electric effect on Emerson" of *Aids to Reflection,* "the book that more than any other single volume catalyzed the synthesis" between the "new ideas" Emerson was ingesting and the "old ideas" he had found in Plato, Plutarch, Montaigne, and the seventeenth century. What emerged was the concept of an active "power that resides in each individual soul," a power higher than the senses, higher than the understanding dependent on input from the senses. "What matters here is not whether Coleridge exactly follows Kant or whether Marsh or Emerson fully understood the nuances of either Coleridge or Kant. What matters is the idea of reason itself and what Emerson does with it." That is true, though it is worth noting that Coleridge probably *knowingly* deviated from Kant, and that Emerson followed Coleridge, not just Marsh on Coleridge—to whose thinking Marsh was judged, even by contemporary admirers, to be too subservient.[18]

This is not at all to denigrate a man for whom being and knowing, faith and reason, were reconcilable, and whose own conversion in 1815 was accompanied by a continued pursuit of knowledge. Despite his essentially religious project in the "Preliminary Essay," Marsh emphasized how Coleridge (like Bacon and Kant) centered attention on the human mind, the "laws of our own being," wherein philosophy, ethics, and religion must find their "first principles" and "ultimate grounds." Slightly misquoting

18. For an informed account of these matters, see Harding, "James Marsh as Editor." For Miller's comment, see *The Transcendentalists: An Anthology,* 34. Richardson risks making Emerson, who deplored even "second-hand" knowledge, a learner at thirdhand. Although that is not at all his intention, he may underestimate Coleridge's role somewhat by suggesting that his American editor was even more significant to the Transcendentalists than the thinker whose book he was introducing. Quoting Marsh on Coleridge's account of the active power of intuitive Reason residing in "each individual soul," Richardson concludes: "Marsh's formulation became for the next few years a conviction Emerson would hold for the rest of his life" (*Mind on Fire,* 93–94). For a full account of the responses of Emerson, Alcott, and other Transcendentalists to Marsh's edition of *Aids to Reflection,* see Peter Carafiol, *Transcendent Reason: James Marsh and the Forms of Romantic Thought.*

Saint Bernard of Clairvaux ("We must retire inward if we would ascend upward"), Marsh in effect, and unintentionally, aligned himself with centripetal Romanticism, its psychological and metaphorical movement inward rather than outward, its placement of creativity, even divinity, deep within us in a center that somehow unifies the two motions. For Coleridge, for example, the Atonement was a matter of "subjective change," an emphasis offensive to his more orthodox readers, even Henry Hedge. Marsh himself believed that Christ was to be known outwardly ("historically") as well as "inwardly and spiritually." What he did *not* accept, and could not be expected to foresee, was the Transcendentalist appropriation: the reorienting of Pauline Christological language so that it applied—directly, without the mediation of historical Christianity—to the autonomous human soul itself.

In the crucial part of his introduction, Marsh takes up the distinction upon which Coleridge, and Emerson after him, most adamantly insists. Synopsizing Coleridge, Marsh explains that the "fixed laws" are not, as the empiricists thought, to be found in the "understanding," but in "Reason." The "keys" to Coleridge's "system" will be found

> in the distinctions . . . he makes and illustrates between *nature* and *free-will*, and between *understanding* and *reason* . . . . A truth may be mysterious, and the primary ground of all truth and reality must be so. But though we may believe what *passeth all understanding,* we can *not* believe what is absurd, or contradictory to *reason* . . . . It must be observed by the reader . . . that I have used several words, especially *understanding* and *reason,* in a sense somewhat diverse from their present acceptation.

From the "habit of using, since the time of Locke, the terms . . . indiscriminately, and thus confounding a distinction clearly marked in the philosophy and in the language of the older [classical and English] writers," has come not only "an inconvenient ambiguity of language" but also consequences truly "deplorable." The "misfortune" is that

> the powers of understanding and reason have not merely been blended and confounded in the view of our [Lockean] philosophy;—the higher and far more characteristic [power], as an essential constituent of our proper humanity, has been . . . obscured and hidden from our observation in the inferior power, which belongs to us in common with the brutes which perish. According to the old, more spiritual, and genuine philosophy, the distinguishing attributes of our humanity—that *image* of God in which man alone was created . . . was said to be found in the *reason* and *free-will.* [But we have], if the system of Locke and the popular philosophy of the day be true, neither the one nor the other.

Since neither free will, the image of God in the soul, nor "any of those laws or ideas which spring from, or rather constitute reason, can be authenticated by the sort of proof which is demanded," we must, says Marsh, tongue firmly in cheek, "therefore relinquish our prerogative, and take our place with becoming humility among our more unpretending companions," that is, with "the irrational animals." But, Marsh continues, there *is* an empirically unprovable but indisputable superior power: "In the ascending series of powers, enumerated by Milton, with so much philosophical truth, as well as beauty of language, in the fifth book of Paradise Lost, he mentions '*Fancy* and *understanding,* whence the soul / REASON receives. And reason is her *being,* / Discursive or intuitive.' "

These pivotal lines are, as we have seen, prominently featured in both *Aids to Reflection* and *Biographia Literaria,* and Marsh is clearly reading Milton by the light of Coleridge. In his very next comment, he laments that "the highest power," constituting "the being of the soul, considered as anything differing in kind from the understanding, has no place in our popular metaphysics. Thus we have only the *understanding,* 'the faculty judging according to sense,' a faculty of abstracting and generalizing, of contrivance and forecast, as the highest of our intellectual powers; and this we are expressly taught belongs to us in common with the brutes."

Milton—attacked by Coleridge on this point—posits continuity as well as a distinction between understanding and Reason; he also refuses to make a distinction "in kind" between discursive and "intuitive" Reason." The Romantics and Transcendentalists, privileging that all-important "intuitive" Reason, found the merely "discursive" faculty too close for comfort to "mere" understanding. Marsh chooses Coleridge over Milton. Though he has no wish to dwell on the errors of "great or good men" whose philosophy on this point may blur "that *image* of God in which we are created," Marsh, following his mentor, feels compelled to attack such opinions because "the distinction in question" and the assertion of intuitive Reason as the highest and "essential constituent of our being" are "vitally important to the formation and support of any rational system of philosophy," as well as to "the interests of truth, in morals, and religion, and indeed of all truth." In accord with Coleridge—who in *Aids to Reflection* allies understanding with nature and Reason with spirit—Marsh argues that without this crucial distinction, humans would be just another species among the other "inferior and irrational animals." And this, he says, would be an absurdity, because brutes, unlike men, are unable to arrive at the "intuition" of "universal truths," unable to "form and contemplate" that noumenal Kantian triad, "the *ideas* of the *soul,* of *free-will,* of *immortality.*" To clinch his point, Marsh quotes from a letter sent him by a friend, a letter with which he concurs: "If you can get the attention of thinking men fixed on his distinction between the reason and the understanding, you will have done enough to reward the labour of a life. As prominent a place as it holds in the writings of Coleridge, he seems to me far enough from making too much of it."[19]

A few pages later, criticizing the contemporary avoidance of "Coleridge's Metaphysics" as being "too deep," and rejecting the common allegation of obscurity, Marsh insists on the linguistic precision of Coleridge, in whose hands "language becomes," to a rare degree, "a living power, 'consubstantial' with the power of thought, that gave birth to it, and awakening and calling into action a corresponding energy in our own minds. . . . [Of the] magnificence of his intellectual powers, and the vast extent of his accumulated stores of knowledge, I shall not venture to speak." He does speak of them, of course, but, given the ineffable, Marsh concludes his synopsis and celebration of Coleridge by repairing to what comes to seem an inevitable quarter: lines from Wordsworth's Intimations Ode. The "few" among us who have

> read his works with the attention which they deserve, are at no loss what rank to assign him among the writers of the present age. . . . The character and influence of his principles as a philosopher, a moralist, and a Christian, and of the writings by which he is enforcing them, do not ultimately depend upon the estimation in which they may now be held; and to posterity he may safely intrust those "productive ideas" and "living words"—those
>
> —truths that wake
> To perish never.[20]

It was with this phrase that Marsh had, three years earlier, capped the peroration of his inaugural address laying out the organic Coleridgean curricular model through which he, as the incoming president of the University of Vermont, intended to lead his college out of the darkness of Lockean and Scottish commonsense epistemology into the clear intellectual and moral light of "those truths that wake to perish never."[21] There as in the "Preliminary Essay," Marsh quotes, of course, from the indispensable ninth stanza, in which Wordsworth raises the song of thanks and

19. Marsh is quoting from a letter of October 28, 1829, from his close friend Ebenezer C. Tracy, who also refers (two years before Marsh's edition) to wide readership by Andover students of Coleridge's *Friend* (Duffy, *Coleridge's American Disciples,* 97–99).

20. Marsh's "Preliminary Essay" is reprinted in its entirety in *Aids to Reflection* (*AR* 489–529; for Beer's own introductory remarks on the Marsh edition, see cxiv–cxxiii). I quote from pp. 492–93, 496, 517, 519, 520, 524, 528–29. Marsh ends by quoting these lines from the ninth stanza of the Intimations Ode.

21. Duffy, *Coleridge's American Disciples,* 36, 55. The address, delivered in October 1826 in Montpelier, was later published in Burlington.

praise, not for the "simple creed / Of Childhood," but "for those obstinate questionings / Of sense and outward things,"

> Fallings from us, vanishings;
> Blank misgivings of a Creature
> Moving about in worlds not realized,
> High instincts before which our mortal Nature
> Did tremble like a guilty Thing surprised;
> But for those first affections,
> Those shadowy recollections,
> Which, be they what they may,
> Are yet the fountain light of all our day,
> Are yet a master light of all our seeing;
> Uphold us, cherish, and have power to make
> Our noisy years seem moments in the being
> Of the eternal silence: truths that wake,
> To perish never. . . .
> (137–43, 144–57; *WP* 1:527–28)

Marsh's climactic allusion, however inevitable, unintentionally undermined in advance his own later criticism of what Emerson and his Transcendentalist colleagues made of the intuitive Reason celebrated by Coleridge and Wordsworth. For Marsh, Coleridgean "intuition" was not only introspective but analytic and systematic as well. Emerson, he later concluded, had reduced it to mere feeling, the impulse of a moment. He found Transcendentalism, Marsh wrote a correspondent in 1841, a rather "superficial affair," having no pretense to a "system of unity," each member of the cult uttering "the inspiration of the moment, assuming that it all comes from the universal heart, while ten to one it comes only from the stomach of the individual."[22] Marsh had a telling point; on the other hand, what seemed to him anarchic individualism was the direct heritage of the Romantic philosophy of intuition he inadvertently helped bring to the United States: a doctrineless doctrine most memorably enshrined in the very stanza of Wordsworthian poetry from which Marsh quoted in concluding the essay in which he introduced Coleridge's *Aids to Reflection* to Emerson and his circle. They must have been pleased to note that Marsh, by quoting from a stanza that had almost talismanic significance for many of them, had reaffirmed one of their foundational beliefs, namely, that, for Coleridge and Wordsworth, however religiously conservative they became, however imperishable the truths they believed had been revealed to them, the intuitive revelatory power remained mysteriously "Transcendentalist":

22. Ibid., 276.

high instincts and first affections that issue in a luminous fountain, shadowy recollections that somehow become a—indeed, *the*—master light.

As if to counter Marsh's criticism about the "superficiality" of Transcendentalism and his reduction of the source of their intuitional truths, found not in any "universal heart" but in the "stomach of the individual," Emerson later cited the same stanza *and* drew his illustration from the very book Marsh was introducing. The passage I am focusing on for the remainder of this section may be found in the opening pages of a late essay titled "Character."[23] "The moral discipline of life is built," he says there, on "the perpetual conflict between the dictate of the universal mind and the wishes and interests of the individual." But, contra Marsh and in accord with Coleridge, he goes on to draw a sharp distinction between the superficial, merely private self and the deep foundation of our "moral nature," between "the biographical Ego" and "the grand spiritual Ego."

This contrast (which appears in Emerson's project, ongoing from around 1848, called "Natural History of Intellect") has both Coleridgean and Wordsworthian roots. On several occasions, Emerson copied into his journals (*JMN* 9:369, 15:115) Coleridge's Latin aphorism "*Quantum sumus, scimus*" (As much as we are, we know). In *Aids to Reflection,* Coleridge supplied his own gloss, one with immense implications for Emerson: "*Quantum sumus, scimus.* That which we find *within ourselves,* which is *more* than ourselves, and *yet the ground* of whatever is good and permanent therein, is the substance and life of *all other knowledge*" (*AR* 30n; italics added). Emerson found in the axiom and its gloss sanction for his concept of a self-reliance at once immanent *and* transcendent, biographical *and* grandly spiritual: a power, even divinity within, that is the ground, substance, and life of our permanent ethical nature and of all we can come to know. This is a Self neither anarchic nor arbitrary; indeed, it is a stern Self whose internal moral depths puts to shame the merely private good we associate with our superficial selves. "Compare all that we call ourselves," says Emerson in "Character," all "our private and personal venture in the world, with this deep of moral nature in which we lie, and our private good becomes an impertinence, and we take part with hasty shame against ourselves" (*W* 10:94). Juxtaposing two phrases separated graphically by only a single letter, Emerson explicitly contrasts our deep "moral nature" with what Wordsworth refers to in the ninth stanza of the Intimations Ode as "our mortal nature" whose "hasty shame" takes the form of guilty trembling. Hence, Emerson immediately evokes those Wordworthian "High

23. This is not the essay of that title in *Essays: Second Series,* nor the eighth chapter, "Character," in *English Traits,* but rather a lecture first published in the *North American Review* in April 1866 and reprinted in the important posthumous collection of Emerson's work titled *Lectures and Biographical Sketches* (1889).

instincts, before which our mortal nature / Doth tremble like a guilty thing surprised."

Having (either inadvertently or to insist on a timeless present) replaced Wordsworth's "Did" with "Doth," Emerson continues to quote from the stanza, probably from memory, since he omits without ellipsis the immediately following appositional phrases ("But for those first affections, / Those shadowy recollections") before quoting the next seven lines. Aside from not adhering to Wordsworth's indentations and precise punctuation, Emerson cites accurately—with one significant exception; he makes "*a* master light" a more emphatic and exclusive "*the* master-light of all our seeing."

Either way, *that* was the line, and *this* the passage, that for Emerson and for the Transcendentalists in general illuminated their own intuitive, spontaneous, instinctual "truths": mysterious in origin but imperishable precisely *because* they were derived from the internalized "spirit" and deep "moral nature" of the individual, not from his "stomach"—Marsh's dismissive anatomical term being precisely what an even more dismissive Emerson refers to in "Fate" as "mere order of nature," man's "ignominious baggage" of perishable "belly and members" (*E&L* 953). Emerson, like Wordsworth in the ninth stanza of the ode, dismisses the NOT ME, or what are called in this stanza material "Fallings from us," celebrating instead their polar opposites, those immaterial and ineradicable "High instincts, before which our mortal nature" trembles in shame, "like a guilty thing surprised." That "guilty" mortal nature resembles not only the ghost of King Hamlet startled by the cockcrow "like a guilty thing / Upon a fearful summons," and Milton's fallen Adam and Eve quaking before the Lord, but also, even more immediately, the "guilty serpent" who—having corrupted Eve, now gorging on the forbidden fruit without knowing she was "eating death"—"Back to the thicket slunk" (*PL* 9:780–92). And "be they what they may," those high instincts are, above all, redemptive. In the lines of the ode as quoted by Emerson in "Character," they are

> the fountain-light of all our day,
> Are yet the master-light of all our seeing,—
> Uphold us, cherish, and have power to make
> Our noisy years seem moments in the being
> Of the eternal silence,—truths that wake
> To perish never.
>
> (*W* 10:94–95)

As in the prior case of Marsh, Emerson's original model in citing, as the climax of his "argument," the ninth stanza of Wordworth's Intimations

Ode was Coleridge himself. He does so both in *Biographia Literaria* (2: 151–53) and in the eleventh and concluding number of "Essays on the Principles of Method," essays he told his son Derwent in 1818 "in point of *value* outweigh all my other works, verse or prose. I therefore urge you to a thoughtful perusal of them. I entreat you to *study* them" (*CL* 4:885–86). Emerson neither received nor required a paternal admonition. Encountering the "Essays on Method" in one of his favorite books, the third volume of *The Friend,* he *had* perused them thoughtfully, concurring with Coleridge on their excellence. Following Emerson in that perusal leads us, as all paths seem to lead, to the ultimately inexplicable mysteries of intuitive Reason and the crucial lines of the ninth stanza of Wordsworth's ode.

Opening the climactic essay by identifying the "two main directions of human activity" as "trade and literature," Coleridge turns to his characteristic contrast of Within and Without. Pursuing commerce, a man is called "into action from without," appropriating the "outward world . . . to the purposes of his senses and sensual nature" with his "ultimate end . . . appearance and enjoyment." The contrasting inner "quest," with its final aim the "nurture and evolution of humanity," is "to find the one principle of permanence and identity, the rock of strength and refuge, to which the soul may cling amid the fleeting surge-like objects of the senses." He goes on to fuse the imagery of the Intimations Ode with the Ovidian myth of Narcissus:

> Disturbed as by the obscure quickening of an inward birth . . . , man sallies forth into nature—in nature as in the shadows and reflections of a clear river, to discover the originals of the forms presented to him in his own intellect. Over these shadows, as if they were the substantial powers and presiding spirits of the stream, Narcissus-like, he hangs delighted: till finding nowhere a representative of that free agency which yet is a *fact* of immediate consciousness [intuition] sanctioned and made fearfully significant by his prophetic *conscience,* he learns at last that what he *seeks* he has *left behind,* and but lengthens the distance as he prolongs the search. (*F* 1:508–9; italics in original)[24]

24. The fate of Ovid's Narcissus—predicted by Tiresias; invoked by one who, like Echo, has been spurned by the boy; and endorsed by Nemesis—begins to be fulfilled when, bending over the clear waters of a forest pool, "to quench one thirst, he feels another rise." Enamored with his own reflected image, he thinks "that what is but a shade must be / a body." In a turn Milton will adapt in having a divine "voice" warn the newly created Eve, similarly infatuated with her own reflected watery image, the Ovidian narrative voice addresses Narcissus directly: "But why, / O foolish boy, do you persist? Why try / to grip an image? . . . If you turn / away he'll fade; the face that you discern / is but a shadow, your reflected form." But Narcissus, cursed that what he sees and loves he "cannot find," wastes away, as Echo had, with futile desire. See Ovid, *The Metamorphoses of Ovid,* 90–97 (3:340–510).

Our end is in our beginning. Coleridge's quest for unity between his mind and nature takes the form, as it does for so many High Romantic thinkers, of what M. H. Abrams has called a "circuitous journey," one ending in the discovery that what we sought was always already there at the outset and that we have left behind what we seek. The specific irony—that the longer we prolong the search for what we have left behind, the more we lengthen the distance between ourselves and "the originals" we seek—adopts the perspective of Wordsworth in the ode. Coleridge positions himself as though looking back from that poem's ninth stanza to its fifth, where we are said to come from God, in neither "entire forgetfulness" nor "utter nakedness, / But trailing clouds of glory"—an eternal radiance gradually encroached upon until "At length the man perceives it die away, / And fade into the light of common day" (62–76). How then do we scientifically validate what is, intuitively, a fact of *immediate* consciousness, presented to man "in his own intellect"? What is the source, Within or Above, of that "obscure" but undeniable (elusive but ever sought and in fact permanent) principle to which (as the originals we seek recede into the distance) the soul may cling amid the fleeting surgelike objects of the senses?

Noting that man employs a form of scientific analysis perhaps "first given to him by express revelation," Coleridge juxtaposes, for neither the first nor the last time, a line, in Latin, from Juvenal's eleventh satire ("from heaven it descends") with, in Greek, the famous Delphic and Socratic dictum. The result is a fusion of Above and Within: "*E coeli descendit,* KNOW THYSELF."[25] Under the tutelage of this scientific analysis perhaps descended from heaven, man "separates the *relations*" created by his own intellect and "at once discovers and recoils from the discovery, that the *reality,* the *objective* truth, of the objects he has been adoring, derives its whole and sole evidence from an obscure sensation, which he is alike unable to resist or to comprehend, which compels him to contemplate as without and independent of himself what yet he could not contemplate at all, were it not a modification of *his own being*" (*F* 1:509; italics in original).

We are—epistemologically, spiritually, and poetically—at the center of the Romantic project, the intersection of what Coleridge, most precisely

25. These ancient texts, coupled not long before his death as the epigraph to his poem "Self-Knowledge," had first been juxtaposed by Coleridge in a letter of March 25, 1801. The context—a self-disparaging Coleridge in the Wordsworthian shadow—is revealing, and sad. "If I die," he wrote to William Godwin, "and the booksellers will give you anything for my life, be sure to say, 'Wordsworth descended on him like the [Know Thyself] from Heaven; by shewing to him what true poetry was, he made him know, that he himself was no Poet'" (*CL* 2:714).

in chapter 12 of the *Biographia,* distinguished as, on the one hand, the "OBJECTIVE" world of "NATURE," Kantian "phaenomena" without consciousness, and, on the other, the "sum of all that is SUBJECTIVE": the conscious and exclusively representative power, "the SELF or INTELLIGENCE," what Emerson, also capitalizing the key terms, calls the "Soul" as distinguished from "NATURE" or "the NOT ME" (*E&L* 8). In doing so, he is following both Coleridge and Carlyle, who, in turn, are "Englishing" Fichte's famed *Ich* and *Nicht-Ich.* All acts of positive knowledge require, says Coleridge, a "reciprocal concurrence" of the two, which is no problem experientially since, during the cognitive act itself, the "objective and subjective are so instantly united"—"coinstantaneous and one"—that we cannot determine precedence. Only when we attempt to "explain this intimate coalition" do we find it necessary to suppose the union dissolved, alternately assigning primacy. If we make the objective primary, we must account for the supervention of the subjective; if the subjective is taken as antecedent, the problem then is "how there supervenes to it a coincident objective" (*BL* 1:254–62).

Coleridge, though always insistent on "reciprocal concurrence" in what Emerson called this "galvanic circuit," unsurprisingly ceded essential primacy to mind, "the intellectual or mental initiative, as the motive and guide" of all our inquiries.[26] There is, according to the ninth essay in the group, "potentially if not actually, in every rational being, a somewhat, call it what you will"—pure reason, the spirit, Bacon's *lumen siccum* or *Lux Intellectus,* the "intellectual intuition" of Fichte and Schelling—as indispensable to science as it is to every form of contemplation of the relation between subject and object, the real and the ideal. "Philosophy being necessarily bi-polar," Bacon will treat primarily of the truth manifested at one pole,

26. Emerson's phrase occurs amid some charming but serious questions in "Experience." Perhaps recalling the "clouds that gather round the setting sun," clouds that, in the final stanza of the Intimations Ode, "take a sober coloring" from the eye of one who has kept watch over human mortality, Emerson states that the universe inevitably "wear[s] our color, and every object fall[s] successively unto the subject itself. . . . As I am, so I see." He then asks, do we "see that kitten chasing so prettily her own tail? If you could look with her eyes, you might see her surrounded with hundreds of figures performing complex dramas, with tragic and comic issues, long conversations, many characters, many ups and downs of fate,—and meantime it is only puss and her tail. How long before our masquerade will end its noise of tambourines, laughter, and shouting, and we shall find it was a solitary performance?—A subject and an object,—it takes so much to make the galvanic circuit complete, but magnitude adds nothing. What imports it whether it is Kepler and the sphere; Columbus and America; a reader and his book; or puss with her tail?" (*E&L* 489). Ever engaged in the tension between real and ideal, Emerson remains a Romantic idealist. Although the effort to connect the two is operative on every level, from the most ordinary instance to the most sublime, there is no doubt about primacy.

the "real," Plato of the same truth manifested at the other, the "ideal" (*F* 1:491–92). But in our quest, truth "must be found within us before it can be *intelligibly* reflected back on the mind from without." In terms of "the mirror and the lamp" (Yeats's phrase, made even more famous by M. H. Abrams), truth is to be found not in the merely reflective, and distorting, external Mirror of Narcissus, but in the inner Lamp: luminous, expressive, Romantic, imaginative, divine. If we are, says Coleridge, "blind to the master-light" recommended to us not only by Wordsworth but by ancient and modern philosophy as well, we can never attain true knowledge, true wisdom (*F* 1:494–95).

In our present text, the climactic essay in the series, Coleridge goes on to quote the whole of the sixth and ninth stanzas of the Intimations Ode. In the sixth, Earth, at once benign and amnesia inducing, does all she can within her limits "To make her Foster-child, her Inmate Man, / Forget the glories" he has known and that "imperial palace whence he came" (82–86). Here, as in the fifth and ninth stanzas, immersion in nature, however beautiful nature may be, lengthens the distance from what Coleridge calls the "originals of the forms," originals left further and further behind as we, Narcissus-like, prolong our search for them among the shadowy reflections of the natural world. Yet those shadows, however inadequate as representatives, retain vestiges of what we seek, and the intimations of our immortality are themselves described by Wordsworth as "*shadowy* recollections" (150).

The ninth stanza begins with an abrupt shift, from the "earthly freight" and custom that, at the end of the eighth stanza, lie upon us "with a weight / Heavy as frost, and deep almost as life!" The quickened rhythm introduces not only a recuperated but also a transformed and deepened joy, a shift in imagery from frost to not quite extinguishable sparks amid the ashes and an emphasis on a *positive* aspect of the depths of human life:

> O joy! That in our embers
> Is something that doth live,
> That nature yet remembers
> What was so fugitive!
> The thought of our past years in me doth breed
> Perpetual benediction. . . .
>
> (130–35)

As the personification, reinforced by the last lines quoted, makes clear, it is Wordsworth, not a merely material "nature" unpartnered by the human mind, who "remembers." And his perpetual blessing is not—though these are "most worthy to be blest"—for delight and liberty, the "simple creed of childhood" marked by "new-fledged hope." Not for these does he raise the "song of thanks and praise," but "for those obstinate questionings / Of sense and outward things, / Falling from us, vanishings. . . ." Questionings "of sense and outward things," vanishings, worlds "not *real*ized": this is that "abyss of idealism" of which Wordsworth speaks in the famous comments on the ode made to Isabella Fenwick in 1843. In childhood, it was an abyss at once glorious and terrifying. "At that time," he says, "I was afraid of such processes. In later periods of life I have deplored, as we have all reason to do, a subjugation of an opposite character, and have rejoiced over the remembrances," expressed, as he says, in the lines just quoted (*WP* 1:978). He is thankful, above all, for those "High instincts," those affections and recollections that are "the fountain light of all our day," a "master light of all our seeing." Whatever the provenance and ontological status of these *noumenal* intimations ("be they what they may"), they are "truths that wake / To perish never," possessing—despite Hume's dismissal of imagination's power of "instant transport"—the "power" to take us back, so that,

> Though inland far we be,
> Our Souls have sight of that immortal sea
> Which brought us hither,
> Can in a moment travel thither,
> And see the Children sport upon the shore,
> And hear the mighty waters rolling evermore.
> (163–68)

For Coleridge, this stanza of his friend's ode became one of the touchstones for the "Dynamic Philosophy" he sought. Predictably, "philosophers of the schools," who only "live and move in a crowd of phrases and notions from which human nature has long ago vanished," know nothing of such a philosophy. But "you"—Coleridge continues in this, the twelfth chapter of the *Biographia*, addressing directly those of his readers "who reverence yourselves, and walk humbly with the divinity in your own hearts"—are "worthy of a better philosophy! Let the dead bury the dead, but do you preserve your human nature, the depth of which was never yet fathomed by a philosophy made up of notions and logical entities" (*BL* 1:262–63). For all his theorizing, Coleridge ends up *asserting* rather than rationally demonstrating that "better philosophy," since one cannot prove, by means of the understanding or even the discursive reason, unfathomable truths that can be revealed only through the master light of intuitive Reason.

As epigraph to the sixth essay in "Essays on Method" Coleridge had quoted in Greek from the *Metaphysics* (8:26) of Theophrastus. As Coleridge knew (*CN* 3:3574), the passage had earlier been translated accurately by Hooker in *The Laws of Ecclesiastical Polity:* "They that seek a reason in all things, do utterly overthrow Reason." In his own translation, Coleridge slightly embellishes the Greek in order to get in his Within-Without contrast: "Seeking the reason of all things from without, they preclude Reason" (*F* 1:464). As Pascal said, "The heart has reasons reason knows not of," or, in the words of the German idealist philosopher Jacobi, words probably echoed by Coleridge in the passage just cited about the divinity in your own hearts, "The Light is in my heart: as soon as I try to carry it to my intellect, it goes out." Coleridge's project was to affirm the heart's truth *and* to try "to carry" that light to the intellect by means of that Miltonic intuitive Reason possessed by men of genius whose imaginative insight allowed them to grasp truths beyond the range of the Enlightenment, whether it was the critical analytic intellect of the empiricists or *Vernunft,* the pure reason of Kant. When De Quincey, famously distinguishing between "the literature of *knowledge*" and "the literature of *power,*" makes the further distinction between "the *mere* discursive understanding" and "the higher understanding or reason," associated with "Scripture's *understanding heart,*" the "great *intuitive* (or nondiscursive) organ," he is reading Milton's Raphael through the filter of "many years' conversation with Mr. Wordsworth," who was himself the beneficiary of many years' conversation with Mr. Coleridge.[27]

A thinker may be cognitively compelled, as Coleridge says in the eleventh essay, "to contemplate as without and independent of himself what yet he could not contemplate at all, were it not a modification of *his own being.*" It is this calling into doubt, the "obstinate questionings / Of sense and outward things" (Coleridge's "fleeting surge-like objects of the senses"), that evokes Wordsworth's gratitude in the ode. He, too, places his faith and reliance on vestigial feelings and memories, those "High instincts," that, however numinous, "uphold" him, becoming what Coleridge called the "one principle of permanence and identity, the rock of strength and refuge, to which the soul may cling" amid the surge of sensuous images. Coleridge's observation that "our whole and sole evidence" of the *true* "reality"—Platonic, Plotinian, spiritual, Romantic, imaginative—of the objects we have been "adoring" derives from an "obscure sensation," incomprehensible yet irresistible, precisely mirrors what Wordsworth refers to as primal affections, shadowy recollections, and high instincts that provide our guiding light. Inevitably, these quintessential intimations and intuitions

27. De Quincey acknowledged his "obligation" to Wordsworth for the knowledge-power distinction in 1823 (*Letters to a Young Man,* in *Collected Writings,* 10:48). The full development of that distinction, along with the distinction between mere discursive understanding and the higher intuitive Reason associated with Scripture's (1 Kings 3: 9; Isa. 6:10) understanding heart, comes in 1848, in De Quincey's essay on Pope (10: 55–56; all italics in original).

remain, by definition, mysterious and "obscure." It is that mixture of indeterminacy, permanence, and indispensability that is emphasized in these crucial lines of the ninth stanza of the Intimations Ode, in the Coleridgean gloss on those lines in the last of his essays on Method, and in the subsequent commentaries of both Marsh and Emerson.

Every syllable of this ninth stanza of the ode resonated with Emerson, from the questioning of sense and outward things through the dialectic of Within and Without and Above, and the universalizing of individual experience, to the seemingly throwaway but highly significant caveat. Because he cannot test the authenticity of the report of his senses, Emerson asks rhetorically in the "Idealism" chapter of *Nature,* "What difference does it make, whether Orion is up there in the heaven, or some god paints the image in the firmament of the soul?" Emerson may be fusing Kant's twin objects of "ever increasing admiration and awe, the starry heavens above and the moral law within" (in the peroration of *The Critique of Practical Reason*); more certainly, he concludes this pivotal paragraph by echoing Wordsworth's admission of ultimate ignorance. "Whether nature enjoy a substantial existence without, or is only in the apocalypse of the mind," claims Emerson in the "Idealism" chapter, "it is alike useful and venerable to me. *Be it what it may*" (*E&L* 32; italics added). Along with Coleridge's concession of ultimate mystery ("a somewhat, call it what you will"), Emerson is remembering Wordsworth's even less philosophical acknowledgment that he does not know the precise nature of his ode's intimations: "be they what they may."

We are on the verge of mystical experience, the ineffable. In the Simplon Pass episode, in book 6 of *The Prelude,* Wordsworth is reduced, through "sad incompetence of human speech," to describing as "Imagination" that mysterious and "awful Power" that rose unconsciously "from the Mind's abyss" (*P* 6:593–95). As with Emerson's speculation as to whether nature has external substance "or is only in the apocalypse of the mind" (*E&L* 32), one recalls Saint Paul, who is "caught up" into the paradise of the third heaven, "whether in the body, or out of the body, I cannot tell" and hearing "unspeakable words, . . . not lawful for a man to utter" (2 Cor. 12: 1–4).[28] The lines in the Intimations Ode immediately following "be they what they may" provide my subtitle, for, *whatever* they are, these intuitive instincts constitute "the fountain light of all our day." In the very last of his innumerable allusions to that Wordworthian light, in a letter written when he was sixty-five, Emerson looked back thirty years to that significant moment when all "mean egotism vanishes" and, his head "uplifted into

28. J. Robert Barth, S.J., connects the Pauline and Wordsworthian passages (*Romanticism and Transcendence: Wordsworth, Coleridge, and the Religious Imagination,* 63–64).

infinite space," he became a transparent eyeball. In the letter, reflecting Wordsworth's subordination of educational courses to "spontaneous wisdom" and mysterious intimations, his elevation of "intuition" above "tuition," Emerson declared: "We live among hints from the gods, & are often more lifted & guided by a hint than a course of study or practice. These may make us solid & satisfactory, but the other is the light of all our day, & having seen it, we never can be quite mean" (*L* 4:14).

Emerson echoes the same line from the ode in his essay "History," where he asserts that all the facts of history "preexist in the mind." This "human mind"—at once "individual" and incarnating the "universal Mind"—"wrote history, and this must read it. The Sphinx must solve her own riddle. If the whole of history is in one man, it is all to be explained from individual experience." Thus, each fact in one's "private experience flashes a light" on all of human history. The Emersonian imperative to read *creatively,* as urged in "Self-Reliance" and the "American Scholar," here takes the form of advice to the student "to read history actively and not passively; to esteem his own life in the text, and books the commentary." The text is us, ourselves the riddle posed to be self-solved; everything is within us, "of the soul." This, says Emerson, is his "claim of claims," and "the obscure consciousness of this fact is the light of all our day" (*E&L* 237, 239).

"Obscure" in all particulars but one, that Wordsworthian light is, for Emerson, virtually identical with self-reliance—though it is a "self" that remains distinguishable from what we "call ourselves": those impertinent, superficial, merely private selves shamed in the presence of our deep "moral nature," which participates in the "universal Mind." Without that qualification (and the observation in "Character" seems less an altering afterthought than one of many clarifications of Emerson's original conception of self-reliance), this assertion in "History" would confirm the judgment of James Marsh about the Transcendentalists being "superficial" and particularly deluded in considering as an inspiration that "comes from the universal heart" what is far likelier to derive "from the stomach of the individual." In fact, since he was writing in March 1841, the month *Essays: First Series* was published, he may very well have been responding to "History," the opening essay in the volume, as well as to the essay that immediately follows, "Self-Reliance." Though Marsh would disagree, Emerson's own tempering of the more extreme readings of his core doctrine was achieved with the help of Wordsworth and, especially, Coleridge. In the two chapters that follow, on "Emerson's Discipleship," we turn to the more general question of the American thinker's sometimes denied but indisputable debt to his major transatlantic precursors.

Chapter 3

Emerson's Discipleship

RESISTANCE

Many things I owe to the sight of these men. I shall judge more justly, less timidly, of wise men forever more. . . . [I]t is an *idealized* portrait which we always draw of them.

—EMERSON after his 1833 visits to Coleridge, Wordsworth, and Carlyle

Had Emerson expected gods in trousers?

—ROBERT WEISBUCH on Emerson's response, *Atlantic Double-Cross: American Literature and British Influence in the Age of Reason*

The Transatlantic pathways opened up (though not necessarily explored) by recent criticism make it more readily possible to find, at least in outline, most of Emerson's mature stances of self-reliance and orphic originality already prescribed in the work of his romantic forebears. All this makes the issue of Emerson's foundational role in American literary life a more complex one, as the boundaries between what Emerson founded and what he imported become harder to see.

—LEE RUST BROWN, *The Emerson Museum*

Emerson visited Europe three times: in 1833, in 1847–1848, and, as an old man accompanied by his daughter Ellen, in 1872. Though he met, among others, Robert Browning and John Ruskin during that final vacation, only the first two visits are part of Emerson's intellectual history. He came, the first time, to meet a number of writers who had influenced him—above all, Coleridge, Wordsworth, and Carlyle—and he revisited the latter two (Coleridge had died in 1834) during his second trip. The psychodrama of Emerson's response both to the men he met and to the impact of their work upon him is well synopsized in the final two epigraphs above: the delightful rhetorical question of Weisbuch and the judicious comment of Brown on the difficulty of drawing clear boundaries between "what Emerson founded and what he imported." Much of what he imported came through the transatlantic pipeline of Coleridge. To anyone familiar with the Romantics, in particular with the multifaceted phenomenon of Coleridge—as thinker and poet, transmitter to England and the United States of German idealist philosophy, and cocreator of an equally exportable Wordsworth—that transatlantic role seems reasonably obvious. Yet, as noted earlier, it tends to be acknowledged and, until quite recently, dismissed. Frank Thompson's perceptive tracing of Emerson's indebtedness to Coleridge had no more impact on most students of American literature than did the work of those who had earlier noted the Coleridgean influence.

The most advanced current thinking about transatlantic Romanticism is epitomized in the reciprocal emphasis with which Richard Gravil concludes his introduction to *Romantic Dialogues:* "Any study" of the major nineteenth-century American writers "that contents itself with a passing nod to English Romanticism, and the odd footnote to Coleridge, as many such studies still do, is both misleading and self-deluding," he insists. "Equally, however, any study of English Romanticism that ignores the centrality of 'America' to Romanticism's self-definition . . . is offering a bowdlerized literary history." That "many studies still do" ignore or play down the transatlantic dialogue is largely attributable to two causes. One cause is simply academic: the "specialization" factor in professional scholarship. Sacvan Bercovitch has referred to "the chronic resistance of Americanists, in their zealous search for National Character, to give due attention to 'foreign' influences." And Lawrence Buell, surveying responses to New England literary culture, particularly the Transcendentalist movement, protests "the excesses of contemporary scholarship, which sometimes stress Transcendentalism's indigenous roots at the expense of its international connections." More recently, Buell has observed a cultural forgetting involving specifically the Coleridge-Emerson connection:

> The tendency for Americanists to concentrate on the inner coherence of our literary history has caused many of us to lose sight of the fact that no precursor had a more formative influence on Emerson's thinking than the English Romantic Samuel Taylor Coleridge, from whom he derived the liberating distinction between Reason (which intuitively apprehends Truth)

and Understanding (the faculty of empirical deduction and rational calculation) traditionally called "reason."[1]

But the second, and more interesting cause, has to do with an initial—and then critically reiterated—pattern of denial. Until fairly recently, most critics of American literature followed the major nineteenth-century writers themselves in their aggressive-defensive insistence on their own "American" originality. In Emerson's case, the strategy took the form of significant silence and erasure, especially in published texts most adamant in their assertion of originality. The second half of this chapter will focus on three such silences or erasures in *Nature,* all having to do with Coleridge and Wordsworth, benefactors whose presence is repeatedly emphasized in the privacy of contemporary journal entries, even as they are denied entrance into the very public forum of Emerson's first and foundational book. The writers of *Old* England might be visited and vamped from, but, if Emersonian power and originality were to be preserved, readers in *New* England must find "no foot-track in the field" traversed by Emerson (*EPP* 330), no overt trace of Coleridge, Wordsworth, and Carlyle.

We can track this Emersonian division between acknowledgment and attempted erasure or supersession of Old England in many places, most starkly, perhaps, in those passages having to do with Emerson's actual journeys to England. Since we will be spending some time on the first pilgrimage, I will mention here two passages in *English Traits* having to do with the second journey. In the "Stonehenge" chapter, we find Emerson in conversation, in late 1847, with his old friend Carlyle, who criticizes visiting Americans for running off to France instead of "staying manfully in London, and confronting Englishmen, and acquiring their culture, who really have much to teach them." Emerson concedes English virtues, the "sense and spirit" of a nation of men that "have everything, and can do everything,"

> but meantime, I surely know, that, as soon as I return to Massachusetts, I shall lapse at once into the feeling, which the geography of America inevitably inspires, that we play the game with immense advantage; that there and not here is the seat and centre of the British race; and that no skill or activity can long compete with the prodigious natural advantages of that country, in

1. Gravil, *Romantic Dialogues,* xx; Bercovitch, ed., *Typology and Early American Literature,* 4; Buell, "The Transcendentalist Movement," 8; Buell, ed., *Ralph Waldo Emerson: A Collection of Critical Essays,* 5. In his new full-length study, Buell accepts the portrait of Emerson as an American "icon." But the fact that our culture has been "shaped in interaction with transatlantic, transpacific, and hemispheric influences" makes it all the "more crucial to appreciate how canonical figures like Emerson have been oversimplified" in being thought of *simply* "as icons of U.S. national culture" (*Emerson,* 3).

> the hands of the same race; and that England, an old and exhausted island, must one day be contented, like other parents, to be strong only in her children. (*E&L* 916)

It was, he immediately adds, a "proposition which no Englishman of whatever condition can easily entertain," and, indeed, Emerson himself can go so far, in chapter 3 of *English Traits,* as to reinforce the point about the "same race" by generously yet rather grimly conceding that "we are met by a civilization already settled and overpowering. The culture of the day, the thoughts and aims of men, are English thoughts and aims. . . . The American is only the continuation of the English genius into new conditions, more or less propitious" (*E&L* 784–85). And once he was back in the United States, Emerson, despite his emphasis on the strong "children" of "that country," found that, in fact, it was no country for young men. In debating the relative merits of England and the United States with Thoreau in 1850, Emerson, disagreeing with the protégé with whom he was increasingly out of tune, took Carlyle's side of the debate. A "rambling talk with H. T.," initially an attempt to mend fences, soon reverted to their differences. Of American lack of accomplishment, Emerson confides to his journal: "Yes, we have infinite powers, but cannot use them. When shall we attain our majority, & come to our estate[?]" (*JMN* 11: 286). In the case of the United States and his dream of the American Scholar and the great native Poet, neither of whom he believed to be incarnated in the young man who had graduated the year after the astonishing "American Scholar" address had been delivered in 1837, Emerson was still waiting for that "true romance" that (he claimed at the end of "Experience") "the world exists to realize," namely, "the transformation of genius into practical power" (*E&L* 492). Emerson insists in his pragmatic mode, "Genius is not a lazy angel contemplating itself and things. . . . Thought must take the stupendous step of passing into realization" (*W* 12:43).

By the time he returned from England in 1848, Emerson was, if anything, even more under the shadow of that supposedly exhausted "parent" from whom he had tried to declare independence in the 1830s. Yet defenders of Emerson's American originality, for whom such admissions are beside the point, find the tracing of influence, especially Emerson's reception of the entanglements of Coleridge and Carlyle with German idealism, reductive—simply inadequate as an "explanation" of the phenomenon of Emerson. And so it is, when it is allowed to overshadow the "more or less propitious" development of British Romanticism on the expansive native ground, the immense "geography," of America. My intention is not to reduce Emerson to a simple disciple of the British Romantics or to what Bloom preempts as a "weak descendent" of the German idealist tradition that came to Emerson through Coleridge. Although the ideational lineage seems indisputable, nothing can account for the inflections of the individual talent: in the case of Emerson, as Milnes noted in 1840, the remarkable *style* in which that mind on fire expresses itself, and what he makes, in an American context, of his intellectual-intuitive heritage. Fully aware of that heritage, he would yet insist (in "Considerations by the Way" in *The Conduct of Life*) that although "all America seems on the point of embarking for Europe," we "shall not always traverse seas and lands" as cultural tourists. "One day we shall cast out the passion for Europe, by the passion for America" (*E&L* 1090). Eventually, if later than Emerson anticipated, that day came. But in his own context, though the Emerson traced here remains largely his own man, we cannot overlook his debts and appropriations.

Harold Bloom will disagree, but as the author of *The Anxiety of Influence* himself has explained to us at length, the ways of influence are labyrinthine indeed. To quote not Bloom, but a great poet, Paul Valéry, "Influence is clearly distinguishable from imitation. . . . [W]hat a man does either repeats or rejects what someone else has done—repeats it in another tone, refines or amplifies or simplifies it, loads or overloads it with meaning, or else rebuts, overturns, destroys and denies it, but thereby assumes it and has invisibly used it." Applying such an approach in attempting to work through Emerson's harvesting from Coleridge and Wordsworth, I follow in the wake not only of critics from Thompson and Miller to Weisbuch and Ellison, Gravil and Buell, but of one other expansive treatment of the impact of European Romanticism on the major nineteenth-century American writers: Leon Chai's *Romantic Foundations of the American Renaissance*. The subject of this sweeping synthesis is "the assimilation and transformation"—in the work of such major American authors as Emerson, Poe, Hawthorne, and Melville—"of the cultural legacy of European Romanticism." Chai tracks the American writers' creative appropriation and reinterpretation of "certain governing concepts or tendencies"—principally, the secularization of religion and the revelation through Nature of an immanent divine presence, the relationship between mind and external Nature, and the role of the creative and perceiving consciousness. His chief concern is with "the different forms Romantic thought assumes in the course of its development, the nature and process of its transmission, the alterations it experiences—in short, the whole course of its growth and transformation."[2]

2. Valéry, *Collected Works,* 8:241; Chai, *Romantic Foundations,* xi, xii, 423. Chai singles out Wordsworth as the major figure who "looms over" his book "as a numinous presence." He surmises that Wordsworth's full relation to American Romanticism

That said, transmission necessarily precedes transformation. Not even Emerson is sui generis, and more than a hint of the anxiety of influence hovers over his meetings with Wordsworth and Coleridge (the younger Carlyle was another matter) in the summer of 1833, his first trip to Europe. Nothing, asserts Chai, better typifies the "historical and intellectual continuity" between Romanticism and the American Renaissance than these visits. In characterizing the meetings with the first two as "full of hope and, unfortunately, disappointed expectations," Chai is registering Emerson's own account—and, presumably unconsciously, replicating the trajectory of Wordsworth and Coleridge in their evolving response to the French Revolution, the very paradigm of hope and disappointed expectations.[3] In both cases, it is dangerous to take things at face value. To simply accept Emerson's account is to overlook his need *to be* disappointed in order to preserve the autonomy of his own "aboriginal Self" (*E&L* 268). This crucial point was nicely made by Bloom's former student Julie Ellison, in her perceptive *Emerson's Romantic Style,* a study published three years before Chai's book; then by Robert Weisbuch, both in the opening pages of *Atlantic Double-Cross* and in the earlier-cited 1999 article; and, most recently by Richard Gravil.

The primary evidence lies, of course, in Emerson's published accounts of his visits to Wordsworth, Coleridge, and Carlyle, long available in *English Traits,* narratives that, shaped in hindsight, can now be measured against and supplemented by the journal comments he made at the time. There can often be a marked disparity. For example, the entries on Wordsworth, written within hours of his visit on August 28, 1833, record every detail of Wordsworth's conversation. Except when it came to defending Carlyle and Goethe from Wordsworthian assault, Emerson listened in the respectful silence dictated by tact, deference to age, and genuine admiration. He was understandably flattered by his host's "great kindness," especially by the invitation to walk in his garden where he recited to him, "with great spirit," his recent and—Emerson thought—"beautiful" sonnets on Fingal's Cave (sonnets Emerson later included in *Parnassus*). He inquired, as he would again during his 1848 visit, about the unpublished autobiographical epic,

---

could be expressed only "by confronting the totality of his oeuvre with that of Melville or Emerson." In the case of the latter, "much might be said" about Wordsworth's "exploration of the nature of consciousness and the experience of divine presence compared to Emerson's." A full treatment, however, would "require juxtaposing a comprehensive interpretation of *The Prelude* with that of *Nature* (rather than treating concepts or *topoi* from these works), a procedure quite different from mine" (5). I do some of this sort of juxtaposing, but the present book is hardly "comprehensive" in the sense Chai intends.

3. Chai, *Romantic Foundations,* 6.

extracts of which had spurred excitement to see the "promised" poem. As for the famous Wordsworthian "egotism," Emerson found it neither "displeasing" nor "intrusive." He concluded of the visit: "I spoke as I felt, with great respect of his genius" (*JMN* 4:223–26). Over time, Emerson would be less deferential, but even in *English Traits* Wordsworth's "genius" was never in doubt, and, once Emerson had himself emerged as a major figure, he was freed to express both an admiration and a criticism less burdened by the anxiety of influence and the fear of imitation.

Of course, Emerson had defensively armed himself against awe from the outset, as we can also see from the journals. Given their availability we do not, in exploring Emerson's relationship to Coleridge and Wordsworth, have to venture all that far into what Valéry called the realm of the "invisible." Before he set foot on land, still aboard the brig *Jasper*, Emerson had laid out the parameters of his American encounter with Europe: the coming of vigorous youth to a venerable but superannuated and even invalided parent. "Well blithe traveller what cheer?" he opens his infectious entry for January 14, 1833.

> What have the sea & the stars & the moaning winds & your discontented thoughts sung in your attentive ears? Peeps up old Europe yet out of his eastern main? hospitably ho! Nay the slumberous old giant cannot bestir himself in these his chair days to loom up for the pastime of his upstart grandchildren as now they come shoal after shoal to salute their old Progenitor[,] the old Adam of all. Sleep on, old Sire, there is muscle & nerve & enterprise enow in us your poor spawn who have sucked the air & ripened in the sunshine of the cold West to steer our ships to your very ports & thrust our inquisitive American eyes into your towns & towers & keeping rooms. Here we come & mean to be welcome. So be of good cheer now, clever old gentleman. (*EPP* 490–91)

But the clever one here is Emerson. In the Anglo-American struggle for cultural priority, a favorite American strategy, certainly one adopted by Emerson in this journal entry, is "to make decrepitude and its signs the characterization of Britain and its writers, and to contrast with this British anxiety, the promise of a free American future." The immediate occasion prompting this comment (by Weisbuch and quoted by Gravil) was Emerson's "American Scholar" address, but it is if anything even more germane to this journal entry. After stopping at Malta and Sicily, Emerson went to Naples to visit Walter Savage Landor. Even entering the famous bay (March 12), the upstart grandchild, asserting Adamic priority, refuses to be "overawed." Such names as "Baiae & Miseneum & Vesuvius, Procida & Pausilippo & Villa Reale sound so big that we are ready to surrender at discretion & not stickle for our private opinion against what seems the human race. Who cares? Here's for the plain old Adam, the simple genuine Self against the whole world. Need is, that you assert yourself or you will find yourself overborne by the most paltry things" (*EPP* 491). It is hard to resist that nonchalant "Who cares?" but the final adjective, *paltry,* gives away part of the aggressively defensive game: the provincial Yankee as an audacious second Adam at once flaunting and feigning bravado in the presence of something anything *but* paltry: European civilization and the impending visits to Coleridge, Wordsworth, and Carlyle.[4] With the partial exception of the vigorous Carlyle, the valetudinarians he met at Highgate and Rydal Mount would also prove, predictably, underwhelming.

To be sure, Emerson had help from the principals in diminishing their stature. Unless one grants Yeats's great spiritual-imaginative "unless"—and, for his own purposes, Emerson often was not willing to grant it—"an aged man *is* but a paltry thing." The aged men Emerson sought out on this first trip to Europe were, by then, conservative Christians far removed from, respectively, the early dissenting Unitarian Coleridge had once been and—in Coleridge's term—the then "at least . . . *Semi*-atheist" Wordsworth.[5] After meeting with John Stuart Mill, Emerson called on Coleridge, reduced by time and Emerson's prose to a "short, thick old man," snuff stained and preoccupied by sectarian squabbles. The "Sage of Highgate" treated his young guest, the future "Sage of Concord," to a typically Coleridgean monologue, sounding like "printed paragraphs." The religiously obsessed old man made it abundantly clear during Emerson's interview of an hour or so that it was "a wonder . . . after so many ages of unquestioning acquiescence" in the "doctrine of the Trinity" that "this handful of Priestleyans should take on themselves to deny it." Of course, Joseph Priestley had been a religious and political hero of the youthful Coleridge, who once dreamed of emulating his emigration to the United States. But, as Coleridge told Emerson, he "knew all about Unitarianism

4. Gravil, *Romantic Dialogues,* 62. Between Italy and England there was Paris. At first "sorry" to leave Italian towns with their "antiquity & history" to "come to a loud modern New York of a place" (*JMN* 4:197), he soon found himself enjoying Paris—and learning. He took in the Louvre and lectures at the Sorbonne and, most significantly for his future career, visited the Jardin des Plantes.

5. Coleridge so described Wordsworth in May 1796 to his fully atheist friend, the radical John Thelwall. Five weeks later, in the postscript of a letter inviting Thelwall to visit him in Stowey, Coleridge added: "We have an hundred lovely scenes about Bristol, which would make you exclaim, O admirable *Nature!* & me, O Gracious God!" (*CL* 1:216, 222).

perfectly well, because he had once been a Unitarian," indeed "had been called 'the rising star of Unitarianism,'" and consequently "knew what quackery it was." He referred to the visit, eleven years earlier, of Boston pastor William Ellery Channing. Coleridge had been impressed by Channing (as had Wordsworth, who read aloud to him from his unpublished epic).[6] But it was neither Channing's intellect nor his attunement to Romanticism that engaged Coleridge during this interview with Emerson, who reports that his host "spoke of Dr. Channing," insisting that it was "an unspeakable misfortune"

> that he should have turned out a Unitarian after all. On this he burst into a declamation on the folly and ignorance of Unitarianism,—its high unreasonableness; and taking up Bishop Waterland's book, which lay on the table, he read with vehemence two or three pages written by himself in the fly-leaves—passages, too, which, I believe, are printed in the "Aids to Reflection." When he stopped to take his breath, I interposed that, "whilst I highly valued all his explanations, I was bound to tell him that I was born and bred a Unitarian." "Yes," he said, "I supposed so;" and continued on as before. (*E&L* 771)[7]

Obviously, whether it was Channing's Unitarianism (gradually but fully accepted) or Emerson's (at first embraced and now wavering), it was a creed well beyond the Christian pale of this "old man, with bright blue eyes and fine clear complexion," a seer grown crotchety who "was old and preoccupied, and could not bend to a new companion and think with him" (*E&L* 770, 773). The ironic twist in this intellectual comedy—"rather a spectacle than a conversation," says Emerson—is that Coleridge's "new companion" was beginning to think that much conventional Unitarianism was precisely, as Coleridge called it, "quackery." But, of course, Emerson was moving beyond that sect in a radical, not as Coleridge had, in a conservative, trinitarian direction.

From London, Emerson journeyed to Scotland—first to Edinburgh, where he preached at a Unitarian chapel and where he met Alexander Ireland, who was later to become one of his first biographers, then on to Craigenputtock in the Highlands, where he stayed the night at the invitation of Thomas and Jane Carlyle.

6. Wordsworth read from the unpublished "Poem for Coleridge," according to Elizabeth Palmer Peabody, whom Channing introduced to the poetry of Wordsworth. See her *Reminiscences of William Ellery Channing,* 80–81.

7. Both of Daniel Waterland's books—*A Vindication of Christ's Divinity* and *The Importance of the Doctrine of the Holy Trinity*—contained ardent defenses of trinitarianism, and Coleridge annotated both. See *AR* 564–65, and, for Coleridge's annotations, *Marginalia,* 6:54–93.

Emerson was intellectually prepared for the visit. He had been profoundly impressed by three of Carlyle's brilliant early essays. The first, "State of German Literature" (1827), called upon literary men rather than theologians to become the "dispensers and living types" of a wisdom embodying the all-pervading "Divine Idea," and explained the distinction between Reason and understanding: the former "discovers truth itself, the absolutely and primitively true," whereas the latter "discovers only relations," a distinction to be found in Coleridge's *Friend, Biographia Literaria,* and *Aids to Reflection.* In "Signs of the Times" (1829), Carlyle denounced the submission of mind to matter, creative freedom to mechanism and mediocrity, and called for a "dynamic" reversal based on a shift of perspective from outer to inner, since the current "deep paralyzed subjection to physical objects comes not from nature, but from our own unwise mode of viewing nature." But because "we are fettered by chains of our own forging," they are Blakean mind-forged manacles we "ourselves can rend asunder." In "Characteristics" (1831), the third, and most embryonic of these essays, Carlyle, like Coleridge, emphasized the role of "intuitive" rather than merely "logical" or "argumentative" reason, a celebration of the "inner sanctuaries" of the Unconscious with "its abysses of mystery and miracle." Armed with the mental capacity to overcome a "diseased" hyperconsciousness and recover a spiritual and affirmative vision, we can, says Carlyle, advocating a proto-Nietzschean stance of "heroic joy," attain a non-Nietzschean fusion of religious faith and the "scientific mind." Those seeking the sacred in an age of negation must "realize a worship for themselves, or live unworshipping." But "out of Evil comes Good," and already we can detect "streaks of a dayspring . . . in the east. It is dawning; when the time shall be fulfilled, it will be day."[8]

Rhetorical power aside, and despite his own extensive reading of German philosophy, much of this is to be found in Coleridge, particularly the take on Kant. But whatever Carlyle's indebtedness, it *never* seems to be acknowledged. Like Emerson in his shipboard notebook before setting foot on European soil, Carlyle was defensive from the outset. It was through his friend Edward Irving that Carlyle met Coleridge in 1824, though he had joked prior to the meeting that Irving seemed to think he would experience "some strange development of genius" and, having conversed with Coleridge, would "soon learn to speak in tongues." When he did finally visit Highgate, he found "the Kantian metaphysician and quondam lake poet" a man with "a good soul, full of religion and affection." But he also thought Coleridge physically unimpressive and lazy, "a man of great and

8. These essays appear in Carlyle, *Critical and Miscellaneous Essays,* 1:26–83, 462–87, 2:344–83.

useless genius," and judged the meeting "unprofitable, even tedious," even though "we parted very good friends" and Carlyle "promised to go back and see him some other evening—a promise I fully intend to keep."[9]

This caveated dismissal hardly prepares us for the gratuitous and venomous intellectual and ad hominem attacks on Coleridge to be found in Carlyle's journals and letters over the years. Though even into the 1860s and '70s Carlyle was ridiculing Coleridge's reputation as a magus, even denying his knowledge of Kant, his sustained antipathy to the Sage of Highgate ("a mass of richest spices, putrefied into a dunghill") may be said to culminate in a hostile yet remarkably ambivalent passage in his 1851 *Life of John Sterling.* The ostensible justification for the character assassination is that Coleridge's was chief among the malign influences from which Carlyle's friend Sterling (who had also visited Highgate in the mid-1820s) was saved by the real hero of the book, the biographer! But it is hard to miss the envy and anxiety of influence looming beneath the surface of this nevertheless fascinated portrait of the magnetic man who had anticipated Carlyle in bringing German philosophy to England and whose oracular conversation cast a magical spell on the "rising spirits of the young generation"—young men who might otherwise have been disciples of Carlyle himself. Though on this occasion Carlyle is not bombastic, he does succeed, with his characteristic verve, in putting palpably before us a living person in unforgettable prose. The highlights are worth repeating, not only to savor Carlyle's stylistic brilliance, glittering with malice and wit, but also to see how crucial the German connection was. The opening passage is a deservedly famous set piece of Victorian prose:

> Coleridge sat on the brow of Highgate Hill, in those years, looking down on London and its smoke-tumult, like a sage escaped from the inanity of life's battle; attracting towards him the thoughts of innumerable brave souls still engaged there. His express contributions to poetry, philosophy, or any specific province of human literature or enlightenment had been small and sadly intermittent; but he had, especially among young inquiring men, a higher than literary, a kind of prophetic or magician character. He was thought to hold, he alone in England, the key of German and other Transcendentalisms; knew the sublime secret of believing by "the reason" what "the understanding" had been obliged to fling out as incredible. . . . A sublime man; who, alone in those dark days had saved his crown of spiritual manhood; escaping from the black materialisms, and revolutionary deluges, with "God, Freedom, Immortality" still his: a king of men. . . .
>
> He distinguished himself to all that ever heard him as at least the most surprising talker extant in this world,—and to some small minority, by no means to all, as the most excellent. . . . I still recollect his "object" and "sub-

9. Carlyle, *The Collected Letters of Thomas and Jane Welsh Carlyle,* 2:459–60, 3:90.

> ject," terms of continual recurrence in the Kantian province; and how he sang and snuffled them into "om-m-mject" and "sum-m-mject," with a kind of solemn shake or quaver, as he rolled along. . . . [Despite the challenges of atheism and materialism, the English Church, which was not dead but "tragically asleep only," could be "brought to life again"]. But how, but how! By attending to the "reason" of man, said Coleridge, and duly chaining-up the "understanding" of man: the *Vernunft* (Reason) and *Verstand* (Understanding) of the Germans, it all turned upon these, if you could well understand them,—which you couldn't.[10]

To judge from the essays summarized above, Carlyle *could* "understand," and apply, Coleridge's principal emphases and distinctions. In fact, shortly after encountering the Coleridgean rather than Kantian distinction between Reason and mere understanding in *Aids to Reflection,* Carlyle noted in a journal entry (December 1826): "Yes, it is true! The decisions of Reason (Vernunft) are superior to those of Understanding (Verstand)," the latter being variable whereas the former "last forever." And in a later entry (August 1829), though he retains his originality with a strikingly *specific* image from nature, he draws a Coleridgean analogy employing *both* of his precursor's paramount distinctions: "Understanding is to Reason as the talent of a Beaver (which can build houses, and uses its tail for a trowel) to the genius of a Prophet and Poet. Reason is all but extinct in this age: it can never be altogether extinguished."[11]

I am going into some detail here because, given my focus on Coleridge and Wordsworth, I treat Carlyle only peripherally—though I *do* note his influence on the Divinity School Address and suggest that the conclusion of "Threnody" is indebted to the "Everlasting Yea" chapter of *Sartor Resartus.* In any case, the loving if often contentious relationship between the two is well known. Emerson was to carry on a long and notable correspondence with Carlyle, whose *Sartor Resartus* he introduced to the United States, getting it serialized in *Fraser's Magazine* and published in Boston—in 1836, in time to influence the introduction to Emerson's own *Nature.*[12]

10. Carlyle, *The Life of John Sterling,* 54–60. As Charles Richard Sanders has said, Carlyle "might have been a happier man if there had never been a Coleridge" (*Coleridge and the Broad Church Movement,* 151). See also Sanders, "The Background of Carlyle's Portrait of Coleridge in *The Life of John Sterling,*" in *Carlyle's Friendships and Other Studies,* 36–60.

11. Carlyle, *Two Notebooks of Thomas Carlyle: From 23rd March 1822 to 16th May 1832,* 83–84, 142.

12. As Gravil remarks, "Emerson fuses three of *Sartor*'s themes in his own introduction: the adjuration to escape the bondage of old clothes; the theme of the supernatural bases of the natural, which emerges in later chapters as a major thesis; and a Fichtean definition of nature as encompassing 'all which philosophy distinguishes as the NOT ME'" (*Romantic Dialogues,* 94).

Carlyle's "bold and original" history, *The French Revolution,* that phoenix risen from his friend Mill's fireplace, was also published in the United States with the help of Emerson, who reviewed it in 1838, praising the author for his assertion that history is essentially biography[13] and for his insight into the "high and beautiful laws which exist in the reason of man," even in the midst of the spate of pain and horror minutely detailed by Carlyle. There we have a glimpse of the famous, or infamous, Optimist, the saintly Emerson of the serene smile, ignorant of, or unwilling to face, the true nature of evil—an understandable and persistent image, but still a caricature.

As the years passed, Emerson would, like other friends including John Stuart Mill, find Carlyle more and more eccentric, indiscriminately committed to the worship of strength, regardless of whether it was "divine or diabolic" (*JMN* 4:291), a charge to which Emerson himself may seem vulnerable, given his hyperbolic claim that he will follow his impulses, even if others think they come from the devil (*E&L* 61–62). Carlyle became increasingly reactionary and racist, his growing social and political anger reflected in a proportionately more furious rhetoric. Years later, in 1888, Emerson's German disciple would locate that rage in religious displacement. In the ninth chapter of *Twilight of the Idols,* Nietzsche, comparing Carlyle and Emerson, diagnosed the former as "a man of strong attitudes and words, a rhetor from *need,* constantly lured by the craving for a strong faith and the feeling of his incapacity for it (in this respect, a typical romantic!)." In his "heroic-moralistic interpretation of dyspeptic states," Carlyle "drugs something in himself with the fortissimo of his veneration of men of strong faith. . . . At bottom, Carlyle is an English atheist who makes it a point of honor not to be one." Nietzsche's characterization of Carlyle's friend was in sharp contrast:

> *Emerson.* Much more enlightened, more roving, more manifold, subtler than Carlyle; above all, happier. One who instinctively nourishes himself only on ambrosia, leaving behind what is indigestible in things. Compared with Carlyle, a man of taste. Carlyle, who loved him very much, nevertheless said of him: "He does not give us enough to chew on "—which may be true, but is no reflection on Emerson. Emerson has that gracious and clever cheerful-

13. In his own essay "History," Emerson states: "All history becomes subjective; in other words there is properly no history, only biography"; indeed, "the whole of history is in one man" and is "all to be explained from individual experience" (*E&L* 237). Though Emerson out-Carlyles Carlyle, this audacity is, initially, indebted to the author whose passionate and now no less passionately condemned formulation—"the history of the world is the biography of great men"—appeared in the same year (1841) as Emerson's essay. See Carlyle, "Hero as Divinity," in *On Heroes, Hero Worship, and the Heroic in History.*

ness which discourages all seriousness; he simply does not know how old he is already and how young he is still going to be; he could say of himself, quoting Lope de Vega: "*Yo me sucedo a mi mismo*" [I am my own heir].[14]

These conflicting temperaments, splendidly contrasted by Nietzsche (who illuminates rather than reduces Emersonian "cheerfulness" as *gaya scienza*), explain the growing gulf between the two men. From the outset of their deep if troubled relationship, Emerson found Carlyle so brilliant, so energetic, so "amiable," that he could not but "love him" (*JMN* 4:79). Yet over the years, the two old friends found less and less in common. "'Tis curious," concluded Emerson, "the magnificence of his genius, & the poverty of his aims" (*JMN* 10:553).[15]

In comparison with the exciting visit to Carlyle, Emerson's journey to the Lake District and the long-anticipated pilgrimage to Rydal Mount were somewhat anticlimactic. Still, here was the Poet in the flesh. After decades of misunderstanding, abuse, and ridicule at the hands of the Edinburgh reviewers, especially the once formidable Francis Jeffrey, Wordsworth had triumphed.[16] Though the 1824 edition of his poems had not sold out in Boston, he was, by 1833, a transatlantic institution: the author

14. Nietzsche, *Twilight of the Idols,* 9, secs. 12–13, in *The Portable Nietzsche,* 521–22.

15. Emerson was never exasperated enough to refer to Carlyle as William Morris once did in response to a question by Yeats. Carlyle was, said Morris, a genius who should have had someone standing beside him to "punch his head every five minutes." Still, during Emerson's second visit to England, the old friends found their mutual attraction fading. To Emerson, Carlyle seemed increasingly "morbid"; Carlyle now found Emerson "somewhat moonshiny" (Simon Heffer, *Moral Desperado: A Life of Thomas Carlyle,* 262). On one occasion, the two almost came to a parting of the ways. Emerson's unpublished account catches the Carlylean fury ("Powers and Laws of Thought," Houghton Library manuscript [cited in Richardson, *Mind on Fire,* 445]). When, discussing the character of one of Carlyle's heroes (and Milton's "chief of men"), Oliver Cromwell, Emerson differed with his host, the latter "rose like a great Norse giant from his chair—and, drawing a line with his finger across the table, said, with terrible fierceness, 'Then, sir, there is a line of separation between you and me as wide as that, and as deep as the pit.'" It was instead the friendship that proved deep, too deep not to survive, though in a sort of afterglow.

16. The evolution of Wordsworth's reputation in New England has been traced in two dissertations: by Armida Jennings Gilbert (1989) and, more thoroughly, by Joel Pace (1999). The focus of Pace's thoughtful full-scale study is clear in his title, "Wordsworth in America: Publication, Reception, and Literary Influence, 1802–1850." In the central and most valuable portion of her dissertation, her chapters on Wordsworth and Emerson, Gilbert sifts through the periodical literature on Wordsworth, most of it familiar to Emerson. Everyone has noted the wild swings in Emerson's own comments on Wordsworth, fluctuating between what Rusk has called "disgust" and "veneration" (*L* 1:xxxiv). The "inconsistency" can in large part be explained by the unevenness of the poetry itself and by the particular standard being applied: comparative (in which

of some celebrated lyrics familiar, it seems, to almost every reader in New England, and the philosopher-poet who had produced an edifying epic, *The Excursion* (1814), prefaced by that "Prospectus" rightly admired by Emerson and his aunt. The sixty-three-year-old poet proved a considerably more cordial host than Coleridge, though Emerson was being only partially unfair (the judgment was based on what he admits was "a single conversation") in later describing Wordsworth as "one who paid for his rare elevation by general tameness and conformity," a figure, in short, of what Emerson would later call the Establishment, not of the Movement. Or, to employ the names given to the characters in *The Excursion* among whom Wordsworth had parceled out and dramatized different aspects of himself: the wise if sententious Wanderer had won out over the "heathen" and disillusioned but salvageable Solitary, and even, to some extent, over the Poet. It was not a recent development. Wordsworth's epic, especially its fourth book, had provided Keats with some of his own mythology in *Endymion.* Yet when, in 1817, he had read Wordsworth his "Hymn to Pan," from book 1, the self-demythologized older poet had famously sniffed (though we will never know upon which word his *chief* emphasis fell), "a very pretty piece of paganism."

Given the dismissive remark he made in 1841 (noted below), the now orthodox Wordsworth, a man increasingly touchy about his own early "pantheism," might have said the same about American Transcendentalism in 1833. Apparently, he did not, but his thinking can be gauged by his responses to Emerson and Transcendentalism registered in the years immediately following. Though, in 1837, he had been sent copies of Emerson's *Nature* and "The American Scholar," Wordsworth never read them. This time, it was not a case of receiving a book and shelving it unread (the painful case with Keats's 1817 *Poems,* left at Rydal Mount by his young admirer and found, with the leaves still uncut, at the time of Wordsworth's death, almost three decades after Keats's). The Emerson texts sent across the ocean by his American admirer, the remarkably accomplished Elizabeth Palmer Peabody, seem not to have arrived—a great misfortune for anyone interested in the transatlantic dialogue. Whatever his reaction to

---

case Wordsworth emerges as second only to Shakespeare and Milton) or Ideal, an Emersonian standard against which *no* poet survives unscathed, especially no contemporary poet, even Goethe and Wordsworth. Gilbert's distinctive contribution has been to analyze the reviews Emerson read (those by Jeffrey and other Edinburgh reviewers, as well as favorable reviews, most important by Henry Taylor) and persuasively demonstrate that such secondary reading was "a major influence" on Emerson's responses to, and occasionally contradictory opinions on, Wordsworth's poetry ("English Romantic Poets," esp. 64–311).

the declaration of independence made in "The American Scholar," Wordsworth would surely have read *Nature* with a shock of recognition, finding there much of his own Romantic *naturphilosopie,* along with some of his now rejected thoughts returning with a certain alienated majesty. *Too* alienated, perhaps. Wordsworth did receive the copy of Emerson's *Essays: First Series* sent him by Peabody in March 1841. Writing to his American publisher, Henry Reed, in August of that year, Wordsworth described the *Essays* as exemplifying, along with the work of Carlyle, "the weakness of our age."[17]

What seems to have been uppermost in his mind was the so-called theological ideas of the man who had emerged as the leading American Transcendentalist. "Where," Wordsworth asked archly, "is the thing which now passes for philosophy at Boston to stop?" This letter to Reed, printed ten years later, when Wordsworth was dead but the Boston pseudophilosopher very much alive, was almost certainly read by Emerson, who would have encountered it in his copy of the Boston edition of Christopher Wordsworth's two-volume *Memoirs of William Wordsworth* (1851). His awareness of Wordsworth's criticism might well have affected his disparagement, five years later in *English Traits,* of Wordsworth's "narrow and very English mind." Emerson's much admired Wordsworth, for all his greatness, had—"off his own beat," poetry—degenerated in every other way into the very model of "conformity" (*E&L* 778). And for the elderly and orthodox Wordsworth, American Transcendentalism was just another, and not so pretty, piece of paganism.[18]

In contrast to the interview with Coleridge, Emerson and Wordsworth did not discuss religion in 1833. They discussed instead literature (they concurred that *The Excursion* was superior even to the more popular "Tintern Abbey"), science (Wordsworth prophetically anticipated that "Newtonian theory... might be superseded" [*JMN* 4:224]), and education. Indeed, his main subject on this as on many other occasions, including the visit of William Ellery Channing in 1822, was his concern that book

17. Leslie Nathan Broughton, ed., *Wordsworth and Reed: The Poet's Correspondence with His American Editor, 1836–50,* 57. Margaret Neussendorfer has published (in *Studies in the American Renaissance,* ed. Myerson) eight of the letters Peabody sent to Wordsworth between 1825 and 1845, in two of which (February 1838 and March 29, 1841) she discussed the Emerson texts she was sending Wordsworth.

18. Broughton, *Wordsworth and Reed,* 57. Reed concurred, finding Emerson's principal defect "an intolerable corruption of our mighty language" (60). The letter was first printed in Christopher Wordsworth's *Memoirs of William Wordsworth,* 2:390. In his 1999 dissertation, Pace plausibly surmises that Emerson's awareness of the letter affected his description of Wordsworth in *English Traits.* Pace's "Wordsworth in America," 313, is cited in Gravil, *Romantic Dialogues,* 230n33.

learning was being preferred to the intuitive wisdom to be gleaned from our experiential intercourse with nature.[19] On that point, despite a brief and long-since-dropped enthusiasm for the Bell system of education, Wordsworth was in 1833 as he had been during the Great Decade. Not so in other respects. No longer the rebel of the 1790s, he was now a politically conservative thinker long since disillusioned by the bloody excesses of the French Revolution, transformed into an ardent nationalist by the need to defeat Napoléon, and, most recently, driven to political apoplexy by the Reform Bill of 1832. With wit and indignation (unfortunately confined to an unpublished manuscript titled "Reform and Chartism," intended for, but omitted from, *English Traits*), Emerson praised the Reform Bill, which "took away the right of election from a stone wall, a green mound, and a ruined house" and allowed two members of Parliament for Birmingham and Manchester, which previously had no members, despite the fact that their "mills" had paid for "the coalitions of Europe." Though a fierce supporter of the long national struggle of the British-led coalitions against Napoleonic France, Wordsworth was disturbed not only by some of the bill's provisions enlarging the franchise of the newly activist middle class but also by what he considered the corrupt political means (the creation of peerages) employed to turn that bill into law.[20] Still, one longs for the younger Wordsworth, who had found rather more corruption in the representation of rotten boroughs.

But, again, Emerson's host was the Wordsworth of 1833: Hazlitt's un-Miltonic turncoat from the cause of the Revolution, the "apostate" of Shelley and Byron, the "lost leader" of Browning (whose poem of that title Emerson printed in *Parnassus*), the antidemocratic reactionary so brilliantly savaged in 1839 by Orestes Brownson (who, a year after *that,* would himself turn conservative and, four years later, mystify Emerson by converting to Catholicism!).[21] The man Emerson encountered—physically hardy

19. The following remarks in Channing's European journal would seem to reflect the conversation with Wordsworth: "The intellectual education of the poor is talked of. Can the poor, as they are now situated, be taught much? What idea does the poor child get in a common school? The true school of human nature is the sphere opened to its faculties and affections in daily life" (*Memoirs of William Ellery Channing,* 1:496, 497).

20. He was right, and he no doubt had in mind his own poem on how even a good purpose is defeated when the end is achieved through corrupt and corrupting means. That poem, "Dion," was a favorite of Emerson, who would later, in the case of Daniel Webster, be no less exercised by the betrayal of principles in the name of political expediency. The unpublished praise of the Reform Bill (in Houghton Library) is cited in Richardson, *Mind on Fire,* 452.

21. His conversion to "popery" perplexed Emerson, who thought it had to do with the rituals and "symbolism"; it had to do, said Brownson, with what lay *behind* the

but suffering from eye problems that forced him to wear "green goggles"—was, despite his chanting of several recent sonnets, in relative poetic dotage. But he was still capable of prophetic utterance, and not only about the supersession of Newtonian physics by some future theory. Exercised by the societal breakdown he saw as inherent in the 1832 legislation, Wordsworth made a paradoxical, and eerily clairvoyant, remark to his guest. Americans, said Wordsworth a quarter century before the crucial event of our history, "needed a civil war . . . to teach them the necessity of knitting the social ties stronger." Wordsworth and his organicist friend Coleridge had long deplored the loss of communal cohesion, but the visitor from the United States must still have been taken aback by this rather drastic proposal as a remedy for the unraveling of the social fabric (*E&L* 775–76).[22]

But it was, Emerson reports in *English Traits,* education that dominated Wordsworth's discourse: "He had much to say of America, the more that it gave occasion for his favorite topic,—that society is being enlightened by a superficial tuition, out of all proportion to its being restrained by moral culture. Schools do no good. Tuition is not education. He thinks more of the education of circumstances than of tuition"—more, that is, of intuitive interaction with living Nature than of book learning (*E&L* 775). As we will see in examining book 5 of *The Prelude,* true education meant for Wordsworth the enhancement of freedom and power, "knowledge not purchased with the loss of power." Wordsworthian "power," the call to "Let Nature be your Teacher," even Wordsworth's specific criticism of a systematic education "*out of all proportion*" to the intuitive, spontaneous intercourse with Nature: all seem recalled in a single sentence of Emerson's late essay "Inspiration," which employs as well the Romantics' aeolian

---

symbolism. But back in 1839, before his conversion and his revulsion from the elections of 1840, Brownson found Wordsworth a reactionary in poetics (legislating at the expense of "spontaneity") and in politics: a sycophant to aristocrats, a traitor to himself and to the principles of the French Revolution, which contained within it, Brownson thought as late as 1839, "the cause of Humanity." See his "Wordsworth." Brownson seems a less mystifying figure when viewed in the dual light of Romantic "disenchantment" with, or "apostasy" from, the French Revolution and twentieth-century turns from the communist God that failed. Brownson was at one stage an American precursor of Marx, at another what the conservative thinker Russell Kirk (in his introduction to Brownson's *Selected Essays*) has called "the most convincing American opponent of Marxism," perceived as "a Christian heresy."

22. It became a constant Wordsworthian theme that America's sectional contradictions arising from the slavery issue could be resolved only by a civil war. In 1861, Emerson, committed to "the most absolute abolition," went further. Following the attack on Fort Sumter, he visited Charleston Naval Yard and, declaring that "sometimes gunpowder smells good," said of the imminent civil war that "amputation is better than cancer."

harp: "The depth of the notes which we accidentally sound on the strings of nature is out of all proportion to our taught and ascertainable faculty, and might teach us what strangers and novices we are in this universe of pure power" (*W* 8:278). Emerson left Rydal Mount, as Channing had a decade earlier, with the word *teach* ringing in his ears: what sectionally divided *Americans* needed to be taught, what and how *children* needed to be taught, primarily *outside* the schoolroom.

Looking back as he completed his nine months in Europe, Emerson thanked "the great God who has led me through this European scene, this last schoolroom in which he has pleased to instruct me from Malta's isle, thro' Sicily, thro' Italy, thro' Switzerland, thro' France, thro' England, thro' Scotland, in safety & pleasure & has now brought me to the shore & the ship that steers westward." For all his insistence on his American independence, Emerson's journeys to and from Europe seem flanked by the poet most crucial to him as well as to Coleridge and Wordsworth. On the stormy Atlantic crossing from the United States, Emerson, confined much of the time to his stateroom, filled the hours by reading Goethe's *Italian Journey* and reciting to himself from memory "nearly the whole of Lycidas, clause by clause" (*JMN* 4:103, 111). Now, about to embark for his return, he sounds like nothing so much as Milton in the exordium to book 3 of *Paradise Lost* (lines 15–19). Like Milton, Emerson was thanking the heavenly powers that had enabled him to survive the perils of a flight from one world to another. That guiding divinity, Emerson records in his journal,

> had shown me the men I wished to see—Landor, Coleridge, Carlyle, Wordsworth—he has thereby comforted & confirmed me in my convictions. Many things I owe to the sight of these men. I shall judge more justly, less timidly, of wise men forever more . . . [I]t is an *idealized* portrait which we always draw of them . . . Especially are they all deficient all these four—in different degrees but all deficient—in insight into religious truth. They have no idea of that species of moral truth which I call the first philosophy. (*EPP* 491)

Conveniently forgotten, at least for the moment, were Carlyle's Fichtean intuition of the Divine Idea, Coleridge's elaboration of a more-than-Kantian, even divine intuitive Reason, Wordsworth's visionary power and capacity to provide consolation in distress. What he "owes" to these men is here reduced to the sobering realization that he had rather too easily idealized them! It is as if he had never read the prose of Carlyle and Coleridge, never perused Wordsworth's "Tintern Abbey" or the "Prospectus" to *The Recluse,* or even the Great Ode and its intimations of immortality. Emerson must have been particularly thankful to have encountered the aging men he conversed with at Highgate and Rydal Mount. "Had Emerson expected gods in trousers?" asks an amused and amusing Weisbuch in the opening sentence of the first chapter of *Atlantic Double-Cross.* "At thirty, unaccomplished, unemployed, and incompletely focused, he visited the greatly accomplished English writers—Landor, Coleridge, Carlyle, Wordsworth—and tenderly cherished his disappointment." Weisbuch uses the journal entry just cited to launch, in his opening chapter, "ten observations" that may be said to "characterize the negotiations between American and British writers in the nineteenth century." To crudely reduce his thirty-two pages of nuanced elaboration to a sentence: he describes an originality-stifling British domination, both individual and national, and the one-sided need, on the part of the dominated, not only to resist but also to debunk, a fear-masking denial of continuing influence taking an antagonistic form in the hope that insult might prove a catalyst to native imagination.[23] Depicting Wordsworth and, particularly, Coleridge as tottering valetudinarians remarkably like Europe itself (that old giant barely able to "stir himself in these his chair days to loom up for the pastime of his upstart grandchildren") made it easier, for the moment, for Emerson to repress the truth that the Coleridge and Wordsworth that mattered to him, and mattered immensely, were not the old gentlemen with whom he had recently conversed, but those figures of capable imagination: the critical genius and the great poet whose work was just beginning to profoundly influence him and his circle back in the United States.

Emerson made that ungratefully grateful journal entry three days before he boarded the brig *New York* for his return voyage; aboard ship, as the coast of Ireland receded into the distance, he jotted in that same notebook: "I like my book about nature & wish I knew where & how I ought to live. God will show me" (*JMN* 4:237). Where and how he was going to live may well have been in the hands of Providence; the ways in which he was going to get on with the book that would eventually emerge as *Nature* had been laid out for him by the three men he had most "wished to see": Coleridge (and to a considerable extent "Coleridgeans" themselves), Carlyle, and Wordsworth. They are all present on every page of *Nature*—all the more present in their nominal absence. This is not the sort of absence that deconstruction seeks out and invariably finds—the gaps and silences that subvert and unravel a text—but, rather, what might be called a *structuring* absence. Their very names may have been erased from the text itself by a troubled Emerson, but he is engaged in what has recently and cogently been termed an act of "transparently inefficacious denial."[24] It

23. Weisbuch, *Atlantic Double-Cross,* 3–35.
24. Gravil, *Romantic Dialogues,* 67.

is inefficacious because, however occluded, the great British Romantics remain, under erasure yet still shining through: master lights in darkness visible.

❧ A half century after Thompson, in 1978, R. A. Yoder briefly explored the influence on *Nature* of the British and German Romantics.[25] Seven years later came Weisbuch's *Atlantic Double-Cross,* a book that made it possible for the same author, writing thirteen years after *that,* to confidently and concisely present "Post-colonial Emerson and the Erasure of Europe." Here we find such penetrating synopses as the one quoted in the third epigraph to my introduction and, even more graphically, an "erasure" of Wordsworth (whose name is never mentioned in *Nature*) that extends to the most celebrated moment in that book. To cite the familiar preamble to the epiphany of the transparent eyeball: "Crossing a bare common, in snow puddles, at twilight, under a clouded sky, without having in my thoughts any occurrence of special good fortune, I have enjoyed a perfect exhilaration. I am glad to the brink of fear" (*E&L* 10). Weisbuch's commentary, from its opening rhetorical question to its sweeping but completely persuasive final assertion, needs to be quoted in full:

> Is it possible to imagine that experience in that way without having read William Wordsworth? And yet the democracy of the experience, its astonishing availability, its confessional statement, all would be undermined by the very notion of a learned idea. Emerson, simply, is covering his tracks in the New England snow, in part because any acknowledgement of influence will damage the freshness of the assertions and wreck his rhetoric. What startles in *Nature* as new is the declamatory voice, a writing strategy whereby logic is always ready to sacrifice a sequence of thought for a moment of aphoristic revelation. This is a voice against memory, which is also the personal counterpart of history. Emerson wants every moment to be a booming Now, each instant open to the farthest heaven. Writing itself is always a record of a thought, belated in that sense, and so Emerson needs a prose that pulls itself vertically from the chronological, the voice of unfallen Adam now, the first namer confronting phenomena as if for the first time. Such a new beginning would become a ruin were Emerson to acknowledge the history of European romantic poetics and philosophy as a chief presence in his thought.[26]

By echo and omission, Weisbuch reinforces the point he is making. That Adamic confrontation of phenomena "as if for the first time" echoes the

25. Yoder, *Emerson and the Orphic Poet in America,* 29–39.
26. Weisbuch, "Post-colonial Emerson," 206–7.

charge made by "Matthew" (in "Expostulation and Reply," a poem Emerson frequently cites) against Wordsworthian "William," who looks around on his

> "Mother Earth,
> As if she for no purpose bore you;
> As if you were her first-born birth,
> And none had lived before you!"
> (*WP* 1:355)

And Weisbuch sacrifices the aphoristic moment that culminates Emerson's own sequence of thought; he does not feel the need (or perhaps thought he would blur his own point about Emerson's track-covering erasure of Wordsworth) to go on to actually quote the epiphany of the transparent eyeball: "My head bathed by the blithe air, and uplifted into infinite space,—all mean egotism vanishes. I become a transparent eye-ball; I am nothing; I see all; the currents of the Universal Being circulate through me; I am part or particle of God."[27] It would be too curious to consider all the possible "sources" or analogues of this, the first published appearance of the Emersonian doctrine of what he would call in his essay of that title the "Over-Soul." But, unique as it is, there is axial alignment with what Coleridge called the sense of "Divine Omnipresence" in the sublime passage of "Tintern Abbey." He believed in the "omni-presence," Emerson wrote in 1839, "that is, that the all is in every particle; that entire nature reappears in every leaf & moss" (*JMN* 7:186). As it is hard *not* to think of analogous texts, I will mention several, of which the most obvious remains "Tintern Abbey."

Emerson describes an uplifting into infinite space and a rapturous self-transcending unity with the divine in which the currents of the Universal Being "circulate through" him and he becomes a "particle" of God. There are several analogous moments, three of them singled out by Emerson himself, in *The Excursion*. The first, from book 1, is discussed in chapter 4; the second, from book 9, also later discussed, describes an "*active* Principle" that "circulates" through and "animates all things" (*E* 9:1–26). But the most immediately relevant may be the Wanderer's speech in the opening section of book 4, a sustained passage well known to Emerson and a treasured favorite of his aunt Mary. "How beautiful this dome of sky," the sage begins his prayer to the God who "hast built, / For thy own glory, in

27. Though for an 1856 printing of *Nature* Emerson replaced *particle* with *parcel,* most readers, myself included, prefer the original choice, which appears in both the original edition and the 1849 reprinting. *Particle* is restored, both in the Library of America edition (*E&L* 10) and in the *Collected Works* in progress (1:10).

the wilderness!"[28] God has constituted him "a priest of thine," perhaps one reason the Wanderer reminded Emerson of Bronson Alcott, that "God-made priest" (*L* 2:30). Despite his poverty, he has, the Wanderer insists, been rescued from ignorance and debasement. "By thy grace / *The particle divine* remained unquenched" (*E* 4:34–43, 48, 50–51). He, too, is part or particle of God—and in the context of a longer passage of great importance to Emerson. Two lines in particular—emphasizing, significantly enough, the flashing brevity of rhapsodic spiritual moments—became almost an obsession with him. So much so that, quite aside from the resemblance to the epiphany of the transparent eyeball, the lines and Emerson's repeated references to them deserve some scrutiny—especially since they were singled out for ridicule by the most influential and savage reviewer in England.

Emerson marked the passage in his copy of Wordsworth's poems (4: 134), and he quoted it from memory in a journal entry recorded at sea on September 17, 1833, as he was sailing back to the United States fresh from his visit to Wordsworth three weeks earlier. After referring to a love of "moral perfection" no less intense than that of Milton, Emerson describes it as his "angel from childhood until now," an angel that had alienated him from men and tortured him with guilt yet "inspired me with hope. It cannot be defeated by my defeats." The reference to "hope" amid even repeated defeats signals what is probably Emerson's most significant Wordsworthian legacy: consolation in moments of crisis. Appropriately, he turns in this journal entry to Wordsworthian lines offering hope and the ultimate victory of ever defeated man: "As the law of light is fits of easy transmission & reflexion [Newton's phrase] such is also the soul's law. She is only superior at intervals to pain, to fear, to temptation, only in raptures unites herself to God and Wordsworth truly said, 'Tis the most difficult of tasks to keep / Heights which the soul is competent to gain'" (*JMN* 4:87).[29]

28. This is the passage (*E* 4:34–42) quoted by Emerson's aunt in 1815 (Cole, *Mary Moody Emerson,* 151–52). Mary treasured her "sublime Wordsworth," and it is particularly unfortunate that pages in the "Almanack" in which she had transcribed passages from Wordsworth are among the many pages missing from the manuscript in the Houghton Library (119).

29. The lines were pronounced incomprehensible by Francis Jeffrey in that brutal review of *The Excursion* beginning famously, "This will never do," an opening note of "vulgar exultation" attacked by Coleridge (*BL* 2:115). Of the entire passage, Jeffrey observes: "If our readers can form the slightest guess at its meaning, we must give them credit for a sagacity to which we have no pretensions" ("Wordsworth's *Excursion,*" *Edinburgh Review* 24 [1814]: 10). These lines are quoted, in a very different spirit, by Oscar Wilde in *De Profundis.* The brilliant comedy of his life having turned to tragedy, the Wit and Aesthete once enamored of artifice and surface now condemns "everything" (whether in life or art, which ought to be organic in the Coleridgean sense) "that is

The allusion is to *The Excursion* (4:139–40). As part of his attempt to correct the despondency of the Solitary, the stoic Wanderer insists that it is "not arduous" to relinquish earthly things "and stand in freedom loosened from this world" but that it *is* hard for a creature of dust to *sustain* "ethereal hopes." He himself confesses that it is "impossible" to frame conceptions equal to his "soul's desires" and "the most difficult of tasks to *keep* / Heights which the soul is competent to gain." Emerson cited these lines again, in April 1834 (*JMN* 4:274), and several times subsequently, once (four months after little Waldo's death) as "a sort of elegy on these times" (*JMN* 8:242, 9:123). In his late essay "Inspiration," he quoted them yet again in lamenting the "want of consecutiveness . . . 'Tis with us a flash of light, then a long darkness, then a flash again. . . . This insecurity of possession, this quick ebb of power . . . tantalizes us."[30] Thus, Wordsworth's Wanderer, in addition to providing consolation in distress (see *JMN* 5:160–61), plays his part in the celebrated moment at the "heights," when Emerson, his soul inspired and united in momentary rapture with God, becomes a transparent eyeball. Emerson himself looks back to that rare moment seven years later in his great essay "The Poet." Every time he reads what seems an inspired poem, he says, he joyfully anticipates breaking his chains and mounting "above these clouds and opaque airs," attaining a heavenly perspective—those Wordsworthian "Heights"—that will "reconcile me to life and renovate nature. . . ."

---

made from without and by dead rules, and does not spring from within through some spirit informing it." In general, the trajectory of *De Profundis* is from the superficial to the profound, from Without to Within. In one section, the spiritually reborn Wilde reveals his reading of Wordsworth (along with Walter Pater on Wordsworth), seeming to fuse aspects of stanza 9 of the Intimations Ode with the Wanderer's lines, in book 4 of *The Excursion,* as well as the Solitary's vision of a heavenly city in book 2: "Far off, like a perfect pearl, one can see the city of God. It is so wonderful that it seems as if a child could reach it in a summer's day. And so a child could. But with me and such as I am it is different. One can realize a thing in a single moment, but one loses it in the long hours that follow with leaden feet. It is so difficult to keep 'heights that the soul is competent to gain.' We think in Eternity, but we move slowly through Time" (116).

30. All poets, he says, "have signalized their consciousness of rare moments . . . when a freedom, a power came to them." Unfortunately, it is "impossible to detect and wilfully repeat the fine conditions to which we have owed our happiest frames of mind." He then quotes Wordsworth: " 'Tis the most difficult of tasks to keep / Heights which the soul is competent to gain." (Emerson proves his point in an unpublished poem in which he feebly echoed these lines: to be "free," as "Few are," but "All might be," is "the *height / Of the soul's flight.*") There are, however, he concludes his essay, "some hints" that, combining human autonomy *and* receptiveness, emphasize the "right obedience to the powers of the human soul. Itself is the dictator; the mind itself the awful oracle. All our power, all our happiness consists in our reception of its hints, which ever become clearer and grander as they are obeyed" (*W* 8:272–73, 277, 284).

> Such is the hope, but the fruition is postponed. Oftener it falls that this winged man, who will carry me into the heaven, whirls me into mists, then leaps and frisks about with me as it were from cloud to cloud, still affirming that he is bound heavenward; and I, being myself a novice, am slow in perceiving that he does not know the way into the heavens, and is merely bent that I should admire his skill to rise, like a fowl or a flying fish, a little way from the ground or the water; but the all-piercing, all-feeding and ocular air of heaven that man shall never inhabit. (*E&L* 451–52)

The actual moment of Transcendentalist vision, the "ocular" moment of the transparent eyeball, is the part of the Emersonian epiphany that clinches beyond reasonable doubt Emerson's recollection of a no-less-celebrated passage, the work of a poet who, sometimes at least, met Emerson's impossible criterion for poetic greatness. In "Tintern Abbey," in lines Emerson doubtless knew by heart (45–49), Wordsworth, speaking as an imperial "we," describes how, "laid asleep / In body," we become "a living soul,"

> While, with an *eye* made quiet by the power
> Of harmony, and the deep power of joy,
> We *see* into the life of things.
> (*WP* 1:359; italics added)

As Milton's archangel would know, that is to enter into a state of pure intuition (*intueri:* to look into), to see into things directly, apprehending truth without ratiocinative process. Wordsworth may or may not be consciously following Milton; Emerson is surely conscious at this point of "an immediate precedent" in Wordsworth.[31]

But Emerson does not simultaneously erase and covertly acknowledge just *one* great Romantic precursor; there is another, indisputable erasure

31. As Mark Edmundson has noted, Emerson "here retreats to one of the received discourses he was attempting to overcome" in the interest of having "a poetry and philosophy of insight and not of tradition, and a religion by revelation to us, and not the history of theirs." There can be "little primary 'insight' from a vision that derives so directly from Wordsworth. . . . To cast the burdens of selfhood by becoming the eyeball that renders all things transparent may be an appealingly grotesque modification of Wordsworth's tranquil visions, but it is only that. The American newness—if it existed at all—required something without an immediate precedent to sum it up" (*Towards Reading Freud: Self-Creation in Milton, Wordsworth, Emerson, and Sigmund Freud,* 131). Myra Jehlen presses a legitimate distinction too far when she insists that Emerson's ecstasy on this occasion "is of another order entirely from Wordsworth's in nature," an "opposite experience" since it involves "not a heightening of his own separate and autonomously creative consciousness but a merging into universality." The very dissolving of egotism paradoxically projects "an intensification of the self," but this self "is yet not actively a poet" (*American Incarnation,* 96–97).

in the immediate preamble to the epiphany of the transparent eyeball, a preamble that quotes, without attribution or even quotation marks, Coleridge—and not only Coleridge but Coleridge *on* Wordsworth. "There is a property in the horizon," says Emerson, "which no man has but he whose *eye* can integrate all the parts, that is, the poet." Certain farmers may own the land, "yet to this their warranty-deeds give no title" (or, as Frost would later say, "Whose woods these are I think I know," but the owner lives in the village, and it is the *poet* who, responding aesthetically and imaginatively, stops "to *watch* his woods fill up with snow"). "To speak truly," Emerson continues in his focus on seeing, few adults can see nature, most do not see the sun, or have only "a very superficial seeing. The sun illuminates only the eye of the man, but shines into the *eye and the heart of the child. The lover of nature is he whose inward and outward senses are still truly adjusted to each other; who has retained the spirit of infancy even into the era of manhood*" (*E&L* 10; italics added).

After quoting this passage, Merton M. Sealts Jr. immediately adds, "Emerson is not merely echoing the commonplaces of Romantic theory about nature and childhood that he could have picked up in reading Wordsworth and Coleridge; he is speaking out of his own experience, just as he does again and again throughout *Nature*." With the last point, I completely agree. But Professor Sealts, to whose book I am otherwise indebted, is aiding and abetting Emerson's attempts at erasure when he directs us to a journal entry in which Emerson quotes Coleridge's remark that "Infancy... is body & spirit in unity" (*JMN* 5:363).[32] This is, consciously or unconsciously, to *mis*direct, since the sentence he has just quoted from *Nature*—about the retention of the spirit of infancy even into the era of manhood—is lifted verbatim from Coleridge. Both in *The Friend* and in *Biographia Literaria,* Emerson encountered—as part of his mentor's distinction between Genius and mere Talent—Coleridge's equally emphatic celebration of the capacity of poetic genius "to carry on the feelings of childhood into the powers of manhood, to combine the child's sense of wonder and novelty" with a response to things we have been accustomed to seeing, "and so to represent familiar objects as to awake the minds of others to a like freshness of sensation concerning them" (*F* 1:109–10). He slightly varies the formula—"the carrying on of the freshness and feelings of childhood into the powers of manhood"—in a postscript later in *The*

32. Sealts, *Emerson on the Scholar,* 68. In attributing to the subjective assertiveness of Milton's Satan ("Myself am Hell") Emerson's crucial and repeated insistence, especially in *Nature* and "Experience," that "Nature always wears the colors of the spirit," Sealts also seems (278–79n2) to be avoiding the more proximate influences: Coleridge and Wordsworth, especially in the final stanza of the Intimations Ode, where the clouds take their "coloring / From" the eye of the perceiver.

Friend (1:419). Yet another expanded version was subsequently incorporated by Coleridge into his discussion of "Wordsworth's Earlier Poems" in *Biographia Literaria.* Let me establish the context for the words of Coleridge lifted by Emerson.

What made "so unusual an impression" on his feelings immediately, and subsequently on his judgment in encountering Wordsworth's poetry, was, says Coleridge in the *Biographia,* "the union of deep feeling with profound thought; the fine balance of truth in observing with the imaginative faculty in modifying the objects observed." As Emerson says immediately *following* the transparent-eyeball passage, "The greatest delight which the fields and woods minister is the suggestion of an occult relation between man and the vegetable. . . . Yet it is certain that the power to produce this delight does not reside in nature, but in man, or in a harmony of both," for "Nature always wears the colors of the spirit" (*E&L* 11). Coleridge, who had earlier noted that "the man of genius lives most in the ideal world" (*BL* 1:43), goes on to say that what impressed him in Wordsworth's poetry, "above all," was "the original gift of spreading the tone, the *atmosphere,* and with it the depth and height of the ideal world around forms, incidents, and situations, of which, for the common view, custom had bedimmed all the lustre and dried up the sparkle and the dew drops." Later in *Nature,* fusing that "lustre" with the "solemn imagery" of Wordsworth's Boy of Winander passage (not to mention "Tintern Abbey," "I Wandered Lonely as Cloud," and much of Wordsworth in general), Emerson describes the "advantage which the country-life possesses for a powerful mind, over the artificial and curtailed life of cities." The lesson learned in nature shall not be lost "altogether in the roar of cities or the broil of politics. Long hereafter, amidst agitation," even in "the hour of revolution,— these solemn images shall reappear in their morning lustre" as the poet bred in the woods "saw and heard them in his infancy." And thus, "the keys of power are put into his hands" (*E&L* 23).[33]

Having anticipated his own paraphrase of what Wordsworth had proposed to himself as his object in *Lyrical Ballads,*[34] Coleridge now inserts into the *Biographia* discussion the passage from *The Friend:*

33. Emerson was fond of another artistic variant on the image of perpetual continuity between manhood and youth. In a journal entry of early 1847, he says: "Ancora impero—I carry my satchell still." He is transcribing an apparent motto of Michelangelo, cited in a lecture on the artist, and again in "Poetry and Imagination": "The aged Michelangelo indicates his perpetual study as in boyhood—'I carry my satchel [schoolbag] still'" (*EL* 1:102–3; *EPP* 298–99).

34. According to Coleridge's summary in *Biographia Literaria,* chapter 14, devoted to *Lyrical Ballads,* Wordsworth proposed "to give the charm of novelty to things of everyday, . . . by awakening the mind's attention from the lethargy of custom, and directing it to the loveliness and the wonders of the world before us; an inexhaustible

> To find no contradiction in *the union of old and new;* to contemplate the ANCIENT of days and all his works with feelings as fresh, as if all had spr[u]ng forth at the first creative fiat; characterizes the mind that feels the riddle of the world, and may help to unravel it. *To carry on the feelings of childhood into the powers of manhood; to combine the child's sense of wonder and novelty with the appearances, which every day for perhaps forty years had rendered familiar... this is the character and privileges of genius, and one of the marks which distinguish genius from talents.* And therefore is it the prime merit of *genius*... so to represent familiar objects as to *awaken in the minds of others* a kindred feeling concerning them and that *freshness of sensation* which is the constant accompaniment *of mental, no less than of bodily, convalescence.* (*BL* 1:80–81, incorporating *F* 2:73–74; italics added)

Emerson's version of convalescence ("In good health," he says, "the air is a cordial of incredible virtue") leads directly to the famous crossing of the "bare common" and to the sudden shift to the woods, where the Coleridgean image of renewed "childhood" (the Wordsworthian insistence that "the Child is Father of the Man") is again evoked: "In the woods too, a man casts off his years, as the snake his slough, and at whatever period soever of life, is always a child. In the woods, is perpetual youth" (*E&L* 10). "Why in age, / Do we revert so fondly to the walks of Childhood?" asks Wordsworth's Wanderer. Because "there the soul discerns / The dear memorial footsteps unimpaired / Of her own native vigour" (*E* 9:36–40). There is no need to repeat the image of the transparent eyeball, but it is interesting to note that Coleridge—who probably gave Emerson as well as Shelley the image of purging from our inward sight the "film of familiarity" (which clouds our vision so that "we have eyes, but see not")—also insisted, in that memorable passage from *Aids to Reflection* earlier quoted in full, that "Nothing is wanted but the eye, ... the light which is the eye of this soul"; this "*seeing* light, this *enlightening* eye" (*AR* 16), is, precisely, the Wordsworthian "master light of all our seeing."

This is what Emerson meant, years later, in "Poetry and Imagination," in contrasting the physical eye to what he calls here, as in the "Idealism" chapter of *Nature* and in the Divinity School Address, the imaginative "eye of Reason," going on to quote Blake, of whose work he was unaware when he wrote *Nature.* Emerson leads into the quotation by citing a poet of whose work he was well aware: Blake's "abnormal genius, Wordsworth

---

treasure, but for which in consequence of the film of familiarity and selfish solicitude we have eyes, yet see not, ears that hear not, and hearts that neither feel nor understand" (*BL* 2:7, fusing Jer. 5:21 with Isa. 6:10). Shelley, who read *Biographia Literaria* shortly after it was published, echoed Coleridge's "film of familiarity" four years later in his *Defense of Poetry:* "Poetry... purges from our inward sight the film of familiarity which obscures from us the wonder of our being" (*Shelley's Poetry and Prose,* 505).

said, interested him more than the conversation of Scott or Byron" (an equally impressed Coleridge, on his first reading of Blake's *Songs* in early 1818, pronounced him a "Genius" and "mystic" [*CL* 4:833–34, 836–38]). Emerson then quotes the peroration from Blake's *Vision of Judgment,* the most remarkable of the passages selected by Dante Gabriel Rossetti for Alexander Gilchrist's *Life of William Blake* (1863): "He who does not imagine in stronger and better lineaments and in stronger and better light than his perishing mortal eye can see, does not imagine at all. . . . I assert for myself that I do not behold the outward creation, and that to me it would be a hindrance, and not action. I question not my corporeal eye any more than I would question a window concerning a sight. I look through it, and not with it" (*EPP* 303).[35] Here as in Emerson's own "transparent eye-ball," the emphasis is on transparency; we see *through,* not *with,* the eye—Coleridge's "seeing light, this enlightening eye."

Blake was dead before Emerson published *Nature,* and Nietzsche not yet born. But the German philosopher—an Emersonian and a thinker who (according to Yeats) "completes Blake and has the same roots"—also has an observation reminiscent of, and in part indebted to, this crucial trope of the "eye." Describing a "mood, for which I long above all others," the twenty-two-year-old Nietzsche begins a letter to a young friend by recalling the opening of that other "Nature," the sixth of the essays in *Essays: Second Series:* "There are days," Emerson had written, ". . . wherein the world reaches its perfection," especially the "halcyons" of "Indian summer," when "the day, immeasurably long, sleeps over the broad hills and warm wide fields. To have lived through all its sunny hours, seems longevity

35. Emerson was unaware of Blake other than as a painter prior to the publication of Gilchrist's *Life,* a book he repeatedly borrowed from the Boston Atheneum. In this famous passage Blake dismisses the "Outward Creation" as "Dirt upon my feet . . . no part of Me." Questioned if he does not see the rising sun as a "round disk somewhat like a Guinea," the visionary replies, "O no no I see an innumerable company of the Heavenly host crying Holy Holy Holy is the Lord God Almighty[.] I question not my Corporeal or Vegetative Eye any more than I would Question a Window concerning a Sight[.] I look thro' it & not with it." Blake repeated the distinction in sec. 5 (lines 101–4) of *The Everlasting Gospel:* "This life's dim windows of the soul / Distorts the heavens from pole to pole / And leads you to believe a lie / When you see with, not through, the eye" (*The Poetry and Prose of William Blake,* 555). Strangely, Richard R. O'Keefe (in his "Blakean reading" of Emerson) notes the resemblance to the description of the transparent eyeball, but does not add that Emerson later quoted this very passage. Even more strangely, though he notes a Blake-Emerson connection (Emerson's "Man" is "original man or unfallen Adam, which is to say America, in the transcendental sense, just as Blake's Albion is the unfallen form of Man") and has offered a Gnostic reading of the transparent-eyeball passage, Bloom makes no connection between the Emersonian epiphany and Blake's strikingly similar image. See his *Agon,* 158–59, and his introduction to *Ralph Waldo Emerson: Modern Critical Views,* 6.

enough." At such times, "in the presence of" what Emerson follows Coleridge in calling "*natura naturata,* or nature passive," we "quit our life of solemn trifles" and "our eyes are bathed in these lights and forms" (*E&L* 541, 542, 543). Fusing this tranquil opening—what Wallace Stevens would later evoke as the credences of summer—with the pure seeing of the transparent eyeball, Nietzsche begins his letter:

> Sometimes there come those quiet meditative moments in which one *stands above one's life* with mixed feelings of joy and sadness, like those lovely summer days which spread themselves expansively and comfortably across the hills, as Emerson so excellently describes them. Then *nature* becomes *perfect,* as he says, and *we ourselves* too; then we are set *free from the spell of the ever-watchful will; then we are pure, contemplative, impartial eye.*[36]

"With an *eye* made quiet by the power / Of harmony, and the deep power of joy, / We *see* into the life of things," Wordsworth had said, anticipating the Emersonian transparent eyeball. Replicating that famous moment, Nietzsche, in this early letter, also anticipates his own version of infinite space and currents circulating. Caught up in the euphoric inspiration in which he composed *Zarathustra,* conceived high in the Engadine, he felt himself "6000 feet beyond man and time." That epiphanic moment, related—as we will see—to his Emerson-inspired recovery from grief, came when, as Yeats put it in his presentation of Nietzsche in *A Vision,* "the doctrine of the Eternal Recurrence *drifts before his eyes.*"[37]

36. Nietzsche, letter of April 7, 1866, to Carl von Gersdorf, in *Selected Letters of Friedrich Nietzsche,* 10–11; italics added. This calm suspension of the will and the Emersonian emptying out in the "eye-ball" passage ("I am nothing; I see all") seem replicated not only in Nietzsche but also in Margaret Fuller and William James, who speaks, in *The Varieties of Religious Experience,* of that momentary state in which "the will to assert ourselves and hold our own has been displaced by a willingness to close our mouth and be nothing in the floods and waterspouts of God." Fuller's epiphany resembles Emerson's in its unspectacular natural setting, its emptying out and simultaneous affirmation of the self. On Thanksgiving Day, 1831, Fuller attends church but experiences "a disunion from the hearers and dissent from the preacher." Feeling that her gifts were "all unrecognized," yet experiencing "within myself great power," she walks out into the fields on a "sad and sallow day of the late autumn." Slow processions of clouds pass over a "cold blue sky," the earth is dull colored, "with sickly struggles of the late green here and there," a wind blowing "reluctant leaves," "no life else." Like Keats's Saturn—in *Hyperion,* a poem also admired by Emerson (*E&L* 527–28)—she stops and sits, thoughtlessly, by a "stream, shrunken, voiceless, choked with withered leaves . . . all was dark, and cold, and still." Suddenly, there "passed into my thought a beam from its true sun . . . which has never since departed from me." As in the moment in Emerson when "all mean egotism vanishes," she felt "there was no self; that selfishness was all folly," yet the awareness remained rooted in that inner power (*Memoirs of Margaret Fuller,* 1:139–41).

37. Nietzsche, *Ecce Homo,* section on *Thus Spoke Zarathustra,* 1. Yeats, *A Vision,* 299; italics added.

Nietzsche's contemplative eye is the eye of genius. A contemporary reports that in October 1811, Coleridge "drew the distinction between talent and genius by comparing the first to a watch and the last to an eye. . . . [O]ne was a piece of only ingenious mechanism, while the other was a production above all art." Anybody, properly instructed, could make a watch, but "nobody could make an eye."[38] Two months later, in a Shakespeare lecture, ocular genius was joined with the childlike wonder of the "poet," a man "who carries the feelings of childhood into the powers of manhood" and so "can contemplate all things with the freshness and wonder of a child & connecting with it the inquisitive powers of his manhood, adds as far as he can final knowledge, admiration, & where knowledge no longer permits admiration gladly sinks back again into the childlike feeling of devout wonder."[39]

Reading the Intimations Ode, philosophic Coleridge was predictably critical of Wordsworth's credulity-straining apotheosis of the child as "thou best Philosopher." Equally predictably, he concurred with the ocular celebrations of that child of glory as "thou *Eye* among the blind," a "*Seer* blest" (echoing Adam's grateful description of Milton's archangel Michael, after he prophesied our finding of a "paradise within" as compensation for Eden lost), and, finally, as a "little Child, yet *glorious* in the might / Of heaven-born freedom. . . ." Noting the "enormous influence of novelty—the way in which it quickens observation, sharpens sensation, and exalts sentiment," John Ruskin would later say, "I think that what Wordsworth speaks of as a glory in the child, because it has come fresh from God's hands, is in reality nothing more than *the freshness of all things to its newly opened sight.*" We lose that initial visionary power as we grow older. To illustrate the "vanishing" of "the old childish feeling," Ruskin immediately quotes from "the same poem," indeed the same stanza (8) of the ode: "Custom hangs upon us with a weight / Heavy as frost and deep almost as life."[40] The task of the writer, and the glory of the Great Ode, is to compensate for that loss by presenting—with an intensification rather than "any severing of [the] loves" that bind the human perceiver with "Fountains, Meadows, Hills, and Groves" (stanza 11)—a vision, still exalted but colored by a mature "final knowledge," of human suffering and mutability:

38. Quoting John Payne Collier's report of an October 17, 1811, conversation with Coleridge. See T. R. Raysor, ed., *Coleridge's Shakespeare Criticism,* 2:124.

39. Manuscript quoted from lecture 8 (December 12, 1811), in *Lectures 1808–1819: On Literature,* 1.

40. Ruskin, in the remarkable seventeenth chapter, "The Moral of Landscape," in *Modern Painters* 367; italics added.

The Clouds that gather round the setting sun
Do take a sober colouring from an *eye*
That hath kept watch o'er man's mortality.
(197–99)

By acknowledging that "the radiance which was once so bright" is "now forever taken from my *sight*" (stanza 10), but denying "any severing" of the emotional bond between the perceiver and the natural world (176–77, 189), the emphasis falls as much on continuity as change. Thus, a version of what Emerson calls the "original relation to the universe" enjoyed by "foregoing generations" (*E&L* 7) can be enjoyed by an integrated self that, in the process of maturing, has "retained the spirit of infancy even into the powers of manhood." Those powers, epitomized in the visionary form of a "transparent eye-ball," define a manhood shaped and quickened into new creation by traveling in the not quite erasable tracks of Wordsworth and Coleridge in the New England snow. Although a true poet, he insists, "finds no foot-track in the field he traverses" (*EPP* 330), Emerson himself *had.* Yet he *tried* to erase those tracks, perhaps "glad to the brink of fear" in another sense: anxious, despite the striking originality of this extraordinary visual and visionary moment in *Nature,* about the extent of his indebtedness.

Though there are several instances of Emersonian effacement of Coleridge in *Nature,*[41] I will focus for the remainder of this chapter on one example of more than passing interest. As in the preamble to the transparent-eyeball passage, we again have to do with the "spirit of infancy," this time "infant minds." In his 1831 and 1832 journals and in the

41. Toward the end of the "Beauty" chapter, we are told that the standard of beauty is "the totality of nature; which the Italians expressed by defining beauty *'il piu nell' uno.'* Nothing is quite beautiful alone; nothing but is beautiful in the whole" (*E&L* 18). But Emerson is borrowing his foreign tag (Italian for "the many in one") from Coleridge, whose concept of "multeity in unity" is aligned with his "each-and-all" formulation (*F* 1:511). In 1834 Emerson had ended his Coleridge-influenced poem of that title, whose theme is that "Nothing is fair or good alone," with the couplet: "Beauty through my senses stole; / I yielded myself to the perfect whole." But Coleridge is not mentioned in the "Beauty" chapter of *Nature.* His name is similarly omitted in the "Idealism" chapter, a section of which, beginning "Whilst thus the poet *animates nature* with *his own thoughts,*" attributes to "Plato" the statement, "The problem of philosophy is, for all that exists conditionally, to find a ground unconditioned and absolute" (*E&L* 36). Emerson has lifted that "Platonic" statement from a sentence in *The Friend* (1:460) in which Coleridge, in the course of abridging a passage from book 5 of *The Republic,* in effect turns Plato into Kant and then romanticizes Kant by making the thinker a "poet."

1833 lecture "The Uses of Natural History," Emerson refers to a passage of Coleridge, poetry for once, lines that epitomized one of his own crucial concepts. Because he quotes them repeatedly in his notebooks and in a lecture, only to delete them when it came to an 1835 expansion of the earlier lecture and, more significantly, to the far more public forum of his book *Nature,* both the emphasis and the erasure seem worth dwelling on for a few moments.

First, in 1831, in notes under the heading "POETRY," Emerson describes poetry's "very essence" as consisting in "the fine perception & vivid expression of that subtle & mysterious analogy which exists between the physical & the moral world," an analogy "which makes *outward* things and qualities the natural types & emblems of *inward* gifts & emotions, & leads us to ascribe life & sentiment to every thing that interests us in the aspects of external nature." As early as 1826 Emerson had read and been impressed by Sampson Reed's *Observations on the Growth of the Mind,* a treatise on Platonic and Swedenborgian "correspondences" between nature and spirit. But in illustrating his point about an outer-inner analogy and the poet's ascribing of "life & sentiment" to things in external nature, Emerson cited neither Reed nor Wordsworth (whose project—at epic length in *The Prelude,* writ smaller in the Intimations Ode—was synopsized in Reed's title), but Coleridge:

> For all that meets the bodily sense I deem
> Symbolical, one mighty alphabet
> For infant minds.
>
> (*JMN* 6:173–74)

The following year, as his first entry under the heading "NATURE," he copied out the same three lines. He glossed them with his own observation: "The universe is transparent; the light of higher laws than its own, shines through it" (*JMN* 6:218–19), a formulation that will be repeated in *Nature* (*E&L* 24) and anticipates the more Kantian-sounding axiom underlying his 1837 series of lectures called "Human Culture": "The obscure attraction which natural objects have for [each individual] are only indications of the truth which appears at last, that *the laws of nature preexisted in his mind*" (*L* 2:221; italics in original). In the "Idealism" chapter of *Nature,* fusing the Kantian Copernican Revolution in epistemology with Coleridge's emphasis on the "shaping spirit of Imagination," a power "Undreamt of by the sensual and the proud" ("Dejection: An Ode," 70, 86), Emerson compares the imaginative to the unimaginative mind: "The sensual man conforms thoughts to things; the poet conforms things to his thoughts." And he defines the "Imagination" as the "use which the Reason makes of the material world," investing "dust and stones with humanity"

(*E&L* 34). Emerson goes on, quite rightly, to praise the "imperial muse" of Shakespeare, who, above all other poets, possessed the "power" to subordinate nature "for the purposes of expression," illustrating the point by quoting five passages from the sonnets and plays (*E&L* 35–36). Nevertheless, his language makes it perfectly clear that he is following, precisely, Coleridge's alteration of Kant, with the correspondence of things to thoughts effected through the shaping spirit of imagination. He even seems to be recalling that "*active* Principle" that—the Wanderer claims, in one of the crucial passages in *The Excursion*—subsists in all of nature, even "in every pebbly stone / That paves the brooks" (*E* 9:7–8). By restricting his examples to Shakespeare—as he had in his December 1835 lecture on Shakespeare, in which these same thoughts occur—Emerson effectively erases Wordsworth and, even though he cites the three lines from *The Destiny of Nations,* the Coleridge of "Dejection: An Ode."

Back in 1833, Emerson allowed Coleridge's three lines to make a *public* appearance, in "The Uses of Natural History," a well-received lecture riddled with allusions. We speak, he says

> in continual metaphors of the morn, the noon and the evening of life... because the whole of Nature is a metaphor or image of the human Mind. The laws of moral nature answer to those of matter as face to face in a glass. "The visible world," it has been well said, "and the relations of its parts is the dial plate of the invisible one." In the language of the poet, "For all that meets the bodily sense I deem / Symbolical, one mighty alphabet / For infant minds." (*EL* 1:23–24)

Having alluded to, and altered, Saint Paul and borrowed Swedenborg's "dial plate,"[42] Emerson concludes not by identifying, but at least by citing "the poet." The lines come from Coleridge's early fragment *The Destiny of Nations* (lines 18–20), and the "poet" will turn up absent rather than merely anonymous in *Nature,* where all of these allusions, with the single exception of the lines from Coleridge, reappear. Once restored to their original context, one can see why Emerson would have thought them a fitting "clincher" to his emphasis on the metaphoric and even legislative and constitutive relation between the "visible" and "invisible" worlds. Appropriately enough, coming from a man whose writings, according to

42. His immediate source (*JMN* 4:33) was Hedge's 1832 essay "Emmanuel Swedenborg." The image (later to provide the title for the *Dial*) is cited again in notes grouped under "NATURE" (*JMN* 6:219). Much of Emerson's knowledge of Swedenborg, almost as crucial an influence on *Nature* as Coleridge, came through Hedge's articles and through the editor of the *New Jerusalem Magazine,* Sampson Reed, whose Swedenborgian conception of "correspondences" between visible and invisible realms is well synopsized by Emerson in his essay on Swedenborg in *Representative Men.*

Theodore Parker, "did great service in New England, helping to emancipate enthralled minds," Coleridge's passage—which looks back to the Bible and to Milton, and ahead to Wordsworth at his most sublime—also had the advantage for a man with Emerson's project, of being a paean to liberation, the unleashing of "Man's free and stirring spirit," presently "entranced." For "what is Freedom, but the unfettered use / Of all the powers which God for use had given?"

> But chiefly this, him First, him Last to view
> Through meaner powers and secondary things
> Effulgent, as through clouds that veil his blaze.
> For all that meets the bodily sense I deem
> Symbolical, one mighty alphabet
> For infant minds. . . .
>
> (15–20; *CPW* 1:132)[43]

When Emerson took up the passage we have been discussing and reworked it for the opening lecture in his new winter 1835–1836 series, he continued to instrumentally define language as "a naming of invisible and spiritual things from visible things. The use of natural history is to give us aid in supernatural history. The use of the outer creation is to give us language for the beings and changes of the inward creation" (*EL* 1:220). Though he acknowledges that it is seldom the case in the modern world, language, in its "infancy," is "all poetry," the representation of "spiritual facts" by "natural symbols." And that is still so with those masters of lan-

43. These lines, which open by looking back to Revelations 1:11 and to Adam's description of God in *PL,* also anticipate Wordsworth's vision at the imaginative climax of the Simplon Pass episode in book 6 of *The Prelude.* Coleridge's "unfettered" freedom and "mighty alphabet" symbolical of divine power are transmuted into "unfettered clouds" and a revelation of the "one" in nature. Torrents and crags and raving stream, the "unfettered clouds and region of the Heavens," tumult and peace, darkness and light were "like workings of one mind," the features of "the same face, blossoms upon one tree; / Characters of the great Apocalypse, / The types and symbols of Eternity, / Of first, and last, and midst, and without end" (*P* 6:628–40). The Wordsworthian vision in the Gorge of Gondo—the words of Revelation written into mutable natural objects—has its Emersonian analogues in the symbolic interpretation of the natural world in *Nature,* and in the peroration of the essay on Goethe that concludes *Representative Men.* The Wordsworthian "Characters of the great Apocalypse" take the form of what Emerson calls, in the "Idealism" chapter of *Nature,* the "apocalypse of the mind" (*E&L* 32). At the end of the Goethe essay, Emerson insists that it is the task not of the divine but of the *human* spirit to "write Bibles," and not merely to report but to reconfigure the "signatures" in nature. Though *Representative Men* was published in 1850, the same year as *The Prelude,* it ends no less audaciously than *Nature* had begun, a decade and a half earlier: "We too must write Bibles, to unite again the heavens and the earthly world. . . . and first, last, midst, and without end, to honor every truth by use" (*E&L* 761).

guage, the "poets, orators, and philosophers" who "most sharply see and most happily present emblems, parables, and figures" (*EL* 1:221). Though he has now deleted specific reference to external nature as "Symbolical, one mighty alphabet / For infant minds," Coleridge's thought and imagery are precisely restated in Emerson's imaginative conversion—by those attuned to the primordial power of language in its "infancy"—of things, a mere "alphabet," into thoughts. After a partial reappearance in his first lecture on Shakespeare, these thoughts reached their best-known expression in the "Language" chapter of *Nature.* Emerson still insisted that parts of speech "are metaphors because the whole of nature is a metaphor of the human mind" (*E&L* 24). The "powers" given by God allow "human minds" to perceive nature as "one mighty alphabet"—Coleridge's very point in the lines Emerson kept quoting in his earlier formulations. But however much they haunted him, those lines are not to be found in the text of *Nature.* Emerson kept them out as part of his deliberate policy of erasure. Coleridge is mentioned once in the book, and innocuously (*E&L* 30), Wordsworth not at all.

In 1805, in chapter 4 of *Anima Poetae,* Coleridge reprised his own image of a "symbolical . . . alphabet," placing even greater emphasis on what was "within" the self: "In looking at objects of Nature while I am thinking, as at yonder moon dim-glimmering through the dewy window-pane, I seem rather to be seeking, as it were *asking* for, a symbolical language for something within me that already and forever exists, than observing anything new." In this interaction of Within, Without, and Above, Coleridge sees divine agency. The inscription within the self of what "already and forever exists" recalls a letter he sent around the time he wrote *The Destiny of Nations.* Reacting to his radical friend John Thelwall's atheistic rhapsodizing about the sublime beauties of nature, Coleridge said that his own response to nature—unlike that of Godless Thelwall and that "*Semi*-atheist" Wordsworth—was less immediate than mystically religious. In fact, it was, in the language of *The Destiny of Nations,* "symbolical," everything that meets the eye being part of "one mighty alphabet," indivisible and infinite. He can "*at times,*" he says, feel the "beauties" Thelwall described "in—themselves & for themselves." But Coleridge stresses his more characteristic perspective, that of a man whose sense of nature's limitations reflects a vision of infinitude, with emphasis on the potentially infinite capacity of the mind, or at least of "my mind." Thus, as he says in the letter,

> More frequently *all things* appear little—all the knowledge, that can be acquired, child's play—the universe itself—what but an immense heap of *little things*?—I can contemplate nothing but parts, & parts are all *little*—!—My mind feels as if it ached to behold & know something *great*—something

> *one & indivisible*—and it is only in the faith of this that rock or waterfalls, mountains or caverns give me the sense of sublimity or majesty!—but in this faith *all things* counterfeit infinity! (*CL* 1:349; italics in original)

Confirming the religious core of his philosophy, Coleridge then cites his own lines, from the original version of "This Lime-Tree Bower My Prison," in which, anticipating the sublime passage of "Tintern Abbey" (and resembling the Emersonian epiphany of the transparent eyeball), he stands "*Silent*... *gazing round* / On the wide landscape" until all seems "a living Thing," clothing the "almighty Spirit, when he makes / Spirits perceive his presence" (*CL* 1:49–50; italics added). Unlike the pantheistic "presence" and syntactically mysterious "something far more deeply interfused" of "Tintern Abbey," the activating "almighty Spirit" here is clearly God. No wonder that years later, in two passages of *Aids to Reflection,* a far more orthodox Coleridge was worried about the lines in his play *Osorio* (a play read in manuscript and admired by Wordsworth in the autumn of 1797) in which Ferdinand is described by his wife, Alhadra, as one who "worships Nature in the hills and valleys, / Not knowing what he loves, but loves it all!" This pantheistic nature worship was, he admits, "for a brief period... my own state," though he strains to absolve the Wordsworth of "Tintern Abbey" of any such guilt by association (*AR* 404). Earlier in the book, and in an even more orthodox vein, he had drawn a sharper distinction between himself and his character Ferdinand. "The Reader will, of course, understand, that I am here speaking in the assumed character of a mere Naturalist, to whom no light of revelation has been vouchsafed" (*AR* 353).

Though Coleridge would remain obsessed by what Carlyle mocked as his Kantian "om-m-mject" and "sum-m-mject," it is to the poetic, the Romantic, Coleridge, rather than the theologian, that we can best apply the "displacement" thesis of M. H. Abrams: the Romantics "undertook, whatever their religious creed, or lack of creed, to save the traditional concepts, schemes, and values which had been based on the relation of the Creator to his creature and creation, but to reformulate them within the prevailing two-term system of subject and object, ego and non-ego, the human mind or consciousness and its transactions with nature."[44] Emerson fits the pattern better than later Coleridge. In "The Uses of Natural History," he announces that "the laws of moral nature answer to those of matter as face to face in a glass" (*EL* 1:24). Paul had famously said that although "now we see as through a glass, darkly," partial vision will be

44. Abrams, *Natural Supernaturalism: Tradition and Revolution in Romantic Literature,* 13.

replaced by "face to face" knowledge in eternity (1 Cor. 13:9–12), when we will, by allusive implication, attain the unmediated vision of Jacob: "I have seen God face to face" (Gen. 32:20). When Emerson repeated his Pauline alteration, that personal meeting in eternity was displaced into a correspondence—through a glass still partly dark—between the laws of moral nature and those of matter, that "occult relation between man and the vegetable" he refers to in *Nature* (*E&L* 11).

Thus, in "Language," he still cites Swedenborg's "dial plate" of the invisible: an image comparable to Coleridge's vision of the perceived world as "symbolical," a "mighty alphabet," and to Wordsworth's apocalyptic "characters," the "types and symbols of Eternity" (*P* 6:638–39). Although he drops the three lines from *The Destiny of Nations,* almost as if to make up for that deletion, he *does* quote a passage from Plotinus he had borrowed from *Biographia Literaria.* He also ends his chapter by quoting, without attribution, a statement—"every object, rightly seen unlocks a new faculty of the soul"—that commentators invariably but unconvincingly trace to Coleridge's *Aids to Reflection.*[45] That attribution almost seems a reiteration of what I have just suggested was Emerson's own unconscious making-up for deletion. Though that speculation is admittedly far-fetched, there would certainly be ample justification for editorial recompense to Coleridge, who, along with Wordsworth, suffered Emersonian erasure from the surface text of *Nature:* victims of the same resistance registered in Emerson's journal as he set sail from Europe following his visits to the two men he privately acknowledged elsewhere to be, respectively, the major critic and the major poet of the age.

45. They include the editors of vol. 1 of the ongoing edition of Emerson's *Collected Works* (1:250n) and of *EPP* (39n). But Emerson's statement translates Goethe's "Jeder neue Gergenstand, wohl beschaut, schließt ein eeues Organ in uns auf" "almost verbatim while it shows hardly any resemblance" to the passage cited by Emerson's editors (Van Cromphout, *Emerson's Modernity,* 32). Emerson had purchased a fifteen-volume set of Goethe's posthumously published works and was reading through the set at the time he made the first of several journal entries (August 12, 1836) on his reading. Goethe's phrase occurs in vol. 10, but Emerson might well have read ahead, given that that volume is the only one in the set with "Nature" in the title.

Chapter 4

Emerson's Discipleship

SHEDDING BENIGNANT INFLUENCE

I know no such critic. Every opinion he expresses is a canon of criticism that should be written in steel, & his italics are the italics of the mind.

—EMERSON on Coleridge, 1836 journal

the truly great
Have all one age, and from one visible space
Shed influence.

—COLERIDGE, "To William Wordsworth"

Emerson returned from Europe having convinced himself of the inadequacies of those he had been so anxious to meet. Above all, he had found Coleridge and Wordsworth "deficient." This was a judgment that could not long stand. And, indeed, a fairer assessment than the dismissive journal entry he recorded as he was setting sail back to the United States was imminent. I have already quoted the seminal letter written to his brother Edward eight months later, in which Coleridge's distinction between Reason and understanding was revealed as the foundation of Emersonian Transcendentalism. Whatever mixed feelings he had about the poetic unevenness of Wordsworth and the mind-narrowing Anglicanism of Coleridge, he had no doubt about the nobility of their "aims" and, in the case of Coleridge, actual intellectual eminence. If, in January 1835, Emerson could pronounce Carlyle "the best thinker of his age," it was only, as he noted, "since Coleridge is dead" (*L* 1:432). The man he had met two years earlier, living with the protective Gillmans and looking corpulent but well despite the earlier ravages of opium and drink, was, said Emerson, too old to be open to the ideas of others. But, then, of course, so many of Emerson's ideas were Coleridge's to begin with! Years later, less anxiously and far more honestly, Emerson could, in *English Traits,* register his conviction that

> Coleridge, a catholic mind with a hunger for ideas, with eyes looking before and after to the highest bards and sages, and who wrote and spake the only high criticism in his time,—is one of those who save England from the reproach of no longer possessing the capacity to appreciate what rarest wit the island has yielded. [But even the Brahmins] can no longer read or understand the Brahminical philosophy [offered them by] the best mind in England. (*E&L* 901–2)

Though he may have been tin-eared when it came to Coleridge's poetry, Emerson was fully attuned to the prose critic and thinker. His 1836 lecture "Modern Aspects of Letters" featured as its centerpiece a commentary on the recently deceased Coleridge, celebrated as our preeminent critic and reverer of the intuitive or divine "Reason." As the editors remark of these early lectures in general, they reflect Emerson's wide reading of classical and canonical English authors and "favorite 'new lights' such as Goethe, Coleridge, Wordsworth, and the local Swedenborgians—above all, as always, Coleridge." This particular lecture was worked up during "the period when he was most immediately under the spell of Coleridge's philosophy, and there are many evidences of a close reading of *The Friend* and other volumes." More recently, Eric Carlson has rightly observed that the "incisiveness of those pages testifies to the depth of Emerson's absorption of Coleridge's ideas and to the unique greatness of Coleridge as a critical mind."[1]

In two journal entries, later incorporated in his discussion of Coleridge in "Modern Aspects of Letters," Emerson epitomized Coleridge in a phrase of Plato: "He is a god to me who shall rightly define & divide" (*JMN* 6: 209, 5:79).[2] Emerson seized on the pivotal Coleridgean distinctions and on Coleridge's valuation. Reason is superior to Understanding, as the Organic is to the Mechanic, Genius to Talent, Imagination to Fancy, Symbolism to Allegory, Whole to Part—the inferior term in each case being limited to the reception of the objective world, the external realm perceived through the senses, whereas the superior terms pertain to the

1. For "Modern Aspects of Letters," see *EL* 1:371–85, and, for the editorial comments, *EL* 1:4, 207. For Carlson's remarks, see the introduction to his revised edition of *Emerson's Literary Criticism,* xxv.

2. The phrase (from Plato's *Phaedrus,* 266), may be cited from Bacon's *Novum Organum.*

subjective world, the realm of ideas. In his journals, Emerson had frequently commented on the Coleridgean dialectical "method" (see, for example, *JMN* 3:229, 299, 5:114, and 6:222), a method that depended on precise definitions and—he said in the 1836 lecture—had "enriched the English language and the English mind with an explanation of the object of Philosophy." Coleridge had provided "admirable definitions, and drawn indelible lines of distinction between things heretofore confounded"—such distinctions as those between "an Idea and a Conception; between Genius and Talent; between Fancy and Imagination; of the Idea of a State." Emerson here alludes to *Biographia Literaria, Aids to Reflection, The Friend,* and, in the last item, *On the Constitution of the Church and State.* Coleridge's term *Genius* plays a role in Emerson's thought second only to what he called in this lecture the "all-important distinction between Reason and Understanding." These definitions and these specific texts of Coleridge gave Emerson the precise terminology *he* needed to express an American version of the British Romantic revolution.

The prime distinction remains that between Reason (an intuitive, visionary, imaginative, quasi-divine faculty, a *via illuminativa* to the Truth) and "mere" understanding (a faculty capable of rational calculation but sense derived and thus limited to empirical deduction), in short what those in the dominant Lockean tradition meant by "reason." As earlier noted, Coleridge's deliberate or at least creative misreading of Kant's terms—*reason, understanding,* and especially of what he meant by *intuition*—provides much of the theoretical basis of British Romanticism and American Transcendentalism. Perhaps never fully aware of the *precise* ways in which Coleridge had altered Kant, Emerson consistently adopts, and deploys, this Coleridgean version of Kant, of whom he knew little or nothing before reading Coleridge, Carlyle, and Hedge.

In his 1836 lecture, Emerson commemorates Coleridge as the "solitary scholar" who had revealed "genius and depth of thought to be still possible" in even this uncongenial age, one who shared Emerson's radical faith in the divinity of each person, a Temple housing the Inner Light in the form of intuitive Reason:

> He was of that class of philosophers called Platonists, that is, of the most Universal school; of that class that take the most enlarged and reverent views of man's nature. His eye was fixed upon Man's Reason as the faculty in which the very Godhead manifested itself or the Word was anew made flesh. His reverence for the Divine Reason was truly philosophical and made him regard every man as the most sacred object in the Universe, the Temple of Deity. (*EL* 1:377, 379)

No lecture or essay is devoted exclusively to Coleridge; this 1836 tribute remains Emerson's only sustained public treatment of the man and his work. But complimentary references are scattered throughout Emerson's letters, journals, and notebooks, and there are frequent allusions, attributed and unattributed, to Coleridge's prose and translations from the German. In hindsight, he reports being disappointed, during his 1833 visit, by his host's theological conservatism; attempting to "reconcile the gothic rule and dogma of the Anglican Church with eternal ideas," the former religious radical had, Emerson later remarked in *English Traits,* "narrowed his mind" (*E&L* 902). But in a journal entry made in 1836, the same year as the lecture just cited, he recorded his appreciation of the range and incisiveness of that mind, undiminished by any such narrowing: "I told Miss Peabody last night [November 23] that Mr. Coleridge's churchmanship is thought to effect the value of his criticism &c. I do not feel it.... I know no such critic. Every opinion he expresses is a canon of criticism that should be writ in steel, & his italics are the italics of the mind" (*JMN* 5:252).

Man's "every act," says Emerson in his essay on Goethe in *Representative Men,* "inscribes itself in the memories of his fellows" (*E&L* 746). In this 1836 journal entry, we have another inscription in characters that endure because inscribed by one formidable mind upon another. As so often in Emerson, it is unforgettably expressed; it is also eminently just and a personal acknowledgment. Like many others, Emerson had abundant reason to attest to the impression upon his own mind of the italics of Coleridgean criticism. An oracular dialectician rather than a systematic philosopher, Emerson nevertheless needed a reasonably sophisticated epistemological vocabulary. His Transcendentalist revolution required, as it happened, a specifically *Coleridgean* vocabulary, a dialectical process complex (indeed, paradoxical) enough to synthesize the Emersonian Me and NOT ME, what Coleridge called, to reverse the order, the "objectively Real" (experience, things without, nature) and the "subjectively Real" (intuitive Reason, somehow including a nature nuptially reconciled and internalized).

When we describe the Romantic and Transcendental revolutions as *subjective, inner, psychological, aesthetic, intuitive, organic,* and characterized not by mere *Understanding* but by a higher *Reason* inseparable from *Intuitive Knowledge,* or *Instinct,* or *Insight,* or *Imagination,* or *Spirit,* we are using terms either coined, reintroduced, plagiarized, or transformed by Coleridge. If we adapt what Whitman said of his indebtedness to Emerson, we might—remembering that according to Emerson "we boil at different degrees"—say that he himself was "simmering, simmering, simmering," until Coleridge and Wordsworth brought him to a "boil." But it was Coleridge who supplied the philosophic grounding, for Emerson as he had for Wordsworth before him.[3] Though in private letters and conversation Wordsworth praised Coleridge's wonderful mind, publicly (aside from the "Essay, Supplementary, to the Preface" of his 1815 *Poems*) he celebrated only his love for his friend, most notably in the tribute in the revised version of the final book of *The Prelude*. Emerson, too, and for similar reasons, was reluctant to publicly acknowledge his incalculable intellectual debt to Coleridge.

Much of the critical—also, the more numinous—vocabulary of the movement, in particular the distinction between Reason and understanding and the more paradoxical relationship between inherent and bestowed enlightenment, initially derived from a single book. "The most immediate force behind American Transcendentalism was Coleridge, who gained many ardent readers in New England following the edition of *Aids to Reflection* that was brought out in 1829 by President Marsh of the University of Vermont." Any historian of the period (I have already referred to Perry Miller and Robert Richardson) might have been cited to make this sweeping yet indisputable point. I have quoted F. O. Matthiessen, from the opening pages of his landmark study *American Renaissance* (1941), to make my own point: that Matthiessen, perhaps the leading Americanist of his period, participates in the general failure, with the notable exception of Frank Thompson, to develop tangible and specific implications of the Coleridge-Emerson connection.[4]

Matthiessen's fourth chapter ("The Organic Principle") opens with an eight-page section titled "From Coleridge to Emerson," which itself opens with Coleridge's famous distinction (largely plagiarized from A. W. Schlegel, the unnamed "Continental critic" he refers to in this the ninth of his 1817 Shakespeare lectures) between "mechanic and organic form." But despite his section title, Matthiessen stays at a general level and, indeed, brings in Thoreau and Whitman—quite appropriately, of course, since, along with Emerson's own essays, *Walden* and *Leaves of Grass* provide remarkable examples of organic growth and development. Matthiessen's discussion illuminates a shared commitment, in their best work, to the organic principle distilled in the Coleridgean axiom, "Such as the life is, such the form." In a "work of true genius," the innate forming power, "acting creatively under

3. In addition to other material already cited, see Barry Wood, "The Growth of the Soul: Coleridge's Dialectical Method and the Strategy of Emerson's *Nature*." Whitman's famous tribute to Emerson is quoted from J. T. Trowbridge, *My Own Story*, 367. Emerson's remark about boiling at different degrees occurs in "Eloquence," in *Solitude and Society* (1870).

4. Matthiessen, *American Renaissance*, 6. For the section discussed in the following paragraphs, see pp. 133–40.

laws of its own origination," is, says Coleridge in the passage Matthiessen quotes, "one and the same" with "the perfection of its outward form." Perhaps because he wants to maintain his focus on "form," Matthiessen refrains from connecting this formulation with a related, and more momentous, form of autonomy: the self-reliant Emersonian individual—aboriginal rather than derivative, active rather than passive, creative rather than imitative, and obeying laws only of his own making. Indeed, Emerson's whole theory of *human* progress, as outlined in "Intellect," is organic, with instinct—intuitive Reason—as both origin and end: "All our progress is an unfolding, like the vegetable bud. You have first an instinct, then an opinion, then a knowledge, as the plant has root, bud, and fruit. Trust instinct to the end, though you can render no reason" (*E&L* 419).

Even when it comes to his prime poetic illustration of the Coleridgean organic principle at work, Matthiessen, in the course of an insightful explication of one of Emerson's best and best-loved poems, "The Snow-Storm," does not connect the poem back to the originating passage he cited from Coleridge and, again, despite his section title, either never notices or passes over as irrelevant two possible precursor poems by Coleridge. Though differences as well as similarities link "The Snow-Storm" with "Frost at Midnight," the "north wind's *masonry*" and the memorable final line, "The frolic *architecture* of the snow," do seem reminiscent of Coleridge's opening where, though unhelped by any wind, "The frost performs its secret *ministry*," a discreet and mysterious ritual repeated in the rondural closing, where the eave drops either fall, heard only "in the trances of the blast," or are hung up "in silent icicles" by means of that "secret ministry of frost" (*CPW* 1:240–42). Emerson presents us with the varieties of "form" produced by the savage masonry of the "north wind," that "*fierce artificer,*" organic forms that leave

astonished Art
To mimic in slow structures, stone by stone,
Built in an age, the *mad wind's night-work,*
The *frolic* architecture of the snow.
(*EPP* 442; italics added)

The raving "wind" in the seventh stanza of Coleridge's "Dejection: An Ode" is also a fierce artisan, though a bard rather than an architect: a "*Mad Lutanist!*" a "*mighty Poet,* e'en to *frenzy* bold!" (*CPW* 1:367). Such personifications stress that crucial nexus for the Romantics and the Transcendentalists, the analogy between the human and the natural world. In addition, the variety of forms in which the Emersonian snow is sculpted by the wind ("Parian wreaths," "swan-like form," "a tapering turret") would seem to demonstrate Coleridge's clinching point in Matthiessen's orienting text: "Such as the life is, such the form. Nature, the prime *genial artist,* inexhaustible in diverse powers, is equally *inexhaustible in forms.*"[5]

Perhaps such resemblances-within-difference are no more than coincidental. Emerson sometimes refers directly to Coleridge's poetry: to the music of "To William Wordsworth" or to "Alph," the sacred river in "Kubla Khan" (*E&L* 921), the one original Coleridge poem printed in *Parnassus,* or to *The Ancient Mariner*—not even excerpted in *Parnassus,* but to which he once touchingly alluded, describing the recently drowned Margaret Fuller as "the wedding guest to whom the long pent-up story must be told" (*JMN* 11:495).[6] Emerson was impressed by a passage in Coleridge's translation of a Schiller play, a passage he quotes (*JMN* 4:325) in a significant personal context: the death of his brother Edward. And, as noted earlier, he several times cites important lines from Coleridge's *Destiny of Nations* about all things sensory being "Symbolical, one mighty alphabet" revealing God in nature. His important allusion to "Dejection: An Ode" in the "Prospects" chapter of *Nature* is silent. For the most part, what engages Emerson is the ideational content; in general, aside from "Kubla Khan," he seems oblivious to Coleridge's poetry *as* poetry. For him, the Coleridge that mattered was the Thinker: England's greatest post-Kantian religio-centric epistemological philosopher and most formidable literary critic. As a poet, Coleridge was for Emerson less a practitioner than a "professor of the art" (*JMN* 4:312), and he has virtually nothing to say even of that handful of poems in which, leaping forward from the pseudo-Miltonic turgidity that deformed his ambitious early work, Coleridge had actually become a great practitioner. I mean that holy trinity of terrible beauty, *The Ancient Mariner, Christabel,* and "Kubla Khan," as well as the

5. In contrast with Coleridge's quietude, though these silences are "trances in the blast," the Emersonian snow arrives "Announced by all the trumpets of the sky." Their farmhouse veiled by snow, Emerson's "housemates sit / Around the radiant fireplace, enclosed / In a tumultuous privacy of storm" (*EPP* 442). The "inmates" of Coleridge's cottage are "at rest," leaving him to commune with the only other "unquiet thing," and thus a "companionable form," the flake of soot fluttering on the "grate" of *his* fireplace (*CPW* 1:240).

6. This description of Fuller as the ideal confidante occurs in the 1851 notebook in which Emerson collected materials for his contribution to a memoir following her tragic death (along with that of her husband and child) in a shipwreck off Fire Island. Revealingly, in *Parnassus*—the anthology of poems and favorite passages labored over by Emerson for a half century and finally published with the help of his daughter in 1874—Coleridge is represented by only six selections, half of them translations from Schiller's *Wallenstein,* the other half composed of "A Character," the ballad "Genevieve," and—the one great lyric to make it—"Kubla Khan." The sole reference to his work in the preface takes the form of a passage of Coleridge's prose *on* poetry, a comment Emerson immediately applies to Wordsworth's poetry.

great poems in the "conversation" mode: from "The Nightingale" and "Frost at Midnight" to "Dejection: An Ode," originally a more conversational verse epistle to Sara Hutchinson. Emerson was familiar with all these, as well as with "To William Wordsworth."

One would expect, especially in the case of the last two, some comment, or at least inclusion in *Parnassus,* if for no other reason than that they bring Coleridge and Wordsworth together. "Dejection," both as ode and private epistle, covertly responds to the opening four stanzas of the then incomplete Intimations Ode, recently read to Coleridge by Wordsworth; "To William Wordsworth" is an overt response, with Milton as intermediary, to Wordsworth's extended reading of the 1805 version of the "Poem for Coleridge," the epic we know as *The Prelude.* As psychodramatic distillations of the personal, poetic, and philosophical interaction between Coleridge and Wordsworth, both poems foreground the mobile dynamic between inner and outer, mind and matter, creative power and passive reception—the post-Kantian epistemology at the center of German idealism, British Romanticism, and American Transcendentalism.

This dichotomy between subject and object and their inevitable interrelationship is implicit in any systematic philosophy. But Emerson's handling of the dialectic reflects less an immersion in, say, Schelling than in Coleridge's prose and Wordsworth's poetry. Depending on context, Coleridge and Wordsworth seem unsure, and therefore formulatively ambiguous, as to whether the dominant power comes from within or without. In "Tintern Abbey," Wordsworth is a lover

> of all that we behold
> From this green earth; of all the mighty world
> Of eye, and ear,—both what they half create
> And what perceive.
>
> (104–7; *WP* 360)

That "*half*-create" was later emphasized by Bloom as an instance of deep reservation, Wordsworth's repression of his own "preternatural self-reliance," a reservation earlier detected, and echoed, by Yeats, who claims that when we artists are abashed by our own sense of limitation, "We are but critics, or but half create."[7] At other times, sure of his own power of imagination and "Not prostrate, overborne, as if the mind / Itself were

7. See Bloom's essay on Wordsworth in *Poetry and Repression: Revisionism from Blake to Stevens,* 75. Bloom concludes his discussion of the lines quoted by alluding to Emerson. "Having invoked directly his eye and ear," Wordsworth registers, "even more surprisingly, a deep reservation about his own perpetual powers, or rather an admission of limitation. The mighty world of eye and ear is not a balance of creation and perception, but of half-creation and full perception. . . . What is being repressed here is

nothing, a mean pensioner / On outward forms" (*P* 6:736–38), Wordsworth can adumbrate his most assertive formulation, in the "spots of time" passage of *The Prelude*. That statement—"The mind is lord and master—outward sense / The obedient servant of her will" (12:222–23)—parallels Coleridge's "we receive but what we give, / And *in our life alone* does nature live" ("Dejection: An Ode"). Together they are, prior to Emerson, perhaps the most daring assertions (at least in English, since Fichte and the youthful Schelling seek unity in the "absolute I" and Schiller insists, in *On the Sublime*, on "the *absolute* greatness *within us*") about the subordination of external nature to the subjective Self. Though Coleridge, in "Dejection," emphasizes human emotion even more than that intuitive Reason he had made indistinguishable from his "shaping spirit of Imagination," such texts, taken together, lead directly to the oracular finale of Emerson's own *Nature*, which, however misleading his book's title, ultimately celebrates not the phenomenal world, but the shaping power of the sovereign mind or "Spirit" (essential, ideal) over what is, in comparison, "an accident and an effect"—in short, "the kingdom of man over nature" (*E&L* 49).

In the relation between Coleridge and Emerson, we do have, I believe, a case of what Bloom has called "the anxiety of influence" in an ephebe's confrontation with a precursor. But, aside from the manifest impact of the Dejection Ode on the "Orphic Poet" at the end of *Nature* (the repetition of a key word, *blank*, a word with, as usual, Miltonic reverberations, confirms a conscious connection), the debt has to do with Coleridge's *prose*, not his poetry—a debt not always acknowledged publicly and sometimes not even privately. Anyone reading through Emerson's voluminous journals and notebooks will notice how often he quotes an original when his immediate and sometimes "filtering" source is Coleridge. Though it was Coleridge's prose that mattered, there may be an Emersonian version of the Coleridge poem he *did* value. Yet Emerson (intoxicated at the time by his reading of the Persian Sufi poet Hafīz) may simply not have been aware of the resemblance between "Kubla Khan" and his own marvelous "Bacchus," that source of inspiration for Emily Dickinson. Emerson's rhapsodic, Dionysian chant, petitioning the pagan god for a "wine which never grew / In the belly of the grape" and for "water and bread" that "need no transmuting" (a fully humanized and apocalyptic eucharist rather than the conventional Lord's Supper) seems to fuse Coleridge's inspired and transgressive bard, who has "fed on honeydew / And drunk the milk of

---

Wordsworth's extraordinary pride in the strength of his own imaginings, his preternatural self-reliance" (75). The Yeats poem quoted is "Ego Dominus Tuus": the dramatic speaker, "Ille," is translatable, as Ezra Pound once pointed out, to "Willie."

Paradise," with (as I suggest at the end of this chapter) the details of the Creation of Light in book 7 of *Paradise Lost.*[8]

If, for Emerson, Coleridge was the preeminent Thinker and Critic of the age, Wordsworth was its outstanding Poet. Comments to that effect are to be found in *English Traits,* in his 1840s essays in the *Dial,* and in remarks scattered in the journals. There is also *Parnassus.* In addition to the preface, which praises Wordsworth, the volume itself includes forty-three selections from Wordsworth, second only to Shakespeare (presumably Milton would have been second had Emerson not ruled out *Paradise Lost,* which "goes so surely with the Bible on to every book-shelf, that I have not cited a line").

As with most of his early readers in England and the United States, it took some time for Emerson to warm up to Wordsworth. He began to read his poetry while a junior at Harvard, four years before the first Boston edition appeared, the four-volume *Poetical Works* published by Cummings, Hilliard in 1824. In his early twenties, reflecting the neoclassical biases of many of the reviews he read before genuinely engaging the poet himself under the aegis of Coleridge, Emerson found Wordsworth insufficiently elegant and was understandably wary of his tendency to "pantheism." Familiar with *The Excursion* as early as 1821, Emerson, five years later, read "Dion," a poem also "much applauded" by his brother Charles (*JMN* 6: 272), and the Intimations Ode. Thereafter, as his letters and journals reveal, he returned to Wordsworth regularly, recording a lifelong pattern of sublime praise leavened by often harshly negative criticism.

In June 1826, he wrote an important letter to his aunt Mary, an admirer who had read Wordsworth "before every or any body liked him" and whose insights into the Intimations Ode exceeded his own at the time. Mingling misjudgment and insight, Emerson faults Wordsworth—"a lover of all the enchantments of wood & river" but "seduced by an overweening confidence in the force of his own genius"—for having "discarded that modesty under whose influence all his great precursors have resorted to external nature," humbler bards unwilling "to tamper with the secret and metaphysical" essence of "evanescent" nature. Later Emerson would champion precisely what he here condemns: the assertion, by Coleridge as well as Wordsworth, of the supremacy of Mind in the nuptial relationship with Nature. Despite Wordsworth's condemnation of those who "murder to dissect," Emerson rather perversely accuses him of picking to pieces and pouncing

8. Emerson probably came to Hafīz by way of Goethe, having read "The Book of Hafiz" in Goethe's *West-Eastern Divan* (1819).

on "the pleasurable element he is sure is in" natural things, "like the little boy who cut open his drum to see what made the noise." A rhetorical question follows, reflecting the Edinburgh reviewers in substance and neoclassical stance if not quite in wit, with Emerson again attacking precisely what he would later come to value and Mary already appreciated: Wordsworth's characteristic finding of significance in the commonplace. "Is it not," asks Emerson rhetorically, "much more conformable to that golden middle line in which all that is good and wise in life lies, to let what Heaven made small and casual remain the objects of a notice small and casual, and husband our admiration for images of grandeur in matter or in mind?" In a passage that tallies with Keats's identification of the "Wordsworthian or egotistical sublime," and reveals his early groping with such major texts as the Intimations Ode and the "Prospectus" to *The Recluse,* he provocatively informs his aunt that he would not bother to abuse Wordsworth,

> not even for his serene egotism whereby he seems at every turn thunderstruck to see what a prodigious height human genius has headed up in *him,* but that he has occasionally written lines which I think truly noble. He would be unworthy of your notice but that now & then comes from him a flash of divine light and makes you uneasy that he should be an earthen vessel. . . . He has nobly embodied a sentiment which, I know not why, has always seemed congenial to humanity[:] that the soul has come to us from a preexistence in God; that we have a property in the past which we do not ourselves recognize, & a title to the future of which we should be little thankful. . . . [L]et the glory & virtue of other worlds be as they may, in parting with our identity we part with happiness. (*L* 7:148–50)[9]

Barely twenty-three, Emerson already values the self's "identity" and "happiness"—the "flash of divine light"—above the supposed "glory and virtue of other worlds." Further, in doing so, he transcends the derivative prejudices expressed earlier in the letter, rising to a recognition of the distinction between mere "egotism" and what he would later valorize as self-

9. Mary's rebuttal, ignoring the charges, ecstatically proclaimed Wordsworth poetry's "priest," he who, "alone of poets, since Milton, deserves to be called *a hermit in the fields of thought.*" Though there is a reference in this letter to *The Excursion* ("the staff of the wanderer"), Mary's allusions are mostly to the Intimations Ode. She speaks of a "celestial Guest," a female form of nature revealing to her male seeker such "loftiest gifts" as "rainbows" but sometimes "decked with the humblest flowers" (*The Selected Letters of Mary Mood Emerson,* 217–18). Mary copied many passages from *Lyrical Ballads* into her "Almanack" (pages now missing). When Emerson offered her a copy of the ballads in 1829, she whimsically reported to his brother Charles, presumably alluding to Wordsworth's early "pantheism," "I read them in 1805 and don't wish to again tell the Priest" (Cole, *Mary Moody Emerson,* 119).

reliance and self-trust. Though still far less sensitive than his aunt in responding to the poem, he also signals the crucial importance the Intimations Ode would gradually and permanently assume in his life and thought.

But his evaluation, though generally in line with the positive evolution of Wordsworth's reputation, would remain in flux, oscillating between "disgust" and "veneration" (Rusk's terms; *L* 1:xxxiv). In comments made in journal entries in the 1830s, Wordsworth is said to suffer from occasional "imbecility of mind," and seems "a genius that hath epilepsy, a deranged archangel" (*JMN* 3:307, 4:63). Even into the 1840s, in essays in the *Dial*, Emerson continued to express serious reservations, attributing Wordsworth's fame—and his "great and steadily growing dominion" was "a leading fact in modern literature"—to "the idea which he shared with his coevals," to his "moral perception" and role as a consoler in distress, rather than to his undoubted but uneven talents; his merits, Emerson insisted, did not consistently include deft poetic expression. To be sure, Emerson, in his 1840 *Dial* essay "Thoughts on Modern Literature," is hard on *all* the writers he discusses—even the much admired Goethe, who finally "must be set down as the poet of the Actual, not of the Ideal; the poet of limitation, not of possibility; of this world, not of religion and hope; in short, if I may say so, the poet of prose, and not of poetry" (*EPP* 346). By those nonaesthetic idealist standards, who shall 'scape whipping? But one paragraph from that essay should be quoted in full. Beginning with harsh criticism of Wordsworth, it moves through some highly complimentary but still critical remarks, only to end with praise that places him, by association, in the visionary company of Shakespeare and Milton. After the opening critical remarks, quoted above, Emerson continues:

> The Excursion awakened in every lover of nature the right feeling. We saw stars shine, we felt the awe of mountains, we heard the rustle of wind in the grass, and knew again the ineffable secret of solitude. It was a great joy. It was nearer to nature than anything we had before. But the interest of the poem ended almost with the narrative of the influences of nature on the mind of the Boy, in the first book. Obviously for that passage the poem was written, and with the exception of this and of a few strains of the like character in the sequel the whole poem was dull. (*EPP* 342)

Readers unfamiliar with *The Excursion* may think Emerson has confused that text with reports and scattered samples of the opening book of what would eventually be published, a decade after Emerson was writing, as *The Prelude*. In fact, however, he is rightly praising the *Prelude*-paralleling lines (1:118–62, 191–234) in which the "Author" describes the response to Nature of the Boy destined to become the major figure of *The Excursion:*

the Pedlar, better known as the Wanderer. In recounting the transfer to the reader of a sense of solitude beneath the shining stars, Emerson is remembering that that Boy

> many an evening, to his distant home
> In solitude returning, saw the hills
> Grown larger in the darkness; all alone
> Beheld the stars come out above his head,
> And travelled through the wood, with no one near
> To whom he might confess the things he saw.
> (*E* 1:126–31)

The "awe of mountains" to which Emerson refers was an essentially emotional and, again, *visual* experience. The Boy knew his Bible, "But in the mountains did he *feel* his faith," a feeling of sublimity in which

> littleness was not; the least of things
> Seemed infinite; and there his spirit shaped
> Her prospects; nor did he believe,—he *saw.*
> (*E* 1:223–32)

What is in every sense the central passage comes between the two I have cited. Though he had not yet experienced

> the pure delight of love
> By sound diffused, or by the breathing air,
> Or by the silent looks of happy things,
> Or flowing from the universal face
> Of earth and sky,
> (187–91)

the Boy had "felt the power / Of Nature," and so was being prepared "to receive / Deeply the lesson deep of love": a lesson that he, "Whom Nature, by whatever means, has taught / To feel intensely, cannot but receive" (191–96):

> Such was the Boy—but for the growing Youth
> What soul was his, when, from the naked top
> Of some bold headland, he beheld the sun
> Rise up and bathe the world in light! He looked—
> Ocean and earth, the solid frame of earth
> And ocean's liquid mass, in gladness lay
> Beneath him:—far and wide the clouds were touched,
> And in their silent faces could he read

Unutterable love. Sound needed none,
Nor any voice of joy; his spirit drank
The spectacle: sensation, soul, and form,
All melted into him; they swallowed up
His animal being; in them did he live,
And by them did he live; they were his life.
In such access of mind, in such high hour
Of visitations from the living God,
Thought was not; in enjoyment it expired.
No thanks he breathed, he proffered no request;
Rapt into still communion that transcends
The imperfect offices of prayer and praise,
His mind was a thanksgiving to the power
That made him; it was blessedness and love!
(197–218)

It is hardly surprising that the author of *Nature,* he who had been rapt into the still communion of the epiphany of the transparent eyeball, should respond so intensely to such a blessed moment and even think that "obviously for that passage the poem was written." And Emerson is prescient in singling out lines (and one manuscript version of them actually went into *The Prelude*) that parallel Wordsworth's account of the formative experience of the influence of nature on his own mind. But there is more to *The Excursion* than this one passage, however sublime. It seems revealing that Emerson says nothing about the celebrated tale embedded later in book 1, the moving story the Wanderer tells of Margaret and the ruined cottage. And his own qualification of the statement that "the whole poem was dull" has a significant caveat: dull "with the exception of this [the "narrative of the influences of nature on the mind of the Boy"] and a few strains of like character in the sequel." The charge of dullness, though certainly more than occasionally applicable to *The Excursion,* does not accurately reflect Emerson's own deeply personal response to some of the speeches of the Wanderer, "strains of like character" to be found especially, as we shall see, in books 4 and 9.

In the very next sentence of this 1840 essay, Emerson characteristically gives back most of what he has just taken away, and goes on to conclude with a full-throated encomium. Apparently still referring to *The Excursion,* he states: "Here was no poem, but here was poetry, and a sure index where the subtle muse was about to pitch her tent and find the argument of her song." His allusions are, of course, not to *The Excursion* itself, but to the "Prospectus," the 107 lines of poetry excerpted from the conclusion of *Home at Grasmere* and appended by Wordsworth to his prose preface to *The Excursion.* Emerson, to whom these lines were immensely important, is referring specifically to the passage (quoted in his journals as well) in which Wordsworth, having invoked a "greater Muse" even than the Urania of Milton, announces his own "high argument," identifying neither heaven nor hell but "the mind of Man" as "My haunt and the main region of my Song." The lines that follow immediately in the "Prospectus," the source of Emerson's reference to the "muse about to pitch her tent," are also, in part, a reversal of the archangel Raphael's hierarchy of forms:

> Beauty—a living Presence of the earth,
> Surpassing the most fair ideal Forms
> Which craft of delicate Spirits hath composed
> From earth's materials—waits upon my steps;
> Pitches her tents before me as I move,
> An hourly neighbour.
>
> (42–47; *WP* 2:38)

The very *next* lines of the "Prospectus" directly influenced the opening paragraph of Emerson's *Nature*, especially the famous rhetorical questions raised in response to the assertions that "Our age is retrospective. It builds the sepulchres of the fathers" (*E&L* 7; this connection is later discussed in full). Though those assertions themselves are indebted to "sources" (the opening sentence of Hazlitt's essay on Coleridge and Webster's address dedicating the Bunker Hill monument), the most salient precursor text is the "Prospectus," the poem alluded to here in "Thoughts on Modern Literature." But it was too early, even in 1840, for Emerson to acknowledge *this* patent a debt. It was easier to parcel out blame and praise. The paragraph I have been citing and glossing certainly ends with the latter. Armed with Coleridge's concept of intuitive Reason and his elucidations of that divine faculty in Wordsworth, Emerson identifies the central argument of the muse about to pitch her tent: It was

> the human soul in these last ages striving for a just publication of itself. Add to this, however, the great praise of Wordsworth, that more than any other contemporary bard he is pervaded with a reverence of somewhat higher than (conscious) thought. There is in him that property common to all great poets, a wisdom of humanity, which is superior to any talents which they exert. It is the wisest part of Shakespeare and of Milton. For they are poets by the free course which they allow to the informing soul, which through their eyes beholdeth again and blesseth the things which it hath made. The soul is superior to knowledge, wiser than any of its works. (*EPP* 342)

In the end, the muse's crucial "argument" in Wordsworth, as it had been, says Emerson, in Shakespeare and Milton before him, is that the "informing soul," being the creative power, is superior to its "works," the things *it* "hath made" and "blesseth." For Yeats, a poet in this same tradition,

> man made up the whole,
> Made lock, stock and barrel
> Out of his bitter soul.
> ("The Tower," 149–51)

And he insists in the climactic lines of "A Dialogue of Self and Soul," arguably his central poem, not only that "We are blest by everything" but also that "Everything *we look upon* is blest" (71–72; italics added). Such a poet, whatever the inferiority of his talents to his innate genius, would eventually triumph. And, as Emerson notes, Wordsworth had.

Adhering closely to Coleridge's discussions in *Biographia Literaria* and *The Friend,* Emerson described Wordsworth's gradual achievement of a wide audience. In 1834, Emerson reminded himself to "transcribe from the Quarterly Review the sentences on the progressive influence of the man of Genius" (*JMN* 4:328). The man of "genius" was Wordsworth, both the term and the identification those of Coleridge, author of the *Quarterly Review* essay. His image of a progressively expanding influence may have affected Emerson's essay "Circles": "The life of a man is a self-evolving circle which, from a ring imperceptibly small, rushes on all sides outward to new and larger circles and that without end" (*E&L* 404). One such circle was the originally tiny but widening gyre of readers created by Wordsworth, a self-reliant man who endured incomprehension, hostility, and downright ridicule to eventually create a large and attentive audience, that "great and steadily growing dominion" he enjoyed in England and the United States. His correspondent Elizabeth Peabody told him in 1839 that "whereas your audience was once as *few* as *fit* in this country—now it is coextensive with the country—and nowhere have you a deeper power." Peabody, who knew many of Wordsworth's poems by heart and who loved to allude, is here echoing Wordsworth's own allusion to Milton (*PL* 7:31) in the "Prospectus" "'fit audience let me find though few!' / So prayed, more gaining than he asked, the Bard" (lines 23–24). The expansion from a minute to an immense audience was a phenomenon repeated in the career of Emerson himself, who became, by the 1850s, the best-known lecturer in the United States, with significant audiences as well in England and Scotland, where he lectured in 1847–1848. He had succeeded by trusting his own instincts, even in the face of the widespread condemnation following his "blasphemous" Divinity School Address of 1838.

In this he resembled Wordsworth, praised by Emerson for "stick[ing] close to his own thought" (*JMN* 3:306). That thought mingled "sanity" with "inspiration," coalescing in a meditative interaction with nature. It is obvious enough why Emerson would stress Wordsworth's having learned from brooding on direct experience rather than from books, and any mystery about his persistent commendation of Wordsworth for his "sanity" is cleared up by realizing that *both* emphases derive from Coleridge, who notes, as a "characteristic excellence of Mr. W's works . . . a correspondent weight and sanity of the Thought and Sentiments,—won, not from books; but—from the poet's own meditative observation" (*BL* 2:144–45). In the preface to *Parnassus,* characteristically mingling criticism and praise, Emerson asserts:

> Coleridge rightly said that "poetry must first be good sense, as a palace might well be magnificent, but first it must be a house." Wordsworth is open to ridicule of this sort; and yet, though setting a private and exaggerated value on his compositions and taking the public to task for not admiring his poetry, he is really a master of the English language; and his best poems evince a power of diction that is no more rivalled by his contemporaries than is his poetic insight. But his capital merit is, that he has done more for the sanity of his generation than any other writer.[10]

In one of his finest late tributes, Emerson said of Wordsworth: "This rugged rough countryman walks & sits alone, assured of his sanity & his inspiration, & writes to no public—sneered at by Jeffrey & Brougham, branded by Byron, blackened by the gossip of Barry Cornwall & De Quincey . . . for they all had disparaging tales of him, yet himself no more doubting the fine oracles that visited him than if Apollo had brought them visibly in his hand." After years of misrepresentation, he had become recognized, even in "obese material England," as "the genuine, & the rest the impure metal" (*JMN* 15:443). Wordsworth had in effect become his own Simeon and happy warrior, fulfilling and witnessing the revolution he had announced in the preface to *Lyrical Ballads.* Toward the end of *English Traits,* Emerson pointedly observes:

> I do not attach much importance to the disparagement of Wordsworth among London scholars. Who reads him well will know, that in following the strong bent of his genius, he was careless of the many, careless also of the few, self-assured that he should "create the taste by which he should be enjoyed." He lived long enough to witness the revolution he had wrought, and "to see what he foresaw." (*E&L* 928)

Emerson ends by connecting Wordsworth with his own composite hero, that inspired man who, having "wrought / Upon the plan that pleased his boyish thought," perseveres and, "through the heat of conflict, keeps the

10. Emerson, *Parnassus,* viii–ix.

law / In calmness made, and *sees what he foresaw.*"[11] The first phrase placed in quotation marks is the more significant. As his remarks confirm, Emerson (either from having read Wordsworth's "Essay, Supplementary to the Preface" to the 1815 *Poems* or from having perused Christopher Wordsworth's two-volume *Memoirs* of 1851) was familiar with the most celebrated of Wordsworth's letters to Lady Beaumont. On May 21, 1807, responding to her concern that he may have been hurt by the immediate reaction to *Poems in Two Volumes* (1807), Wordsworth seeks to reassure her that he "distinctly foresaw" and dismissed in advance this "present reception" of his poems. "Of what moment is that compared with what I trust is their destiny, to console the afflicted, . . . to teach the young and the gracious of every age, to see, to think and feel, and therefore to become more actively and securely virtuous; this is their office, which I trust they will faithfully perform long after we (that is, all that is mortal of us) are mouldered in our graves."[12]

"Careless" of both the "few" (the "London scholars") and the "many," as Emerson put it, Wordsworth reports himself disturbed neither by the malice of the "London wits and witlings" nor by the "uncomprehending condemnation" his poems may have incurred from "that portion of my contemporaries who are called the Public." Instead, he expresses a "calm," even "invincible confidence," that his poems would, in time, "co-operate with the benign tendencies in human nature and society" and prove "efficacious in making men wiser, better, and happier." Having echoed his own, as yet unpublished, "Prospectus" to *The Recluse,* with its confident hope that his song "With star-like virtue in its place may shine / Shedding benignant influence," Wordsworth goes on to quote Coleridge, who had earlier reassured Lady Beaumont in this matter of Wordsworth's reputation. People in "the senseless hurry of their idle lives do not *read* books, they merely snatch a glance at them that they may talk about them. And even if this were not so, never forget what I believe was observed to you by Coleridge, that every great and original writer, in proportion as he is great or original, must create the taste by which he is to be relished; he must teach the art by which he is to be seen."[13]

11. Wordsworth, "Character of the Happy Warrior," lines 3–4, 53–54; *WP* 1:660–61 (italics added).

12. Wordsworth, *The Letters of William and Dorothy Wordsworth: The Middle Years,* pt. 1: 145–46.

13. In the "Essay, Supplementary," after reviewing the reception of his predecessors, Wordsworth concludes: "If there be one conclusion more forcibly pressed upon us than another by the fortunes and fate of Poetical Works, it is this,—that every Author, as far as he is great and at the same time *original,* has had the task of *creating* the taste by which he is to be enjoyed. This remark was long since made to me by [my] philosophical Friend" (*WP* 2:944).

A considerable portion of the letter is devoted by Wordsworth to such a teaching, in the form of a full explication of his sonnet, "With ships the sea was sprinkled far and nigh." But the creation of that taste by which Wordsworth was eventually enjoyed, the teaching through which his art was properly seen, was, in large part, the task and accomplishment of the friend he cites here. Emerson too, quoting these very phrases, was aware that those who read Wordsworth "well" had acquired that skill with the indispensable help of Coleridge. Emerson's own appreciation of Wordsworth's poetry intensified dramatically after he began to read Coleridge in 1829. After his initial desultory encounters, he returned to Wordsworth, as Frank Thompson says, "with the praise of Coleridge ringing in his ears." Emerson was speaking both for the many, and for himself, when he said of Wordsworth in 1843, "We have learned how to read him" (*E&L* 1253). That informed reading led Emerson to a fuller appreciation, for example, of what he had earlier rejected as Wordsworthian egotism. Although that egotism had its "private" dimension, Emerson understood the implications of the noun in Keats's formulation of the "Wordsworthian or egotistical sublime." Wordsworth's "noble distinction," notes Emerson in a journal entry, "is that he seeks the truth & shuns with brave self-denial every image and word that is from the purpose—means to stick close to his own thought & give it in naked simplicity & so make it God's affair not his own whether it shall succeed" (*JMN* 3:306).

❧ Wordsworth's best "thought" and best poetry did eventually "succeed" among those who "have learned how to read him." And what did Emerson read? Throughout his life the single Wordsworth poem most persistently mentioned, quoted, and alluded to is the Intimations Ode, profound in its impact on Emerson as on all the Transcendentalists. But aside from the ode and "Tintern Abbey," Emerson, as the editor of his letters accurately notes, most frequently praised "the more austere poems and not, curiously enough, those of [what Rusk hyperbolically labels] extreme mystical quality" (*L* 1:lxxxiv). Aside from portions of *The Excursion,* and the great "Prospectus" published with it (printed in toto under the title "Outline" in *Parnassus*), the two austere poems that most impressed Emerson—who was, as his brother Charles said, "enamoured of the severe beauty of the Greek tragic muse"—both draw upon classical sources: "Laodamia" (1814) and "Dion" (1816). Given their evident significance for Emerson and the fact that neither (especially "Dion") is likely to be among the Wordsworth poems familiar to most readers, I have supplied synopses of both in an appendix, in which I also suggest that "Dion" gradually took on something of the political weight it had for

Wordsworth, and that "Laodamia," second only to the Intimations Ode in Emerson's estimation, may have had personal reverberations for both men.

Other persistent Emersonian favorites included "Character of the Happy Warrior," "The Old Cumberland Beggar," "Ode to Duty," "Rob Roy's Grave," and a considerable number of "noble sonnets." As for *The Prelude:* when it was posthumously published in the United States (by Appleton) in 1850, Emerson purchased copies for himself and for his aunt Mary and made some notes in his own copy. Despite reservations about the epic as a whole, he admired portions that had been earlier extracted—notably the lines Wordsworth himself published in 1835 on upstanding men whose self-reliance was developed "In Nature's presence" (eventually part of book 13) and the great skating scene, the winter episode in the seasonal cycle of book 1, featured by Coleridge in the Christmas 1809 issue (number 19) of *The Friend.* Both these lengthy excerpts were included by Emerson in *Parnassus,* along with the "Boy of Winander" episode, first published in the 1800 edition of *Lyrical Ballads* and later quoted and singled out as distinctively Wordsworthian by Coleridge (*BL* 2:103–4). In 1868, when he "read for the first time, I believe, carefully" Wordsworth's *White Doe of Rylstone,* Emerson pronounced it "tender, wise, & religious, such as only a true poet could write, honoring the poet & the reader" (*JMN* 16:105).

Also included in *Parnassus,* and elsewhere praised by Emerson, were three autumnal but affirmative poems: "Ode to Lycoris" (ending "Still, as we nearer draw to life's dark goal, / Be hopeful Spring the favourite of the Soul!"), "September, 1819" (celebrating the song of birds, unchecked in the face of "winter storms," confident in the God who provides for "all His creatures"), and the "Lines" written in 1806 on hearing of the approaching death of Charles James Fox, with its important Plotinian peroration, obviating, when "the great and good depart," the need to "mourn" (*WP* 2:354, 400, 1:721). These are impressive as well as comforting poems. Other Emersonian favorites had less to do with poetic merit than straightforward spiritual and consolatory content. One, "The Force of Prayer" (printed in *Parnassus* as "The Boy of Egremond"), concludes that even the worst "sorrow of heart" will end, "If but to God we turn, and ask / Of Him to be our friend" (*WP* 1:741). Another, "Fidelity," I discuss in the final section of this book, in connection with what many would see as the fact-suppressing religious "affirmation" shared by Wordsworth and Emerson—though I also note, along with Emerson's profound gratitude to Wordsworth's healing doctrine of compensation and consolation in distress, a certain impatience, in the wrenched aftermath of the early death of his wife, Ellen, with the vocabulary of conventional piety that occasionally intruded into even the best of Wordsworth's poems.

Notably omitted from *Parnassus,* though imitated by Emerson (see Chapter 7), are the famous quatrain poems from *Literary Ballads.* Wordsworth had been subject to ridicule—not only for memorializing Simon Lee and his "swollen ankles" and the idiot boy and his adventures but also for these early lyrics advocating an "anti-intellectual," even irrational, preference of nature to "mere" book knowledge. Even granting the obvious truth that such poems deployed a dialectic, this was no mere poetic gesture, a playing of the fool for the song's sake. However he changed over the years, Wordsworth never revised his sense of *relative* merits, never renounced the *substance* of his intuitive faith in an ennobling intercourse with vital Nature, what he called—in the original, less pious, version of "Lines Written in Early Spring"—his personal and unorthodox "creed."[14] And when it came to Wordsworth's contrast between Intuition and Tuition, Emerson clearly privileges the first term—rather like Blake in preferring infernal Energy to angelic Order, or early Nietzsche the Dionysian to the Apollonian, or Yeats the Antithetical to the Primary. This is especially so when the tuitional is epitomized in those restricting "systems of education" condemned in "The American Scholar."

But it is a matter of elevating rather than excluding. Our inquiry into the identity of the "Trustee" behind "self-trust" leads us, says Emerson in "Self-Reliance," to that "source, at once the essence of genius, of virtue, and of life, which we call Spontaneity or Instinct. We denote this primary wisdom as Intuition, whilst all later teachings are tuitions. In that deep force, the last fact beyond which analysis cannot go, all things find their common origin" (*E&L* 269). Since "all things," notably including intuition and tuitions, find a "common origin," implicit in all these polarities is an eventual fusion or reunion. Emerson is demoting, not debunking, belated but significant additional learning, those "later teachings" he followed Wordsworth in calling "tuition." As Stanley Cavell never tires of reminding us, intuition and spontaneous instinct, though superior to tuition, are not the whole of Emersonian wisdom.[15] Coleridgean Emerson, for all his emphasis on Intuition and instinctual Spontaneity, identified, as

14. Later he changed the lines to reflect a more orthodox, or Coleridgean, hypothesis: "If this belief *from heaven be sent,* / If such be Nature's *holy* plan." Emerson always praised Wordsworth's "self-reliance," his grounding of everything on his own moods and beliefs as he encountered a world of circumstances without help from Christianity or Platonism. Though Emerson might have been disturbed by this revision, Wordsworth retained, as Plotinus at least metaphorically does in the fifth Ennead, the spiritual-natural correspondence, and a caveat: *if* the belief was sent from "heaven," the holy "plan" was still "*Nature's,*" a nurturer always ready to "bless" our minds and hearts (*WP* 1:312).

15. Cavell cites the passage from "Self-Reliance" in order to "commemorate my annoyance at having to stand the repeated, conforming description of Emerson as a

the most sophisticated weapon in his "magazine of power," *conscious knowledge*. In this context, it is worth noting the divided implications of the adjective in the Wordsworth phrase perhaps uppermost in Emerson's mind: "*spontaneous* wisdom." Etymologically bracketing "independence" (*spontaneus*) and "binding" (*spons, spondere*), "spontaneous" epitomizes the polar tension we will be exploring. That is the sort of paradox that would be appreciated by the Emerson who devoted a significant part of the "Language" chapter of *Nature* to the tracing of linguistic roots. Whether he traced these particular roots or not, it is only apparently paradoxical that Emersonian "spontaneity," even that aspect of it that dismisses "books," is in fact largely derived from his *reading of* Wordsworth.

But even as he read him, Emerson remained critical of Wordsworth's unevenness, his uninspired descents into the "garrulous" and mere "platitudes" (*JMN* 5:335). "'Tis one of the mysteries of our condition," he wrote in a note in mid-1871, "that the poet seems sometimes to have a mere talent—a chamber in his brain into which an angel flies with divine messages, but the man, apart from this privilege, common-place. Wordsworth is an example." In the note that follows, Emerson was still capable of taking his contradictory estimates to the extreme of diagnosing Wordsworth as "a lame poet" who "suffers from asthma of the mind," only to add a correction to this very note five years later (*JMN* 16:244). His overall assessment, first publicly registered in 1856 in *English Traits*, was, like his astute commentary on England in general, characteristically two-sided but, finally, judiciously celebratory: "The exceptional fact of the period is the genius of Wordsworth. He had no master but nature and solitude.... His voice is the voice of sanity in a worldly and ambitious age. One regrets that his temperament was not more liquid and musical. He has written longer than he was inspired. But for the rest he has no competitor" (*E&L* 906; cf. *JMN* 13:352).

That is to say, his only competitors were among the mighty dead. Though he also revered Chaucer and loved Herbert, for Emerson as for his mentor Coleridge, the three preeminent English poets were, in descending order, Shakespeare, Milton, and Wordsworth. In the autumn of 1864, Emerson "read with delight" a perceptive if "casual notice" in the *London Reader* with which he thoroughly concurred, an assessment of Wordsworth in which "his highest merits were affirmed, & his unquestionable superiority to all English poets since Milton." What "struck"

---

philosopher of intuition, a description that uniformly fails to add that he is simultaneously the teacher of tuition, as though his speaking of all later teachings as tuitions were a devaluing of the teachings rather than a direction for deriving their necessary value" (*In Quest of the Ordinary*, 115).

Emerson as he read the piece was "the certainty with which the best opinion comes to be the established opinion. . . . 'And thus the world is brought / To sympathy with hopes & fears it heeded not'" (*JMN* 15:443, slightly misquoting lines 39–40 of Shelley's "Ode to a Skylark").

In this note Emerson refers to Arthur Clough as the one person who had impressed him, during his 1847–1848 travels in England, as a proper judge of Wordsworth, "admiring him aright" despite the cultic status of Tennyson. But by then the most acute judge, Coleridge, was long since dead. The pivotal role of Coleridge in shaping the critical thinking behind Emerson's own placement of Wordsworth in the near vicinity of Shakespeare and Milton is confirmed when we realize that it was he who opened up to Emerson not only Wordsworth but Shakespeare and Milton as well.[16] Milton's privileged niche in Emerson's pantheon was almost shared by Wordsworth—for Emerson, the paramount contemporary poet, "the manliest poet of his age." On the basis of his best work, and he did compose some "puerile poems," Wordsworth, Emerson wrote in his journal in 1875, "has established his claim to the highest thought in England in his time" (*JMN* 16:136–37). This repeated emphasis on Wordsworth's "thought" and "intellect" reminds us, again, that Emerson seldom engaged in close, or intrinsic, reading, attending to such poetic details as sound, cadence, rhyme, tone. It is therefore good to know that when in 1868 it was proposed that he offer a "private class" for young men to discuss literature, Emerson's first thought was that it would allow him, in distinguishing between "good poetry" and mere "eloquence" that "passes for good poetry," "to vindicate the genius of Wordsworth & show his distinctive merits," a manifestly American version of Coleridge's project, particularly in *The Friend,* and in *Biographia Literaria,* which Emerson thought the preeminent critical work of the age (*JMN* 16:137–38).[17]

16. Though preposterously said (by a former classmate) to have known "almost all of Shakespeare by heart" even before he arrived at Harvard, Emerson did not seriously engage the plays until he started to read Coleridge. Though Emerson's youthful Puritanism created resistances, "before the end of the 1820s, he became excited over reading Coleridge, whose idolatrous attitude toward Shakespeare was soon infective, abetted as it was by the enthusiasm of Emerson's brother Charles" (Sanford Marovitz, "Emerson's Shakespeare: From Scorn to Apotheosis," 124, 128). Echoing Shelley's recent sonnet "Ozymandias," and a favorite passage from Coleridge's *Friend,* young Emerson depicts Shakespeare as possessing "surpassing genius" marred by detestable immorality: "This statue is colossal but its diabolical features poison our admiration for the Genius which conc[ei]ved and the skillful hand which carved it." Yet Shakespeare possesses "singular power, singular among men," because his poetry "never halts, but has what Coleridge defines [as] Method"—echoing Coleridge's statement in the "Essays on Method" in *The Friend* that "unprogressive arrangement is not Method" (*JMN* 1:297, 3:229, 5:114, 6:222).

17. Unfortunately, this opportunity for practical criticism never materialized. The private-class proposal, made by William Forbes, Emerson's son-in-law, eventually took

The "genius of Wordsworth" could be fully appreciated, both Coleridge and the poet himself believed, only in the context of his admiring but competitive interaction with Milton, a judgment subsequently endorsed by many perceptive readers, Keats and Emerson among them. Much of this book, for good or ill, is a kind of echo chamber, and given the fact that all three of my major figures—Wordsworth, Coleridge, and Emerson—were saturated in the poetry and prose of John Milton, many of the echoes in that chamber are necessarily Miltonic. Milton was second only to Shakespeare in the Emersonian scale of greatness. Indeed, Milton's function was especially valuable in modifying the mean "descent" of the "English genius" from the "Parnassian" heights of the Elizabethan age "into the lower levels" typified by "Locke, to whom the meaning of the idea was unknown" and whose "understanding" became "the measure, in all nations, of the English intellect." As Emerson beautifully put it in this passage of *English Traits,* Milton was "the stair or high-table land to let down the English genius from the summits of Shakespeare" (*E&L* 899)—and, it might be added, to lift that genius again to the new summits of Romanticism. Twenty years earlier, in his splendid lecture on Milton, Emerson said: "We think no man can be named, whose mind still acts on the cultivated intellect of England and America with an energy comparable to that of Milton" (*EL* 1:149).

Yet Milton, too, was a creative borrower, and not only from the Bible and the ancients. Even as he audaciously vowed to take on "Things unattempted yet in prose or rhyme" (*PL* 1:16), he was, even more audaciously, borrowing his very formulation from an earlier epic poet, Ariosto.[18] Emerson thought Wordsworth "a more original poet" than Milton—worthy to be crowned with "the poet's garland," he wrote in a journal entry on August 17, 1834, since he "speaks by the right that *he has somewhat yet unsaid to say*" (*JMN* 4:312–13; italics added). There was nothing of greater importance in Emerson's increasingly "Romantic" estimation. In fact, this comment was described, by G. R. Elliot three-quarters of a century ago, as marking "a significant crisis in the story of Emerson's inner development": a willingness to take Wordsworth as "Romantic *vates* more and more into favor, putting up with the deficiencies of his art for the

---

the form of a series of ten readings, largely devoted to Wordsworth's poetry, in Chickering's Hall, Boston, between January 2 and March 20, 1869.

18. See the opening chapter, "The Originality Paradox," of McFarland's *Originality and Imagination.* "As brief but choice illustration," adopted "as a kind of microcosmic symbol of the paradox," McFarland quotes a commentator's observation: "Milton's pledge to pursue 'things unattempted yet in prose or rhyme' . . . is itself a quotation from the *Orlando Furioso*" (14n47). The "commentator" is David Quint in his *Origin and Originality in Renaissance Literature: Versions of the Source* (216).

sake of his 'originality' as a seer," and going on to apply the lesson to his own situation. The imperative to say the "yet unsaid" adumbrates Emerson's own dilemma as a young writer—and illustrates yet again, to a degree Elliot seems not to notice, the paradox of originality. Emerson's "multifarious genius" wanted

> to say everything, and indeed was doing so, more or less, in the Journal. But as poet and essayist, he was trying to concentrate upon "somewhat yet unsaid to say." In this process Wordsworth proved to be a very present help: he did much to concentrate Emerson's vision in the direction of naturistic individualism. His shaping influence was exerted upon Emerson's first book, *Nature,* which just at this time, with much difficulty, was beginning to assume publishable form.[19]

But if Emerson found *his* path to the "yet unsaid" with the help of Wordsworth, he was only repeating Wordsworth's own point of departure in finding *his* originality. Emerson thought Wordsworth more "original" than Milton in large part because he was less bookishly "learned," less in thrall to what Wordsworth, and after him Emerson, referred to as "tuition," as contrasted with intuition. Protective of that "originality," and seldom generous in praising poets other than "Shakespeare, or Milton, Labourers divine!" (*P* 5:165), Wordsworth, for all his reverence of Milton, found it hard to praise without competing, or could truly praise only *by* competing, his creativity stimulated by his great precursor. Thus, Wordsworth's own poetry is pervaded by Miltonic echoes. This is *especially* true—as has been demonstrated briefly by Elizabeth Sewell in *The Orphic Voice* and by M. H. Abrams throughout his seminal *Natural Supernaturalism*—of the crucial "Prospectus" to *The Recluse,* the poem in which Wordsworth lays out an agenda requiring him to absorb and surpass the mighty bard who inspires in him both idolatry and rivalry. Milton's "great argument" is superseded by Wordsworth's "high argument," theodicy yielding to Romantic epistemology, the relationship between mind and nature becoming more immediately germane than that between God and man. It is in the famous introduction to *Nature,* and in its "Orphic" peroration, two of the texts in which Emerson is at his boldest, that we find him most indebted to Wordsworth's "Prospectus." In the introduction Emerson claims utter originality, while, in the final chapter, he asserts the sovereignty of the human mind, which takes dominion over the external world. With Wordsworth's "Prospectus," and Coleridge's Dejection Ode, covertly brought to bear at precisely these assertive points, intertextuality *does emerge, pace* Bloom himself, as a Bloomian power struggle.

19. G. R. Elliot, "On Emerson's 'Grace' and 'Self-Reliance,'" 101.

The "Prospectus" mapped out Wordsworth's entire triadic project, the first completed portion of which, the posthumously published *Prelude,* is almost as riddled with functional Miltonic allusions as is the "Prospectus." Let me, in concluding this chapter on overt and covert discipleship, pursue just one recurrent image, seemingly slight but, in its ramifications, significant: the "shedding" of light as a form of influence.

In the opening book of *The Prelude,* Wordsworth dropped one Miltonic phrase ("It is an injury...", discussed in Chapter 6), only to add another to the same passage. The addition, in which the evening sun becomes a "*mellowing* sun, that *shed / Mild influence*" (*P* 1:102–3; italics added), also echoes Milton. In its immediate Wordsworthian context, the echo seems insignificant, until we restore it to its *Miltonic* context, thus revealing that even the movement toward a pleasurable if temporary indolence contains within it the potential of new creation. The mellowing sun that "shed / Mild influence" recalls Raphael's description to Adam of Creation itself, specifically the creation of light, including our "glorious Lamp," the "jocund" sun, that "all the horizon round / Invested with bright rays," while "the Pleiades before him danced / *Shedding sweet influence*" (*PL* 7:370–74; italics added). Milton is himself alluding to "the sweet influence of Pleiades" (Job 38:31), but the revealing verb is *shed,* repeated far more significantly in Wordsworth's "Prospectus" and, at an equally momentous and parallel point, in the canon of Emerson, this time his poetry.

In the "Prospectus" Wordsworth hopes that, inspired by "genuine insight," his song "With star-like virtue in its place may shine / Shedding benignant influence" (88–90): a hope and phrase endorsed by Coleridge, who tells us, in "To William Wordsworth," that "the truly great / Have all one age, and from one visible space / Shed influence" (50–52). As that echo suggests, this "shedding" has an intricate lineage—one worth tracing in the concluding section of this chapter since the shedding of "light," as my subtitle indicates, is at the heart of the present project.

In "Bacchus," his most ecstatic poem, Emerson calls for wine "that is *shed,* / Like the torrents of the *sun* / Up the *horizon* walls," wine inspiring the poet to write (and these are the concluding lines) with the equivalent of that divine

> pen
> Which *on the first day* drew,
> Upon the tablets blue,
> *The dancing Pleiads* and eternal men.
> (64–67; *EPP* 453)

This intoxicating, luminous wine may gush from the Persian jug of Hafīz, but, imagination mattering more than wine, the verbal details derive from English Milton's Creation scene.[20] Of course, Emerson secularizes Milton, replacing divine creation with a rival creation by the inspired poet, the Emersonian Self as liberating God. He could not have done so without having absorbed that Wordsworthian "Outline" he so admired: the "Prospectus," which, anticipating "Bacchus," replaced Milton's depiction of God's creation with man's: "the *creation* (by no lower name / Can it be called)" that "the individual Mind" and "the external World" (each "fitted" to the other, with mind dominant) "with blended might accomplish" (69–71).

This is a more austere but still recognizable version of what he refers to earlier in this poem as the marriage, accompanied by a projected "spousal hymn," of mind and the external world—what Coleridge will describe in the Dejection Ode in terms of a ministering Joy, "Which, *wedding Nature to us,* gives in dower / A new Earth and new Heaven" (67–69). Apocalyptic Blake may have been indignant in the margins of his copy of the "Prospectus" ("You shall not bring me down to believe such fitting and fitted[.] I know better and Please your Lordship"), but, his Kant filtered through Coleridge, this is Wordsworth's "high argument," a secular displacement of Milton's "great argument," which was to "assert Eternal Providence, / And justify the ways of God to men" (*PL* 1:24–26), and even of his "higher argument" in book 9, where Milton's subject is "Not less but more heroic than the wrath / Of stern Achilles, . . . or rage of Turnus." Whether Homeric or Virgilian, "Wars, hitherto the only argument / Heroic deemed," are inadequate themes to Milton, to whom "*higher argument* / Remains, sufficient of itself to raise" the "name" of heroic epic (*PL* 9:14–18, 42–44; italics added).

And just as Milton must supersede Homer and Virgil, Wordsworth must supersede Milton, advancing, though retaining the same terms of heroic quest, into new regions with the indispensable help of the very precursor who must be surpassed. Once again, the mighty dead have quickened a new, and altered form, of creation, with Wordsworth using Milton as a Coleridgean "*fulcrum* for a further propulsion" (*BL* 1:124). Milton had opened book 7 by invoking his Muse to inspire him so that he might prove worthy of his impending and daunting poetic task, the up-

20. In his great essay "The Poet," Emerson explains that poets' flirtation with intoxication derives from their desire to transcend the limits of individual consciousness, to tap into some more profound and wider source of power. But, like Keats in the "Ode to a Nightingale" (the penultimate stanza of which Emerson printed in *Parnassus*), the Emersonian poet finally chooses imagination rather than wine to access "a new energy. . . by abandonment to the nature of things," going beyond "his privacy of power" to "draw on a great public power" (*E&L* 459–61), presumably *anima mundi,* or the Over-Soul.

coming description of Creation: "Descend from Heaven, Urania." Wordsworth will need "Urania," or "a *greater* Muse, if such / Descend to earth or dwell in highest heaven!" for his theme is that matrix of human creativity, the "Mind of Man," a region higher (more sublime) than any Miltonic heaven of heavens, deeper (more profound) than any hell, even "the darkest pit of Erebus." He needs a "gift of genuine insight," related to that "gift" that alone "consecrated" his liberty in book 1 of *The Prelude,* an intuitive power, imagination, that fuses soul, mind, and heart:

> Descend, prophetic Spirit! that inspir'st
> The human soul of universal earth,
> Dreaming on things to come; and dost possess
> A metropolitan temple in the hearts
> Of mighty Poets: upon me bestow
> A gift of genuine insight; that my Song
> With star-like virtue in its place may shine
> Shedding benignant influence. . . .
> (83–90; *WP* 2:39–40)

In keeping with Romantic and Emersonian duality, this shed light may have its source Within or derive ultimately from Above. Either way, its function, when shed by a great poet, a "benefactor" or "friend to man" (Keats's description of Milton before he applied it to the Grecian Urn), is to illuminate human darkness, to lift the burden of the mystery. The light is at once earthly and celestial, humane and transcendent, solitary and social. Depending on context, it may emanate from what Coleridge, in retiring from political activism in December 1796, referred to as "the taper in my cottage window" or beam out from what he called—in describing the "homeward" reorientation and internalization of the political hopes Wordsworth had invested in the French Revolution—"The dread watch-tower of man's absolute self" ("To William Wordsworth"). Yet, as retiring Coleridge added in encouraging the greatest of the English Jacobins, John Thelwall, to "uplift the torch dreadlessly" in continuing to publicly resist government repression, "the Light shall stream to a far distance from the taper in my cottage window" (*CL* 1:277). Thus, Coleridge anticipates what Emerson called the polarity between Solitude and Society. And Wordsworth's shattered political hopes would, out of the nadir of despair, be reconstituted internally, becoming the source that, through poetry, would shed benignant influence—even "joy" (as he also says in the "Prospectus") "in widest commonalty spread" (18).

The purpose, cooperating (as Wordsworth said in the 1807 letter to Lady Beaumont) "with the benign tendencies in human nature and society," would be consolation and benefaction, to be a benignant and compensatory light to others, shining with "star-like virtue," illuminating the darkness. Of his own spiritual and consolatory doctrine of "compensation" Emerson said, in the opening paragraph of the essay of that title, that he hoped that "in it might be shown men a ray of divinity. . . . It appeared, moreover, that if this doctrine could be stated in terms with any resemblance to those *bright intuitions* in which this truth is sometimes revealed to us, it would be *a star* in many dark hours and crooked passages in our journey that would not suffer us to lose our way" (*E&L* 285; italics added).

Emerson's discreet response to the Wordsworthian shedding of light is overt in Keats. In describing Wordsworth's progress through darkness to light in his remarkable "Mansion-of-Many-Apartments" letter to John Hamilton Reynolds, on May 3, 1818, Keats had in mind not only "Tintern Abbey," whose "burthen of the mystery" he specifically quotes, but also the "Prospectus," with its advance beyond Milton and its shedding of benign influence and "star-like" light. We are in darkness, Keats tells his friend, and Wordsworth's "Genius is explorative of those dark Passages. Now if we live & go on thinking, we too shall explore them. [H]e is a Genius and superior [to] us, in so far as he can, more than we, make discoveries, and *shed a light* in them." Anticipating his sublimatedly heroic phrase later in the letter, "a *grand march* of intellect," Keats immediately adds, "Here I must think Wordsworth is deeper than Milton—though I think it has depended more upon the general and gregarious advance of intellect, than individual greatness of mind."[21] Wordsworth is deeper—more "modern," we would say—than the Milton he advances on in the "Prospectus," since his predecessor's arena of action—God and the angels, heaven and hell—is psychologically internalized, replaced by the "Mind of Man," identified by Wordsworth in the "Prospectus" as "my haunt, and the main region of my song" (lines 40–41).

The equivalent psychological inward turn in Keats, adumbrated in this letter to Reynolds, occurs in the first of the great odes. Like the "Prospectus," the "Ode to Psyche" assimilates and supersedes Milton, in this case by restoring and internalizing the pagan worship extirpated by the Christ child in Milton's Nativity Ode, repeatedly echoed by Keats in "Psyche." As the neglected goddess's priest and choir all in one, "see[ing] and sing[ing] by my own eyes inspired," Keats will, in the extraordinary final stanza of his own ode, "build a fane / In some untrodden *region of my mind*" (50–51), that "Mind of Man" chosen by Wordsworth as his haunt and the "main region" of his song, with a further echo of Wordsworth's "Temple in the hearts / Of mighty Poets" (86–87). In the mysterious

21. Keats, *Letters of John Keats,* 1:281–82. Keats's argument is based on the "stages" of life recapitulated by Wordsworth in "Tintern Abbey."

stanza of the Intimations Ode that most haunted Keats, as it would Emerson and many others, "High instincts" and "shadowy recollections, / . . . be they what they may," emerge as a "master light of all our seeing." In Keats's erotic variation in the finale of "Psyche," "*shadowy* thought" kindles to a "bright torch," the light of seeing that proved tragic in the original Greek myth, with, in Keats's happy restitution, the casement window left open "at night to let the warm Love in." Related to the nuptial in the "Prospectus," the "great consummation" in which "the discerning intellect of man" is "wedded to this goodly universe / In love and holy passion," and dramatizing the provisionally separate emphases in the concluding stanzas of the Intimations Ode ("thought" and the "philosophic mind" in stanza 10, and feeling, heart, and "thoughts . . . too deep for tears" in the final stanza), Keats's revisiting and revising of the old Psyche-Cupid story gives us what is at once the most amusing and most touching of all the innumerable Romantic reconciliations of mind and heart, thought and feeling. And since the contraction or psychological internalization of the myth is accompanied by a diastolic expansion outward in two related and generous impulses, of service to the neglected and of open-windowed and openhearted love, Keats seems to glance again at the "Prospectus," this time its benign vision of "joy in widest commonalty spread."

This is the humanistic, mortal dimension of that Wordsworthian *shedding* of "benignant influence." At the same time, behind all this "shedding" of light there are issues of life, death, and, in some form, resurrection. "Let perpetual light shine upon them," goes the prayer for the dead, echoed and altered in the Intimations Ode, in which Wordsworth tells us that the thought of his past years breeds in him "perpetual benediction," that last the word Emerson once mistakenly transposed to "Tintern Abbey" (*JMN* 4:63). That is terminus, with the hope of renewal beyond the grave. But there is also genesis itself, Milton's description of the Creation of Light. The whole procession takes its most resonant form, in terms of shed light, in the ancestral image familiar to Milton, Coleridge, Wordsworth, Emerson, and Yeats: the Plotinian fountain of emanation, an overflow, bounteous and luminous, cascading or radiating down from the divine One through *Nous* (mind or intellect) and on to and through the darkling and divisive world of generation, with the potential of an epistrophic return of the individual soul to mystical and ecstatic reunion with the originating One, the oft-repeated "flight of the alone to the Alone."[22]

22. This, the final sentence of the *Enneads,* is alluded to by Emerson (*JMN* 7:430; *E&L* 663); by Lionel Johnson in the final lines of "The Dark Angel" ("Lonely unto the Lone I go, / Divine to the Divinity"); and by Yeats in the widely misread central stanza of the best of the "Crazy Jane" poems: "A lonely ghost the ghost is / That to God shall come" (*W. B. Yeats: The Poems; A New Edition,* 258).

One of Emerson's favorite Wordsworth poems, the "Lines" on the expected death of Charles James Fox, poses a self-answering question: is it not the case

> That Man who is from God sent forth,
> Doth yet again to God return?
> Such ebb and flow must ever be,
> Then wherefore should we mourn?
> (21–24; *WP* 1:721)

As "the sun flows (or radiates), and the mind is a stream of thoughts, so was the universe an emanation of God," Emerson asserts in 1841 (*JMN* 7:428–29). The fusion of liquid and light is behind the numinous image that dominates the present project: Wordsworth's "fountain light of all our day," that "master light of all our seeing." Aquatic imagery flows into the luminous, the luminous into the ocular. In *Aids to Reflection,* that early guidebook for the Transcendentalists, Coleridge refers to "the light which is the eye" of the soul. "This *seeing* light, this *enlightening* eye, is Reflection," though meaning more than "what is ordinarily meant by that word," since we "ought . . . to know . . . whence it first came, and still continues to come—of what light even this light is *but* a reflection. This, too, is THOUGHT; and all thought is but unthinking that does not flow out of this, or tend towards it" (*AR* 15–16; italics in original). Even in this overtly Christian account, we have the usual paradox of inner light that yet has its Plotinian origin in the divine, a "divinity within," immanent yet somehow indistinguishable from the transcendent source of all illumination.

And that is the appropriate image with which to end this opening section. Here and throughout the chapters that follow, my intention is not to reduce the rich complexity of intellectual and literary history to mere *Quellenforschung* (or source hunting), inevitably overstating the particular echoes and "influences" with which I am concerned, or to reduce the "erect" Emerson to a state of dependency. The man who emerges from this study is more deeply indebted to Coleridge and Wordsworth than, until quite recently, most readers since Frank Thompson have been willing to concede. But it is also true that to be indebted is not necessarily to be dominated, especially when one is reading, as Emerson so often was, not to be instructed, but to be confirmed and stimulated by encountering one's own thoughts in the mind of another, thoughts that bear no individual copyright. His characteristic emphasis is on both the collective pool in which all ideas swim and on each reader's own readiness and creativity. The thinker, says Emerson, "is to give himself to that which draws him out, because that is his own" (*JMN* 7:349). And he asks himself, and us, much earlier, in the autumn of 1831: "Were you ever instructed by a wise and eloquent man? Remember then, were not the words that made your blood run cold, that brought the blood to your cheeks, that made you tremble or delighted you,—did they not sound to you as old as yourself? Was it not truth that you knew before . . . ? It is God in you that responds to God without or affirms his own words trembling on the lips of another" (*JMN* 3:302).

Perhaps *everything* one reads with passionate intensity constitutes one's own rejected thoughts returning with a certain alienated majesty. But, for the purposes of this book, what has emerged as *most* "true" (however problematic and mysterious that truth), and of greatest thematic importance, is what Emerson called (in a crucial journal entry of May 1836) "the true light of all our day." Radiating, as it so often does in Emerson, from that Wordsworthian "fountain light of all our day," this is principal among the intimations of *some* form of Transcendentalist immortality. Derived ultimately from Plato, Plotinus, and Milton, but filtered through Coleridge and Wordsworth, this light constitutes the intuitive "argument for the spiritual world," for the "spirit" of such men—and, in one paramount instance, the spirit of Emerson's own "wonderful" little boy, Waldo—is what Emerson usually *means* by what he calls in this journal entry "the spiritual world" (*JMN* 5:160–61).

Part II

POLARITIES

Chapter 5

Powers and Pulsations

QUOTATION AND ORIGINALITY

I know at least one who has been deemed worthy of the Gift; who has received the Harp with Reverence, and struck it with the hand of Power.

—SAMUEL TAYLOR COLERIDGE on William Wordsworth, *The Friend*

❧

I had better never see a book, than to be warped by its attraction clean out of my own orbit, and made a satellite instead of a system.

—RALPH WALDO EMERSON, "The American Scholar"

❧

There is no pure originality. All minds quote. . . . only an inventor knows how to borrow.

—RALPH WALDO EMERSON, "Quotation and Originality"

❧

Nature hates calculators; her methods are salutary and impulsive. Man lives by pulses . . . ; and the mind goes antagonizing on, and never prospers but by fits.

—RALPH WALDO EMERSON, "Experience"

Whether he is describing the pulsating movements of nature or of the mind, Emerson habitually thinks in terms of that most pervasive of Romantic concepts, the doctrine of polarity. Of the education of the American scholar "by nature, by books, and by action," Emerson says that

> The final value of action, like that of books, and better than books, is, that it is a resource. That great principle of Undulation in nature, that shows itself in the inspiring and expiring of the breath; in desire and satiety; in the ebb and flow of the sea; in day and night; in heat and cold; and as yet more deeply ingrained in every atom and every fluid, is known to us under the name of Polarity,—these "fits of easy transmission and reflection," as Newton called them, are the law of nature because they are the law of spirit. The mind now thinks; now acts; and each fit reproduces the other. (*E&L* 62)

The concept of polarity was familiar to Emerson from his reading, especially, of Goethe, one of his "Representative Men," and of Coleridge. Though there are precedents (in, for example, the Eastern yin-yang concept and in the Hebrew Kabbalah), Coleridge himself, in a passage Emerson knew, accurately traced the lineage back to the Greek pre-Socratic Heraclitus and his Hermetic heir, Giordano Bruno. Reading *The Friend,* Emerson could hardly have missed this explosion of capitals and italics: "EVERY POWER IN NATURE AND IN SPIRIT *must evolve an opposite, as the sole means and condition of its manifestation:* AND ALL OPPOSITION IS A TENDENCY TO RE-UNION. This is the universal Law of Polarity or essential Dualism, first promulgated by Heraclitus, 2000 years afterwards republished, and made the foundation both of Logic, of Physics, and of Metaphysics by Giordano Bruno" (*F* 1:94n).

Coleridge might have added "literature" and "criticism" to his list of disciplines founded on the principle of polarity. As he said in a letter of 1820, "In all subjects of deep and lasting interest, you will detect a struggle between two opposites, two polar forces, both of which are alike necessary to our human well-being & necessary each to the continued existence of the other" (*CL* 5:35). In fact, this polar rhythm—notably in terms of the heart's systole and diastole—plays out in many of Coleridge's own most characteristic poems: a psychological and aesthetic movement from intimate focus on an immediate scene, expansion to take in a wider landscape with correspondingly ampler intellectual reflections, ending in a rondural return to the local, particular scene. Such a dialectical polarity, manifest in the "conversation poems" of 1795–1798, is not only topographical and psychological but also political, traceable in the Coleridgean oscillating rhythm of commitment and quietistic withdrawal. Coleridge himself posited a dilating "Yea" and contracting "Nay" in "an attempt to delineate the arc of oscillation" in his alternating mental state, a political dialectic acceptable to some commentators; condemned by others as indicative of instability of character or, in dialectical terms, the slippery equivocations epitomizing the "problem of Romantic apostasy"; and praised by others, who perceive a reconciliationist consistency underlying the shifting forces driving, and dividing, Coleridge Agonistes.[1]

This dialectical-polar-reconciliationist concept is at the "heart" of Coleridge's thought and work, of the "Dynamic philosophy" he inherited from the German idealist philosophers, Kant and Schelling above all. Deriving his Kant from Coleridge, Emerson learned that "the understanding," which "distinguish[es] without dividing," prepares the way "for the intellectual re-union of the all in one" in the "eternal reason," and that the reciprocity between "each and all" could be translated into his own terms: Self and the Over-Soul, in turn a version of the relationship between the individual talent and its creative interaction with received tradition (*F* 1:522). From his reading of Coleridge, Emerson might have known indirectly about one of the source texts for both his mentor and Schelling. Like so many others at the time, Coleridge, buttressing Heraclitus and Bruno, had found an authoritative modern text in Kant's dynamic conception of matter founded on the tension between "attraction and repulsion." Goethe, Hegel, and Schelling, whom Coleridge pronounced "the most successful improver of the Dynamic system," all cite this passage, and the short Kantian treatise of 1786, *Metaphysische Angfangsgrunde der Naturwissenschaft* (Metaphysical elements of natural philosophy), in which the passage appears, was, even beyond his norm for marginalia, heavily annotated by Coleridge, who also praises it in *Biographia Literaria* (*BL* 1:153).

"Strange alternation of attraction and repulsion!" Emerson exclaims in "Character" (in *Essays: Second Series; E&L* 503). Four paragraphs earlier, he had established the superior pole in this alternating pulsation, a hierarchy based on a primary "power" and its resistant force. "Character" has its natural place in the North; "feeble souls are drawn to the south or negative pole." Whereas the person of character fearlessly and autonomously exercises power over mere circumstance, the feeble souls, governed by forces from without rather than within, "worship events" and ask no more than to find a factual connection, "a chain of circumstances." But the "hero sees that the event is ancillary: it must follow *him.* A given order of events has no power to secure to him the satisfaction which the imagination attaches

1. Those who have contributed most to the discussion of these issues include Albert Guerard, Kelvin Everest, Carl Woodring, Max Schulz, David Erdman, and (speaking for the prosecution), David Simpson, E. P. Thompson, and Alan Liu. The texts directly alluded to include Everest's *Coleridge's Secret Ministry: The Context of the Conversation Poems;* Schulz's "Coleridge Agonistes"; Erdman's introduction to his edition of Coleridge's *Essays on His Times,* 1:lxxxv; and Liu's *Wordsworth: The Sense of History,* 416, 422, 427. See also John Beer's recent introduction to *The Rime of the Ancient Mariner,* 2–3.

to it; the soul of goodness escapes from any set of circumstances, whilst prosperity belongs to a certain mind, and will introduce that power and victory which is its natural fruit, into any order of events." Such a person is immune from merely external forces. On the other hand, no change of circumstances can repair a defect of character. Rather than iconoclastically breaking idols of superstition, those lacking character merely transfer the idolatry:

> What have I gained, that I no longer immolate a bull to Jove, or to Neptune, or a mouse to Hecate; that I do not tremble before the Eumenides, or the Catholic Purgatory, or the Calvinistic Judgment-day,—if I quake at . . . public opinion . . . or at the threat of assault, or contumely, or bad neighbors, or poverty, or mutilation, or at the rumor of revolution, or of murder? If I quake, what matters it what I quake at? . . . [I]f we are capable of fear, [we] will readily find terrors. The covetousness or the malignity which saddens me, when I ascribe it to society, is my own. I am always environed by myself. On the other part, rectitude is a perpetual victory, celebrated not by cries of joy, but by serenity, which is joy fixed or habitual. (*E&L* 499–500)

To employ the language of three of his favorite Wordsworth poems, Emerson here presents the "character" of a "happy warrior," one secure in the belief, amid the selfishness and cruelties encountered in the "dreary intercourse of daily life," that no malignity shall "prevail against us" ("Tintern Abbey"). Such a person of character is not terrified by pagan superstitions, by "the darkest pit of lowest Erebus," even by "Jehovah—with his thunder, and the choir / Of shouting Angels, and the empyreal thrones—I pass them unalarmed" ("Prospectus" to *The Recluse*). This is self-reliance at its most idealist, the Within impervious to the Without. Yet because there is a relationship between self and circumstances, the Me and the NOT ME, and because, for those who can attain this truth, "Within and Above are synonymous" (*JMN* 4:365), Emerson repeatedly calls for a reuniting of the "heavens and the earthly world" (*E&L* 761), the Kantian "starry heavens above me and the moral law within me"—the Emersonian polarity between the "firmament of the soul" and "the other firmament" (*E&L* 32; *L* 1:330).

There is no end to the dialectic, and the range is infinite, not only from inner to outer firmament but from the celestial to the infernal as well. That range is revealed, as usual allusively, in a remarkably inclusive sentence in the essay "Circles." Once again, Milton provides the key. "Our life," says Emerson, "is an apprenticeship to the truth, that around every circle another can be drawn, that there is no end in nature, but every end is a beginning; that there is always another dawn risen on mid-noon, and under every deep a lower deep opens" (*E&L* 403). The polarity encompassed by that single climactic clause ranges, by way of allusion to *Paradise Lost*, from highest to lowest, the angelic through the human to the demonic. "Another dawn risen on mid-noon" echoes the human response to the glorious arrival in Paradise of the archangel Raphael. A "Seraph winged" and with "Lineaments divine," Raphael is sent by God to warn Adam and Eve (who has had a troubling dream) about their Satanic enemy, his origins and the imminent threat he poses. At the moment of the angel's arrival, a moment vividly evoked by Wordsworth as well as Emerson, a dazzled and exuberant Adam tells Eve to haste hither and "behold" something "worth thy sight":

> Eastward among those trees, what glorious shape
> Comes this way moving; seems another Morn
> Ris'n on mid-noon.
>
> (*PL* 5:309–11)

As with Emerson, it was the last phrase that registered with Wordsworth, who, restored to the beloved sister from whom he had been parted since the death of their mother nine years earlier, feels blessed with a joy above all others, "that seemed another morn / Risen on mid-noon" (*P* 6:195–98). And Thoreau, in the final sentence of *Walden* may also be recalling Adam's words: "There is more day to dawn; the sun is but a morning-star."

At the other extreme, Emerson's second and final phrase is borrowed, appropriately enough, from Raphael's opposite and humankind's great Enemy. "Under every deep a lower deep opens" recalls the words of Satan in book 4, a fallen angel reduced to "infinite despair," and wound in ever deepening convolutions of his own misery and complicating deception:

> Which way I fly is hell; myself am hell;
> And in *the lowest deep a lower deep,*
> Still threatening to *devour* me, *opens* wide,
> To which the hell I suffer seems a heaven.
>
> (*PL* 4:75–78; italics added)

Traditionally symbolic both of perfection and of limitation, the ever beginning, ever ending circle here becomes something of a bipolar, almost vertiginous, figure, ranging from blessed radiance, eternity and hope, on the one hand, to infernal darkness and "infinite despair," on the other. There could hardly be a more dramatic revelation of Emersonian "optimism" now opposed by forces that threaten to devour *all* hope. Though "Circles" is finally more expansive than restricting, Emerson has moved from the largely unchallenged assertiveness of "The American Scholar" and "Self-Reliance" to a recognition of limitation that would fully emerge later in the essay "Fate"—though even there what is "known to us as limitation" is overcome by its conquering angel: the power of human thought, the soul's "impulse of choosing and acting." Even as he acknowledges circumscribing Necessity, dialectical Emerson counters it with the liberating power of the human mind: "Intellect annuls Fate. So far as a man thinks, he is free" (*E&L* 949, 953).

Emerson's polar vacillation in "Circles" is clear in two additional passages. "The life of man is a self-evolving circle, which, from a ring imperceptibly small, rushes out on all sides to new and larger circles, and that without end. The extent to which this generation of circles, wheel without wheel, will go, depends on the force or truth of the individual soul." It is, we are told, "the inert effort of each thought, having formed itself into a circular wave of circumstance,"

> to heap itself on that ridge, and to solidify and hem in the life. But if the soul is quick and strong, it bursts over that boundary on all sides, and expands another orbit on the great deep, which also runs up into a high wave, with attempt again to stop and to bind. But the heart refuses to be imprisoned; in its first and narrowest pulses, it already tends outward with a vast force, and to immense and innumerable expansions. (*E&L* 404–5)

That is the limitation-refusing equivalent of another dawn risen on midmorn. The opposing sense that under every deep a lower deep opens darkens the conclusion of the second passage, a few paragraphs further on. "Our moods do not believe in each other," Emerson continues, all too aware that the "power" of thought and verbal expression alternates with a "dreary vacuity," an influx and reflux, an "ebb" and "flow," resembling, though more ominously, the usual polar systole and diastole: "Alas for this infirm faith, this will not strenuous, this vast ebb of a vast flow. I am God in nature; I am a weed by the wall" (*E&L* 406). Here Emerson oscillates wildly between self-deification and self-annihilation, creative energy and the dreaded loss of inspiration: "the flash of light, then a long darkness, then a flash again," as he says in "Inspiration" (*W* 8:272–73). And even when, in this the final paragraph of "Circles," he says that "nothing great was ever achieved without enthusiasm," he chooses to omit (for he has just silently quoted Coleridge) the rest of Coleridge's remark in *The Statesman's Manual:* "For what is enthusiasm but the oblivion and swallowing up of self in any object dearer than self, or in an idea more vivid." We can be sure the omitted phrase was in Emerson's mind, for he had just noted: "In nature every moment is new; the past is always *swallowed* and forgotten." Perhaps, taken out of Coleridge's *positive* context, the momentarily grim "oblivion and *swallowing* up of self" threatened the preacher of self-reliance, a man alternating between power and vacuity, assertion and anxiety, and thus was too close for comfort to Satan's "lower deep, / Still threatening to *devour* me" (*LS* 23).[2]

Though "Circles" expands to encompass Milton and Coleridge, Emerson's exclamation about the "strange alternation of attraction and repulsion" may echo Goethe's notation on the passage in Kant about "attraction and repulsion." Goethe's response reveals more than one polarity: "Since our excellent Kant says in plain words that there can be no material without attraction and repulsion (that is, without polarity), I am much reassured to be able, under this authority, to proceed with my view of the world according to my own earliest convictions, in which I have never lost confidence."[3] This statement wonderfully compresses a further tension: that between tradition and the individual talent, the spirit of the age and the particular thinker, quotation and originality. Goethe had recognized, as Emerson said we so often do, a "truth that [he] knew before, . . . his own words trembling on the lips of another" (*JMN* 3:302). Coleridge said the same of *his* reading of Kant, Fichte, and Schelling (*BL* 1:160; *CN* 3:2375). Indeed, in citing the crucial distinction Milton's Raphael makes between understanding and Reason, "discursive or intuitive," Coleridge insists that he felt "*confirmed* by authority so venerable: for I had previous and higher motives in my own conviction" of the necessity of the distinction "to all sound speculation in metaphysics, ethical or theological" (*BL* 1:173–74). In the same way, Goethe, reassured by authority without injury to "my view" of the world, based on "my own earliest convictions," preserved *power* in order to generate further striving and—his vision being dialectical and spiritual rather than cyclical and material—ever higher ascent.

Whether in his study of nature (from optics to botany) or in his presentation of man in his poetry, Goethe adopted the polar dynamic of contraction and expansion issuing in an "advance into the infinite," through the exercise of what he too calls "intellectual intuition." We do not have to accept his mythic conjectures (his primal phenomenon, the *Urphanomen,* or primal plant, the *Urpflanze*) to be attracted to the Goethean conception

2. The passage as a whole influenced Emerson's "enlarged" concept of self-reliance; see Chapter 8.

3. Goethe, *Gedenkausgabe der Werke, Briefe und Gesprache,* 19:732. Subsequent parenthetical references are to this edition, quoted in McFarland, "Complex Dialogue," 76.

of ceaseless striving, *Steigerung.* In the course of that "ever-striving ascent" (16:925), everything from plants to human beings, from flora to Faust, struggles to achieve its innate "higher intention." Apparently illuminating Goethe's *Urpflanze* with Coleridge's "Imagination, or Esemplastic Power" (*BL* 1:168) and his reciprocal concept of "each and all" (*F* 1:511), Emerson, in a note of May 3, 1834, remarks that truly comprehending the "beauty" of phenomena requires that they be seen not "separately," but as constituent parts of a harmonious "composition." All subclassifications must be looked on as "temporary," with "the eye always watching for the glimmering of that pure plastic Idea. . . . This is evidently what Goethe aimed to do, in seeking the Arch plant, which, being known, would give, not only all actual, but all possible vegetable forms" (*JMN* 4:288, 289).

Among the litany of polarities Goethe offers at one point, several—"Ourselves and objects . . . Mind and matter . . . light and dark . . . ideal and real . . . Imagination and understanding" (16:863–64)—were of particular interest to Coleridge and Emerson. And all involve *power,* the issue at the center of *all* polarities and pulsations. In German idealism, British Romanticism, and American Transcendentalism, the dynamic transaction between subject and object, mind and nature, inner and outer, is a dialectic of relative power. This shifting Power underlies Emerson's many discussions of Polarity, Undulation, Pulsation, the dialectic between Motion and Rest, in the interrelationship of nature and the human mind. For Emerson, the devotee of darting, shooting energy, activity is nevertheless but half of a creative polarity that includes rest in the form of wise passivity or diligent indolence. At the highest level, there is a bond between such seeming polar opposites as passively accepted "Fate" and actively affirmed "Power": a linkage reinforced by the dialectical juxtaposition of the essays thus titled at the beginning of *The Conduct of Life,* "Fate" followed immediately by "Power."

The key word, *power,* comes up twice in "To William Wordsworth," still the most brilliantly condensed synopsis and interpretation of *The Prelude.* Responding to his friend's reading of the whole poem over two weeks in 1807, Coleridge refers to the higher or intuitive "Reason" that transcends mere understanding and to that dynamic flux and reflux of "tides" either "obedient to external force," or "currents self-determined," alternately impelled

> by some inner *Power;* of moments awful,
> Now in thy inner life, and now abroad,
> When *power* streamed from thee, and thy soul received
> The light reflected, as a light bestowed.
>
> (13–19; italics added)

These lines are echoed in "Prospects," the remarkable conclusion of *Nature.* Discussing (without mentioning Coleridge) the major Coleridgean distinction, Emerson dismissed mere understanding, celebrating instead a more than Kantian intuitive Reason, and its "exertions of a power which exists not in time or space, but an instantaneous *in-streaming causing power*" (*E&L* 47; italics added). And Emerson immediately goes on to allude to a crucial Coleridgean variation on Milton's reference to his physical blindness. "And still I gaze—and with how blank an eye!" cried Coleridge in "Dejection: An Ode." Echoing despondent Coleridge's ability to look at but "not feel" the beauty of nature, Emerson insists that "the ruin or the blank that we see when we look at nature, is in our own eye." The asserted polarity between one's inner life and the world without has broken down; Emerson deplores the fact that, in "actual life," the Coleridgean-Wordsworthian "marriage" between man and nature is "not celebrated" (*E&L* 47).

For Coleridge and Wordsworth—and after them Emerson—power ultimately resides in the subject, the sovereign Mind of Man. We hear in *Nature* of "the kingdom of man over nature," a dominion received by that "mediate" servant "as meekly as the ass on which the Saviour rode" (*E&L* 49, 28). Even for *this* High Romantic Emerson and for the Wordsworth who could declare that "The mind is lord and master—outward sense / The obedient servant of her will" (*P* 12:222–23) and the Coleridge for whom "we receive but what we give, / And in our life alone does Nature live" ("Dejection: An Ode," 47–48), the mind-nature relation remains in fruitful fluctuation—between passive yet receptive perception and active, energetic creation. That dialectic is reflected in the tension between imagination and education. The Wordsworthian ideal, "Knowledge not purchased with the loss of power" (*P* 5:425), helps explain his intuition-tuition distinction. Early and late, Wordsworth stressed the growth of the mind through "wise passiveness" as a stage of creativity, part of the imaginative and intuitive intercourse of the mind and heart with nature. It was a process antithetical to "tuition," classroom instruction and book learning.[4]

4. Since intuition was a relatively superior way to build up a human spirit, why did he (and, in book 9 of *The Excursion,* his Wanderer) embrace the regularized discipline of the Bell or Madras system of national education? It has been suggested that Wordsworth recognized that the imposition of power from above "is not entirely separable from the forms of imaginative power with which he identifies—imaginative power that imbues its objects with 'life.'" Thus, the poet's differing ideas on the subject of informing the mind (and his personal endorsement of the Bell system was enthusiastic but brief) may be less a matter of confusion than "a function of the very structure of power" and of the dialectic that "leaves open the question of whether what is involved is an uprising from below or an imposition from above[.] What from one perspective

Power is also involved in the tension between what Emerson, a man who both cherished *and* dismissed books, calls "Quotation and Originality." The two opening sentences of his most audacious claim to originality—the introduction to *Nature*—are themselves quotations or allusions. The very first—"Our age is retrospective"—echoes William Hazlitt's essay (in *The Spirit of the Age*) on Coleridge, the man who, personally and intellectually, opened Hazlitt up to the world of thought and imagination, and the principal intellectual influence on Emerson himself. It was Hazlitt who first pointed out that Coleridge was not only a master of quotation and allusion but all too often guilty of plagiarism—a charge Emerson acknowledged but dismissed as trivial compared to Coleridge's role as "benefactor" to a whole age. This accuser was himself, of course, a great master of quotation and allusion.[5] The most penetrating student of Hazlitt's critical mind, a mind telepathically attuned to the various forms of power, emphasizes what he calls "the politics of allusion," the role of power in quotation and allusion. A critic's wish, explains David Bromwich, "is to take possession of what he was possessed by. No interesting act of quotation therefore can imply a simple gesture of homage; the reader cannot help being interested in more than the accuracy of the result." A critic, "when he quotes is interrupting the text to which his chosen passage belongs, and exhibiting *his power* in relation to an author he cares for, at the same time that he acknowledges *the author's mastery over him.*"[6]

Such power shifts and apparent "contradictions" are familiar to students of Emerson, an omnivorous reader who denounces books; a herald of the "close" of America's "long apprenticeship to the learning of other lands" (*E&L* 53) in profound debt to his transatlantic Romantic precur-

looks like democratization appears from another to be indoctrination." The tension, therefore, between the knowledge gained through instinctual interaction with nature and that gained from tutorial instruction and books is another instance of differing forms of empowerment. See Alison Hickey, *Impure Conceits: Rhetoric and Ideology in Wordsworth's "Excursion,"* 113. She takes issue with Carl Woodring, the R. A. Foakes article cited below, and James K. Chandler's more extended account in "Rousseau and the Politics of Education," chap. 5 of *Wordsworth's Second Nature: A Study of the Poetry and Politics.*

5. Hazlitt insists, in "On the Aristocracy of Letters," that "true superiority" can arise only "out of the presupposed ground of equality," the liberty that produces neither "submission nor condescension." True "progress" is dialectical, based on resistance between two worthy forces: "The mind strikes out truth by collision, as steel strikes fire from flint!" (*The Complete Works of William Hazlitt,* 4:208). Appropriately enough, Hazlitt is here adapting an image of Samuel Johnson, perhaps the only literary critic to whom he would have to concede superiority as well as priority. "Genius," said Johnson in *The Rambler* (no. 25), "whatever it be, is like fire in the flint, only to be produced by collision with a proper subject."

6. Bromwich, from *Hazlitt: The Mind of a Critic,* 175.

sors, a defender of the fiercely "independent" Self who also insists that we must transcend mere "private" impulses, a self-reliant individualist who, in keeping with the paradox of originality, recognizes as well that we are all part of a larger tradition. This is the polarity embraced in the very terms of Emerson's 1859 lecture "Quotation and Originality." Here (and elsewhere) the decrier of dependence, imitation, and the dead past admits that "all minds quote" (*W* 8:178), that "all originality is relative. Every thinker is retrospective" (*E&L* 715). Like the other Romantic tensions, that indebtedness-independence polarity will play out dialectically throughout Emerson's lectures and essays.

In the earlier work, however, and especially in the public documents, the debt to his immediate precursors and "benefactors" must be played down, even effaced in order to preserve his claims to self-reliant independence and the power that comes with originality. Thus, there is a marked difference in the forms, early and late, of Emersonian allusion. When Henry James said of Emerson that he "liked literature as a thing to refer to, liked the very names of which it is full," he was referring "especially" to such "later writings" as the essays in *The Conduct of Life,* where the Sage of Concord "mentions . . . authorities" with the profusion of "his well-loved and irrepressibly allusive Montaigne." In Emerson's "own bookishness," as James says in noting the paradox, "there is a certain contradiction. . . . Independence, the return to nature, the finding out and doing for oneself, was what he mostly highly recommended; and yet he is constantly reminding his readers of the conventional signs and consecrations—of what other men have done."[7] Yes, but *not* when those "other men"—Coleridge and Wordsworth prominent among them—had done things too directly anticipating what Emerson himself was doing. When the resemblance was too close for comfort, especially in the earlier writings, those "authorities" were *not* mentioned, their "very names" expunged. Originality required erasure, yet the polar tension between innovation and indebtedness continued. That paradoxical relationship—what a leading twentieth-century expounder of the principle of polarity, in which opposites involve each other, called the tension between "immediacy and mediation"—can be traced in any number of Emersonian texts.[8]

Two of them are the seminal documents in which Emerson's call for originality and self-reliance is most emphatic: the opening of *Nature,* that wonderful if vertiginous "little azure-coloured" book published in 1836,

7. James, *Partial Portraits* (1888), reprinted in James's *Literary Criticism,* 262.

8. See M. R. Cohen in his major work, *Reason and Nature: An Essay on the Meaning of Scientific Method.* This is the first pair Cohen gives in his list of "Opposites" that "all involve each other when applied to any significant entity," all of them demonstrating a "necessary copresence and mutual dependence" (165).

and the essay "Self-Reliance" itself. *Nature* begins by reversing both Saint Paul and Ezekiel, and in ways that at first seem antithetical to his theme. As Denis Donoghue reminds us, 1 Corinthians 13 "prophesied the supersession of prophecy and knowledge: the time will come when we shall see God face to face, without mediation." In contrast, Emerson places that unmediated vision in the *past:* "The foregoing generations beheld God and nature face to face." But in doing so, he is echoing not only Paul but also the text Paul himself is echoing, Jacob's "I have seen God face to face" (Gen. 32:30). After saying that our forefathers beheld God and nature "face to face; we, through their eyes," Emerson asks, "Why should not we *also* enjoy an original relation to the universe?" This "also"—as in the next assertion, that the "sun shines to-day *also,*" which presupposes an earlier shining, indeed that there really *is* "no new thing under the sun" (Eccles. 1:9)—deconstructs originality by acknowledging that an earlier generation of "seers" *did* enjoy such a primary, "original" revelation (*E&L* 7). Emerson is buttressing Jacob with Coleridge. It was "revelation" by which "the earliest teachers of humanity [were] *inspired,*" says Coleridge in the last of his essays on method: "They alone were the true seers of GOD, and therefore prophets of the human race" (*F* 1:516).

Though face-to-face with belatedness, Emerson's challenge to us is to assert *our own* "original relation to the universe." In this opening paragraph of his introduction, after lamenting that "our age is retrospective. It builds the sepulchres of the fathers," he famously predicts, and calls for, an unmediated revelation in which "the living generation," having ceased to build those sepulchres, or to "grope about the dry bones of the past," will no longer masquerade in the "faded wardrobe" of that dead past (*E&L* 7). Emerson's dismissal of "groping among the dry bones of the past" constitutes, as Donoghue says, "another reversal, since Ezekiel 37 has always been interpreted by Christian readers as a sign of resurrection."[9] Exactly. But, although Emerson's allusion certainly *sounds* like a decisive dismissal of all patriarchal legacies, the break from the past is, as usual, complicated by the fact that he is asserting an originality, a resurrection from the dead past, that takes the form of *quotation,* one form of groping among the bones of the past—in this case, the recent past.

The earliest, most crucial of the recent texts to which Emerson alludes at the opening of *Nature* is Wordsworth's "Prospectus," an affirmative connection already noted and to which I will return. The other two texts appeared in 1825 and, presenting as they did an age of belatedness, must have been troubling to Emerson, especially the first: Hazlitt's chapter "Mr.

9. Donoghue, "Emerson at First," 23.

Coleridge" in *The Spirit of the Age.* Once we recognize the power politics involved in allusion, the need for the mind, like steel striking flint, to strike out truth by collision, we can see why Emerson might have borrowed the opening sentence of *Nature* from the sentences opening a chapter on Emerson's own—but here unmentionable—precursor. In a *perspectival* collision with Emerson's own project, Hazlitt begins his essay by lamenting the intimidating burden of a monumental past.

> The present is an age of talkers, and not of doers; and the reason is, that the world is growing old. We are so far advanced in Arts and Sciences, that we live in retrospect, and doat on past achievements. The accumulation of knowledge has been so great, that we are lost in wonder at the height it has reached, instead of attempting to climb or add to it. . . . What is the use of doing anything, unless we could do better than all those who have gone before us? What hope is there of this? We are like those who have been to see some noble monument of art, who are content to admire without thinking of rivalling it.[10]

After complaining that "our age is retrospective," Emerson adds: "It builds the sepulchres of the fathers." This second sentence echoes the second of the texts referred to, this one deriving from native ground. In referring to "the sepulchres of the fathers," Emerson is remembering not only Luke 11:47 but also the words of that great son of Massachusetts, Daniel Webster (a titan not yet disfigured, in Emerson's eyes, by his support of the Fugitive Slave Law as part of the 1850 Compromise). Once again echoing in order to alter perspective, Emerson recasts Webster's 1825 speech on the occasion of the laying of the cornerstone of the Bunker Hill Monument, an address Emerson listed in his 1826 journal (*JMN* 3:38). Webster addressed his audience as a "race of children" who, "standing among the sepulchres of the fathers" and filled by the "pious feeling of dependence and gratitude" inspired by "this column, rising towards heaven among the pointed spires of so many temples dedicated to God," must feel themselves looked down upon by the watchful eyes of their dead forebears.

But just as he had reversed Hazlitt's originality-stifling reverence of some past "noble monument of art," so Emerson subverts Webster's emphasis on the weight of the past and the originating power of the ancestral dead. He celebrates instead "the living generation": Webster's "children" who, by their active reception of the example of the Founding Fathers, are vitally renewed, *em*powered, and liberated. Emerson's disciple Nietzsche makes precisely this point in his essay on the life-enhancing use of history,

10. Hazlitt, *Complete Works,* 11:28–29.

an essay influenced by Emerson's "American Scholar." After celebrating the "strong artistic spirits" who "transform" their heritage, Nietzsche adds, "Their path will be barred, their air darkened, if a half-understood monument to some great era of the past is erected as an idol and zealously danced around, as though to say: 'Behold, this is true art: pay no heed to those who are evolving and want something new!' " It is precisely to that something new that Emerson pays heed in liberating "the living generation" from idolatry of the mighty dead. As Harold Bloom notes, agreeing with D. H. Lawrence, "America had started European and venerable, and then grew back to become new and youthful."[11] In Nietzsche's uncanny insight, noted earlier, Emerson "simply does not know how old he is already and how young he is still going to be." But Nietzsche, like Lawrence and Bloom, was following Emerson (who in turn was following Wordsworth and Coleridge) in emphasizing the retention of "the spirit of infancy" into the era of manhood in the second chapter of *Nature,* and in his later rhetorical question: "Whence then this worship of the past?" since the parent has "cast his ripened being" into "the child" (*E&L* 270).

Yet the child remains aware of its parent; the renewer always knows that there is an *it* to be made new. Emerson may scorn to be a "secondary man," yet he can erase the past only subjectively. By definition, no "second Adam," no "second Temple," can, despite defiant claims of originality, really be the first. Writing in 1835 to Henry Hedge, Emerson referred to recent work, "chiefly upon Natural Ethics," that was the seedbed of the essays that—following his working-through of the trauma he experienced in the aftermath of the death of his brother Charles—would be published the following year as *Nature.* Emerson described his efforts as his attempt to bring "a pebble or two to the edification of the new temple whilst so many wise hands are demolishing the old" (*L* 1:447). But his very language, echoing less the Solomonic temple of Hebrew Scripture than the "new temple" of one of his (and Coleridge's) favorite English writers, Francis Bacon, reveals his awareness that he was hardly the first to announce a "new philosophy" based on the relation between man and nature. Indeed, Emerson's ultimate relation, "the kingdom of man over nature" (*E&L* 49), echoes Bacon's "the empire of man over things." At the same time, the fact that he was writing to the author of a crucial Transcendentalist document, Hedge's seminal 1833 essay on Coleridge, the aging genius

11. Bloom, *The American Religion: The Emergence of the Post-Christian Nation,* 41. For the earlier references in this paragraph, see Nietzsche, "On the Uses and Disadvantages of History for Life," in *Untimely Meditations,* 71. Webster is quoted in *The Works of Daniel Webster,* 1:59–60, 72–73. The allusion is also noted in Donald E. Pease, *Visionary Compacts: American Renaissance Writings in Cultural Context,* 214.

Emerson had himself visited that very year, also suggests that, just as he was echoing Bacon in order to supersede him, he wanted to incorporate and supersede his Romantic precursors, Coleridge and Wordsworth.[12]

Coleridge is at the heart of this seemingly paradoxical but actually inextricable relationship between tradition and innovation, what Emerson, the high priest of self-reliance and unmediated vision, recognized as the necessary connection between what he called benefaction and reception, or originality and quotation. Anticipating the Adamic opening of *Nature,* as well as the fierce independence of "Self-Reliance" and "The American Scholar," a young and prescient Emerson (only twenty-seven at the time) wrote in his journal: "Every man has his own voice, manner, eloquence. Let him scorn to imitate any being, let him scorn to be a secondary man" (*JMN* 3:199). Shortly thereafter (April 1831), he inscribed in the same journal a ringing endorsement of what he would later call self-trust and self-reliance, a conviction that

> In your own bosom are your destiny's Stars[.]
> Confidence in yourself, prompt resolution[,]
> This is your Venus! & the sole malignant[,]
> The only one that harmeth you[,] is *Doubt*!
> (*JMN* 3:251)

But the words are not Emerson's; they are, at one remove, Schiller's, placed inappropriately in a foolish man's mouth but part of a speech containing—as the translator said—"profound moral insight." And the translator and transmitter was, again, Coleridge.[13]

12. Part of Bacon's projected "Great Instauration," the fragmentary utopian fantasy known as *The New Atlantis* (ca. 1617), is best known for its description of a repository of natural science he called "Solomon's House," a formative idea that found a local habitation and a name when the Royal Society was established some forty years later. "Quotation confesses inferiority," Emerson tells us in "Quotation and Originality." ". . . If Lord Bacon appears already in the preface, I go and read the 'Instauration' instead of the new book" (*EPP* 324). Emerson's visit to the Jardin des Plantes in Paris in this same year, 1833, a momentous experience that made him decide to become a "naturalist," in part confirmed Bacon, who was also, of course, steeped in Plato. But the mechanics and mathematics, the inductive and scientific method, that constituted the "riches" of "Solomon's House" in *The New Atlantis* had also yielded, in Emerson's case, to the "intuitive" Reason Coleridge had quarried out of his distinctive blend of Plotinus, Milton, Kant, and his own Romanticism.

13. The words are spoken by Illo, Wallenstein's brutal and less than brilliant Field Marshall. Revealingly, Emerson referred to Schiller's text as "Coleridge's Wallenstein" (*JMN* 2:251). See Coleridge's translation of *The Piccolomini; or, The First Part of Wallenstein,* 1:11.82–85 (*CPW* 2:628). For Emerson's association of lines from the second part of this translation with the death of his brother Edward, see *JMN* 4:325.

In a similarly distanced affirmation of self-reliance, in "The Transcendentalist," Emerson again cites a German "source." Though this time he reveals (in a virtually unprecedented footnote) that he is using "Coleridge's Translation," Emerson does not reveal his double deviation from Coleridge: an assertion of self-reliance that takes the form of silent alteration of both the original text, by F. H. Jacobi, and the translation, not to mention creating the false impression that he is simply following Jacobi and Coleridge. The Transcendentalist, Emerson tells us, "resists all attempts to palm other rules . . . on the spirit than its own" on the ground—and again we have the Emersonian conviction that thought is not a private possession—that "the spiritual measure of inspiration is the depth of the thought, and never, who said it." Having, under Kantian and post-Kantian auspices, transferred "the world into the consciousness," internalized the spiritual or unwritten law within his own shaping mind, such an idealist "easily incurs the charge of antinomianism by his avowal that he, who has [within him] the Lawgiver, may with safety not only neglect, but even contravene every written commandment." Emerson then cites, as Jacobi had, the scene in *Othello* in which "the expiring Desdemona absolves her husband of the murder, to her attendant Emilia. Afterwards, when Emilia charges him with the crime, Othello exclaims, 'You heard her say herself it was not I.' Emilia replies, 'The more angel she, and thou the blacker devil' " (*Othello* 5:2, 128, 130–31). Emerson continues, quoting, at least at first, from Coleridge's translation of Jacobi's 1799 "Open Letter to Fichte":[14]

> Of this fine incident, Jacobi, the Transcendentalist moralist, makes use, with other parallel instances, in his reply to Fichte. Jacobi, refusing all measure of right and wrong except the determinations of the private spirit, remarks that there is no crime but has sometimes been a virtue. "I," he says, "am that atheist, that godless person who . . . would lie as the dying Desdemona lied [and as others have in obeying the spirit of a higher law] . . . [f]or, I have assurance in myself, that, in pardoning these faults according to the letter, man exerts the sovereign right which the majesty of his being confers on him; he sets the seal of his divine nature to the grace he accords." (*E&L* 196–97)

In that final sentence, Emerson has embellished Jacobi's "das Gesetz um des menschen willen gemacht ist, nicht der Mensch um des Gesetzes

14. This was the most personally wounding of the tracts written against Fichte during the controversy of 1799 in which he was accused of atheism—having identified God with the moral world order, an order in turn grounded in the *Ich,* "posited" as the source of all cognition and thus "the only absolutely valid objective reality." It began as a long private letter accusing Fichte of "nihilism," though Jacobi published it in expanded form several months later (September 1799). Between these dates, Fichte fled from the university at Jena to Berlin, where he stayed for most of the rest of his life. A translation of the public letter (by Diana I. Behler) may be found in Ernst Behler, ed., *Philosophy of German Idealism,* 119–41.

willen," literally translated by Coleridge as "the Law was made for Man and not Man for the Law" (*F* 1:313, epigraph to essay 15 in vol. 2). More interestingly, having gone beyond both Jacobi and Coleridge (though not beyond Fichte, with his Divine *Ich*) in asserting man's sovereign right, even a divinity within, Emerson, on this occasion, implies that there is complete accord among the original, the translator, and himself. But Coleridge's essay-opening sentence, responding directly to Jacobi's point in the epigraph, asserts an emphatic caveat: "If there be no better doctrine, I would add!" That "better doctrine" is disclosed at the end of the essay: it is, unsurprisingly, "to be found unalloyed and entire in the Christian system, and is there called FAITH" (*F* 1:313, 325). Whatever he thought of this final paragraph (Coleridge himself had misgivings),[15] Emerson was clearly determined—altering Jacobi, Coleridge, and "the Christian system" itself—to set the seal of *his own* divine nature on man's exertion of "the sovereign right which the majesty of his being confers upon him."

Though occasionally, as here, Emerson trumps his sources, he usually adheres to them, even as he asserts his independence. The paradox of self-reliant individuality relying on quotation is, as Stanley Cavell has said, "a gag that especially appeals to contemporary sensibilities," and that gag is never more overt than in the famous essay itself. "Self-Reliance" is prefaced by a Latin epigraph, from Persius, "Ne[c] te quaesiveris extra" (*Satires* 1:7, elsewhere translated by Emerson as "Thou art sufficient unto thyself" [*JMN* 4:318])—followed by a passage from Beaumont and Fletcher, beginning "Man is his own star . . ." (from the epilogue to *Honest Man's Fortune*). The essay itself opens on a derivative rather than self-reliant note: "I *read* the other day some verses . . . which were original" (*E&L* 259). One of its most nonchalantly daring passages begins, "I shun father and mother and wife and brother, when my genius calls me. I would write on the lintels of the door-post, *Whim*" (*E&L* 262). Here, in the very act of audaciously asserting his independence and "genius," Emerson is fusing words of Jesus with passages in both Exodus (12:23) and Deuteronomy (6:9). And if he is, in a sense, troping God, he does so under the auspices of that higher term—"Genius" as opposed to mere "Talent"—in the "grand . . . distinction" he had set himself to "quickly learn" from Coleridge (*JMN* 3:211).

Given the need to quote in the very act of asserting one's autonomy, it seems fitting that Emerson's most enthusiastic and exciting disciple, Nietzsche, should replace his original epigraph to *The Gay Science* (an important

15. Those misgivings were rhetorical, not cognitive or theological. Annotating his son's copy, he noted that the paragraph "*falls off* from all the preceding," just, but "*dimly* stated; not *brought out,* nor urged to the point" (*F* 325n2).

passage from Emerson's essay "History") with four lines of his own doggerel asserting total independence and directing laughter "at any master who lacks / The grace to laugh at himself." But the very title of the quatrain ("Ueber meiner Häusthur" [Over my house-door]) echoes Emerson's writing on "the lintels of the door-post" and the opening lines themselves, with their jaunty, deliberately ungrammatical double negative—

Ich wohne in meinem eignen Häus,
Hab Niemandem nie nichts nachgemacht

(I live in my own house,
Ain't never imitated nothing or nobody)—

are, if anything, even more Emersonian than the original epigraph. Of his copy of Emerson's *Essays* (in German, including both the first and second series), Nietzsche said, in 1881–1882, when he was working on *The Gay Science,* "Never have I felt so much at home in a book, and in *my* home." His declaration of independence in the revised motto to *The Gay Science,* his living "in my own house," simultaneously and paradoxically affirms that he really *did* feel "at home" in a "house" of self-reliance at once Emersonian *and* Nietzschean.[16] He may have thought that "we have lost a philosopher" in Emerson, "the author who has been richest in ideas in this century so far" but who, lacking strict discipline and a scientific education, was "unfortunately made obscure by German philosophy—frosted glass." But Nietzsche could still see the essential Emerson, that "glorious, great nature, rich in soul and spirit," through the obscuring *Milchglas* (milky, frosted, clouded glass). "Other men are lenses through which we read our own minds," said Emerson in "Uses of Great Men" (*E&L* 616). A German critic, taking this sentence as motto, points out, "Nietzsche, from the very beginning of his philosophic career in 1862 through 1888, the end of his rationally conscious life, used Emerson's writing as a lens . . . to read the possibilities of his own philosophic future."[17]

16. The 1882 and 1887 title pages of *The Gay Science* are reproduced, both in Kaufmann's edition (27–29) and in Michael Lopez, ed., *Emerson/Nietzsche,* 58, 60. The remark about feeling "at home" in Emerson's *Essays* is in the complete German Musarion edition of Nietzsche: "*Emerson*—Never have I felt so much at home in a book, and in *my* home, as—I may not praise it, it is too close to me" (*Gesammelte Werke: Musarionausgabe,* 11:283). This is among the notes (the *Nachlass* of 1881–1882) made by Nietzsche when he was simultaneously rereading Emerson and writing *The Gay Science,* a work influenced and originally prefaced by an epigraph from Emerson, who on several occasions numbered himself among the "professors of the Joyous Science."

17. Herwig Friedl, "Emerson and Nietzsche, 1862–1874." In a letter of 1884 to his friend and fellow Emersonian Franz Overbeck, Nietzsche said, "I do not know how much I would give if only I could bring it about, *ex post facto,* that such a glorious, great nature, rich in soul and spirit, might have gone through some *strict* discipline, a

Philosophy, German and French, figures in another famous paragraph, also from "Self-Reliance," but with reverberations going back to a crucial distinction in *Nature.* The paragraph begins, "Man is timid and apologetic; he is no longer upright; he dares not say 'I think,' 'I am' but quotes some saint or sage" (*E&L* 270). But of course Emerson is at that very moment, as Cavell points out, not only *saying* his "I," but *quoting,* and agreeing with, the Cartesian *cogito* (I think, therefore I am), especially as expressed by Descartes in the *Second Meditation:* "I am, I exist, is necessarily true every time that I pronounce it or conceive it in my mind." Similarly, in *Nature,* distinguishing between the Soul and Nature, Man Thinking and the external world, between the famous Me and "the NOT ME, that is, both nature and art, all other men and my own body" (*E&L* 8), Emerson seems to be echoing the Cartesian distinction between *res cogitans* and *res extensa,* and, more important, the *Ich* and *Nicht-Ich* of Fichte, Schelling, and Novalis. More immediate sources include the German subject-object distinction as parodied by Coleridge (*BL* 1:159–60) in his satiric poem on "the Fichtean Egoismus" in *Biographia Literaria* ("I, I, I! I itself I!") as well as the Fichtean polarity as reformulated by the Diogenes Teufelsdröckh of Emerson's friend Carlyle: "our ME *[Ich],* the only reality: and Nature, with its thousandfold production and destruction, but the reflex of our own inward Force." Referring in retrospect to his resurrection from "The Everlasting No," Carlyle says, "Then was it that my whole ME stood up, in native God-given majesty."[18] Like Emerson in "Self-Reliance," Carlyle echoes Milton's description of unfallen Adam and Eve, "erect and tall, / Godlike erect," with "native honor clad / In naked majesty. . . lords of all" (*PL* 4:288–90).

By reading and quoting, as well as saying the self, by mixing book knowledge, or "tuition," with the "primary wisdom" he followed Plotinus, Milton, Fichte, Schelling, Coleridge, and Wordsworth (but *not* Kant) in calling "intuition," Emerson is not simplistically contradicting or dismantling the whole "upright" and individualistic thesis of "Self-Reliance," a text that is nothing if not a rejection of suppliant dependence and an expression of what he repeatedly calls the "sovereignty" or "majesty" of "the erect position"—though even here, as just noted, Emerson's language echoes, and

---

really scientific education. As it is, in Emerson we have *lost a philosopher*" (*The Portable Nietzsche,* 441). For Nietzsche, the strict discipline was clearly *not* German metaphysics, which, whatever its undoubted benefits, was capable of clouding the glass of Coleridge, Carlyle, and Emerson. A variant of the obscuring effect of *Milchglas* occurs in Emerson's remark on Carlyle: the merit of glass is not to be seen, but to be seen through, "but every crystal & lamina of the Carlyle glass shows" (*TN* 2:169).

18. Cavell, "Being Odd, Getting Even," in his *In Quest of the Ordinary,* 106–7, 113–15; Carlyle, *Sartor Resartus,* 126.

more emphatically than Carlyle's, Milton's description of prelapsarian Adam and Eve. Emerson's observation, in "Self-Reliance," that "the virtue in most request is conformity. Self-reliance is its aversion" (*E&L* 261), is the text behind Cavell's advocacy of what he has called "aversive thinking." Yet, as the examples just given confirm, Cavell is also right to simultaneously insist that Emersonian self-reliant intuition does not eradicate connections with tradition, books, tuition. In fact, the familiar representation of Emerson as the simple apostle of intuition is itself an instance of conformity, an understandable depiction but finally as reductive as the related caricature of the smiling optimist oblivious, or indifferent, to evil and suffering. Instead of contradicting himself in buttressing intuition with tuition, Emerson is instead unapologetically acknowledging the linguistic and intellectual heritage to which we are all necessarily indebted, and demonstrating Blake's axiom that the thankful receiver bears a plentiful harvest—to which Emerson would add, as in fact he *did* add in the final paragraph of "Quotation and Originality," that the harvest itself becomes *materia poetica* for the next generation of creators:

> We cannot overstate our debt to the Past, but the moment has the supreme claim. The Past is for us; but the sole terms on which it can become ours are its subordination to the Present. Only an inventor knows how to borrow, and every man is or should be an inventor. We must not tamper with the organic motions of the soul. 'Tis certain that thought has its own proper motion, and the hints which flash from it, the words overheard at unawares by the free mind, are trustworthy and fertile when obeyed and not perverted to low and selfish account. This vast memory is only raw material. The divine gift is ever the instant life, which receives and uses and creates, and can well bury the old in the omnipotency with which Nature decomposes all her harvest for recomposition. (*EPP* 330)

Here Emerson anticipates Nietzsche on the three metamorphoses of the spirit and on the creative "use" of history (discussed later). He also reaffirms, echoing Wordsworth's Intimations Ode, the intuitional "hints that flash" from the soul or mind as a divinity within and—recalling, I suspect, the Child of stanza 7 of the ode, who merely mimics, "as if his whole vocation / Were endless imitation"—endorses Wordsworth's warning about the dangers of borrowing at the expense of invention, a perversion of the vital, "divine gift" that "receives and uses and *creates*." Yet, as he says in "Quotation and Originality," the debt to the past is immense. "None escapes it. The originals are not original. There is imitation, model and suggestion, to the very archangels, if we knew their history." Thus, we are in danger of being reduced to literary "eavesdropping, . . . our life a custom, and our body borrowed, like a beggar's dinner, from a hundred charities" (*EPP* 320, 324).

We might, for the moment, end this dizzying but perfectly understandable dualism regarding books and reading, and therefore intellectual and imaginative indebtedness, with the sort of comment (again, from "Quotation and Originality") to be found throughout Emerson's work—no less frequently than the arch dismissal of books we encounter in passages such as those cited by Laura Furman and Elinore Standard in their 1997 compendium, *Bookworms: Great Writers and Readers Celebrate Reading,* about which more in a moment. "We prize books, and they prize them most who are themselves wise. . . . Our debt to the past, through reading and conversation, is so massive, our protest or private addition so rare and insignificant,—and this is commonly on the ground of other reading and hearing,—that, in a large sense, one would say that there is no pure originality. All minds quote" (*EPP* 320).

It is no wonder that, when on other occasions he insists on originality and denounces "books," vamping Emerson "doth protest too much." As he here acknowledges, "our private addition" to the massive inheritance we gain is "so rare and insignificant" that we cannot help but be anxious about the debt we incur. We are in danger of becoming parasitic, the dwarfs of ourselves, a fate Emerson resolutely refuses even as he acknowledges the giants of the all too immediate past. In "Uses of Great Men," while he echoes "The American Scholar" and "Self-Reliance" in pointing out the "danger" of excessive influence (the "attractions" of a "great man" can "warp us from our place," making us "underlings and intellectual suicides"), he had just praised the great man, one of whom is an "indemnification . . . for populations of pigmies," and praised especially the great man who "can abolish himself, and all heroes, by letting in this element of reason, irrespective of persons," an "upward force" and "power so great" that it destroys "individualism" (*E&L* 627, 625). That is because, finally, "society is a Pestalozzian school: all are teachers and pupils in turn. We are equally served by receiving and by imparting," and "great men exist that there may be greater men" (*E&L* 629, 632). That no sayer, no writer, can be utterly "original" is a truth that embraces the three English poets most frequently praised by Emerson: Shakespeare, Milton, and Wordsworth. Necessarily, it applies as well to Emerson.

❧ Then there is the more familiar advocate of unmediated experience, originality, and self-reliant individualism. "What are books?" Emerson asked in 1839. A year earlier, in the Divinity School Address, he had shocked the stern old war gods of Unitarianism; now, perhaps even more dramatically than in his 1837 lecture "The American Scholar," he was about to shock those who worshiped that other external god, the book. The occasion was the second of two lectures on literature delivered at the Masonic Temple in Boston on December 18, 1839, a talk unpublished until a century and a third later. "What are books? They can have no permanent value."

> When we are aroused to a life in ourselves, these traditional splendors of letters grow very pale and cold. Literature is made up of a heap of nouns and verbs enclosing an *intuition* or two. . . . Why should I quit the task . . . assigned to me by the Soul of Nature, to go gazing after the tasks of others or listening to the rumor of their performance? There is other peeping beside setting the eye to chinks and keyholes [as in] this everlasting reading . . . of what *others* have done. . . . Let us think more nobly. Let us, if we must have great actions, make *our own* so. . . . Let us do *our own* duties. Why need I go gadding into the scenes and philosophy of Greek or Italian history, before *I have built my own house* and *justified myself to my own benefactors*? (*EL* 3:230–31; italics added)

His thoughts here, even that memorable "peeping," were anticipated in the January 1820 entry with which the seventeen-year-old Emerson inaugurated what would become a lifelong series of journals. The "Common Place book" he was starting would "contain a record of new thoughts (when they occur)" and serve as a "receptacle of all the old ideas that partial but peculiar peeping at antiquity can furnish or furbish" (*JMN* 1:3–4; *EPP* 484). The language of the 1839 literature lecture also echoes, along with the Divinity School Address and "The American Scholar," the introduction and conclusion of *Nature.* In reprinting the passage quoted above as the primary Emersonian contribution to their compendium, Laura Furman and Elinore Standard accurately register a major aspect of Emerson, an aspect that, of course, undermines their titular emphasis on those who "celebrate" reading. As they note in their introduction, themselves echoing the opening paragraph of *Nature,* "Bookworms sometimes regret that they do not live in what Ralph Waldo Emerson called an 'original relation' to the world." Thus, it is "no wonder" that Emerson, "who valued direct experience, should have protested the intermediary nature of reading," or that, in "defending the reader against the book," he should have "expressed an extreme, and modern, view" of the reader's relation to what he or she reads.

Overlooking the reference to his "own benefactors" in the very passage they cite, they see Emerson—with considerable, yet only partial, accuracy—as foreshadowing our modern (variously appropriative, psychoanalytical, receptive, affective, subjective, even self-absorbed) theories of reading and creative misreading. What Emerson "meant," they tell us, and it was a belief "repeated... with variations throughout his life," is that "we each bring to our reading the images, sensations, emotions, and experiences that constitute us as individuals; we populate the world of the book with our unique selves." (As Stendhal liked to remind his audience, "A novel is like a bow, and the violin that produces the sounds is the reader's soul.") An omnivorous reader with a gift for finding what tallied with his own needs and skipping what did not, Emerson thought of himself as belonging to the rich and enriching fourth of "Coleridge's four classes of Readers. 1. The Hour glass sort, all in & all out; 2. The Sponge sort, giving it all out a little dirtier than it took it in; 3. of the Jelly bag, keeping nothing but the refuse; 4. of the Golconda, sieves picking up the diamonds only" (*JMN* 4:360).[19] Of course, those diamonds were often his own rejected thoughts coming back to him with a certain alienated majesty. As he asked, again rhetorically, this time at the beginning of a journal entry (also quoted in *Bookworms*), "What can we see, read, acquire, but ourselves? Take the book, my friend, and read your eyes out; you will never find there what I find.... To introduce a man to a good book is like introducing him to fine company. It is nothing if he is nothing."[20]

This affective or reader-centered theory of reading was passed down, as from one liberated liberator to another, from Emerson to Nietzsche, and, I suspect, from Nietzsche to *his* disciple, W. B. Yeats. Because portions of the present book trace a lineage from Coleridge and Wordsworth to Emerson, and from Emerson to Nietzsche and so on to Yeats, who read *all* of these precursors, I will pause to make a few connections regarding the point at issue before returning to the specific case of Emerson.

"There is then creative reading as well as creative writing" (*E&L* 59). This, along with much else in "The American Scholar," Emerson's declaration of literary independence, is taken up by Harold Bloom, who repeatedly apotheosizes the "strong reader," especially when that reader is also a poet. "Really strong poets can read only themselves," Bloom has often told us. "For them to be judicious is to be weak." In "Why I Write Such Good Books," that good European *and* good Emersonian, Nietzsche, claimed, "Ultimately, nobody can get more out of things, including books, than he already knows" from personal experience; of course, he added (amused, but with a trace of that tone of—only partially—inconsistent

19. Suggesting an evolution from the semblances of understanding to the Ideal reality apprehended by the intuitive Reason, the entry is headed "House of Seem and house of Be."

20. Furman and Standard, *Bookworms*, xxiii, 85–86. This passage was later incorporated, with revisions, in "Spiritual Laws" (*E&L* 314).

exasperation evident in all such creative readers, including Derrida) that anyone who claimed to understand *his* work "had made up something out of me after his own image." Here as in so many other ways, Nietzsche proved prophetic. The "Nietzsche" many sophisticated postmodernists know is largely the construct of Martin Heidegger, based not on what Nietzsche himself chose to publish, nor even on the *Nachlass* on which Heidegger almost exclusively relies, but, finally, on Heidegger's own "interpretation," an interpretation at once insightful, influential, and often profoundly arbitrary. The reductio ad absurdum comes from Michel Foucault, who can claim both to understand Nietzsche's thought and to honor it by knowingly distorting it: "The only valid tribute to thought such as Nietzsche's is precisely to use it, to deform it, to make it groan and protest. And if commentators then say that I am being faithful or unfaithful to Nietzsche, that is of absolutely no interest." Of course, it *is* of "interest" to those who, while aware of the creative element in reading, remain disturbed by tortured readings handed down as legitimate interpretations of Nietzsche's texts—texts that must have *some* determinate meaning even for Foucault, who can speak of willfully "deforming" them.[21]

In his 1930 diary, W. B. Yeats declared, "We do not seek truth in argument or in books, but clarification of what we already believe." As if to prove both Yeats's and Nietzsche's point, though I suspect not to validate either Heidegger's brilliant but often distorted "interpretation" or Foucault's deliberate deformations, Erich Heller, discussing Yeats's annotations on Nietzsche, claims that many of Yeats's glosses "ride rough-shod over Nietzsche's meanings." It is "certainly not the mind of the *poet* but rather the mind of the thinker that tends to vanish as soon as Yeats becomes entangled, in the margin, with Nietzsche's ideas." It is hard to resist the considerable truth, and the light charm, of Heller's image for creative misprision: "He who has bees in his bonnet reads not so much for the love of what he reads as for the honey to be made from it; and not since Blake has there been, in the history of great English poetry, a bonnet like Yeats's, buzzing with so many agile bees."[22]

Still, it is important to register a caveat. In annotating Nietzsche, Yeats

21. See Nietzsche, "Why I Write Such Good Books," in *Ecce Homo,* 1; Heidegger, *Nietzsche;* and Foucault, "Nietzsche, Genealogy, History," in *Power/Knowledge: Selected Interviews and Other Writings, 1972–1977,* 53–54.

22. Heller's remarks first appeared in a 1968 *Encounter* article, later reprinted in the expanded edition of his *Disinherited Mind: Essays in Modern German Literature and Thought,* 329–47. For Yeats's remark about reading for clarification of what we already believe, see *Explorations,* 310. At the time Yeats was reading Swift and may be recalling his observation in *Thoughts on Various Subjects* (1711): "'That was excellently observed,' say I when I read a passage in another where his opinion agrees with mine. When we differ, then I pronounce him to be mistaken."

was certainly seeking clarification of what he already believed *and* confecting the "honey" of poetic generation. But closer study of those annotations reveals a genuine engagement with Nietzsche's ideas. This mixture of insight and creative appropriation is typical of Yeats's response to the work—the ideas, the form, the individual tone—of those who mattered to him most, from Plato and Plotinus, through Swift and Burke, Blake and Shelley, to Pater and Nietzsche. "Yeats's encounters, when his imagination meets the words or work, consciousness or presence," of his significant others, lie, as Douglas Archibald has said, "at the heart of his poetry." And at the heart of that heart, I would add, is the linking of Blake with Nietzsche, who, said Yeats, "completes Blake and has the same roots." Such Yeatsian interactions and encounters sometimes take the form of what Bloom has called *clinamen* or *tessera:* the creative swerving from, or "completion" of, a precursor. More simply—on most occasions, and like most artists—Yeats varies, alters, modifies, bends the inherited materials to his own aesthetic purposes. But despite his reputation as an autodidact as idiosyncratic as he was brilliant, Yeats tends to know what he is doing. That is to say, his creative appropriations are often less a matter of hubristic dominance, narcissistic self-reading, or exploitative irresponsibility than an example of Coleridge's opulent "Golconda" class of reader, illustrating Blake's axiom that "the thankful receiver bears a plentiful harvest."[23]

The same is true of Emerson. Because, as he says in "Experience," nature and books alike "belong to the eyes that see them," we may stipulate to his figure of speech that introducing a reader to a good book is like introducing someone to "fine company. It is nothing if he is nothing." But if that reader *is* something, then what he reads *does* constitute "fine company"—in the case of Emerson, an individualist who yet had "the shades of all the good and great for company" (*E&L* 71), a visionary company of "benefactors." That was the word, an Emersonian favorite, with which, nonchalantly and even inconsistently, he ended his overt dismissal of "books" in the passage quoted at the outset of this section.

Emerson's term may derive from a coalescence of the two "benefactors" he actually singled out as his own contemporary examples. As a close reader of Coleridge's periodical *The Friend,* Emerson may well be remembering Wordsworth's reference (in his essay "Upon Epitaphs," which first appeared in the February 1810 issue; *F* 2:336–46) to the "mighty

23. Archibald, *Yeats,* xii. See also Keane, *Yeats's Interactions with Tradition,* xiii–xvii, 151–55, 166–73. Yeats claims that "Nietzsche completes Blake and has the same roots" in a 1903 letter (*Letters of Yeats,* 379). For Bloom, see the related studies of the mid-1970s, especially *Anxiety of Influence, A Map of Misreading,* and *Poetry and Repression.* Blake's axiom, my motto for much of this book, occurs in the "Proverbs of Hell" section of *The Marriage of Heaven and Hell,* pl. 9 (*Poetry and Prose of Blake,* 36).

benefactors of mankind" who stand in no need of "biographic sketches" to ensure a posterity "already done by their Works, in the memories of men." Among the gifts of such English benefactors most worthy of our gratitude is their "utterance of some elementary principle most essential to the constitution of true virtue," or "an *intuition,* communicated in adequate words, of the sublimity of intellectual power." Bringing together the two mightiest of his own benefactors, a coupling he clinches by quotation, Wordsworth illustrates the only appropriate "tribute" to such mighty benefactors, the "only offering that upon such an altar would not be unworthy," by citing as the conclusion of his essay lines 1–8 and 15–16 of Milton's first published poem, the "Epitaph upon Shakespeare," which first appeared in the *Second Folio* (1632) of Shakespeare's plays. That "Dear Son of Memory," Shakespeare ("my Shakspeare," as Milton tenderly addresses him in the opening line), needs no "weak witness" of an elaborate pyramid to ensepulchre him since (in what are, unfortunately, the least vigorous lines in the poem), "Thou in our wonder and astonishment / Hast built thyself a livelong monument" (*F* 2:346).

Derived from Wordsworth or not, Emersonian "benefactors" are those who, having been thankful if perhaps covert receivers, become themselves generous givers. This emphasis on giving is crucial; again and again Emerson asks, how does a writer *give,* how does he or she *add*? On the basis of this criterion of benefaction and magnanimity, he repeatedly celebrates Plato, Chaucer, Montaigne, Francis Bacon, Shakespeare, Swedenborg, and Goethe. But among contemporaries he chose—in 1850, the year of Wordsworth's death—just two: "Wordsworth almost alone in his times belongs to the giving, adding class, and Coleridge has also been a benefactor" (*JMN* 11:273). Margaret Fuller, the most brilliant conversationalist in the Transcendentalist circle, was not only a pioneer feminist but also a pioneer in venerating Coleridge as a benefactor. Within months of the publication of Marsh's edition of Coleridge's *Aids to Reflection,* she records in her journal "a conviction that the benefits conferred by him on this and future ages are as yet incalculable," adding, with the consciousness of being part of an elite chosen to penetrate sublime mysteries: "To the unprepared he is nothing, to the prepared, everything"—precisely the point Coleridge had made about Wordsworth's Intimations Ode, apprehensible, he thought, only by a select group of readers (*BL* 2:147).[24]

When he has "built my own house," says Emerson, he will have "justified myself to my own benefactors" (*EL* 3:231). But literary "monuments" can also be impediments, "mighty benefactors" formidable rivals who

24. Fuller is quoted by Miller in the preface to his excerpts from Marsh's "Preliminary Essay," in *The Transcendentalists: An Anthology,* 35.

threaten to reduce even their most original heirs to imitation and quotation. That Emerson's is an original voice seems beyond dispute, but paradox and anxiety remain implicit in the tense but fruitful relationship with his immediate Romantic predecessors, a relationship marked by genuine gratitude but leavened by concern at the prospect of belatedness. The same uneasiness characterizes Wordsworth's stance toward Milton, an idol whom he venerated as man and poet but with whom, as he and so many of his contemporaries realized, he was engaged in a lifelong competition. "Milton is his great idol," said Hazlitt of Wordsworth in 1808, "and he sometimes dares to compare himself with him."[25]

But it was more than "sometimes." In this competition, an agon he both welcomed and dreaded, Wordsworth was *always* conscious of Milton as the formidable angel with whom he had to wrestle. Of the following three anecdotes, all illustrative of Wordsworth's literary possessiveness as a form of the egotistical sublime, the first two specifically relate to his competition with Milton. Having asked a friend in 1825 what he thought was the finest elegiac composition in the language, and receiving the perfunctory response "Lycidas," Wordsworth boldly ventured to enter the lists with one of his own poems—not, as one might expect, the "Lycidas"-haunted Intimations Ode, but the poem Emerson himself ranked second only to the ode. Wordsworth announced: "It may, I think, be affirmed that Milton's 'Lycidas' and my 'Laodamia' are twin Immortals."[26] In *English Traits,* Emerson offers his own homely anecdote, its Harold Pinter–like anticlimax nevertheless making the competitive point: "A gentleman in London showed me a watch that once belonged to Milton, whose initials are engraved on its face. He said, he once showed this to Wordsworth, who took it in one hand, then drew out his own watch, and held it up with the other, before the company, but no one making the expected remark, he put back his own in silence" (*E&L* 928).

The third anecdote, reported to Emerson by Thomas De Quincey, has been mentioned: the fact that "Wordsworth, as soon as he heard a good thing, caught it up, meditated upon it, and very soon reproduced it." When, on at least one occasion, De Quincey said, "That is what I told you," Wordsworth replied, "No, that is mine,—mine, and not yours." "On the whole, we like the valor of it," said Emerson, who was approving *his own* valor as well as Wordsworth's. "As soon as I read a wise sentence anywhere," he once confessed, "I feel at once the desire of appropriation"

25. Hazlitt, *Complete Works,* 11:92. But for Hazlitt, the comparison was also political. Wordsworth was an apostate, lacking Milton's "deep and fixed" principles. Milton would neither "worship the rising sun," that recurrent image for the early promise of the French Revolution, "nor turn his back on a losing and fallen cause" (8:177–78).

26. Alaric Alfred Watts, *Alaric Watts: A Narrative of His Life,* 1:240.

(*JMN* 4:336). As he noted in *Representative Men,* anticipating T. S. Eliot's dictum (in *The Use of Poetry and the Use of Criticism*) that "bad poets imitate, good poets steal": "It has come to be practically a sort of rule in literature, that a man, having once shown himself capable of original writing, is entitled thenceforth to steal from the writings of others at discretion. Thought is the property of him who can adequately entertain it; and of him who can adequately place it. A certain awkwardness marks the use of borrowed thoughts; but as soon as we have learned what to do with them, they become our own" (*E&L* 715).[27]

As for Wordsworth specifically, Emerson had no doubt that he was still the most original poet in English since Milton. As usual, he was in accord with Coleridge, the critic who had first taught him, and the generation before him in England, to properly appreciate the poet who "in imaginative power . . . stands nearest of all modern writers to Shakespeare and Milton; and yet in a kind perfectly unborrowed and his own" (*BL* 2:151). At the conclusion of the June 1809 essay with which he launched *The Friend,* Coleridge records his gratitude to the principal poetic predecessors he shares with Wordsworth, benefactors whose influence has, in his own case, not been "in vain." As usual, however, conscious for almost a decade now of the gradual loss of his own shaping power of imagination, he awards the poetic palm to Wordsworth: "I am content and gratified, that Spenser, Shakespere, Milton, have not been born in vain for me: and I feel it as a Blessing, that even among my Contemporaries I know one at least, who has been deemed worthy of the Gift; who has received the Harp with Reverence, and struck it with the hand of Power" (*F* 2:15).

The harp Emerson received had been struck with power by both Milton *and* Wordsworth, with Coleridge standing by, not only to remind him of his bardic belatedness but also with a set of critical distinctions bearing the prints of any number of accomplished fingers even before Emerson began to play. As an American and a New Englander, Emerson was acutely aware of both his English and his continental heritage. As "The American

27. In the course of this Shakespeare essay, Emerson digresses to discuss Chaucer's influence, one that charms us "with the opulence which feeds so many pensioners." But, Emerson continues, "Chaucer is a huge borrower" as well, drawing on a multitude of "benefactors." Back in an 1835 lecture already referred to, "The Age of Fable," Emerson had said that whereas Shakespeare, Pope, and Dryden "borrow from Chaucer and shine by his borrowed light," Chaucer himself reflects Boccaccio and Colonna, who in turn reflect the "elder Greek and Roman authors, and these in their turn others if only history would enable us to trace them! There never was an original writer. Each is a link in an endless chain" (*EL* 1:284–85). Let Chaucer's "apology," says Emerson in *Representative Men,* be that "what he takes has no worth where he finds it, and the greatest where he leaves it" (*E&L* 114–15). Or, as Emerson's valorous Wordsworth cried out: "Mine,—mine, and not yours."

Scholar" and *Representative Men* demonstrate, he bore the burden of the European past boldly yet with an anxiety of influence all the more significant because it is so often qualified or even repressed, or too defensively protested in an assertion of self-reliance. Emerson feared above all being reduced to the dreaded subservience of "imitation," for him, as he says in "Self-Reliance," a form of "suicide" (*E&L* 259). We saw that tension actually played out in his 1833 pilgrimage to Highgate and Rydal Mount, the visits to Coleridge and Wordsworth modulating from disappointment to a relieved, if rather too much protesting, recovery of autonomous power allegedly undiminished by actually confronting his shaping forces in the flesh. The solution, for Emerson as for every master of creative reception, is to work through the dialectic between tradition and innovation, a pragmatic use of the received past becoming a stimulus to creative power in the present. We must accept, absorb, and then, and only then, transmute. And *even* then, when Emerson has in fact "built my own house," he will, as he rather remarkably concludes the passage with which we began, have "*justified myself to my own benefactors.*"

This is a far cry from the "extreme" modern or postmodern view according to which readers are given carte blanche to use *and* abuse previous writers and their texts—a solipsistic process, indifferent to the past and to the benefactors themselves, that simply finds the self narcissistically mirrored, or "validated," in every defenseless text. Though we hear less these days about "the death of the author," it is still thought by some to be an intolerable infringement of our freedom to concede that those writers and those texts retain, or ought to retain, *their own* inalienable rights—the freedom, for example, not to be violated or trampled over by the newcomer, especially the reader who, failing to go through the reverential stage of submission in which we allow a writer or a text to inhabit us so that we *can* repossess it as our own, has not yet earned the privilege of engaging in selective, let alone distortional, interpretation. But, finally, strong readers *do* earn that right—for Emerson and Nietzsche, it is a "duty"—moving from gratitude for the benefactions of the past to the sine qua non: new creation. As Nietzsche's Zarathustra famously put it, shifting from texts to teachers, "One repays a teacher badly if one remains only a pupil," and Emerson himself took delight in claiming he had no disciples.[28]

There are many illustrations of this dialectical progression of reception, use, and new creation. In "The American Scholar," Emerson refers

28. With these thoughts compare the following: "The true teacher defends his pupils against his own personal influence. He inspires self-trust. He guides their eyes from himself to the spirit that quickens him. He will have no disciple." It might be Nietzsche's Zarathustra or Nietzsche's mentor, Emerson. Actually, it is Emerson's friend Bronson Alcott, holding forth on "The Teacher," in "Orphic Sayings."

to the "strange process"—and for him it is a crucial process associated, as we will see, with his reading of Coleridge and Wordsworth—"by which experience is converted into thought, as a mulberry leaf is converted into satin" (*E&L* 60). Going beyond what he would later note as the imitative danger implicit in a merely parasitic sucking, this transmutation of the roughage of experience into something rich and strange comes close to making the silkworm a feeding-and-secreting metaphor for literary reception and assimilation leading to new creation. In "To William Wordsworth," Coleridge describes the stages of his response to the recitation of the 1805 *Prelude:* It was at first acquiescent, "*driven* as in surges," preceding an activation of "stars *of my own birth,*" constellated foam creatively "*darting off.*" A similar darting off occurs at the end of Keats's pivotal "On Sitting Down to Read *King Lear* Once Again," though Keats emphasizes from the outset his active involvement in the reading process: "once again the fierce dispute / Betwixt damnation and impassioned clay, / Must I burn through." In strapping himself to that wheel of fire, Keats is experientially immersing himself in Lear's pain and participating, knowledgeably, in that agonizing trajectory of learning. Far from freeplaying with the text, he knows in advance that he will be "consumed" by it, but he also anticipates his ultimate emergence, liberated to greater creativity of his own: "But when I am consuméd in the fire / Give me new Phoenix-wings to fly at my desire." That hypermetrical final line, an alexandrine that breaks the previously constraining cage of the sonnet's pentameter, signals this new-born, and *earned,* freedom.[29]

Another memorable dramatization of this three-stage process is to be found in the opening speech of Nietzsche's Zarathustra, "On the Three Metamorphoses of the Spirit," from camel to lion to child. In the first two stages, we move from a "reverent" bearing of the burden of the past ("What is most difficult," asks the camel-like spirit that would freely submit and "bear much, that I may take it upon myself and exult in my strength"), through Leonine defiance of tradition by one who would be "master in his own desert." But for the ultimate task, not only preservation and destruction but the *creation* of values as well, the child and his "sacred 'Yes' is needed." The child "is innocence and forgetting, a new beginning, a self-propelled wheel," the spirit who "conquers his own world." This creative new beginning Nietzsche calls the "innocence of becoming," Blake "infant joy," and Hart Crane, even more beautifully and in a phrase close

29. Keats, *The Poems of John Keats,* 225. Louise Rosenblatt was right, a third of a century ago and well before the advent of "reader-response criticism," to quote Keats's sonnet as illustrative of her "transactional" (a term also used by Emerson) "model of reading" (Coda: A Performing Art" [1966], now included in the most recent edition of *Literature as Exploration,* 263–64, 276–77).

to Coleridge, "an improved infancy."[30] There is a "remedial force of spirit," a new and "innocent" creation that redeems man, who is otherwise a "god in ruins," says Emerson's Orphic Poet. "Infancy is the perpetual Messiah, which comes into the arms of fallen men, and pleads with them to return to paradise" (*E&L* 45–46).

Taking the opposed pairings in toto—on the one hand, imitation, books, quotation, baldpated scholarship, tuition, calculation, what De Quincey calls "the literature of *knowledge,*" the "mere" understanding, tradition, the past; on the other, childlike new creation, self-reliance, originality, instinct, the intuitive Reason, spontaneity, life, De Quincey's "literature of *power,*" innovation, the present oriented toward the future—it is difficult not to juxtapose Emerson with Wordsworth immediately before him and Thoreau immediately after, as well as with another text of Nietzsche. I will return to Wordsworth, but the chapter that follows begins with Emerson and Nietzsche.

30. Blake, final plate of *Visions of the Daughters of Albion* (*Poetry and Prose of Blake,* 50); Crane, "Passage," in *The Complete Poems and Selected Letters and Prose of Hart Crane,* 21.

Chapter 6

Intuition and Tuition

READING NATURE AND THE USE AND ABUSE OF BOOKS

Books are for the scholar's idle hours.

—RALPH WALDO EMERSON, "The American Scholar"

You shall no longer take things at second or third-hand . . .
nor look
through the eyes of the dead . . . nor feed on the spectres in
books.

—WALT WHITMAN, "Song of Myself"

To read a book early in the morning, at daybreak, in the vigor and dawn of one's strength—that I call viciousness.

—FRIEDRICH NIETZSCHE, on bookworms

Will you be a reader, a scholar merely, or a seer?

—HENRY DAVID THOREAU, *Walden*

How we mislead each other, above all,
How books mislead us.

—WILLIAM WORDSWORTH, *The Prelude*

It is appropriate that Harvard University, the nation's premier seat of learning, should have been the setting for Emerson's two most electrifying orations, the speeches in which he rose most dramatically to the challenges presented both by the public occasions and by his own need, often self-suppressed, to speak out boldly and without reservation. If the immediate and local impact of the second speech, the July 1838 address to the Harvard Divinity School, was the most explosive, the reverberations of the first, "The American Scholar" address (August 1837), were the more widespread. The lecture, marked by what Kenneth S. Sacks has aptly described as "passion, intensity, and towering integrity," established Emerson's fame not only in New England but also (thanks to the ringing endorsement of Thomas Carlyle) in England itself. Assaulting intellectual constraint in the United States, especially restrictive educational philosophy and cultural dependence on Europe, Emerson confronted—directly and on the solemn occasion of the annual Phi Beta Kappa Lecture—his own Unitarian-dominated alma mater, an institution he considered pedagogically unimaginative, derivative, conformist, reduced to feeding on what Walt Whitman would call the "spectres in books." Since the whole conception of what it meant to be an "American scholar" had to be changed, where better to start than here? And Emerson certainly succeeded in shaking up the elite academic establishment. "I don't know what the world is coming to, if such a voice as that can be heard in old Harvard," Orestes Brownson wrote him two months after the address. "You bearded the lion in his den."[1]

That bearding took place under Romantic auspices, with Emerson insisting, as Coleridge had, that first truths were to be derived from the mind's observation of, and interaction with, nature: an "intuitive" interchange that, Emerson agreed with Wordsworth, was of proportionately greater value than "tuition," or book learning. Thus, Emerson was in accord with both Wordsworth and his most perceptive critic. Coleridge had praised, as a "characteristic excellence" of his friend's poetry, "a correspondent weight and sanity of the Thought and Sentiments,—won, not from books; but—from the poet's own meditative observation" (*BL* 2: 144–45). In *English Traits,* an echoing Emerson pronounced Wordsworth the "exceptional . . . genius" of his age, one who had "no master but nature

1. Brownson to Emerson, unpublished letter (November 10, 1837), quoted in Sacks, *Understanding Emerson: "The American Scholar" and His Struggle for Self-Reliance,* 19. For the earlier-cited characterization of the address, see p. 4. In this full-scale study, Sacks places the address in a multilayered context: the milieu of both the Transcendentalist rebels and the Unitarian elite, as well as the contemporary state of institutional education, especially at Harvard. In addition, drawing on Emerson's journals, Sacks explores private thoughts that reveal "the hesitation and ultimate courage of an insecure intellectual" trying, simultaneously, to live up to the expectations of his friends and to preserve his own self-reliance (2).

and solitude" and whose voice "is the voice of sanity in a worldly and ambitious age" (*E&L* 906; cf. *JMN* 13:352). Emerson was consciously Wordsworthian in celebrating direct experience, "an original relation to the universe" (*E&L* 7), unmediated by reading. Books had their value, of course, but not when they came between Man Thinking and his response to nature, in the process undermining both self-reliance and originality of thought. For intercourse with nature need not be thoughtless. Coleridge emphasized his friend's powers of "*meditative* observation." In "The American Scholar," an oration alternately titled "Man Thinking," these proportions are maintained: our first teacher is Nature, our second Books, since the "mind of the Past" is there "best inscribed." But books are to be taken up in "the scholar's idle times," when inspiration flags and he is not enjoying the precious hour "when he can read God directly" (*E&L* 57–58).

If the "American Scholar" address looks back to Coleridge's Wordsworth, it also "looks forward" (*E&L* 57), most strikingly, to Nietzsche. The present theme—the tension between intuition and tuition, genius and dependence, originality and imitation, the use and abuse of books—may be illuminated by the juxtaposition of two texts in particular. Here, then, is Emerson, in "The American Scholar," delivered at Harvard in the thirty-seventh year of the nineteenth century, and, precisely thirty-seven years further on in the century, Nietzsche, in the second essay of his *Untimely Meditations,* the one titled "On the Uses and Disadvantages of History for Life." Thoreau I add as a kind of confirming coda.

Emerson greeted his audience, on August 31, at "the re-commencement of our literary year," an anniversary "of hope," though not enough of labor, since we seem "too busy to give to letters" any more than is required to ensure their bare "survival." At least literature *has* survived, "the sign of an indestructible instinct." But perhaps "the time is already come," when "the sluggard intellect of this continent will look from under its iron lids and fill the postponed expectation of the world with something better than the exertions of mechanical skill. Our day of dependence, our long apprenticeship to the learning of other lands, draws to a close. The millions that around us are rushing into life, cannot always be fed on the sere remains of foreign harvests" (*E&L* 53). This opening theme is reverted to in the final paragraph: "We have listened too long to the courtly muses of Europe," as a result of which "the spirit of the American freeman is . . . suspected to be timid, imitative, tame" (*E&L* 70). It was time for that spirit to exert its native genius, to break its bonds. "We will walk on our own feet; we will work with our own hands; we will speak our own minds." The climactic sentence echoes Coleridge's democratic phrases, "each and all," with "every man . . . the Temple of Deity." Emerson announced: "A nation of men will for the first time exist, because *each* believes himself inspired by the Divine Soul which also inspires *all* men" (*E&L* 71; italics added).

We can still appreciate the rapture with which Carlyle read such words: "Out of the West comes a clear utterance, clearly recognizable as a *man's,* and I *have* a kinsman and brother: God be thanked for it! I could have *wept* to read that speech; the clear high melody of it went tingling through my heart . . . My brave Emerson!" Even the retrospective assessments of Emerson's own countrymen capture the drama of the moment. "We were socially and intellectually moored to English thought," said James Russell Lowell in 1871, "till Emerson cut the cable and gave us a chance at the dangers and glories of blue water." That speech, a third of a century earlier, "was an event without parallel in our literary annals." And Emerson's first biographer gave "The American Scholar" the label it has had ever since. "This grand oration," said Oliver Wendell Holmes in 1885, "was our intellectual Declaration of Independence," probably the most inspired and inspiring address "among all the noble utterances of the speaker" and one that "no listener ever forgot." Yet, as Perry Miller has noted in pointing up the familiar paradox: "In this spirit he announced that the day of our dependence on the learning of other lands was drawing to a close—just in the very day that he and his contemporaries were finding a resolution to achieve independence in a voluminous absorption of the new learning of Romantic Europe!"[2]

For all its greatness, "The American Scholar" is both belated and derivative. Not only had Emerson's declaration of independence been anticipated by Cooper and Channing but it also depends, as Richard Gravil notes, "so much" upon "the major figures of English Romanticism" as to amount to a "comprehensive raid on Romantic articulations." Ironically, when Emerson *does* quote an English poet, it is not a Romantic, but Edward Young, cited in support of the dangers of influence, since "illustrious Examples engross, prejudice and intimidate." In remarking the dangers of influence and imitation, Emerson illustrates the usual paradox by *quoting*—from a book titled *Conjectures on Original Composition* (1759), a text that, further compounding the irony, celebrates the polar tension in which originality necessarily participates in the very tradition one is supposedly no

2. Miller, "New England's Transcendentalism" (*EPP* 676). The comments from Carlyle, Lowell, and Holmes are synopsized in Donald McQuade et al., *The Harper Single Volume American Literature,* 526. Margaret Fuller was less hopeful than Emerson in his oration. "Books which imitate or represent the thoughts and life of Europe do not constitute an American literature." For that to exist, "an original idea must animate this nation and fresh currents of life must call into life fresh thoughts along its shores." We can have no expression "till there is something to express" ("American Literature: Its Position in the Present, and Prospects for the Future," in *Margaret Fuller, American Romantic: A Selection from Her Writings and Correspondence,* 323).

longer imitating: "For may not this Paradox pass into a Maxim?" asks Young rhetorically. Namely, "The less we copy the renowned Ancients, we shall resemble them the more."[3]

Unsurprisingly, then, even in declaring independence, this herald of the new is characteristically of two minds about books and tradition. The time *may* have come when Americans will no longer be content with European remnants, yet any vital present and future are rooted in the past, and "the mind of the Past" is "best inscribed" in books. Hence, Emerson concedes, the "theory of books is noble"—at least as once practiced, in some originary past. "The scholar of the first age received into him the world around; brooded thereon; gave it the new arrangement of his own mind, and uttered it again," transforming "dead fact" into "quick thought." Here, drawing on the not quite "sere remains of foreign harvests," Emerson rehearses—in Kantian terms he had found reformulated in Coleridge, in Carlyle, and in Wordsworth's "Prospectus"—mind's interaction with its first "great influence," Nature, whose beauty and laws "correspond" to the beauty and laws of that very mind (*E&L* 56, 54). The second "great influence into the spirit of the scholar is the mind of the Past." But because our renovative purpose is to transform dead fact into quick thought, each age "must write its own books," each "generation" preparing "the next." Thus, "the books of an older generation will not fit this," at least not if they continue to be passively received and fetishized, thwarting the imperative "to yield that peculiar fruit which each man was created to bear" (*E&L* 71).

As an illustration of the saying that "All things have two handles; beware of the wrong one," we are warned that there is a right and wrong way to read. A "grave mischief" arises when the "sacredness which attaches to the act of creation,—the act of thought,—is transferred to the record. The poet chanting, was felt to be a divine man; henceforth the chant is divine also." Thus—and here Emerson follows Young's distinction between the "Man" and the "Composition"—is love of the "hero" corrupted into "worship of the statue"; reverence of "the book," become "noxious" and tyrannical, is institutionalized: "The sluggish and perverted mind of the multitude, slow to open to the incursions of Reason, having once so opened, having once received this book, stands upon it, and makes an outcry, if it is disparaged. Colleges are built on it by thinkers, not by Man

3. Gravil, *Romantic Dialogues,* 59–60; Young, *Conjectures on Original Composition,* 20–21. Though he insists that "*Originals* are the fairest Flowers: *Imitations* are of quicker growth, but fainter bloom," Young realizes that we inevitably mimic our precursors. "Imitate them, by all means; but imitate aright," imitating "not the *Composition,* but the *Man.*" By drinking at the same inspiring spring, "the true *Helicon,*" we imitate not the *Iliad,* but Homer himself (9, 20–21).

Thinking; by men of talent, that is, who start wrong, who set out from accepted dogmas, not from their own sight of principles" (*E&L* 57).

Earlier in the lecture, employing Coleridge's distinction between Reason and mere understanding, Emerson had described "Man Thinking" as the integrated human being who remains open to the influxes of intuitive Reason; in the "degenerate state," he becomes "a mere thinker, or, still worse, the parrot of another man's thinking" (*E&L* 53). As he will say later, in "Uses of Great Men," when we fail to guard against the overinfluence of those who have brought us truths, "our delight in reason degenerates into idolatry of the herald" (*E&L* 623). Conformist, derivative scholars, basing themselves on received dogmas rather than their own principled "sight," their own vision, are, he says in "The American Scholar," but "men of talent." The distinction is, again, that of Coleridge, this time between mere Talent and Genius. As early as 1830, Emerson had referred to the "grand definition Coleridge gives" (in *The Friend*) "of Talent," which employs its means to "vulgar conventional ends," as opposed to "Genius," which "on the contrary finds its ends in the means. It concerns our peace," Emerson concluded this journal entry of November 19, 1830, "to learn this distinction as quick as we can" (*JMN* 3:211). He *had*—as is demonstrated by *Nature*, "The American Scholar," "The Method of Nature," and "Uses of Great Men."[4]

This Genius-Talent distinction is elaborated on in the long-unpublished commencement address delivered at Middlebury College in 1845, eight years after "The American Scholar." Just as much of *Nature* was based on the Reason-understanding distinction, the Middlebury address is essentially structured on *this* Coleridgean distinction. Emerson concludes by telling the graduating students in his audience, you will be "happy for more than yourself, a benefactor of men," if you can answer two questions, questions that speak "to Genius, to that power which is underneath and greater than all talent, and which proceeds out of the constitution of every man," but whose "private counsels are not tinged with selfishness."

4. In the introduction to *Nature,* Emerson lifted his image of retaining "the spirit of infancy even into the era of manhood" (*E&L* 10) from the passage in *The Friend* in which Coleridge defined "GENIUS, as originality in intellectual construction; the moral accompaniment, and actuating principle of which consists, perhaps, in the carrying on of the *freshness and feelings of childhood* into the *powers of manhood.* By TALENT, on the other hand, I mean the comparative facility of acquiring, arranging, and applying the stock *furnished by others* and already existing in *books or other conservatories of intellect*" (*F* 1:419; italics added). In "Uses of Great Men," Emerson says that although it is "the delight of vulgar talent to dazzle and to bind the beholder, . . . true genius seeks to defend us from itself. True genius will not impoverish, but will liberate, and add new senses" (*E&L* 622, 623). In "The Method of Nature" (1849), we are told that "talent finds its models, methods, and ends in society," whereas "Genius is its own end, and draws its means and the style of its architecture from within."

"Men of talent fill the eye with their pretension"; they contentiously and "noisily persuade society. . . . But Genius has no taste for weaving sand or in trifling; but flings itself on real elemental things, which are powers, self-defensive; which first subsist and then resist unweariably forevermore all that opposes."[5]

This self-reliant yet unselfish resistance of genuine genius to "all that opposes" its own development clarifies the argument, in "The American Scholar," against originality-stifling dependence on books, the lecture's most patently Wordsworthian thesis. Having condemned those who parrot the thinking of others, Emerson goes on to emphasize the *mistaken* "duty" of scholars. The sentence that follows is at the genetic core of the address. Less than two weeks before he was to give the talk, a thus far uninspired Emerson suddenly (following a visit by Hedge and then Alcott) saw his theme. "One thing is plain," he wrote in his journal, the young student must have his own training. "The training of another age will not fit him. He himself & not others must judge what is good for him. . . . Meek young men grow up in colleges & believe it is their duty to accept the views which books have given & grow up slaves" (*JMN* 5:364–65). Scholars, we learn toward the end of the lecture, *do* have true "duties," which "may be comprised in self-trust," enabling us to cut through our own doubts and guilty uncertainties, those "nettles and tangling vines in the way of the self-relying and self-directed" (*E&L* 63). But instead of an integrated scholar, Man Thinking, we have "bookworms," the "restorers of readings, the emendators, the bibliomaniacs of all degrees," who devote themselves to a fatally misconceived duty: "Meek young men grow up in libraries, believing it their duty to accept the views which Cicero, which Locke, which Bacon, have given, forgetful that Cicero, Locke, and Bacon were only young men in libraries when they wrote these books" (*E&L* 57). In his poem "The Scholars," Yeats would later play a characteristically erotic variation on this sentence, mocking the conventional old baldpates who "cough in ink" as they lifelessly "edit and annotate" lines of love-tormented poetry written by such passionate "young men" as Catullus.[6]

5. Emerson, untitled discourse delivered at Middlebury College, July 22, 1845 (*LL* 1:96). Much of what preceded this moment had foreshadowed the full development of the Talent-Genius distinction.

6. Unforgetful of Emerson's young men forgetting that the classical writers dutifully pored over by restorers, emendators, and other bibliomaniacs were themselves once "young men," Yeats mocked the "Old, learned, respectable bald heads," who, forgetful of their own sins, "Edit and annotate the lines / That young men, tossing on their beds, / Rhymed out in love's despair / To flatter beauty's ignorant ear." The pedants all "cough in ink," "think what other people think," and wear the carpet with their shuffling—"Lord, what would they say / Did their Catullus walk that way?" Criticism can be, and has been, directed against this poem, by W. H. Auden (in *The Dyer's Hand*)

❧ Emerson now makes his central point. "Books are the best of things, well used; abused, among the worst." What is "the right use, . . . the one end, which all means go to effect?" Books "are for nothing but to inspire. I had better never see a book," says Emerson (resembling Los, Blake's blacksmith god of creative imagination, who "must create a system or be enslaved by another man's"), "than to be warped by its attraction clean out of my own orbit, and made a satellite instead of a system" (*E&L* 57). The one thing of value is "the active soul," which "sees" truth and "utters" it, that is to say, "creates." And it is on self-reliant action and creativity, and on the Coleridgean distinctions—between Understanding and intuitive Reason, between Fancy and Imagination, Talent and Genius—that Emerson's emphasis falls:

> In this action, it is genius. . . . In its essence, it is progressive. The book, the college, the school of art, the institution of any kind, stop with some past utterance of genius. This is good, say they,—let us hold by this. They pin me down. They look backward and not forward. But genius looks forward: the eyes of man are set in his forehead, not in his hindhead: man hopes, genius creates. Whatever talents may be, if the man create not the pure efflux of the Deity is not his;—cinders and smoke there may be, but not yet flame. . . . Instead of being its own seer, let it receive from another mind its truth, though it were in torrents of light, without periods of solitude, inquest, and self-recovery, and a fatal disservice is done. Genius is always sufficiently the enemy of genius by over influence. . . .
>
> Undoubtedly there is a right way of reading, so it be sternly subordinated. Man Thinking must not be subdued by his instruments. Books are for the scholar's idle times. When he can read God directly, the hour is too precious to be wasted in other men's transcripts of their readings. But when the intervals of darkness come, as come they must,—when the sun is hid, and the stars withdraw their shining,—we repair to the lamps which were kindled by their ray, to guide our steps to the East again, where the dawn is. (*E&L* 57–58)

---

and Lionel Trilling (in "On the Modern Element in Literature"), both of whom express gratitude for the scholarly editing and annotating of our classic texts, including the codices of Catullus. The fact that Emerson and Yeats would *also* agree with that critique does not obviate the problem they expose: the deadliness of conformity and the dangers to vital creativity posed by the pedantic, disembodied thought of what Yeats called in 1899 "an academic class," which is "always a little dead and deadening" in its "preoccupation with words rather than ideas, with facts rather than emotion" ("The Academic Class and the Agrarian Revolution," in *Uncollected Prose by W. B. Yeats,* 150). But, of course, Yeats is no more an enemy of books, rightly used, than is Emerson—as is demonstrated in a related poem, "To a Wealthy Man . . . ," celebrating a Renaissance library, written at the same time as "The Scholars." See *W. B. Yeats: The Poems,* 107–8, 140–41.

But even when, cut off from the light of all our day, we repair to books, the lamps kindled by that light, we must be active. Since Man Thinking "grudges every opportunity of action past by, as a loss of power," there can be no "true scholar" without "the heroic mind." The "preamble of thought, the transition through which it passes from the unconscious to the conscious, is action. Only so much do I know, as I have lived." Grounding himself on Coleridge's Latin axiom, according to which knowledge is contingent on vital being, Emerson embraces passionate intensity—autonomous, intuitive, even savage:

> The scholar loses no hour in which the man lives. Herein he unfolds the sacred germ of his instinct, screened from influence. What is lost in seemliness is gained in strength. Not out of those on whom systems of education have exhausted their culture, comes the helpful giant to destroy the old or to build the new, but out of unhandselled [ungrateful] savage nature, out of terrible Druids and Berserkers, come at last Alfred and Shakespeare. (*E&L* 60, 62)

This tribute to savage nature, it is always worth remembering, comes from a man afflicted with the tuberculosis that had debilitated his father and killed his young wife and brothers. With Emerson as with Nietzsche, the worship of health, vigor, an almost barbarous vitality, stemmed from a realization of his own bodily infirmity. In "Terminus," a poem of old age (though written when Emerson was only in his fifties), the "Berserker" image (in the form of the Viking word *Baresark*) recurs in the observation (attributed to "the god of bounds") that Emerson's own ancestors, when they gave him breath, failed to bequeath, along with needful sinew, the "Baresark marrow to thy bones," leaving

> a legacy of ebbing veins,
> Inconstant heat and nerveless reins,—
> Amid the Muses, left thee deaf and dumb,
> Amid the gladiators, halt and numb.
> (29–32; *EPP* 479)

As the poignant reference to "the Muses" confirms, the point of the passage in "The American Scholar" celebrating the "terrible Druids and Berserkers" is that savage strength is a prerequisite to *artistic* greatness. We may be reminded of the later insistence by Nietzsche's disciple Yeats that "terrible *beauty*" ("Easter 1916") arises from violence, which, since it *is* the prerequisite as well of artistic greatness, compels us (in one of Yeats's most Nietzschean poems, "Ancestral Houses") to "take our greatness with our violence." At such Dionysian or Berserker moments, Emerson clearly anticipates his heir, and Yeats's mentor, Nietzsche, who counted himself a loyal disciple of a precursor guided by "intuitive" Reason, and who was nothing if not "wild"—the author, at his most ecstatic, of "Bacchus" and the "Orphic Poet" peroration of *Nature*. "O celestial Bacchus! Drive them mad,—this multitude of vagabonds, hungry for eloquence, hungry for poetry, starving for symbols, perishing for want of electricity to vitalize this too much pasture." It might be Nietzsche, crying out in *The Birth of Tragedy* for Dionysus to enter into creative fusion with the god of form, Apollo, and denigrating the green-pasture happiness of the herd. Actually, it is Emerson, in "Poetry and Imagination" (*EPP* 317–18).[7]

Even as readers, therefore, we must assert virile, autonomous power. Reciprocally, the purpose of books is to invigorate, to *enhance* power. In "History," an essay cited by Nietzsche, Emerson declares that "the student is to read history actively, and not passively; to esteem his own life the text, and books the commentary. Thus compelled, the Muse of history will utter oracles, as never to those who do not respect themselves" (*E&L* 239). This is the ideal reader. But, says Emerson in the final sentence, even the unschooled and the illiterate "stand nearer to the light by which nature is to be read, than the dissector or the antiquary" (*E&L* 256). Antiquarian history is both a stage and a target of Nietzsche's own essay on history, a meditation on the right and wrong use of the past. He opens with Goethe, the great representative man he shared with Emerson, quoting a phrase that highlights the affinity binding all three: "I hate everything that merely instructs me without augmenting or directly invigorating my activity."[8]

This is *his* "opinion" as well, Nietzsche announces in initiating an essay arguing that we need history, but not for the reasons "the idler in the garden of knowledge needs it," not "so as to turn comfortably away from life and action." (As Emerson had said, books were to be relegated to the true scholar's "idle hours.") We want to serve history, says Nietzsche, "only to

7. In his Dionysian manifestations, Emerson anticipates not only his direct disciple, Nietzsche, but the counter-Enlightenment revolt against Freud by *his* sometime disciple, Jung, who, around 1910, invoked—in a letter to the shocked master—a neopagan, Mithraic, Dionysian cult based on archetypal memories sedimented deep within the "collective unconscious." He wanted, Jung told Freud, "to revive among intellectuals a feeling for symbol and myth, ever so gently to transform Christ back into the soothsaying god of the vine, which he was, and in this way absorb those ecstatic, instinctual forces of Christianity for the one purpose of making the cult and the Sacred myth what they once were—a drunken feast of joy where man regained the ethos and the holiness of an animal. This was the beauty and purpose of classical religion." It was, more immediately, the beauty and purpose of Nietzsche—whose Zarathustra Jung quoted to Freud in asserting autonomy: "One poorly repays a teacher if one remains only the pupil" (W. McQuire, ed., *The Freud/Jung Letters*, 491).

8. Nietzsche, *Untimely Meditations,* 59–123. Subsequent references are made parenthetically in the text.

the extent that history serves life; for it is possible to value the study of history to such a degree that life becomes stunted and degenerate."[9] History is not to be studied as a dead, immutable past; rather, it is to be fully experienced, in Nietzsche's central and sustained organic metaphor, as a living being, a plant that can either grow rampant, overgrowing and obliterating the present, or be pruned and cultivated so as to be of "use" to "life." Sometimes, it even has to be forgotten; for "*there is a degree of sleeplessness, of rumination, of the historical sense, which is harmful and ultimately fatal to the living thing, whether this living thing be a man or a people or a culture.*" To preserve individual and cultural health, "*the unhistorical and the historical are necessary in equal measure*" (59–63; italics in original).

Those "historical men," for whom "looking to the past impels them towards the future and fires their courage to go on living," filled with "hope," are unaware of the fact that they "think and act unhistorically" since their preoccupation with history "stands in the service, *not of pure knowledge, but of life*" (65; italics added). Yeats, who makes precisely this Life-Knowledge contrast in his central annotation on Nietzsche, is unknowingly in debt to Nietzsche's precursor, Emerson, as is Emerson to his own precursor, Coleridge.[10] "Only as much do I *know* as I have *lived*," says Emerson in "The American Scholar," paraphrasing Coleridge's Latin axiom in *Aids to Reflection*, "*Quantum sumus, scimus*" (we *know* what we *are*). "Instantly we know," Emerson adds, "whose words are loaded with life, and whose not" (*E&L* 60). His *were;* as James Russell Lowell once said, thinking back to the crisp winter nights when Emerson's voice thrilled the young, "He brought us *life*, which, on the whole, is no bad thing."[11] When caught up in the

9. On the basis of how they enhance or diminish life, Nietzsche distinguishes three kinds of history, the "monumental," the "antiquarian," and the "critical," which roughly correspond with another triad, the "historical," the "unhistorical," and the "suprahistorical." Progress is oriented toward the final stage in each triad.

10. Crystallizing his annotations on Nietzsche in a virtually career-synopsizing diagram, Yeats set "Night" (associated with Christ and Socrates) against "Day" (associated with Homer). The first, or "primary," pole, Night, he equated with "*denial* of self, the soul turned towards spirit seeking *knowledge*"; the second (the vitalistic Yeatsian-Nietzschean "antithetical") he equated with the "*affirmation* of self, the soul turned away from spirit to be its mask & instrument when it seeks *life.*" Yeats's antitheses reflect Nietzsche's contrast between the pursuit of "knowledge" at the expense of "life," as well as his distinctions between Dionysus and the Crucified, Homer and Socrates/Plato, slave morality and master morality, between "power" issuing in affirmation and *ressentiment* issuing in denial. The diagram (originally drawn in the margin of a 1901 anthology of Nietzsche compiled by Thomas Common, *Nietzsche as Critic, Philosopher, Poet and Prophet*) is reproduced and fully discussed in my *Yeats's Interactions with Tradition,* 117–24.

11. In *My Study Windows* (1871), James Russell Lowell stresses the *vitalizing* power of Emerson, whom he pronounces "one of the few men of genius whom our age has produced," as proved by "his masculine faculty of fecundating other minds. . . . We

influx of incalculable energy, Emerson himself says in "Circles, "I cast away in this new moment all my once hoarded knowledge," sure of the new truth as "divine and helpful; but how it shall help me I can have no guess, for *so to be* is the sole inlet of *so to know*" (*E&L* 413; italics in original).

In this same passage, Emerson, appalled that "we grizzle every day," sees no need, in the presence of "life, transitions, the energizing spirit," for this "old age . . . to creep on a human mind. In nature every moment is new; the past is always swallowed and forgotten; the coming only is sacred" (*E&L* 412–13). Anticipating his own Zarathustra, whose value-creating Child is "innocence and forgetting, a new beginning," Nietzsche advocates a similar forgetting in his history essay. For him, Life, the impulse of creative vitality, when it is in danger of being overgrown or buried beneath a heap of dry-as-dust academic scholarship, may require of us either a "temporary destruction of the past" or a more active "*a posteriori*" reconstruction. The paramount point is that the "use" of history is to preserve and enhance (against their monumentalistic or antiquarian "arch-enemies") those "strong artistic spirits," who "are alone capable of learning from that history in a true, that is to say life-enhancing sense, and of transforming what they have learned into a more elevated practice" (71). These three species of history may either flourish or turn into a "devastating weed." If the man "who wants to do something great has need of the past at all, he appropriates it by means of monumental history." He, on the other hand, who "likes to persist in the familiar and the revered of old, tends the past as an antiquarian historian." Only the man "who is oppressed by a present need, and who wants to throw off this burden at any cost, has need of critical history, that is to say a history that judges and condemns. Much mischief is caused through the thoughtless transplantation of these plants: the critic without need, the antiquary without piety, the man who recognizes greatness but cannot himself do great things, are such plants, estranged from their mother soil and degenerated into weeds" (72).

Antiquarian history is to be admired, within limits. He who "looks back to whence he has come," with love and loyalty, piety and gratitude, reveres and preserves for those who come after the "conditions under which he himself came into existence—and thus he serves life" (73). It was this tendency that directed the Italians of the Renaissance and awoke in their poets the genius of ancient Italy to what Nietzsche's hero, Jakob Burckhardt

---

used to walk in from the country to the Masonic Temple . . . through the crisp winter night, and listen to that thrilling voice of his, so charged with subtle meaning and subtle music, as shipwrecked men on a raft to the hail of a ship that came with un-hoped for food and rescue. Did our own imaginations transfigure dry remainder-biscuit into ambrosia? At any rate, he brought us *life,* which, on the whole, is no bad thing" (381, 383).

(to whom he sent this essay), called a "wonderful new resounding of the primeval strings" (73), another reverentially received harp struck with the hand of power. To convey the nature of the true historical sense, Nietzsche recurs to his own—archetypal, Romantic, organic—metaphor: "The contentment of the tree in its roots, the happiness of knowing that one is not wholly accidental and arbitrary but grown out of a past as its heir, flower and fruit, and that one's existence is thus excused and, indeed, justified—it is this which is today usually designated as the real sense of history" (75).

This celebration of the past, of tradition, is repeatedly overlooked by those who, focusing exclusively on the radical element in his polar thinking, have made Nietzsche philosophy's poster-child perspectivist and deconstructionist, the initiator, *theoretically,* of "a fundamental break from the past," dismissing in the process Nietzsche's actual (often more traditional than deconstructive) interpretive *practice,* as well as "his pervasive use of traditional notions of truth, moral virtue, and reason."[12] But, of course, bipolar Nietzsche also agrees with his mentor, Emerson, that the "profound apprehension of the Present is Genius, which makes the Past forgotten," and that original genius "believes its faintest presentiment against the testimony of all history" (*EPP* 329). Accordingly, two paragraphs later in the essay we are examining, Nietzsche warns against the historical sense when it serves to petrify rather than vitally preserve. The "imminent danger" comes when "the senses of a people harden," when the study of history

> serves the life of the past in such a way that it undermines continuing and especially higher life, when the historical sense no longer conserves life but mummifies it, when the tree gradually dies unnaturally from the top downwards to the roots—and in the end the roots themselves usually perish too. Antiquarian history itself degenerates from the moment it is no longer animated and inspired by the fresh life of the present. (75)

He makes the same point, in perhaps his most direct assault on the potentially deadening effect of books, in the passage that ends with the sentence quoted in the third epigraph to this chapter, "To read a book early in the morning, at daybreak, in the vigor and dawn of one's strength—that I call viciousness." The whole of the passage, in part a philologist's protest against philological pedantry, seems directly indebted to Emerson's warnings about books, especially in the "American Scholar" address. Emerson,

12. Peter Berkowitz, from the preface (ix–xi) of his antipostmodern *Nietzsche: The Ethics of an Immoralist.*

in turn, was remembering Wordsworth's provisional advice to "come forth into the light of things" and to "bring no book"—since books, as Emerson says, threaten to crush rather than stimulate creativity by drawing even an inherently original thinker out of his "own orbit." The scholar, says Nietzsche,

> who actually does little else than wallow in a sea of books . . . finally loses completely the ability to think for himself. He cannot think unless he has a book in his hands. When he thinks, he responds to a stimulus (a thought he has read)—and finally all he does is react. The scholar devotes all his energy to affirming or denying or criticizing matter that has already been thought out—he no longer thinks himself. . . . In him the instinct of self-defense has decayed, otherwise he would defend himself against books. The scholar is a decadent. With my own eyes I have seen gifted, richly-endowed, free-spirited natures already "read to pieces" at thirty—nothing but matches that have to be struck before they can emit any sparks—or "thoughts."[13]

This potentially mummifying dominance of books is, for the pedantic and antiquarian mind, the burden of the Past and of belatedness. In the history essay, Nietzsche goes on to lament the "implanting" of the belief, harmful at any time and especially in an oversaturated and belated age, that "one is a latecomer and epigone" (83). In an image anticipating Frye, Bate, and Bloom on belatedness, Nietzsche argues: "The guests who come last to table have to be content with the last places." If you wish to have a place at the table, perhaps at its head, then "perform some high and great deed." Emerson had called for Genius, operating in the Present, to either absorb or forget the Past in order to expedite the Future. "*If you are to venture to interpret the past,*" says Nietzsche, "*you can do so only out of the fullest exertion of the vigour of the present.*" Aspire to the goal of "a great and comprehensive hope, of a hope-filled striving. Form within yourself an image to which the future shall correspond, and forget the superstition that you are epigones. You will have enough to ponder and to invent when you reflect on the life of the future" (93–94; italics in original).

Unsurprisingly, given its Emersonian character, we find the same emphasis in Thoreau's chapter "On Reading," and the opening paragraph of the chapter that follows it, in *Walden.* "We should be as good as the worthies of antiquity," says Thoreau, "but partly by first knowing how good they were." An accomplished classicist who was also deeply read in Indian literature, a man for whom (echoing Milton's *Areopagitica*) "books are the

13. Nietzsche, in *Friedrich Nietzsche: Werke in drei Bänden,* 2:1094, cited in McFarland, *Originality and Imagination,* 16.

treasured wealth of the world and the fit inheritance of generations and nations," Thoreau anticipated the day when the libraries "shall be filled with Vedas and Zenavestas and Bibles, with Homers and Dantes and Shakespeares, and all the centuries to come shall have successively deposited their trophies in the forum of the world. By such a pile we may hope to scale heaven at last."

Thus far, he seems a venerator of books and the past, but the key to the direction of his Emersonian argument is in that final sentence: books and the inherited tradition are finally a "pile," a launching pad to our own heaven-scaling innovations. Thoreau also agreed with Wordsworthian Emerson in ranking books below "nature," even getting in a joke at the expense of the greatest of "nature poets." "Looking over the dry and dusty volumes of the English poets," he found it hard to believe, Thoreau confided in an 1841 journal, "that those fresh and fair creations I had imagined are contained in them." Compared with the "commonest nature" seen "from the library window" the whole of English poetry "seems very mean." Earlier in this journal, he made an entry the final often-quoted sentence of which anticipates that *almost* irresistible essay "Wordsworth in the Tropics," in which Aldous Huxley argues that a "few months in the jungle," away from Europe's "tamed and temperate Nature," would have "cured" Wordsworth of his "too easy and comfortable pantheism." The "best poets, after all," notes Thoreau, "exhibit only a tame and civil side of nature—They have not seen the west side of any mountain. Day and night—mountain and wood are visible from the wilderness as well as the village—They have their primeval aspects—sterner savager—than any poet has sung. It is only the white man's poetry—we want the Indian's report. Wordsworth is too tame for the Chippeway."[14]

As insistent as Wordsworth and Emerson on the provisional "superiority" of nature to books, even one's own books, Thoreau was no less acutely aware than they, and Nietzsche, of the need for "strong readers" rather than powerless pedants. In remarks that carry over from "On Reading" to the opening of the following chapter of *Walden,* "Sounds," Thoreau points out, as Emerson does, the "danger" and confinement of books when the past ceases to inspire the present and prepare the future, when reading becomes a substitute for ever alert living, when the All is lost in the particular, when bleary-eyed scholarship becomes a detriment to vision. "There

14. Huxley, "Wordsworth in the Tropics," 113, 128; Thoreau, *Journals,* 1:337–38, 321. Four years later, however, we find Thoreau praising Wordsworth for having achieved a dignified old age, leading "a simple epic life" in times of "confusion and turmoil." Wordsworthian serenity and contentment, the dotage that struck Yeats as a terrifying prospect to be avoided by a poet, seemed to Thoreau a "cheering" prospect.

is," as Emerson had said in warning about "this everlasting reading," "other peeping beside setting the eye to chinks and keyholes" to see "what others have done." Are we, asks Thoreau, to be mere scholars or transcendental "seers"?

> The works of the great poets have never yet been read by mankind, for only great poets can read them. . . . [O]f reading as a noble enterprise [most men] know little or nothing; yet this only is reading, in a high sense, not that which lulls us as a luxury and suffers the nobler faculties to sleep the while, but what we have to stand on tip-toe to read and devote our most alert and wakeful hours to. . . .
>
> But while we are confined to books, though the most select and classic, and read only particular written languages, which are themselves but dialects and provincial, we are in danger of forgetting the language which all things and events speak without metaphor. . . . The rays which stream through the shutter will be no longer remembered when the shutter is wholly removed. No method or discipline can supersede the necessity of being forever on the alert. What is a course of history or philosophy, or poetry, no matter how well selected . . . compared with the discipline of looking always at what is to be seen? Will you be a reader, a student merely, or a seer? Read your fate, see what is before you, and walk on into futurity.[15]

Far from categorically consigning books to the ash heap, Thoreau, like Emerson before him and Nietzsche after, was instead warning that grateful reception must not deteriorate into worship of a dead past, incapable of quickening new creation. In Emerson's case, the crucial interaction was with European Romanticism, balancing tradition and revolutionary innovation. His thankful yet troubled relationship to the prose of Coleridge and Carlyle and the poetry of Wordsworth was further problematized by this tension between life and knowledge, the vital present and the burden of the past, especially as represented by the dead weight of "books." It is fine to read, but to worship the texts of the past is to be not a scholar but a bookworm. And the attack on bookworms goes back as far as there have been libraries, including the most famous in the ancient world. At the heart of the library at Hellenistic Alexandria was the Mouseion, the "home of the Muses," which housed and supported invited scholars, poets, and scientists from all over the Mediterranean. One disgruntled Greek scholar, doubtless among the uninvited, anticipated Thoreau's "mere" students and Emerson's vamping pedants by cynically describing those contentiously poring over and codifying the great collection of papyrus

15. Thoreau, *Walden: An Annotated Edition,* 100–101, 104, 108.

texts as "scribbling bookworms" found "in Egypt's populous nation," endlessly debating "as they flock around / the muses' feeding stations."[16]

That age-old mockery of bookworms was advanced, most famously or notoriously, by Wordsworth and Emerson—and, perhaps, most outrageously, by two great modern poets (and admirers of Emerson) writing in English: Robert Browning and William Carlos Williams. There is, of course, Browning's "Grammarian's Funeral," whose titular figure, "famous calm and dead," was a man who, deciding "not to Live but Know" and "dead from the waist down," postponed life in favor of learning and so died without ever having lived. Less well-known is "Sibrandus Shafnaburgensis." There, out-Wordsworthing the Wordsworth of *Lyrical Ballads,* Browning contrasts the lifeless pedantry of a bookworm with the squirming sexual vitality represented by the spiders, worms, and slugs that invade a tome he left in the vaginal "crevice" of a plum tree. "How did he like it," the whimsical speaker wonders, "when the live creatures / Tickled and toused and browsed" his precious volume?

> All that life and fun and romping,
> All that frisking and twisting and coupling,
> While slowly our poor friend's leaves were swamping,
> And clasps were creaking and covers suppling!

Back he brings what has survived the spawning vitality of prodigal life, back to his bookshelves where it will "Dry-rot till the Judgment-day!" As the frank if displaced sexuality of the poem indicates, Browning was hardly the sort of "moral eunuch" depicted in Shelley's parody of Wordsworth in "Peter Bell the Third": "He touched the hem of Nature's shift, / Felt faint—and never dared uplift / The closest, all-concealing tunic." Yet as an exercise in spirited hyperbole (the dialectical playing off of one partial truth against another, half of a polarity), "Sibrandus Shafnaburgensis" is in the direct line of Wordsworth's nature-celebrating, book-spurning dialogue poems in *Lyrical Ballads.*[17]

16. As translated by Lionel Casson in his *Libraries in the Ancient World,* quoted in Bernard Knox, "Tablets to Books," 42.

17. For the lines cited (314–17) from "Peter Bell the Third," see Shelley, *Shelley's Poetry and Prose,* 335. For "A Grammarian's Funeral" and "Sibrandus Shafnaburgensis," see Browning, *The Poems and Plays of Robert Browning,* 167–72, 11–13. As one might guess from the opening exclamation of the latter poem, ("'Plague take all your pedants,' say I!"), to say nothing of its title, Browning's satirist is himself an extremist. The author of the book he holds was "so good as to die" centuries earlier, leaving behind the encumbrance of "this rubbish." Bringing the book into his garden, the speaker reads it "From title page to closing line," then takes his "revenge," dropping the volume, in a flurry of double entendres, into the "crevice" of a plum tree, a moist cleft with "lap of moss" and "lip of gum." Having procured cheese and a bottle of wine, he

Yeats's poem "The Scholars" is in this general mode, as is George Eliot's depiction in *Middlemarch* of the Reverend Edward Casaubon, that "dried bookworm" laboring "as in a treadmill fruitlessly." But one has to wait a century before finding something approximating Browning's energy enlisted in the same cause. William Carlos Williams, who can sound remarkably like the antibook side of Emerson, *does* seem to go to the book-burning extreme in the library-destruction scene in book 3 of *Paterson.* The place "sweats of staleness and of rot," the "stagnation and death" emanating with a "library stench" from books that "cannot penetrate and cannot waken, to be again / active but remain—books." Thus, the conflagration in which papers are blackened, consumed, and "scattered to the winds" is both a necessary and a "beautiful thing." In what almost seems an organic anticipation of that fire, the destruction of what is stagnant and rotten as the necessary—Romantic and Nietzschean—prerequisite to new creation, Williams asserts in his 1939 essay "Against the Weather": "To stop the flames that destroy the old nest prevents the rebirth of the bird itself. All things rot and stink, nothing stinks more than an old nest, if not recreated."[18]

Despite his more (literally) incendiary language, Williams—like Wordsworth, Emerson, Thoreau, Nietzsche, and Browning—warns not against books per se, but the misuse to which they are put by readers who fail to draw from them inspiration for their own creative efforts. Emerson might cry out in a notebook poem of the late 1840s, "Burn up the libraries!"

---

next "Lay on the grass and forgot the oaf / Over a jolly chapter of Rabelais" (he is *still* "reading," but from a text remarkable for vitality rather than pedantry). But "this morning," taking "pity, for learning's sake," he "fished" up the "delectable treatise" from its crevice, only to find it nearly absorbed by Nature. Invaded by spider, worm, slug, and eft, by all the teeming creative forces ignored or perverted by bookworm pedantry, it is spotted and streaked, discolored by droppings, a "toadstool" sprouting from "chapter six"! As in the case of the corpse in "The Grammarian's Funeral," Browning's assault on life-denying pedantry is serious. At the same time, his rollicking delight in the irrepressible energies of life makes the poem comical (it first appeared in the July 1844 issue of Thomas Hood's new *Hood's Magazine and Comic Miscellany*) or, as Joyce would say, "jocoserious."

18. Williams, *Paterson (1946–58),* 101–3, 116, 117; Williams, "Against the Weather," in *Selected Essays,* 208. See chap. 5, "Inclusions and Redundancy: William Carlos Williams in the Emersonian Grain," in Charles E. Mitchell's *Individualism and Its Discontents: Appropriations of Emerson, 1880–1950.* In the library scene, Williams sounds like both Emerson and Nietzsche, a dynamic duo coupled by Alexander Star in a review of Nicholson Baker's *Double Fold: Libraries and the Assault on Paper* (2001). Baker quotes Verner Clapp (first president of the American Council on Library Resources), who, though a serious reader, increasingly finds books "dingy, dreary, dog-eared, and dead," things that, unlike their authors, have "a way of lingering on." Let modern libraries extract, through microfilm, the "profit and usefulness" from printed texts and stop them from "clogging the channels of the present." Though Baker "understandably finds it disturbing in a librarian," it is, Star remarks, "a sentiment that Emerson or Nietzsche would have understood" ("The Paper Pusher," 39).

raze the foundations of the colleges, rout the philosophers and critics, who "narrowing niggardly / Something to nothing / . . . End in the Néant" (*CPT* 411). But though he might say, in "The American Scholar," it would be better never to see a book than to be warped by its attraction out of his own orbit, and "made a satellite instead of a system," he adds, two pages later, "I would not be hurried by any love of system, by any exaggeration of instincts, to underrate the Book" (*E&L* 57). We always have to remember that Emerson valued his own "pedantic cartload" of books, that this celebrator of a fierce vitalism was the same man who took issue in his 1838 journal with the rejection of books in favor of nature in Wordsworth's "Tables Turned" (*JMN* 7:69). He obviously loved and learned from all those books that stimulated him to record his responses and creative extrapolations in thousands of pages of meticulously organized journals and notebooks, the larders from which he drew in writing his own lectures and essays. As he says in "The American Scholar," just as the body needs to be "nourished," so the human mind "needs to be fed by . . . knowledge." What is required is "a strong head to bear that diet," an ability to "read well," that is, inventively, creatively (*E&L* 59).

As we have seen, Emerson's call for a specifically *American* originality was being made by a man whose diet was transatlantic. Even as he celebrated an independent American future in "The Poet" and "The American Scholar," Emerson looked across the ocean for literary and philosophic models. He may, as in "The Poet," have been prophesying the advent of a Whitman, but he was not quite ready for the Whitmanian "barbaric yawp" of uninflected Americanism. The man who anticipated the end of "our long apprenticeship to the learning of other lands" (*E&L* 53), who cried out for independence and indigenous poetic voices, "was himself deeply and openly indebted to European thought and literature." Not a single one of his later exemplars, in *Representative Men,* was an American. "The American Scholar," as Richardson notes, "was written by a man who read daily in Goethe, Plutarch, Montaigne, Shakespeare, and Wordsworth."[19]

19. Richardson, *Mind on Fire,* 263. Just how ingrained the phenomenon was may be gauged by an incident having to do with the mid-nineteenth-century "Young America" movement, centered in New York City. Its leader, John L. O'Sullivan, inventor of the term that epitomized American exceptionalism and expansionism, *Manifest Destiny,* was also the editor of the movement's principal organ, the *United States Magazine and Democratic Review* (Elizabeth Peabody's review of *Nature* appeared here). Though determined to usher in a new generation of writers who would find their voice by breaking free of the literary and cultural standards of both Old and New Englands, O'Sullivan successfully lured Nathaniel Hawthorne into writing for his new journal by promising him, in a letter of April 19, 1837, that it would be "designed to be of the highest rank of magazine literature, taking its *ton* of the first class in England." A British ship was always looming on the cultural horizon. See Edward L. Widmer, *Young America: The Flowering of Democracy in New York City,* 71–72.

In the Transcendentalist version of "the perennial problem of Europe and America," we have what Perry Miller calls "a test-tube model of the process of assimilation that had been at work even before the declaration of political independence": how the American artist or thinker, working in conditions that to some extent shape his or her character and work, nevertheless "reaches out for the results of an older and more complex culture, how he reworks them and refashions them to suit his own needs, and so perturbs and enriches the life of America." All this is illustrated, notes Miller, "in the emergence and formulation" of Transcendentalism. "Because they desperately needed forms and concepts in which to embody a passion that arose out of domestic pressures, the Transcendentalists appropriated with avidity the new literature of 'romanticism' that came to them through Wordsworth and Coleridge and the new philosophy of German idealism that came to them at second-hand."[20]

The inevitable conclusion in the case of Emerson is that, despite his emphasis on "our own" creativity as opposed to the tasks of "others" and the "rumor of their performance," despite the celebration of our arousal "to a life in ourselves" compared to which books seem no more than heaps of "pale and cold" verbiage enclosing the all-important "intuition or two," Emerson saw himself as part of a transatlantic movement, a connection he spent his life alternately denying and confirming but always embodying. His alternating celebrations and reservations about Wordsworth and Coleridge reflect not only an appraisal of their considerable yet uneven merits but also the uneasy relationship of a paladin of self-reliance who knew just how reliant he had been on the theoretical and critical distinctions of Coleridge and governing ideas he encountered in the poetry of Wordsworth. As an example of the unspoken but manifest presence of Wordsworth in this matter of books, take the following complaint of Emerson, which occurs, as it happens, in the opening lecture in the series from which Laura Furman and Elinore Standard quote. The "decay of learning" in (and this is the title of the lecture) "the present age" is in part, Emerson grumps, attributable to a sad and remarkable, even paradoxical, state of affairs: "The fine geniuses of the day decry books" (*EL* 3:194).

Here we have paradox piled on paradox because, leaving aside *his own* decrying of books, the foremost of these fine geniuses of the present age is, of course, that Wordsworth who warns against excessive book learning, the denigrator of tuition and celebrator of intuition—Coleridge's intuitive Reason, of which Wordsworth becomes the great *poetic* spokesman. Emerson

20. Miller, *The Transcendentalists: An Anthology,* 10. Over the half century since, Miller's brief account of the process of assimilation has been fleshed out by Yoder, Ellison, Harding, Chai, Packer, Brown, Weisbuch, and Gravil.

never forgot his conversation with Wordsworth on August 28, 1833, and the old man's complaint that society was being "enlightened" not by "moral" training engendered by an intuitive intercourse with nature, but by a disproportionate "superficial tuition. . . . Schools do no good. Tuition is not education." Wordsworth "thinks more," Emerson reported, "of the education of circumstances" than of books and the classroom (*E&L* 775). In middle age Wordsworth had temporarily endorsed the Bell system of regularized national, and nationalistic, education.[21] But at the age of sixty-three, when Emerson met him, he felt toward "education" as he had when he first "began to inquire, / To watch and question those" he met on "lonely roads," those "open schools in which I daily read / With most delight the passions of mankind" (*P* 13:159–63). Wordsworth would have agreed with Mark Twain, who confided in his 1898 notebook that "education consists mainly in what we have unlearned" and who is purported to have said, famously, "I have never let my schooling interfere with my education." Like Twain, Wordsworth was a thoughtful observer who, in the process of walking through the long schoolroom of life, became

> convinced at heart
> How little those formalities, to which
> With overweening trust alone we give
> The name of Education, hath to do
> With real feeling and just sense;
> . . . .
> How we mislead each other; above all,
> How books mislead us. . . .
> (*P* 13:167–72, 207–8)

He learned a similar lesson in revolutionary France in 1791, when "the soil of common life, . . . too hot to tread upon," taught Wordsworth the utter inadequacy of written history to the felt reality of events, events that mocked history, whether past or to come. Now he *felt* "how all men are deceived / Reading of nations and their works," and he has only "laughter for the page that would reflect / To future times the face of what now is!" (*P* 9:166–74). Books, education, were as nothing compared to direct experience, whether of political "earthquakes" (*P* 9:179) or of the manifesta-

21. That personal endorsement was reflected in the doctrine espoused by the Wanderer: a systematized tuition whereby "The whole people should be taught and trained" (*E* 9:358). As the language suggests, Wordsworth's advocacy of a notably *nationalistic* system of education cannot be divorced from Britain's need, in a dark time, to struggle on against Napoleonic tyranny—a call for educational reform resembling the U.S. response to the launching of *Sputnik* by a tyranny with which the United States was then engaged in a life-and-death struggle.

tions of a fostering and educating Nature herself, what Wordsworth calls in the opening book of *The Prelude* her dual "ministry" of beauty and of fear (*P* 1:301, 468).

Such education, whether it derives from within or from an intuitive interaction with external nature, is incalculable, sublime, luminous. In "Self-Reliance," Emerson proposes as the "highest merit" ascribable to "Moses, Plato, and Milton," that they "set at naught books and traditions, and spoke not what men but what they [themselves] thought. A man should learn to detect and watch that gleam of light which flashes across his mind from within, more than the lustre of the firmament of bards and sages" (*E&L* 259). The same imagery—spontaneous intuitions as gleams of light—recurs in an 1845 journal entry, in which Emerson focuses, as he had in the opening paragraph of "The Over-Soul" (*E&L* 385), on the uninventoried residual mystery of man, the intriguing "remainder" of which "no tongue can tell" but that tantalizes us with a "glimpse or guess of the awful Life that lurks under" the surface self. "For the best part, I repeat," of "every mind is not that which he knows," the "firm recorded knowledge" that "soon loses all interest for him," but rather "that which hovers in gleams, suggestions, tantalizing unpossessed before him."[22] These mysterious "gleams" and "suggestions" emanate, like that self-reliant "gleam of light," from the "visionary gleam" and "master light of all our seeing," in the ninth stanza of the Intimations Ode. "Be they what they may" (and Wordsworth is no more sure than Emerson, given that such illuminations are beyond rational argumentation and proof), these tantalizing gleams are the true and only sources of our genuine power, intuitions and intimations transcending any and all "recorded knowledge." Or so the Romantics and Transcendentalists would have us believe.

Thus, we are, as so often, back to the teaching of Milton's archangel on intuitive Reason, at least as interpreted by Coleridge. The speech of Raphael in *Paradise Lost* remains a constant touchstone, and both Wordsworth and Emerson could also use the charming passage, discussed in the next chapter, from Milton's *Tractate on Education,* to support their experiential engagement with nature and reliance on intuition rather than education through the study of books. But Wordsworth, unlike nonchalant Emerson, could never depict Milton as setting "at naught books and traditions." Though he could hardly hope to find in that man of unparalleled

22. Emerson goes on to say that while man's life "is of a ridiculous brevity and meanness," this "dancing chorus of thoughts & hopes is the quarry of his future, is his possibility, & teaches him that" mortal life is the "first age & trial only of his young wings," and that "vast revolutions, migrations & gyres on gyres in the celestial societies invite him." The entry, dated "Autumn 1845," is most familiar as the coda to Stephen Whicher's influential "organic anthology" (*Selections from Emerson,* 406).

erudition a consistent case against reading, he could not help interacting with his great precursor. And so we have him, in the book of *The Prelude* actually titled "Books," employing Milton's Satanic architects to condemn rigid, book-centered education, a tuition that overwhelms and devalues fruitful, intuitive intercourse with our first and truest teacher, Nature.

Of course, book 5 of *The Prelude* does include a genuine (if somewhat perfunctory) tribute to the titular "books." Wordsworth commemorates "all books which lay / Their sure foundations in the hearts of Man," especially the Bible, Homer, English ballads, and "more varied and elaborate," "Those trumpet-tones of harmony that shake / Our shores in England"—a reference to Milton, obvious enough in its very sound, but confirmed by the allusion to the final lines of his own "Scorn not the sonnet," a poetic short form Milton *trans*formed into a mighty "trumpet" (5: 198–206). Nevertheless, the announced topic is almost neglected in favor of Wordsworth's actual theme: the development of a race of "real" children, children "not too wise, / Too learned, or too good; but wanton, fresh," often

> Bending beneath our life's mysterious weight
> Of pain, and doubt, and fear, yet yielding not
> In happiness to the happiest upon earth.
> Simplicity in habit, truth in speech,
> Be these the daily strengtheners of their minds;
> May books and Nature be their early joy!
> And knowledge, rightly honored with that name,
> Knowledge not purchased with the loss of power!
> (*P* 5:411–25)

This passage, capped by the celebrated last line, follows the archetypal description of such a child of Nature, the Boy of Winander. It is a haunted and haunting presentation since this boy was Wordsworth himself before he shifted from autobiography to distanced third-person narration and, in an added coda, killed and buried the child he once was; hence, the famous opening: "There *was* a boy." That youth would blow "mimic hootings to the silent owls," who, "Responsive to his call," would answer with "concourse wild / Of jocund din"—until he was greeted with a silence that defeated his best efforts.

> Then sometimes, in that silence while he hung
> Listening, a gentle shock of mild surprise
> Has carried far into his heart the voice

Of mountain torrents; or the visible scene
Would enter unawares into his mind,
With all its solemn imagery, its rocks,
Its woods, and that uncertain heaven, received
Into the bosom of the steady lake.

(5:373–88)

This was a favorite passage of Emerson—who printed it, under the title "The Boy-Poet" in *Parnassus*—and of Coleridge, who cited the lines to illustrate Wordsworth's distinctive gifts (*BL* 2:103–4). He had felt that way from the outset. Referring to the final lines shortly after they were written, Coleridge observed in a December 1798 letter to Wordsworth, "I should have recognized them anywhere; and had I met these lines running wild in the deserts of Arabia, I should have instantly screamed out, 'Wordsworth!'" (*CL* 1:452–53). He was responding to the imaginatively revealed unity of water and heaven, the "steady" lake receiving into its bosom the unsteady reflection of a cloudy sky, a transfiguration rendering the transitory enduring. Aside from the great skating scene, which traces a similar trajectory from excitement to tranquillity (a passage also admired by Emerson), Wordsworth never surpassed this description of active reciprocity with Nature and, even more, of the wise passiveness of a suspended listening in which the mind and the human heart (to which "space and its infinities are attributed," as De Quincey finely points out, by the sublime expression "far") are unconsciously ("unawares," as in the Mariner's blessing of the water snakes) opened up to the voice and to the vast and solemn imagery of Nature. The organic sequence—an initial exertion of energy, followed by tense waiting and then relaxation and a sudden, unexpected flash of sublime revelation—was stressed by Wordsworth himself, in language applicable, *mutatis mutandis,* to the skating scene. The "Boy," he notes in his 1815 preface, is "listening, with something of a feverish and restless anxiety, for the recurrence of the riotous sounds which he had previously excited; and, at the moment when the intenseness of his mind is beginning to remit, he is surprized into a perception of the solemn and tranquillizing images which the Poem describes" (*WP* 2:918).[23]

23. This was included in the first volume of Emerson's edition of Wordsworth. De Quincey wrote in 1839: "This very expression, 'far,' by which space and its infinities are attributed to the human heart, and to its capacities of re-echoing the sublimities of nature, has always struck me as with a flash of sublime revelation" (*Recollections of the Lakes and of the Lake Poets,* 161). In "Literary and Lake Reminiscences," De Quincey tells a parallel anecdote in which Wordsworth, expecting important news, awaited the mail coach with his ear to the road to catch the first sound of the approaching wheels. After much expectant tension, he abandoned hope, raised his head with relaxed senses—and suddenly perceived a bright star in the heavens, an unexpected sight that brought to him "a pathos and a sense of the Infinite" (*Collected Writings,* 2).

We encounter in the Plotinian opening of Emerson's "Over-Soul," an essay Oliver Wendell Holmes rightly said would be better called "An Over-*flow* of a spiritual imagination," a similar sense of sublimity and submission to a higher and deeper power that—mysterious and incalculable—balks and baffles our individual talents:

> Man is a stream whose source is hidden. Our being is descending into us from we know not whence. The most exact calculator has no prescience that somewhat incalculable may not balk the very next moment. I am constrained every moment to acknowledge a higher origin for events than the will I call mine. As with events, so it is with thoughts. When I watch that flowing river, which, out of regions I see not, pours for a season its streams into me, I see that I am a pensioner; not a cause, but a surprised spectator of this ethereal water; that I desire and look up, and put myself in the attitude of reception, but from some alien energy the visions come. (*E&L* 385)[24]

"That great nature in which we rest" is the Over-Soul, within which we are all made one, "a common heart" whose proper "action is submission" to "that overpowering reality which confutes our tricks and talents." Coleridge's celebration of intuitive Reason over the merely quantifying and calculating understanding (*L* 1:412–13; *E&L* 26) is here fused by Emerson with Wordsworth's insistence that the most profound education comes not from tuition, but is arrived at unawares, and with "a gentle shock of mild surprise," when we attend upon nature, silently listening or suddenly seeming to see into the life of things. "The best read naturalist who lends an entire and devout attention to truth, will see that there remains much to learn of his relation to the world, and that it is not to be learned by any addition or subtraction or other comparison of known quantities, but is arrived at by untaught sallies of the spirit, by a continual self-recovery, and by entire humility" (*E&L* 43). Emerson here resembles not only the Boy of Winander, "hung / Listening" to the vast silence, but the "curious child" in the Wanderer's tale in *The Excursion.* That boy, illustrating the truth that "Nature fails not to provide / Impulse and utterance" (*E* 4: 169–70), put to his ear a shell, to which, "in silence hushed, his very soul / Listened intensely," his face brightening with joy to hear from within "Murmurings, whereby the monitor expressed / Mysterious union with its

24. Holmes makes this perceptive remark in his biography of Emerson, though the "Over-flow" reminded him less of Plotinus than of another philosopher who influenced Coleridge, Wordsworth, and Emerson. Reading "The Over-Soul," says Holmes, quoting the famous adjective of Novalis, "we cannot help thinking of the . . . 'God-intoxicated' Spinoza" (*Ralph Waldo Emerson,* 173). Many have said the same in responding to the "sublime" passage of "Tintern Abbey," perhaps Wordsworth's closest approximation to Spinozistic pantheism.

native sea." The Wanderer, a man of faith, informs the skeptical Solitary (in a borrowed simile, but one that would resonate with Emerson and, later, and magnificently, with Melville):

> Even such a shell the universe itself
> Is to the ear of Faith; and there are times,
> I doubt not, when to you it doth impart
> Authentic tidings of invisible things;
> Of ebb and flow, and ever-during power;
> And central peace, subsisting at the heart
> Of endless agitation.
>
> (*E* 4:1141–47)

There is, says Emerson in "Circles," a "central life" within and above "incessant movement and progression," endless activity that "could never become sensible to us but by contrast to some principle of fixture or stability in the soul. Whilst the eternal generation of circles proceeds, the eternal generator abides." That central stability is, explains Emerson, completing his image of repose at the core of endless generation, "superior to knowledge and thought" (*E&L* 412). The same is true for the Wanderer, who, completing his seashell simile, insists that

> The estate of man would be indeed forlorn
> If false conclusion of the reasoning power
> Made the eye blind, and closed the passages
> Through which the ear converses with the heart.
>
> (*E* 4:1152–55)

Again, this is the "understanding heart," De Quincey's "intuitive organ," the guarantor that we are reading, not the lesser "literature of *knowledge*," but the "literature of *power*," a Keatsian "quiet power," or, as he put it elsewhere, "the supreme of power, / . . . might slumb'ring on its own right arm." And this is precisely what Melville's Ishmael—having experienced, at sea and within himself, the central calm at the heart of circumscribing tumult—finds in his first sighting of Moby-Dick himself: "a mighty mildness of repose."[25]

25. Keats, "Sleep and Poetry" (236–37), in *Poems of Keats,* 74. In chap. 87 of *Moby-Dick; or, The Whale,* the same passage of *The Excursion* registered by Emerson in "Circles" is movingly elaborated by Melville, who also seems to be remembering Wordsworth's Intimations Ode. When his boat is hauled by a harpooned whale past the churning ring of "the outermost whales" and into the "innermost heart of the shoal," Ishmael finds himself in a satin-smooth "central expanse," "that enchanted calm which they say lurks at the heart of every commotion." Hemmed in by "the tumults of the outer concentric circles," they come upon the cows and calves, gentled as

Despite the Wanderer's religiously orthodox coda to the seashell passage,[26] later Wordsworth, in his own revisionary voice or the echoing voice of the devout Wanderer, checks and mutes without ever eradicating his early evocations of a vital and passionate "over-flow," and of a less orthodox quiescence or quiet power at the heart of endless agitation. One thinks again of the ode's "shadowy recollections," which, "be they what they may," have the power to make "Our noisy years seem moments in the being / Of the eternal Silence" (150–56), or of "that serene and blessed mood" (41) of "Tintern Abbey," in which, anticipating the Emersonian epiphany of the transparent eyeball,

> even the motion of our human blood
> Almost suspended, we are laid asleep
> In body, and become a living soul:
> While with an eye made quiet by the power
> Of harmony, and the deep power of joy,
> We see into the life of things.
> (44–49; *WP* 1:358–59)

The polar movement—for, as Wordsworth says in the 1800 preface to *Lyrical Ballads,* "we must attend the fluxes and refluxes of the mind"—is

---

by a spell. But far beneath this calm surface, another and still stranger world met our eyes as we gazed over the side." Through the transparent water, they see the infant whales feeding, gazing away from their mothers' breasts, "as if leading two different lives at the same time," seeming, "while yet drawing mortal nourishment," to be "still spiritually feasting upon some unearthly reminiscence" (398). Following this unlikely yet highly probable echo of the Intimations Ode, Melville alludes to yet other intimacies, "young Leviathan amours in the deep." "And thus, though surrounded by circle upon circle of consternations and affrights, did these inscrutable creatures at the centre freely and fearlessly indulge in all peaceful concernments; yea, serenely revelled in dalliance and delight. But even so, amid the tornadoed Atlantic of my being, do I myself for ever centrally disport in mute calm; and while ponderous planets of unwaning woe revolve around me, deep down and deep inland there I still bathe me in eternal mildness of joy" (399).

Reading chap. 87 as "Melville's great response" to the Coleridgean-Wordsworthian "one life," Richard Gravil traces Ishmael's phrase "deep inland" to "Tintern Abbey" and its "soft *inland* murmur" (*Romantic Dialogues,* 156–57). But his own lovely allusion (he describes the infant whales "trailing clouds of glory") suggests that "deep inland" also comes from the Intimations Ode. "Hence in a season of calm weather," says Wordsworth in stanza 9, "Though inland far we be, / Our souls have sight of that immortal sea / Which brought us hither. . . ."

26. You, he informs the Solitary, unconsciously "Adore, and worship," and are "pious" and "devout" beyond your intent (*E* 4:1148–50). One recalls Wordsworth's pious alteration of the final stanza of "Lines Written in Early Spring" or of passages in *The Prelude*. An example related to the Emersonian overflow initiating "The Over-Soul" is the apostrophe, "Oh! Soul of *Nature!* that dost *overflow / With passion and with life*" (*P* [1805], 11:138–39), tamed by Wordsworth to "Powers on whom I daily waited," powers "*by laws divine* / Sustained and *governed*" (*P* 12:93–104; italics added).

from submission (*"an eye made quiet"*) to active agency: "*We see . . .*" The same shift occurs in "The Over-Soul." Praising man's "wisdom, and virtue, and power, and beauty," which come "not from his tongue" but from a Wordsworthian "deep power," Emerson adds that although fallen man may live "in succession, in division, in parts," nevertheless his innate potential power makes him more than a passive "spectator" and "pensioner," his mind, as Wordsworth would say, more than a "mean pensioner / On outward forms" (*P* 6:737–38). This is the other half of the polarity, the Me or "Soul" becoming interfused with the NOT ME in the very "act of seeing": "Within man is the soul of the whole; the wise silence; the universal beauty, to which every part and particle is equally related; the eternal ONE. And this deep power in which we exist, and whose beatitude is all accessible to us, is not only self-sufficing and perfect in every hour, but the act of seeing and the thing seen, the seer and the spectacle, the subject and the object, are one" (*E&L* 386).

In this unification, attended by a Wordsworthian "wise silence" and "deep power," Emerson follows Coleridge's analytical unification of the objective and subjective, which coalesce in the experiential act of knowledge itself, when they become "coinstantaneous and one" (*BL* 1:254–62). Emerson's healing of dismemberment and "division," the relocation "within man" of the "soul of the whole," also recalls the Coleridgean distinction between the "intuition of things which arises when we possess ourselves, as one with the whole," and the alienated state in which "we think of ourselves as separated beings, and place nature in antithesis to the mind, as object to subject, thing to thought, death to life" (*F* 1:520).

The man chosen to effect the required healing and reintegration was, Coleridge believed, Wordsworth—who, of course, concurred in his friend's judgment. Indeed, the words just cited from "The Over-Soul" are as Wordsworthian as they are Coleridgean. Less rhapsodic than *Nature*'s epiphany of the transparent eyeball, in which "the currents of the Universal Being circulate through me; I am part or particle of God" (*E&L* 10), this passage from "The Over-Soul"—with its integration of seer and spectacle, subject and object, knower and known, thing and thought—seems another, and linguistically closer, version of the sublime passage of "Tintern Abbey" evoking that mysterious "presence," or "something," or *primum movens,* that dwells everywhere, including "the mind of man." This dynamic spirit, at once inner and universal, permeating and giving quasi-divine life to the whole interrelated cosmos, never attained more glorious poetic expression than in these celebrated lines that haunted the Transcendentalists, and Emerson more than most. They are worth placing in context. Though he has lost much, says Wordsworth, namely, the "aching joys" and "dizzy raptures" of youth, he will not "mourn nor murmur," believing that "other gifts have followed; for such loss, I would believe, / Abundant recompense."

For I have learned
To look on nature, not as in the hour
Of thoughtless youth; but hearing oftentimes
The still, sad music of humanity,
Nor harsh, nor grating, though of ample power
To chasten and subdue. And I have felt
A presence that disturbs me with the joy
Of elevated thoughts; a sense sublime
Of something far more deeply interfused,
Whose dwelling is the light of setting suns,
And the round ocean and the living air,
And the blue sky, and in the mind of man:
A motion and a spirit, that impels
All thinking things, all objects of all thought,
And rolls through all things.
(84–102; *WP* 1:360)

In submitting ourselves to this indispensable passage, as in reading the Emerson of *Nature,* "The Poet," and "The Over-Soul" (or, for that matter, such German Romantics as Schiller and Schelling, and even the Hegel of *The Phenomenology of Mind* and *The Lectures on the Philosophy of Religion*), we, too, are made to "feel" a "presence" and "motion": an organic, dynamic, harmonious, animating force that permeates the universe, including the human mind—as Wordsworth, influenced by Coleridge, emphasizes no less than Kant before him, and Emerson after him. Nevertheless, *as* thinkers, not just feelers, questioners engaged in the definitional analysis Coleridgean Emerson often reduces to the hackwork of the mere understanding, or Carlylean Emerson sometimes dismisses as diseased inquiry, we may find ourselves asking *precisely what* is being affirmed at this sublime moment of unity and transport. Is it pantheism, "panentheism," or, as Coleridge insisted a quarter century later, rendering his "*Semi*-atheist" friend of 1798 retroactively orthodox, nothing less than the idea of "Divine Omnipresence"?

But because Wordsworth is here deliberately vague and syntactically unparseable, that mysterious "something far more deeply interfused" remains, as the poet doubtless intended it should, resistant to *any* attempt at definitional limitation.[27] Some will wish to dismiss it all (and this is at

27. The extraordinary syntax of the sublime passage in "Tintern Abbey" has been analyzed in William Empson, *Seven Types of Ambiguity,* 151–54, and by the linguist H. G. Widdowson, in *Stylistics and the Teaching of Literature,* 43–45, 61–62. Empson's

the heart of condescension toward Emerson as well) as prescientific or prephilosophical intuitionalism, subjective ecstasy at the expense of conceptual comprehension: the familiar Romantic elevation of "feeling" over "thinking." Wordsworth's very vagueness, this nebulous if majestic "sense sublime," may have caused Emerson to rank that "favorite poem with the public" lower than certain books of *The Excursion* and some of the sonnets, a judgment, he reports, with which Wordsworth concurred (*E&L* 777). But the same qualities may have enhanced the passage's appeal to Emerson, whose own position, even before the Divinity School Address, certainly seemed like the very pantheism he had once deplored in Wordsworth.

But is he any more a "philosopher" than Wordsworth? Resistant to "system," Emerson himself spoke of his incapacity for methodical writing, his preference for a more poetic, or "fluxional," utterance, and, as we have seen, Nietzsche regretted losing him as a genuine philosopher. For the most part, Emerson seems a sublime prose poet, a mythmaker to be read as we read Blake or, at their most sublime in their poetry, Wordsworth and Coleridge. Thus, although it is a distortion of Emerson, as it long was of Nietzsche, to seize on his poetic, dialectical, aphoristic, and often ludic brilliance as a stylist to deny him the capacity for philosophic thought, it is no less a misreading to seek system, and to become dismissive, irritated, even furious when we fail to find it—as William Empson *almost* does with Wordsworth, responding to the *poetic* power of the sublime passage of "Tintern Abbey," even as he condemns its "loose rhetoric" and theological, philosophical "shuffling." Still, though he was hardly Coleridge's intellectual equal, Wordsworth is not averse to thinking. To some, the sublime passage of "Tintern Abbey" may seem Romantic afflatus, vague "feeling." But should we simply dismiss as *un*thinking the climactic epistemological emphasis on the mind of man, on the Kantian-Coleridgean dialectic between "all thinking things, all objects of all thought"?

Whatever tentative conclusion we reach, few can doubt the importance of these lines to Emerson, and especially to *Nature.* It is no wonder that Samuel Osgood, author of a perceptive 1837 review of *Nature*—a review noting the "strong hold" of "Coleridge and Wordsworth" on Emerson's among other contemporary minds—should have chosen as his epigraph most of the "sublime" passage (he quoted lines 88–102), or that Emerson

---

analysis, which first appeared in 1930, has, he admits in a footnote in the later edition (153n), been disliked by the critics for its "meanness and fussiness." But as much as he admires the passage as poetry, he still finds Wordsworth's expression of his doctrine ("as much pantheism as would not shock his readers") a matter of "shuffling" and "loose rhetoric."

himself excerpted even more of it (lines 88–109) for *Parnassus.*[28] The connection with *Nature,* as with "The Over-Soul," especially the passage quoted above, is obvious enough. And although, in his essay "The Poet," Emerson was, in effect, prophesying the bard who would soon appear in the form of Walt Whitman, and claiming "I look in vain for the poet whom I describe," it is hard to imagine these lines of Wordsworth *not* resonating in the rolling sublimity of Emerson's evocation of his ideal poet, not a man of mere "talents," but a "genius," a "winged man" through whom "the ethereal tides . . . roll and circulate , . . . then is he caught up into the life of the Universe, his speech is thunder" (*E&L* 450, 452, 459). From the sublimities of "Tintern Abbey," Emerson, with that last metaphor, has in effect turned to Coleridge on Wordsworth: "Quem quoties lego, no verba mihi videor audire, sed tonitrua" (Whenever I read him, it seems to me not words that I hear, but thunder [*F* 1:182]).[29] But Emerson has reason, as Robert Weisbuch has cogently observed, to be mute about Coleridge and Wordsworth, especially this aspect of power and interfusion with the Universe; as he says of *Nature,* though there is a "compelling" and "compelled," personal and national, reason for the silence, Emerson's own "sense of a dynamic, flowing universe, and of a commerce between nature, mind, and God all secure a New England home for a transplanted romanticism."[30]

28. Osgood, "Emerson's *Nature,*" 385; Emerson, *Parnassus,* 29. Osgood stresses Emerson's Christian position as well as his Romanticism—the latter allied with his opposition to "practical" men (bankers, railroad executives), who exploit nature with no appreciation of either its "intrinsic" or its "emblematic character" (387)—that is to say, men of mere understanding. The author of the *most* perceptive contemporary review of *Nature* also quoted Wordsworth at the outset—in that case, the sixth stanza of "Expostulation and Reply," ending with the celebrated advocacy of "a wise passiveness." See Elizabeth Palmer Peabody's "Nature—a Prose Poem" (reprinted in *EPP* 590–97).

29. Though Coleridge was here referring not to Wordsworth's poetry, but to the prose of his *Convention at Cintra* pamphlet, Emerson in an 1831 journal entry applied Coleridge's Latin phrase to one of his favorite Wordsworth poems, "Character of the Happy Warrior." He was not alone in recalling Coleridge's image. Later in *The Friend,* a letter to the editor (signed "Mathetes" ["Learner"], written by John Wilson and Alexander Blair), concurred in Coleridge's praise of Wordsworth: the times require a teacher, and "of one such teacher who has been given to our own age, you have described the power when you said, that in his annunciation of truths he seemed to speak in thunders. I believe that mighty voice has not been poured out in vain: that there are hearts that have received into their inmost depths all its varying tones: and that even now [1818], there are many to whom the name of WORDSWORTH calls up the recollection of their weakness, and the consciousness of their strength" (*F* 1:387). Wordsworth responded—importantly and at length—to this letter (*F* 1:388–405).

30. Weisbuch, "Post-colonial Emerson," 206.

❧ Though Emerson speaks in "The Over-Soul" of an influx of "alien *energy*" at those moments when we are in a state of quiet, suspended receptivity, the thrust of these passages is from energy toward quiescence and what Wordsworth calls in his comment on the Boy of Winander episode "tranquillizing images." Later in *The Prelude,* Wordsworth illuminates this climactic emphasis on Nature's tranquillity as well as his famous definition of poetry as "emotion recollected in tranquillity," while retaining the original excitement. Book 12 of the 1805 *Prelude* (book 13 in 1850) opens with a celebration of nature as the source of both "emotion" and "calmness," gifts of reciprocal "peace and excitation" that lead, when "unsought," to a "happy stillness of the mind":

> From Nature doth emotion come, and moods
> Of calmness equally are Nature's gift:
> This is her glory—these two attributes
> Are sister horns that constitute her strength;
> This twofold influence is the sun and shower
> Of all her bounties, both in origin
> And end alike benignant. Hence it is
> That genius, which exists by interchange
> Of peace and excitation, finds in her
> His best and purest friend—from her receives
> That energy by which he seeks the truth,
> Is rouzed, aspires, grasps, struggles, wishes, craves
> From her that happy stillness of the mind
> Which fits him to receive it when unsought.
> (*P* [1805], 12:1–14)

Wordsworth is doubtless intellectually indebted to Coleridge's philosophic conversation about Genius and the dynamic polarity between energy and rest, this "interchange / Of peace and excitation." But whereas Coleridge increasingly couched these distinctions and finally interrelated polarities in the prose later pored over by Emerson, for whom "each thing is a half and suggests another thing to make it whole; as . . . motion, rest" (*E&L* 287), it was Wordsworth who became their principal *poetic* spokesman. In an 1827 note Emerson, perhaps locating the *literary* "source" of what would become the Over-Soul's "stream whose source is hidden," recalls "a poet represented as listening in pious silence 'To hear the mighty stream of Tendency.'" He is recalling the elevated tranquillity of age praised by Wordsworth's Wanderer in the opening speech of the final book of *The Excursion.* Upon such a man, unlike those doomed "To run the giddy round of vain delight, / Or fret and labour on the Plain below," may be conferred

> Fresh power to commune with the invisible world,
> And hear the mighty stream of tendency
> Uttering, for elevation of our thought,
> A clear sonorous voice, inaudible
> To the vast multitude....
>
> (*E* 9:86–92)

Alluding as well to the obscure "intimations" of the Great Ode, Emerson, emulating in youth the piety of Wordsworth in age, goes on in this note to praise the "wisdom" of the Wanderer's words: "We may learn much, a practised ear may learn more of the counsels & operations of Providence by watching with pious curiosity the obscure intimations of design that[,] coming from every corner tho' slight in particulars[,] bear a mighty Confederate testimony to His being & character" (*JMN* 3:80–81). In that earlier and less orthodox Wordsworthian version of quiet listening and watching in man's interaction with nature, the Boy of Winander (a younger Wordsworth himself), benefiting from the bountiful interchange between the receptive self and the external world, receives as a gift—"Unawares" and with a gentle shock of mild "surprise"—that happy "stillness of the mind" that comes from Nature when most "unsought."

Magnificent even in isolation, the Boy of Winander passage, in context, constitutes Wordsworth's dramatic contrast to the narrow and restricted modern education, which, neglecting a receptive and energizing intercourse with the natural world, and its twofold influence, produces a "monster birth," a grotesque "prodigy," a deprived and shrunken "dwarf child" (*P* 5:293–363). Such a deformed child is the victim of educational "experts" whom Wordsworth finds infernal—as is revealed by his extended allusion to *Paradise Lost* in book 5 of *The Prelude.* Our modern practitioners of supposedly "enlightened" systematic education—"These mighty workmen of our later age," those workmen "Who, with a broad highway have *overbridged* / The froward *chaos* of futurity" (*P* 5:347–49; italics added)—have their demonic precursors in Milton's Satanic architects, the bridge builders Sin and Death, referred to in book 3 and, most relevantly, in book 10 of *Paradise Lost.* In Milton's cosmic geography, the vexed gulf between Hell and Earth is "Chaos," spanned by a bridge, a "ridge of pendent rock," of "length prodigious" anchored to the base of Hell and fastened "with pins of adamant / And chains" (*PL* 10:313–19). The terrible sense of perdurable inflexibility, of mechanical restriction, is caught by Wordsworth in his description of the "pinfold" to which students are confined, young victims of systematic education "fenced round" by these "Wardens of our faculties," "watchful men" who would control "All accidents, and to the very road / Which they have fashioned," that overbridging highway, "would confine us down / Like engines" (*P* 5:355–58).

In "The American Scholar" Emerson says of "the book, . . . the college, the institution of any kind," "They pin me down" (*E&L* 57–58). In "History," universalizing his own painful personal experiences as the slowest (aside from poor Bulkeley) of the children of a father who seems to have been as tyrannical an educational taskmaster as the father of John Stuart Mill, Emerson deplores the "cramping influence of a hard formalist on a young child in repressing his spirits and courage, paralyzing the understanding, and that without producing indignation, but only fear and obedience, and even much sympathy with the tyranny." When he grows up, the child sees that the tyrant-educator was himself a former victim of authoritarianism. The enlightened man sees "the oppressor of his youth is himself a child tyrannized over by those names and words and forms, of whose influence he was merely the organ to the youth" (*E&L* 250). In "Self-Reliance," Emerson uses the same cramping language in attacking educators who allow their classifications to become "idolized" by their pupils, systematizers whose own confining "walls" they mistake for "the walls of the universe." Such masters cannot imagine how we self-reliant ones "have any right to see" on our own, indeed how we "can" see. We must, goes the accusation, have stolen "the light" from them, the systematizers, who "do not yet perceive, that light, unsystematic, indomitable, will break into any cabin, even into theirs. Let them chirp awhile and call it their own. If they are honest and do well, presently their neat new pinfold will be too strait and low, will crack, will lean, will rot and vanish, and the immortal light, all young and joyful, million-orbed, million-colored, will beam over the universe as on the first morning" (*E&L* 277).

Wordsworth, prophet of the "master light of all our seeing," would applaud. But the obstacles are formidable, and the prospects are often less light than dark, less open than imprisoning. Once these false educational premises are enforced, there seems to be almost no possibility of escape. The very "discourse" of such a systematically educated "prodigy" inevitably "moves slow, / Massy and ponderous as a prison door" (*P* [1805], 5:320–21). This curious image, though later dropped by Wordsworth, links the "dwarf child" of book 5 with the "pigmy" child of the Intimations Ode, whose "whole vocation" is "endless imitation," and, especially, with the rather startling intrusion of the prison image in stanza 5 of the ode: "Shades of the prison-house begin to close / Upon the growing boy." Wordsworth may be recalling the "straitened," contracted condition of Milton's fallen angels at the end of book 1 of *Paradise Lost.* They had seemed until their fall gigantic. "Now less than smallest Dwarfs, in narrow room" confined, they resemble a "Pigmean Race" (*PL* 1:776–80). In any case, the prison-house image in the ode is just one of many similar images associated in both Wordsworth and Coleridge with unnatural, imprisoning systems of education.[31] Just as Satan had usurped divine prerogatives, and with the help of his demonic architects imperiled Eden, so the sinister "wardens" of systematic education have usurped the maternal and educational role of our true teacher, Nature, leaving the child deprived, while a nurturing

> Earth is grieved to find
> The playthings which her love designed for him
> Unthought of—in their woodland beds the flowers
> Weep, and the river-sides are all forlorn.

While he never read these lines (confined to the 1805 version of *The Prelude,* 5:346–49), Emerson was of course familiar with related lines written at the same time (ca. February 1804). In the sixth stanza of the Intimations Ode, Earth fills her maternal lap with pleasures designed to console her foster child for the lost glories of eternity. Here, in the 1805 *Prelude,* she is grieved to find those proffered pleasures neglected, her woodland flowers and riversides left forlorn. This is the bitter fruit of a misguided, tyrannical system of education that produces pedantic prodigies rather than vital children, "scholars" that anatomize and botanize rather than love Nature, Emerson's "beautiful mother," for whom he professes, even in the "Idealism" chapter of *Nature,* "a child's love" (*E&L* 38). Providing we understand where the final supremacy lies, love is the key to "man's connection with nature."

> But these young scholars, who invade our hills,
> Bold as the engineer who fells the wood,
> And travelling often in the cut he makes,
> Love not the flower they pluck, and know it not,
> And all their botany is Latin names.

This is Emerson, in "Blight" (*EPP* 454–55), a blank-verse poem of 1843 that reads in part like a palinode on the "Commodity" chapter of

31. Attacking the methods of educator Joseph Lancaster, Coleridge (in an 1808 lecture) compared harsh and humiliating discipline of students to "fear of Newgate" and "horror at the thought of a slave ship!" (*CN* 3:3291n). Recalling the latter comparison, Wordsworth, four years later, described the establishment of the more humane Bell-system schools as, "with the exception of the abolition of the slave trade, the most happy event of our times." In 1807, the year the slave trade was abolished, Coleridge ended a notebook poem titled "Coeli Enarrant" with the literally striking image of "a child beneath its master's" blow, who "Shrills out at once its task and its affright." Such images may clarify apparent "intrusions" in greater works: *The Prelude* begins with the poet's own escape "from a house of bondage," a "prison where he hath been long immured" (1:7–8); the ocean, calmed beneath the moon in *The Ancient Mariner,* is "Still as a slave before his Lord"; in the Great Ode, Immortality broods over the Child (in a simile criticized by Coleridge) like "a master o'er a slave." See Foakes, "'Thriving Prisoners': Coleridge, Wordsworth, and the Child at School."

Nature. These lines (18–22), and what follows, recall "Nutting," in which the penitent Wordsworthian speaker, having "ravaged" a virginal forest nook bearing no previous "sign / Of devastation," admonishes us to

> move along these shades
> In gentleness of heart; with gentle hand
> Touch—for there is a spirit in the woods.
> (54–56; *WP* 1:369)

Emerson catches, even more directly, the contempt expressed, in Wordsworth's "Poet's Epitaph," for the cold "Philosopher! a fingering slave," one that would "peep and botanize / Upon his mother's grave" (*WP* 1: 396). No connection with nature is possible for the botanizing "young scholars" of "Blight"; in such loveless circumstances, the very elements

> haughtily return us stare for stare.
> For we invade them impiously for gain;
> We devastate them unreligiously,
> And coldly ask their pottage, not their love.
> Therefore they shove us from them, yield to us
> Only what to our griping toil is due;
> But the sweet affluence of love and song,
> The rich results of the divine consents
> Of man and earth, of world beloved and lover,
> The nectar and ambrosia, are withheld;
> And in the midst of spoils and slaves, we thieves
> And pirates of the universe, shut out
> Daily to a more thin and outward rind,
> Turn pale and starve.
> (36–49; *EPP* 455)

Emerson's mentor, Wordsworth—whose "fingering slave," a cold analyst asleep in his "intellectual crust," is "an ever-dwindling soul"—would certainly have approved of this account of the ecological and moral blight that follows when vision has gone awry, when we cannot perceive that there is a spirit in the woods. Even in "A Poet's Epitaph," the Wordsworth poem closest to "Blight," man's supremacy to nature is never in doubt. But the relationship remains, in the language of "Blight," a "sweet affluence of love and song," a bond of earthly "beloved" and human "lover," a wedding without which we starve. "I count the genius of Swedenborg and Wordsworth as the agents of a reforming philosophy," notes Emerson, "the bringing poetry back to Nature,—to the marrying of Nature and mind, undoing the old divorce in which poetry had been famished and false, and Nature had been suspected and pagan" (*W* 8:66). We must be receptive to Nature, which, in turn, becomes absorbed into her human lover. What Wordsworth calls the "dwindling" of the soul occurs when the invading and loveless scholars replace "The harvest of a quiet eye / That broods and sleeps on [man's] own heart." Such a man of quiet power "murmurs near the running brooks / A music sweeter than their own" and views "the outward show of sky and earth, / Of hill and valley," while "impulses of deeper birth / Have come to him in solitudes" ("A Poet's Epitaph," 39–52). Those shut out from the cultivation of such intuitive "impulses" are said to be "smooth-rubbed" souls to which no "form or feeling" can "cling" because they have been subjected to an education that produces, instead of an integrated human being, "a reasoning, self-sufficing thing, / An intellectual All-in-all" (30–32; *WP* 1:396–97).

Such a bloodless specimen, denied the "harvest" of the quiet eye and the quasi-divine "nectar and ambrosia" attending the marriage of man and earth, reduced to the thin sustenance of nature's "outward rind," must necessarily "Turn pale and starve," a deprived and famished form reflecting what Emerson follows Wordsworth in considering a confined and confining education overemphasizing "tuition" at the expense of intuitive, instinctual intercourse with nature. The latter is precisely what Wordsworth embodies in the Boy of Winander and in the "curious child" whom the Wanderer describes applying to his ear the seashell to which "in silence hushed, his very soul / Listened intensely."

Unmediated communion with Nature is most fully represented in the Wanderer himself, the chief figure of *The Excursion* and the character in whom Wordsworth concentrated most of his own thoughts and feelings. The Wanderer, he told Isabella Fenwick, was what he himself would have been "had I been born in a class which would have deprived me of what is called a liberal education" (*WP* 2:952). By now we recognize the irony in that "*deprived*" and "what is *called*. . ." Since this characteristic, if provisional, dismissal of "tuition" includes both Wordsworth's years at Cambridge and, more generally, the inevitable influence upon him of reading, it is worth noting that the Wanderer, in consoling the Solitary in the pivotal fourth book, in fact *includes* books, these sources of hoarded "truth," among those consolations:

> books are yours,
> Within whose silent chambers treasure lies
> Preserved from age to age; more precious far
> Than that accumulated store of gold
> And orient gems, which, for a day of need,
> The sultan hides deep in ancestral tombs.
>
> (*E* 4:564–69)

The echo here of Milton's description of a good book as the precious lifeblood of a master spirit "treasured up on purpose to a life beyond life" (in *Areopagitica*) might remind us of the reading Wordsworth attributes to the Wanderer when he was a boy. Back in book 1, we learned that "while yet a child, with a child's eagerness," that boy did not fail "Incessantly to turn his ear and eye / On all things which the moving seasons brought"; that, as an adolescent, sitting in caves and "in the hollow depths of naked crags," he traced in their "fixed lineaments" an "ebbing and a flowing mind / Expression ever-varying!"; and that, "Thus informed, / He had small need of books" (149–62). Nevertheless, he did read imaginative romances and, most significantly, saved enough hard-earned money to buy a volume he had seen in the reading stalls, "the book that had most tempted his desires." Now, "Among the hills / He gazed upon that mighty orb of song, / The divine Milton" (247–50).

Predictably, he is reading *in* Nature, among the hills. Still, it was not for their celebration of ageless and precious wisdom treasured up between leather covers that the Wanderer's speeches in book 4 of *The Excursion* were revered by perceptive readers on both sides of the Atlantic. They included, in the United States, Emerson, his aunt Mary, and his young friend, the poet Jones Very, and, in England, Charles Lamb, Keats, and John Ruskin. Along with the Intimations Ode, book 4 of *The Excursion* was, for many of his contemporaries, this poet's crowning achievement, and what they were responding to was Wordsworth's most sustained exposition, through the speeches of the Wanderer, of the power of the human Imagination interacting directly with Nature, and, especially, of the superiority of the intuitive Reason to mere understanding. In his essay on the poem in the *Quarterly Review,* Charles Lamb singles out "the fourth book, entitled 'Despondency Corrected', . . . as the most valuable portion of the poem." He praises the Wanderer's speeches for their "moral grandeur," "wide scope of thought" and "lofty imagery," and cherishes his "tender personal appeals" to the despondent Solitary. Then, seizing on his friend Coleridge's central distinction, Lamb addresses what he rightly took to be the main theme of *The Excursion,* and the central target of the Wanderer's Wordsworthian assault: "The general tendency of the argument (which we might almost affirm to be the leading moral of the poem) is to abate the pride of the calculating *understanding,* and to reinstate the *imagination* and the *affections* in those seats from which modern philosophy has laboured but too successfully to expel them."[32]

32. Lamb, review of *The Excursion.* The text, with revisions by the *Quarterly* editor, William Gifford, is reprinted in *Lamb as Critic,* 197. Though Coleridge was in many ways disappointed by *The Excursion,* above all because it was not *The Recluse,* he did

There is no place here to closely examine the Wanderer's speeches—in the first and last books and, especially, in book 4, of *The Excursion*—on the intuitive interaction of the human mind and spirit with the natural world. But we have already looked into *The Prelude,* specifically Wordsworth's attack on institutional educators as the *worst examples* of that "modern philosophy" and "calculating *understanding*" that would alienate us from Nature and from our own affections and intuitive impulses of deeper birth. "When," asks Wordsworth in book 5 of *The Prelude,* will these deformers and shrivelers of the young, these presumptuous "teachers"—hyperrational and ever watchful, niggardly and unnatural—themselves be taught, and come to "learn"

> That in the unreasoning progress of the world
> A wiser Spirit is at work for us,
> A better eye than theirs, most prodigal
> Of blessings, and most studious of our good,
> Even in what seem our most unfruitful hours?
> (*P* 5:359–64)

With these final lines, which lead directly to the Boy of Winander episode, Wordsworth returns us to the dialogue poems from *Lyrical Ballads,* where Milton again figures. We can best approach those poems—gnomic dramatizations of the polarity between intuition and tuition, wise passiveness and restless activity—by establishing a context provided, first, by Coleridge, then by the opening book of *The Prelude.*

---

admire much that was in it. Writing to Lady Beaumont on April 3, 1815, he said that "proofs meet me in every part of *The Excursion* that the poet's genius has not flagged," indeed that "one half of the number of its Beauties would make all the beauties of all his Contemporary Poets collectively mount to the balance" (*CL* 4:564).

Chapter 7

Passivity and Activity

There are evidently two powers at work, which relatively to each other are active and passive, and this is not possible without an intermediate faculty, which is at once active and passive.

—SAMUEL TAYLOR COLERIDGE, *Biographia Literaria*

The regular course of studies, the years of academical and professional education, have not yielded me better facts than some idle books under the bench at the Latin school. What we do not call education is more precious than that which we call so.

—RALPH WALDO EMERSON, "Spiritual Laws"

I do not judge men by anything they can do. Their greatest deed is the impression they make on me. Some serene, inactive men can do everything.

—HENRY DAVID THOREAU, *Journal,* 1840

In the hollow vale,
Hollow and green, he lay on the green turf
In pensive idleness.

—THE WANDERER as a Boy, *The Excursion*

By way of preamble to exploring the productive tension between apparent idleness and creative power, between the passive and the active, as played out in the opening book of *The Prelude,* we might take up two

Coleridgean texts offering memorable examples of negative passivity and of that very different "passive motion" that is an integral part of progression. The two examples, both from chapter 7 of *Biographia Literaria,* had a demonstrable impact on Yeats and registered as well with Emerson. In a passage of "Circles" replete (as we saw in Chapter 5) with unattributed allusions to Coleridge, Emerson speaks of a loss of creative power, a passive, negative "ebb," or "dreary vacuity," that reduces the godlike self to impotent insignificance: "I am a weed by the wall" (*E&L* 406). Negative passivity, one of the "necessary consequences of the Hartleian theory of associationism," reduces us, exclaims an even more indignant Coleridge, to "the mere quicksilver plating behind a looking-glass; and in this alone consists the poor worthless I!" (*BL* 1:119). Yeats, who would later influentially contrast passive mechanical mimesis to Romantic organic creativity in terms of "the mirror and the lamp," inserted at this point in his copy of the *Biographia* a small piece of paper on which he wrote, "plating behind a looking glass," and in correspondence with a friend deplored the turning of the "mind . . . into the quicksilver at the back of the mirror." He finally went public in his essay on George Berkeley: "Something compels me to reject whatever—to borrow a metaphor of Coleridge's—drives mind into the quicksilver."[1]

He went even more memorably public in a late poem that amounts to a sustained response to Coleridge's example from nature a few pages later in this seventh chapter. Dramatizing passive-active contraries producing systolic-diastolic progression, Coleridge describes

> a small water-insect on the surface of rivulets [and how] the little animal *wins* its way up against the stream by alternate pulses of active and passive motion, now resisting the current, and now yielding to it in order to gather strength and a momentary *fulcrum* for a further propulsion. This is no unapt emblem of the mind's self-experience in the act of thinking. There are evidently two powers at work, which relatively to each other are active and passive, and this is not possible without an intermediate faculty, which is at once active and passive.

And he quickly adds that this faculty is, "in philosophical language, . . . the IMAGINATION" (*BL* 1:124), also described in *The Statesman's Manual* as "that reconciling and mediatory power," the creative crux between sensory apprehension and active thought (*LS* 29).

1. Yeats inserted the piece of paper at p. 57 of his (the 1876) edition of *BL.* See Yeats, *A Descriptive Catalog of W. B. Yeats's Library,* item 401. For the letter to the friend, see Yeats, *W. B. Yeats and T. Sturge Moore: Their Correspondence, 1901–1937,* 67; and, for the public pronouncement, see Yeats, *Essays and Introductions,* 407.

Emerson's response, incorporating Coleridge's "momentary fulcrum," came in journal entries. "A fact is only a fulcrum of the spirit. It is the terminus of a past thought but only a means now to new sallies of the imagination & new progress of wisdom," and again, this time with emphasis on the contraction-expansion polarity between private inactivity and public activism: one who seems "quite withdrawn into himself" may be "hiving knowledge & concentrating powers to act well hereafter" (*JMN* 5:177; 4: 368). Yeats's approving response came in the form of "Long-legged Fly," a poem imaginatively expanding on Coleridge's emblem of the mind in the process of thinking. Yeats offers three historical examples of civilization-altering figures in moments of quiet, creative reverie: Julius Caesar in his war tent, "His eye fixed upon nothing, / A hand under his head"; a youthful Helen of Troy, quietly dancing, lost in reverie in "a lonely place"; Michelangelo, in a trancelike state, almost spontaneously producing *The Creation of Man* on the Sistine Chapel ceiling, his hand moving "to and fro" with "no more sound than the mice make." Though Michelangelo is actually painting, all three dramatic vignettes are essentially illustrative of silent, momentary repose, or wise passivity, as a component of creative "new sallies," a dialectical process in which, "Like a long-legged fly upon the stream, / [The] mind moves upon silence." Thus, as Emerson says, "a silent thought" can inaugurate an epoch. One of his most memorable versions of the dialectic between repose and action occurs in "Self-Reliance." "Power," he asserts, "ceases in the instant of repose." But that cessation is, dialectically, preparation, since power "resides in the moment of transition from a past to a new state, in the shooting of a gulf, in the darting to an aim" (*E&L* 271). Thus, repose and action (shooting, darting) are not opposed "negatives" but Blakean "contraries," and, as dialectical Blake tells us in plate 3 of *The Marriage of Heaven and Hell,* "without Contraries is no progression."[2]

Equivalent to intuitive Reason, Coleridge's capitalized IMAGINATION, the intermediate and reconciling power in the water-insect passage, reveals opposing forces—which the merely logical and reductive faculty of understanding perceives as a simple, contradictory dualism—to be interrelated parts of a larger and dynamic unity. In the important essay "Nature," in *Essays: Second Series,* Emerson follows Spinoza, Bacon, Schelling, and—most directly—Coleridge (*BL* 1:240–41) in distinguishing, as Averroës first had, between "*natura naturata,* nature passive," and *natura naturans,* nature active, protean, volatile, creative. This Emerson calls "the Efficient

2. Blake, *Poetry and Prose of Blake,* 34. For "Long-Legged Fly," see *W. B. Yeats: The Poems,* 339.

Nature, *natura naturans,* the quick cause, before which all forms flee as the driven snows, itself secret, its work driven before it in flocks and multitudes" (*E&L* 546). Despite the immediate and unexpected linguistic homage here to Shelley—"Mont Blanc" and the opening movement of the "Ode to the West Wind"—Emerson continues to pay primary homage to Coleridgean polarity by subdividing *natura naturans* into two apparently opposing but actually interdependent properties. Because we bring to every experiment the "innate universal laws" that reveal the "whole" underlying diverse "particulars," we can unriddle nature's "secrets." There are two. "Motion or change, and identity or rest, are the first and second secrets of nature," says Emerson. This polarity, the "whole code of her laws," constitutes Coleridgean simultaneity-within-difference, or Wordsworthian rest-within-motion, for nature, says Emerson, modulating from plain to high style,

> has but one stuff,—but one stuff with two ends, to serve up all her dream-like variety. Compound it how she will, star, sand, fire, water, tree, man, it is still one stuff, and betrays the same properties. . . . The uneasiness which the thought of our helplessness in the chain of causes occasions us, results from our looking too much at one condition of nature, namely, Motion. But the drag is never taken from the wheel. Wherever the impulse exceeds, the Rest or Identity insinuates its compensation. (*E&L* 546–47, 554)

By this time, the 1840s, Emerson was reading (along with his beloved Goethe) the newly translated German theorists of *Naturphilosophie,* as well as reading and often conversing with prominent Anglo-American biologists and geologists.[3] Thus, in "Experience," when he says that we, like all of nature, live "by pulses," he is, of course, not thinking exclusively of Coleridgean dialectic and of Wordsworthian reciprocal impulses from the self and from the vernal wood. Nevertheless, Emerson's abiding mentors when it comes to the pulsations at the crux of both natural and mental processes remain—along with Goethe—Coleridge and a Wordsworth intellectually influenced by Coleridge. The mental polarity or antagonism in Coleridge, as in his German precursors, Goethe and Kant and Schelling, is between the natural and the ideal, the objective and the subjective, the surface and the "ulterior consciousness," each constituting "one of the two Polar Sciences," which are, says Coleridge, to be brought together at "their equatorial point," resulting in "a total and undivided philosophy" (*BL* 1:282). And the "first principle" of such a philosophic system is "to

3. For details, see William Rossi, "Emerson, Nature, and Natural Science," 136, 149n89.

render the mind intuitive of the *spiritual* in man (i.e., of that which lies *on the other side* of our natural consciousness)" (*BL* 1:243).

All undulating roads, all polarities, lead back to "the *spiritual* in man," apprehensible by the intuitive Reason. But the pulsations and polarities remain to dominate both the natural and the intellectual worlds. Combining science with the Romantic-Transcendental preference of intuition to the calculations of mere understanding, Emerson says, "Nature hates calculators; her methods are salutary and impulsive. Man lives by pulses; our organic movements are such; and the chemical and ethereal agents are undulatory and alternate; and the mind goes antagonizing on, and never prospers but by fits" (*E&L* 483).

The pulsation that initiates *The Prelude* is that of the inspiring wind, or *spiritus*—later described as "Nature's self, which is the breath of God" (*P* 5:221). That *spiritus* is invoked in the opening line—"O there is a blessing in this gentle breeze"—a breeze that "beats" against the poet's cheek almost like his own heartbeat and is endowed with feeling by the poet himself; it "seems half-conscious of the joy it brings." Thirty lines later, this rising breeze provokes "within / A correspondent breeze" that becomes "a tempest," a superabundant "energy, / Vexing its own creation" (*P* 1:33–38). In this reciprocity of breezes within and without ("Whether from *breath of outward* circumstance, / Or from the Soul—an *impulse to herself,*" as Wordsworth puts it in the "Prospectus" to *The Recluse*), the poet seems at once harp and wind. These oscillating impulses, replicated in the duality of the breeze, capture the whole dynamic between Wordsworthian freedom and labor.

In his well-known essay "The Correspondent Breeze," M. H. Abrams, tracing that prominent Romantic metaphor, notes that "air-in-motion"—whether as "breeze or breath, mind or respiration"—is not only a "property of the landscape, but also a vehicle for radical changes in the poet's mind." Though this venerable metaphor is hardly unique to the Romantics, there is, as Abrams says, "no precedent for the way in which the symbolic wind was called upon by poet after poet, in poem after poem, all in the first few decades of the nineteenth century." And not only in well-ventilated poems. "The Over-Soul," in Emerson's essay of that title, "can inspire whom it will, and behold! their speech shall be lyrical and sweet, and universal as the rising of the wind" (*E&L* 386). Abrams quotes this passage and, of course, both the "Ode to the West Wind" and *The Defence of Poetry*—on creative mental states subject to impressions likened by Shelley to "the alternations of an ever-changing wind over an Aeolian lyre which move it by their motion to ever-changing melody." Abrams does not cite two late poems ("The Harp" and "Maiden Speech of the Aeolian Harp") by

Emerson, who, though not particularly responsive to music, loved a wind harp given him as a gift. Oddly, Abrams also omits the one text both Shelley and Emerson, as well as Wordsworth, would have had in mind: Coleridge's "Eolian Harp," the poem that may, in its original (1795) version, have inaugurated this Romantic metaphor and whose undulatory alternations make it particularly germane to the present focus on passive-active polarities and pulsations in Wordsworth and Emerson.[4]

The strings of the wind harp in Coleridge's poem alternately are caressed by a "desultory breeze" or, "Boldlier swept," produce notes that "Over delicious surges sink and rise." At the prompting of the "breeze," the "mute still air" becomes (in the final "Keatsian" line of the famous passage inserted in 1817 beginning "O, the one Life within us and abroad") "Music slumbering on her instrument."[5] In two related moves, the harp is compared to the mind and the mind (more radically) to the diverse harps said to constitute the whole of harmonious nature—indeed, the consciousness of all living things, that "one Life" within us and abroad. Stretched out on a hillside at noon, "tranquil and mus[ing] upon tranquillity," the languid yet receptive poet experiences spontaneous thoughts, "many idle flitting fantasies" traversing his

> indolent and passive brain,
> As wild and various as the random gales
> That swell and flutter on this subject Lute!
> (38–43)

In the speculation that immediately follows (a sublimely pantheistic surmise shortly, and ominously if anticlimactically, to be checked by the reproving eye of his religiously orthodox fiancée), Coleridge hypothetically but audaciously identifies the indolent-active brain's response to the breeze with nature's own response to a mysterious and all-pervading force—a *spiritus* or *anima* that anticipates the deeply interfused "some-

4. Abrams, "The Correspondent Breeze: A Romantic Metaphor" (1960), in *Correspondent Breeze,* 25, 26, 41–42. In the 1972 "Coleridge's 'A Light in Sound,'" also printed in this collection (158–91), Abrams studies "The Eolian Harp," focusing, however, on the imagery of light rather than breeze. *The Defence of Poetry* is quoted from Shelley, *Shelley's Poetry and Prose,* 277.

5. Coleridge, "The Eolian Harp," 15, 19–20, 33–34 (*CPW* 1:101). In a historical anomaly, Keats's 1816 lines on poetry as "the supreme of power, / . . . might half slumb'ring on its own right arm" ("Sleep and Poetry," lines 236–37, p. 74) may have influenced a poem dated 1795! Coleridge visited the shop of his (and Keats's) publisher and perused the galleys of "Sleep and Poetry" *before* composing, and inserting into the revised version of "The Eolian Harp," the passage ending with "Music slumbering on her instrument." Reciprocally, Coleridge's windswept notes that "over delicious surges sink and rise" may reappear in the mournful music of the insects "borne aloft / Or sinking as the light wind lives or dies" in Keats's "To Autumn."

thing" that "rolls through all things," including "all thinking things," in "Tintern Abbey," as well as through such Emersonian prose texts as *Nature,* "The Over-Soul," and "The Poet":

> And what if all of animated nature
> Be but organic Harps diversely fram'd
> That tremble into thought as o'er them sweeps
> Plastic and vast, one intellectual breeze,
> At once the Soul of each, and God of all?
> (45–49)

That last phrase is one of the more notable appearances of the Coleridgean Each and All, that unified coupling that inspired Emerson in various ways—not least in his Coleridge-entitled poem, "Each and All," in which river and sky, sparrow-song and seashell, cannot be taken out of their context in nature, where "all are needed by each one; / Nothing is fair or good alone." The poem ends with the poet standing amid oaks and firs, pinecones and acorns, actively seeing and hearing yet finally passively yielding himself to the All:

> Over me soared the eternal sky,
> Full of light and of deity;
> And I saw, again I heard,
> The rolling river, the morning bird;—
> Beauty through my senses stole;
> I yielded myself to the perfect whole.
> (46–51; *EPP* 433)

The all-encompassing wind that plays upon us, the "one intellectual breeze" of "The Eolian Harp," recurs in two later poems in which Coleridge specifically responds to Wordsworth. In the Dejection Ode, his response to the then four-stanza fragment that would become the Intimations Ode, the wind that, at first, barely played "Upon the strings of this Aeolian lute" later becomes a "Mad Lutanist." Integrating mind, soul, and heart, and echoing and altering the final line of the Intimations Ode, Coleridge tells us—in the second poem, "To William Wordsworth" (*CPW* 1:403–8)—that his friend had dared to tell

> what within the mind
> By *vital breathings* secret as the soul
> Of vernal growth, oft quickens in the heart
> Thoughts all too deep for words.
> (8–11)

Toward the end of this poem, in which the auditing of another's words inspires creative hope in the auditor, Coleridge mingles reception and activity, along with breeze, stars, and sea. In "silence listening" to the recitation of Wordsworth's autobiographical epic,

My soul *lay passive,* by the various strain
Driven as in surges now beneath the stars,
With momentary stars *of my own birth,*
Fair constellated foam, still *darting off*
Into the darkness. . . .
(96–100; italics added)

This enactment of the rhythm between passive reception and active creation (Emerson may have echoed that "darting" in his own "shooting of a gulf, . . . darting to an aim" [*E&L* 271]) is particularly touching. Even more touching, indeed heartbreaking, is a letter of 1828. There, echoing his own earlier poems (and, as usual, Milton) along with the opening of Wordsworth's *Prelude,* Coleridge tells Lady Beaumont that, although he could never "resume Poetry," he still felt the old alternating pulsations, "air" in movement, the lulls and surges and swells of breeze and correspondent breeze:

Is the power extinct. No! No! As in a still summer Noon, when the lulled Air at irregular intervals wakes up with a startled *Hush-st,* that seems to re-demand the silence which it breaks, or heaves a long profound Sigh in its Sleep, and an Aeolian Harp has been left in the chink of the not quite shut Casement—even so—how often!—scarce a week of my Life shuffles by, that does not at some moment feel the spur of the old genial impulse—even so do there fall on my inward Ear swells, and broken snatches of sweet Melody, reminding me that I still have within me [that] which is both Harp and Breeze. (*CL* 6:73)[6]

"Lulled air" can be stirred into momentary life by the "spur of the old genial impulse." That "spur" echoes "Lycidas" on Fame, and "genial"—borrowed for "Tintern Abbey" by Wordsworth, who refuses to "suffer my genial spirits to decay"—reappears in Coleridge's Dejection Ode, where "My genial spirits fail." The ultimate source, cited by Coleridge himself in a 1797 letter to his publisher, Joseph Cottle (*CL* 1:319), in which he describes a deeply depressed, breezeless state, is *Samson Agonistes:* "I feel my genial spirits droop, / My hopes all flat . . ." (594–95). Though applied to

6. In a letter written a decade earlier, this time with a volcanic image and philosophy the explicit enemy of the Muse, the poetic impulse was also depicted as suppressed but not quite extinguished: "The Philosopher, tho' pressing with the weight of an Etna, cannot prevent the Poet from occasionally . . . manifesting his existence by smoke traversed by electric flashes from the Crater" (*CL* 4:879).

Shakespeare, Emerson's phrase "genial power" (*E&L* 711) probably has the same Miltonic lineage, filtered through Wordsworth and Coleridge.

In the letter to Lady Beaumont, Coleridge acknowledges that the breeze-stimulated reawakening can also seem "to re-demand the silence which it breaks." Emerson, too, is driven by more than "a single impulse," indolence *and* action, ebb *and* flow, release *and* responsibility, independence *and* obligation. His freedom is charged, as Milton's and Wordsworth's were, by a self-imposed and ambitious task, the need to prove oneself capable of accomplishing a heroic undertaking. The "world" was "all before" postlapsarian Adam and Eve," the "earth . . . all before" liberated but burdened Wordsworth; a whole "eternity" of conflicting impulses, the very "air" throbbing with provocations to indolence and action, "opens before" the American Adam and Orpheus: "The air . . . invites man with provoking indifference to total indolence and to immortal actions. . . . [T]he vast Eternity of capacity, of freedom, opens before you, but without a single impulse."

The divided impulses of indolence and activity that provoke Emerson and shape the opening pages of *The Prelude* are at the heart of the creative process, and they seem, in some sense, as Seamus Heaney says in describing Wordsworth's conception of the poetic act, peculiarly "feminine." Recently, three women waxed Wordsworthian in our most widely distributed magazines by calling for summer liberation for our children. In a 2004 issue of the *New York Times Magazine* focused entirely on "The Ever More Carefully Arranged, Artfully Blueprinted, Technologically Devised, Painstakingly Organized American Childhood," Melissa Fay Greene uses the example of ad hoc sandlot baseball to show how "hyper-scheduled, overachieving" kids still manage to have fun. "The outdoor lives of today's children—like their inner lives—have fallen to adult dictatorship," she argues. But although "vast tracts of children's lives" have been claimed by grownups, the "good news is that children—true to the spark of Tom Sawyer or Br'er Rabbit within them all—subvert adult designs at every opportunity." Writing in *Time* in 2003, in "Free the Children," Nancy Gibbs had also called for summer liberation from rules and schedules to enable children to develop "the gifts that freedom brings." Arguing that summer should be "a state of grace" and "a time when rules can be bent," she longs for her daughters "to have a whole summer" when they can play and "read for fun, even books that don't appear on the officially sanctioned summer reading list." Be "bored," she advises them, "and see where it takes you, because the imagination's dusty wilderness is worth crossing if you want to sculpt your soul." Memories of her own stretched summers persuade her that we ought to be "listening to all the warnings from social scientists about our Hurried Children who for the rest of the year wear their schedules like clothes that are too tight. The experts have long charted the growing stress and disappearing downtime of modern children," a trend that now "extends across class and region."[7]

Greene and Gibbs had been anticipated by a *Newsweek* "Last Word" essay titled "Doing Nothing Is Something," in which novelist and Pulitzer Prize–winning columnist Anna Quindlen speaks out more than nostalgically about the dangers of children being "systematically stunted by scheduling," and especially about the need for summer, which used to be "a time apart for kids, a respite from the clock and the copybook, the organized day." If "downtime cannot be squeezed during the school year into the life of the frantic and often joyless activity with which our children are saddled while their parents pursue frantic and often joyless activity of their own," and if the kind of summer she remembers is perhaps "gone for good," we have, she rightly believes, lost something of immense value, experiences that, in her own case, were "the making of me, as a human being and a writer," for downtime is "where we become ourselves." She concludes: "I don't believe you can write poetry, or compose music, or become an actor without downtime, and plenty of it, a hiatus that passes for boredom but is really the quiet moving of the wheels inside that fuel creativity. . . . There is ample psychological research suggesting that what we might call 'doing nothing' is when human beings actually do their best thinking, and when creativity comes to call."[8]

Her title suggests that Quindlen is quietly alluding to the passage in *A Room of One's Own* in which—seeking to enhance the creative opportunities of those, women in particular, with little or no "downtime"—Virginia Woolf urges the need to discover "what alternations of work and rest they need, interpreting rest *not as doing nothing but as doing something* but something that is different."[9] Woolf was aware of the psychological discoveries of Wordsworth a century earlier, and Anna Quindlen herself, though she has Woolf in mind, might have supplemented the ample research to which she and Gibbs refer with some of the most heartfelt passages of Emerson, or of Keats—writers even more directly aware than Woolf that Wordsworth was the great mentor on this crucial subject, the genesis of creative power in "what seem our most unfruitful hours" (*P* 5:364), so-called downtime when we appear to others, and sometimes to ourselves, to be "doing nothing."

7. Greene, "Sandlot Summer," 40; Gibbs, "Free the Children," 80.
8. Quindlen, "Doing Nothing Is Something," 76.
9. Woolf, *A Room of One's Own,* 2195. I will return to Heaney and Woolf.

The Prelude begins with Wordsworth caught in a dialectical tension that is at the paradoxical heart of the creative impulse—and certainly at the heart of that interplay, shared by Emerson, between reverence and denunciation of books, between receptive openness to nature and the demands of the intellect and of one's gifts and ambition. The first three hundred lines of *The Prelude,* leading up to the scenes of bird snaring, boat stealing, cliff scaling, and ice skating, offer a sustained pattern of what Coleridge called in the water-insect passage "alternate pulses of active and passive motion." Wordsworth's autobiographical epic opens with release and tension: carefree liberation and a temptation to voluptuary indolence quickly challenged by a self-imposed creative task. Unlike expelled Adam and Eve at the end of *Paradise Lost* ("The world was all before them" [*PL* 12: 646]), Wordsworth is *entering* his paradise: "The earth is all before me," the "servile yoke" cast off (*P* 1:14, 105). At the same time, spurred by his equivalent of Miltonic "zeal and just ambition" to attain "Fame" ("Lycidas"), he feels the need to begin the task he has set himself: the creation of a work the world should not willingly let die. Feeling himself "a renovated spirit singled out," Wordsworth fears betraying his genius, the "gift" that alone "consecrates" his "liberty" and "joy." In terms of the biblical parable (Matt. 25:14) he invokes (like Milton before him in the sonnet "When I consider how my light is spent"), Wordsworth dreads the prospect of "unprofitably travelling toward the grave, / Like a false steward who has much received / And renders nothing back" (*P* 1:53, 31–32, 267–69). At once liberated and burdened, he is torn between the need to "brace myself to some determined aim, / Reading or thinking," and the desire to luxuriate in the season and his newfound freedom. He temporarily refuses "to bend the sabbath of that time / To a servile yoke": "'It is an injury,' said I, 'to this day / To think of any thing but present joy'" (*P* [1805], 1:107–13).

Embodying the usual paradox of supposedly unmediated response taking the form of quotation, spontaneous receptivity in the form of literary allusion, that phrase echoes Milton's 1644 *Tractate on Education,* written in response to a request for a description of an ideal academy. Finally cutting his hypothetical young students some slack, respite from his proposed (and dauntingly rigorous) curriculum, taskmaster Milton observes that, in addition to scheduled exercise, "there is another opportunity of gaining experience to be won from *pleasure itself* abroad. In those *vernal seasons* of the year when the air is calm and pleasant, it were an *injury and sullenness against nature* not to go out and see her riches, and *partake in her rejoicing* with heaven and earth." Milton may be recalling Dante's lines about those lost, willfully sad souls, fixed in the mire and forever sighing, "Tristi fummo / ne l'aere dolce che dal sol s'allegra, / portando dentro accidioso fummo" (*Inferno,* 7:121–23; in John Ciardi's succinct translation:

"Sullen were we in the air made sweet by the sun"). But Wordsworth is more likely to be recalling Milton's "sullenness" than Dante's *triste* and *accidioso.* He echoes this passage again in the first of the pastoral stanzas of the Intimations Ode, in his initial and premature recovery from alienation and despondency—"No more shall grief of mine the *season wrong*"—as well as in his attempt, in the next stanza, to persuade himself that he actually *has* recovered and now experiences the joy he vicariously describes: "Oh evil day!" he cries. "If I were *sullen* / While earth herself is adorning / This sweet May-morning" (stanzas 3, 4; italics added). And another passage from book 4 of *The Excursion,* which attains rhetorical afflatus in the imagining of a "solitary raven, flying / Athwart the concave of the dark blue dome," ends with the Wanderer, having descended from "these imaginative heights" to the fields and bowers of the terrestrial world, admonishing the Solitary to acknowledge that even "to Nature's humbler power / Your cherished *sullenness* is forced to bend" (*E* 4:1178–91; italics added).

The passage from *On Education* resonated with Emerson as well, doubtless connected in his mind with such lines and with Wordsworth's invitations, in the dialogue poems of *Lyrical Ballads,* to put books aside and come forth into the air. In "John Milton," the most important of his early biographical lectures, Emerson praises the bard's "love of nature," his "rare susceptibility to impressions from external nature." Milton believed, Emerson rightly notes, that his "poetic vein only flowed from the autumnal to the vernal equinox; and in his essay on Education he doubts whether, in the fine days of spring, any study can be accomplished by young men. 'In those vernal seasons of the year, when the air is calm and pleasant, it were an injury and sullenness against nature, not to go out and see her riches and partake in her rejoicing with heaven and earth'" (*EL* 1:151).[10]

Of course, this familiar passage, however rhapsodic, is not simply an anomaly. Contemplation of nature, the sensible world, is the necessary first step in learning, and thus in right teaching. From the outset of the *Tractate on Education,* Milton, in accord with Renaissance doctrine traceable (in all but its specifically Christian aspects) to Aristotle's *On the Soul,* had insisted that the "end of learning" is to "repair the ruins of our first parents by regaining to know God aright, and out of that knowledge to love him, to imitate him." We strive for perfection by uniting virtue with the grace of faith. "But because our understanding cannot in this body

10. Though published posthumously (in 1893), "Milton," the fourth of the six 1835 "Biography" lectures, initiated Emerson's career as a literary critic and pioneered the biographical approach brought to fruition a decade later in the 1845 lectures later published as *Representative Men* (1850). *The Tractate on Education* (edited by Thomas Hartmann) is quoted from *The Prose of John Milton,* 239. I have modernized a few archaic spellings.

found itself but on sensible things, nor arrive so clearly to the knowledge of God and things invisible, as by orderly conning over the visible and inferior creature, the same method is necessarily to be followed in all discreet teaching."[11] The archangel Raphael, in his first teaching, had given Adam the same instruction about a loving contemplation of sensible things as part of his *scala,* a teaching to which the pupil gratefully replies:

> Well hast thou taught the way that might direct
> Our knowledge, and the scale of Nature set
> From center to circumference, whereon
> In contemplation of created things
> By steps we may ascend to God.
>
> (*PL* 5:508–12)

In short, *not* to put our books and ambitions aside at times, *not* to rejoice in God's creation, is to sin against the spirit; the "injury or sullenness against nature" is a moral issue. Of course, one *could* sullenly injure the season by accepting what Wordsworth calls a "servile yoke," initiating the laborious study required to accomplish a major creative work. But, again echoing Milton, Wordsworth procrastinates in this opening book:

> Ah! better far than this, to stray about
> Voluptuously, through fields and rural walks,
> And ask no record of the hours, resigned
> To vacant musings, unreproved neglect
> Of all things, and deliberate holiday:
> Far better never to have heard the name
> Of zeal and just ambition.
>
> (*P* 1:250–56)

Better far... voluptuously... far better... just ambition: this time the Miltonic text alluded to is rather more familiar. Since these lines from *The Prelude* were not published until 1850, Emerson was long unaware of this specific playing out of the systolic-diastolic pulsation between liberty and responsibility, yielding to the delights of the moment, on the one hand, exerting authorial will, spurred by just ambition, on the other. But like Coleridge and Wordsworth, he knew by heart ("clause by clause") the poem in which a youthful Milton, masked as shepherd-poet, overcomes "denial vain, and coy excuse" and reluctantly but decisively takes up the task of writing the elegy for Edward King. Aside from implicit commitment to the spiritual consolation that will eventually resolve the issues of

11. Milton, *The Prose of John Milton,* 230. Hartmann notes the provenance of Aristotle's treatise *On the Soul,* specifically 2.2 and 3.8.

premature death, divine justice, and literary ambition raised in the poem, young Milton is driven to write not only by "Bitter constraint, and sad occasion dear," but by his own just desire for "Fame," the

> spur that the clear spirit doth raise
> (That last infirmity of noble mind)
> *To spurn delights and live laborious days.*
> (70–72; italics added)

Still, he does briefly wonder (thus allowing a voluptuous carpe diem music to momentarily enter "Lycidas") if it were "*not better done*" to put aside the "incessant care" of studying poetry ("the thankless Muse") in order "To sport with Amaryllis in the shade, / Or with the tangles of Neaera's hair?" (67–69).

The more demure dallying of Wordsworth, Coleridge, and Emerson takes the form of sublimated intercourse with Nature herself. Along with "The Eolian Harp," the best instance in Coleridge, a passage in "The Nightingale" exhibiting the now familiar paradox, incorporates a double quotation from "Lycidas." "He, too, knew how to build the lofty rhyme," wrote Milton of Edward King. Coleridge criticizes the

> Poet who hath been *building up the rhyme*
> When he had *better far* have stretched his limbs
> Beside a brook in mossy forest-dell
> By sun or moonlight, to the influxes
> Of shapes and sounds and shifting elements
> Surrendering his whole spirit.
> (24–29; *CPW* 1:264–65)

In this surrendering mood—most memorably captured in Wordsworth's youthful book-spurning exercises in the hyperbolic in *Lyrical Ballads*—we come to Nature directly, intuitively, a resurrection from the dead. In "To My Sister," the poet invites Dorothy to "Come forth and feel the sun," and to "bring no book: for this one day / We'll give to idleness" (12, 15–16). In "Expostulation and Reply," the response to, "Where are your books?" is that "we can feed this mind of ours" by communing with living and eloquent Nature, "this mighty sum / Of things for ever speaking" (5, 23, 25–26). In a poem Emerson specifically endorsed *and* criticized, "The Tables Turned," the pedant-friend is advised to "quit your books," connected with "dull and endless strife," and instead accept the gift of "Spontaneous wisdom." Again secularizing Jesus' command to Lazarus to "come forth" from the tomb, the imperative is to "Come forth into the light of things, /

Let Nature be your Teacher." Taking deliberate holiday, we are to leave our books behind and "bring" with us instead "a heart that watches and receives" (1, 9, 19, 31–32).

That is the first step, not sufficient, but necessary and foundational. Seamus Heaney, the modern poet most profoundly influenced by both Wordsworth and Yeats, in an essay contrasting their differing "musics," describes Wordsworthian composition not as "an active pursuit," but as "listening . . . , a wise passiveness, a surrender to energies that spring within the centre of the mind." In words that Emerson would have endorsed, Heaney points out that Wordsworth's "strength and originality as a writer came first of all from trusting the validity of his experience." But he still had to become a poet, to discover the proper "sounds" to animate a philosophy of nature that in merely paraphrasable content would be inert. "Nature forms the heart that watches and receives but until the voice of the poet has been correspondingly attuned, we cannot believe what we hear." Wordsworth's "distinctive music, and what was definitive of that music," his "sympathetic," almost "feminine" conception of "the poetic act as essentially an act of complaisance with natural impulses and tendencies," differs sharply from "Yeatsian control and mastery"—what Heaney characterizes, borrowing what he rightly calls Denis Donoghue's "finely-tuned adjective," as Yeats's "equestrian authority." In this, "the Wordsworthian process differs radically from the Yeatsian, just as the satisfaction and scope of their musics differ."[12]

Such comments deserve the praise lavished on them by Helen Vendler: Heaney's "essays on his predecessors—bravura pieces of characterization, the best in recent memory—end up defending a Wordsworthian and Keatsian 'wise passiveness' (absorptive, hidden, receptive, yielding) against the Hopkinsian and Yeatsian tendency to force-march language into compliance with authorial will." True—but true of only half the polarity. For the "language" that describes and "claims" the lyrical Wordsworthian moment, the proper "music" and "voice" that give the poet's experience its "appropriate expression and enactment," has—as Frank Kermode points out—its own "force and authority." Thus, poetically as well as philosophically, Wordsworth simultaneously submits receptively to nature and *also* asserts mind's active power as "lord and master."[13]

In Romantic interactions between subject and object, man and nature,

12. Heaney, "The Making of a Music: Reflections on Wordsworth and Yeats," given as the first Kenneth Allott Memorial Lecture at Liverpool (1978), in *Preoccupations: Selected Prose, 1968–1978,* 69–71.

13. Vendler, *Soul Says: On Recent Poetry,* 193; Kermode, "Memory" (1994), in *Pieces of My Mind: Essays and Criticism, 1958–2002,* 304, 306.

the mind at times passively receives, or modifies, or cocreates, or exerts an imperious supremacy. The most characteristic instances involve a polarity, passive receptivity alternating with the assertion of the more active power of the shaping imagination. The arc can swing from an idealism verging on solipsism to pantheism. In a splendid passage of his 1874 essay on Wordsworth, collected in *Appreciations,* Walter Pater, after alluding to the final stanzas of the Intimations Ode, registers the Romantic polarity—and *replicates* it by noting, in an appreciation qualified by skepticism, the relative character of these two very different yet related forms of the Wordsworthian sublime:

> Sometimes as he dwelt upon those moments of profound, imaginative power, in which the outward object appears to take colour and expression, a new nature almost, from the prompting of the observant mind, the actual world would, as it were, dissolve and detach itself, flake by flake, and he himself seemed to be the creator, and[,] when he would[,] the destroyer of the world in which he lived—that old isolating thought of many a brain-sick mystic of ancient and modern times.
>
> At other times, again, in those periods of intense susceptibility, in which he appeared to himself as but the passive recipient of external influences, he was attracted by the thought of a spirit of life in outward things, a single, all-pervading mind in them, of which man, and even the poet's imaginative energy, are but moments—that old dream of the *anima mundi,* the mother of all things and their grave. . . . The network of man and nature was seen to be pervaded by a common, universal life: a new, bold thought lifted him above the furrow, above the green turf of the Westmoreland churchyard, to a world altogether different in its vagueness and vastness, and the narrow glen was full of the brooding power of one universal spirit.[14]

In his lyrics of "intense susceptibility," exhibiting and advocating a "wise passiveness," Wordsworth interacts, as in *The Prelude,* with Milton, to agree and to differ. In the poem in which the famous phrase actually occurs, "Expostulation and Reply," Wordsworth's interlocutor, Matthew, an unconscious representative of what Milton condemned as "an injury and sullenness against nature," urges the supposedly idling poet to read books in order to be illuminated by "that light bequeathed / To beings else forlorn and blind," to "drink the *spirit breathed* / From *dead men* to *their kind*" (6–8; italics added). Milton's description of a "good book" as "the precious life-blood of a master *spirit, embalmed* and treasured up on purpose to a life beyond life," is here subverted by Wordsworth, who has his opponent, deaf to his own self-defeating irony, equate reading to the transmission of

14. Pater, "Wordsworth," 54–55.

corpse breath to the living, who are as moribund as the literally "dead men" they read. Echoing (consciously or unconsciously) both Wordsworth's breath-death pun and Coleridge's "life-in-death," James Cox has acutely observed that "getting over the deaths of loved ones" was no mere spiritual cliché in the case of Emerson; extended mourning was for him "a literal breathing in, or inspiration, of the death in life."[15]

In *The Prelude,* Wordsworth describes great writers as

> Powers
> For ever to be hallowed; only less
> For what we are and what we may become
> Than Nature's self, which is the breath of God.
> (*P* 5:218–21)

Stripped of its functional irony, the spirit "breathed from dead men to their kind" is to be valued, but *not* above the spontaneous wisdom and truth "breathed by" the health and cheerfulness imparted to us by Nature, which is itself "the breath of God." Emerson's position was in accord with Wordsworth's, both in the emphasis on the preeminent value of the mind's interaction with nature, where "man can read God directly" (*E&L* 58), and in the recognition of the genuine but secondary value of books. Thus, it is not contradictory that Emerson should, in one of the lectures in his 1839–1840 winter series, quote one of his favorite Wordsworth poems, "Dion," to make a point *supporting* education and books (*EL* 3:297). As Emerson knew, the two Matthew-and-William poems, "Expostulation and Reply" and "The Tables Turned," were—like the dialogue between "Hermit" and "Poet" bridging the chapters "Higher Laws" and "Brute Neighbors" in *Walden* (218)—jocoserious debates between an interlocutor and a Wordsworthian speaker intended to redress a prior imbalance by overstating his own partial truth.

In "Expostulation and Reply" (*WP* 1:355–56), in a charge that would be remembered by Emerson as a belated but would-be American Adam looking upon the natural world as if for the first time, "Matthew" criticizes precisely the fresh vision Wordsworth advocates and embodies:

> "You look upon your Mother Earth,
> As if she for no purpose bore you;
> As if you were her first-born birth,
> And none had lived before you!"
> (9–12)

15. Cox, "R. W. Emerson: The Circles of the Eye," 72.

Wordsworth's spokesman, "William," responds that in reading Nature rather than books his senses are vitally if not aggressively engaged, since "The eye . . . cannot choose but see," the ear must hear, and "our bodies feel . . . / Against or with our will" (17–20). He is no less certain

> that there are Powers
> Which of themselves our minds impress;
> That we can feed this mind of ours
> In a wise passiveness.
>
> (21–24)

Elizabeth Peabody, the most astute and allusive Wordsworthian among Bronson Alcott's disciples, began her luminously intelligent contemporary review of Emerson's *Nature* by quoting this stanza of "Expostulation and Reply." Identifying neither poet nor poem, rightly assuming her audience would be familiar with both, she quoted the lines as illustrative of "Reason, from the top of the being" (or what Wordsworth more felicitously called, in the Intimations Ode, "thy being's height"), looking "into the higher nature of original truth, by Intuition."[16] Though youthful Emerson had dismissed Wordsworth's quatrain poems in *Lyrical Ballads* as "the poetry of pygmies" (*JMN* 1:162), he would later feel differently. And, as Peabody assumed, "wise passiveness" *was* a concept congenial to the intuitive side of Emerson. Reenacting the Wordsworthian dialogue by taking issue with the idea expressed by his brother William and a friend in an 1851 conversation to the effect that one should focus industriously on a single useful skill, Emerson bridged the false dualism between external utility and inner power and joy. Let a man "listen & obey, & by a wise passiveness accept & use his several powers & health & symmetry will be kept for him, sufficient variety of power & expression," producing "joy to himself & utility to men" (*JMN* 11:336). Emerson's precise phrasing ("accept & use," "power & expression") straddles the shifting terms of the Coleridgean-Wordsworthian power dialectic.

In "The Tables Turned" (*WP* 1:356–57), Nature brings us "sweet lore" in the form of nourishing gifts as opposed to cold analysis, the "meddling intellect" that disfigures "the beauteous forms of things," so that we "murder" those natural forms in order "to dissect." It is not the "young scholars" of Emerson's Wordsworthian poem "Blight," nor "sages" nor books conveying that "spirit breathed" from dead men to their kind, but a blessed and blessing feminine Nature that is our true instructress, the impulsive

16. Peabody, "Nature—a Prose Poem," *United States Magazine and Democratic Review* 1 (February 1838): 319–29, reprinted in *EPP* 590–97; quote on 590.

source of a genuine, "spontaneous" wisdom and truth "breathed by" health and happiness and productive of that instinctual health marking the person of integrated faculties. We are therefore to "Come forth into the light of things, / Let Nature be your teacher."

> She has a world of ready wealth,
> Our minds and hearts to bless—
> Spontaneous wisdom breathed by health,
> Truth breathed by cheerfulness.
>
> One impulse from a vernal wood
> Can teach you more of man,
> Of moral evil and of good,
> Than all the sages can.[17]
>
> . . . .
>
> Enough of Science and of Art;
> Close up those barren leaves;
> Come forth, and bring with you a heart
> That watches and receives.
>
> (17–24; 29–32)

This was, of course, a partial truth—hyperbole memorably expressed, meant to dramatize the dialogue and to rectify a disproportion. But as Emerson noted, recalling Milton's distinction between licence and liberty, "always a licence attends reformation. . . . We now say with Wordsworth to the scholar 'Leave your old books: Come forth into the light of things let nature be your teacher.'" Tongue in cheek, and making it clear that "wise passiveness" was no excuse for unproductive laziness, Emerson continued this 1838 journal entry: "Out upon your pedantic cartloads of grammars & dictionaries & archeologies. The Now is all. Instantly the indolence & self-indulgence of the scholar is armed with an apology. Tush[,] I will have a good time" (*JMN* 7:69).

17. This is close to the thought expressed in the best-known letter of Saint Bernard of Clairvaux. A mystic who claimed a higher intuitive knowledge, Bernard also communed with nature and could say (as he does in Epistle 106), "Believe me, for I know, you will find something far greater in the woods than in books. Trees and stones will teach you that which you can never learn from the masters." Shakespeare's banished Duke Senior, who found in the Forest of Arden "tongues in trees" and "Sermons in stones" (*As You Like It*, 2.2.16–17), echoes Bernard; perhaps Wordsworth does as well. Coleridge quotes the duke's words as an instance of "method" resulting "from the religious instinct" (*F* 2:497). Whatever its immediate "source" (Bernard or the duke, Coleridge or Wordsworth), Emerson's doctrine is Wordsworthian in his early poem "The River": "Oh, call not Nature dumb; / These trees and stones are audible to me" (*W* 9:385).

Nevertheless, Emerson remained susceptible to the lure of Wordsworth's "favorite topic" (*E&L* 775) during their 1833 conversation. Emerson's weighing of the comparative merits of tuition and intuition reflects as well the early poetry of Wordsworth, their sentiments confirmed by that interview—and, incidentally, reconfirmed a dozen years later in Wordsworth's critique (in a letter of December 16, 1845, to Seymour Tremenheere) of a contemporary educational report. He asked, purely rhetorically, is "too little value . . . not set upon the occupations of Children out of doors . . . comparatively with what they do or acquire in school? Is not the Knowledge inculcated by the Teacher, or derived under his management, from books, too exclusively dwelt upon, so as almost to put out of sight that which comes, *without being sought for, from intercourse with nature* . . ."[18] Again, Wordsworth was not dismissing "tuition," or book knowledge, only its being dwelt on "out of all proportion" or "too exclusively." Here, almost half a century after he wrote the dialogue poems in *Lyrical Ballads* and briefly considered, and rejected, Tom Wedgwood's "nursery of genius" educational scheme (and, later, the Bell system), the Tory humanist was still, however "conservative" he had become, celebrating "wise passiveness," "spontaneous wisdom" that comes without being frantically sought. What is to be sought instead is an ennobling interchange—even a sublimatedly sexual relation—between mind and nature as a comparatively far more valuable source of "wisdom" than the knowledge derived from "books and sages" and, certainly, from the sort of tyrannical and spirit-crushing teachers he had so furiously condemned in book 5 of *The Prelude:* those "mighty workmen" of a Satanic educational system.

For Coleridge as for Wordsworth and, through them, for Emerson himself, Nature remains the indispensable other in the nuptial relationship, and—whatever the secondary value of books and tuition—our true Teacher. That theme recurs often, including in "The American Scholar," that challenge to the Harvard intelligentsia, where, again, in the context of his most ardent declaration of America's need to assert literary independence from England, Emerson, paradoxically as usual, was at his most Wordsworthian, relegating "books" to the "idle times" of the true scholar, who attains genuine wisdom through intuitive intercourse with divinity's midwife, Wordsworthian Nature. The embrace of this doctrine, comparative but nevertheless passionate, is not restricted to Emersonian prose. The sequence within *Lyrical Ballads* that includes "Expostulation and Reply" and "The Tables Turned," "Lines Written in Early Spring" and "To

18. Wordsworth, *The Letters of William and Dorothy Wordsworth: The Later Years,* 3: 1268; italics added.

My Sister," was poetically revisited by Emerson, first in "The Humble-Bee" (1837), in "Woodnotes" (1841), then in "Monadnoc" (ca. 1845), with its Wordsworthian and Goethean imperative—

> Bookworm, break this sloth urbane;
> A greater spirit bids thee forth
> Than the gray dreams which thee detain.
> (16–18; *CPT* 49)

—and finally in "Waldeinsamkeit," written in 1857 and collected in *May-Day* (1867).

"The Humble-Bee," to begin with the earliest poem, is Wordsworthian from its title on. Though "the solitary humble-bee / Sings in the bean-flower" in Coleridge's "This Lime-Tree Bower My Prison," Emerson's choice of humble-bee rather than bumblebee would seem to signal a Wordsworthian cherishing of the humble things of nature. The inspiration of the poem is recorded in Emerson's May 1837 journal. "The humble-bee & the pine warbler seem to me the proper objects of attention in these disastrous times," he wrote. He had just followed a bee into the woods, and exclaimed: "I . . . feel a new joy in nature" (*JMN* 5:527), a joy not unlike that of Wordsworth who, in "Lines Written in Early Spring," contrasted the "pleasure" felt by the birds and blossoms and twigs and transmitted to receptive humans, who have ample reason to grieve "What man has made of man." Emerson even out-Wordsworths Wordsworth. The "best philosopher" and "Seer blest" of the Intimations Ode is at least a human child; Emerson's whimsical apostrophe to his bee is rather more endearingly hyperbolic: "Wiser far than human seer, / Yellow-breeched philosopher!" (52–53; *EPP* 441).

"Woodnotes" falls into a structural pattern we associate, in brief compass, with the Petrarchan sonnet and, in a sustained form, with Wordsworth: the immediate presentation of a scene followed by an explicit interpretation of that presentation. This is the dialectic we find repeatedly in *The Prelude,* especially in the seasonal activities in book 1, the crossing of the Simplon Pass in book 6 and the related "spots of time" in book 12, culminating in Wordsworth's ascent of Mount Snowdon in the final book. But "Woodnotes" more closely resembles those earlier instances of Wordsworthian dialectic, the dialogues in "Expostulation and Reply" and "The Tables Turned."

In June 1841, walking almost every day in the vernal woods surrounding Walden Pond, Emerson, in a "Waldenic" poem inspired, like "Monadnoc," by Goethe and Wordsworth, and foreshadowing Thoreau, composed his own preference for the book of Nature. "Woodnotes, II," takes the form of literal woodnotes. Its speaker, Emerson's favorite tree, the white pine, condenses the most memorable quatrain of "The Tables Turned"—about the single "impulse from a vernal wood" being able to "teach you more of man," of "moral evil and of good, / Than all the sages can"—to "the wood is wiser far than thou" (compare the opening of his unpublished 1839 prose sonnet, "Woods": "Wise are ye, O ancient woods! Wiser than man" [*JMN* 7:248]); expands "spontaneous wisdom breathed by health" to two lines: "The hills where health with health agrees, / And the wise soul expels disease"; and urges us, in an arboreal equivalent of Wordsworth's imperative to "bring no book," to

> leave thy peacock wit behind;
> Enough for thee, the primal mind
> That flows in streams, that breathes in wind:
> Leave all thy pedant lore apart;
> God hid the whole world in thy heart.
> Love shuns the age, the child it crowns,
> And gives them all who all renounce.
> (*CPT* 45, 47)

Recalling the response of "William" to the bookish and busy inquirer convinced that "nothing of itself will come, / But we must still be seeking" ("Expostulation and Reply," 27–28), Emerson, who had warned in *Nature* that things of natural beauty mock us "if too eagerly hunted" (*E&L* 16), has his speaking pine advise such an eager hunter "thread[ing] the woods in vain / To find" what species of bird is piping: "*Seek not,* and the little eremite / Flies gayly forth and sings in sight." The upshot amounts to a fusion of the position of "William" in the dialogue poems and of Wordsworth's crowning of the "child" in the Intimations Ode: "And thou,—go burn thy wormy pages,— / Shall outsee seers, and outwit sages" (*CPT* 47). If the jaunty tetrameters and the imperatives to "leave . . . pedant lore apart" and burn such pages as do not come from the book of Nature, look back to the book-spurning "simple" Wordsworth of the quatrain poems just cited from *Lyrical Ballads,* the image of the "child," or the child within us, who can "outsee seers" and "outwit sages" once again resembles the Wordsworthian apotheosis of the Child, the "Seer blest" and "best philosopher" of the Intimations Ode, a redemptive Emersonian "infancy" now associated by the proud father with his own wondrous child, Waldo.

Though, unlike his prose, Emerson's poetry is generally free of direct literary allusions, these poems are exceptions, especially "Waldeinsamkeit," its echoes, as well as its quatrain form, confirming the direct influence of Wordsworth's dialectical ballads, those "simple songs," as the poet himself called them, for "thinking hearts." In these related texts, the poets are committed to the immediate joys for which, as Emerson says, "the day was made" (12), echoing Wordsworth's taking "Our temper from today" and his putting aside of other concerns "For this one day" ("To My Sister," 32, 39). The poet claims of the "breeze" that opens *The Prelude* that it "seems half-conscious of the joy it brings." In these poems, Wordsworth less tentatively attributes to inanimate nature consciousness and a capacity for pleasure. In "Lines Written in Early Spring," it is his "faith that every flower / Enjoys the air it breathes," and—watching the "budding twigs spread out their fan, / To catch the breezy air"—he insists, "I must think, do all I can, / That there was pleasure there" (11–12, 17–20). In his own poem, whose title (derived from the German Romantics) means "forest solitude," Emerson is equally insistent that "The woods at heart are glad" (20). Wordsworth's sister is told to "bring no book" on the "first mild day of March" ("To My Sister," 1, 15, 39), and Matthew is exhorted to "quit your books," to close those "barren leaves," and "Come forth, and bring with you a heart / That watches and receives" ("The Tables Turned," 1, 30–32). An echoing Emerson states:

> Aloft, in secret veins of air,
> Blows the sweet breath of song,
> O, few to scale those uplands dare,
> Though they to all belong.
>
> See thou bring not to field or stone
> The fancies found in books;
> Leave authors' eyes, and fetch your own
> To brave the landscape's looks.
> ("Waldeinsamkeit," 37–44)

Emerson's final stanza completes the echo of Wordsworth's advice to Dorothy to "bring no book; for this one day / We'll give to idleness" (in "To My Sister"):

> Oblivion here thy wisdom is,
> Thy thrift, the sleep of cares;
> For a proud idleness like this
> Crowns all thy mean affairs.
> (45–48; *EPP* 478)

The final adjective recalls the "mean egotism" that "vanishes" when Emerson himself, having "become a transparent eye-ball," feels the "currents of the Universal Being circulate" through him (*E&L* 10). Like Emerson's "mean affairs," Wordsworth's refrain in "Lines Written in Early Spring" lamenting "What man has made of man" evokes the grievous condition in which attunement to the pleasure-filled, vital universe has been displaced by a busy, desiccated rationalism that, incapable of an unmediated response to natural beauty, is subservient to the materialistic and political "world" that is too much with us. That world, during the 1850s, was increasingly disturbing to Emerson, particularly in terms of slavery and the abolitionist movement, to which he was now adamantly committed. But the old polarity, the pull between Solitude and Society, had not disappeared; it intrudes even into this poem of forest solitude.[19] A decade or so before Emerson wrote "Waldeinsamkeit," the struggle against slavery and its spread had finally given him a cause that, mingling hope and heartache, resembled the great historical event that had defined his Romantic precursors. In spring 1798, when the dialogue poems that would appear in *Lyrical Ballads* were written, Wordsworth and Coleridge—disheartened and disillusioned by the French invasion of democratic Switzerland, the oppressed having become oppressors in their turn—had withdrawn from the political world to poetry and nature, recanting (publicly in Coleridge's case) their former commitment to the French Revolution. For Wordsworth, lamenting "what man has made of man," the endorsement of "wise passiveness" was, in part, a conversion from revolutionary to imaginative energy and an embrace of Romantic *waldeinsamkeit* and of political quietism.

Emerson recognized the political dimension of the language in these poems. Indeed, his own polarity between his characteristic aloofness and reluctant but driven commitment on behalf of certain reforms was often summarized in the language of these Wordsworthian poems. Even before the public outcry stirred by the Divinity School Address, he had backed away from active involvement in social reform, longing, even as he was engaged in public protest, to "let the republic alone until the republic *comes* to me" (*JMN* 5:479), and he concluded his 1845 commencement address at Middlebury by challenging each of the students present to take home with him "this, that he need *not seek* anything; that power, and love, and friendship shall *come* to the great." As he had said in the peroration of "The American Scholar," if "the single man plant himself indomitably on his instincts, and there abide, the huge world will *come round to him*" (*E&L*

19. It does so in the oblique, syntactically awkward but clearly paradoxical fourth stanza: "Cities of mortals woe-begone / Fantastic care derides, / But in the serious landscape lone / Stern benefit abides." The woe of crowds pent up in cities is treated with contemptuous mirth since it derives from a cluster of sociopolitical concerns, a "care" that *seems* nothing if not serious and realistic but is in fact unreal, "fantastic." In contrast, the "benefit" that abides from solitude in the *truly* "serious" landscape is, in keeping with the law of Emersonian self-reliance, "stern." But even this lonely sternness does not preclude sociopolitical engagement, however oscillating and subject to change that commitment may become.

70).[20] Such language seems a more than oblique endorsement of Wordsworth's condemnation of the overbusy conviction that "*nothing of itself will come, / But we must still be seeking*" ("Expostulation and Reply," 27–28). As we will see, in an 1840 lecture, Emerson actually cited Wordsworth's most resonant quietist phrase in telling the abolitionists present that, although he too abhorred the crime of slavery, he would persist in wearing his loose and unbecoming "robe . . . of inaction, this *wise passiveness,* until my hour *comes* when I can see how to *act with truth as well as to refuse*" (*EL* 3:266; italics added). That hour *would* come, the republic would seem to Emerson to have "come" to him, when the question of slavery, and the danger of its extension, epitomized in the enactment of the Fugitive Slave Law, moved Emerson to eloquence on behalf of a republic threatened by the spread of what he slowly but surely perceived as an abomination.[21]

Such allusions, in the immediate context of increasing pressures to become politically active, confirm the importance to Emerson of this cluster of "simple" Wordsworth poems. That these lyrics affected Emerson is clear. That he could not match their gnomic brilliance in verse, even when he tried, may be one clue to his omission of them in his ample selection from Wordsworth in *Parnassus.* The double conclusion reached by Carlos Baker seems beyond dispute: "It is true that Emerson's lines do not always achieve the prosodic polish of Wordsworth's simple but not simplistic phrasings. Yet no one can read 'Waldeinsamkeit' without concluding that many quatrains of both poets are virtually interchangeable."[22]

As Baker had noted in the preceding sentence, the position adopted in "Waldeinsamkeit" resembles not only Wordsworth but Keats as well: Emerson's "'proud idleness' comes close to Wordsworth's 'wise passiveness' and even approaches the 'diligent indolence' of John Keats." He is right, of course, though it seems odd that he omits the significant point that *both* Keats and Emerson are consciously and transparently Wordsworthian in these formulations. Wordsworth's exaltation of nature over books, of idleness over the busy intellection convinced that nothing of itself will come,

20. The "huge world" here resembles those seekers of the writer of a "better book" or the "maker of a better mousetrap than their neighbor," to whose door, "though he builds his house in the woods, the world will make a beaten path." The saying is attributed to Emerson (in Sarah S. B. Yule and Mary S. Keene, *Borrowings* [1889]), and he probably *did* say it in a lecture; it is close to a February 1855 journal entry—which, however, omits the memorable mousetrap.

21. The trajectory of Emerson's early reticence and gradual, but finally passionate, commitment to political and social reforms, above all, the abolition of slavery, has been clarified by the publication of *Emerson's Antislavery Writings,* edited by Len Gougeon and Joel Myerson, and, most recently, by *The Political Emerson,* edited by D. M. Robinson.

22. Baker, *Emerson among the Eccentrics: A Group Portrait,* 468–69.

but we must still be seeking, blossoms beautifully in Keats. For Emerson, Shakespearean "genial power" consists "in being altogether receptive, in letting the world do all, and suffering the spirit of the hour to pass unobstructed through the mind" (*E&L* 711). Adumbrating the specifically Shakespearean "quiet power" he finally and fully attained in the ode "To Autumn," Keats wrote to his friend John Hamilton Reynolds on February 18, 1818: "Now it is more noble to sit like Jove tha[n] to fly like Mercury—let us not therefore go hurrying about and collecting honey-bee-like, buzzing here and there impatiently from a knowledge of what is to be arrived at; but let us open our leaves like a flower and be passive and receptive—budding patiently under the eye of Apollo and taking hints from every noble insect that favors us with a visit."[23] Wordsworth had urged Dorothy to "give" the day to "idleness," and presented that Boy who became the Wanderer as he "lay on the green turf / In pensive idleness" (*E* 1: 260–61). Doubtless remembering both passages, Keats tells Reynolds that he had been "led into these thoughts by the beauty of the morning operating on a sense of Idleness—I have not read any Books—the Morning said I was right—I had no idea but of the Morning and the Thrush said I was right." And he copies out his unrhymed sonnet, "Thou Whose Face Hath Felt the Winter's Wind," in which the thrush, having advised us to "fret not after knowledge," concludes:

> He who saddens
> At thought of idleness cannot be idle,
> And he's awake who thinks himself asleep.

❧ The passive receptivity of the open and budding flower, and this Keatsian emphasis on an "idleness" not quite nameable but something other than being idle, together with Seamus Heaney's apt description of Wordsworth's conception of the poetic act, in "complaisance with natural impulses," as "sympathetic," almost "feminine," might be compared with an almost identical conception in Virginia Woolf's *Room of One's Own,* the passage Anna Quindlen had in mind in the *Newsweek* essay earlier quoted. At the moment just before her "rambling" thoughts are (almost passively) "given another turn," and she pivots (from chapter 4 to chapter 5) from considering women writers of the past to those of the present, Woolf anticipates the books to be written by women in the future. They will be different from those of men because of both "physical conditions" (the likelihood of being interrupted at work) and differences in the "psychology of women," rooted, she suspects, in the very "*nerves that feed the brain.*" To

23. Keats, *Letters of John Keats,* 1:232–33.

facilitate the productivity of women, one would have to "find out . . . *what alternations of work and rest* they need, *interpreting rest not as doing nothing but as doing something but something that is different; and what should that difference be?* All this should be discussed and discovered."[24] It hardly dims the luster of that essay, still luminous after three-quarters of a century, to note that these alternating pulsations—especially the function of moments of "rest" that are not at all the same as doing nothing, moments when we "*feed* this mind of ours / In a wise passiveness"—*had* been discussed and discovered, and discovered—by Wordsworth and Coleridge, Keats and Emerson—to be a part of male as well as female psychology: constituent elements in that polar dialectic, mediated by imagination, indispensable, whatever the gender differences in the bicameral brain, to human creativity in general.

Keats's Wordsworth-based "diligent indolence," Emerson's "proud idleness" in the Wordsworth-saturated "Waldeinsamkeit," and Woolf's productive "alternations" of work and a "rest" that is more than idleness all converge in confirming that "wise passiveness" is not a carte blanche for laziness. In the "Cambridge" section of book 6 of *The Prelude,* Wordsworth distinguishes between productive indolence and what, taking blame for his own largely wasted time at Cambridge, he refers to as

> multitudes of hours
> Pilfered away, by what the Bard who sang
> Of the Enchanter Indolence hath called
> "Good-natured lounging."
>
> (*P* 6:179–82)

(Even here, Wordsworth alludes to literature, though, for once, the Bard is not Milton, but James Thompson, author of *The Castle of Indolence.*) Still, earlier in this section, he acknowledges an evasion of systematic education that tallies with his observation, in book 5, that much may be accomplished in what may *seem* our most unfruitful hours. Abandoning "indolent society," including "Frank-hearted maids of rocky Cumberland" and their "not unwelcome days of mirth" and "nights of revelry" (the rural equivalent of Milton's Amaryllis and Neaera),[25] Wordsworth—with "no settled

24. Woolf, *A Room of One's Own,* 2194–95.

25. "Lycidas," of course. Not even Milton, Wordsworth's great predecessor at Cambridge, was immune to fun. According to his nephew Edward Phillips, the young Milton, aside from rejoicing in nature, also took holidays from his studies (a Cambridge curriculum he gradually found unsatisfying), enjoying the more than occasional "Gawdy-day" with other youthful playgoers and fellows about town (Helen Darbishire, ed., *The Early Lives of Milton,* 612). Of course, back at his father's house and with that father's support, Milton followed his college career with five years of sustained, concentrated study.

plan," but possessing a "Poet's soul"—remained "detached / Internally from academic cares," and, indulging his own "over-love / Of freedom," rebelled against all "restraints and bonds."

> Yet who can tell—
> Who knows what thus may have been gained, both then
> And at a later season, or preserved;
> What love of nature, what original strength
> Of contemplation, what intuitive truths,
> The deepest and the best . . . ?
>
> (*P* 6:14–42)

This is the Wordsworth who wrote the dialogue poems in *Lyrical Ballads,* and who might have written much of "The American Scholar" and parts of "Circles." In the latter, after quoting Edward Young's observation that "smaller faults" were forgivable since they were often "half converts to the right," Emerson declares: "It is the highest power of divine moments that they abolish our contrition also. I accuse myself of sloth and unprofitableness day by day; but when these waves of God flow into me, I no longer reckon lost time" (*E&L* 411).[26] By the time he wrote these words, Emerson had, to a considerable extent, overcome a tendency that had appalled him from youth. At the age of seventeen, at the commencement of his journal keeping, he had noted: "I find myself often idle, vagrant, stupid, & hollow. This is somewhat appalling & if I do not discipline myself with diligent care I shall suffer severely from remorse & the sense of inferiority hereafter. All around me are industrious & will be great, I am indolent & shall be insignificant. Avert it heaven! avert it virtue! I need excitement" (*JMN* 1:39, October 24, 1820). To Wordsworth Emerson may have owed, along with other benefactions, a life-preserving gift enabling him to avoid the tragic fate of his brilliant but *too* ambitious and industrious brothers, Edward and Charles. However much he may have disciplined himself with "diligent care," Emerson had also learned to incorporate, as part of his "magazine of power," a Wordsworthian and Keatsian diligent and productive indolence. "Some serene, inactive men *can,*" as Thoreau said, "do everything."

Though in their mode of passive receptivity to "intuitive truths" Emerson, like Keats, is thoroughly Wordsworthian, Emerson was also familiar—on his own but, in this case, powerfully reinforced by Coleridge—with two "intuitive" Enneads of Plotinus that advocate the same quiet power

26. Emerson quotes from Young's *Night Thoughts,* 9:2316–17. Another of Young's "half" formulations, in which the human senses "*half create* the wondrous *world* we see" (*Night Thoughts,* 6:427), influenced Wordsworth's "mighty world / Of eye, and ear,—both what they half create, / And what perceive" ("Tintern Abbey," 105–7).

and patience rather than relentless inquiry. The "relation between the mind and matter," contends Emerson in the "Language" chapter of *Nature,* "is not fancied by some poet, but stands in the will of God, and so is free to be known by all men. It appears to men or it does not appear" (*E&L* 24). The phrase of Plotinus alluded to in that final sentence[27] had appeared earlier, in an 1835 journal entry on the unlawful inquiry about the highest, or "intuitive knowledge," and "whence it sprang as if it were a thing subject to place and motion for it neither approached hither nor again departs from hence, to some other place, but it either appears to us, or it does not appear" (*JMN* 5:103).

Emerson is quoting the fifth Ennead (5.5.7), Coleridge's favorite saying of Plotinus. He quotes it in full in English (and, partially, in Greek) in *Biographia Literaria,* leading up to it by quoting from the third Ennead (3.8.4), in which Plotinus imagines Nature responding to her importunate questioners: "Should any one interrogate her, how she works, if graciously she vouchsafes to listen and speak, she will reply, it behoves thee not to disquiet me with interrogatories, but to understand in silence, even as I am silent, and work without words." Employing the terms of Milton's angel Raphael in the crucial passage (*PL* 5:469–90) he had cited two chapters earlier, Coleridge goes on to associate Plotinian thought with "intuitive" rather than "discursive" Reason, associating that intuitive knowledge, in turn, with the Wordsworthian master light, here what Wordsworth referred to in *The Excursion* as "The vision and the faculty divine" (*E* 1:79). Coleridge cites Plotinus:

> Likewise in the fifth book of the fifth Ennead, speaking of the highest and intuitive knowledge as distinguished from the discursive, or in the language of Wordsworth, "The vision and the faculty divine," he says: it is not lawful to enquire whence it sprang, as if it were a thing subject to place and motion, for it neither approached hither, nor again departs from hence to some other place; but it either appears to us or it does not appear. So that we ought not to pursue it with a view to detecting its secret source, but to watch in quiet till it suddenly shines upon us; preparing ourselves for the blessed spectacle as the eye waits patiently for the rising sun. (*BL* 1:241)

The Emerson of proud idleness agrees that, just as the "eye" awaits the rising sun, we should watch in quiet, waiting patiently for the sudden

27. In her 1838 review of *Nature,* Peabody, referring to that sentence, chides a reviewer (Francis Bowen, in the *Christian Examiner*) for his inability to understand "what it means." Though she does not recognize the source in Plotinus, she asks, "Where lies the obscurity? . . . In other words, *to people with open eyes there are colors, to people with shut eyes, at least, to those born blind, there are no colors*" ("Nature—a Prose Poem," 593; italics in original).

illumination, the appearance of the intuitive or divine wisdom, which comes when we least expect it. As he put it in "Experience," perhaps echoing Wordsworth's "whether busy or at rest" in the ninth stanza of the Intimations Ode: "We do not know today whether we are busy or idle. In times when we thought ourselves indolent, we have afterwards discovered that much was accomplished, and much was begun in us" (*E&L* 471). Responding in 1843 to a letter from Emerson, Margaret Fuller began: "Thy letter, o best Waldo, displays the wonted glorious inconsistency, beginning as a hymn in praise of indolence, and ending with demands of work" (*L* 2: 220n). Fuller's guide was hardly in thrall to "a foolish consistency," that "hobgoblin of little minds" (*E&L* 265), but indolence and productivity were, for him as for Wordsworth and the Keats of "diligent indolence," not inconsistent but complementary, two sides of the creative coin. As we have seen, for Wordsworth, the mystery was explained by a power higher than any dreamt of in the philosophy of those "mighty" educationalists and torturing "wardens" who would mechanistically confine us down, too presumptuous to learn that a "wiser spirit" and "better eye" is at work for us,

> most prodigal
> Of blessings, and most studious of our good,
> Even in what seem our most unfruitful hours.
> (*P* 5:560–64)

Emerson's finest ode to a productive indolence may be the prose of "Spiritual Laws." The second paragraph of that essay both synopsizes this section's theme and, through allusion, illustrates the paradox of originality. Celebrating the "preponderance of nature over will," instinct rather than a restless and "perplexed" struggle and striving, Emerson alludes again to that quiescent Ennead of Plotinus (either "God is there, or he is not there"). He alludes as well to Adam's response, in book 7 of *Paradise Lost,* to his great teacher, the archangel Raphael; to an attempt by Carlyle, in a fallen and infected age, to return, on a higher level, to something resembling prelapsarian instinct; and—actually quoting this time—to a little-known poem of Wordsworth. All these allusions are intended to reinforce Emerson's own "Wordsworthian" valuing of "impulsive and spontaneous" intuition over tuition, the value of the "health" of a self-reliant nature undiseased by incessant "seeking" and by what we too often "*call* education."

The Wordsworth allusion reinforces the teaching both of Milton's archangel and of Carlyle, in his seminal 1831 essay, "Characteristics." Basing himself in part on his own 1825 study of Schiller, Carlyle insists that "inquiry" into such abstruse considerations as "the Origin of Evil" is a form of "Disease," and calls, in an age of self-consciousness and perplexed doubt, for unconscious spontaneity, an immersion in vital experiences, and (echoing "Tintern Abbey") the appreciation of "a certain instinct of *something far deeper* that lies under such experiences." He laments that the "memory of that first state of Freedom and paradisiac Unconsciousness," the state urged upon Adam by Raphael, has "faded away into an ideal poetic dream," while its supposed remedy, postlapsarian "Science," both in its origin and continuation, is nothing "but Division, Dismemberment, and partial healing of the wrong."[28] The "wise soul expels disease," says Emerson in "Waldeinsamkeit," his poetic fusion of natural and human "health." In his version of the Angelic and Carlylean dismissal of diseased inquiry presented in "Spiritual Laws," Emerson claims:

> The intellectual life *may* be kept clean and *healthful, if man will live the life of nature,* and not import into his mind difficulties which are none of his. No man *need be perplexed in his speculations.* Let him *do* and *say* what *strictly belongs to him, and, though very ignorant of books, his nature shall not yield him any intellectual obstructions and doubts.* Our young people are *diseased* with the theological problems of original sin, origin of evil, predestination, and the like. These never . . . darkened across any man's road who did not go *out of his way to seek them.* These are *the soul's mumps, and measles, and whooping-coughs,* and those who have not caught them will not know these enemies. It is quite another thing that he should be able to give account of his faith, and expound to another the theory of his self-union and freedom. This requires rare gifts. Yet, without this self-knowledge, there may be *a sylvan strength and integrity in that which he is. "A few strong instincts and a few plain rules" suffice us.* (*E&L* 305–6; italics added)

This apparently *anti*-intellectual version of "the intellectual life," its infectious audacity bordering on an endorsement of the notion that ignorance

28. Carlyle, "Characteristics," in *Critical and Miscellaneous Essays,* 2:343–47, 361–63. Disease requires healing, as Matthew Arnold recognizes in referring to "Wordsworth's healing power" in "Memorial Verses," written shortly after Wordsworth's death. For Carlyle, the healing—the restoration of spiritual life at a dialectically higher stage than its original—had been prophesied by Schiller, whose life and work Carlyle had studied in a book (Emerson owned a later copy) published six years before he wrote "Characteristics." According to Schiller, spiritual life in its innocent form—"instinctive and natural life"—has been "sunder[ed]" by "the spiritual itself" in the act of "self-realization," and thus "the spirit has *by its own act* to win its way to concord again." It was "civilization itself that inflicted this wound upon modern man," says Schiller, in a figure that, as M. H. Abrams has noted, is patently echoed by Hegel, who famously observed in *Logic* that the "principle of restoration is found in thought, and thought only. The hand that inflicts the wound is also the hand which heals it." For both passages, see Abrams, *Natural Supernaturalism,* 221.

is bliss, would seem to provide ammunition for an animus against any and all books. Yet Emerson's language is riddled with the literary allusions mentioned, and there *is* the concession about the "rare gift" of being able to "account" for and "expound to another" one's intuitive faith in one's "self-union and freedom." But Emerson falls back on the "sylvan" strength of integrated and instinctual life and on Adam's new-taught wisdom. Advised by Raphael to be "lowly wise: / Think of what concerns thee and thy being" (*PL* 8:173–74), Adam, "cleared of doubt," thanks that "pure / Intelligence of heaven, angel serene," for his having now been

> freed from intricacies, taught to live,
> The easiest way, nor with *perplexing thoughts*
> To interrupt the sweet of life, from which
> God hath bid dwell far off all *anxious cares,*
> And not molest us, unless we our selves
> Seek them with wandering thoughts, and notions vain.
> (*PL* 8:179–87; italics added)

Raphael is warning Adam about the dangers of what both Saint Augustine and John Donne were to term *curiositas,* learning that is not directly related to one's salvation. But although he condemned *curiositas,* Donne (a man almost as erudite as the incomparably learned Milton) also recognized the thirst for knowledge, what he called, in a phrase echoed by Browning in "The Grammarian's Funeral," "an hydroptic immoderate desire of human learning." Similarly, Milton's prescient Adam realizes that the restless mind tends to range far afield, leaving the things that should most concern us "still to seek," while we dissipate our energies in fanciful imaginings—what later ages would call scientific curiosity, intellectual speculation, arcane knowledge. Though not without value, these are all idle pursuits if, substituting for life itself a futile quest for remote knowledge, they distract us from both instinctual integrity and "the prime wisdom," what Emerson calls "the first philosophy." The "mind or fancy," says Adam, is apt

> to rove,
> Unchecked, and of her roving is no end;
> Till warned, or by experience taught, she learn
> That *not to know* at large of *things remote*
> From use, obscure and subtle, but to know
> *That which before us lies in daily life,*
> Is the prime wisdom, what is more, is fume,
> Or emptiness, or fond impertinence.
> (*PL* 8:188–95)

Empty fume, inhaled, dulls the brain, and Emerson agrees with Raphael's pupil, Adam, and with Carlyle that (in Keats's phrase) "the dull brain perplexes and retards." Still, Raphael's teaching is meant only to limit idle and dangerous speculation about what it is needful for us to know. Some knowledge is a dangerous thing. Adam and Eve, tempted by that "false Worm," Satan, to whom Eve gave ear, are soon to eat of the Tree of the Knowledge of Good and Evil, which leads to their Fall, later epitomized by Adam as "Bad fruit of Knowledge" (*PL* 9:1067–73). If Raphael's doctrine is salvationist rather than anti-intellectual, Emerson's seems, in this passage, more dubious. Yet even here, in this supposedly natural, spontaneous, sylvan text, the scholar-reader is present. In affirming the superiority of that curiously incurious "intellectual life" (clean, healthy, unperplexed, and apparently unspeculative) and in setting "strong instincts" against mere "books," literary Emerson *alludes* (to Milton and Carlyle) and ends by actually *quoting* (Wordsworth, though without attribution). And this by now familiar paradox of originality is compounded by the fact that the poem he quotes, the sonnet beginning "Alas! What Boots the Long Laborious Quest," itself alludes to the question—"Alas! what boots it with uncessant care . . ."—initiating Milton's momentary turn (in "Lycidas") against the "laborious days" required to "strictly meditate . . . the thankless Muse." Milton had begun with an exclamation and question; Wordsworth's echoing sonnet is structured on three interrelated questions, ending in an affirmation incorporating a freedom fighter related to William Tell, a hero celebrated by Carlyle's Schiller.

Writing in the dismal historical context of Napoléon's 1809 victory over the Germans, including the defeat of the Tell-like peasant rebel Andreas Hofer, Wordsworth questions the point of the "long laborious quest" (accompanied by Germanic-Coleridgean "abstruse" pains) to attain "that transcendent rest" in which the passions come under the sway "Of Reason, seated on her sovereign hill." Is it not all in vain

> If sapient Germany must be deprest
> Beneath the brutal sword?—Her haughty Schools
> Shall blush; and may not we with sorrow say
> A few strong instincts and a few plain rules,
> Among the herdsmen of the Alps, have wrought
> More for mankind at this unhappy day
> Than all the pride of intellect and thought?
> (8–14; *WP* 1:836)

Though Wordsworth's expression of political sorrow at this unhappy time is profoundly sincere, the champion of rural freemen and instinctive strength cannot resist chastising intellectual hubris in the form of the haughty and now humbled "Schools" of sapient Germany, endorsing instead (as does Emerson, by quoting) the strong instincts and plain rules of the Alpine herdsmen led by Hofer, whose peasant uprising in the forests of the eastern Alps recalled for some the earlier Alpine exploits of "Arnold Winkelried, in the high Alps" (*E&L* 17) and of Tell in leading Switzerland's forest cantons to victory over the Hapsburgs. Together, these courageous "nationalist" independence movements against imperial tyranny explain Emerson's placement of Wordsworth's sonnet in the "Heroic" section of *Parnassus* (221), as well as his reference to "sylvan" strength—an adjective reinforced by the concluding lines of Wordsworth's sonnet "Hofer," in which we are to see, "beneath this godlike Warrior . . . / Hills, Torrents, woods, embodied to bemock" the tyrant Napoléon (*WP* 1:829).[29]

Finally, to come to the end of this vertiginous labyrinth of quotation and allusion, it should be noted that this sonnet of 1809 is illuminated by the major work Wordsworth wrote in that year: his prose tract *On the Convention of Cintra,* a bitter attack on the British betrayal of the rebelling Spaniards. Significantly, here too, Wordsworth pays eloquent tribute to the polar reciprocity and final fusion of calm and activity, a "union of peace with innocent and laudable animation"—even if the animation that is the necessary prerequisite to peace here takes the form of hunting out and utterly destroying the French army in Spain. In less bloodthirsty terms, Wordsworth praises the life-sustaining "genial and vernal inmate of the breast, which at once pushes forth and cherishes," the "elastic" expan-

29. Emerson would have encountered both sonnets in Coleridge's *Friend.* "Hofer" appeared in the October 26, 1809, number. "Alas! What Boots the Long Laborious Quest" was first published (November 16, 1809) as "Sonnet, Suggested by the Efforts of the Tyrolese, Contrasted with the Present State of Germany" (*F* 2:183). The rapidly shifting military and political context of 1809 would require an appendix; suffice it to say that the "contrast" Wordsworth draws is between, on the one hand, Germany following Napoléon's devastating military victories over the Prussian army in 1806 and the humiliating "reorganization" after the Peace of Tilsit and, on the other, the Tyrolese uprising led by the remarkable Andreas Hofer. Despite the intellectual but ineffectual patriotic fervor whose chief center was the University of Berlin, founded in 1809, Germany remained prostrate, resistance to Napoléon shifting to a well-led Austria. That resistance, too, had been crushed by the time Wordsworth wrote his sonnet, leaving only the peasant insurrection led by Hofer, a Tyrolean reincarnation of the legendary leader of the fourteenth-century Swiss-German uprising against Hapsburg rule recently glorified in Schiller's drama *Wilhelm Tell* (1804). In his sonnet "Hofer," Wordsworth transforms the Tyrolean hero into "Tell's great Spirit, from the dead / Returned to animate an age forlorn" (*WP* 1:829). Schiller's nation-rousing justification of violence against tyranny reflected Sturm und Drang Romanticism in general. But in volatile combination with the particular stimuli of Fichte's stirring *Addresses to the German Nation* (1807–1808) and, above all, the 1808 guerrilla war of the Spanish against the occupying French, Schiller's masterpiece had helped fire up Germany against the tyrant Napoléon, only to result, in sharp contrast to Tell's victory over the tyrant Gessler, in ignominious defeat.

siveness of man's heart ending in a tranquillity oriented "towards his Creator." It is a matter of head as well as heart; as he had said earlier in the tract, "all knowledge of human nature leads ultimately to repose." Thus, in the *Cintra* essay, Wordsworth, in effect, restores what had been brutally crushed in the sonnet: "that transcendent rest" sought through sovereign Reason by the German idealists. And, in envisioning a resurrection of Germany itself, Wordsworth, in the pamphlet, bases that eventual victory on the contributions of *both* "strong instincts" *and* "sapient" schools—Germany's "peasants, *and* its philosophers."[30]

Still, it is those strong instincts that Emerson endorses in "Spiritual Laws." To return to that essay: having quoted Wordsworth on "plain" rules and those "few strong instincts" that have wrought more for mankind "than all the pride of intellect and thought," Emerson immediately launches into a paragraph that sounds like nothing so much as a tallying paraphrase of Wordsworth's "favorite topic" during their 1833 conversation: the comparative superiority of education by intuition rather than tuition, an insistence to be found not only in the dialogue poems in *Lyrical Ballads* and in book 5 of *The Prelude* but throughout much of Wordsworth's poetry and prose as well. We cannot calculate in advance, through systematic learning and "assigned" books, what will be of paramount importance to us later in life, says Emerson, as convinced as Wordsworth

> How little those formalities to which
> With overweening trust alone we give
> The name of Education, hath to do
> With real feeling and just sense.
> (*P* 13:169–72)

30. Wordsworth, on the *Convention of Cintra,* in *The Prose Works of William Wordsworth,* 1:341. Whether or not he actually read Wordsworth's essay on Cintra, Emerson was certainly aware of it—as usual via Coleridge, whose praise (in Latin) of the pamphlet's rhetoric was, as we have seen, transferred by Emerson to his own praise of "Character of the Happy Warrior," another work of Wordsworth celebrating heroism even in the face of apparently insurmountable odds. Wordsworth's pamphlet has a great visual equivalent. The French scorched-earth policy in Spain was marked by widespread atrocities—the usual rape and pillage, widespread reprisals, ever busy firing squads. The spectacle of a powerful, authoritarian, imperial regime crushing a weak, disorganized but valiant guerrilla resistance (the term *guerrilla,* Spanish for "little war," was coined at this time) is nowhere more powerfully represented than in Goya's dramatic masterpiece *The Third of May, 1808, in Madrid: The Shooting on Principe Pio Mountain.* Recall Goya's vivid scene: the French firing squad a line of regimented automatons; the victims dead, dying, or waiting their turn; the focal point a white-shirted peasant, kneeling on the bloodstained earth, his face and posture a remarkable mixture of human horror, nationalist pride, and fatalistic resignation in the face of death. No one can contemplate that painting without having his or her imagination stirred. And that is the crucial agency appealed to in Wordsworth's pamphlet as well.

His "will," says Emerson,

> never gave the images in my mind the rank they now take. The regular course of studies, the years of academical and professional education, have not yielded me better facts than some idle books under the bench at the Latin School. What we do not call education is more precious than that which we call so. We form no guess, at the time of receiving a thought, of its comparative value. And education often wastes its effort in attempts to thwart and balk this natural magnetism, which is sure to select what belongs to it. (*E&L* 306)

This "natural magnetism," which mysteriously selects what "belongs to" the self-reliant spirit unthwarted by book-centered education, is the least dispensable half of that polarity we have been exploring—though, understood correctly, both halves of the polarity (intuition, spontaneity, and wise passiveness on the one hand, tuition, will, and laborious intellectual seeking, on the other) play a needful part in the creative process. No one who criticizes him, says Emerson later in "Spiritual Laws," can "excite me to the least uneasiness by saying, 'He acted, and thou sittest still.' I see action to be good, when the need is, and sitting still to be also good" (*E&L* 321). "Let us not rove," he says in "Self-Reliance"; let us rather "sit at home with the cause . . . for God is here within" (*E&L* 272). Having developed self-trust, aligning ourselves with "natural magnetism," that intuitional truth of the "self-relying soul," we approach Emersonian Frost's later couplet: "We dance round in a ring and suppose, / But the Secret sits in the middle and knows." Sounding like Keats in his distinction between flying Mercury and "sitting" Jove, between the busy bee and the patiently budding flower, Emerson goes on to ask in "Spiritual Laws": "Why should we be busybodies and superserviceable? Action and inaction are alike to the true." As he had just noted: "We call the poet inactive," failing to realize that "real action is in silent moments," the "epochs of our life" occurring not in external visible actions, but "in a silent thought by the way-side as we walk" (*E&L* 320–21). Such walks—the sort we associate with Wordsworth and Coleridge, Emerson and Thoreau—explain the pun (preambling) in Emerson's insistence, in "The American Scholar," that "the preamble of thought, the transition through which it passes from the unconscious to the conscious, is action. Only so much do I know, as I have lived" (*E&L* 60).

As noted earlier, that final phrase echoes a passage from Coleridge that, in turn, can lead us as it led him to an appreciation of one of Words-

---

Had the British held out in Spain, he insists, they would have administered "a shock to the enemy's power, where that power is strongest, in the imaginations of men."

worth's supreme accomplishments: the skating scene, connected with the Boy of Winander episode and sharing with it a trajectory leading from the expenditure of excited energy to an all-encompassing tranquillity—a rondure, as in "A Slumber Did My Spirit Seal," from individual motion to rest to participation in a diurnal and cosmic motion. The interconnections require a bit of tracing, especially since they reveal a countertruth to Emerson's celebration of apparently unconscious spontaneity.

Coleridge's Latin axiom from *Aids to Reflection*—"*Quantum sumus, scimus*" (We are what we know, or know what we are)—was synopsized by Emerson as the transformation of "unconscious truth" into the powerful "domain" of conscious knowledge (*E&L* 25; *JMN* 5:189). Reflecting Carlyle's celebration of anti-self-consciousness in "Characteristics," Emerson had first used this phrase in a negative way. In a journal entry of December 2, 1834, the "passage from the Unconscious to the Conscious" is "from careless receiving to cunning providing; from beauty to use; from omnivorous curiosity to anxious stewardship; from faith to doubt; from maternal Reason to hard short-sighted Understanding; from Unity to disunion" (*JMN* 4:348). Even there, he was employing Coleridgean terminology; later, glossing the Coleridgean axiom in *Nature,* the Conscious becomes a positive term and development.

In "The American Scholar," echoing Paul on the corruptible putting on incorruption, the mortal putting on immortality (1 Cor. 15:53), and Wordsworth on "emotion recollected in tranquillity," Emerson says that "the actions and events of our childhood are now matters of calmest observation," whereas a more recent "deed" will remain temporarily "immersed in our unconscious life" until in "some contemplative hour it detaches itself . . . to become a thought of the mind. Instantly it is raised, transfigured: the corruptible has put on incorruption. Henceforth, it is an object of beauty, however base its original neighborhood" (*E&L* 60–61). Earlier that same year (January 1837), in his lecture "Philosophy of History," he had said: "Whoever separates for us a truth from our unconscious reason, and makes it an object of consciousness, . . . must of course be to us a great man." Coleridge and Wordsworth would seem to qualify, for, as Emerson's language confirms, he is recalling both the Coleridgean (Freud-anticipating) movement from the Unconscious to the Conscious and Wordsworthian emotion recollected in pensive tranquillity. But Emerson would later discover in Wordsworth even more memorable dramatizations of that doctrine and of the poetic conversion of experience into thought. We find that conversion repeatedly embodied in such "spots of time" as the childhood events of the seasonal cycle in book 1 of *The Prelude* and the retrospective meditations that illuminate the mountain epiphanies in books 6 (the crossing of the Simplon Pass) and 14 (the nocturnal ascent of Mount Snowdon).

The Boy of Winander episode and the skating scene—two of the "spots of time" with which Emerson was familiar prior to his acquisition in 1850 of the posthumously published *Prelude*—had both been printed as excerpts from the longer poem years before, the first by Wordsworth himself (in the 1800 *Lyrical Ballads* and later in the 1815 *Poems*), the second, and intimately related episode, by Coleridge, who quoted it in full (prefaced by three lines of his own) as the conclusion to an essay in the Christmas 1809 issue of *The Friend.* It was there that Emerson encountered the sixty-line skating passage, a passage he also quoted in full, both in his 1839 lecture, "Genius," and, thirty-five years later, in *Parnassus.* His account in "Genius," about how a gifted poet "seizes on a circumstance so trivial that an inferior writer would not have trusted himself to detach and specify" (*EL* 1:77–78), echoes Coleridge, who, in *Biographia Literaria,* praises the skating episode as a particularly effective example of "the perfect truth of nature in [Wordsworth's] images and descriptions as taken immediately from nature," details that "escape the eye of common observation, thus raising to the rank of gems, what had been often kicked away by the hurrying foot of the traveller on the dusty high road of custom" (*BL* 2:148–49).

On at least three occasions, Emerson parallels that "raising to the rank of gems": First, he does so in his remark (just cited from "The American Scholar") about a deed being "raised, transfigured." In a more extended comment, he recalls Coleridge's "hurrying foot" and—endorsing Wordsworth's leveling Muse and the displaced political-poetical revolution announced in the 1800 preface to *Lyrical Ballads*—looks back to Wordsworth and ahead to Whitman. And Emerson rejoices in being born in "an age of Revolution," when (in an echo of the political hopes and fears expressed in *The Prelude* and in Coleridge's "France: An Ode"), "the energies of all men are searched by fear and by hope." In this revolutionary context, Emerson embraces "the common":

> I read with joy of the auspicious signs of the coming days, as they glimmer already. . . . One of these signs is the fact, that the same movement which effected the elevation of what was called the lowest class in the state, assumed in literature a very marked and as benign an aspect. Instead of the sublime and beautiful; the near, the low, the common, was explored and poeticized. That which had been negligently trodden under foot . . . is suddenly found to be richer than all foreign parts. The literature of the poor, the feelings of the child . . . are the topics of the time. . . . It is a sign,—is it not? of new vigor. . . . I ask not for the great, the remote, the romantic; what is doing in Italy or Arabia; what is Greek art, or Provencal minstrelsy; I em-

> brace the common, I explore and sit at the feet of the familiar, the low. (*E&L* 68–69)

Of course, this renunciation of "the romantic" takes the form of an embrace of *Wordsworthian* Romanticism. In *Nature,* Emerson declares that "the invariable mark of wisdom is to see the miraculous in the common" (*E&L* 47). We can hardly *not* think of Coleridge on Wordsworth, but aboriginal Emerson names neither. When in "The American Scholar" Emerson finally allows the repressed to return by casually referring to three of his four great Romantic precursors ("Goethe, Wordsworth, and Carlyle"), his praise is limited to their part in the trend to "embrace the common" in such a way that "things near" are recognized as "not less beautiful and wondrous than things remote," that "the near explains the far" (*E&L* 69). Although Emerson goes on to praise Goethe and Swedenborg, he is thinking even more of the poetry of Wordsworth and the critical insights of Coleridge in which the polarity between simple fact and sublime and sublimating thought is united and animated by genius. The "low" alone is not enough; what is required is polarity, the union of low and high, the trivial and the sublime, a unifying "idea" Emerson associates, in this "newer time," with the genius of Goethe, Wordsworth, and Carlyle. Show me, he says, the "ultimate reason" underlying apparent trifles.

> Show me the sublime presence of the highest spiritual cause lurking, as always it does lurk, in these suburbs and extremes of nature; let me see every trifle bristling with the polarity that ranges it instantly on an eternal law, . . . referred to the like cause by which light undulates and poets sing;—and the world lies no longer a dull miscellany . . . but has form and order; there is no trifle; there is no puzzle; but one design unites and animates the farthest pinnacle and the lowest trench. (*E&L* 69)

A journal entry of June 21, 1838, has, in recent years, become celebrated as the first instance, almost seventy years before James Joyce, of the use of the theological term *epiphany* to denote a trifling fact that radiates out into higher significance, a privileged moment, a Wordsworthian "spot of time." "Day creeps after day," says Emerson, "each full of facts, dull, strange, despised things. . . . [P]resently the aroused intellect finds gold and gems in one of these scorned facts, then finds . . . that a fact is an Epiphany of God" (*JMN* 7:29). Anticipating Joyce, Emerson is looking back to Wordsworth—but then so is Joyce! Although he associates his "epiphanies" with Aquinas, Joyce actually seems less Thomistic than Wordsworthian in declaring (in *Stephen Hero*) that "the soul of the commonest object . . . seems to us radiant. The object attains its epiphany." In fact, in 1905, at the very time that he was working out his concept of the epiphany, Joyce was thinking about the radiant "moments" and "spots of time" in Wordsworth, to whom, "in my history of literature I have given the highest palms," grouping him with Shakespeare and Shelley. Shortly thereafter, in a second letter to Stanislaus, he credited his brother for a "word" that virtually belongs to Coleridge, who most often lavished it on the very poet now being praised by Joyce: "I think Wordsworth," wrote Joyce to his brother, "of all English men of letters best deserves your word 'genius.'"[31]

Coleridge and Wordsworth coalesce as well in Emerson's description of the aroused intellect's discovery of "gold and gems" in despised and scorned facts that turn out to be epiphanies, an association confirmed by Emerson's echoing of Coleridge—the third of the three instances referred to—on commonly observed details raised "to the rank of gems" by Wordsworth, especially in that epiphanic episode, the skating scene. In another journal entry, Emerson, too, specifies an element of that scene as exemplifying the common, the familiar, the low. He focuses on an observation that would be beneath all but the most self-trusting poet and certainly *was* beneath the notice of pre-Wordsworthian poets: "How much of self-reliance it implies to write a true description of any thing, for example, Wordsworth's picture of skating; that leaning back on your heels and stopping short in mid-career. So simple a fact no common man would have trusted himself to detach as a thought" (*JMN* 5:454). Admirers of the ice-skating scene, recognized by readers from Coleridge on as one of Wordsworth's supreme achievements, might well ask, is that all there is? But we can at least acknowledge that Emerson has a point. It may seem a small point, but the transfiguration of so simple a fact as stopping on skates emphasizes one important aspect of two-voiced Wordsworth. If the rooting of our most profound experiences in simple, even humble things, base in origin and neighborhood, has long since become a poetic commonplace, it is Wordsworth and what Hazlitt called his "levelling" Muse who made it so, he who showed "How verse may build a princely throne / On humble truth" ("At the Grave of Burns," 35–36). As Pater remarks in his essay on the poet in *Appreciations,* "The peculiar function of Wordsworth's genius" was "a power to open out the soul of apparently little or familiar things."[32]

31. Joyce, *Stephen Hero,* 213; Joyce, *Selected Letters of James Joyce* (May 3, June 11, 1905), 62–63. I suspect that schoolboy Stephen's anticipation of Christmas in *Portrait* plays off the similar situation in *The Prelude* (12:287–323). Emerson's journal entry on the "epiphany" has been cited as paralleling the Wordsworthian "spots of time" and anticipating the Joycean epiphany by both M. H. Abrams (*Natural Supernaturalism,* 413, 421) and Robert Langbaum ("The Epiphanic Mode in Wordsworth and Modern Literature," in *The Word from Below: Essays on Modern Literature and Culture,* by Langbaum 37). See also Emerson's lecture "Education" (*W* 10:132).

32. Pater, "Wordsworth," 48.

But there is more to it than that, both in terms of the full ramifications of self-reliance, originality, and spurning of convention and in the full profundity of that "opening out." For example, in "Poetry and Imagination," characterizing one of Coleridge's most celebrated distinctions, Emerson observes that "fancy is wilful; imagination a spontaneous act, . . . a perception and affirming of a real relation between a thought and some material fact; fancy amuses; imagination expands and exalts" (*EPP* 304). In his 1843 essay on Wordsworth in the *Dial,* Emerson again pays tribute to this poet's "self-reliance" and confidence in "his own mood," to his astonishing originality in seizing on occasional incidents. In his reliance on his private moods and commonplace events, Wordsworth "called in question" both literary and social convention, normative "social theories on the conduct of life." And these were called in question "on wholly new grounds," not from Platonism or from Christianity, but from "the lessons which the country muse taught a stout pedestrian climbing a mountain, and in following a river from its parent rill down to the sea" (*E&L* 1255). And that's true, too—though a Mark Twain–like reader, honed on the faulty woodlore of a Fenimore Cooper, might be tempted to point out that when the stalwart pedestrian put on skates, his country muse would have taught him that if he *simply* leaned back on his heels without angling those skates, he would quickly find himself hissing along the polished ice on his sibilant if less than sibylline ass. Wordsworth, a famously skilled skater even at sixty (when, Dorothy informed Mary Lamb, her brother was "still the crack skater on Rydal Lake"), would have dug his heels in at an oblique angle. Emerson, a comparatively inexperienced and awkward skater, might not.[33]

Moving from the mundane to the sublime, from the simple "material fact" to the imagination that "expands and exalts us," it is time to quote the skating scene in full. I do so in the form in which Emerson encountered it in *The Friend* (2:258–59), placing in brackets the few later revisions, all improvements. Identified by Coleridge as Wordsworth's and "extracted, with its author's permission, from an unpublished Poem on the Growth

33. For Dorothy's letter of January 9, 1830, to Mary Lamb, see Wordsworth, *Letters: Later Years,* 1:443. Wordsworth's skill as a skater was well known among his rural neighbors; there was "noan better in these parts," according to one local contributor to "Reminiscences of Wordsworth among the Peasantry of Westmoreland," *Wordsworthiana* (1889), 98–99, cited in R. D Havens, *The Mind of a Poet,* 304. Hawthorne's daughter tells an amusing and revealing anecdote about the skating skills of Emerson, in comparison with those of Thoreau (an experienced skater who figured "dithyrambic dances and Bacchic leaps on the ice") and of her own cloaked father (moving like "a self-impelled Greek statue, stately and grave"). In contrast, Emerson, always on the verge of toppling, seemed "barely able to hold himself erect, pitching headforemost, half lying on the air" (Rose Hawthorne Lathrop, *Memories of Hawthorne,* 53).

and Revolutions of an Individual Mind," the excerpt is titled "Growth of Genius from the Influences of Natural Objects, on the Imagination in Boyhood, and Early Youth," and prefaced by Coleridge with a three-line epigraph from his own poem "To William Wordsworth." Those lines—"an Orphic Tale indeed, / A Tale divine of high and passionate thoughts / To their own music chaunted!" (45–47)—allude to the skating scene's context, the opening book of *The Prelude.* Even more appropriately, they allude to Wordsworth's lofty aspiration—under the relentless urging of Coleridge himself!—to write *The Recluse,* an intended fusion of thought and passion, philosophic truth and lyricism, "wisdom married to immortal verse" (*E* 7:536). In *The Prelude,* Wordsworth, in a double echo of Milton, tells us that he yearns toward "some philosophic song / Of Truth," one that

> cherishes our daily life;
> With meditations passionate from deep
> Recesses in man's heart, immortal verse
> Thoughtfully fitted to the Orphean lyre.
> (*P* 1:229–34)[34]

Coleridge begins his excerpt with Wordsworth's elevated apostrophe to "The Wisdom and Spirit of the Universe," as close as the man who wrote the lines in 1798 could get to saying "God." The lines, describing how that Spirit intertwined for the poet the passions that "build up our human soul," are echoed in Emerson, as the "incalculable," hidden "masterpieces of God, the total growths and movements of the soul," which mysteriously "help" us "when we are building up our being" (*E&L* 415). We build up our human soul, says Wordsworth, with "enduring things" that purify the elements of feeling and of thought, "sanctifying by such discipline" both "pain and fear, until we recognize / A grandeur in the beatings of the heart." Following a transitional reference to "November days," when "vapours rolling down the vallies made / A lonely scene more lonesome," Wordsworth moves into the skating episode itself, perhaps the paradigmatic example of the polar interaction between activity and wise passivity. It is an evening in "the frosty season, when the sun / Was set," and distant cottage windows blazed through the twilight gloom. All were happy; for young Wordsworth, it was "a time of rapture," as (exhibiting the "glad animal movements" of "Tintern Abbey") he "wheel'd about, / Proud and exulting, like an untir'd horse." All "shod with steel," the boys "hiss'd along the polished ice," playing games charged with folk memories of the woodland hunt.

34. For the double Miltonic reference, see below, Chapter 10 note 24.

So through the darkness and the cold we flew
And not a voice was idle; with the din
Meanwhile the precipices rang aloud; [Smitten]
The leafless trees and every icy crag
Tinkled like iron; while *the* distant hills [far]
Into the tumult sent an alien sound
Of melancholy not unnoticed, while the stars
Eastward, were sparkling clear, and in the west
The orange sky of evening died away.

In a visual and auditory drawing back anticipating the final lines of Keats's "To Autumn," we recede from the "din" of the excited boys on the lake to the ringing precipices, from the leafless trees and icy crags that tinkled like iron to the somber reverberations of the distant hills, ending, as in Keats, with the "sky"—here, the simultaneously emerging stars of evening and the dying sunset. Commenting on this passage, Emerson, too, fused the visual with the auditory, noting "the *sound* of the stars" on a snowy night (*JMN* 5:454), which chimes with his Wordsworth-inflected notation, in the "Beauty" chapter of *Nature,* of "the charm, last evening, of a January sunset" and how the "leafless trees become spires of flame in the sunset, with the blue east for their back-ground . . . and stubble rimed with frost, contribute something to the mute music" (*E&L* 15).

Amid these melancholy reverberations of the otherness of Wordsworth's cherished but sublime Nature, and the subtle intimations of mortality, one boy skates away from the "tumultuous throng," in pursuit of a gleam, an elusive ideal in the form of a star reflected on the ice. It is another instance, to quote the lines that so excited Coleridge in the Boy of Winander episode, of the "heaven received / Into the bosom of the steady lake," here the glassy surface of a frozen lake. In one of his finest revisions, Wordsworth added, sometime after 1809, a Miltonic cadence. Visually echoing the heavenly chorus of angels in "Lycidas" that "sing, and singing in their glory, move," the reflected star "fled, and flying still before me, gleamed." In the original passage, the boy "cut[s] across the image [later, *reflex*] of a Star"

That gleam'd upon the ice; and oftentimes,
When we had given our bodies to the wind,
And all the shadowy banks on either side
Came sweeping through the darkness spinning still
The rapid line of motion, then at once
Have I, reclining back upon my heels,
Stopp'd short; yet still the solitary Cliffs
Wheel'd by me even as if the earth had roll'd
With visible motion her diurnal round!
Behind me did they stretch in solemn train,

Feebler and feebler, and I stood and watch'd
Till all was tranquil as a *summer sea.* [dreamless sleep].

The boy who had "wheel'd about," and was one of those who "hiss'd" and "flew" along the ice, is now motionless as the cliffs "wheel" by *him.* He becomes a still center of the turning world, earth's "diurnal round." No longer energetically active, in a state of wise passivity, he now watches and receives, absorbed into a tranquillity anticipating the Wanderer's evocation of motionless "power" and "central peace, subsisting at the heart / Of endless agitation" (*E* 4:1145–47) and dwarfing even the imagery of the visible scene in which the Boy of Winander hung listening—"surprized," as Wordsworth said in his own gloss, "into a perception of the solemn and tranquillizing images which the Poem describes." It is at the pivotal moment, the one that so engaged Emerson, when the skater abruptly "Stopped short," ending his own rapid "motion," that Nature unexpectedly but fully reveals to him her grander "motion," of which he is a small part or particle, yet a motion in which, as a participant, he is imaginatively expanded and exalted. Thinking of the seasonal episodes of the opening book of *The Prelude* (robbing birds' nests, rowing the stolen boat, above all the ice-skating scene, the one episode known to Emerson prior to 1850), Barbara Packer rightly remarks: "The most valuable experiences Wordsworth discovered in his childhood as he looked back on it were not the incidents a biographer would be likely to record but rather certain uncanny moments of heightened perception that occurred unexpectedly in the midst of ordinary childish sports."[35]

Though Emerson's focus on Wordsworth's observation of a "simple fact" beneath the notice of lesser poets does provide an "opening out" to larger issues, it also, I think, represses more than it expresses. In "The Poet," having just described a bard remarkably like the Wordsworth of the sublime passage of "Tintern Abbey," Emerson sweepingly announces, "I look in vain for the poet I describe." Similarly, faced with a scene epitomizing the motion/rest/motion dialectic he inherited critically from Coleridge and poetically from Wordsworth (as well as their larger shared dialectic between nature, the human mind, and a haunting quasi-divine presence), Emerson also (as Elizabeth Peabody once regretted) "stopped short."[36] His commentary, focused on the skater's stopping in midcareer,

35. Packer, *Emerson's Fall,* 163. For the final version of the ice-skating scene, see *P* 1:416–63.

36. In concluding her splendid 1838 review of *Nature,* Peabody wishes Emerson would not "accuse us of ingratitude, in that after he has led his readers to this high point of view [she refers to the penultimate paragraph of "Spirit," which she glosses in language riddled with Coleridge's major distinctions], they crave more, and accuse

exemplifies what New Historicists and other critics susceptible to the hermeneutics of suspicion would call a "significant silence"—or what Robert Weisbuch, referring to early and middle Emerson's silence regarding his immediate Romantic precursors, has termed "erasure."

There *is* that synesthetic registration of the "sound of stars" on a snowy night. But in essentially limiting himself to the stopping short on skates (even if it *is* a "common" or "near" fact that expands to explain "the far"), Emerson represses these truly expansive connections to his benefactors—as he did throughout *Nature,* where, to preserve his individual and national originality, he deliberately avoids mentioning Wordsworth and restricts himself, as we have seen, to that single harmless reference to Coleridge's lecture on the Gothic mind in the Middle Ages.[37] Thus, we are left to exercise our own imaginations in surmising the skating episode's deeper and higher impact on Emerson, a prose poet and recorder of the pathos and grandeur that couple us with the diurnal and annual cycles of nature (*E&L* 21–22), a man who, though as self-reliant a being as Wordsworth, was nevertheless so often, like him, swept up into the self-transcending, circulating immensity of the universe, an all-encompassing dialectic of motion and rest.

❧ Explaining the ubiquitous "alternation of attraction and repulsion," the polarity between action and passivity, motion and rest, Emerson contends: "Everything in nature is bipolar, or has a positive and negative pole. There is a male and a female, a spirit and a fact, a north and a south. Spirit is the positive, the event is the negative. Will is the north, action the south pole" (*E&L* 499, 503). The full range of polarities is laid out in the essay "Compensation." Enumerating such opposites as darkness and light, heat and cold, the ebb and flow of waters, male and female, the inspiration and expiration of plants and animals, the systole and diastole of the heart, the undulations of fluids and of sound, centrifugal and centripetal gravity, Emerson observes, "Polarity, or action and reaction, we meet in every part of nature. . . . An inevitable dualism bisects nature, so that each thing is a half, and suggests another thing to make it whole; as, spirit, matter; man, woman; odd, even; subjective, objective; in, out; upper, under; motion, rest; yea, nay" (*E&L* 286–87). Such polarities—like the flux and

---

him of stopping short, where the world most desires and needs further guidance" ("Nature—a Prose Poem," *EPP* 596).

37. "'A Gothic church,' said Coleridge, 'is a petrified religion.'" Here, in the "Discipline" chapter of *Nature* (*E&L* 30), Emerson quotes (from *Literary Remains* [1836]) Coleridge's "Lecture on the General Characteristics of the Gothic Mind in the Middle Ages"—not exactly one of the texts to which he was most indebted.

reflux of the Wordsworthian "interchange / Of peace and excitation"—embrace passivity and action, indolence and labor, spirit and matter, self-reliance and necessity, or—to cite Stephen Whicher's influential identification of *the* defining tension in Emerson's "inner life"—Freedom and Fate. Just as he felt the demands of ambition straining against his freedom, so, reciprocally, even within the stringent restrictions of Fate, Emerson, in his grimly exhilarating essay of that title, asserts his limited but irrepressible "power." He was, in Yeats's oxymoron, "predestinate *and* free."[38]

Two Coleridgean texts that particularly influenced Emerson—the reciprocity between "each and all" and the axiom "*Quantum sumus, scimus*"—illuminate two interrelated polarities, each containing mighty opposites to be reconciled. I mean the tension—at the heart of Romantic and Emersonian dialectic—between the individual and his communal responsibilities and between the Self and God. The next chapters focus on the ambiguous ramifications of the concept of Divinity Within, particularly in terms of the doctrine of Self-Reliance: the problematic relation between the merely private self and the enlarged Self, as well as between that Self and God, whether considered as immanent or transcendent. Coleridge's Latin axiom became, with the help of his own gloss in *Aids to Reflection,* a momentous source for Emerson's finding, "within ourselves," a self paradoxically "more than ourselves," the ground of our moral life and of "all other knowledge." This concept of Self-Reliance clarifies the tension between Solitude and Society, the pull between withdrawal into the realm of one's own creative labor and the need to engage politically, which Emerson presents (again using Coleridge's term) as a tension between the "individual genius" and the "universal genius." This polarity illuminates Emerson's reluctant but not insubstantial sociopolitical activism in the great issues of the day, particularly the crisis brought about by the resuscitation of the old Fugitive Slave legislation, while the Self-God polarity engages the very definition of that elastic term, *Self-Reliance,* and its theological ramifications.

These issues are taken up in the next chapter. We may conclude the present chapter, and the whole of this middle section on "polarities," by agreeing with Thomas McFarland and Stanley Cavell. At the pivotal moment in his lecture "Emerson, Coleridge, Kant," Cavell turns "to Coleridge, the figure from whom the American Transcendentalists would have learned much of what they know about Kant, and about German philos-

38. See "'Predestinate and Free': Yeats and the Nietzschean Paradox of Exultant Freedom within Compulsion and Constraint," chap. 6 of my *Yeats's Interactions with Tradition.*

ophy generally, and by whom Emerson would have been preceded in his emphasis on polarity in human thinking. . . . That Coleridge is part of a tradition obsessed with the polarity of human thought needs no confirmation from me," says Cavell, and he directs us to McFarland's "Complex Dialogue: Coleridge's Doctrine of Polarity and Its European Contexts."[39] The point remains that those European philosophic contexts, and the emphasis on polar thinking, came to Emerson essentially through Coleridge.

More than enough has been said in this section on "polarities" to clarify this pattern of alternating pulsations, the interplay of the active and the receptive implicit in wise passiveness, perhaps even to shed light on other elements in the omnipresent binary pattern Emerson shares with so many creative spirits. Clearly, Emerson—with important consequences for the Transcendentalist movement and for much subsequent American literature and thought—found most of his favorite distinctions and polarities in the books of Samuel Taylor Coleridge, the pivotal thinker who opened up to him the vitalistic and healing poetry of Wordsworth and who taught him the supreme value of the passive-active polarity, along with those crucial distinctions between Genius and Talent, Imagination and Fancy, and, above all, intuitive Reason and mere Understanding, the latter the distinction upon which both British Romanticism and—for all its vaunted originality and self-reliant autonomy—American Transcendentalism may fairly be said to be founded.

39. Cavell, *In Quest of the Ordinary,* 40–41, 46–47.

Part III

DIVINITIES

Chapter 8

Solitude and Society

SELF-RELIANCE AND COMMUNAL RESPONSIBILITY

Quantum sumus, scimus. That which we find within ourselves, which is more than ourselves, and yet the ground of whatever is good and permanent therein, is the substance and life of all other knowledge.

—SAMUEL TAYLOR COLERIDGE, *Aids to Reflection*

❧

The poet Wordsworth asked, "What one is, why may not millions be?" Why not? Knowledge exists to be imparted.

—RALPH WALDO EMERSON, "The Progress of Culture"

❧

If I live my life according to my God-given insights, then I cannot go wrong, and even if I do, I know I have acted in good faith.

—ADOLF HITLER, in conversation, 1941

❧

Power is one great lesson which Nature teaches Man. The secret that he can not only reduce under his will, that is, conform to his character, particular events but classes of events & so harmonize all the outward occurrences with the states of mind, that must he learn.

—RALPH WALDO EMERSON, *Journal,* June 15–16, 1836

The relation between the solitary self and the larger community can be understood, in Romantic terms, as another form of the distinction and ultimate interchange, or "marriage," between Fichte's *Ich* and *Nicht-Ich,* the Me and NOT ME of Carlyle and Emerson, subject and object, spirit and matter—the Channing Ode's "Law for man, and law for thing." The first set of terms in this bipolarity constitutes an imaginative and—for Fichte, Coleridge, Wordsworth, and especially Emerson—a "moral" realm, either asserting a divinity within or enshrining a symbolic reflection of a transcendent God. This internal "moral nature," in the face of which, Emerson says, the private self can become a mere "impertinence" (*W* 10: 94–95), in turn engages the Coleridgean Each and All, with each of us—in what Emerson described as Coleridge's "enlarged and reverent" view of human nature and of the "Divine Reason"—"the most sacred object in the Universe, the Temple of Deity" (*EL* 1:377, 379).

In the course of these important 1836 remarks on Coleridge, Emerson casually dismissed *Aids to Reflection* as "the least valuable" of his mentor's works, "though a useful book I suppose" (*EL* 1:379). In practice, the themes and formulations of this useful book sank deep into his consciousness. To cite a prime example, much of Emerson, especially the emphasis on an expansion of consciousness from "within" that yet transcends its source, is encapsulated in Coleridge's Latin axiom and his attendant explanation in *Aids to Reflection:* "*Quantum sumus, scimus.* That which we find *within ourselves,* which is *more* than ourselves, and *yet the ground* of whatever is good and permanent therein, is the substance and life of *all other knowledge*" (*AR* 30n; italics added).[1]

That mysterious something within yet above and beyond our individual, merely "personal" self ("*I* am *nothing,* I *see all,*" Emerson affirms in becoming a transparent eyeball) is the ground of all morality and permanent knowledge, a knowledge that is substantial and vital, not abstract and weighed down by the inherited burden of history, tradition, and the passively accepted dicta of others—everything that he rejects, in "Self-Reliance," as conforming to "the world's opinion," instead of his own imperative. "To believe your own thought, to believe that what is true for you in your private heart is true for all men—that is genius" (*E&L* 259). "I celebrate myself," Emersonian Whitman announces, more nonchalantly but no less momentously, in introducing himself to us: "And what I assume you shall assume / For every atom belonging to me as good belongs to you." In these opening words of "Song of Myself," and therefore the opening words of *Leaves of Grass,* Whitman strikes more emphatically the note of cosmic democracy only implicit in what sounds like Emerson's more egocentric proclamation. Here, in any case, we are at the triumphant yet prob-

1. Inadvertently reversing it ("*Quantum scimus sumus*"), Emerson copied the aphorism into his journals twice (*JMN* 9:369, 15:115).

lematic center of Transcendentalist "individualism," a simultaneously self-affirming and self-transcending "power" center we will have to ponder for a moment.

The Emersonian imperative just cited is yet another variation on Kant, this time on the Kantian Categorical Imperative; nevertheless, this form of "genius" is also dangerous, as much subsequent trouble has demonstrated. The following celebrated (or notorious) passage in "Self-Reliance" embodies an idea with consequences for many—perhaps most powerfully for Nietzsche:

> Nothing is at last sacred but the integrity of your own mind. . . . I remember an answer which when quite young I was prompted to make to a valued adviser who was wont to importune me with the dear old doctrines of the church. On my saying, What have I to do with the sacredness of traditions, if I live wholly from within? my friend suggested—"But these impulses may be from below, not from above." I replied, "They do not seem to me to be such; but if I am the Devil's child, I will live then from the Devil." No law can be sacred to me but that of my nature. Good and bad are but names very readily transferable to that or this; the only right is what is after my own constitution, the only wrong what is against it. (*E&L* 261–62)[2]

Though Emerson was troubled by the "diabolical" potential in Carlyle, he was himself capable of adopting what ironic Blake in *The Marriage of Heaven and Hell* called "the Voice of the Devil," a voice echoed by Nietzsche, who partially transcribed this passage of "Self-Reliance," and who has his prophet say (in the first part of *Thus Spoke Zarathustra):* "I whisper this advice in the ear of him possessed of a devil: 'Better for you to rear your devil!'" Emerson chose as the chapter title of a projected book "the mind as its own place" (*JMN* 3:316). In doing so, he was, of course, alluding to Milton's Satan (*PL* 1:253). Margaret Fuller—a woman who seemed, for most of her truncated life, nothing if not sure of the power "within herself"—acknowledged that it was from Emerson "that I first learned what is meant by the inward life. . . . that *the mind is its own place* was a dead phrase until he cast light upon my mind." Her allusion to Satan, perhaps unconscious, is certainly not intended to denigrate her mentor.[3] Emerson's trust in his impulses partakes of virtue since those impulses seem to him "right." But in advocating an ethic generated "wholly from within," from the mind as its own place, he moves not only beyond the

2. Nietzsche's transcription of the last and the third-from-last sentence of this passage has been documented by Eduard Baumgarten in tracing Emerson's influence ("Mitteilungen und Bemerkungen . . . ," 111).

3. For Fuller's comment, see Moncure Daniel Conway, *Emerson at Home and Abroad,* 89.

constraints of received doctrine, social conformity, and tradition but also, as Nietzsche would later say, "beyond good and evil," at least as conventionally understood. Coleridge cannot have known what he was unleashing when he assured Emerson that what "we find within ourselves" is "the ground of whatever is good and permanent therein and the substance and life of all other knowledge." And Emerson, in turn, cannot have known what the impact of the doctrine of self-reliance would be on the German youth who began to read him at the age of seventeen. Himself a great liberator, Nietzsche found his own liberating god in Emerson.

What *gets* liberated—that "Nietzschean" or "Emersonian" aberration, Hitler, for example—is another matter. One distinguished American critic, Alfred Kazin, reports in *God and the American Writer* that he "once heard" another distinguished critic, the conservative southerner Cleanth Brooks, "charge that 'Emerson led to Hitler.'"[4] Evidently, Emerson—that glorifier of the liberated self, celebrator of one's "sacred impulses," equator of infinitude and the individual, champion of the god within—retained his power to infuriate the religiously orthodox mind, no matter how brilliant that mind.

Of course, Brooks was not being utterly irresponsible. More than one scholar has traced the metapolitical roots of Nazism and the phenomenon of Hitler to German Romanticism, including German idealist philosophy, the same philosophy that found its way to Emerson by way of Carlyle and, especially, Coleridge. Ideas can have the most horrifically unintended consequences. In his own perverse way a product of German thought, Hitler was a selective student in this tradition. The future führer carried with him throughout World War I a copy of Schopenhauer's *World as Will and Representation* (not, interestingly enough, Nietzsche's *Zarathustra,* the German soldier's typical knapsack book). In the 1930s, he read and annotated passages on the godlike self in the eight-volume set of Fichte given him by Leni Riefenstahl, the filmmaker who also gave the world in 1934 the greatest of all propaganda films, *The Triumph of the Will.* Hitler's growing messianic conviction that he was predestined for greatness providing he followed the dictates of his infallible inner voice was in part attributable to his acceptance of the myth he himself created. But he also seems to have genuinely believed himself an instrument of Providence, inspired by divine powers. Though he thought Christianity "an outgrowth of the Jews" and father of that bastard Bolshevism, he may, with hints from Fichte, have identified himself with Christ's assertion of divinity. It seems ominously appropriate that the Fichte volumes should have been given him by Riefenstahl, the opening shot of whose masterwork features a plane

4. Brooks quoted in Kazin, *God and the American Writer,* 14.

bearing Hitler descending from the clouds: deus ex machina, the führer as God.

As Carlyle noted, and Emerson remembered, the "foundation of what Fichte means by his far-famed *Ich* and *Nicht-Ich* (I and Not-I)" is his idealist conviction that the whole of the material universe consists of "Impressions produced on *me* by something *different from me.*" It is the "impact" (*Anstoß*) upon you of the external obstacle that makes you aware of the *Ich,* as something different from the *Nicht-Ich,* the Other that the imperial Self seeks not only to understand but also to alter, to mould, to dominate. Thus, the *Ich* tends to assume the role of an "absolute" or "pure I" akin to deity, or what Fichte calls the "Divine-Me." It was precisely this that Emerson's aunt Mary—perhaps recalling Coleridge's caricature of "the Fichtean Egoismus" as "myself God" in a satiric poem identifying the *Ich* with "the God imperativus"—sarcastically condemned in Fichte's philosophy: the "hypothesis" that "in recognizing a divine idea—a God within—banishes the only God who self-exists," the Judeo-Christian God "in whom we live and move," and whose independent ontological status, for her and other believers, is not in doubt.[5]

At one point Fichte, in one of the volumes that engaged Hitler, asks rhetorically: "Where did Jesus derive the power that has held his followers for all eternity?" Hitler drew a heavy line beneath the answer: "Through his absolute identification with God." In another passage, a three-sentence paragraph also highlighted by Hitler, Fichte (anticipating Emerson's insistence that each of us can be as Christ was in the moment of inspiration when he identified himself with the "I am") claims, "God and I are One. . . . His life is mine; my life is his. My work is his work, and his work my work." In 1939, Hitler was given a manuscript, *The Law of the World: The Coming Religion,* by an enthusiast named Maximilian Riedel. Again, he read with pen in hand. A version of one underlined sentence reappeared, in 1941, during one of his monologues. "Mind and soul ultimately return to the collective being of the world," a metaphysical führer informed his enthralled guests. "If there is a God, then he gives us not only life but also consciousness and awareness. *If I live my life according to my God-given insights, then I cannot go wrong, and even if I do, I know I have acted in good*

5. Mary Moody Emerson, "Almanack," in Cole, *Mary Moody Emerson,* 208–9. Carlyle's remarks on Fichte occur in his essay "Novalis," in *Critical and Miscellaneous Essays,* 2:25. The *Ich* and *Nicht-Ich* of Fichte and Novalis, filtered through Carlyle, become Emerson's Me and NOT ME. The Latin opening line of Coleridge's poetic parody (*BL* 1:160) may be translated as "Huzzah! God's vice-regent, myself God." Of this "burlesque," Coleridge himself said that it conveyed "as tolerable a likeness of Fichte's idealism as can be expected from an avowed caricature" (*BL* 1:159–60n). I will return to this poem in the next chapter.

faith." Not only did Hitler believe in divine powers; he also believed "that the mortal and the divine were one and the same: that the God he was seeking was in fact himself."[6]

This is High Romanticism gone sour. That the Romantic concept of divinity within, like the doctrine of self-reliant individualism, is not only liberating but potentially anarchic or tyrannical or both, was acknowledged by some Romantics and Transcendentalists themselves, especially in their later "conservative" years. But Wordsworth, Coleridge, and Emerson—unlike the advocates of a rugged individualism or will to power that is mindlessly or brutally self-assertive—retained a belief in autonomy, freedom, and idealism without forgetting that the needs of a humane society, knit by ties of reciprocal obligation, were incompatible with selfish (unrestrained, merely private and therefore petty) individualism.

Emerson was quite explicit about the moral dangers of the unrestrained will; once again he would seem to have gone to school to his principal Romantic mentor. In its reprobate form, says Coleridge in appendix C of *The Statesman's Manual,* "the WILL becomes Satanic pride and rebellious self-idolatry in the relation of the spirit to itself, and remorseless despotism relatively to others," the consequence of the will's "fearful resolve to find in itself alone the one absolute motive of action, under which all motives from within and from without must be either subordinated or crushed" (*LS* 65). Emerson made a similar point in his late essay "Character." There, in sharply distinguishing self-reliant individualism from the trivially personal, he is at once qualifying his earlier concept of self-reliance and repudiating its understandable but extremist interpretation. An "intensely focused thinker who kept returning lifelong to his core idea," Emerson was, notes Lawrence Buell, "forever reopening and reformulating it, looping away and back again, convinced that the spirit of the idea dictated that no final statement was possible." Nevertheless, like George Kateb, perhaps the most penetrating analyst of the theory of Self-Reliance, Buell insists on the importance to Emerson of what Kateb calls "impersonal individuality," a formulation that subsumes the apparent or actual "contradiction" between the god within and the Over-Soul, between the assertion of an autonomous, intuitive self and the absorption of that self in an all-encompassing universal, and impersonal, life force:

> The Me at the bottom of the me, the "Trustee" or "aboriginal Self" on which reliance may be safely grounded, is despite whatever appearances to

6. This is the conclusion of Timothy W. Ryback, in "Hitler's Forgotten Library: The Man, His Books, and His Search for God," 80, 81, 88–90. In 2001, Ryback studied Hitler's annotations in these and other volumes in his personal library, volumes now housed in the Hitler Collection in the Library of Congress, Washington, D.C.

> the contrary not a merely personal interest but a universal. The more inward you go, the less individuated you get. Beneath and within the "private" is a "public" power on which anyone can potentially draw. So Self-Reliance involves not a single but a double negative: resistance to external pressure, then resistance to shallow impulse.[7]

In "Character," Emerson explores this idea in depth. "Morals is the direction of the will on universal ends," he explains. "He is immoral who is acting to any private end. He is moral—we say it with Marcus Aurelius and with Kant—whose aim or motive may become a universal rule, binding on all intelligent beings." Having linked the correspondence sought by the Roman stoic between the universe and his own moral impulses with the modern ethicist's Categorical Imperative, Emerson quickly buttresses Marcus Aurelius and Kant with the Wordsworth of the Intimations Ode, again quoting those lines about "truths that wake / To perish never," the "fountain-light of all our day" and "master-light of all our seeing," which lead, in moral men, "to great enlargements" (*W* 10:94–97). In "Uses of Great Men," he had said that "these enlargements" liberate "elastic" man from his "bounds" so that he is "exalted" by "ideas" transcending his individual self (*E&L* 622, 623). As in the phrase just quoted from "Character," Emerson seems to have in mind a passage from *The Statesman's Manual,* evasively alluded to in "Circles." The phrase he quoted, without quotation marks let alone attribution—"nothing great was ever achieved without enthusiasm" (*E&L* 414)—was immediately followed, in Coleridge's text, by this: "For what is enthusiasm but the oblivion and swallowing-up of self in an object dearer than self, or in an idea more vivid?" There is, to be sure, a "wicked" enthusiasm (which Coleridge analyzes in the famed passage of appendix C to which he directs us, and which I discuss later in this chapter). "But in the genuine enthusiasm of morals, religion, and patriotism, this *enlargement and elevation of the soul above its mere self* attest the presence, and accompany the intuition of[,] ultimate PRINCIPLES alone." Only these "enlargements" can "deeply and enduringly" interest the "undegraded human spirit . . . because these alone belong to its essence, and will remain with it permanently" (*LS* 23; italics added).

Much hostile discussion—most, not all, coming from the Left, and most though not all of it focused on "Emersonianism," as opposed to the personally benign Sage of Concord—has seized on the ambiguous legacy of Emersonian individualism in order to stress what Coleridge called "wicked" enthusiasm, immoral rather than moral "enlargements": the dangers of a detached, egoistic, antisocial, unlimited, avaricious, anarchic, or

7. Buell, *Emerson,* 2, 65.

solipsistic Self, valorized and privileged at the expense of solidarity, association, community. Morse Peckham speaks for many in saying of Emerson, he "created a doctrine of 'self-reliance' which could be and was absorbed by the anarchic individualism of the socially irresponsible middle-class Philistine."[8] And by worse forms of unbridled, even demonic, individualism, if we are to give credence to charges made against Emerson by intelligent readers such as Cleanth Brooks, Yvor Winters (discussed later in this chapter), and A. Bartlett Giamatti, disturbed above all by Emerson's separatist impulse and admiration of "power."

❧ In a celebrated address as president of Yale University, Giamatti condemned Emerson as a dangerous worshiper of "self-generated, unaffiliated power," a "brazen adolescent" determined "to sever America from Europe, and American culture and scholarship from whatever humankind had fashioned before." Giamatti was accurate in emphasizing Emerson's setting of "the strong, healthy, unfettered" man against the "implicitly effete and bookish." It is even, perhaps, understandable that he would raise (speaking to students in the wake of both the then recent war in Vietnam *and* of certain excesses of the attendant student movement) the dangers of either politicians or protesting students "being freed . . . from any sense of restraint," of appearing—as Emerson does in the late essay that most disturbed Giamatti—to glorify the "bruisers" of the world. In that essay ("Power," in *The Conduct of Life*), Emerson certainly expresses admiration for those whose superfluity of virile, "coarse energy" and fierce "power" makes them leaders. In general history, as well as in individual or industrial life, the strength of those who succeed "rests at last on natural forces, which are best in the savage, who, like the beasts around him, is still in reception of the milk from the teats of Nature" (*E&L* 979).

Yet although "this power, to be sure, is not clothed in satin," it "brings its own antidote; and here is my point," says Emerson, "that all kinds of power usually emerge at the same time; good energy, and bad" (*E&L* 976), or what Coleridge contrasted as "wicked" and "genuine" enthusiasm. Giamatti was hardly alone, among those writing between, say, 1968 and the present, in being disturbed by bad energy and wicked enthusiasm—the negative implications of *power.* Particularly suspicious have been the historicist and materialist critics, Foucault's demystifying critique being, of course, the most ubiquitous and influential. Power has become increasingly suspect not only in military, political, and socioeconomic terms

8. Peckham, *Beyond the Tragic Vision: The Quest for Identity in the Nineteenth Century,* 236.

but also in the creative work of writers who—like Wordsworth and Carlyle, Emerson and Nietzsche and Yeats—seem most taken with, even infatuated by, the concept. But we can still wonder, to go back to Giamatti, if this is sufficient justification to scapegoat Emerson as at once the underwriter of the Vietnam War and of the incivility of those who protested against it.[9]

For one thing, Emerson—like Blake, Wordsworth, and Carlyle before him, and Nietzsche and Yeats after him—employs the language of power, strength, struggle, and heroism in, if not exclusively, essentially, a displaced, internalized form. His heroes are quintessentially warriors of the spirit, wielding the sword of what Blake calls "mental fight." The distinction between what Blake, following Milton, contrasts as "spiritual" and "corporeal warfare" crosses cultural boundaries—as we have been recently rereminded. Although there are, in the Qur'an, a considerable number of so-called sword passages, in America's post-9/11 debate about the meaning of jihad, Emerson, an advocate of Within rather than Without, would doubtless stress the positive interpretation: jihad as an internal striving rather than the external "holy war" against the infidel preached and practiced by Islamist extremists. If so, he would be following, if not Mohammed's exclusive interpretation, at least his own prioritizing distinction; coming home from a battle, he famously told his followers that they were returning to the "greater *jihad*" from the "lesser *jihad.*" Similarly, Yeats was following his own paired mentors, Blake and Nietzsche, when he once asked in an unpublished lecture: "Why should we honour those that die on the field of battle; a man may show as reckless a courage in entering into the abyss of himself."[10] In an unpublished lecture of his own, Emerson makes the same point in rhetoric of a lower register but, if anything, even more graphically: "The speculative man, the scholar, is the right hero," he told the 1845 graduating class at Middlebury College.

> Is there only one courage, and one warfare? I cannot manage sword and rifle; can I not therefore be brave? I thought there were as many courages as men. Is an armed man the only hero? Is a man only the breech of a gun, or the hasp of a bowie-knife? Men of thought fail in fighting down malignity because they wear other armour than their own. . . . It seems to me that the thoughtful man needs no other armour but this one,—concentration. One thing is for him settled, that he is to come at his ends. He is not there to defend himself, but to deliver his message; if his voice is clear, then clearly; if husky, then huskily; if broken, he can at least scream; gag him, he can still

9. Giamatti's 1981 address was printed later that year in *The University and the Public Interest;* see 172–76.

10. The lecture has since been edited and published; see Joseph Ronsley, "Yeats's Lecture Notes for 'Friends of My Youth,'" 81.

> write it; bruise, mutilate him, cut off his hands and his feet, he can still crawl towards his object on his stumps. (*LL* 1:91)

Nothing "effete" here, to be sure, but rather than the Emersonian "bruisers" understandably troubling to Giamatti we find instead the bruised but unconquerable, and the power at issue remains what Emerson refers to in the next paragraph as "power in the mind," a force that should inspire awe rather than suspicion, something to be cherished rather than demystified.

This question of *power* is at the center of Emerson's thought, even at the center of his supposed indifference to death. In the final chapters of this book, I take up the effect of his reading of Wordsworth on Emerson's response to the deaths of those he loved: the nature of his mourning, or famous "refusal to mourn." When it comes to the danger either of their originality being eclipsed by their great precursors or of losing themselves in excessive mourning over the loss of loved ones, neither Wordsworth nor Emerson is willing—in the words of perhaps their greatest joint heir, the Wallace Stevens of "Sunday Morning"—to "give [his] bounty to the dead." To do so would be to sacrifice that supposedly "self-generated, unaffiliated power" deplored by Giamatti. But such power ought not to be condemned by equating it with mere brute force or the utter rejection of tradition. It has been rightly noted that "in Emerson the power that matters most is always the power to reinvent the self at the expense of whatever conformity impedes quickened life," a formulation that distinguishes between tradition and conformity and straddles the insistence on self-reliant autonomy and the resistance to giving way to self-destroying grief.[11] In both cases, the dead, including the dead weight of the past, yields to the Wordsworthian "something that doth live," the fire seed in the embers that feed quickened life, originality, and the "power" that so troubled Giamatti.

Not that so intelligent a man as Giamatti was being obtuse. He was, in fact, following the path laid out in what was still the most influential contemporary study of Emerson. According to Stephen E. Whicher, despite his response to so many "cross-influences," especially Carlyle and "Coleridge more than anyone else," Emerson "yet strikes one of the most startlingly new notes . . . ever to be struck in American literature." In a sentence that suggests familiarity with the distinction made by Wordsworth,

11. Edmundson, *Towards Reading Freud,* 145. Emerson inscribed his journal entry on "Power" as the "great lesson which Nature teaches Man" (*JMN* 5:174; see the final epigraph to this chapter) in the immediate aftermath of the death of his brother Charles. The passage was later used in *Nature.*

Hazlitt, and De Quincey between "the literature of *knowledge*" and "the literature of *power,*" and a sentence that I suspect registered with Giamatti, Whicher insists that "the lesson" Emerson "would drive home is man's *entire independence.* The aim of this strain in his thought is *not virtue, but freedom and mastery.* It is *radically anarchic,* overflowing *all the authority of the past, all compromise or cooperation* with others, in the name of the *Power* present and agent in the soul."[12]

In this sense, Emerson *did* try, in Giamatti's word, to "sever" America's dependent connection with Europe—and power *is* a dangerous element. The Emersonian texts to which Giamatti was responding—*Nature,* "Self-Reliance," "The American Scholar," and, above all, "Power"—certainly make claims to and for unaffiliated "power," a radically anarchic force that, to be sure, is potentially destructive not only of high culture but of simple cooperation with others, or what William Hazlitt calls "the cause of the people." In a public polemic defending his view of Shakespeare's *Coriolanus,* and in the process revealing that the sublime is not necessarily humane, Hazlitt insists that the people's cause "is but little calculated for a subject for Poetry," since "the language of Poetry naturally falls in with the language of power." He affirms, in this letter to the editor of the *Quarterly Review,* "that Poetry, that the imagination, generally speaking, delights in power, in strong excitement, as well as in truth, in good, in right, whereas pure reason and the moral sense approve *only* of the true and good." This tendency toward power, strength, excitement, he concludes, is such that it "gives a Bias to the imagination often [in]consistent with the greatest good, that in Poetry it triumphs over Principle, and bribes the passions to make a sacrifice of common humanity."[13]

Notably impressed by Hazlitt's distinction, John Keats was, like others, also aware that the subject of power and poetry had been addressed by Coleridge and was central to Wordsworth's thinking. And, again, Milton—specifically, his Satan—was at the heart of it all. After attending the last of Hazlitt's Tuesday evening lecture series in early 1818, Keats ascribed our admiration of "such a beast of prey" as Milton's Satan (was he alluding to Shelley and Byron, those Promethean poets of the "Satanic School"?) to

12. Whicher, *Freedom and Fate,* 56; italics added.

13. A few years later, in 1829, Carlyle, for all the theatrical excitement and rugged strength of his own prose, was unhappy that we now "praise a work, not as 'true,' but as 'strong'; our highest praise is that it has 'affected' us." Though he despised Hazlitt's journalistic livelihood, Carlyle may have been responding directly to him on this occasion. Both Hazlitt's *Letter to Gifford* and Carlyle's comment (from "Signs of the Times," 1829) are quoted in Morris Dickstein, *Keats and His Poetry,* 255; italics added.

the temporary separation of "the principle of power" from "the sense of good," a principle "that makes us read with admiration and reconciles us in fact to the triumphant progress of the conquerors and mighty hunters of mankind." For all his evil, Milton's Satan is given, said Coleridge in 1816, "the qualities that have constituted the COMMANDING GENIUS, . . . that have characterized the Masters of Mischief . . . and mighty Hunters of Mankind, from NIMROD to BUONAPARTE." As his echo indicates, Keats is fusing Hazlitt's lectures on power with Coleridge on Satanic self-idolatry as "sublimely embodied in the Satan of . . . *Paradise Lost,*" and, on the historical stage, by Napoléon. Is it "not true," Keats asks in conclusion, "that here, as in other cases, the enormity of the evil overpowers and makes a convert of the imagination by its very magnitude?"[14]

On the question of Napoléon Bonaparte, at once the champion of the French Revolution and its betrayer, Emerson, like so many of his Romantic forebears, is typically divided, and in a way immediately germane to the ambiguities inherent in the doctrine of self-reliance. Napoléon is one of Emerson's "Representative Men" (*E&L* 727–45): he is at once "the incarnate Democrat," since he was "the destroyer of prescription," and the great nemesis of "the rich and aristocratic." Yet in one of his characteristic turns in this book from celebration to criticism, Emerson depicts Napoléon as the democrat become demagogue—not magnanimous but selfish, his concept of immortality reduced to a lust for fame. He becomes, in short, an exemplar or "representative" not of greatness but of that self-idolatry castigated by Coleridge. Buell is right in reading the essay on Napoléon in *Representative Men* as "an addendum to 'Self-Reliance' that spells out the ethic by celebratory illustration but cautions against its single most characteristic abuse, overweening self-assertion. It is the Emersonian equivalent of *Moby Dick*'s Captain Ahab. . . . Just as Melville creates a narrator, Ishmael, who both feels Ahab's power and recoils against it, so too with the Emersonian persona" who first celebrates Napoléon and then turns from praise to faultfinding, as he does in all his portraits in *Representative Men,* but never so abruptly and violently as here.[15]

In "Power," though Emerson's admiration seems more straightforward, there may still be a subtle fusion of Napoléon with Milton's Satan: "What a force was coiled up in the skull of Napoleon!" he marvels. But despite the resemblance of his image to Milton's powerful description of Satan entering the heart and head of the serpent, coiled in "many a round self-

14. Keats, *Letters of John Keats,* 2:75–76; Coleridge, appendix C of *The Statesman's Manual,* in *LS* 65–66.

15. Buell, *Emerson,* 82–84. Nietzsche attacks the Romantic and Carlylean hero cult of Napoléon in *Daybreak,* § 298.

rolled," Emerson, though as a youthful moralist he had condemned the warrior-emperor, is clearly impressed (*PL* 9:179–91).[16] Able to command and control an army of blackguards, Napoléon "dragged them to their duty and won his victories by their bayonets." But Emerson's emphasis falls even more on those, like "Pericles and Phidias," whose natural strength—at a historical moment when savagery, "just ceasing to be," began to yield to an "opening sense of beauty"—is wed with civilized virtues: "Everything good in nature and the world is in that moment of transition, when the swarthy juices still flow plentifully from nature, but their astringency or acridity is got out by ethics and humanity." The sense of beauty as sublimation leads to Emerson's other artistic example: Michelangelo, in whose case "this aboriginal might gives a surprising pleasure when it appears under conditions of supreme refinement" (*E&L* 980, 981).

Of course, superabundant power, when the Coleridgean "commanding genius" is a great artist, is not always accompanied by ethics and humanity, at least as conventionally understood. Hazlitt knew that; so did Emerson. Indeed, the core of Nietzsche's philosophy, based to some extent on Emersonian insights, is the enhancement of the conditions under which "higher individuals," those of greatest "creativity," may emerge unhindered by the obstacles of conventional morality. Second only to his incomparable Goethe, Beethoven was singled out by Nietzsche as an example, that Beethoven who, at the age of twenty-eight, told a friend, "The devil take you. I refuse to hear about your whole moral outlook. *Power* is the moral principle of those who excel others, and it is also mine." (Of course, the same Beethoven, having dedicated his *Eroica* symphony to Napoléon, effaced that dedication, so violently that he tore the title page, when the hero's exertion of power took the form of occupying the composer's Vienna.) As for Wordsworth: both in his poetry and as asserted in the "Essay, Supplementary to the Preface" to the 1815 edition of his *Poems,* he insists that "every great poet," if he is a truly "original" writer, "has to call forth and communicate *power*"—power "of which *knowledge* is the effect." The ideal, again, is "Knowledge not purchased with the loss of power!" (*P* 5:425). Echoing Wordsworth on the distinction though not the ideal fusion, Thomas De Quincey, in 1823, insists that, in literature, "the true antithesis to *knowledge* is not *pleasure,* but *power.* All that is literature seeks to communicate *power;* all that is *not* literature, to communicate *knowledge.*" For this "distinction," he tells us in a note, "as for most of the

16. Milton's description stirred Keats's empathetic imagination; he concluded his annotation on the passage (in an 1807 pocket edition of Milton's poems): "Whose head is not dizzy at the possibl[e] speculations of Satan in the serpent prison—no passage of poetry ever can give a greater pain of suffocation."

sound criticism on poetry, or any subject connected with it that I have ever met with, I must acknowledge my obligation to many years' conversation with Mr. Wordsworth."[17]

These speculations finally crystallize in the remarkable pages, from the essay on Pope, in which De Quincey distinguishes between the literature of knowledge and the literature of power in language that brings together virtually all of the terms and concepts that define Coleridgean-Wordsworthian Romanticism *and* Emersonian Transcendentalism. Though revised a decade later, this essay was written in 1848, shortly after De Quincey was visited (and Wordsworth *re*visited) by Emerson, during his second trip to England. Did De Quincey and Emerson discuss the distinction between the merely provisional, accretional, didactic "literature of *knowledge,*" and the altogether higher "literature of *power,*" ultimately equated with "exercise and expansion to your own latent capacity of sympathy with the infinite"? It would be equally fascinating to know if they discussed the related distinction, also made repeatedly by De Quincey in this section of the essay, between "the *mere* discursive understanding" and "the higher understanding or reason," associated with "Scripture's [1 Kings 3:9; Isa. 6:10] . . . '*understanding heart,*'" that is, "the great *intuitive* (or nondiscursive) organ."[18]

Whatever they did or did not discuss, it would have all been familiar to Emerson from his reading of Coleridge—specifically, the distinction between Reason and understanding, as well as Coleridge's equally insistent subdistinction (based, as Emerson fully realized, on the celebrated passage in book 5 of *Paradise Lost*) between the merely discursive and the all-important *intuitive* Reason. As noted in Chapter 2, De Quincey's source—"many years' conversation with Mr. Wordsworth"—itself had a source: Wordsworth's many years' conversation with Mr. Coleridge. In just a few pages, De Quincey manages to distill the Miltonic speculations and Kantian epistemology that, via Coleridge, came to inform the thought and work of Wordsworth and that—once filtered through the transatlantic conduit of Coleridge (with some help from Carlyle and Cousin)—came out as Emersonian Transcendentalism.

❧ The question, in the present context, is that raised by Coleridge, Hazlitt, and Keats, and largely prescinded from by Wordsworth and De Quincey: how does "power" play out in the polarity between individual

17. De Quincey, *Letters to a Young Man,* in *Collected Writings,* 10:48. Beethoven's 1798 letter to his friend Zmeskall is quoted in Maynard Solomon, *Beethoven,* 86 (Beethoven underlines the word *Power*).

18. De Quincey, *Collected Writings,* 10:55–56; italics in original.

self-assertion and communal responsibility, between the autonomy of the commanding genius and the cause of common humanity? Consider again those qualities most highly valued by Emerson: intuitive Reason, self-reliance, freedom from conventional restraints and externally imposed "duties"—the liberation, in particular, of what an Emersonian Nietzsche calls "higher," creative individuals. However exhilarating, the roll call is also bristling, as Giamatti and others have stressed, with potential dangers. Those dangers are inherent in, rather than invented by readers of, Emerson's volatile texts. His is certainly, in the phrase of one critic, "an *uneasy* solitude," as we realize every time we renegotiate the relationship in his work between the individual and society.[19] Whatever his earliest impulses, and even they were more private than public, there can be little doubt that as the result of the widespread public condemnation of the Divinity School Address, a shaken but unrepentant Emerson moved away from certain communal emphases to assert all the more defiantly the self-reliant individual averse to conformity. But even before the outrage stirred by that event, he generally tried to avoid active involvement in public affairs, including social reform, preferring to "let the republic alone until the republic comes to me" (*JMN* 5:479). He made that entry in his journal in April 1838, the very morning after he had, with some reluctance, written and mailed his "Letter to President Van Buren" regarding the Cherokee question. That reluctance was in keeping with what he had called in a journal entry of December 21, 1834, his "Philosophy of *Waiting,*" a selective philosophy that "needs sometimes to be unfolded. Thus he who acts is qualified to act upon the public, if he does not act on many, may yet act intensely on a few." Such a man may seem "quite withdrawn into himself, still if he know & feel his obligations, he may be (unknown & unconsciously) hiving knowledge & concentrating powers to act well hereafter & a very remote hereafter" (*JMN* 5:368).[20] Though in such a "hiving" and contentment to let the republic "come" to him Emerson might have been in complacent accord with Wordsworth's condemnation of the busy notion that "Nothing of itself will come, / But we must still be seeking," others found his "wise passiveness" either potentially culpable or a sanction for the inactivity of others.

In the face of certain momentous social concerns, above all the question of slavery and abolition, Emerson's reluctance to go beyond individual condemnation, his aloofness from organized action, was, as some well

19. Maurice Gonnaud, *An Uneasy Solitude: Individual and Society in the Work of Ralph Waldo Emerson.* On the rich and ambiguous legacy of Emersonian self-reliant individualism, see Mitchell, *Individualism and Its Discontents.*

20. On Emerson's "Philosophy of Waiting," see Sealts, *Emerson on the Scholar,* 42–45, 107, 136–38.

disposed toward him feared, easily misconstrued as teaching that, "in the great struggles between right and wrong going on in society, we may safely and innocently stand neuter." Six years after that assessment in 1838 by his friend Ellis Gray Loring, the Boston abolitionist Maria Weston Chapman described Emerson's "contemplative rather than active" role as that of "a philosophical speculator rather than a reformer." For her, though she does not make the identification, the Wordsworthian "light of all our day" valorized by Emerson was the wrong guiding light for *this* day. By endlessly "talking about the clear light," though not doing much to apply it in the affairs of the day, Emerson was, intentionally or not, giving "hundreds of young persons" an "excuse for avoiding the Anti-Slavery battle."[21] Emerson's response to such concerns, given between the friendly admonition of Loring and the pointed criticism of Chapman, took a Wordsworthian form. In his 1840 lecture "Reform," following his mentor William Ellery Channing, Emerson argues that particular reforms should be seen as part of a universal transformation—a point Wordsworth had made, in describing the slave trade, "this most rotten branch of human shame," as destined "to fall together with its parent tree" (*P* 10:244–62). Thus, engagement in particular reformist activities must not be permitted, says Emerson, to reduce the self-reliant individual to "an instrument." He tells the abolitionists in his audience that although he shares their abhorrence of the "crime" they assail, "yet I shall persist in wearing this robe, all loose and unbecoming as it is, of inaction, this *wise passiveness,* until my hour *comes* when I can see how to act with truth as well as to refuse" (*EL* 3:266; italics added).

As I have already suggested, Emerson is employing Wordsworth's language to explain his resistance to political activism; and, at times, it can seem a cop-out under Wordsworthian auspices. Yet with some undeniable exceptions, the point of what Donald Pease has called the Transcendentalists' "visionary compact" was *not* to sanction selfishness, but to enhance the sense of human relatedness and spiritual harmony with the divine as experienced in nature. The epistemological attempt to reconcile subject and object, mind and nature, was not the only reconciliationist aspect of Emerson's thought—as is demonstrated by his mobile dialectic between such apparent polar opposites as Freedom and Fate, Each and All, Self and Society. As David M. Robinson puts it in concluding the introduction to his 2004 selection of Emerson's writings on politics and social reform: "Self-reliance was not, finally, a stance of isolation, but a description of the means by which one could creatively engage the world. The trajectory

21. See Len Gougeon, "Historical Background," introduction to *Emerson's Antislavery Writings,* edited by Gougeon and Myerson, xxiv, xxv.

of Emerson's thinking encompasses an increasingly direct engagement with politics, embodying his recognition that membership in a social community entailed a profound moral responsibility."[22] Here, too, the Romantics, this time Coleridge, provide the required formulation.

Coleridge's reciprocity of "Each and All" impressed Emerson, who understood that, in Coleridge's own case, conservative politics, even retirement from activism, did not mean abandonment of communal responsibilities. Early and late, Emerson himself was obviously aware that the autonomous individual could not exist alone, nor could society exist without individuals. What was required was an alternative that would be creative and progressive, what dialectical Blake meant when he insisted, "Without Contraries is no progression." Emerson speaks, in his essay "The Conservative," of mighty opposites in society, the two great "metaphysical antagonists" of Reform and Conservatism. Individually they are failures. "Conservatism makes no poetry, breathes no prayer, has no invention; it is all memory. Reform has no gratitude, no prudence, no husbandry," and, in its injudicious "antagonism inclines to asinine resistance, to kick with hoofs. . . . Each exposes the abuses of the other, but in a true society, in a true man, both must combine" (*E&L* 175). If Conservatism and Reform require symbiotic balance, Solitude and Society require creative alternation. In June 1838, a month when Emerson was beset with visiting friends (Margaret Fuller, Caroline Sturgis, Bronson Alcott) who had "talked for days," he sought "*Alternation,*" taking his own advice to "go lie down, then lock the study door; shut the shutters, then welcome the imprisoning rain, dear hermitage of nature. Recollect the spirits. Close up the too expanded leaves." This evolved into an axiom recorded in his journal for June 13: "Solitude is naught and society is naught. Alternate them and the good of each is seen. . . . Undulation, Alternation is the condition of progress, of life" (*JMN* 7:14). But if the "too expanded leaves" sometimes need to be closed up, at other times, in keeping with the progressive law of alternation, they are to be opened. Indeed, the autonomous, self-reliant individual is, in an Each-and-All paradox, responsible "for the guardianship and education of every man." Here is Transcendentalism's version of that imaginative institutionalization of the conception of every man as a temple of deity: the Coleridgean "clerisy," a term "invented by Coleridge and adopted by Emerson."[23]

Emerson's emphasis at the conclusion of his 1836 tribute to Coleridge falls on his precursor's conviction that each man is the "Temple of Deity."

22. Robinson, *The Political Emerson,* 22.

23. Frank Kermode, "Changing Epochs," 173. For Coleridge's definition of the term, see *On the Constitution of the Church and State,* 46–47. Ben Knights analyzes this Coleridgean concept with legs in *The Idea of Clerisy in the Nineteenth Century.*

This "most republican of all principles" made Coleridge, even as a Tory "aristocrat in his politics," value "lowly and despised men the moment a religious sentiment or a philosophic principle appeared" (*EL* 1:379). Emerson's persistent emphasis on Coleridge's intuitive Reason as man's highest faculty, the divinity within, is familiar. But this final point, about Coleridge's imaginative or spiritual republicanism in designating every man as housing divinity ("not one of human kind, so poor and destitute, but there is provided for him, even in his present state, *a house not built with hands*" [*AR* 15–16]) seems to have served a significant purpose for Emerson, providing an exemplary and much needed bridge between Each and All, between self-reliant individualism or natural aristocracy and a republican companionship, not of "such men as do not belong to me and to whom I do not belong," as Emerson says in a famous passage in "Self-Reliance," but of "noble" types bound by "spiritual affinity" (*E&L* 262, 273).

There is a provocative passage on this point of the relationship of "great" individuals to the community in "The American Scholar," a lecture read by Nietzsche and in many ways a precursor of his own untimely meditation "On the Uses and Disadvantages of History for Life." At several points, both texts unreservedly exalt individualism—specifically the "great" individual above the "masses," a community reduced to "dwarfs" or "bugs." But even in these cases, there is a larger teleological purpose. Nietzsche's aristocratic ethics and *Übermensch* are implicit in the history essay's most momentous statement. "The time will come," he says, when our primary attention will be given not to

> the masses but individuals, who form a kind of bridge across the turbulent stream of becoming. These individuals . . . live contemporaneously with one another; thanks to history, which permits such a collaboration, they live as that republic of genius of which Schopenhauer once spoke; one giant calls to another across the desert intervals of time and, undisturbed by the excited chattering dwarfs who creep about beneath them, the exalted spirit-dialogue goes on. It is the task of history to be the mediator between them and thus again and again to inspire and lend the strength for the production of the great man. No, the *goal of humanity* cannot lie in its end but only *in its highest exemplars.*[24]

24. Nietzsche, *Untimely Meditations,* 111; italics in original. The paramount point of Nietzsche's critique of morality, here anticipated, is the enablement of the emergence of nascent higher types, of which the greatest exemplars are Beethoven and, above all, Goethe. "The really great men to my understanding," says Nietzsche, are "the men of great creativity." Such a higher man has Emersonian self-reliance and self-trust. Possessing "a solitude within him that is inaccessible to praise or blame, his own justice that is beyond appeal," he has "the ability to despise, and reject everything petty about him" (*The Will to Power,* §957, 962).

Rejecting Marx, adapting Darwin, and marshaling Emersonian individualism and Schopenhauer's "republic of genius" in the cause of developing "great communities" not based on what is "good for the majority," Nietzsche develops the argument further in the next essay in *Untimely Meditations*, "Schopenhauer as Educator." He establishes, as his "fundamental idea of *culture*," that it "sets for each one of us but one task: *to promote the production of the philosopher, the artist, and the saint within us and without us and thereby to work at the perfecting of nature*" (161; italics in original). Since, left to itself, nature has not yet produced one of these paragons, we must work consciously with it. Nietzsche advances the following as a proposition to reflect on: "Mankind must work continually at the production of individual great men—that and nothing else is its task." Thus, the conscious goal of human evolution must lie not in those who happen to come last in time, "but rather in those apparently scattered and chance existences which favourable conditions have here and there produced." Distinguishing between "here" (our contemporary utilitarian and egalitarian ethos) and "there" (the achievement of our evolutionary goal), Nietzsche proposes that "mankind ought to seek out and create the favourable conditions" under which

> those great redemptive men can come into existence. But everything resists this conclusion: here the ultimate goal is seen to live in the happiness of all or of the greatest number, there in the development of great communities. . . . How can your life, the individual life, receive the highest value, the deepest significance? How can it be least squandered? Certainly only by living for the good of the rarest and most valuable exemplars,[25] and not for the good of the majority, that is to say those who, taken individually, are the least valuable exemplars. And the young person should be taught to regard himself as a failed work of nature but at the same time as a witness to the grandiose and marvelous intentions of this artist: nature has done badly, he should say to himself; but I will honor its great intentions by serving it so that one day it may do better.

Coming to that resolve, he places himself within the circle of culture, for "culture is the child of each individual's self-knowledge and dissatisfaction with himself." Anyone who believes in "culture," says Nietzsche, is "thereby saying: 'I see above me something higher and more human than

25. This portion of Nietzsche's text is cited, somewhat out of context, by John Rawls (sec. 50 of *A Theory of Justice*) as violating his principles of justice, a violation either "strict" (slavery justifying) or "moderate" (justifying an antiegalitarian distribution of wealth and income). In "Emerson's Aversive Thinking" (235, 237–39), and more recently and extensively in *Cities of Words* (13, 211–26), Stanley Cavell, while admitting that Nietzsche's comments "can sound bad," demonstrates the "mismatch between Rawls's and Nietzsche's concerns."

I am; let everyone help me to attain it, as I will help everyone who knows and suffers as I do: so that at last the man may appear who feels himself perfect and boundless in knowledge and love, and who in his completeness is at one with nature, the judge and evaluator of things.' "

In images resembling Emerson's deploring of modern man (in the climactic chapter of *Nature*) as "the dwarf of himself," who has "shrunk" so that the structure externalized by "the laws of his mind" still "fits him, but fits him colossally," or at best "once" fit him (*E&L* 46), Nietzsche claims that Love alone can bestow on the soul the desire to look beyond itself and to seek "for a higher self as yet still concealed from it." In short, Nietzsche's *most* valuable "exemplar" is not some "other" to be emulated and sacrificed for (Schopenhauer himself is here superseded, barely mentioned in the essay that bears his name), but the higher self *within us,* liberated and so capable of transforming the culture. The great man serves as a model for the greatness potential in each of us. Those attached to some great man, and "by that act *consecrated to culture,*" come to "hate" their "own narrowness and shrivelled nature" and to develop sympathy for "the genius who again and again drags himself up out of our dryness and apathy," an exemplar for "all those who are still struggling and evolving." Nature presses "toward man," repeatedly fails to "achieve him," yet succeeds in "producing the most marvelous beginnings," fragments that call to us: "Come, assist, complete, bring together what belongs together, we have an immeasurable longing to become whole."[26]

This magnanimous desire to "look beyond" the narrow self tallies with the "impersonal individuality" (the subordination of what Emerson calls the "biographical Ego" to the "grand spiritual Ego") that George Kateb rightly finds at the heart of Emersonian Self-Reliance. Indeed, Kateb, though he never mentions Coleridge, finds Nietzsche ("Emerson's best reader") close enough to his mentor to conclude his preface by asserting that "friends of democratic individuality have much to learn from Nietzsche—as much as he learned from Emerson." Not that Nietzsche is to be simplistically located in the camp of democratic individualism. That is hardly the intention of Kateb, who in fact suggests approaching Emerson after having been "immersed in Nietzsche" as "a way to disregard Emerson's reputation for softness, or to dispel the ignorant familiarity that surrounds him." Precisely. Many, for example, will think the tone as well as the substance of some of the passages I have just quoted from Nietzsche—especially that image, from the "History" essay, of giants undisturbed by the "chattering dwarfs who creep about beneath them" and the scenario in which the inferior happily sacrifice themselves to expedite the emer-

26. Nietzsche, "Schopenhauer as Educator," in *Untimely Meditations,* 162–63.

gence of the superior—distinctively Nietzschean, hardly Emersonian. Indeed, in later and more notorious pronouncements, which he himself recognized as "most alien and embarrassing to the present taste," the prophet of the will to power and of an ethic beyond conventional good and evil insists that "noble values" depend on the principle that "one has duties only to one's peers" and that although noblesse oblige and even "pity" have their place in such an ethic, the fact remains that "a good and healthy aristocracy... accepts with a good conscience the sacrifice of untold human beings who, *for its sake,* must be reduced and lowered... to instruments." To the "noble soul... other beings must be subordinate by nature and have to sacrifice themselves."[27]

Surely *this* counter-Kantian, "Hitler-anticipating" master morality is far removed from the benign Emerson, isn't it? Well, here, whatever the German's other possible "sources," is Nietzsche's primary American mentor lamenting the current condition of man, and in no less salient a text than "The American Scholar":

> Men in the world to-day are bugs, are spawn, and are called "the mass" and "the herd." In a century, in a millennium, one or two men... [approximate] to the right state of every man. All the rest behold in the hero or the poet their own green and crude being,—ripened, yes, and are content to be less, so *that* may attain to its full stature.... The poor and the low are content to be brushed like flies from the path of a great person, so that justice shall be done by him to that common nature which it is the dearest desire of all to see enlarged and glorified. (*E&L* 66)

Yet just as Nietzsche summons such great individuals to flower into "greater communities," Emerson insists—employing Coleridge's "enlargement and elevation of the soul above its mere self" (*LS* 23), and his reciprocity of Each and All—that we "all" have a stake in developing the potential of "each" for the greater good. And despite the elitist brushing aside of the "poor and the low," he can also declare in this same essay, "I embrace the common, I explore and sit at the feet of the familiar, the low" (*E&L* 68–69). We associate this mental republicanism, or potential natural aristocracy of every man, even the lowliest, perhaps less with Coleridge than with Wordsworth, for whom the poet, inspired by a leveling Muse, was a man speaking to other men. In the "Progress of Culture," his second Phi Beta Kappa lecture (delivered thirty years after the first), Emerson discusses a number of "benefactors," all "exceptional men, and

27. The "Ego" contrast occurs in Emerson's ongoing lecture "Natural History of Intellect." Kateb, *Emerson and Self-Reliance,* xxix, 33, xxix; Nietzsche, *Beyond Good and Evil,* in *Basic Writings of Nietzsche,* § 260, 258, 265.

great because exceptional." But then he adds a point reflecting his reading of book 13 of *The Prelude,* in which Wordsworth, contemplating the exceptional man, rhetorically asks,

> Why is this glorious creature to be found
> One in ten thousand only? What one is
> Why should not millions be?
>
> (87–89)

"The question," says Emerson, "which the present age urges with increasing emphasis, day by day, is whether the high qualities which distinguish [such men] can be imparted. The poet Wordsworth asked, 'What one is, why may not millions be?' Why not? Knowledge exists to be imparted" (*W* 8:226).

Emerson's formulation, suggesting a kind of trickle-down theory in which wisdom is bestowed by the exceptional upon the unwashed, may lack the nobility of Wordsworth's democratic faith that genuine liberty and imaginative power can and should be widespread because all are endowed with these as their birthright. At least, however, there is the clear sense that heroes and great men have a responsibility to others: the task of lifting *them* to fulfill their potential. The pride of the exceptional individual need not rule out a balancing humility. In the case of the great who also happen to be Christians, evangels can take many forms, high and humble. As Milton says, in a passage quoted by Emerson, "Notwithstanding the gaudy superstition of some still devoted ignorantly to temples, we may be well assured, that he who disdained not to be born in a manger, disdains not to be preached in a barn." As evidence of Milton's "perception of the doctrine of humility," and his willingness to serve his "revolutionized country" by assuming "an honest and useful task," Emerson cites a genuine rather than rhetorical question from the great Puritan's *Reason of Church Government:* "Who is there . . . that measures strength by suffering, dignity by lowliness?" Emerson comments: "Obeying this sentiment, Milton deserved the apostrophe of Wordsworth," and he quotes (accurately except for the substitution of "itself" for "herself" in the last line) the conclusion of Wordsworth's sonnet "London, 1802" (*WP* 1:580), which Emerson later included in *Parnassus* under his own title, "To Milton":

> Pure as the naked heavens, majestic, free,
> In cheerful godliness; and yet thy heart
> The lowliest duties on itself did lay.
>
> (*EL* 1:152–53)

As early as January 1826, Emerson copied in his journal oxymoronic lines of Wordsworth recalled (and altered) by Yeats, whose Crazy Jane celebrates truth "Learned in bodily lowliness / And in the heart's pride." In the peroration of "Lines, Left upon a Seat in a Yew-Tree," Wordsworth asserts that "pride," "Howe'er disguised in its own majesty, / Is littleness" and that he who "feels contempt / For any living thing," even the "least of Nature's works," is unwise. We are to be "instructed," in the lines quoted by Emerson with obvious approval (*JMN* 2:12), that "true knowledge leads to love" and that

> True dignity abides with him alone
> Who, in the silent hour of inward thought,
> Can still suspect, and still revere himself,
> In lowliness of heart.
>
> (60–64; *WP* 1:256)

At such moments, Wordsworth invests such terms as *low* or *humble* or *common* with a significance at once sociopolitical *and* spiritual. Emerson would, of course, have recognized Wordsworth's (and Milton's) biblical precedent in this subversion of the high and mighty, what Hazlitt brilliantly characterizes as the revolutionary implications of Wordsworth's "Muse, . . . a levelling one . . . distinguished by a proud humility." Saint Paul tells us that "base things of the world, and things which are despised, hath God chosen" so that "no flesh should glory in his presence" (1 Cor. 1:23–29). In the words of M. H. Abrams, who quotes both the Pauline text and Hazlitt's famous remarks from the essay on Wordsworth in *The Spirit of the Age:* "The insistent transvaluations of Scripture—'blessed are the meek: for they shall inherit the earth,' 'many that are first shall be last, and the last first'—translated into the literary domain, reappear in Wordsworth's characteristic oxymorons: the glory of the commonplace, the loftiness of the lowly and mean, the supreme import of the trivial, and the heroic grandeur of the meek and the oppressed."[28]

As usual, Milton and his archangel are involved. In his Miltonic "Ode to Duty," Wordsworth explicitly prays to be made "lowly wise," a direct echo of Raphael's advice to Adam to be "lowly wise" (*PL* 8:173). The striking word in the Wordsworthian tribute to Milton, a "deserved" tribute as Emerson rightly says, is of course *lowliest,* echoing (as Emerson noticed)

28. Abrams, *Natural Supernaturalism,* 395–96. The sense in which Wordsworth was "the most original poet now living" is made clear in Hazlitt's discussion of that leveling Muse who "takes the commonest events and objects, as a test to prove that nature is always interesting from its inherent truth and beauty." In his choice of subject as in his style, which "gets rid (at a blow) of all the trappings of verse," Wordsworth "elevates the mean by the strength of his own aspiration." He has "struck into the sequestered vale of humble life . . . and endeavored (not in vain) to aggrandize the trivial and add the charm of novelty to the familiar. No one has shown the same imagination in raising trifles into importance" ("Mr. Wordsworth," in *Complete Works,* 11:86–88).

Milton's "dignity by lowliness." Wordsworth's "lowliest" was in turn echoed by Hart Crane. A modern democratic rhapsode, Emersonian by way of Whitman, Crane cries out in the climactic lines of the proem to *The Bridge:* "Unto us lowliest sometime sweep, descend / And of the curveship lend a myth to God."[29]

Emerson would have been only mildly surprised, Whitman not at all, by God's mythological incarnation in the harplike Brooklyn Bridge. That something could sweep and descend even "Unto us lowliest" remains a potent and unifying democratic vision. "A nation of men will for the first time exist," Emerson concludes "The American Scholar" on a Coleridgean point, "because each believes himself inspired by the Divine Soul which also inspires all men" (*E&L* 71). In that central passage of *The Friend* indelibly impressed on Emerson and reflected in his comment about every man as the Temple of Deity, Coleridge had spoken of the "common centre, of the universal law," which (and here he too echoes Milton), "inspiring humility and perseverance," will lead one to "comprehend gradually and progressively the relation of each to the other, of each to all, and all to each" (*F* 1:511). In that final sentence of "The American Scholar," Emerson seems to join Coleridge's Miltonic "republican" principles with his discussions of the "each" and the "all," Coleridgean terms that inform not only Emerson's poem "Each and All" but, as well, much of his fluctuating thought on the relationship between the individual and the community, Solitude and Society.

❧ Directly, and as a shaping influence on Wordsworth, Coleridge was an appropriate guide for Emerson. Coleridge's desire to spread knowledge, to illuminate the "lowly," predated his conceptualizing of a clerisy. Even at his most radically activist, he was intent on shedding enlightenment instead of, or at the very least prior to, any bloodshed. As wary of the "mob" as he was of the hated Pitt government, he insisted, in his 1795 "Bristol Addresses to the People" (printed, significantly under an "elitist" Latin title, *Conciones ad Populum*), that he was "pleading *for* the Oppressed, not *to* them," and that "general Illumination should precede Revolution." We might be listening to Emerson, who shared Coleridge's distrust of the "lower classes" and his fear of the mob. When, in 1836, Carlyle complained to him that British politicians were in the process of destroying the country, Emerson responded that things were just as bad in the United States:

> We have had in different parts of the country mobs and moblike legislation, and even moblike judicature, which have betrayed an almost godless state of

29. Crane, "To Brooklyn Bridge," in *Complete Poems of Crane,* 46.

> society; so that I begin to think even here it behoves every man to quit his dependency on society as much as he can, as he would learn to go without crutches that will soon be plucked away from him, and settle with himself the principles he can stand upon. There is reading, and public lecturing too, in this country, that I could recommend as medicine.[30]

On the last day of 1796, having just moved to Nether Stowey and announcing his retirement from the "*public* life" for which "I am not *fit*," Coleridge wrote to the great activist, the "English Jacobin" John Thelwall, urging *him* "to uplift the torch dreadlessly" in the good fight. His own, said Coleridge, was a different course on the path of human liberation, "yet the Light shall stream to a far distance from the taper in my cottage window" (*CL* 1:277). Among the recipients of that light was Emerson and all the rest of Coleridge's American disciples. Wordsworth, another of Emerson's "benefactors," also insisted on a reciprocal relationship between what Emerson called Solitude and Society. Wordsworth's invocation in the "Prospectus" of a prophetic Spirit to bestow upon him a gift of genuine insight, so that his poetry, "With star-like virtue in its place may shine, / Shedding benignant influence" (*WP* 2:39), in effect celestializes Coleridge's earlier and recurrent image of a benign light streaming from the taper in his cottage window to illuminate and liberate others.

Of course, both of these assertions also involve quietism, "retreat" from political activism. The letter to Thelwall was written on the eve of the first of Coleridge's oscillating "retirements" from political life, in December 1796. Wordsworth was writing in 1798, the year that saw the French invasion of democratic Switzerland (in February), the mass arrests of English Jacobins and other radicals in the panic over an invasion of England itself (in March and April), and the decision of Wordsworth and Coleridge (whose associations and loyalty were dubious enough to have a government spy assigned to observe their activities) to set sail for Germany (a March plan, carried out in September), where over the following months Coleridge ingested German beer and German philosophy and Wordsworth mapped out his poetic master plan—while both escaped (to quote the title of the poem that, along with his formal recantation in "France: An Ode," marked Coleridge's second "retirement") such "fears in solitude" as being drafted, as suspected subversives and thus eminently expendable, into the militia back home. The Pitt government need not have worried. By then the commitment of Wordsworth and Coleridge to the French Revolution was, essentially if not decisively, over. The ideals (*liberté, égalité, fraternité*) had been overwhelmed by too many bloody realities following

30. Coleridge, *Lectures 1795: On Politics and Religion,* 43; Emerson, *The Correspondence of Emerson and Carlyle,* 84–85.

the declaration of war between France and England: the September massacres, the Reign of Terror with all the horrors of the guillotine, a French war of defense transformed into "one of conquest" and imperialism with the ascendancy of Bonaparte. Here was the spectacle, as Wordsworth put it in *The Prelude,* of the "oppressed," the French, having "become oppressors in their turn" (*P* 11:206–16), and so betraying principles to which Wordsworth and Coleridge claimed to remain loyal. Nevertheless, it remains an endlessly debated question as to whether the internalization of revolution in Wordsworth and the oscillating retreat of Coleridge from the barricades of political commitment, leading in both cases to the dread watch tower of the individual self, are matters—in the influential terms of E. P. Thompson—of "Disenchantment or Default."[31]

What, essentially, Thompson said of Wordsworth and Coleridge—that their apostasy took the form of a regression to paternalism and conservative fear of the potentially anarchic "masses"—has been said of Emerson, not by Thompson, but by another Marxist scholar, and not in comparison with original but withdrawn sympathies with revolutionaries in France, but with Menshevik revolutionaries in czarist Russia. Writing in 1932, in the midst of the U.S. Great Depression, V. F. Calverton, having identified the "petty bourgeois individualism" of the American frontier as "the basic psychological determinant in our national ideology," argued that the "false consciousness" attendant on the obscuring of class-based analysis by rugged individualism is to be laid at the door of Emerson. He conceded that Emersonian faith in the common man, in self-reliant individualism, and in democracy was "thoroughly sincere" and, initially, liberatory. However, when the actual, as opposed to the abstract or ideal, "common man arose in his might," a bourgeois "Emerson became alarmed, and was moved to defend caste against mass." That was so with Wordsworth and Coleridge as well.

Not only—to continue with Calverton's analysis—did Emerson not practice what he preached; he also metaphysically buttressed himself against the social implications of his apparently liberatory doctrine, resisting the revolutionary ramifications of his own "anarcho-individualism." In this he resembles, for Calverton, the Mensheviks, who, "when they saw a revolution in reality, became horrified, and who, because they were not prepared for the ruthless tasks of carrying a revolution to its inevitable conclusion, became the most bitter opponents of the Bolsheviki who put

31. Thompson's 1969 lecture is now available in his posthumous collection, *The Romantics: England in a Revolutionary Age,* 33–74. Scholars of the developments traced in this paragraph include David Erdman, Carl Woodring, Marilyn Butler, Alan Liu, Paul Magnuson, Nicholas Roe, and David Simpson. See also my own *Coleridge's Submerged Politics.*

the revolution into actual practice and made it work." This intrusion of the real into the ideal may remind those familiar with J. M. Synge's tragicomic masterpiece, *The Playboy of the Western World,* of the pivotal scene in act 3 in which Christy—having "actually" seemed to kill the father he has already been romanticized for having allegedly killed—is ferociously turned on by the woman whom he loves and who loves him: "There's a great gap," declares Pegeen, "between a gallous story and a dirty deed."[32] In the light of what was to come in the next decade and a half of Irish history (the Easter Rising, the Anglo-Irish War, and the tragic Civil War), this turn in Synge's play inevitably evokes the connection between endless Irish talk of a romanticized revolution and the bloody realities of revolution "put . . . into actual practice."

Of course, Calverton was himself romanticizing revolution. Just how ruthlessly the Bolshevik revolution worked, or, rather, *did not* work, we now know. Nor do we have to blithely concede, as historically "necessary" and "inevitable," the employment of such allegedly end-justifying means as the guillotine and the gulag. Whatever their later disenchantment or default, and their insistence that England and the other reactionary monarchies had goaded the French into excess, Wordsworth and Coleridge always denied such revolutionary "justification." Hardly immune to the millennial promise of the French Revolution, Wordsworth was appalled by the "enormities" of the Reign of Terror. He alluded, as Emerson later would, to the grotesque ceremony in which the Jacobins, in late 1793, untenanted the Virgin Mary with a streetwalker and renamed Notre Dame the "Temple of Reason." In a gesture reflecting Coleridge's distinction between Reason and the all too limited human understanding, Wordsworth refused to concede the name of the highest human faculty to perpetrators of and apologists for insatiable "domestic carnage" ("and never heads enough / For those that bade them fall") as a required purging. Those "who throned / The human understanding paramount / And made of that their God" were all too teleologically "content to barter short-lived pangs / For a paradise of ages" (*P* 10:362–63, 341–45, 356).[33] True, Wordsworth did not spill tears at news of the death of Louis XVI and Marie Antoinette, and he did applaud *one* "purging." But his motivation was humane. At news of

32. Synge, *Playboy,* 116.

33. In "American Slavery," a lecture delivered several times in 1855 but not published until 1995 (in the Gougeon and Myerson edited collection, *Emerson's Antislavery Writings*), Emerson chose two "moments of greatest darkness, and of total eclipse." One was Congress's passage of the Fugitive Slave Law, the other that day during the French Revolution "when the Parisians took a strumpet from the street, seated her in a chariot, and led her in procession, saying, 'This is the Goddess of Reason'" (Robinson, *The Political Emerson,* 128).

the death of Robespierre and his associates, Wordsworth was transported with joy, again filled with hope that "The glorious renovation would proceed" with this sweeping away of those who had produced a "river of Blood," and preached that "nothing else / Could cleanse the Augean stable" (*P* 10:584–93).

Thus, for all their early radicalism, we can claim Wordsworth and Coleridge as imaginary allies in rejecting some of Calverton's Marxist premises and, certainly, his prescriptive and discredited conclusion that "the faith of Emerson and Whitman belongs to the past, and not to the future. Their belief in the common man was a belief in him as a petty bourgeois individual; our belief must be in him as proletarian collectivist." But we can hardly dismiss the following out of hand:

> Eternally, . . . Emerson's stress is upon the self, the individual self, the personal ego. Society can take care of itself, or go hang, as the frontiersman would have put it. It is the individual who must be stressed, the individual who must learn to stand alone, and become sufficient within himself. . . . [W]ithout wishing it, Emerson gave sanction by virtue of his doctrines to every type of exploitation which the frontier encouraged.[34]

Emerson has, of course, been blamed for almost every subsequent American excess, whether entrepreneurial, ethical, or aesthetic. Emersonian individualism supposedly sanctioned the post–Civil War robber barons—J. P. Morgan, Jay Gould, Andrew Carnegie, Commodore Vanderbilt, John D. Rockefeller—who lengthened their individual shadows into the institutions of corporate aggrandizement. It is true that, for example, in the "Discipline" chapter of *Nature,* Emerson anticipates the Nietzschean Will to Power by asserting, "The exercise of the Will or the lesson of power is taught in every event" (*E&L* 28), and in the essay "Power" itself, we are told that the "energy" of business leaders "usually carries a trace of ferocity," that those who learn to control "steam, fire, and electricity" are vigorous men who "cannot live on nuts, herb-tea, and elegies" and cannot "satisfy all their wants" by attending public lectures. Hungry for adventure, they would rather "die by the hatchet of a Pawnee" than spend their days at a desk. Such roughriders are "made for war, for the sea, for mining, hunting, and clearing; for hair-breadth adventures, huge risks, and the joy of eventful living" (*E&L* 977, 979).

Still, as we have discussed earlier, and this is true in the case of Nietzsche as well, the true exponent of power for Emerson is not the "rugged individual," whether plutocrat or tyrant, but "Man Thinking." Though, in *The Conduct of Life,* discussion of the higher virtues is deferred to two

34. Calverton, *The Liberation of American Literature,* 247–49, 258, 479–80.

later essays ("Culture" and "Worship"), even in "Power" (though not until the penultimate paragraph) Emerson insists that "I have not forgotten that there are sublime considerations which limit the value of talent and superficial success. We can easily overpraise the vulgar hero" (*E&L* 985). His supreme exemplar of power is that liberated and liberating god the Poet. But even here Emerson has been found culpable. In this more rarefied area of the aesthetic, one example may stand for many, since it is the most excessive and comes from a distinguished literary critic notable for the lucidity with which he usually defends reason against Romanticism. I mean the raging exorcism of Yvor Winters, who verges on the madness he attributes to Emerson in blaming the unrestrained verbal and autobiographical excesses of Hart Crane, including his suicide, on the "insane" Emersonianism he absorbed by way of Whitman.[35]

To be sure, given his proclivity toward ambiguity, paradox, equivocation, even contradiction, Emerson is open to an unusually wide spectrum of interpretation and misprision; in common with writers as different as Rousseau and Nietzsche, he invites creative appropriation, use, and abuse. He can be thought of as the enabler, even the Dionysian prophet, of individualistic excess, even, perhaps more legitimately, as the father of the heroic individualism of Nietzsche, whose Superman is set over and against the "herd." But even the Superman's precursor, Zarathustra, descends from the solitary mountain heights to interact with and help men. Emerson's admitted lack of sympathy for many reformers, "miscellaneous popular charities," and "the thousandfold Relief Societies" (*E&L* 262–63), has been much noted and duly deplored. And, as Cornell West has demonstrated, those aspects of Emerson's thought reflecting ethnic stereotypes and racial determinism represent serious limitations. Even in these cases, however, Emerson's moral sentiments and compassion are partially redemptive, and, in general, the argument has been well made, by Len Gougeon, that a good deal of the negative criticism, stemming in large part from Oliver Wendell Holmes's influential depiction of Emerson as a

35. Winters, "The Significance of *The Bridge* by Hart Crane" (1947), in *In Defense of Reason,* 589–602. Though Winters had praised *White Buildings* in 1926 and had been corresponding with Crane, he wrote, when it appeared in 1930, a critically and personally devastating review of *The Bridge,* the emotional excess and structural incoherence of which he attributed to Crane's having become besotted with Whitman. When he later repeated the assault, the major culprit was revealed as the influential but unwise Sage of Concord. "We have," Winters wrote of Crane in 1947, "a poet of great genius who ruined his life and his talent by living and writing as the two greatest teachers of our nation recommended." The primary blame for Crane's mindless Romanticism and, later, for his verbal, alcoholic, and sexual excesses, culminating in his suicide, was laid by Winters at the Dionysian doorstep of Whitman's progenitor, Emerson.

social conservative, has been overstated.[36] In addition, though Emerson remained divided when it came to the pull between commitment to his own intellectual work and public engagement in the great issues of the day, he saw that dilemma too as a reconcilable polarity; like Coleridge and Wordsworth, he believed that the light he produced in solitude would radiate to illuminate society as a whole.

Concentrating on his own development and lifework, Emerson cultivated a certain aloofness from national affairs. But his conscience was a powerful force; it kept dragging him into the public arena. As he puts it in his characteristically reticent way in his late essay "The Fortunes of the Republic," it is simply impossible "to extricate yourself from the questions in which the age is involved" (*W* 11:539). But Emerson's natural preference in the polarity between Solitude and Society, scholarly detachment and political activism, was clear even before the clamor following the Divinity School Address.

The tension between activism and quietism takes the form, in Emerson as in Coleridge, of oscillation and ambivalence. For example, in April 1838, three months prior to the Divinity School Address, Emerson wrote an open letter to President Van Buren protesting—in vain—the carrying out of the brutal and unconstitutional Jacksonian policy of uprooting the Cherokees from their ancestral lands (*W* 11:87). That is well known; what is still rather less well known is that, although he "fully sympathize[d]" with the sentiments he expressed, he "hated" writing the letter, deeming it a "deliverance that does not deliver the soul." As an exponent of self-reliance, he was determined to do only what "concerns my majesty & not what men great or small think of it.... I write my journal, I read my lectures with joy—but this stirring in the philanthropic mud, gives me no peace. I will let the republic alone until the republic comes to me." Like Robert Lowell, who rejected an invitation to the White House during the Vietnam War because urged to do so by his friends, Emerson agreed with the cause but accepted the activist role "rather from my friends" than

36. See Gougeon's comprehensive and groundbreaking study of Emerson's involvement in the abolitionist cause, *Virtue's Hero: Emerson, Anti-slavery, and Reform,* as well as his earlier-noted prefatory essay to *Emerson's Antislavery Writings,* coedited with Myerson. Though Holmes was a perceptive biographer, he was also a paragon of the "genteel school" and has been rightly criticized for muting Emerson's belated but uncompromising abolitionist position. For an argument closer to Holmes than to Gougeon, see *Yankee Saints and Southern Sinners,* by Bertram Wyatt Brown, who claims that, as a lecturer, Emerson, sensitive "to public opinion,... never spoke against slavery when he was on tour" (30).

from his own dictate: "It is not my impulse to say it & therefore my genius deserts me, no muse befriends, no music of thought or of word accompanies. Bah!" (*JMN* 5:479). The violence of his language reveals his sense that no matter the justice of the cause, he had, by submitting to public pressure from his neighbors, betrayed his own intuition, his nonconformist creed of self-reliance.

Two years later, less opposed to national expansion than worried about the extension of slavery implicit in the annexation of Texas (*JMN* 9:64), Emerson publicly opposed the Mexican War as immoral, though he did not engage, as Thoreau did, in civil disobedience. Whatever we make of the apocryphal exchange between Emerson and the incarcerated Thoreau ("What are you doing in there?" "What are *you* doing *out* there?"), Emerson did have reservations about Thoreau's decision to go to jail (a one-night affair) rather than pay his poll tax at this time. According to Bronson Alcott's journal for July 25, 1846, "E[merson] thought it mean and skulking, and in bad taste. I defended it on the grounds of a dignified non-compliance with the injunction of civil powers."[37] It is possible that the "it" Emerson thought "mean and skulking" refers to the action of the civil authority (Sam Staples, the local tax collector and warden of the county jail) rather than the action taken by Thoreau, which Emerson, with characteristically divided feelings, considered at once dubious and noble. In a journal entry at the time, he plays a variation on his old Within-Without contrast: "Build your prison walls thicker. It needs a firmer line of demarcation to denote those within from those without." The abolitionists denounced the Mexican War but paid the tax. And Daniel Webster's only protest regarding the war was its cost. "They calculated rightly on Mr. Webster. My friend Mr. Thoreau has gone to jail rather than pay his tax. On him they could not calculate" (*JMN* 9:444–46).

The incalculable difference was that between a materialist and an idealist approach to political events. One of Emerson's best-known poems takes up this issue. Quite aside from the Transcendentalist and general New England distaste for the crasser forms of American materialism, the "relation between mind and matter," the Me and the NOT ME, can be so out of balance that the world of "things" assumes a dangerous dominance. Political engagement, even in causes to which Emerson was sympathetic, can seem, or be made to seem, a question of the lower usurping the position of the higher, reversing priorities so that "*things* are in the saddle, / And ride *mankind.*" The famous lines are from Emerson's "Ode: Inscribed to W. H. Channing" (1846), in which we are also told, in the lines immediately

37. Alcott, *The Journals of Bronson Alcott,* 1:183.

following, that there are two "discrete" laws, "Not reconciled— / Law for man, and law for thing" (50–54; *EPP* 445). This is another playing out of the Emersonian agon between Power and Fate, moral freedom and material necessity. Addressing Channing, who had been urging his *too* self-reliant friend to participate more directly in abolitionist politics, Emerson insists on maintaining his distance:

I cannot leave
My honied thought
For the priest's cant,
Or statesman's rant.
(3–6)

Referring obliquely to Channing, who now advocated separating from the South, Emerson asks (echoing the "What boots it . . ." of both "Lycidas" and that "What-boots-it" Wordsworth sonnet he had quoted in "Spiritual Laws"):

What boots thy zeal,
O glowing friend,
That would indignant rend
The northland from the south?
(36–39)

He wonders "what good end" would be served by disunion, since Boston, linked commercially to the South, "would serve things still"—material "things" that are Satanic, "of the snake" (43).

At the same time, Emerson is disturbed by the spectacle of "the famous States / Harrying Mexico / With rifle and with knife!" (16–18), especially given the predictable impact of the war on the extension of slavery. In a concise registration of its opposing pulls, Lawrence Buell has remarked, "The poem can scarcely contain itself, so galling are its competing aversions: toward the Mexican War as an instrument of slavocracy, toward being hectored into wasting energy denouncing it." The tension is never reconciled. The ode ends celebrating "freedom," in which cause "The astonished Muse finds thousands at her side" (96–97), but that resonant flourish does not overcome Emersonian antipathy to political activism nor his emphasis on *individual* freedom: "Every one to his chosen work" (75). The Ode to Channing is an important and, in its defense of one's own work and the detachment necessary to accomplish it, for many readers a disturbingly quietist poem. This is especially the case since it was written in response to the death in prison of the Salem abolitionist Charles Turner Torrey, whose funeral (at which Channing spoke) Emerson attended in Boston on May 19, 1846, a week after the U.S. declaration of war on Mexico.[38]

In the first-generation Romantics, Coleridge and Wordsworth, their American cousin found a political quietism that had, however, been *earned* following ardent activism. For a time, Emerson could rely on his Romantic precursors to justify his preference for the Within rather than the Without. We have seen how he employed Wordsworth's advocacy of a "wise passiveness" to explain his political aloofness and relative "inaction." A crucial statement—in a crucial place, the climax of *Nature*—confirms his alignment with transatlantic Romanticism, especially with Coleridge, Wordsworth, and Carlyle. Like them, Emerson calls for an internal revolution, that of "mind" or "spirit," an imaginative revolution higher and antecedent to any external revolution of "things" and destined to assert its dominion. There is even an analogue of the Wordsworthian "correspondent breeze" within:

> Build, therefore, your own world. As fast as you conform your life to the pure idea in your mind, that will unfold its great proportions. A correspondent revolution in things will attend the influx of spirit. . . . The sordor and filths of nature, the sun shall dry up, and the wind exhale. As when the summer comes from the south; the snow banks melt, and the face of the earth becomes green before it, so shall the advancing spirit create its ornaments along its path, and carry with it the beauty it visits, and the song which enchants it . . . until evil is no more seen. The kingdom of man over nature, which cometh not with observation, . . . he shall enter without more wonder than the blind man feels who is gradually restored to perfect sight. (*E&L* 48–49)

Compelling as it is, such a teleological allegory can depoliticize even a revolutionary ideology. Why be a reforming activist engaged in the minutiae of "things" when all the material changes desired will attend the influx of spirit and evil be seen no more? This is the serene, determinist morality of a man endorsing (*JMN* 3:80; *E&L* 709) what Wordsworth's Wanderer calls the beneficent "stream of tendency" (*E* 9:82). And Emerson's response to another famous passage in *The Excursion* exemplifies this quietist "millennialism" as an excuse not to act. But in part at least, Emerson is reading this second passage selectively in order to come to what may seem a preordained, idealist conclusion.

38. Buell, *Emerson,* 137; see also Len Gougeon, "The Anti-slavery Background of Emerson's 'Ode Inscribed to W. H. Channing,'" and David Bromwich, *A Choice of Inheritance: Self and Community from Edmund Burke to Robert Frost,* 133–41.

The passage is a tale told not by the Wanderer but by the Solitary, 170 lines culminating book 2 of *The Excursion* and famous for the splendid mountain vision he describes. The morning after a storm, with the hills "still shrouded in impenetrable mist," the Solitary, descending the mountain, takes a "single step," which, freeing him from the "blind vapour, opened to my view / Glory beyond all glory ever seen." What the Solitary sees through the opening in the clouds and mist amounts to a prophetic vision of a "mighty city" of "diamond and of gold, / With alabaster domes, and silver spires." Though a natural phenomenon (wrought by "earthly nature"), it becomes (paradoxically, since the transformation is attributable to the power of the creative imagination) an "unimaginable sight," and what he "*saw* was the revealed abode / Of Spirits in beatitude." He stands entranced and gazes: "The apparition faded not away, / And I descended" (*E* 2:829–81).

Unsurprisingly, the vision portion of the passage registered with Emerson, who quoted its opening lines in an important if conflicted journal entry of September 1841:

> We are all of us very near to sublimity. As one step freed Wordsworth's Recluse on the mountains from the blinding mist & brought him to the view of "Glory beyond all glory ever seen" so near are we all to a vision of which Homer & Shakespeare are only hints & types and *yet cannot we take that one step. It does not seem worth our while to toil for anything so pitiful as skill to do one of the little feats we magnify so much, when presently the dream will scatter & we shall burst into universal power.* (*JMN* 8:51; italics added)

Characteristically, Emerson's statement is complex, even "contradictory." He is saying several things at once. First, that action is but a minute and meaningless step in a much larger, hopeful, and inevitable fulfillment; but that, second, our failure to take that "step" can become an excuse for idleness; and, third, that—as he makes clear three years later, when much of this passage was repeated in "Nominalist and Realist" (the final item in *Essays: Second Series*)—the "deferring of our hopes" through "idleness" has its risks: "Whilst we are waiting, we beguile the time with jokes, with sleep, with eating, and with crimes" (*E&L* 580). Still, reading the original note, we are essentially left wondering if all our individual toil takes place in the mist of a dream destined to scatter in the face an all-encompassing vision. Such a conclusion is only partly relevant to the state of the Solitary as presented by Wordsworth in this passage. A former enthusiast long since disillusioned by the French Revolution, the Solitary has lost faith in all political activism, and despite his glorious experience following the mountain storm, he remains a tempest-tossed and dejected man. But he is also revealed as a *compassionate* man, despondent yet apparently still believing that it *is* (to contradict Emerson's journal entry) "worth our while to toil," to engage in at least some individual "little feats," even if they *do* take place in a mundane dream destined to scatter when, as Emerson predicts in his note, "we shall burst into *universal* power."

The crucial fact that Emerson neglects to mention is that the Solitary was on the mountain in the first place because he and several shepherds had gone up to try and save a poor and aged neighbor who, digging for winter turf, had been caught in a storm and stranded on the heights. Rebuffed by the storm on their first attempt, the rescue party tries again the next morning. That they made the effort and were successful *matters.* And the fact that the rescued man, despite seeming uninjured, died some days later, clinches the lesson Wordsworth *wants to teach,* as opposed to the lesson Emerson, and after him, John Ruskin, *chooses to learn.* Jonathan Bate, who has nothing to say of Emerson but who is interested in Ruskin's response to this episode, makes my point:

> In the vision, the Solitary seems to see "the revealed abode / Of Spirits in beatitude": the phenomenon of nature has offered a momentary glimpse, an intimation of immortality. This causes him to [momentarily] forget the old man's suffering. But human pain and mortality are quickly asserted as we learn that the quest for fuel and the exposure to the storm have cost the old man his life. As in the story of the ruined cottage [in the opening book of *The Excursion*], Wordsworth has juxtaposed the heartlessness and the beauty of nature. He does not rest with mountain glory; his is also the poetry of human suffering.

Bate persuasively argues that Ruskin produces, in a passage eventually dropped but originally intended for the second volume of *Modern Painters,* a "precise analogue" of the Wordsworthian vision, at once the effect of earthly nature and a revelation of divine presence. Ruskin also has a sublime mountain vision featuring a storm and the apparition of a "celestial city," but, Bate accurately notes, unlike the Solitary's apparition, which is "but an interlude in the course of a narration that is focused on humanity rather than nature and on suffering rather than glory," the passage intended for *Modern Painters* "works towards the obliteration of" what Ruskin himself calls "the associations of humanity" and the annihilation of the individual subject (again in Ruskin's words) "before, and in the presence of, the manifested Deity." Ruskin always attributed his "eye" and ability to "see" to Wordsworth, particularly the Wordsworth of *The Excursion,* but his meditation on the experience of being in the divine presence ("It was only then that I understood that to become nothing might be to become more than Man . . . the immortal soul might be held for ever—impotent as a leaf—yet greater than tongue can tell—wrapt in the one contemplation of the infinite God") sounds remarkably reminiscent of the epiphany of "the transparent eye-ball," in which, dissociated from humanity, indeed, "nothing" himself, Emerson *sees* all, caught up in a rapture in which he is "part or particle of God."[39]

That celebrated moment has been cited as illustrative of a Transcendentalist solitude verging on solipsism and an abdication of communal responsibility. For Carolyn Porter, for example, Emerson is the pivotal figure in the idealized and intuitive subjectivity (epitomized in the transparent eyeball) that leads to the quietism and alienation of the American writer in a socioeconomic world of individualistic competition. There is obviously much to be said for this reading. Emerson's native penchant for internalizing both the divine and the societal surely found authorization not only in the quietest aspect of Coleridge and Wordsworth but also in mentors as different as Milton, Montaigne, and Carlyle. Emerson agreed with Milton that, since it derives from the God within, liberty is to be found principally *there*—within. Although the heaven of *Paradise Lost,* as Northrop Frye puts it in "The Garden Within," is a "city and a society, the pattern established for man on earth by God was not social but individual and not a city but a garden." To be of any use, social and political revolution "has to be related to the vision of what it is to achieve. And we find that the goal of man's quest for liberty is individualization: there is no social or ideal state in the human mind." As Montaigne announces in the final book of the *Essays,* though Emerson, in discussing his favorite skeptic, does not quote the passage: "The world looks always outward, I turn my gaze inward; there I fix it. Everyone looks before him; I look within. I have no business but with myself. Others . . . are always going elsewhere. . . . But I revolve within myself." Carlyle proclaims, rather more grimly than Voltaire's Candide: "The world's being saved will not save us; nor the world's being lost destroy us. We should look to ourselves."[40]

My juxtaposition of the responses of Emerson and Ruskin to the Solitary's vision would seem to ally me with the interpretation of Emerson as an unequivocal supporter of this kind of total internalization. Yet Montaigne remained, like Coleridge and Wordsworth, acutely aware of his civic responsibilities, and Milton, anything but uncommitted, retains, though "compassed round" with the dangers of the Restoration, something of his politically subversive voice even in *Paradise Lost.* Emerson, too, neither

39. Bate, *Romantic Ecology: Wordsworth and the Environmental Tradition,* 69–71. He cites Ruskin from *Modern Painters,* 364.

40. Porter, *Seeing and Being: The Plight of the Participant Observer in Emerson, James, and Faulkner;* Frye, *The Return of Eden: Five Essays on Milton's Epics,* 110, 114; Montaigne, *Essays,* in *The Works of Michel de Montaigne,* 219–20; Carlyle, "The Hero as Man of Letters," in *On Heroes.*

simplistic Utopian nor rationalizing shirker, feels the pull between, on the one hand, his desire to engage in the solitary seeing and thinking of a man who builds his own world and, on the other, the demands of an external world often groaning for deliverance from evil. It was, of course, the crisis of slavery that finally compelled Emerson to address the difficulty at the heart of his theory of history and of politics. He had to overcome his own deep-rooted historical vision, one that may be variously described as optimistic, providential, or deterministic but which, in any case, entailed the crucial issue just raised in discussing Emerson's "millennialist" conclusion to *Nature* and his selectively "quietist" response to the *full* experience of Wordsworth's Solitary at the conclusion of book 2 of *The Excursion.* The dilemma can be succinctly stated. If an evil such as slavery is against the moral constitution of the universe itself, is it not destined, *inevitably,* to fail? Wordsworth himself thought the slave trade, "this most rotten branch of human shame," was fated, in the coming revolution, "to fall together with its parent tree" (*P* 10:244–62). Though Emerson, too, often insists that this is so, such a view obviously

> undermines the felt necessity to take direct political responsibility and action. Any consistent theory of political reform must be based on the conviction that history is open, not determined—but that, of course, means that the progress of justice is not guaranteed. . . . As the national struggle over slavery grew in intensity, Emerson's inner struggle over the course of history intensified. He saw more and more clearly that one could not easily or confidently assume the triumph of the good, unless one became an agent of the good.

Or, to employ the more activist axiom attributed to Edmund Burke, and which David Robinson here appears to be playing off: "The only thing necessary for the triumph of evil is for good men to do nothing."[41]

❧ Either seduced by Coleridge's word *Genius* into overdramatizing his lifelong Solitude-versus-Society dilemma or registering the individual (Within) and universal (Without) implications of the term, Emerson in 1844 twice invoked the crucial word *genius.* In his March lecture, "New England Reformers," he contrasts abolitionist activism—anticipating Thoreauvian civil disobedience ("We refuse the law, we go to jail")—to an individual's "obedience to his genius," which "is the only liberating influence." Collective action is "all in vain; only by obedience to his genius; only by the freest activity in the way constitutional to him, does an

41. Robinson, introduction to *The Political Emerson,* 14–15.

angel seem to arise before a man, and lead him by the hand out of all the wards of the prison" (*EPP* 233). In a contemporary journal entry, he wrote: "My Genius loudly calls me to stay where I am, . . . whilst the Universal Genius beckons me to the martyr's and redeemer's office" (*JMN* 9:61–62). Emerson, however, was no more suited to martyrdom than was Coleridge, who took political chances in the repressive 1790s but who always reacted with caution to real danger. Though Emerson's *primary* task was not (at least not *consistently*) national redemption, his activism, selective and usually reluctant, was not negligible; he did not let society—in Calverton's dismissive phrase—"go hang." The following examples, focused on slavery and abolition and covering two decades during which Emerson was at the height of his creative powers and the nation at its most turbulent, reveal a continuing polarity between sociopolitical engagement and withdrawal to the self in the form of commitment to his true vocation.

In January 1838, Emerson addressed a meeting in Concord protesting the murder of the Illinois abolitionist Elijah Lovejoy; his notes (the talk itself has not survived) reveal his stance as antislavery, though not yet abolitionist and less than enlightened on the question of racial egalitarianism. Though still not a full-fledged abolitionist, in the same year, 1844, in which he described the tension between his internal genius and the universal genius that beckoned him to a politically redemptive role, Emerson commemorated the emancipation of black slaves in the West Indies, delivering in Concord a powerful attack on the evils of America's peculiar institution (*W* 9:97). The following year, he refused to give a scheduled lecture at the New Bedford Lyceum on learning that the membership had voted to exclude blacks (*L* 8:61–62), a decision that seems to have initiated his slow but inexorable movement toward total commitment to the abolitionist cause. That the decision was *his own* reflects his belief that, morally and strategically, *social* reform was dependent on *individual* moral action. He was, as the Channing Ode reveals, well aware of the hypocrisy of Bostonians who preached liberation yet engaged in commerce with Southern slaveholders. In the antislavery writings, awareness turns to a mixture of revulsion and sarcasm: "The sugar they raised was excellent: nobody tasted the blood in it." A youthful Coleridge, also convinced that individual illumination and moral choice were the necessary prerequisites to social reform, urged his audience, in his own 1795 lecture "On the Slave Trade," to boycott sugar and rum, products "polluted with the blood" of innocent slaves. Unfortunately, he continued in this indignant harangue, people prefer to look away, providing "the dunghill be not before their parlour window" (a memorable image later imported into *Aids to Reflection*). Hence "the continuance of the Slave-trade. The merchant finds no argument against it in his ledger: the citizen at the crouded feast is not nauseated by the stench and filth of the slave-vessel—the fine lady's nerves are not shattered by the shrieks! She sips a beverage sweetened with blood, even while she is weeping over the refined sorrows of Werter or of Clementina."[42]

Emerson had his disagreements even with abolitionists who were *not* hypocritical, but it was not on the central question; as he said in 1858, he was, and by then had been for some years, an abolitionist of "the most absolute," though less than fully activist, kind. His opposition to slavery and its possible extension reached its peak as it became undeniably clear that this was *the* "question" in which his "age was involved," a contradiction at the heart of the U.S. Constitution that was now threatening to tear the nation apart. For Emerson as for many other New Englanders, things came to a head when the old Fugitive Slave Law, enacted in 1793 but largely ignored in the Northern states, was strengthened as part of the Compromise of 1850. Emerson now bitterly condemned a man he once admired, Daniel Webster, whose controversial or "infamous" speech of March 7, 1850, defended the whole package that went into the Compromise. Alluding to Webster's famous trademark speech two decades earlier when he had championed "Liberty and Union now and forever, one and inseparable!" Emerson now wrote in disgust: "The word *liberty* in the mouth of Mr. Webster sounds like the word *love* in the mouth of a courtezan" (*JMN* 11:345–46).[43]

Emerson praised the courage, in public speeches and sermons denouncing the law, of his activist friend Theodore Parker. "Every drop of your blood and every moment of your life is a national value," he wrote his friend in praising his "brave harangue," Parker's April 1851 sermon "The Chief Sins of the People." He received an equally magnanimous, and significant, response, in which Parker, unlike Channing, begged Emerson

42. Gougeon and Myerson, *Emerson's Antislavery Writings,* 20; Coleridge, "On the Slave Trade," in *The Watchman,* 139. The fine lady who weeps over Goethe's hero and Richardson's heroine but is unperturbed sipping tea sweetened with the blood of black slaves may have acquired her taste from the third of his friend Robert Southey's six anti–slave trade sonnets of 1794, addressed to "Ye who at your ease / Sip the blood-sweetened beverage."

43. In the equally graphic image of historian Samuel Eliot Morison, "The North could never have been induced to swallow a new fugitive slave law, had not Webster held the spoon; and, even so, it gagged and vomited" (*The Oxford History of the American People,* 572). Though Clay's 1850 Compromise package was intended to calm growing sectional strife and avert fratricidal bloodshed, the consequence for Webster was assault from his native region—by abolitionists and moderates alike. The abolitionist poet John Greenleaf Whittier lamented, in his poem "Ichabod," his "fallen angel's" disgrace but, unlike Emerson, refrained from branding "with deeper shame his dim / Dishonoured brow." Clearly, the former champion of Union and Liberty and the nation's most eloquent orator had, in the eyes of his fellow Northerners, separated the inseparable by subordinating morality to law, Liberty to Union.

not to become even more actively engaged himself, but "to remember how much I have got from yourself. . . . Much of the little I do now is the result of seed of your sowing" (*L* 4:249–50). But if "every drop of [Parker's] blood" was a national honor, Webster's was a national disgrace: "All the drops of his blood have eyes that look downward" (*W* 11:203–4). It is a vivid but surreal phrase—clarified when we recall Milton's fallen angel, Mammon, that "least erected spirit" who fell from heaven; "for ev'n in heaven his looks and thoughts / Were always downward bent" (*PL* 1:679–81).

Declaring that he would never obey this "filthy enactment," Emerson violently attacked the Fugitive Slave Law on May 3, 1851, in a long and powerful speech to his fellow citizens in Concord. Thinking specifically of Webster as a now disgraced native son, Emerson spoke of waking every morning with the "odious remembrance of that ignominy which has fallen on Massachusetts." However reluctantly, the Universal Genius now had greater claim than his own: "The last year has forced us all into politics, and made it a paramount duty to seek what it is often a duty to shun."

> Just now a friend came into my house and said, "If this law shall be repealed I shall be glad that I have lived; if not I shall be sorry that I was born." What kind of law is that which extorts language like this from the heart of a free and civilized people? . . .
>
> An immoral law makes it a man's duty to break it. . . . If our resistance to this law is not right, there is no right. . . . This is not going crusading into Virginia and Georgia after slaves, who, it is alleged, are very comfortable where they are . . . [T]his is befriending, in our own State, on our own farms, a man who has taken the risk of being shot, or burned alive, or cast into the sea, or starved to death, or suffocated in a wooden box, to get away from his driver: and this man who has run the gauntlet of a thousand miles for his freedom, the statute says, you men of Massachusetts shall hunt, and catch, and send back again to the dog-hutch he fled from. . . .
>
> We shall one day bring the States shoulder to shoulder and the citizens man to man to abolish slavery. . . . Let us respect the Union to all honest ends. But also respect an older and wider union, the law of Nature and rectitude. . . . This law must be made inoperative. It must be abrogated and wiped out of the statute-book; but whilst it stands there, it must be disobeyed. (*W* 11:179–212)

He had already underlined in his journal his own exclamation: "*I will not obey it, by God!*" In keeping with his opposition to the Fugitive Slave Law, Emerson actively supported, in the congressional campaign of 1851, the (unsuccessful) Free-Soil candidate, John Gorham Palfrey, and responded to the filthy enactment in a handful of poems in the 1851 *Liberty*

Bell: "The Phoenix," "Faith," "The Poet," "To Himself," and "Word and Deed."[44] In an important address, in New York City on March 7, 1854 (the fourth anniversary of Webster's "infamous" speech and an address that adumbrated a series of antislavery lectures the following year in Boston, Philadelphia, and, again, New York City), Emerson employed a striking metaphor that had first appeared in a journal entry two years earlier. Writing in August 1852, he appears first to evade responsibility for emancipation by passing the task on to God—rather as Robert E. Lee would in a famous 1856 letter to his wife.[45] But then he asserts the more profound duty of a spiritual, intellectual warrior, committed to guarding his post and to liberating other *internal* prisoners:

> I waked at night, & bemoaned myself, because I had not thrown myself into this deplorable question of Slavery, which seems to want nothing so much as a few assured voices. But then, in hours of sanity, I recover myself & say, God must govern his own world, & knows his way out of this pit, without my desertion of my post which has none to guard it but me. I have quite other slaves to free than those negroes, to wit, imprisoned spirits, imprisoned thoughts, far back in the brain of man,—so far retired in the heaven of invention, &, which, important to the republic of Man, have no watchman, or lover, or defender, but I. (*JMN* 13:80)

In the New York City address, he repeated the image, telling the audience whose revulsion from the Fugitive Slave Law he shared, that he disliked abandoning his own creative work to go "meddling" in public affairs, since "I have my own spirits in prison, spirits in deeper prisons, whom no man visits if I do not" (*W* 11:217). One recalls the ghostly solitude of Frost's "Desert Places," along with Yeats's less eerie but more immediately relevant "On Being Asked for a War Poem," in which Yeats—responding to pressure from Edith Wharton and Henry James to contribute a poem

44. See Len Gougeon, "Emerson, Poetry, and Reform" and "Emerson and the Campaign of 1851." By 1851, the rupture had healed with Palfrey, the Harvard dean "hurt" by Emerson's 1838 Divinity School Address.

45. As an American icon, Lee has traditionally been depicted as a tragic figure who condemned the very institution he was called upon to defend militarily. But Lee, though he thought slavery "a moral & political evil in any Country," was, when it came to the South, at best a "gradual emancipationist," willing to remit the task to a divine Providence working with less than deliberate speed. As he wrote his wife, Mary Custis Lee, on December 27, 1856: "While we see the Course of the final abolition of human slavery is onward, & we must give it all the aid of our prayers & all justifiable means in our power, we must leave the progress as well as the result in his hands who sees the end; who Chooses to work by slow influences; & with whom two thousand years are but as a Single day." The letter is quoted in Douglas Southall Freeman's landmark four-volume biography, *R. E. Lee,* 1:371–73.

supporting the Allies in World War I—also dismisses political engagement as "meddling," as well as a distraction from one's more "human" vocation as a writer:

> I think it better that in times like these
> A poet's mouth be silent, for in truth
> We have no gift to set a statesman right;
> He has had enough of meddling who can please
> A young girl in the indolence of her youth,
> Or an old man upon a winter's night.

Emerson's reluctance to "meddle" even in causes in which he believed, and the priority he accorded to his own work, recurred in the case of Anthony Burns. In May 1854, the detention in the Boston Court House of Burns, an escaped slave, caused an uproar in the city. Bronson Alcott and Theodore Parker were actively engaged in the finally futile attempt to protect the fugitive. Though Emerson was supportive, it was from a distance; pleading commitment to his own work, he stayed in Concord, writing. Two years later, he spoke in support of Kansas Relief, a fund to help Kansans impoverished by marauding proslavery mobs, and signed a petition to Governor Henry J. Gardner protesting the unlawful detention of Massachusetts citizens in Missouri. But unlike the petition's initiator, Franklin Benjamin Sanborn, Emerson's commitment was limited to signing.[46] That same year, he heard John Brown's speech in Concord and was much impressed. When, in 1859, Brown acted on his ideals, Emerson, though he at first referred to "the sad Harper's Ferry business," added soon afterward, "I must hope for his escape" (*L* 5:178, 180). Profoundly disturbed by Brown's sentence to be hanged for treason and murder, Emerson started a private letter to the governor of Virginia, Henry Alexander Wise, pleading for the condemned man's life. Though he never finished the letter, after Brown's execution Emerson insisted that it was "the *reductio ad adsurdum* of Slavery, when the Governor of Virginia is forced to hang a man whom he declares to be a man of the most integrity, truthfulness, and courage he has ever met. Is that the kind of man the gallows is built for?"[47] And Emerson's ardor was not simply ex post facto. Ten days earlier, in a lecture titled "Courage" delivered in Boston on the eve of the execution and responding to Brown's eloquent address to the Virginia court, Emerson described him as "a new saint . . . awaiting his martyrdom," and who, if he shall suffer death, "will make the gallows glorious like the

46. See Francis B. Dedmond, "Men of Concord Petition the Governor."

47. Emerson, "Speech at a Meeting to Aid John Brown's Family," in *Emerson's Antislavery Writings,* edited by Gougeon and Myerson, 118–19.

cross." That phrase was omitted when the lecture was published in *Society and Solitude.* But the famous words were publicly spoken: impassioned and nation-polarizing words uttered by that nation's most celebrated orator, and destined to resonate in the history that followed.[48]

In 1862, Emerson met Lincoln, whose election two years earlier he had pronounced "sublime"; he had subsequent misgivings about presidential missteps, but all was forgiven when Lincoln issued the Emancipation Proclamation, that "dazzling success" (*W* 11:317), on the first day of 1863. The event was commemorated that very evening in a "Jubilee Concert" at the Music Hall in Boston. The audience, having waited nervously for the telegram confirming the presidential signature, was brought to its feet by Emerson's program-opening poem—climaxing in an unexpected image of shared liberation in which both "the captive" and the free people of the nation were simultaneously "unbound" and demanding that any "ransom" should be paid not to the slaveholder, but to the true "owner," the "slave" ("Boston Hymn," in *EPP* 465–68). In two 1864 lectures, "American Life" and "Fortunes of the Republic," Emerson, emulating Thoreau's chanticleer cry in *Walden,* intended to "wake" his neighbors, calling on his countrymen to "awake" and, "with energy," correct the injustices of America's political system. Finally, in July of that year, Emerson celebrated Colonel Robert Shaw, killed along with many in his black regiment in the attack on Fort Wagner, with his poem "Voluntaries." The final and famous lines of its third and central movement enlist in the patriotic cause the near divinity of the common dust in which human greatness inheres:

> So nigh is grandeur to our dust,
> So near is God to man,
> When duty whispers low, *Thou must,*
> The youth replies, *I can.*
> (71–74; *EPP* 470)

These lines, later incised on the base of the Soldiers' Monument on Concord Green, would be remembered by many, most significantly by William James.

This brief litany illustrates rather than gainsays the legitimate, and balanced, criticisms of Emerson as public figure: his political impotence, for

48. Emerson, "Courage," *New-York Tribune,* November 8, 1859; cf. *W* 7:427. The passage is quoted in David S. Reynolds, *John Brown, Abolitionist,* 366. Reynolds notes that the famous phrase did not originate with Emerson, who borrowed it from the abolitionist Mattie Griffith, a "brilliant young lady" he admired (*L* 5:83). But Reynolds also insists that when "aired publicly by Emerson, the 'gallows glorious' phrase sped through newspapers North and South like a ricocheting bullet. It outraged Brown's opponents and inspired his supporters," adding "fuel to the already inflamed sectional tensions that led to civil war" (367).

the most part, even when he did act; his reluctance to engage publicly in truly risky ways; his distrust of the masses; his exercise of personal power that stopped short of empowering the less fortunate; a genuine sense of justice and occasional compassion that transcend without erasing the sort of "liberal" racism endemic to the period; his unwillingness to alienate the educated middle classes whose materialism he criticized but whose capitalist profits helped to pay his lecture fees. The combination may make Emerson, in Cornell West's summary, "a petit bourgeois libertarian, with at times anarchist tendencies and limited yet genuine democratic sentiments."[49] The same might be said of Coleridge, though it should be added that, in the intensity of his defense of John Brown, Emerson in his fifties attained a passion and eloquence exceeding even the antislavery fervor of Coleridge in his radical twenties.

What Emerson sought, in theory at least, was a balance between Each and All, Solitude and Society, a fusion of selective public activism and the shedding of what Wordsworth calls "benignant influence" from a starlike eminence and distance. This is precisely what Theodore Parker, in his 1859 pamphlet claimed for Emerson, whose "brilliant genius rose in the winter nights, and hung over Boston, drawing the eyes of ingenuous young people to look up to that star," whose light "led them forward along new paths, and toward new hope." That "hope" included Parker's own cause, abolition, and he himself said that whatever he did in that cause was "seed" of Emerson's "sowing." Predictably, however, travel on those "new paths" illuminated by Emerson was not restricted to kindly high-minded sages; many of the new paths were dominated not by idealistic and humane apostles of intuitive Reason but by materialists, including slave owners, both energetic and rapacious. Like Carlyle, Emerson, when he was not celebrating their virile power, rather naively hoped that the captains of industry would also become socially responsible leaders. But again, it was not the warrior, the politician, or the entrepreneur but, as Emerson said (in the original title of "The American Scholar"), "Man Thinking," or, in the retained title of another lecture, the poet, who was to be, in Emerson's resonant phrase, "a liberating God." The poet, for whom "the world seems always waiting," stands "among partial men" as representative" of "the complete man" who is to come, and who, like the superabundant, overflowing *Übermensch,* "apprizes us not of his wealth, but of the commonwealth" (*E&L* 450, 448).

That is true of Emerson himself, as Man Thinking, as poet, prose poet, and seer. Just as Coleridge thought that the light would stream to a far

49. West, "The Emersonian Prehistory of American Pragmatism," in *The American Evasion of Philosophy: A Genealogy of Pragmatism,* 40.

distance from the taper in his cottage window, so, too, Emerson, working within his own chosen limits, intended his intellectual, aesthetic, and spiritual bounty to pour out to the American commonwealth and beyond—to that "republic of Man" to which, he justifiably believed, his "imprisoned thoughts" were "important" (*JMN* 13:80). And his very terms—obedience to one's "genius" as "the only *liberating* influence," the poet as "*liberating*" divinity, the angel that leads us "out of all the wards of *the prison,*" his own "*imprisoned*" thoughts—suggest that, from at least the midforties on, America's great moral and political crisis, human slavery, was never far from Emerson's thoughts, even at his most "distanced," looking down, almost sub specie aeternitatis, on the benign stream of tendency.

The Emersonian creative man "apprizes us not of his wealth, but of the commonwealth," though at his own self-imposed "dictate." This magnanimity, a free overflow without claims or duties imposed by "others," especially the "masses," appealed enormously to Emerson's disciple Nietzsche, who was largely responsible for passing the ideal on to his own heir, W. B. Yeats. In the opening lines of "Ancestral Houses," the first poem in his sequence *Meditations in Time of Civil War,* we are told that among the flowering lawns of one of Yeats's idealized Anglo-Irish aristocrats, amid the rustle of his planted hills,

> Life overflows without ambitious pains;
> And rains down life until the basin spills,
> And mounts more dizzy high the more it rains
> As though *to choose whatever shape it wills*
> And *never stoop* to a *mechanical*
> Or *servile* shape, at *others' beck and call.*

These may be

> Mere dreams, mere dreams! Yet Homer had not sung
> Had he not found it certain beyond dreams
> That *out of life's own self-delight* had sprung
> The abounding glittering jet. . . .
>
> (6–12)

Here, rather remarkably, Yeats has hammered into unity the organic-mechanical distinction Coleridge borrowed from A. W. Schlegel; Kant's, Coleridge's, and Wordsworth's obedience to self-chosen "inner laws"; and the Nietzschean will to power and distinction between "master morality" and "slave morality," a melange issuing in autonomy and the affirmation of self and life, as opposed to enforcement from without, servile *ressentiment,* and life denial. This is, to be sure, the noblesse oblige of a natural aristocrat, but it is not selfishness, as Yeats clarifies in annotating a passage from *Beyond Good and Evil.* Basing himself on the "stern" cardinal principle of "noble morality," Nietzsche had declared that one has "only obligations to one's equals, that one may act towards beings of a lower rank... according to discretion or 'as the heart desires.'" Underlining "only obligations" and "to discretion," Yeats responds in the right-hand margin: "Yes, but the necessity of giving remains. When the old heroes praise one another, they say 'he never refused any man.' Ni[e]tzsche means that the lower cannot create anything, cannot make obligations to the higher."[50] We may—says Emerson, in one of many observations that influenced Nietzsche and, after him, Yeats—reject "reflex" duties, obligations to others. But though I may "neglect this reflex standard, and absolve me to myself," I have "my own stern claims." Discharging the "debts" placed upon me by this self-imposed obligation "enables me to dispense with the popular code." But the law of autonomy and self-reliance remains, as both Nietzsche and Yeats also insist, "high and solitary and most stern": "If any one imagines that this law is lax, let him keep its commandments one day.... [T]ruly it demands something godlike in him who has cast off the common motives of humanity, and has ventured to trust himself for a taskmaster. High be his heart, faithful his will, clear his sight, that he may in good earnest be doctrine, society, law, to himself, that a simple purpose may be to him as strong as iron necessity to others" (*E&L* 274).

Even an admirer of Emerson as ardent and informed as Harold Bloom may concede too much on the admittedly touchy point of giving based on "noble morality." Responding, in his essay "Mr. America," to the often castigated passage in "Self-Reliance" (*E&L* 262–63) in which Emerson denies his "obligation" to those "poor" with whom he has no "spiritual affinity," even though he confesses "with shame" that "I sometimes succumb" to the call of "miscellaneous popular charities," Bloom remarks that "self-reliance translated out of the inner life and into the marketplace

50. For the Nietzsche passage (*Beyond Good and Evil,* §260, in *Basic Writings of Nietzsche,* 396) and Yeats's annotation, see Keane, *Yeats's Interactions with Tradition,* 262–63. Yeats is clarifying, not rejecting or whitewashing, Nietzsche, who repeatedly insists that "the noble type of man... regards *himself* as the determiner of worth" (a passage marked by Yeats) and has a "solitude within him... inaccessible to praise or blame, his own justice that is beyond appeal" (*The Will to Power,* § 962). Internally motivated, the magnanimity of the *Übermensch* is an overflowing of one's own freely given superabundance. In endorsing Nietzsche's ideal of the autonomous hero, Yeats is unconsciously endorsing Emerson's as well, even to the crucial doctrine of self-absolution. Thus, like Yeats's "No Second Troy" (its heroine "high and solitary and most stern"), his "Irish Airman Foresees His Death," in which the hero rejects all conventional external motivations in favor of an autonomous instinct ("A lonely impulse of delight / Drove to this tumult in the clouds"), is not only consciously Byronic and Nietzschean but unconsciously Emersonian as well (*W. B. Yeats: The Poems,* 91, 135).

is difficult to distinguish from our current religion of selfishness." Subjecting this provocative passage of "Self-Reliance" to a brilliant textual and contextual reading, Cavell out-Bloomed Bloom for once, insisting that the biblical sources on which Emerson is playing reveal him as clearly distinguishable from "those who may be taken as parodies of him." Emerson, at such an apparently pitiless moment, seems a compound of Blake (who reminds us, in his gnomic recognition of condescending pity's root in injustice, that "Pity would be no more / If we did not *make* somebody Poor"), Nietzsche, and Robert Frost. But Emerson seems less an adherent of Frostian social "heartlessness" than of the Nietzschean critique of pity, not in itself, but as a collectively imposed obligation.[51]

The distributive justice in which Emerson *did* believe was spiritual and intellectual rather than economic. Not that Emersonian individualism is *un*related to issues of poverty and wealth. James Russell Lowell, in his perceptive portrait of Emerson in *A Fable for Critics* (a poem revisited in the next chapter), is hardly wrong to speak of "A Greek head on right Yankee shoulders, whose range / Has Olympus for one pole, for t'other the Exchange" (23–24). Emerson could speak, in the elevated prose of "The Poet," of his ideal American singer finding subject matter even in "Banks and tariffs," though he adds, just four paragraphs later, that his liberated and liberating poet "shalt lie close hid with nature, and canst not be afforded to the Capitol or the Exchange" (*E&L* 465, 467). But the old assaults on Emersonian individuality as responsible for both political and economic overreaching do not die easily, as was evident in some of the commentary in the spate of newspaper editorials attending Emerson's bicentennial. For example, extending to the present the kind of charge made by Giamatti in the post-Vietnam era, a June 2003 *New York Times* op-ed piece traced to Emerson not only the financial rapacity of certain corporate executives and their Wall Street accomplices but also (as John Updike noted, two months later in the *New Yorker* and with implicit agreement) the Bush administration's "us-first, go-it-alone foreign policy."[52]

Of course, William James and John Dewey found in Emerson support for their vision of an *anti*-imperialist American future, and, as we have seen, for all his affirmation of "power," Emerson was acutely aware of the dangers of willful self-assertion, especially as exercised by the "vulgar hero"

51. For a response to Bloom and to John Updike (who, in "Emersonianism," had recently reduced the passage to a simple doctrine of "righteous selfishness"), see Cavell's 1984 lecture, "Hope against Hope," reprinted as appendix A of his *Conditions Handsome and Unhandsome: The Constitution of Emersonian Perfectionism,* 134–35. The Blake lines are the opening couplet of "The Human Abstract," in *Songs of Experience* (*Poetry and Prose of Blake,* 27).

52. Updike, "Big Dead White Male," 77.

(*E&L* 985). Similarly, whatever the unintended reverberations of his ringing endorsements of self-reliance, compounded by his observation that, like history, "an institution is the lengthened shadow of one man" (*E&L* 267), Emerson's individualism was not meant to endorse commodification and the Exchange in the form of ruthless corporate aggrandizement. Faced with the spectacle of the corporate and accounting greed and criminality revealed in 2001–2002, Emerson—the *Times* and John Updike notwithstanding—would surely have been as appalled as the rest of us, perhaps more so since he would have seen the officers of Enron, WorldCom, Tyco, Arthur Andersen, and the rest not only as malefactors but also as minions of Mammon, that always downward-oriented, least erect of the fallen angels.[53]

But there remains that *most* "erect" of figures: Emerson's self-reliant man, near angelic and related to Milton's unfallen Adam and Eve, "erect" and "clad / In naked majesty" (*PL* 4:288–90), before they were brought low by Satanic power. According to Eve herself, aside from God's command not to eat of the forbidden tree, she and prelapsarian Adam were to "live / Law to ourselves, our reason is our law" (*PL* 9:953–54). Ironically, considering that it was their corrupted reason (their desire for forbidden knowledge) that led to the Fall of Adam and Eve, it is, for Emerson, precisely the power of intuitive Reason—the inner "law" and inner "light"—that elevates us to near divine status, making it, at privileged or blasphemous moments, hard to distinguish the Emersonian self from any God external to that self. In the next two chapters, I focus on the problematics of the feeling of "divinity within," a lethal fault in Adam and Eve (*PL* 9:1010), in Emerson part of the ambiguous legacy of radically immanent theology mingled with idealist philosophy and the Romantic doctrine of the godlike creative Imagination.

53. For one consequence of transcendental self-reliance taking the form of John D. Rockefeller and monopoly, see Howard Horwitz, "The Standard Oil Trust as Emersonian Hero."

Chapter 9

Divinity Within

THE GODLIKE SELF AND THE DIVINITY SCHOOL ADDRESS

One man [Jesus Christ] was true to what is in you and me. He saw that God incarnates himself in man. . . . He said, in this jubilee of sublime emotion, "I am divine. Through me, God acts; through me, speaks. Would you see God, see me; or see thee, when thou also thinkest as I now think."

—RALPH WALDO EMERSON, Divinity School Address

❧

'Tis refreshing to old-fashioned people like me
To meet such a primitive Pagan as he,
In whose mind all creation is duly respected
As parts of himself—just a little projected;
And who's willing to worship the stars and the sun,
A convert to—nothing but Emerson.

—JAMES RUSSELL LOWELL, *A Fable for Critics*

❧

Emerson believed in having the courage to treat all men as equals. . . . "Shall I not treat all men as gods?" he cries. If you like, Waldo, but we've got to pay for it, when you've made them *feel* that they're gods. A hundred million American godlets is rather much for the world to deal with.

—D. H. LAWRENCE, 1923 book review

As Lawrence said of Emerson's American program of egalitarian divinization, it *is* "rather much," especially when the liberated godlets take their status seriously.[1] And where, in the specific context of the vision of the United States, does the primary emphasis in this formulation fall, on the adjective *egalitarian,* or the noun *divinization*? Cornell West, following William James and John Dewey, traced the "instinctive awareness" they shared back to Emerson, specifically to the first of his seminal lectures at Harvard, "The American Scholar," and its declaration of the nation's cultural independence. For West, Emerson's American scholar, having appropriated "God-like power," employs that power in associating "a mythic self with the very content and character of America." Thus, Emersonian "individualism pertains not simply to discrete individuals but, more important, to a normative and exhortative conception of the individual *as* America." There is much to be said for this specifically American variation on the paradoxical absorption of a defiantly autonomous self within an all-encompassing Over-Soul. But there is even more to be said for aligning the sociopolitical perspective of James and Dewey less with "The American Scholar" than with Walt Whitman's *Democratic Vistas,* written thirty years later, and announcing a vision, as Richard Rorty has recently said, "more secular and more communal than Emerson's," for, "at bottom, . . . Emerson, like his disciple Nietzsche, was not a philosopher of democracy but of private self-creation, of what he called 'the infinitude of the private man.' Godlike power was never far from Emerson's mind. His America was not so much a community of fellow citizens as a clearing in which God-like heroes could act out self-written dramas." Although it is dangerous to say what a man is "at bottom" in the case of a thinker willing to quote Milton's Satan in order to assert that "under every deep a lower deep opens" (*E&L* 403), Rorty's emphasis—and this *is* the Emerson *most* valued by Nietzsche—is, properly, on the apostle of power and divinity within.[2]

Of course, if we each believe ourselves to be driven wholly from within, becoming a kind of Romantic godlike hero, the potential ramifications can be creative or destructive. The explosive doctrine is—unavoidably—self-reliant individualism than which few doctrines and legacies could be more ambiguous, especially given Emerson's habit of emphasizing, depending on the occasion, a single aspect of a larger truth. Not long after Ellen's death, Emerson confided to his notebook a poem that never made it into print—though its God at the "bottom of my heart" anticipates the "deep heart"

1. Lawrence's remarks occur in his review of Stuart P. Sherman's *Americans* (1922), in the *Dial* (May 1923). For both the review and Sherman's chapter on Emerson ("The Emersonian Liberation"), see Konvitz, *Recognition of Emerson,* 162–69.

2. Rorty, *Philosophy and Social Hope,* 26. Rorty quotes Dewey's 1911 essay "Maeterlinck's Philosophy of Life" and West's *American Evasion of Philosophy,* 12–13.

of "Threnody," and the description of that heart as an "Angel" and unerring "wise Seer" once again fuses *Paradise Lost* with Wordsworth's Intimations Ode. Emerson insists that he will not "live out of me," will not see "with others' eyes," that *his* "good is good," his "evil ill." He "would be free," something he cannot be were he to take things as "others please to rate them." Instead, "I dare attempt to lay out my own road," so that whatever

> myself delights in shall be Good[,]
> That which I do not want,—indifferent[.]
> That which I hate is Bad. That's flat[.]
> Henceforth, please God, forever I forego
> The yoke of men's opinions. I will be
> Lighthearted as a bird & live with God.
> I find him in the bottom of my heart[;]
> I hear continually his voice therein
> And books, & priests, & worlds, I less esteem[.]
> Who says the heart's a blind guide? It is not.
> My heart did never counsel me to sin[.]
> I wonder where it got its wisdom[?]
> For in the darkest maze amid the sweetest baits
> Or amid horrid dangers never once
> Did that gentle Angel fail of his oracle[.]
> The little needle always knows the north[,]
> The little bird remembereth his note[,]
> And this wise Seer never errs[.]
> I never taught it what it teaches me[,]
> I only follow when I act aright.
> Whence then did this omniscient Spirit come?
> From God it came. It is the Deity.
>
> (*JMN* 4:47–48)

This fierce celebration of self-reliance and the God within at once fascinates and troubles that devout Emersonian Harold Bloom. He registers his fear of its Pentecostal and political ramifications in the "Evening Land" presided over by George W. Bush, admitting that "in forming the mind of America, [Emerson] prophesied a crazy salad to go with our meat."[3]

It is appropriate that Bloom should echo "A Prayer for My Daughter," which is, as we will see in a moment, Yeats's most radical affirmation of the paradoxical alignment of the autonomous self with the divine will. At such times, one is left wondering whether Emersonian individualism is *nothing but* individualism, or individualism *at all.* In his 1854 lecture attacking the

3. Bloom, *Where Shall Wisdom Be Found?* 200. Denis Donoghue would agree. See his *The American Classics,* 51.

Fugitive Slave Law, he says explicitly of his most celebrated phrase: "Self-reliance, the height and perfection of man, is reliance on God." In the rhetorical question posed by Bliss Perry: "How many of the young persons who have been thrilled by the pages of 'Self-Reliance' have been able to perceive, simply by the evidence offered in that essay, that Emerson always had the higher self in mind, and that, in his son's words,—he really meant 'God-Reliance' when he said 'Self-Reliance'?" But how, to pose our own rhetorical question, can that be if God is *within* man, a divine intuitive principle that makes that indwelling deity a form of "spirit" indistinguishable from mind? In his sermon on man's "Likeness to God," W. E. Channing had insisted both that God "dwells within us" and that, despite this language of immanence, "God's infinity places him beyond the resemblance and approach of man." Emerson, who speaks in the lines earlier quoted of "his voice therein," put it more radically, insisting, in an 1832 sermon, that judging "for ourselves" was a "sacred duty," that no precept was so important "as that a man should get his principles *nowhere but in himself.* There is no other way for you to arrive at *the voice of God* but by patient listening to *your own conscience*" (*CS* 4:79; italics added). Four years later, Emerson's friend George Ripley described the believer as "conscious of an inward nature, which is the source of more important and comprehensive ideas than any which the external senses suggest, and he follows the decision of these ideas as the inspiring voice of God."[4]

Ripley shared Emerson's admiration of Wordsworth's "Ode to Duty," and, as with Emerson, his final phrase may well echo the ode's opening line, addressed to the "Stern Daughter of the Voice of God." Indeed, Wordsworth clung to a vestige of radical autonomy, even in that Senecan and Miltonic poem. The "Ode to Duty," one of Emerson's favorites and a near parallel to his own bowing down, in the essay "Fate," before "Beautiful Necessity," contained in its first printing a sixth stanza, later excised:

Yet not the less would I throughout
Still act according to the voice
Of my own wish; and feel past doubt
That *my submissiveness was choice:*
Not seeking in the school of pride
For "precepts over dignified,"
Denial and restraint I prize
No farther than they breed *a second Will more wise.*
(*WP* 1:606, 1004; italics added)

4. Perry posed this question in the first of his Vanuxem Foundation Lectures at Princeton, March 1931 (*Emerson Today,* 26); Ripley, *Discourse on the Philosophy of Religion Addressed to Doubters Who Wish to Believe,* 9, 10; Channing, "Likeness to God," in *The Transcendentalists: An Anthology,* edited by Miller, 23, 24.

In his own commentary on the poem in *The Friend,* Wordsworth spoke of a person's "act of obedience to a moral law *established by himself,* and therefore he moves then also along the orbit of *perfect liberty*" (*F* 1:405; italics added). Coleridge, alluding to the "Ode to Duty" in his own poem "To William Wordsworth," reiterated the paradox of "chosen Laws controlling choice." But if Wordsworth—insisting on voluntary obedience, the sense that in thy will is our freedom—still believes that we move in "an orbit of perfect freedom," and feels himself to be acting according to "the voice / Of my own wish," who or what, exactly, is "Duty," the "Stern Daughter of the *Voice of God,*" addressed in the ode's opening line? Wordsworth is, of course, echoing Milton, where Eve explains:

> God so commanded, and left that command
> *Sole daughter of his voice;* the rest, we live
> *Law to ourselves, our reason is our law.*
> (*PL* 9:652–54; italics added)

Though faithful to Milton, Wordsworth must have felt, rightly, that the rather willful sixth stanza jarred with his ode's overall emphasis on service and his climactic, obeisant, and (again) Miltonic petition:

> Give unto me, made lowly wise,
> The spirit of self-sacrifice;
> The confidence of reason give!
> And in the light of Truth thy Bondsman let me live!
> (lines 61–64)

Whether or not he was reacting to Wordsworth's ode, Ripley, as the title of his book suggests, is thinking of *On Religion: Speeches to Its Cultured Despisers,* the influential 1799 treatise of his mentor, the German father of hermeneutics, Friedrich Schleiermacher: a predecessor as well of Nietzsche, who also had Emerson as a precursor. But it took Nietzsche, himself the son of a Protestant minister, to articulate the most radical form of immanence and the substitution of autonomous Selfhood for Schleiermacher's (and, apparently, Emerson's) twin theme of individuality paired with ultimate dependence on God, self-reliance equated with "reliance on God."

Another of the last Romantics, Nietzsche's disciple, Yeats, reveals himself as a would-be heir of Nietzschean autonomy and Emersonian self-reliance when he tells us, in his 1909 journal, that, struggling to overcome self-doubt and vacillation and rely instead on his own intuitive and instinctual values, he hopes "at last to keep to my own [impulse] in every situation in life; to discover and create *in myself* as I grow old that one thing which is to life what style is to letters: moral radiance, a *personal* quality of *universal* meaning in action and thought."[5] Ten years later, this Kantian participation of the personal in the universal becomes a spiritual correspondence resembling the Emersonian sense of the self as "part or particle" of divinity. When Yeats insists, in "A Prayer for My Daughter," that the soul, recovering "radical innocence," "learns at last that it is self-delighting, / Self-appeasing, self-affrighting," he is remembering Emerson's celebration (in "Self-Reliance") of the "unaffected, unbiased, unbribable, *unaffrighted innocence*" of children; his claim that, just as honor is "self-dependent, self-derived," so all instances of "power" are "demonstrations of the self-sufficing, and therefore self-relying soul" (*E&L* 261, 266, 272).

And when Yeats adds that the radically innocent soul also learns that "*its own sweet will is Heaven's will,*" he is recalling, along with Emerson's alignment of self-reliance with God-reliance, the river that "glideth at his own sweet will" in what Coleridge rightly calls "Wordsworth's exquisite sonnet on Westminster Bridge at sunrise." Significantly, Coleridge felt it necessary to defend from charges of literalness "the known and felt impropriety" of an expression (the river gliding "at his own sweet will") that merely "seemed," to careless or hostile readers, to attribute conscious will to inanimate nature. Here as elsewhere in *Aids to Reflection,* Coleridge was wary of the slippery slope leading from pantheism (that "worship of nature" to which he himself had once been susceptible) to the complete "untenanting creation of its God" which he had deplored in *The Destiny of Nations.* That untenanting occurs in Yeats's "Prayer," where he is remembering, along with that willful Wordsworthian river, the Romantic, Emersonian, and Nietzschean equation of Self and God, Within and Above, the autonomous and self-determining inner world as the ultimate and creative source of value and "moral radiance." And since divine and demonic are often near-allied, Yeats (for whom the radically innocent soul is self-appeasing, self-delighting, self-affrighting) is also remembering, as his Romantic precursors always do, Milton's Satan, whose power, or imperial "puissance," is "our own" and whose autonomy activates Milton's own rebellious genius, for that liberating Satan is, he himself claims, "Self-begot, self-raised / By our own quickening power" (*PL* 5:860–61).

To whom, then, does Yeats address his "prayer" for his infant daughter? All his "may shes" seem less petitions to *heaven's* will than reflections of his *own,* the will of *Anne's* father, not of any heavenly Father. In one of this poem's two precursors, "Tintern Abbey," Wordsworth deliberately radicalizes *his* immediate precursor text, Coleridge's "Frost at Midnight," in which the father's prayer for his infant son is directed to God as the "Great Universal Teacher." In "Tintern Abbey," Wordsworth himself, to

5. Yeats, *Memoirs: Autobiography—First Draft,* 258; italics added.

Emerson's rather surprising annoyance (*JMN* 4:63), pronounces *his own* benediction upon his sister. "This prayer I make," when he finally makes it, is addressed not to God (there is, despite Coleridge's attempt to convince us otherwise, no clear reference to a supreme being in "Tintern Abbey") but to himself as the prophet invoking "Nature," which "never did betray the heart that loved her":

> Therefore let the moon
> Shine on thee in thy solitary walk;
> And let the misty mountain winds be free
> To blow against thee. . . .
> (134–37; *WP* 1:361)

Of *The Prelude,* M. H. Abrams once asked, "What does God *do* in the poem?" and found the answer to be, "Nothing of consequence," God's "traditional offices" having been "preempted" by the "two generative and operative terms" within which Wordsworth "described the process of his spiritual development . . . : mind and nature." Even when it comes to the more orthodox Wordsworth of most of *The Excursion,* Abrams feels justified in quoting Hazlitt, who, "with his usual acumen," observes: "It is as if there were nothing but himself and the universe."[6] It seems almost pedestrian to note that, readers as brilliant as Hazlitt and Abrams notwithstanding, the author of *The Excursion* is manifestly not only a theist but also a Christian. Their case is stronger in, say, "Tintern Abbey," written before Wordsworth had to deal with Coleridgean alarm about his pantheism and "*Semi*-atheism." In effect, the Wordsworth of "Tintern Abbey," unlike the Coleridgean speaker of "Frost at Midnight" and decidedly unlike his own "Bondsman" of the "Ode to Duty" six years later, usurps the role of Jehovah—not, of course, by becoming a secular Satan, but nevertheless by borrowing what Milton's fallen angel calls "*our own* quickening power."

With Wordsworth as with Emerson, it is seldom easy to demarcate God from Nature's indwelling Spirit and a Supreme Being out of and above oneself from the God within. Reading "Tintern Abbey," we can understand why, in those passages earlier cited from *Aids to Reflection,* Coleridge was so anxious to make his friend Wordsworth retroactively orthodox. Coleridge himself, clearly distinguishing the self from God, speaks in *Biographia Literaria* of an "equatorial point" that would reconcile the polarity between philosophy and religion, a reconciliation he had earlier articulated in the fifth of the Essays on Method in *The Friend,* where "METHOD" *is* the

6. Abrams, *Natural Supernaturalism,* 90, quoting from Hazlitt's review (*Complete Works,* 4:113), a brilliant analysis though essentially limited to the first four books of *The Excursion.*

convergence of philosophy and religion into one integrated whole (*F* 1: 463). In concluding the ninth thesis in the twelfth chapter of the *Biographia,* Coleridge states: "In other words, philosophy would pass into religion, and religion become inclusive of philosophy. We begin with the I KNOW MYSELF, in order to end with the absolute I AM. We proceed from the SELF in order to lose and find all self in GOD" (*BL* 1:283). It was precisely this claim that Emerson was to make in the final line of his elegy for Waldo, "Lost in God, in Godhead found!" But what disturbed, or outraged, those shocked by the Divinity School Address was not only the lecturer's assault on historical Christianity but also Emerson's unwillingness to clearly distinguish the self from God. To that address and its aftermath we turn next.

"'Tis refreshing to old-fashioned people like me / To meet such a primitive Pagan as he" (33–34), joshes James Russell Lowell in his vignette of Emerson, the finest portion of his 1848 *Fable for Critics.* "Pagan!" was among the more genteel accusations leveled at Emerson during the uproar that followed his address to the Harvard Divinity School, delivered in mid-July 1838. Given this book's focus, I will emphasize the connections with the Romantics. As John Updike has recently and accurately observed of Emersonian Transcendentalism, "European Romanticism, rephrased for the American democracy, posed a revolutionary threat to a rationalist elite. At the same time, it upset Christian orthodoxy, even the attenuated Unitarian form."[7] In this cause, even those old revolutionaries Coleridge and Wordsworth could be enlisted. In discussing the aftermath of the Divinity School Address, I will stress the Coleridge connection introduced by "Uriel," the poem, based on another Miltonic angel, in which Emerson allegorically but unmistakably responds to his critics. But we may begin with an Emerson allusion in the text of the address itself, since it is to Wordsworth, whimsically imagining *himself* a potential pagan.

On the significant occasion of this his most public revolt against conformity, and specifically against that "attenuated" form of Christian orthodoxy represented by the Unitarian elite that dominated Harvard, Emerson announced that

> One would rather be
> "A pagan, suckled in a creed outworn,"
> than be defrauded of his manly right in coming into nature, and finding . . . even virtue and truth foreclosed and monopolized. You shall not be a man even. You shall not . . . dare, and live after the infinite Law that is in you, and

7. Updike, "Big Dead White Male," 77.

in company with the infinite Beauty which heaven and earth reflect to you in all lovely forms; but you must subordinate your nature to Christ's nature; you must accept our interpretations; and take his portrait as the vulgar draw it. (*E&L* 81)

The line quoted—here and in an 1834 journal entry (*JMN* 4:380)—is, of course, from one of the greatest of the sonnets Wordsworth wrote shortly after the turn of the century (first published in 1807). The octave begins,

> The world is too much with us; late and soon,
> Getting and spending, we lay waste our powers:
> Little we see in Nature that is ours;
> We have given our hearts away, a sordid boon.
> (*WP* 1:568)

Dulled by crass materialism, we have lost the capacity to respond to the power and beauty of nature; "we are out of tune; / It moves us not." This is the pivot into the sestet, in which Wordsworth exclaims that, if it would allow him to "have glimpses" of a reenchanted world, he would "rather be / A Pagan suckled in a creed outworn" than a modern Christian alienated from a female earth by austere forms of worship, no longer able to respond to the beauty, harmony, and mystery of fecund, vital Nature (*WP* 1:569).

Unlike the "merely spectral" preacher he later refers to, oblivious to the beauty of "the snow storm falling" outside the church (*E&L* 84–85), Emerson, importing Romanticism and experience into his address, had begun by soothing his audience of perhaps a hundred with a deeply responsive description of nature's fecund beauty in "this refulgent summer," in which "it has been a luxury to draw the breath of life. The grass grows, the buds burst, the meadow is spotted with fire and gold" (*E&L* 75). This thankful reception for the gifts of sun and earth, together with his preference for mystery, even superstition, to apathy, suggests another Wordsworthian source, one buttressing the reference to the sonnet's "pagan." In "Despondency Corrected," Emerson's favorite book of *The Excursion,* the Wanderer, following a remark of the Solitary about their Protestant forebears having driven out the "Romish phantasy" (908), compares the zeal of "our brave Progenitors," their experience of a "spiritual presence" (920, 927), with a lesser but still admirable form of spirituality:

> Though favored less,
> Far less, than these, yet such, in their degree
> Were those bewildered Pagans of old time.
> Beyond their own poor natures and above

> They looked: were humbly thankful for the good
> Which the warm sun solicited, and earth
> Bestowed; were gladsome,—and their moral sense
> They fortified with reverence for the Gods;
> And they had hopes that overstepped the Grave.
> (*E* 4:932–40)

In the lines that follow, the modern scientists and philosophers who lovelessly anatomize nature, "Viewing all objects unremittingly / In disconnexion dead and spiritless" (961–62), are said to obtain "less" from sense and reason than did those "misled" but still passionately responsive "pagans." This Wordsworthian context helps explain why Emerson would begin his address with that humbly grateful description of "this refulgent summer" as an example of the beauty that "heaven and earth reflect to you in all lovely forms" and why he would rather be that "pagan, suckled in a creed outworn," than be "defrauded of his manly right in coming into nature" and finding the "virtue and truth" inherent in the "inner law" and "moral sense" foreclosed and monopolized by an external faith, a "corpse-cold" and deadening "historical Christianity" that had, without providing something of compensating value, disenchanted the natural world joyfully embraced in Greek religion and mythology. In the address, Emerson's specific target was historical Christianity, but there was no doubt about the identity of the all-encompassing enemy and the agent of nature's disenchantment. It was, Emerson agreed with Wordsworth and Coleridge, that supposedly enlightened empiricist philosophy, analytical and mechanical, that had probed and violated its "object," rather than entering into a fruitful marriage: the nuptial relationship between mind and nature celebrated throughout the work of Wordsworth, Coleridge, and Emerson.

After his opening reference to radiant summer, and to "the perfection of this world, in which our senses converse," Emerson quickly moved on to the opening of "the mind," revealing "the laws which . . . make things what they are," the laws—universal, supreme, inner—that reveal that natural world, for all its beauty and perfection, as "a mere illustration and fable of this mind" (*E&L* 75). Our perception of these "laws of the soul" awakens, in each and every individual, a "moral sentiment," which results from an "insight" that Emerson follows Plotinus and Milton, Coleridge and Wordsworth, in designating an "intuition." Like the self-executing laws of the soul, such an intuition is without mediation, either historical or institutional (*E&L* 75–76).

Some clergymen in the audience must have been squirming at this point, and Emerson had every intention of once again bearding the elite in their den. Six years earlier, shortly before resigning his pastorate, he had privately pronounced the clergy an "antiquated" profession: "In an altered age," he went on—anticipating this address as well as the introduction to *Nature* and "The American Scholar"—"we worship the dead forms of our ancestors." Substituting a more intellectually respectable brand of paganism for Wordsworth's, associated in the "World is too much with us" sonnet with Proteus and Triton, and in the fourth book of *The Excursion* (in lines that deeply affected Keats) with Apollo and Diana, he asked rhetorically: "Were not a Socratic paganism better than a super-annuated Christianity?" (*JMN* 4:26–27).[8] When he delivered his address to the Harvard divinity students, select faculty, and a roomful of clergymen, it struck at least some of the clerics present as precisely that—paganism.

Given the vehemence and the rhetorical power of his attack on the promulgators, early and late, of "historical Christianity" for neglecting the "inner" Law, it is no wonder that some of the scandalized orthodox clergymen in the audience—not the six graduating students who had invited Emerson to speak—promptly branded their guest lecturer an "infidel," or worse. Here was a man who, having resigned his ministry a half-dozen years earlier, had now gone too far even for Unitarians. Emerson had been decorously disagreed with rather than condemned when he had resigned his ministry because he could no longer in good conscience distribute "the Lord's Supper." But now he was rejecting not only the supernatural interpretation of miracles ("miracles," Emerson grandly informed an audience at the very storm center of the contemporary "Miracles Controversy," were "one with the blowing clover and the falling rain") but also apparently dismissing any concept of a "personal" divinity, indeed any divinity clearly distinguishable from the self.[9] Indeed, the "new Teacher"

8. Though he thought *The Excursion* one of the few things "to be wondered at in this age," Keats, unlike Wordsworth, would not have condescendingly described those ancient poets as "unenlightened swains of pagan Greece." But the future author of the "Ode to a Nightingale" and of all those poems featuring his presiding deity, Apollo, responded gratefully and creatively to the lines in which one of those Greek poets is depicted conjuring up the moon and stars as Diana, "a beaming goddess with her Nymphs," moving "Across the lawn and through the darksome groves," while the fancy of another "fetched, / Even from the blazing chariot of the sun, / A beardless Youth, who touched a golden lute, / And filled the illumined groves with ravishment" (*E* 4:850–66). No lover of Keats's poetry, from *Endymion* on, will be surprised by the touching note of his friend Benjamin Haydon inscribed next to lines 858–64 in his copy of *The Excursion:* "Poor Keats used always to prefer this passage to all others." His reward we know: Wordsworth's dismissal of the "Hymn to Pan" as "a very pretty piece of paganism."

9. Four months earlier, in a journal entry of March 1838, Emerson records talking with a group of friendly theological students who found his insistence on the impersonality of God "desolating & ghastly." He told them that he could not find "when I explore my own consciousness any truth in saying that God is a Person, but the reverse. I feel that there is some profanation in saying He is personal. To represent him as an individual is to shut him out of my consciousness" (*JMN* 5:457).

Emerson envisioned shall, following the "shining laws" within, "see the world to be the mirror of the soul" (*E&L* 92).

Most offensively, Emerson accused the clergy in general of preaching a dead and derivative faith, based on "tradition," which "comes out of the memory, and not out of the soul," out of a historical Christianity that "destroys the power of preaching," by withdrawing it from exploration of "the moral nature of man," giving us "a God of the past." What was required was a revitalized faith, "the breath of new life," that can only derive from personal experience of one's own "indwelling Supreme Spirit," an "ever-present divinity." By reducing a profoundly valuable text, the Bible, to an exclusive and infallible guide to truth, we mortgage ourselves to the past. "Men have come to speak of the revelation as somewhat long ago given and done, as if God were dead." But this is not Nietzsche; it is Emerson, for whom God was not dead but a Presence *in* the present. "God is, not was. . . . He speaketh, not spake" (*E&L* 88).

At the same time, this is to deny "historical" Christianity. Unsurprisingly, the advocate of originality and unmediated vision admonished the graduating ministers before him to refuse even the greatest models and "dare to love God without mediator or veil." We are to be grateful for the great divines and ministers who have gone before, but the novice must be his own man. Imitation of even the greatest models dooms the imitator to "hopeless mediocrity. The inventor did it, because it was natural to him, and so in him it has a charm. In the imitator something else is natural, and he bereaves himself of his own beauty, to come short of another man's" (*E&L* 89). Even the traditional Imitation of Christ is awry, for Jesus, though symbolizing the beauty of spirit, is not its unique embodiment since that spirit is universal. Just as truth is not limited to the Bible, neither does prophecy terminate with Jesus. "Jesus Christ," Emerson told the graduating students, "belonged to the true race of the prophets"; he was the first, seeing with the eye of Reason, to perceive the true mystery of Incarnation: "He saw with *open eye* the mystery of the soul, . . . he lived in it, and had his being there. Alone in all history, he estimated the greatness of man."

> One man was true to what is in you and me. *He saw* that *God incarnates himself in man,* and evermore goes forth anew to take possession of his World. He said, in this jubilee of sublime emotion, "I am divine. Through me, God acts; through me, speaks. *Would you see God, see me; or see thee, when thou also thinkest as I now think.*" But what a distortion did his doctrine and memory suffer in the same, in the next, and in the following ages! There is no doctrine of the *Reason* which will bear to be taught by the *Understanding*. . . . Christianity became a Mythus, as the poetic teachings of Greece and Egypt, before. (*E&L* 80; italics added)

Jesus, then, is great because, himself "a true man," he saw the true greatness of man in general, each and all. As for Jesus being "divine," that proclamation was made in a state of "sublime emotion," a jubilee and claim of divinity within replicable by us, when we think as Jesus had at such moments: he who was the first to realize that "God incarnates himself in man."

"I believe I am more of a Quaker than anything else," Emerson once told his cousin David Greene Haskins. "I believe in the still, small voice, and that voice of Christ is *within us.*" Though even more radical than the Quaker emphasis on the Inward Light, Emerson's insistence on unmediated access to an immanent God has some precedent in both testaments of the Bible. "I will put my law within them," says the Lord in Jeremiah (31:32–33), and an echoing Jesus famously announces in Luke: "The kingdom of God is within you" (17:21). Not to be found "in the sky" or "in the sea," the "Kingdom of God is inside you." That less familiar formulation occurs in an uncanonical text, but one worth citing here. The closest precursor to Emerson's religious radicalism is a text unknown to him, one of the now famous Gnostic Gospels pronounced heretical, but hidden away in a sealed jar (rather than committed to the flames, as they were ordered to be by Athanasius, bishop of Alexandria, in 367) and rediscovered at Nag Hammadi in Egypt in 1945. Of these suppressed texts, the Gospel of Thomas is the most audaciously heterodox in asserting, as Emerson did, that the divine light is not, as in the canonical Gospel of John, incarnate in Jesus alone, but is hidden within each of us. Our goal in seeking that inner light is at once individual illumination and a kind of "twinning" with Christ. Anticipating Emerson's merging of the divine and human "I am," the Jesus of Thomas tells us, "Whoever drinks from my mouth will become as I am." And one of the central texts in Thomas—"If you bring forth what is within you, what you bring forth will save you. If you do not bring forth what is within you, what you do not bring forth will destroy you"—has its parallel in the Divinity School lecture's most dramatic antithesis: "That is always best which gives me to myself. . . . That which shows God in me, fortifies me. That which shows God out of me, makes me a wart and a wen" (*E&L* 81).[10]

Emerson's exclamation about Christianity and Jesus himself—"But what a distortion did his doctrine and memory suffer in the same, in the

10. The passages from the Gospel of Thomas (verses 3, 108, 70) are cited from Elaine Pagels, *Beyond Belief: The Gospel of Thomas,* 49, 32. She quotes the "bring-forth" passage in George MacRae's translation. Harold Bloom has recently remarked that "there is little in the Gospel of Thomas that would not have been accepted by Emerson, Thoreau, and Whitman" (*Where Shall Wisdom Be Found?* 260).

next, and in the following ages!"—seems particularly prescient when we juxtapose the Divinity School Address with this Gnostic Gospel, which, had it not been excluded from the canon and almost from history itself, would have altered, or at least complicated, the received image of Christ and Christianity. Thomas, like Emerson after him, held that Jesus taught that God incarnates himself not in one man in a unique moment of past history, but here and now, and in all men, since we are each endowed with the capacity, should we choose to exercise it, to seek that divinity in whose image we are all made. According to Emerson, this "sublime truth," passed on to those who share the gift of intuitive Reason, is distorted and diminished by conventional men of prose dominated by mere understanding. What is needed is direct, unmediated vision. Thus, each neophyte preacher in the audience, fortified by the God within him, is to go forth on a revolutionary mission: "Yourself a newborn bard of the Holy Ghost, cast behind you all conformity, and acquaint men at first hand with Deity" (*E&L* 89). Ironically, given Emerson's thirty-year ostracism from Harvard following this address, it was voted in 1903 that money left over from the celebration of the centennial of his birth be spent on a marble tablet, placed in the old Divinity School chapel, and inscribed: "Acquaint thyself at first hand with Deity."

❧ This intuitive, firsthand acquaintance with Deity smacks of Carlyle, and of the great precursor whose God, at least in *Paradise Lost,* seems less the Father or the Son than the Inner Light of radical Protestant dissent, the Holy Spirit that made its temple in Milton. But Emerson's principal aid to spiritual reflection, Coleridge, also figures in the Divinity School Address. It was he, Emerson said in 1836, whose "reverence for the Divine Reason . . . made him regard every man as the most sacred object in the Universe, the Temple of Deity" (*EL* 1:379), he who had elevated a noumenal Reason over the merely phenomenal and sensual understanding. Shortly before explaining to his brother Edward the "distinction . . . between Reason and Understanding," Emerson tried in his journal to reconcile this new Coleridgean-Germanic vocabulary with the language of the New Testament:

> Jesus Christ was a minister of the pure Reason. The beatitudes of the Sermon on the Mount are all utterances of the mind contemning the phenomenal world . . . The Understanding can make nothing of [the Sermon]. 'Tis all nonsense. The Reason affirms its absolute verity. . . . A clear perception of [the counteraction of the Reason and the Understanding] is the key to all theology, and a theory of human life. St. Paul marks the distinction by the terms natural man and spiritual man. When Novalis says "It is the instinct of the understanding to counteract the Reason," he only translates into a

scientific formula the sentence of St. Paul, "The Carnal mind is enmity against God."[11]

Though the later Coleridge—Tory and Anglican—would hardly have endorsed the radically immanent theology proclaimed in the Divinity School Address, Emerson reinforced the connection with Coleridge in his poem "Uriel," probably begun in 1839 and published in 1846. Though "Uriel" (*EPP* 436–37) deals overtly with poetic formalists (those preaching "laws of form, and metre just"), it is really Emerson's thinly veiled response to the reaction stirred up by theological formalists and dogmatists unsurprisingly outraged by the Divinity School Address. The situation and the role played by his titular figure, including his "piercing eye," strongly suggest an Emersonian fusion. There is, of course, Milton's angel Uriel, who stands "In sight of God's throne, gloriously bright," an angel even Satan goes out of his way to avoid, his very name meaning the "fire" or "light" of God, and—most significantly, for Emerson's allegory—designated by Milton the "first interpreter" of God's "authentic will" (*PL* 10: 328, 3:654–56). Horace Mann's description of Emerson himself as "a man stationed in the sun" (a description probably known to Emerson and certainly relevant to the poem) had a pictorial parallel, one connecting "Uriel" with Coleridge. Back in 1833, Coleridge had begun and ended his conversation with Emerson by speaking of his old friend of thirty years the American painter Washington Allston. As he was taking his leave of Emerson, the old man showed him an Allston painting of his own and urged his young visitor, himself an admirer of Allston, to convey his regards when he returned to Boston. No doubt he did, and may, in writing "Uriel," have thought of the artist's celebrated painting *Uriel in the Sun.* In any case, in the poem, in which Emerson dramatizes himself as Uriel, Milton's and (possibly) Allston's angel joins forces with that damaged archangel Coleridge himself.[12]

11. Cited from Bliss Perry, ed., *The Heart of Emerson's Journals,* 81–82.

12. Its recent restoration in the Concord Museum reveals that Emerson's study was graced by Allston's etching of Coleridge himself. As it happens, Coleridge declared "Uriel . . . never any great Favorite of mine," an angel "Milton heard cry at the Door of his Imagination, & took in out of charity" (*CL* 2:809). Horace Mann, who lectured in Concord in 1839, had been enthralled by Emerson's own Philosophy of History series, describing the lecturer in terms applicable to the vantage point of Emerson's Uriel and to the "confusion" into which the undiscerning slide in the poem: "As a man stationed in the sun would see all the planets moving round it in one direction and in perfect harmony, while to an eye on the earth their motions are full of crossings and retrogradings; so he, from his central position in the spiritual world, discovers harmony and order when others can discern only confusion" (quoted in Ralph L. Rusk, *The Life of Ralph Waldo Emerson,* 247–48; Rusk suspects that Emerson was aware of Mann's description [272]).

Defying "reverend use" so that he "stirred the devils everywhere," Emerson's Uriel "Gave his sentiment divine." Anticipating Yeats's distinction between the straight line of logic and nature's winding path (symbolized, respectively, by the hawk and butterfly engraved on the ring he always wore), Uriel insists that the "line," that straight line of logical understanding as opposed to what we can see from a solar perspective informed by angelic intuitive Reason, is *contra naturam*, that everything in this "round" universe consists of cyclical energy, a dialectical dynamism that disrupts, even inverts, static opposites:

> "Line in nature is not found;
> Unit and universe are round;
> In vain produced, all rays return;
> Evil will bless, and ice will burn."
> As Uriel spoke with piercing eye,
> A shudder ran around the sky;
> The stern old war-gods shook their heads;
> The seraphs frowned from myrtle-beds;
> Seemed to the holy festival
> The rash word boded ill to all;
> The balance-beam of Fate was bent;
> The bounds of good and ill were rent;
> Strong Hades could not keep his own,
> And all slid to confusion.
>
> (21–34; *EPP* 437)

The cosmic setting and angelic discourse, the shock administered to orthodoxy and the upsetting of conventional bounds of good and evil, the mixture of defiance and humor and the final confusion in which all hell breaks loose—one might think one was reading, if not Nietzsche, Nietzsche's favorite English poet, Byron, specifically his hilarious demolition of theological and political dogmatic cant, *The Vision of Judgment.* Because, in his many comments on Byron, Emerson, who feared imitating his seductive poetry (*JMN* 4:315, 9:373), never mentions this extraordinary poem, the resemblance must be coincidental—though Emerson *was* familiar with this Byronic mixture of convention-ridiculing satire and good humor from reading some of *Don Juan* (*JMN* 6:39, 154, 191, 14:27). In any case, it was just this mischievous mingling of humor and rebellion, not only the heroic contradiction of conventional views but their subjection to good-humored "Byronic" ridicule as well, that appealed to Robert Frost. Judging "Uriel" the best American poem, Frost even allowed one of his characters (Job, who, in *The Masque of Reason* [344] alludes to the line about evil blessing and ice burning) to refer to its source as "the greatest Western poem yet."[13]

Frost was also aware of the poem's personal seriousness. Alluding to the fourth of the lines quoted below, from the final movement, he declared in 1922 his intention to retreat from the world of political controversy. He announced to his friend Louis Untermeyer, "I will take example of Uriel and withdraw into a cloud." That line in "Uriel" alludes to Emerson's own retirement from public controversy in the wake of the charges of heresy and worse leveled at him after the Divinity School Address. Significantly, Uriel's withdrawal includes the proud claim to be a premature prophet, one whose time is yet to come, though for now he can only dazzle and blind those superficial dogmatists incapable of receiving the light:

A sad self-knowledge, withering, fell
On the beauty of Uriel;
In heaven once eminent, the god
Withdrew that hour, into his cloud;
Whether doomed to long gyration
In the sea of generation,
Or by knowledge grown too bright
To hit the nerve of feebler sight.
(35–42)

This description of a Uriel "too bright" for those of "feebler sight," like his earlier speaking with a "piercing eye," suggests an Emersonian identification with Coleridge, whom he had earlier praised for "the piercing sight which made the world transparent to him, and the kindling eloquence with which both in speech and writing this old man eloquently masters our minds and hearts." His lack of a wide audience in his lifetime is to be largely attributed "to the abstruseness of the speculations in which he delighted and which tasked the intellect too sorely to be the favorite reading of the loungers in reading rooms." Essentially, Emerson thought Coleridge's unpopularity supported "the charge we make upon the times, of superficialness or deficiency of interest in profound inquiries" (*EL* 2:377, 380).

Deploying the new "Germanic" modes of theological and epistemological thinking, Coleridge had challenged *his* dazzled contemporaries, only to be greeted, as Uriel-Emerson was, by institutional resistance and incomprehension. His championship of a "Symbolic" interpretation of Religion,

13. Frost, *The Masque of Reason,* 344, in *The Poetry of Robert Frost,* 485. For Frost's letter citing "Uriel" in the paragraph that follows, see *Selected Letters of Robert Frost,* 281.

which would somehow provide a "medium" between the "Literal and the Metaphorical" (*LS* 30, 81), offended the orthodox and evoked charges of sheer "cant" from his former protégé, Hazlitt. Emerson's imagery of a seer grown too bright to hit the nerve of feebler sight is related, as he himself notes, to a simile in his favorite stanza (the only one chosen for *Parnassus*) of Shelley's "To a Skylark": like a poet hidden "In the light of thought, / Singing hymns unbidden. . . ." But the phrase "by knowledge grown too bright" also resembles Shelley's variation on Byron's depiction of the author of *Biographia Literaria* as "a hawk encumber'd by his hood," expounding "metaphysics to the nation— / I wish he would explain his Explanation." Two years later, in his 1820 poem "Letter to Maria Gisborne," Shelley presented an obscured yet dazzling Coleridge as a hooded eagle, an intellect blinded by his own mental light yet superior to the blinking night birds around him: "A cloud-encircled meteor of the air, / A hooded eagle among blinking owls" (207–8). Skeptical of Charles's description of his brother's potential as a "reformer," their aunt Mary, a serious Coleridgean perhaps aware of these references, said of Emerson's "genius" that, "while it invents new universes it is lost in the surrounding halo." That is the way of it with idealist philosophy; even his admirer Nietzsche thought Emerson had been obscured by the clouded glass of German metaphysics, philosophy transmitted to him (though Nietzsche did not know this) primarily through Coleridge, whose prose had, in turn, according not only to Byron but even to Wordsworth (*E&L* 777), been made obscure by his immersion in the same opaque medium. Coleridge seems for once engaging in wry humor when he remarks, "Great indeed are the obstacles which an English metaphysician has to encounter" (*BL* 1:290).[14]

Yet Emerson and others in his circle who valued Coleridge believed, as predicted in the lines quoted above regarding Uriel, that his time would come, though it might take a "long gyration." So would Emerson's own time come (and rather more rapidly), but in the meantime, blinking owls

14. For Mary's characterization of Emerson's genius lost in the "surrounding halo," see Rusk, *Life of Emerson,* 167. For the lines quoted (207–8) from "Letter to Maria Gisborne," see Shelley, *Shelley's Poetry and Prose,* 318. Byron's depiction of Coleridge occurs in the dedication to *Don Juan,* a dedication to Robert Southey that Byron suppressed since the poem's first two cantos were published anonymously and he disdained to "attack the dog in the dark; such things are for scoundrels and renegadoes like himself." As the authors of recently published texts not to his liking, Wordsworth and Coleridge, though never treated with the contempt lavished on Southey, also come in for delicious Byronic ridicule. We have seen his response to the author of *Biographia Literaria;* Wordsworth, too, with his "rather long 'Excursion,'" has "given a sample from the vasty version / Of his new system to perplex the sages; / 'Tis poetry—at least by his assertion." See Byron, *Don Juan and Other Satirical Poems,* 160.

and conventional angels would try to repress the truth that had been revealed by a theological rebel and genuine seer:

> a forgetting wind
> Stole over the celestial kind,
> And their lips the secret kept,
> If in ashes the fire-seed slept.
> But now and then, truth-speaking things
> Shamed the angels' veiling wings;
> And, shrilling from the solar course,
> Or from fruit of chemic force,
> Procession of a soul in matter,
> Or the speeding change of water,
> Or out of the good of evil born,
> Came Uriel's voice of cherub scorn,
> And a blush tinged the upper sky,
> And the gods shook, they knew not why.
> ("Uriel," 43–56)

The Divinity School Address, this poem's originating event, was declared by one of those shaken gods, Andrews Norton, an "incoherent rhapsody," though coherent enough to reveal Emerson as a theologically dangerous radical. In the audience was future Transcendentalist leader Theodore Parker, then a twenty-eight-year-old pastor thrilled by Emerson, who on this occasion "had surpassed himself as much as he surpasses others in general." But there were others present. The clerical war gods gathered in the room included Norton (formerly Dexter Professor of Sacred Literature at Harvard), Dean John G. Palfrey (said to be "hurt" by the talk), and Henry Ware Jr. (whose rejoinder appeared in *The Personality of the Deity*). Had William Ellery Channing, Emerson's "Star of the American Church" (*JMN* 7:470), been present, he might have been quietly supportive, given his locating of final authority for biblical truth in the perception of individuals, whom he, like Emerson, saw as somehow participating in Godhead. The response of others in the room ranged from dismay at the subversion of institutional and community-based faith by Emerson's subjective "theology" through ambivalence to rapture, the latter registering what was to be Emerson's catalytic impact, as poetic as it was theological, on such younger Unitarians as Parker.[15]

15. See David M. Robinson, "Poetry, Personality, and the Divinity School Address," on the willingness of younger Unitarians to accept Emerson's emphasis on, and demand for, "the poetic as the highest expression of the soul" (185). There has been much discussion of the "rhetoric" of the address and of its poetic appeal. Interestingly,

There remained, however, the unenraptured Andrews Norton, a man who had earlier distinguished himself by stopping the publication of Elizabeth Peabody's *Christian Examiner* articles on Marsh's edition of Herder's *Spirit of Hebrew Poetry.* Norton went on the attack; among the majority siding with him was Emerson's aunt Mary, whose reading of Coleridge had enabled her to distinguish between the divine and the human, God and man's intuitive Reason. When, in December 1834, Emerson read to her Coleridge's "defense of prayer" (in *On the Constitution of the Church and State*), she replied, "Yes, for our reason was so distinct from the Universal Reason that we could pray to it, & so united with it that we could have assurance that we were heard" (*JMN* 4:353). Mary had struck a delicate Coleridgean balance. There was nothing delicate about the public fulminations following Emerson's address. To judge from the charges, in newspapers and journals, the shock waves reverberated throughout New England.

Norton's attacks appeared first in the *Boston Daily Examiner* for August 27 and twelve days later in the *Christian Watchman.* By then the critics were in full cry. "Infidelity" was the most frequent accusation, though Emerson was also described as "ignorant," "insane," a "mad dog," a "heretic," a "blasphemer," even a demonic Pan or devil, who had planted the "cloven hoof" of German pantheism and atheism in New England. One anonymous reviewer characterized the address (in the *Christian Watchman* in October) as the "foulest Atheism," all the worse since it was uttered in the sanctuary of an "ancient seat of learning."

In an intelligent but furious assault in the conservative Presbyterian journal the *Biblical Repertory and Princeton Review,* James W. Alexander, Albert Dod, and Charles Hodge attributed the "nonsense and impiety" of the address not only to Emerson but also to the transatlantic sources of the infection, specifically to those adapters of Germanic thought, the "superficial" Victor Cousin and Carlyle. Indeed, Emerson's discourse "was obviously in imitation of Thomas Carlyle, and possessing as much of the vice of his mannerism as the author could borrow, but without his genius." This must have rankled a man for whom imitation was indistinguishable from suicide, and incompatible with "genius" as opposed to mere "talent."

There are, in fact, in the Divinity School Address as in the conclusion of "Threnody," echoes of "The Everlasting Yea" chapter of Carlyle's *Sartor Resartus.* For example, as Alexander, Dod, and Hodge implicitly noticed ("he treats Christianity as a Mythos"), Emerson's claim that, because of

---

an unpublished letter of Longfellow (October 28, 1865) reveals that he read and enjoyed the address. See Gary Scharnhorst, "Longfellow and Emerson's Divinity School 'Address': An Unpublished Letter."

historical distortion, "Christianity became a Mythus," echoes Teufelsdröckh's acknowledgment that because of the enlightened skepticism of Voltaire, "the Mythus of the Christian Religion looks not in the eighteenth century as it did in the eighth." The real issue is, "What next?" But Voltaire, who, unlike Goethe, has "only a torch for burning, no hammer for building," cannot help us "to embody the divine Spirit of that Religion in a new Mythus." Meanwhile, Teufelsdröckh asks rhetorically, "What are antiquated Mythuses to me? Or is the God present, felt in my own heart, a thing which Herr von Voltaire will dispute out of me; or dispute into me?" What is felt within, "in thy heart, . . . is of God. This is Belief; all else is Opinion." Unlike Voltaire, Emerson, to apply to him Carlyle's praise of Goethe, was "not a questioner and a despiser, but a teacher and a reverencer, not a destroyer, but a builder-up; not a wit only, but a wise man." Of course, Emerson's critics at the time saw only the blaspheming destroyer and an anything *but* wise man. To be sure, Emerson had his defenders, principally if anonymously George Ripley, but they had to begin by making a prima facie case that he was in fact intelligent, sane, a reformer rather than a heretic, and imbued with the true spirit of Christianity.[16]

Uriel-Emerson was surprised at the vehemence of the response, but unrepentant. Attending the 1838 Phi Beta Kappa ceremony a month or so after delivering his Divinity School bombshell in July, Emerson noted in his journal: "The young people & the mature hint at odium, & aversion of faces to be presently encountered in society. I say no: I fear it not" (*JMN* 7:60–61). Convers Francis, a minister and moderate Transcendentalist who had attended and admired the address, worried that his inspired friend did not "make the peculiar significance of Jesus so prominent as he ought,"

16. For the Carlyle reference to old and new "Mythuses," see *Sartor Resartus,* 144, and, for his comment on Goethe, his introduction to *Wilhelm Meister's Apprenticeship and Travels,* 1:128. For the cogent attack by the triumvirate of Alexander, Dod, and Hodge, see their "Transcendentalism of the Germans and of Cousin and Its Influence on Opinion in This Country," in *The Transcendentalists: An Anthology,* edited by Miller, 231–40; quotes on 238–39. The essence of the Divinity School Address controversy is distilled in Norton's pamphlet *A Discourse on the Latest Form of Infidelity* (Boston, 1839); Ripley's *"The Highest Form of Infidelity" Examined* (Boston, 1840, and two later letters); and, capping the debate, Norton's reprinting of the *Biblical Repertory* attack in *Transcendentalism of the Germans and of Cousin and Its Influence on the Opinion in This Country* (Cambridge, 1840). George Allen, Marsh's assistant in publishing *Aids to Reflection* and an admirer of *Nature,* was "inclined to side" with Emerson after the Divinity School Address partly "because these ignorant orthodoxists behave so ruffianly towards him, and partly because his Unitarian friends back him so like Sir John's followers [that is, Falstaff's in *1 Henry IV*]. It is delightful to hear *them* crying out infidel and Atheist—the fools! Of the Norton and Ripley controversy, I saw only the first number of each side. I liked Ripley very well, and hated the other man most cordially. I did not see why Ripley was not perfectly in the right in the greater part of his piece" (Duffy, *Coleridge's American Disciples,* 251).

though he was inclined to believe not that Emerson "thought less of Jesus than others do, but more of man, every man as a divine being." A Platonic "winged soul," Emerson was no logician, but "a seer, who looks into the infinite, & reports what he sees." Though aware that "the fluid of malignity had been collecting a good while," and that the "*dii majores* of the pulpit and Divinity School" resented Emerson's popularity, "especially among the brightest young people," Francis was still taken aback by the intensity of the reaction to the address. Taking tea in early September with a family of conservative Bostonians, he discovered that they "abhor & abominate R. W. Emerson as a sort of mad dog," and when he defended "that pure and angelic spirit," they "laughed at me in amazement,—for no such sounds had penetrated their *clique* before." Yet Emerson himself, to Francis's amazement, remained "perfectly quiet amidst the storm."[17]

A letter to Carlyle written three months after the event reveals that the controversy had been reignited by the publication of the address. Sending his friend copies of the offending lecture, Emerson at once belittled the affair, indicated its rancor, *and* insisted on his originality. Publication, he told Carlyle,

> has been the occasion of an outcry in all our leading newspapers against my "infidelity," "pantheism," & "atheism." The writers warn all & sundry against me, & whatever is supposed to be related to my connexion of opinion, &c; against Transcendentalism, Goethe & *Carlyle*. I am heartily sorry to see this last aspect of the storm in our washbowl. For, as Carlyle is nowise guilty; & has unpopularities of his own, I do not wish to embroil him in my parish-differences. You were getting to be a great favorite with us all here, and are daily a greater, with the American public, but just now, in Boston, where I am known as your editor [Emerson had arranged the first publication of *Sartor Resartus*], I fear you lose by the association. . . . Let us wait a little until this foolish clam[or] be overblown. My position is fortunately such as to put me quite out of the reach of any real inconvenience from the panic strikers or the panic struck; & indeed, so far as this uneasiness is a necessary result of mere inaction of mind, it seems very clear to me that, if I live, my neighbors must look for a great many more shocks, & perhaps harder to bear. (*EPP* 548)

The "inaction of mind" is that of the panic mongers and the panicked. But Emerson also felt some guilt about his own intellectual inactivity. Not that he was feeling guilty about what he had said at Harvard, only that he had not said it sooner. Four months prior to the address, in the privacy of his journals, he had recorded his shame at not having already, and vigorously, castigated "the great errors of modern Society in respect

17. Francis, letters to Henry Hedge, August 10, November 12, 1838, in Bosco and Myerson, *His Own Time*, 3–7.

of religion." He wishes, he says, that in the past he had made it uncompromisingly clear that

> you can never come to any peace or power until you put your *whole reliance* in the moral constitution of man *&* *not at all* in a historical Christianity. The belief in Christianity that now prevails is the Unbelief of men. They will have Christ for a lord & not for a brother. Christ preaches the greatness of Man but we hear only the greatness of Christ. . . . I ought to sit & think & write a discourse to the American clergy showing them the ugliness & unprofitableness of theology & churches at this day & the glory & sweetness of the Moral Nature out of whose pale they are almost wholly shut. (*JMN* 4:26–27)

Though much of what he said in the "discourse" he actually delivered to the Divinity School was familiar Unitarian immanence, with which Channing in particular would have been sympathetic, Emerson's rhetoric was altogether more daring, a linguistic "excess" that helps to explain the vehemence of the reaction. That reaction is also attributable to the inability of Emerson, indifferent to dogma and hostile to authority, to empathize with those too attached to outward revelation to succumb to his siren song of inward intuition. Still, being, as he said to Carlyle, "out of the reach of any real inconvenience," Emerson was spared the fate of a man with whom he was associated by contemporaries; the month before Emerson delivered his address, Abner Kneeland had been jailed for blasphemy.[18] Emerson was spared that fate, but he did suffer restriction. As a result of the Divinity School Address, he was shut out of this Unitarian pale and seat of ancient learning; three decades would pass before the infidel would again be invited to speak at Harvard. One can only be surprised at the lecturer's surprise at the reaction, especially from Norton, whose major opus—the just published three-volume *Evidence of the Genuineness of the Gospels*—may have been one unnamed target of Emersonian attack. No wonder Norton counterattacked, launching his own campaign against the Transcendentalists and what he called in the title of his attack in the *Christian Examiner* their "New School in Literature and Religion."

The impact of it all on Emerson was significant. His ideas had not changed. But although in the letter to Carlyle he anticipated afflicting his neighbors with "a great many more shocks, & perhaps harder to bear," he was now impressed with how society "whips" an individual for "nonconformity" (*E&L* 264). The difference between the "strongly pro-community language of earlier lectures and the strident defense of individualism in

18. In "Emerson, Kneeland, and the Divinity School Address," Robert E. Burkholder discusses the atheistic ideas of the jailed Kneeland as background for the reception of Emerson's address.

'Self-Reliance,' is," Robert D. Richardson Jr. thinks, "the result of Emerson's first prolonged exposure to public censure."[19] The idea of self-reliance had enough elasticity to expand beyond the egotistical sublime, just as Emerson's concept of "genius" participates in an ideal at once *within* and *beyond* the self. Still, Richardson's conclusion accurately registers the external pressures reinforcing Emerson's own innate preference for thinking independently and quietly, out of the swing of the sea of public controversy.

Since Wordsworth is cited in the address as preferring "paganism" to a disenchanted world, and Coleridge is enlisted as a model for Emerson's clergy-defying Uriel, I add a final observation on their oblique relation to the Divinity School Address, one that may help put the brouhaha in historical perspective. From our comfortable distance, we are likely to be too hard on the shocked clergymen or too dismissive about the public censure. Though Uriel-Emerson partially identifies himself with Coleridge, the reaction of the man he met at Highgate would not have been markedly different—just more eloquent—had he been alive and in the room where the "cloven hoof" of pantheism had been planted by the young Transcendentalist he had met five years earlier. If Dr. Channing's turning out "a Unitarian after all" had been, for Coleridge, "an unspeakable misfortune" (*E&L* 771), what would he have had to say about Emerson's religious radicalism in the Divinity School Address! Though religion had not come up in Emerson's interview in 1833 with Wordsworth, the author of "Tintern Abbey" had long since been hypersensitive to accusations about his own early "pantheism." I have already quoted his arch remark after reading Emerson's *Essays*—"Where is the thing that now passes for philosophy in Boston to stop?"—and noted that, as early as 1817, he had, no less archly, dampened the enthusiasm of his admirer Keats by greeting the young man's recitation of his "Hymn to Pan" as "a very pretty piece of paganism." Wordsworth was reacting to the poem—even though it was indebted to the Wanderer's critical yet rhapsodic evocation of Greek mythology in book 4 of his own *Excursion*—not as that at least empathetic Wanderer, nor as a great poet or even sensitive critic, but as a man who was, far from being a pantheist or the "*Semi*-atheist" Coleridge thought him in the 1790s, a conservative Christian no longer given, and well before 1838, to speculations about the preferability of being a pagan suckled in a creed outworn.

❧ The Divinity School Address celebrates Jesus not as divine, nor even as Lord, but as the religious thinker who first realized that God incarnates himself in man. In contemplating Self as/or God, we encounter the most

19. Richardson, *Mind on Fire,* 300.

all-encompassing and vertiginous of Emersonian "circles." Emerson begins the splendid essay of that title by announcing that "the eye is the first circle; the horizon, which forms it is the second," and "around every circle another can be drawn" ad infinitum (*E&L* 403). Toward the end of the essay, we may think for a moment that the priority and forming power of the centering human eye have been forgotten, even displaced, when we are told of the "eternal generator of circles" who "abides." But, in context, the still center of the moving world, the peace at the heart of endless agitation, remains, apparently, the *human* soul, for "this incessant movement and progression which all things partake could never become sensible to us but by contrast to some principle of fixture or stability in the soul. Whilst the eternal generation of circles proceeds, the eternal generator abides" (*E&L* 412).

That abiding, eternal generator certainly *sounds like* God. Yet most of Emerson's readers, friendly as well as hostile, have taken Transcendentalist immanence as emphasizing the Self rather than God, Within rather than Above. The following remarks by Richard Henry Dana, an early champion in the United States of British Romantic poetry, provide insight into the reaction to Emerson on this issue even before the Divinity School Address. The penultimate lecture in Emerson's Human Culture series in the winter of 1837–1838, "Holiness," was characterized by Dana, at second- and thirdhand, as typical of the Transcendentalists' "spirit of unbelief." Writing on February 24, 1838, to his friend James Marsh, Dana passes on the reports of his daughter and son, at the time an upperclassman at Marsh's university:

> The *highest* Instinct, that which leads us to a conscious, supreme *Being* was put down as the product of ignorance and weakness of man requiring an Object out of the self. . . . [A]bstract qualities were the all in all. How these exist primarily, and independently of some Being, absolutely, and not as attributes, he has never, that I can learn, attempted to explain, nor has he even alluded to this difficulty. . . . A Unitarian lady told my daughter that in walking home with Mr. Emerson after the lecture, she said to him, I must have an object out of and above myself, which to look at, and on which I may depend. He replied, that if we would but look into ourselves, we should find *there* all we needed. His lecture on Holiness is held by many as equivalent to Atheism.[20]

20. Duffy, *Coleridge's American Disciples*, 214. Dana added that a friend of his reported that Orestes Brownson had declared the "great purpose of man was to aid and elevate his fellow-man and that he who did this was *a christian, though the denial of God were on his lips.* We have all forms of unbelief; and though I wish not to judge, I must say that others, lay and clergy, are covering over an infidelity not essentially short of this, with what they term *spiritual philosophy.* Here is, indeed, a sad state of things amongst us" (215; italics in original).

Emerson would take issue with that characterization, but he could hardly deny the focus on man finding what was needed within himself rather than "out of and above" the self. That is certainly the emphasis in a splendid passage of "The Method of Nature" (1841) that deeply impressed William James. Sounding like the famous Sophoclean chorus on the wonder of man, Emerson asserts that we

> must admire in man, the form of the formless, the concentration of the vast, the house of reason, the cave of memory. . . . The great Pan of old, who was clothed in a leopard skin to signify the beautiful variety of things, and the firmament,—was but the representative of thee, O rich and various Man! thou palace of sight and sound, carrying in thy senses the morning and the night and the unfathomable galaxy; in thy brain, the geometry of the City of God; in thy heart the bower of love and the realms of right and wrong. (*E&L* 122)

In his 1903 "Centennial Address," James saw this conviction epitomized in those lines quoted earlier from Emerson's 1864 poem "Voluntaries": "So nigh is grandeur to our dust, / So near is God to man." For Emerson, notes James, "through the individual fact there ever shone . . . the effulgence of the Universal Reason. The great Cosmic Intellect terminates and houses itself in mortal men and passing hours. Each of us is an angle of its eternal vision. . . . The point of any pen can be an epitome of reality; the commonest person's act, if genuinely activated, can lay hold on eternity. This vision is the head-spring of all his outpourings." Emerson's life, says James, was "one long conversation with the invisible divine, expressing itself through individuals and particulars:—'So nigh is grandeur to our dust, so near is God to man!' "[21] The image of Spirit or Intellect "housing" itself in mortal men, an image that looks back to Coleridge's *Aids to Reflection* and to the final chapter of Emerson's *Nature,* epitomizes the paradoxes of the divinity within: "Man's Reason as the faculty in which the very Godhead manifested itself," Man as the "Temple of Deity," as Emerson synopsized Coleridge's vision in his 1836 tribute.

The ineffable can be sublime or, if not ridiculous, the subject of amused rather than sardonic ridicule. Writing at his epigrammatic best, the author of *A Fable for Critics* spoke for many—so aptly that he might be writing today instead of a century and a half ago:

> All admire, and yet scarcely six converts he's got
> To I don't (nor they either) exactly know what;
> For though he builds glorious temples, 'tis odd
> He leaves never a doorway to let in a god.

21. James, *William James: Writings, 1902–1910,* 1121, 1125.

'Tis refreshing to old-fashioned people like me
To meet such a primitive Pagan as he,
In whose mind all creation is duly respected
As parts of himself—just a little projected;
And who's willing to worship the stars and the sun,
A convert to—nothing but Emerson.[22]

Both in its irregular tetrameters and in its subject matter, Lowell's parody is reminiscent of Coleridge's "burlesque on the Fichtean Egoismus," which also (though Coleridge was as aware of the complexities in Fichte's position as Lowell was of those in Emerson's) conveyed "as tolerable a likeness" of its subject's "idealism as can be expected from an avowed caricature." Coleridge's satiric poem, opening with a burst of Latin translatable as "Huzzah! God's vice-regent, myself God," continues:

The form and the substance, the earth and the sky,
The when and the where, the low and the high,
The inside and outside, the earth and the sky,
I, you, and he, and he, you, and I,
All souls and all bodies are I itself I!

By the end of Coleridge's parody, everything, the Supreme Being included, has become part of "the world's whole Lexicon," with the *I* or *Ich* as the "root." In all "cases," grammatical and philosophic, the Fichtean *Ich* is the "case absolute," self-begot, yet with "Unconstrued antecedence" somehow assigned to "the God infinitivus!" (*BL* 1:160). What Coleridge says of the Fichtean Egoismus, Lowell says, more genially and in more readable verse, of the whole of creation as a projection of "nothing but

22. Emerson leads the procession, the first of the incisive contemporary portraits, which are, by far, the best part of this long poem: "There comes Emerson first, whose rich words, every one, / Are like gold nails in temples to hang trophies on, / Whose prose is grand verse, while his verse, the Lord knows, / Is some of it pr—No, 'tis not even prose." Lowell has brilliantly pithy comparisons (in the best, Emerson is "A Plotinus-Montaigne, where the Egyptian's gold mist / And the Gascon's shrewd wit cheek-by-jowl coexist") and shrewd distinctions: though "There are persons, mole-blind to the soul's make and style, / Who insist on a likeness 'twixt him and Carlyle," C., "shaggy of mind as of limb," and "rapid and slim" E. are very different: "C. labors to get to the centre, and then / Take a reckoning from there of his actions and men; / E. calmly assumes the said centre as granted, / And, given himself, has whatever is wanted" (27–28, 49–59, in F. O. Matthiessen, ed., *The Oxford Book of American Verse,* 250–52). Yet while he can poke infectious fun at the Emerson who has no need of an external God and for whom all creation is a self-projection, Lowell can himself write, in the Wordsworthian or Coleridgean lingo of his poem "The Cathedral," of a quasi-divine intuitive Reason (rapturous "virginal cognitions" that outpace "slower-footed thought" and have "something in them secretly divine") reminiscent of stanza 9 of the Intimations Ode.

Emerson!" It is an old joke, unfair but telling, that the favorite prayer of Unitarians begins, "Paradoxical though it may seem, O Lord..." Reminding us of that alleged prayer, Peter Ackroyd notes that from the perspective of orthodoxy, Unitarianism is in fact "an heretical faith principally because it does not accept the Christian doctrine of the Incarnation—Christ becoming a sort of superior Emerson."[23] The Unitarian-Transcendentalist fusion-distinction of Self and God is nothing if not paradoxical and inexplicable outside the Protestant inner-light tradition, German hermeneutics, or the Within and Without and Above of the Romantic dialectic. And even *within* those traditions and that dialectic, it can all begin to resemble Bottom's dream in *A Midsummer Night's Dream,* since it "hath no bottom." As bottomless Emerson himself says, paradoxically echoing Milton's Satan, "under every deep a lower deep opens" (*E&L* 403). Such depths can only be plumbed, as ebullient and bully Bottom intuitively grasps, by being transmuted into a work of art: "I will get Peter Quince to write a ballad of this dream" (4.1.212–15).

For his part, Emerson would choose as his peculiar genre unstable and destabilizing essays, prose poems of sibylline if sometimes impenetrable depth, impenetrable, at least, on the logical or discursive level, as must be the case on those occasions—and they are not the *only* Emersonian occasions—when we are dealing with the "intuitive" and the sublime. In one sense, the whole paradoxical, even pleonastic, dialectic is epitomized in the final line of "Threnody." "Lost in God, in Godhead found!" rhetorically restores the boy repeatedly lamented as "lost" in the first part of the elegy, but, *philosophically* or "Transcendentally," Emerson could finish the poem, after long delay, only by imagining his son's finite individuality somehow caught up in and merged with an infinite Godhead presiding over an ordered cosmos—the Above, indistinguishable from the Within, somehow subsuming the Within. The dialectical ballet of Self-Reliance and God-Reliance has no ending.

The fusion of, yet distinction between, the Above and the Within, of God and the Self, seems to have been as vertiginous for Emerson as for his readers. The following meditation, recorded on May 26, 1837, begins and ends with questions: "Who shall define to me an Individual? . . . Cannot I conceive the Universe without a contradiction?" Between these genuine questions, Emerson resembles the Coleridge of the Dejection Ode, "whose fountains are within," and the Shelley of the final stanza of the "Ode to the West Wind," vacillating between instrumental dependence ("Make me thy lyre, even as the forest is") and audacious assertion ("Be thou, Spirit fierce, / My spirit! Be thou me, impetuous one"). And, of

23. Ackroyd, *T. S. Eliot: A Life,* 17.

course, along with the Wordsworthian light and "certain moments" when the self becomes indistinguishable from God, there is the ever present polarity, or "contradiction":

> Who shall define to me an Individual? I behold with awe & delight many illustrations of the One Universal Mind. I see my being imbedded in it. As a plant in the earth I grow in God. I am only a form of him. He is the soul of Me. I can even with a mountainous aspiring say, *I am God,* by transferring my *Me* out of the flimsy & unclean precincts of my body, my fortunes, my private will, & meekly retiring upon the holy austerities of the Just & the Loving—upon the secret fountains of Nature.... Yet why not always so? How came the Individual thus armed & impassioned to parricide, thus murderously inclined ever to traverse & kill the divine life? Ah wicked Manichee! Into that dim problem [the perpetual conflict in the world between the forces of darkness and light] I cannot enter. A believer in Unity, a seer of Unity, I yet behold two.... Where is my Godhead now?... Hard as it is to describe God, it is harder to describe the Individual.
>
> A certain wandering light comes to me which I instantly perceive to be the Cause of Causes. It transcends all proving. It is itself the ground of being; and I see that it is not one & I another, but this is the life of my life. That is one fact, then; that in certain moments I have known that I existed directly from God, and am, as it were, his organ. And in my ultimate consciousness Am He. Then, secondly, the contradictory fact is familiar, that I am a surprised spectator & learner of all my life. This is the habitual posture of the mind—beholding. But whenever the day dawns, the great day of truth on the soul, it comes with awful invitation to me to accept it, to blend with its aurora.... Cannot I conceive the Universe without a contradiction? (*EPP* 497)

The "wandering light" that seems to Emerson "the ground of being" and the "life of my life" reveals to him at enraptured and auroral moments that he comes from God, indeed "in my ultimate consciousness Am He." This is the light of which, Coleridge says, even the light of Reason is but a reflection (*AR* 15–16), an illumination at those privileged moments when, he says of his friend in "To William Wordsworth," "power streamed from thee, and thy soul received / The light reflected as a light bestowed." Contrasting understanding with intuitive Reason, an echoing Emerson refers to "Reason's momentary grasp of the sceptre; the exertion of a power which exists not in time or space, but an instantaneous in-streaming causing power" (*E&L* 46–47). This noumenal power (beyond Kantian categories of Time and Space), and its recurrent imagery of light, remains at the crux of the dialectic common to Romanticism and Transcendentalism: the problematic relationship between spirit, nature, mind, and, ultimately between God and the Self. It is a relationship further problematized by often shifting definitions. When, say, we try to make logical sense of the dialectical flow of "Idealism" and "Spirit," those two protean chapters leading up to the sibylline and oracular finale of *Nature,* we can sometimes feel, Coleridgean dialectic notwithstanding, that Emerson—"Cannot I conceive the Universe without a contradiction?"—would have embraced in advance the echoing nonchalance of his two greatest disciples. To Whitman's *sprezzatura* in "Song of Myself"—

> Do I contradict myself?
> Very well then I contradict myself.
> (I am large, I contain multitudes).

—Nietzsche would answer, "It is precisely such 'contradictions' that seduce one to existence."[24]

These protean shifts, "contradictions" to the mere understanding, are part of that "conflict between the forces of darkness and light" Emerson refers to in the journal entry I am glossing. Beyond that duality, there are those auroral visitations issuing in epiphanies of ultimate consciousness when Emerson is not only an "organ" of God but "Am He." Is the source of those luminous moments God or the God within (the human mind in possession of intuitive Reason)? That angelic or divine attribute of man is in opposition to the mere understanding, to say nothing of the belly and members (the body as part of the material NOT ME). At those moments of "mountainous aspiring" when he can "say, *I am God,*" Emerson does so "by transferring my *Me* out of the flimsy & unclean precincts of my body, my fortunes, my private will" (*EPP* 497). The similarity *and* contrast with Whitman is striking. In "Song of Myself," that nondualist egalitarian and reverencer of the body will declare, "Clear and sweet is my soul . . . and clear and sweet is all that is *not* my soul"; cap a hundred-line catalog bristling with instances of human and natural life with, "And these one and all tend inward to me, *and I tend outward to them* / And such as it is to be of *these* more or less *I am*"; and then, celebrating "copulation," the

24. Whitman, "Song of Myself," sec. 51, in *Leaves of Grass,* 88; Nietzsche, *On the Genealogy of Morals,* 3:2, in *Basic Writings,* 535. For just one example of "contradiction" in Emerson, take the peroration of "History." He advances the glorious claim that all of history "shall walk incarnate in every just and wise man," who will epitomize in himself all the ages and become at last "the priest of Pan, and bring with him into humble cottages the blessing of the morning stars and all the recorded benefits of heaven and earth"—only to immediately ask, is there something "overweening in this claim? Then I reject all I have written, for what is the use of pretending to know what we know not. It is the fault of our rhetoric that we cannot strongly state one fact without seeming to belie another" (*E&L* 55–56).

"flesh and the appetites," the "miracle" of the senses and "each part and tag of me," confirm the earlier allusion to divinity ("I am") by announcing:

> *Divine am I* inside *and out,* and *I make the body whatever I*
> *touch or am touched from;*
> The scent of *these arm-pits* is aroma *finer than prayer,*
> *This head* is *more than churches or bibles or creeds.*
> (secs. 3, 15, 24; italics added)[25]

Though Emerson, at times almost detached from his own body, would never dream of elevating those "unclean precincts" of the NOT ME (copulation, let alone the smell of armpits), he would, of course, applaud that final line, as well as Whitman's extension and enlargement of his private self—the "Me Myself" of "Song of Myself," which he identifies with both the "soul" and with God, ecstatic "To be this incredible God I am" ("Song at Sunset," line 29). In a notebook on the Mind, dated 1835 but including material gathered in the period leading up to and following his 1833 visit to England, Emerson had contrasted the private to that enlarged Self, identified with intuitive Reason and divinity, if not quite projected out to encompass the full expanse, political or bodily, of Whitman's democratic vistas:

> Our compound nature differences us from God, but our Reason is not to be distinguished from the divine Essence. We have yet devised no words to designate the attributes of God which can adequately stand for the Universality & perfection of our own intuitions. To call the Reason "ours" or "human," seems an impertinence, so absolute & unconfined it is. The best we can say of God, we mean of the mind as it is known to us. (*JMN* 5:270–71)

Yet there never seems to be complete severance between the two forms of I AM, Divinity and the divinity of the Self. To the extent that the ineffable *can* be clarified, Emerson's thought seems best expressed in the peroration of "The Over-Soul." But even there, with ultimate polarity conveyed in a dialectic between capitals and lowercase, Emerson seems to go beyond Plotinus by playing a variation on his favorite line, the last and most famous, from the *Enneads,* "the flight of the alone to the Alone":

> Ineffable is the union of man and God in every act of the soul. The simplest person, who in his integrity worships God, becomes God.... When we have broken our god of tradition, and ceased from our god of rhetoric, then may God fire the heart with his presence.... Let man, then, learn the revelation of all nature and all thought to his heart; this, namely; that the Highest

25. Whitman, *Leaves of Grass,* 31, 44, 53, and 495 for "Song at Sunset," quoted in the paragraph that follows.

> dwells with him; that the sources of nature are in his own mind. . . . Great is the soul, and plain. It is no flatterer, it is no follower; it never appeals from itself. It believes in itself. . . . The soul gives itself, alone, original, and pure, to the Lonely, Original, and Pure, who, on that condition, gladly inhabits, leads, and speaks through it. Then it is glad, young, and nimble. It is not wise, but it sees through all things. It is not called religious, but it is innocent. It calls the light its own, and feels that the grass grows and the stone falls by a law inferior to, and dependent on, its nature. Behold, it saith, I am born into the great, the universal mind. I, the imperfect, adore my own Perfect. (*E&L* 398–400)

The final step may be taken by Wallace Stevens, a late Romantic who is less a Transcendentalist than a religion-haunted skeptic. "What am I to believe?" asks the Canon Aspirin in the pivotal canto of what is arguably Stevens's central poem, *Notes toward a Supreme Fiction.* Wondering, as he contemplates an "angel" taking flight with spread wings through evening's revelations, if it is "he or I that experience this," the Canon wonders, too, if there is not "an hour / Filled with expressible bliss," in which he is

> satisfied without solacing majesty,
> And if there is an hour there is a day,
> There is a month, there is a time
> In which majesty is a mirror of the self:
> I have not but I am and as I am, I am.[26]

As a poet powerfully influenced not only by Emerson but by his disciples Whitman and Nietzsche as well, Stevens goes beyond Emerson, whose new teacher, in the Divinity School Address, "shall see the world to be the mirror of the soul" (*E&L* 92). For Stevens's Canon, satisfied without the solacing majesty of God, that majesty "is a mirror of the self." Wordsworth, too, is exceeded, even in the *Prelude* passage rightly cited by Bloom as the precursor text to Stevens's sublime evocation, in cantos 7 and 8 of *Notes,* of angelic flight and the achievement of an "expressible bliss." The intuition, provoked by the grandeur of the vision atop Mount Snowdon, of an exalting "under-presence," that "sense of God, or whatsoe'er is dim / Or vast in [the self's] own being" (*P* [1805], 14:71–73), leads to a sense of participation (in the 1850 version) in a visionary company of "higher minds" resembling "angels stopped upon the wing by sound / Of harmony from Heaven's remotest spheres." Such minds "are truly from the Deity," because "they are Powers; and hence the highest bliss / That flesh can know is theirs." That this "consciousness / Of Whom they are," infused through

26. Stevens, *Notes toward a Supreme Fiction,* "It Must Give Pleasure," canto 8 (*Collected Poems,* 405).

"every thought" and through "all affections, by communion raised / From earth to heaven, from human to divine," is yet another reworking of the angel Raphael's speech in book 5 of *Paradise Lost* is confirmed by Wordsworth's concluding reference to Raphael's distinction between the powers of Reason, "Whether discursive or intuitive" (*P* 14:98–99, 112–20).[27]

Neither Milton nor Wordsworth (despite his capitalization of "Whom") *equates* human and divine; Stevens's speaker *does*, audaciously uttering, as Jesus dared to, the Jehovan "I am." God had revealed that divine name to Moses: "Tell them that *I am [ehyeh asher ehyeh]* has sent you" (Exod. 3:14). In John, the one gospel clearly asserting Christ's divinity, Jesus is depicted as greater than Moses and preexisting Abraham, in short God himself in human form. When he announces, "Before Abraham was, *I am*," his listeners take up stones, intending to kill him (John 8:58–59). Stevens manages a triple replication of the forbidden name: "I have not but *I am and as I am, I am.*" Identifying the "single predicament" behind "Stevens's entire body of work," Denis Donoghue asks, echoing the Canon Aspirin, "What is a person of religious sensibility to do in the absence of a doctrine in which he may believe? What is he to believe?" Stevens's poems imply "an answer that is straightforward if seen in one light, desperate if seen in another." Quoting J. S. Cunningham ("In the absence of belief in God, the mind turns to its own creations and examines them"), Donoghue adds: "Instead of meditating on the three cardinal terms God, Nature, and Man, as in the English tradition from Milton to Wordsworth, Stevens conceived God as Major Man, Nature as the world, and Man as the poetic imagination. The trouble with this device, if it feels like trouble, is that God becomes just another name for Wallace Stevens, for the poet's sense of himself at the furthest reach of his invention."[28]

This is not at all what Coleridge meant when he compared the finite human imagination to the infinite I AM (*BL* 1:304), still less what he meant when he said "We begin with the I KNOW MYSELF, in order to end with the absolute I AM. We proceed from the SELF in order to lose and find all

27. Bloom, who had been preceded by Frank Kermode in connecting these passages, notes that the Wordsworth passage "in its conclusion attains its meaning only by an intertextual juxtaposition" with Raphael's speech to Adam in book 5 of *Paradise Lost*, "which distinguishes human from angelic faculties." Since he forbears discussing the Milton passage (as he says, "intertextuality must be kept within some limits if a critical discourse is to sustain itself" [*Wallace Stevens: The Poems of Our Climate*, 213–14]), I add just *one* point. Raphael's speech not only "distinguishes" angelic from human faculties but also indicates one absolutely crucial overlap: humans *can*, at privileged moments, attain normally angelic, intuitive Reason. Not to be outdone, Stevens presents us (in canto 9 of "It Must Give Pleasure," the final part of *Notes toward a Supreme Fiction*) with an "I" that can do all "that angels can," and more (*Collected Poems*, 405).

28. Donoghue, *Reading America: Essays on American Literature*, 221.

self in GOD" (*BL* 1:283). When Stevens, whose formulation would scandalize Coleridge, equates not only the Canon Aspirin but also himself with Jehovah, his audacity, though it exceeds Wordsworth's, parallels that of Fichte and his "Divine-Me" as well as that of Whitman, who identifies "Me Myself" with "this incredible God I am!" And Stevens might have found a precursor in Emerson, who, transferring himself out of his merely private self, can—like Stevens's aspiring Canon—"even with a mountainous aspiring say, *I am God,*" and "in my ultimate consciousness Am He" (*EPP* 497), thus replicating the imaginative breakthrough of his Gnostic Jesus, that each individual, incarnating God, should seek and bring forth the divine light within.

Next, after revisiting Coleridge's distinction between objective "Nature" and the subjective "Self" or "Intelligence," we will move from the extreme subjectivism of Coleridge's Dejection Ode through Wordsworth's psycho-poetic revision of Milton in the "Prospectus" to *The Recluse,* to the similarly humanized revelation in Emerson's introduction to *Nature,* concluding with the assertion of Divinity Within in another poem of Stevens's, "Sunday Morning," the twentieth-century poem that, along with *Notes toward a Supreme Fiction,* most consciously completes these texts by Coleridge, Wordsworth, Emerson—even, in its way, Whitman's "Song of Myself."

Chapter 10

Emerson among the Orphic Poets

We receive but what we give,
And in our life alone does Nature live.

—SAMUEL TAYLOR COLERIDGE, "Dejection: An Ode"

❧

Paradise, and groves
Elysian, Fortunate Fields . . . why should they be
A history only of departed things,
Or a mere fiction of what never was?
For the discerning intellect of Man,
When wedded to this goodly universe
In love and holy passion, shall find these
A simple produce of the common day.

—WILLIAM WORDSWORTH, "Prospectus" to *The Recluse*

❧

Why should not we also enjoy an original relation to the universe? Why should not we have a poetry and philosophy of insight and not of tradition, and a religion by revelation to us, and not the history of theirs? . . . The kingdom of man over nature . . . —a dominion such as now is beyond his dream of God—, he shall enter with no more wonder than the blind man feels who is gradually restored to perfect sight.

—RALPH WALDO EMERSON, *Nature*

❧

Why should she give her bounty to the dead?
What is divinity if it can come

Only in silent shadows and in dreams?

. . . .

Divinity must live within herself.

—WALLACE STEVENS, "Sunday Morning"

For the Romantics, however variously they treat the interaction of nature, the human mind, and a mysterious "presence," it comes down essentially to the old mind-matter conundrum, with the addition that—for men like Coleridge, Wordsworth, and Emerson—there was sufficient theological influence to permit the quasi divinization of consciousness in the form of intuitive Reason, that highest faculty described by Milton's archangel. This power, which Emerson, like Coleridge and Wordsworth before him, exalts over discursive reason and mere understanding, retains vestiges of what we usually mean by rationalism, but it is, of course, much more than that. In "its highest moments such Reason becomes one with consciousness as a form of pure seeing."[1] At such high moments, as Wordsworth says in "Tintern Abbey," exercising this visionary power, we "see into the life of things." This ocular image recurs in the Intimations Ode's "master light of all our seeing" and in Coleridge's *Aids to Reflection,* where spiritual "light" is reflected as THOUGHT," the soul's "eye," this "*seeing* eye, this *enlightening* eye" (*AR* 15–16). It may be said to culminate in *Nature,* which begins with Emerson famously becoming "a transparent eye-ball" and "particle of God," at its center exalts "the eye of Reason," and ends with man's projected entrance into "The kingdom of man over nature," a dominion he "shall enter with no more wonder than the blind man feels who is gradually restored to perfect sight" (*E&L* 10, 33, 49).

Depending on context, this visionary power of mind or soul or imagination engages what is "separate from us, all which Philosophy distinguishes as the NOT ME" (*E&L* 8), in what Wordsworth calls a reciprocal "ennobling interchange / Of action from without and from within" (*P* 13: 375–76), or, at other times, and in accordance with German idealism (that "Philosophy" to which Emerson refers in the introduction to *Nature*), the natural world with which we interact is more expressly subservient to the human mind or imagination. Although there are sublime moments in *The Prelude,* "spots of time" in which there is no doubt about the usurping power of Imagination, of mind's mastery over external sense, Wordsworth is, finally, not Coleridge. In accordance with his idealist interpretation of the famous passage from book 5 of *Paradise Lost,* Coleridge always hoped that Wordsworth was going to accomplish the final overthrow of

1. Chai, *Romantic Foundations,* 286, 333.

Lockean sensationalism, by "demonstrating that the Senses were living growths and developments of the Mind & Spirit in a much juster as well as a higher sense, than the mind can be said to be formed by the Senses" (*CL* 4:574–75).

In this letter, he was referring to the long-envisioned master work *The Recluse,* never written, at least not in the unified form intended, always having been more a Coleridgean than a Wordsworthian project. Though Geoffrey Hartman and Harold Bloom, by emphasizing the dominant power of the Romantic Imagination, have provided brilliant and salutary correctives to traditional—and often, though not always, simplistic—readings of Wordsworth as a "nature poet," Wordsworth *did* believe, contra Coleridge, that "the mind *can* be said to be formed by the Senses." Following those polar impulses earlier discussed, between freedom and responsibility, luxuriating in the season rather than "injuring" it by engaging in the labor demanded by the epic task he had set himself, *The Prelude* really begins at line 301. Wordsworth's initial focus on the "fair seed-time" that his soul enjoyed in his "birth-place" and in the "beloved Vale" to which he was "transplanted" when he was nine—how, in short, "I grew up" (*P* 1: 301–5)—emphasizes his conviction that the formative experiences of his childhood established the theme of the poem as a whole: "the growth of the poet's mind." As we will see later in this chapter, an irascible Coleridge, then in his fifties and estranged from his old friend, confided in the privacy of a letter that this asserted "dependency of the human soul on accidents of birth-place and abode," associated with an unhealthy "nature-worship," was the "trait of Wordsworth's poetic works" he most disliked. But the main project of those poetic works, made clear in the "Prospectus" to *The Recluse*—the very place where Wordsworth most forcefully announces his exploration into the awesome "Mind of Man— / My haunt, and the main region of my song"—was nevertheless to demonstrate that mind's fruitful *marriage* with the objects of sense.

Since he was also wedded to the rhetoric of *power,* Wordsworth is driven to paradox if not oxymoron in several formulations—"mutual domination," "interchangeable supremacy"—in which he attempts to characterize the complex relationship between Nature and the Mind, and Imagination's creative-receptive apprehension of sense experience. The phrases just quoted occur in the aftermath of "that vision" (the "Moon hung naked" in the heavens, the ocean itself seeming to "dwindle, and give up his majesty, / Usurped upon far as the sight could reach," the roar of waters mounting through the rift in the clouds) Wordsworth experienced on Mount Snowdon, when he "beheld" (in the more Miltonic and more orthodox version of 1850) the "emblem of a mind / That feeds upon infinity," a mind "that broods / Over the dark abyss" (*P* 14:70–72), even as the Holy

Spirit had creatively brooded over Chaos at the outset of *Paradise Lost* (1: 20–22). Even at such a mountain moment, amid "circumstances awful and sublime," the *effect* of that Nature symbolic of Mind (and "One function, above all, of such a mind / Had Nature shadowed there") is to return us to the *senses* and *feelings* through which we had mounted to vision in the first place. Emblematic Nature had, by "putting forth"

> That mutual domination which she loves
> To exert upon the face of outward things,
> So moulded, joined, abstracted, so endowed
> With interchangeable supremacy,
> That men, least sensitive, see, hear, perceive,
> And cannot choose but feel.
>
> (*P* 14:79–86)

At the other "high" point of *The Prelude,* that alpine foreshadowing of the ascent of Snowdon, the Simplon Pass episode in book 6, Wordsworth's physical senses actually *fail* him, and the mysterious "Imagination" ("here the Power so called / Through sad incompetence of human speech") rises up from the abyss in the full sublimity of its usurping power (*P* 6:592–95). But even there we achieve transcendence, not by *escaping* the senses, but by mounting *through them* to the sublime. For the most part, though there is always dialectical fluctuation, that is the position taken by Wordsworth, more problematically by Coleridge, and, finally, by their Transcendentalist heir, Emerson. He ends *Nature* by asserting man's dominion *over* nature, yet all three of these writers obviously "love" nature, both because it is the beautiful world with "which our senses converse" (*E&L* 75) and because of the indwelling "presence" or "Spirit" their exercise of intuitive Reason permits them to "see" in it, even when it is a projection.

Before engaging the poetic texts to be discussed in this chapter (Coleridge's "Dejection: An Ode," book 4 of Wordsworth's *Excursion* as well as his "Prospectus" to *The Recluse,* and Wallace Stevens's "Sunday Morning"), we have to look again into this first book of Emerson, a virtual compendium of variations on this dialectic, this vertiginous relationship between man, housing a divinity within, and external nature, the Without, the NOT ME, which also, at times at least, harbors a spiritual presence and is emblematic of the human Mind. In this case, *Nature* may also be the conduit bearing British Romanticism to Stevens's Connecticut.

❧ The divided impulses of *Nature,* that rather misnamed masterpiece, are implicit from the outset, in Emerson's ambivalence about an appropriate epigraph to introduce the work. The original edition opened with a

Neoplatonic epigraph, replaced in all later editions, beginning in 1849, by Emerson's own lines about the upward mobility of aspiring nature. Milton's Raphael seems to join Darwin in a metamorphic and evolutionary poem that ends, "And striving to be man, the worm / Mounts through all the spires of form" (*E&L* 5). Though man is still at the top of the scale, the original, considerably more "Transcendentalist," epigraph was thematically very different. Drawn from Ralph Cudworth's compendium of Platonic and Neoplatonic thought, *The True Intellectual System of the Universe* (1678), that original Plotinian epigraph read: "Nature is but an image or imitation of wisdom, the last thing of the soul; nature being a thing which doth only do, but not know." Lacking *nisus,* any intrinsic capacity to teleologically aspire or strive, nature is dependent on man. Agreeing with the Neoplatonists, Coleridge, discussing human creativity, tells us in his 1808–1819 *Lectures* that, mastering nature's essence (Spinoza's *natura naturans*), "art . . . presupposes a bond between Nature in this highest sense and the soul of Man," but he goes on to insist that nature alone, lacking any human "reflex act," is without knowledge and "without Morality." As Yeats would later put it: "Nature in herself has no power except to die and to forget."[2]

Emerson agrees that, without the "soul of Man," without his intuitive Reason, Nature is barren. And mere understanding, though a human faculty, is not much better than a part of the NOT ME. In *Nature,* he repeatedly depicts understanding as a merely quantitative faculty, far inferior to the intuitive Reason, which imparts to us everything that is "not to be learned by any addition or subtraction, or other comparison of known quantities, but is arrived at by untaught sallies of the spirit, by a continual self-recovery." Understanding "adds, divides, combines, measures. . . . Meantime, Reason transfers all these lessons into its own world of thought, by *perceiving the analogy that marries Matter and Mind*" (*E&L* 43, 26; italics added). In the book's opening chapters, the "greatest delight which the fields and woods minister, is the suggestion of an occult relation between man and the vegetable. . . . Yet it is certain that the power to produce this delight *does not reside in nature, but in man, or in a harmony of both*" (*E&L* 11; italics added). "Nature always wears the color of the spirit," in fact, is in "ministry to man," its beauty visible "as it becomes an object of intellect" (*E&L* 11, 12, 18). An "analogist" who "studies relations in all objects" (this "radical correspondence between visible things and human thoughts"), Man Thinking is "placed in the centre of beings, and a ray of relation passes from every other being to him." Man cannot "be understood without these objects, nor these objects without man. All the facts

2. Coleridge, *Lectures 1808–1819: On Literature,* 2:220–21; Yeats, *Essays and Introductions,* 171.

in natural history taken by themselves, have no value, but are barren, like a single sex. But marry it to human history, and it is full of life" (*E&L* 21, 22).

Though he can sound like Blake ("Where man is not, nature is barren": *Marriage of Heaven and Hell*), Emerson, in insisting on the meaninglessness of "nature alone," can also fall back, not only on Coleridge, always more focused on the spiritual and human than on the natural, but on Wordsworth—sometimes by choosing an unlikely text. In "Compensation," for example, Emerson illustrates his optimistic contention that "disasters of all kinds, as sickness, offence, poverty, prove benefactors," by quoting Wordsworth's "September, 1802, Near Dover" (*WP* 1:579). In that sonnet, gazing out at the Channel, the "span of waters" separating England from the armies of Napoléon (that Wordsworthian bête noire whom, ironically, Emerson had just praised!), Wordsworth speculates on the "power" of the sea, its "mightiness for evil and for good." But the sestet introduces a turn in thought, the belief that "God protects us if we be / Virtuous and wise," since his divine decree "Spake laws to *them,* and said that *by the soul / Only,* the Nations shall be great and free." The antecedent of the pronoun emphasized by Wordsworth, "them," occurs in the lines (10–12) cited by Emerson:

> Winds blow, and waters roll,
> Strength to the brave, and Power, and Deity,
> *Yet in themselves are nothing!*
>
> (*E&L* 297)

Though Wordsworth's point in the sonnet is less epistemological than moral and political, the fact is that these blowing winds and rolling waters, for all their supposed "mightiness for evil and for good," are still, as Coleridge said, part of a nature "without Morality." Such natural elements can bring strength, power, and deity only to *human* agents—here, only to the "brave." Those courageous and virtuous enough to take advantage of the protecting Channel in order to resist Napoleonic power are able to interpret as "benefactors" winds and waters that, like the "meaningless plungings of water and the wind" in Stevens's "The Idea of Order at Key West" (a poem whose more direct Wordsworthian precursor is "The Solitary Reaper"), "*in themselves are nothing*" until symbolically invested with human significance.[3] In "History," Emerson makes the same point: the "preternatural prowess of the hero" and (in another recollection of Cole-

3. In both poems, the speaker and *we* overhear a solitary female singer. In Stevens's version of winds and water "in themselves . . . nothing," it was "she and not the sea we heard," and we know, as "we beheld her striding there alone," that "there never was a world for her / Except the one she sang and, singing, made" (*Collected Poems,* 129–30).

ridge on Wordsworth) "the gift of perpetual youth" alike empower "the human spirit 'to bend the shows of things to the desires of the mind'" (*E&L* 253).

Whether he is idealistically stressing mind's dominance over nature or a harmonious interchange, a fruitful union of polarities, Emerson found authorization in Coleridge and Wordsworth. Like them, and depending on immediate context, he will fluctuate in stressing a passive or active response to nature: receptivity or creativity, even a more violent imposition or usurpation. Emerson's nuptial vocabulary ("relation," "harmony," "ministry," "marry") is obviously that of Wordsworth (especially in the "Prospectus," and in the more temperate work it prefaced, *The Excursion*) and of the Coleridge who, for all his idealism, lamented our alienation from Nature. The very title of Emerson's first book, reinforced by his change of epigraph, suggests a higher valuation of nature than we find in Plotinus or in apocalyptic Blake. "Philosophically speaking," however, "the universe is composed of Nature and the Soul," and his book, weighted toward the natural world only "by turns" (*E&L* 45), makes a point as crucial for Emerson as it is for Coleridge and even the more sense-rooted Wordsworth: Nature's significance lies in its interaction with the human mind, especially under its noblest aspect, intuitive Reason or spirit.

But the same ambiguity that bedevils Emerson's concept of a self-reliance coterminous both with the divinity within and a Universal Self above applies as well to his many engagements with Romantic *naturphilosophie,* the epistemological and emotional relationship between the external world and mind (or "soul" or "spirit"). When we ask, as Emerson does in "Spirit," the penultimate chapter of *Nature,* "Whence is Matter? and Whereto? many truths rise to us out of the recesses of consciousness." The principal truth is that there is, as Coleridge said in the lecture just cited, "a bond between Nature in this highest sense and the soul of Man." Emerson tells us that

> the highest is present to the soul of man, that the dread universal essence, which is not wisdom, or love, or beauty, or power, but all in one, and each entirely, is that for which all things exist, and that by which they are; that spirit creates; that behind nature, throughout nature, spirit is present; one and not compound, it does not act upon us from without, that is, in space and time, but spiritually, or through ourselves; therefore, that spirit, that is, the Supreme Being, does not build up nature around us, but puts it forth through us, as the life of the tree puts forth new branches and leaves through the pores of the old. (*E&L* 41)

It becomes difficult if not impossible to discriminate among the intuitive Reason, the soul of man, spirit, the "dread universal essence," and the Supreme Being; and that Being's putting nature forth "through us" is further complicated by comparing that process to the organic life of the ever renewing tree. The force that drives the green fuse through the flower almost merges with the force that puts nature forth "through us." The "dread universal essence" is not any one thing, but "all in all, and each entirely." Once again echoing Coleridge's Each and All (*F* 1:511), Emerson also seems to be fusing the Coleridgean emphasis on the Supreme Being as an indwelling spirit with the Wordsworthian doctrine that spirit is present not only "behind" but also "throughout nature" and that we mount to transcendence *through* Nature and the senses.

Though Emerson's paragraph may be somewhat confusing, his legerdemain dissolves the separation and alienation from which the Romantics sought to redeem us. Having just read *The Excursion* and the appended "Prospectus" to *The Recluse,* a disappointed Coleridge told Wordsworth that he had been hoping for what the "Prospectus" promised and what he thought they had agreed upon: a mental "revolution," a scheme of "Redemption" from enslavement to mechanistic thinking, and "Reconciliation" from an "Enmity with Nature," an alienation which had substituted Death for "Life, and Intelligence" (*CL* 4:574–75). To reunite what the analytic intellect—understanding or the merely discursive reason—had put asunder, we need, as synthesizing agent, the intuitive Reason. "The groundwork, therefore, of all true philosophy"—Coleridge says in the last of his tracts in "Essays on the Principles of Method" in *The Friend*—"is the full apprehension of the differences between the contemplation of Reason, namely that intuition of things which arises when we possess ourselves, as one with the whole, which is substantial knowledge," and that negative and "ever-varying" half-knowledge that presents itself when "we think of ourselves as separated beings, and place nature in antithesis to the mind, as object to subject, thing to thought, death to life" (*F* 1:520).

In the climactic chapter of *Nature,* which takes up precisely this alienation and the need to heal the rupture, Emerson's Orphic Poet insists that "the foundations of man are not in matter, but in spirit," whose element is "eternity," but since, as Blake would say, "Eternity is in love with the productions of time," the superiority of spirit to matter is at times idealist, at other times reconciliationist. Thus, Emerson, like Coleridge in the letter to Wordsworth, laments our alienation from nature: "We distrust and deny inwardly our sympathy with nature. We own and disown our relation to it, by turns" (*E&L* 45). But by this point in the book, the master in the relation is obviously mind or spirit, a point already made clear in the chapter appropriately titled "Idealism." There Emerson says that the poet, like the philosopher, "animates nature with his own thoughts," the only difference being that "the one proposes Beauty as his main end; the other Truth." Then, echoing Keats's equation, he reconciles the difference: "The true philosopher and the true poet are one, and a beauty, which is truth, and a truth, which is beauty, is the aim of both." Reading Plato or Sophocles, the "charm" in both cases—in a phrase that struck Yeats—is "that a spiritual life has been imparted to nature; that the solid seeming block of matter has been pervaded and dissolved by a thought" (*E&L* 36).[4]

He has approached the *contemptus mundi* tradition of Plotinus, or of Yeats's

> God-appointed Berkeley that proved all things a dream,
> That this pragmatical, preposterous pig of a world, its farrow
> that so solid seem
> Must vanish on the instant if mind but change its theme.

But then Emerson, in a turn as characteristically Romantic as the privileging of Mind or Imagination, suddenly acknowledges that "there is something ungrateful" in casting idealist doubt on the reality of the external world. "I have no hostility to nature, but a child's love to it. I expand and live in the warm day like corn and melons. Let us speak her fair. I do not wish to fling stones at my beautiful mother, nor soil my gentle nest. I only wish to indicate the true position of nature in regard to man" (*E&L* 38). As Emerson knew, Wordsworth had assigned just such a lovely but limited role to "Foster-mother" Earth in the sixth stanza of the Intimations Ode, an image Emerson echoed in order to alter, intensifying the idealist perspective. Whereas, in the ode, "Earth fills her lap with pleasures of her own," Emerson insists that "Earth fills her lap with *splendours not her own.*" Trumping Wordsworth *with* Wordsworth, Emerson borrows the word *splendours* from elsewhere in the ode ("vision *splendid*" and "*splendour* in the grass"), and, perhaps, the second part of his phrase from Wordsworth's description of "objects" transformed either by "light divine" or by the "visionary power" of poetry; thus transfigured, they are "recognized / In flashes, and with *glory not their own*" (*P* 5:601–5). Emerson being—not always, but certainly here—an idealist, the "true position" he assigns nature is secondary to the transfiguring mind of man, what he calls in the passage of "Spiritual Laws" just cited, the "gilding, exalting soul" that confers upon "empty" nature whatever it possesses of "beauty and worth" (*E&L* 313).

4. Compare the following: "Nothing in the universe so solid as a thought" (*JMN* 15:429). The precise analogue in Yeats occurs in the lines from "Blood and the Moon" (quoted below, *W. B. Yeats: The Poems,* 238) on one of his favorite idealist philosophers, Berkeley.

Still, Plotinus must have seemed, on second thought, *too* consistently transcendent to supply the epigraph to *Nature*. The philosopher who his disciple Porphyry tells us was "ashamed of being in the body" was too purely spiritual to serve the turn, on this occasion, of Emerson—an idealist nevertheless wedded, as Wordsworth was, to the concrete world through temperament and a commitment to living metaphors stressing the correspondence of man and nature. But although the original Plotinian epigraph had to go, Emerson insists that this all-important relationship between mind and matter, man and the nature to which he is superior yet wedded, is at once guaranteed and—as Plotinus said—only *potential.* Even we who, unlike nature, *can* "know" are only potential knowers, for, as we learn from the "Language" chapter, the "relation between the mind and matter" is not a question of arbitrary subjectivity. Adapting, as Coleridge had, Kant to Plotinus, Emerson tells us that this relation "is not fancied by some poet, but stands in the will of God, and so is free to be known by all men. It appears to men, or it does not appear" (*E&L* 24). Emerson, like Coleridge, often quotes Plotinus (*Enneads,* 5.5.7) on the unlawful inquiry about the highest knowledge (following Milton and Coleridge, Emerson calls it "intuitive knowledge") and "whence it sprang as if it were a thing subject to place & motion for it neither approached hither nor again departs from hence, to some other place, but it either *appears to us, or it does not appear*" (*JMN* 5:103; italics added).

But another shift has occurred, similar to that involved in replacing the original epigraph to *Nature* with his own poem. In Emerson's creative reading of Plotinus in "Language," what appears or does not appear is *altered.* And the alteration—from spiritual intellect, of which ignorant nature is a mere "image," to the divinely sanctioned yet individually apprehended mind-matter relationship—itself alters his immediate source: *Biographia Literaria,* in which Plotinus is quoted in Greek and English, analyzed, and *not* associated with the mind-matter relation. Indeed, Coleridge, who in his 1803 notebook describes this *Ennead* as a most beautiful expression of what the Quakers call "the inward Light," tells us that he takes Plotinus to be referring to "the highest and intuitive knowledge as distinguished from the discursive," a Miltonic difference "in degree, in kind the same" (*PL* 5:490), which Coleridge comes close at times to suggesting *was* a difference in kind. In any case, Coleridge, as we have seen, identifies Plotinus's higher intuitive knowledge with "The vision and the faculty divine," from the opening book of *The Excursion,* imagery recalling Wordsworth's own "vision splendid" in the Intimations Ode. Though we can, says Plotinus, badger with our importunate interrogatories, we cannot, and ought not, "pursue" this light back to its "secret source." Accordingly, Coleridge employs his favorite Ennead to confirm his argument that we cannot, *pace* Milton's Raphael, trace a matter-spirit "series" back to its divine source (*BL* 1:241).[5]

In the 1834 letter to his brother in which Emerson distinguishes between Reason and understanding, he, like Coleridge, reduces the latter faculty to an incessantly toiling but "near-sighted" and "wrinkled calculator," capable only of "adding and arguing," a degenerate version of understanding repeated in *Nature*. There it dwells in the chimeras of "the present, the expedient, the customary," a mere "steward" of the temporary "house" of our "animal life." Reason, on the other hand, is our "Master," source of the "truth" associated with "Religion Poetry Honor," the "real, the absolute" (*L* 1:312–13). Reason—or Mind, or Soul, or Spirit—is thus divorced from an understanding so closely identified with the body and nature as to be less a part of the Me than of the NOT ME.

At other times, the agon becomes a potential identification, either between us and nature or between mind and the "divine Essence." The goal of art, says Coleridge in "On Poesy or Art," is "to make the external internal, the internal external, to make Nature thought and thought Nature." This goal, reflecting Coleridge's reading of Schelling, was sometimes shared by Wordsworth, who says of the Wanderer's relationship to natural phenomena, "in them did he live, / And by them did he live" (*E* 1:209–10). This symmetrical convergence did not obviate the need for a perennial negotiation of the relationship between mind and nature. Earlier, discussing Coleridge's commentary on the pivotal ninth stanza of the Intimations Ode, I quoted from a passage he first printed in *The Friend,* and rightly thought important enough to repeat. Borrowing not only from himself but from Schelling as well, Coleridge focuses on the "necessary antithesis" yet "reciprocal concurrence" between the central polarities: those of the real and the ideal, the subjective and the objective, conscious intelligence and unconscious nature:

5. Coleridge quotes *Enneads,* 3.8.4, 5.5.7–8. For the connection of the latter with "the inward Light" of Quakerism and radical Christianity, see *CN* 1:1678. See Chapter 7, where I associate Plotinus's advice to await with a patient eye the visionary revelation with those early doctrinal dialogue ballads in which Wordsworth chooses intuition over tuition and receptive-creative "idleness" over busy, ever "seeking," discursive intellect; with the Wordsworthian "idleness" of Keats and Emerson; and with Wordsworth's insistence that, though the wardens of institutional education are blind to it, a "wiser spirit is at work for us, / A better eye than theirs, most prodigal / Of blessings, and most studious of our good, / Even in what seem our most unfruitful hours" (*P* 5:360–63).

> Now the sum of all that is merely OBJECTIVE, we will henceforth call NATURE, confining the term to its passive and material sense, as comprising all the phenomena by which its existence is known to us. On the other hand the sum of all that is SUBJECTIVE, we may comprehend in the name of the SELF or INTELLIGENCE. Both conceptions are in necessary antithesis. Intelligence is conceived of as exclusively representative, nature as exclusively represented. Now in all acts of positive knowledge there is required a reciprocal concurrence of both, namely of the conscious being, and of that which is itself unconscious. Our problem is to explain this concurrence, its possibility and its necessity.
>
> During the act of knowledge itself, the objective and subjective are so instantly united, that we cannot determine to which of the two the priority belongs. There is here no first, and no second; both are coinstantaneous and one. While I am attempting to explain this intimate coalition, I must suppose it dissolved. I must necessarily set out from the one, to which therefore I must give hypothetical antecedence, in order to arrive at the other. But as there are two factors or elements in the problem, subject and object, and as it is left indeterminate from which of them I should commence, there are two cases equally possible. (*BL* 1:254–55)

Coleridge sets out the two cases—either the objective is taken as the first, and then we have to account for the supervention of the subjective, or vice versa. Either way, the act of knowing requires a resolution of the antithesis, "reciprocal concurrence." Coleridge is, of course, and in this twelfth chapter more than anywhere else, deeply indebted to the ideas and the very phrasing of Schelling, whose cognitive revolution, especially in the *Naturphilosophie* (1806), calls for a reversion to an original but now lost unifying vision, in which consciousness or mind or spirit is the subjective equivalent of nature or the world, nature the objective version of mind or spirit. Man has fallen, in the process alienating himself from a world he conceives of as dead and inanimate; what is now required is a cognitive "atonement" and reunification in which "the world of thought becomes the world of nature" and vice versa. More than Schelling and Wordsworth, Coleridge and Emerson were wary of any absorption of the world of thought *by* the world of nature; nevertheless, the Romantic transaction between the two remains a complex and ever changing dialectic between the assertion of active creative power and the recognition of the dangers of *over*assertion, of transgression. The ramifications are many: epistemological, ecological, and political, including what Nietzsche called master-and-slave morality, even sexual politics. It is, in short, the tension between cocreation and perception at the fecund heart of those crucial Emersonian agons (alternately antagonistic and reciprocal) between Man and Nature, Solitude and Society, Power and Necessity, Freedom and Fate.

"Giving and receiving" humanize that polar dialectic. "Thou must give, / Else never canst receive." The phrase is Wordsworth's (*P* 12:276–77), but the dialectical position is that of Emerson's other contemporary "benefactor," Coleridge. The crucial *poetic* text is his emotionalizing of Kant in the central stanzas of "Dejection," a poem that profoundly impressed the Transcendentalists, even when, as in the case of Thoreau's epigraph to *Walden,* it is alluded to in order to stress a dejection-repudiating exuberance.[6] In the ode, originally a verse epistle to Sara Hutchinson, Coleridge both acknowledges and declares: "I may not hope from *outward* forms to win / The passion and the life, whose fountains are *within*" (45–46), for, as he tells his beloved (in the published poem a nameless "Lady"):

> we *receive* but what we *give,*
> And in our life *alone* does Nature live:
> *Ours* is her wedding garment, *ours* her shroud!
> And would we aught behold, of higher worth,
> Than that *inanimate cold world* allowed
> To the poor *loveless* ever-anxious crowd,
> Ah! from *the soul itself* must issue forth
> A *light, a glory,* a fair luminous cloud
> Enveloping the Earth—
> . . . .
> *Joy,* Lady! is the *spirit and the power,*
> Which[,] *wedding Nature to us*[,] *gives* in dower
> A *new* Earth and *new* Heaven,
> Undreamt of by the sensual and the proud—
> Joy is the sweet voice, Joy the luminous cloud—
> We *in ourselves* rejoice!
> (47–55, 67–72; *CPW* 1:365–66; italics added)

In this projected apocalyptic nuptial, vital Joy, overcoming apathy and the consequent alienation between mind and external phenomena, weds us to a now reanimated nature; the marriage dowry is a renovated world, a secular version of the new heaven and new earth of the book of Revelation. This occurs when, through joy, we attain that heightened state of awareness in which sight becomes *insight,* enabling us (as Wordsworth says in "Tintern Abbey") to "see into the *life* of things." And those "things" are quickened *into* "life" by what Coleridge calls "a light, a glory" issuing from the "soul itself" and from we who "in ourselves rejoice." But that inner light and glory also issue from the "visionary gleam" and "glory" described

6. "I do not propose to write an ode to dejection, but to brag as lustily as chanticleer in the morning, standing on his roost, if only to wake my neighbor up." Thoreau lifts his announcement from chapter 2 of *Walden,* a book as affirmative as his epigraph forecasts, but far less distanced from Coleridge than this refutation suggests.

as "fled" at the end of the Wordsworth poem to which Coleridge is here responding: the then-four stanza fragmentary version of what would become the Intimations Ode.

Once again, Coleridge, who could hardly be further removed from the cool lucidity of Kant than he is at this point, is adapting Kantian epistemology to his own imaginative and emotional ends. The thesis of Kant's "Transcendental Idealism" in *The Critique of Pure Reason* is that the generic mind *gives form* to the external objects it *perceives.* The concept of "nature" is "universal," says Kant, because it conforms to "law," to preordained conditions, but those preordained, a priori, conditions "lie," in accord with Kant's Copernican Revolution, *not* in nature itself, but in "*our* sensibility and in *our* understanding." In Coleridge's poem, nature lives in "*our* life alone, . . . / *Ours* is her wedding garment, *ours* her shroud. . . ." In "Dejection," both the ode and the original verse epistle, Coleridge, celebrating joy in the midst of his own profound personal anguish, is expressing a *psychological* rather than a *cognitive* truth: that the capacity of natural beauty to "bring" us pleasure is reciprocally conditioned by what "our" own *individual* subjective state allows us to "give." As Coleridge, and countless others who followed his path in emotionalizing the cognitive revolution of Kant, including John Stuart Mill and William James, have testified, nature is either dead or alive depending on whether *we* are in a state of uncreative dejection or creative inner joy, the "spirit and the power" that actively "gives in dower" a renovated world.[7]

Here, then, the wedding with nature, however indispensable and happy, is not quite between equal partners, nor—in this instance—is the "spirit" transcendent. The "outward forms" of nature are clearly dependent, not upon Plotinus's luminous emanative fountain cascading down from the One, but upon the "inner fountains" of the passionate and loving self and upon the individual soul as the ultimate source of an animating joy and power. Coleridge's formulation, though in accord with the doctrine of immanence and self-determinative autonomy, is more extreme than anything in Wordsworth—though we might, however unfairly, detect its "optimistic" trivialization in Ella Wheeler Wilcox's notorious "Laugh, and the world laughs with you" or in the cliché about seeing the world through rose-colored glasses. Emerson himself, in "Experience," plays some sophisticated optical variations on a "train of moods" resembling "a string of beads," which as we pass through them "prove to be many-coloured lenses which paint the world their own hue, and each shows only what lies in its

7. See Arthur Lovejoy, "Coleridge and Kant's Two Worlds," in *Essays in the History of Ideas,* 254–76, esp. 260–63. Lovejoy does not, however, mention the verbal parallel to which I draw attention. The responses of Mill and James to the poetry of Coleridge and, especially, Wordsworth are discussed in the next chapter.

focus." He may be recalling the "inanimate cold world" of the Dejection Ode when he adds that "we animate what we can and we see only what we animate. . . . It depends on the mood of the man" (*E&L* 473–74). But then, a dozen pages later, he inserts the corrective note that, in a postlapsarian world, our instruments are "suspect." We have learned that "we do not see directly, but mediately, and that we have no means of correcting these coloured and distorting lenses which we are." Perhaps "these subject-lenses have a creative power; perhaps there are no objects. Once we lived in what we saw; now, the rapaciousness of this new power, which threatens to absorb all things, engages us. Nature, art, persons, letters, religions,—objects, successively tumble in, and God is but one of its ideas" (*E&L* 487).

They "tumble" into what Wordsworth calls in the famous Fenwick note on the Intimations Ode "this abyss of idealism" (*WP* 1:978). Among all of Wordsworth's varied formulations of the interplay of the senses, the mind of man, and nature, the closest approximation of Coleridge's extreme position in "Dejection" occurs in *The Prelude,* in the conceptually crucial passage on "the spots of time." These scattered but epiphanic "moments," which retain "with distinct pre-eminence" a "renovating virtue" (208–10), give us access to

> Profoundest knowledge to *what point,* and *how,*
> The mind is *lord and master—outward sense*
> The *obedient servant* of *her will.*
> (*P* 12:221–23; italics added)

Note, even here, the caveat of a question buried within the assertion ("to *what point,* and *how*"), as well as the rather surprising gender shift, from lord and master to "*her* will"—the will, that is, of the creative mind or imagination, depicted, finally, as female. Here we have an actual ennobling "interchange," pronouns shifting to accommodate, if not a "wedding," a curiously androgynous female "lord and master."[8]

There is a passage in an 1826 letter of Emerson reminiscent of the Wordsworthian "spots of time," even of the gendered marital relationship between the mind as female and a Wordsworthian "Presence." "There are in our existence spots of time," Wordsworth had begun the story of revelatory moments in his life (*P* 12:208). "There are . . . in each man's history," Emerson begins,

> insignificant passages which he feels to be to him not insignificant; little coincidences in little things, which touch all the springs of wonder, and

8. Something similar occurs in pt. 6 of *The Ancient Mariner* (lines 314–17), in which a simile employed by the "Second Voice" in effect transforms the female moon ("see! how graciously / *She* looketh down on him") into a "lord" in relation to its "slave," the subservient ocean.

startle the sleeping conscience in the deepest cell of his repose; the Mind standing forth in alarm with all her faculties, suspicious of a Presence which it behoves her deeply to respect—touch not more with awe than with curiosity, if perhaps some secret revelation is not about to be vouchsafed or doubtful if some moral epoch is not just now fulfilled in its history, and the tocsin just now struck that severs and tolls out an irreparable Past. (*L* 1:170)

To be sure, the passages are hardly parallel. Far from a death knell tolling severance from "an irreparable Past," Wordsworth's memorial "spots of time" were part of the process of "enshrining," or so he hopes, "the spirit of the Past / For future restoration" (*P* 12:284–87). Nevertheless, we cannot ignore Emerson's gendered and delicate language: the female Mind standing forth in alarm "with all her faculties," suspicious of the mysterious "Presence" yet filled with "curiosity" as well as "awe." It would seem, as Evelyn Barish has persuasively argued, that the Emersonian tocsin is simultaneously a marriage bell. As the sign of a "secret revelation" in which the dead past is to be left behind as we are summoned to a new life, it would represent a Wordsworthian "renovating virtue" after all.[9]

Such marriage imagery—most notably in the final chapter of *Nature*—confirms certain affinities linking Emerson, Wordsworth, and Coleridge. Though at least some of the resemblance is attributable to their common source in the book of Revelation[10] and in a partially misread Plotinus, Wordsworth's and Coleridge's more overt marriage scenarios seem clear anticipations of Emerson's imagery in *Nature,* the "analogy that marries Matter and Mind" (*E&L* 26), climaxing in the book's final chant of a Fall and nuptial Renovation. In the same year he completed *Nature,* Emerson wrote in his journal: "Man is the point wherein matter and spirit meet and marry," and "The world is full of happy marriages of faculty to object, of means to end; and all of Man marries all of Nature, & makes it fruitful" (*JMN* 5:187, 236).

9. Barish notes Emerson's evocation of "a feminine 'Mind' at a culminating moment, turning her back on the past, ready with awed love to respond to a 'Presence' greater than she. . . . The 'Mind' here is that of a woman on the brink of a mystic marriage," at once "a new bond, and a death knell, signalling that historical Christianity and biblical history are being forsaken in favor of this 'Presence'" (*Emerson: The Roots of Prophecy,* 166). Though she does not mention Wordsworth, his "spots of time" passage was first drafted at a time, 1799, when the mysterious "Presence" he constantly remarks in nature had either usurped or subsumed biblical Christianity.

10. In *Emerson's Rhetoric of Revelation: Nature, the Reader, and the Apocalypse Within,* Alan D. Hodder discusses biblical sources for Emerson's apocalyptic nuptial imagery. Often, especially in *Nature,* Emerson "reinvokes the image of the divine marriage as a way of imaginatively overcoming the separation between Nature and Spirit." Hodder traces allegorical stages, in which Nature is mother, then mate, first an equal then a subservient spouse (27–29).

In the "Prospectus," even "before the blissful hour arrives," Wordsworth says he would "chant, in lonely peace, the spousal verse / Of this great consummation," a Romantic epithalamion that, unlike the spiritual apocalypse in the Bible and unlike traditional readings of Plotinus, takes place between the mind and external nature. Wedding Emerson's own triumvirate of "Milton Coleridge & the Germans," Wordsworth, using "words / Which speak of nothing more than what we are" (58–59), would

> arouse the sensual from their sleep
> Of Death, and win the vacant and the vain
> To noble raptures; while my voice proclaims
> How exquisitely *the individual Mind*
> (And the progressive powers perhaps no less
> Of *the whole species*) to the *external* World
> Is *fitted*—and how exquisite, too—
> Theme this but little heard of among men—
> *The external World is fitted to the Mind;*
> And the *creation* (by no lower name
> Can it be called) which they with *blended might*
> Accomplish—this is our high argument.
> (60–71; italics added)

Blake, annotating this passage in a mood of outraged "mental fight," refused to accept any such mutual "fitting" between the human Mind and a vegetable universe that was a hindrance to vision, the veil (Vala) of nature that had to be consumed away to reveal the infinite that is hidden.[11] Wordsworth's "marriage" struck Blake, here sounding almost Plotinian, as a betrayal of the apocalyptic imagination. As for Wordsworth himself, he wants the marriage to be, as it were, alternately or mutually accommodating, each partner "fitted" to the other, though, as usual, the climactic Kantian-Coleridgean "theme" has the external world "fitted to the mind," things to thought, nature accommodating man, both on an individual and, perhaps, generic level, extending progressively to "the whole species."[12]

11. "You shall not bring me down to believe such fitting & fitted I know better & please your Lordship." And, responding to later lines in the "Prospectus" about hearing "Humanity in fields and groves / Pipe solitary anguish," Blake states: "Does not this Fit & is it not fitting most Exquisitely too but to what[,] not to Mind but to the Vile Body only & to its Laws of Good & Evil & its Enmities against Mind" (*Poetry and Prose of Blake,* 654).

12. Though he is skeptical ("perhaps . . ."), Wordsworth may here have learned from Coleridge not only about Kant's emphasis on the generic mind but also about the second thesis in his "Idea for a Universal History," according to which those natural capacities of Man (the only rational creature on earth) "which are directed to the use of his reason are to be fully developed *only in the race, not in the individual*" (Kant, *On History,* 12–15; italics added).

The peroration of "Prospects," the climactic chapter of *Nature,* is a similarly spousal hymn, with Emerson also placing mankind rather than the things of nature in the saddle. Leading into his finale, he quotes from his beloved George Herbert, from that "beautiful psalmist's . . . little poem on Man," upon whom all of nature attends, a loving servant to a master. The first two lines of the penultimate stanza had been cited earlier in *Nature,* quoted, without attribution, in the "Commodity" chapter, to depict our servant, "Nature, in its ministry to man" (*E&L* 12). Now Emerson quotes five stanzas of the poem, ending with that penultimate verse, in order to once again emphasize the hierarchy, even if the servant is also a friend:

More servants wait on man
Than he'll take notice of. In every path,
He treads down that which doth befriend him
When sickness makes him pale and wan.
Oh mighty love! Man is one world, and hath
Another *to attend him.*

(*E&L* 44–45)

This "mighty love" takes the form, as in Raphael's speech in *Paradise Lost,* of the Chain of Being, "thy great chain," as Herbert calls it elsewhere. On this ascending vegetable-animal-human scale, Man is "ev'ry Thing, / And more." He is "a Tree, yet bears more fruit; / A Beast, yet is, or should be more." The difference—and the justification of that thrice-repeated "more"—is that "Reason and speech we onely bring." As one unified world, "Man is all symmetrie," a microcosm in reciprocal correspondence with the macrocosm. This correlation between man and the universe serves Emerson's purpose. Significantly, however, he omits the final stanza of "Man." That last stanza had rounded back to the first, in which the poet, addressing "God," says he has "heard" that "none doth build a stately habitation, / But he that means to dwell therein." The "stately habitation" is of course "Man," whom all things created serve. But he who is served must in turn serve the Master Builder. As Herbert puts it in the final stanza: since "God" has "So brave a palace built," he should dwell in it until, "at last," *it* may dwell with him. "Till then," just "as the world serves us," *we* should "serve" God, making both the world and us "thy servant."[13]

13. Herbert, *The Poems of George Herbert,* 81–83; italics added. This inconvenient final stanza, omitted from *Nature,* is included by Emerson when he printed the poem in *Parnassus* (144). Emerson praised Herbert's poetry for its intellectual "heat," its "fusion of thought" and "perfect flexibility" (*JMN* 4:428, 432). Coleridge, too, valued Herbert highly and found comfort in him. In addition to comments in *Biographia*

The final stanza of "Man" was omitted for good reason. It was doubtless too personally theistic and too subservient for Emerson's purpose at this point—the peroration of *Nature,* a book whose title, as Harold Bloom insists, "says 'Nature' but means 'Man.'"[14] That book had begun by lamenting a "retrospective age" of outmoded religion that "builds sepulchres to the fathers." Now he is ready, says Emerson, to "conclude this essay with some traditions of man and nature, which a certain poet sang to me; and which, as they have always been in the world, and perhaps reappear to every bard, may be both history and prophecy" (*E&L* 45). That persona, later described as his "Orphic Poet," is, I suspect—historically—a fusion of Plotinus, Coleridge, Wordsworth (playing what Coleridge called his "Orphean lyre"), and Carlyle, together with Emerson's Platonist and Coleridgean friend Bronson Alcott and Emerson himself. A prophetic figure as well, the Orphic Poet seems a precursor of Nietzsche's oracular Zarathustra.

According to Emerson's oracular bard, though "the foundations of man are not in matter, but in spirit," there is still a profound relationship to "nature," a "sympathy" we "distrust and deny inwardly," owning and disowning "our relation to it, by turns." In a biblical image employed as well by Blake, we are likened to "Nebuchadnezzar, dethroned, bereft of reason, and eating grass like an ox. But who can set limits to the remedial force of spirit?" Yet, unremediated, "a man is a god in ruins," the only things preventing total disintegration (a world become "insane and rabid") are death and infancy—the latter, I suspect, a fusion of autobiography (Waldo's imminent birth) with Wordsworth's celebration of the Child in the eighth stanza of the Intimations Ode. But while "Infancy is the perpetual Messiah, which comes into the arms of fallen men, and pleads with them to return to paradise," contemporary "Man is the dwarf of himself" (*E&L* 46).

Emerson's formulation owes much to Wordsworth. This image of contemporary man as "the dwarf of himself" reflects the stunted, imagination-betraying "pigmy" of the seventh stanza of the Intimations Ode; that "dwarf," the monstrous prodigy of systematic education in book 5 of *The Prelude;* and the shriveling consequence of the perverse labors of that "degraded Race" described by the Wanderer in the crucial fourth book of *The Excursion,* those modern scientists and philosophers, "joyless as the blind,"

Literaria (chaps. 19 and 20), he frequently praised Herbert in his letters and notebooks. His annotated copy of the 1674 edition of *The Temple* is now in the Berg Collection of the New York Public Library. For the reference to "thy great chain" ("Employment, 1"), see *Poems of Herbert,* 50.

14. Bloom, *Agon,* 157.

who "pore, and dwindle as [they] pore," that "littleness / May yet become more little" (*E* 4:960–66). John Stuart Mill's reading of Wordsworth is visible in *On Liberty,* in which the human capacities of his era are depicted as "shrivelled and starved." Nietzsche, too, in "Schopenhauer as Educator," lamenting our "narrowness and shrivelled nature," may well have in mind this final chapter of *Nature*. The rest of Emerson's great myth of fall, degeneration, and projected redemption closely resembles four texts, three of which seem cases of direct influence: (1) the lines of Coleridge quoted earlier from "Dejection: An Ode" and (2) his previously cited letter to Wordsworth in response to the publication of *The Excursion,* along with (3) the Wanderer's speeches in the fourth book of that poem and (4) Wordsworth's "Prospectus," published in 1814 as part of the prose preface to *The Excursion,* but actually drafted in 1798—making it the earliest written of the four.

"Once," says Emerson's mythmaking Orphic Poet—in a description of shrinkage *rejected,* incidentally, by Thoreau in the "Conclusion" of *Walden*—man, permeated by spirit, "filled nature with his overflowing currents": "Out from him sprang the sun and moon; from man, the sun; from woman, the moon. The laws of his mind, the periods of his actions externalized themselves into day and night, into the year and the seasons. But, having made for himself this huge shell, his waters retired; he no longer fills the veins and veinlets; he is shrunk to a drop" (*E&L* 46).[15] In Wordsworth's "Prospectus," the individual mind is "*fitted*" to the external world and, in the "little heard of" but more Kantian-Romantic marriage, "The external world is *fitted* to the Mind" (63–66). Emerson's "dwarf," applying to nature mere understanding rather than intuitive Reason, "sees that the structure *still fits* him, but *fits him colossally.* Say, rather, *once it fitted him,* now it corresponds to him from far and on high." No longer a mythic source, man is now the "follower of the sun, and woman the follower of the moon. Yet sometimes he starts in his slumber, and wonders at himself and his house, and muses strangely at *the resemblance betwixt him and it*" (*E&L* 46; italics added).

In this mythological account of modern man's diminution from his ancient greatness, Emerson is remembering, as he often does, book 4 of *The Excursion.* After describing the "bewildered Pagans of old time," who nevertheless responded to the natural world of sun and moon with joy and fortified their "moral sense" with religious reverence of Apollo and Diana (*E* 4:934–39), Wordsworth's Wanderer asks, with uncharacteristi-

15. Compare Yeats, "The Tower" (3:146–51), in *W. B. Yeats: The Poems,* 198, on man creating everything, sun and moon and stars, all "out of" his own soul; again, though supposedly mocked, "Plotinus' thought" (146) figures prominently.

cally sardonic irony, if "our great Discoverers," our ambitious modern scientists and philosophers, who would rather "dive than soar," will obtain "less" from sense and reason than those "misled" pagans:

> Shall men for whom our age
> Unbaffled powers of vision hath prepared,
> To explore the world without and world within,
> Be joyless as the blind?
>
> (*E* 4:944–47)

Let us inquire of "ancient Wisdom," demand of "mighty Nature," if it was ever meant that we should analytically and unimaginatively "pry" from a distance and

> yet be unraised;
> That we should pore, and dwindle as we pore,
> Viewing all objects unremittingly
> In disconnexion dead and spiritless;
> And still dividing, and dividing still,
> Break down all grandeur, still unsatisfied
> With the perverse attempt, while littleness
> May yet become more little; waging thus
> An impious warfare with the very life
> Of our own souls!
>
> (*E* 4:957–68)

This is precisely the shrinking process described by the Orphic Poet of Emerson, who goes on, two paragraphs later, and in his own voice, to employ remedial language that is primarily internal, and in its emphases on alienation and vision, certainly High Romantic—both Coleridgean and Wordsworthian:

> The problem of restoring to the world original and eternal beauty, is solved by the redemption of the soul. The ruin, or the *blank,* that we see when we look at nature, is *in our own eye*. The axis of *vision* is not coincident with the axis of *things,* and so they appear *not transparent but opake*. The reason why the world lacks unity, and lies broken and in heaps, is *because man is disunited with himself.* He cannot be a *naturalist,* until he satisfies all the demands of the *spirit. Love* is as much its demand, as *perception.* Indeed, *neither* can be perfect without the *other.* In the uttermost meaning of the words, thought is devout, and devotion is thought. Deep calls unto deep [Psalms 42:7]. But in *actual life, the marriage is not celebrated.* There are innocent men who worship God after the tradition of their fathers, but their sense of duty has not yet extended to the use of all their faculties. And there are patient naturalists, but *they* freeze their subject under *the wintry light of the understanding.* Is

> not prayer also a study of truth,—a sally of the soul into the unfound infinite? No man ever prayed heartily without learning something. But when a faithful thinker, resolute to detach every object from personal relations, and see it in the light of thought, shall, at the same time, kindle science with the fire of the holiest affections, then will God go forth anew into the creation. (*E&L* 47; italics added)

The Coleridgean distinction between mere understanding and the intuitive Reason, to which Emerson here alludes, as well as the criticism of, and anticipation of a new rekindled "science," is at the heart of the Wanderer's argument in book 4 of *The Excursion.* "If indeed there be / An all-pervading Spirit, upon whom / Our dark foundations rest," then it cannot be that all this "magnificent effect of power," of earth and sky, and

> that superior mystery[,]
> Our vital frame, so fearfully devised,
> And the dread soul within it—should exist
> Only to be examined, pondered, searched,
> Probed, vexed, and criticized. . . .
> I now affirm of Nature and of Truth,
> Whom I have served, that their DIVINITY
> Revolts, offended at the ways of men
> Swayed by such motives, to such ends employed.
> (974–78, 983–86)

In contrast, the man who approaches the human and natural worlds in the proper spirit, who "communes with the Forms / Of Nature," and does so "with an understanding heart / Both knows *and loves*" (*E* 4:1207–10; italics added). Those who contemplate "these Forms / In the relations which they bear to man" will discern how they silently yield innumerable "spiritual presences" (1230–34). For such genuine explorers, once their labors are irradiated by the "light of love" (1244),

> shall be confirmed
> The glorious habit by which sense is made
> Subservient still to moral purposes,
> Auxiliar to divine. That change shall clothe
> The naked spirit, ceasing to deplore
> The burden of existence. Science then
> Shall be a precious visitant; and then,
> And only then, be worthy of her name:
> For then her heart shall kindle; her dull eye,
> Dull and inanimate, no more shall hang
> Chained to its object in brute slavery.
> (1246–56)

This liberation from subservience to objects sounds like a Coleridgean ideal. Nevertheless, when he read *The Excursion,* a disappointed Coleridge, still hankering after the ever elusive *Recluse,* thought that Wordsworth, despite many passages attesting to undiminished poetic power, had not fulfilled their original plan to build a new temple to replace the old. "I supposed you first," he complains,

> to have laid a solid and immovable foundation for the Edifice by removing the sandy Sophisms of Locke, and the Mechanic Dogmatists. Next . . . to have affirmed a Fall in some sense . . . attested to by experience & conscience . . . to point out however a manifest Scheme of Redemption from this Slavery, of Reconciliation from this Enmity with Nature. . . . in short, the necessity of a general revolution in the modes of developing and disciplining the human mind by the substitution of Life, and Intelligence . . . for the philosophy of mechanism which in every thing that is most worthy of the human Intellect strikes *Death.* (*CL* 4:574–75)

That was in May 1815. Charles Lamb, that great friend of both Coleridge and Wordsworth, writing seven months earlier, thought that this was precisely what Wordsworth *had* achieved, especially in the speeches of the Wanderer in book 4—several of which provided Emerson with consolation in distress, especially following the deaths of Ellen, Charles, and little Waldo. Praising *The Excursion* in the *Quarterly Review,* Lamb, as we saw in Chapter 6, cited book 4 as "the most valuable portion of the poem." Employing the prime Coleridgean distinction, he linked its theme to "the leading moral" of *The Excursion* as a whole, which was "to abate the pride of the calculating *understanding,* and to reinstate the *imagination* and the affections in those seats from which modern philosophy has laboured but too successfully to expel them." These expellers of the imagination and the affections, scientists and philosophers of yet unkindled "heart," their collective "eye" still "dull and inanimate," are those "naturalists" who, as Emerson says in the long passage cited from *Nature,* "*freeze* their subject under *the wintry light of the understanding.*" The icy result is precisely what Coleridge called, in "Dejection," an "inanimate cold world." And the internal "ruin or *blank*" that we "see when we look at nature" echoes Coleridge's painful exclamations in the ode: "And still I gaze—and with how *blank* an eye!" as he stares with keen but affectless perception at the "clouds" that, reciprocally, "give away their motion to the stars" and the crescent moon in "its own cloudless, starless lake of blue": "I see them all so excellently fair, / I *see, not feel,* how beautiful they are!" (30–38; *CPW* 1: 364; italics added).

What Coleridge lacks, along with the Wanderer's "light of love," the "Love" Emerson said had to accompany perception, is the "celestial light" whose loss is also lamented in the opening stanza of the poem to which Coleridge is responding: the Intimations Ode. Wordsworth, in turn, was borrowing that "celestial light" from Milton ("So much the rather thou celestial Light / Shine *inward,* and the mind through all her powers / Irradiate"), to whom it was compensation for the physical blindness that had presented him with "a universal *blank* / Of nature's works to me expunged and razed" (*PL* 3:44–55). Whereas Milton's "blank" is literal, what is, as he says, "cut off" or "shut out" in his case by actual blindness anticipates what Coleridge feels to be his severance, by dejection, not from the external beauty of Nature, but from the "passion and the life / Whose fountains are *within*" ("Dejection," 46).

What is required to heal Coleridge's severing blankness of vision is not limited understanding, the "wintry light" of mere observation, but the inner light of intuitive Reason or Spirit, the Wordsworthian "master light of all our *seeing.*" This is what Emerson means by aligned "*vision,*" and Coleridge, quoting the Poet in *The Excursion,* by the "*vision* and the faculty divine" (1:79) possessed by such a man as the Wanderer. It takes the notably Wordsworthian form, in this climactic passage of *Nature,* of the "wisdom *to see the miraculous in the common,*" "poetry" in "facts," phenomena as rooted "in the faculties *and affections of the mind.*" In this way, "shall we come to *look at the world with new eyes*" (*E&L* 47–48; italics added). Then shall "come to pass" the realization Emerson places in the mouth of his "Orphic Poet," the realization that it is not (as in the omitted stanza of Herbert's "Man") *God* who has "So brave a palace built" (Saint Paul's God-given "house not built with hands," Coleridge's "house gloriously furnished"), but the creative spirit of *man* that *builds itself* "a house."

> Nature is not fixed but fluid. Spirit alters, moulds, makes it. The immobility or bruteness of nature, is the absence of spirit; to pure spirit, it is fluid, it is volatile, it is *obedient.* Every spirit *builds itself a house;* and beyond its house a world; and beyond its world, a heaven. . . . The kingdom of man over nature, which cometh *not* with observation,—a dominion such as now is *beyond his dream of God—,* he shall enter *with no more wonder than the blind man feels who is gradually restored to perfect sight.* (*E&L* 48–49; italics added)

The "world" is still a Herbertian "servant" tending on man, but Herbert's God is out of the picture. For Emerson, that creative spirit is Coleridgean; I am thinking not of the theological constructs of the Christian author of *Aids to Reflection,* but of what Coleridge calls in "Dejection" his "shaping spirit of imagination." The Emersonian spirit is also Wordsworthian: a human visionary faculty divine capable of altering, moulding, and building from malleable materials—outward things that are "obedient" not to God, but to the human mind as "lord and master." As Emerson will later say, in the 1842 lecture "The Transcendentalist," "I—this thought which is called I—is the mould into which the world is poured like molten wax." Such a Transcendentalist "believes in miracle, in the perpetual openness of the human mind to new influx of light and power; he believes in inspiration, and in ecstasy" (*E&L* 196). Emerson's climactic references to the "kingdom" or "dominion" of man over nature completes his point, made in the "Discipline" chapter of *Nature,* that the "exercise of the Will or the lesson of power is taught in every event." Man is able to "conform all facts to his character" because

> Nature is thoroughly mediate. It is made to serve. It receives the dominion of man as meekly as the ass on which the Saviour rode. It offers all its kingdoms to man as the raw material which he may mould into what is useful. . . . He forges the subtile and delicate air into wise and melodious words, and gives them wings as angels of persuasion and command. One after another, his victorious thought comes up with and reduces all things, until the world becomes, at last, only a realized will,—the double of the man. (*E&L* 28)

Ecologists may be disturbed by the dominionist implications of such a doctrine, and also implicit here is what Nietzsche, who seems to have registered such passages, would call the Will to Power. But Emerson emphasizes not only the bending of things to thought but also the visionary powers that emerge from turning nature into language, the anticipated capacity to "look at the world with new eyes," and thus to "behold," as Coleridge says, "a new earth and new heaven" that we ourselves have created through an inner joy that weds us to nature—a nature that we, nevertheless, dominate. For Emerson, it culminates in that final image of man coming into his kingdom with no more wonder than a "blind man . . . gradually restored to perfect sight." Emerson, whose tubercular symptoms affected his eyes, is understandably obsessive about sight and blindness, an ocular cluster epitomized in the transparent-eyeball passage at the outset of *Nature.* But the eye and what it sees are also crucial to the Intimations Ode, a compendium of visual imagery and a poem to whose opening four stanzas Coleridge was responding in what became "Dejection." But at this point, I return, for the last time, to a poem almost as crucial to Emerson as the Great Ode: Wordsworth's "Prospectus" to *The Recluse.*

Emerson, who thought Wordsworth not a greater but "a more original poet" than Milton (*JMN* 4:312), would have found direct support for that insight in the "Prospectus," first drafted in 1798 but not published until 1814, when it provided the conclusion of the preface to *The Excursion,* the second epic, though the first to be published, in what was to be a triadic canon capped by *The Recluse.* The latter, though as yet unwritten, was to be followed by the long poem now being published and preceded by the autobiographical epic we know as *The Prelude:* the written but as yet unpublished "Poem to Coleridge" on "the origin and progress of his own powers," a "Work, addressed to a dear Friend, and to whom the Author's Intellect is deeply indebted" (*WP* 2:36). In a remark included in the long essay "Poetry and Imagination" (assembled in 1872 by other hands from earlier texts, especially an 1854 lecture called "English Poetry"), Emerson says that "great design belongs to a poem, and is better than any skill in execution,—but how rare! I find it in the poems of Wordsworth,—Laodamia, and the Ode to Dion, and the Plan of the Recluse" (*EPP* 306). His remarks, in the sentences immediately following, that "We want design," not "enamelling," that we want not "an upholsterer," but "an architect," remind us that Wordsworth conceived of his canon, as he tells us in the prose preface to *The Excursion,* as a "Gothic church," with *The Prelude* as "ante-chapel" and his other poems so many "little cells, oratories," and recesses (*WP* 2:36). "Where else," aside from the Wordsworth poems he enumerates, Emerson asks in the notebook entry in which these thoughts first appeared, "is any great design?" And he adds, "We shall come to value only that excellence of finish that great design brings with it" (*JMN* 9:449).

The "Prospectus," a remarkable poem in its own right, sets out nothing if not a great design. It programmatically announces Wordsworth's entire canonical project, declaring, in the process, that he intends to surpass his master Milton by locating the central scene of Fall and Redemption within the human mind, not in the cosmos of an external hell and heaven presided over by an external God, a "Jehovah—with his thunder, and the choir / Of shouting Angels, and the empyreal thrones." Sinking "deep" and ascending "aloft," Wordsworth will "pass" all such terrors "unalarmed" (28–35), for:

> Not Chaos, not
> The darkest pit of lowest Erebus,
> Nor aught of blinder vacancy, scooped out
> By help of dreams—can breed such fear and awe
> As fall upon us when we look
> Into our Minds, into the Mind of Man,
> My haunt, and the main region of my song.
> (35–41)

This daring journey into the interior, a region more profound than the pit of any hell, more exalted than any conventional heaven, struck a deeply responsive chord in Emerson, who vigorously rejected most orthodox theistic notions in favor of an essentially immanent spiritual vision emphasizing the "moral constitution" of Man Thinking. Robert Weisbuch is right: "It is impossible to imagine Emerson without Wordsworth's relocation of Milton's heaven of heavens within the human mind."[16]

Emerson's repudiation of historical Christianity explains his irritation—often recorded in the journals, and made shockingly public in the Divinity School Address—at boring, spiritually dead preachers whose sermons seemed to him conformist drivel or a dull rehashing of the grim tenets of a decayed Calvinism, of Jehovah with his thunders. But one man's Jehovan thunders is another's spiritual sublimity. If the hardly orthodox William Blake could be driven to fury in the margins of the "Prospectus," even to "a bowel complaint" that, he told Crabb Robinson, "nearly killed me,"[17] it is no wonder that American critics of Transcendentalism, in this case conservative Presbyterians who happened also to be philosophically informed, were driven up the theological wall by what they saw as second- or third-hand Kantianism misused in an attempt to kill the biblical God. One notable post–Divinity School assault of 1839, to which I have earlier referred, was written with the sort of conservative brio one finds in the English *Anti-Jacobin.* The three authors attack Cousin (the "forwarding philosopher" who gets his "new system" and the "newest theology" from Germany and passes it on to the eager Americans), along with Carlyle and Emerson, the author of *Nature* and that "imitator" of Carlyle who had recently delivered the Divinity School Address. "In place of the mysterious and incomprehensible Jehovah, whose infinite perfections will be the study and delight of an eternity," the authors complain, Transcendentalists like Emerson give us a God

16. Weisbuch, "Post-colonial Emerson," 194.

17. There are two famous responses, one in the margin of his copy of Wordsworth, the other in conversation with Robinson. Commenting on Wordsworth's passing by Jehovah, his thunder and his angels, "unalarmed," an exercised Blake wrote in 1826: "Solomon when he married Pharohs daughter & became a Convert to the Heathen Mythology Talked exactly in this way of Jehovah as a Very inferior object of Mans Contemplations he also passed him unalarmed" (*Poetry and Prose of Blake,* 656). In his account of Blake's response to the passage, Robinson reports that Blake, offended equally by Wordsworth's arrogance and naturalism, denounced him "as a Pagan, but still with great praise as the greatest poet of the age" (*Blake, Wordsworth, Coleridge, Lamb, Etc.,* 6). Elsewhere, Robinson reports that the painter Flaxman also "took umbrage" at the passage. Though he thought the lines should be burned, Flaxman did not really smell heresy; indeed, he thought Wordsworth "could not mean anything impious in it." Robinson himself confesses that "I was unable, and am still, to explain the passage," though he rightly dismisses Lamb's sanitizing gloss ("that there are deeper sufferings in the mind of man than in an imagined hell") as "unsatisfactory" (*Henry Crabb Robinson on Books and Their Writers,* 1:156–57).

> whose nature and essence we can now, while seeing through a glass darkly, thoroughly comprehend, and to whom faith is not permitted to transmit any thing of excellence or glory beyond what the human intellect can clearly discern. In place of the God of Abraham, of Isaac, and of Jacob, . . . we are presented with a vague personification of abstract principles, with a God who is described as the reason; . . . the substance of the *me,* or the free personality, and of the fatal *not me,* or nature; who returns to himself in the consciousness of man; of whose divine essence all the momenta pass into the world, and return into the consciousness of man; who is every thing, and, it might with equal significancy be added, nothing.[18]

Though Fichte, with his *Ich* and *Nicht-Ich,* and Cousin along with Carlyle, get the blame, the culprits might well have been the Wordsworth who wrote "Tintern Abbey" and the "Prospectus" or early Coleridge—even if he later recanted and retroactively rectified Wordsworth by excluding him from among those who substitute their own "indefinite sensations" for the biblical Jehovah, while quoting the sublime passage from "Tintern Abbey," which *does* substitute "indefinite sensations" for that Jehovah (*AR* 404)! Surely, earlier Wordsworth was either a pantheist or what K. C. F. Krause would later, in 1828, term a "panentheist." An attempt to avoid the materialistic and atheistic potential of pantheism, panentheism holds that the finite world is incorporated *within* God yet is not only lesser than but also essentially different from God. Coleridge's formula in *Aids to Reflection,* that the Wordsworth of "Tintern Abbey" and the "Prospectus" was, *really,* a more or less devout believer in the "Divine Omnipresence," is a bestowed, and barely defensible, orthodoxy. The *actually* devout Wordsworth of 1825 must have been grateful for his friend's belated, if dubious, seal of approval.

The Wordsworth of 1796–1798 may not have been quite the "*Semi-atheist*" Coleridge described to John Thelwall (*CL* 1:216). But positioning him theologically is hardly simple. Between the views of those who, like M. H. Abrams, see him as a "secular" poet, naturalizing supernaturalism, and those who depict a "Christian" Wordsworth, Robert Barth, who believes that Wordsworth's was *always* an essentially "religious imagination," has recently staked out "a middle ground," arguing that "the truth is somewhere between the two extremes." But however Christian the *man* may have been, Barth doubts, with good reason, that Wordsworth the *poet* was ever, late or early, "fully Christian." His poems, "despite their strong sacramental sense," reveal no "incarnational sense" and "no real sense either of divine redemption or of mankind's need for it."[19]

18. Alexander, Dod, and Hodge, "Transcendentalism of the Germans," in *The Transcendentalists: An Anthology,* edited by Miller, 233, 235.

19. Barth, *Romanticism and Transcendence,* 27–28. For Barth's running argument leading to this conclusion, see pp. 6–7, 13–14, 21–22, and esp. 24–29, and 38n5.

This seems about right, though just barely at odds with Abrams. The author of "Tintern Abbey," Coleridge notwithstanding, was—as Coleridge himself knew better than anyone else—anything but an orthodox theist, let alone an orthodox Christian. Though Wordsworth's phrase in "Tintern Abbey," "whose dwelling . . . ," *does* evoke a numinous sense of what many would call "God," that was a word seldom if ever on the lips of the poet of 1798, and it still located that "presence" in nature and in the mind of man. In *Aids to Reflection,* Coleridge struggles to exonerate his friend (and, not incidentally, his own earlier self) from the quite accurate charge of having substituted this indefinite "sense sublime" for the biblical deity. In citing the lines from "Tintern Abbey," he uses, claims Coleridge, "the language, but not the sense or purpose of the great Poet of our Age." Coleridge claims that he discusses the larger issue—the increasing "unwillingness to contemplate the Supreme Being in his personal Attributes," a "contagion" from which "even the sincerest seekers after light are not safe"—all the more "feelingly" because it describes "that which for a brief period was my own state." And he quotes the indefinite pantheism attributed to Ferdinand, the most "Coleridgean" character in his 1797 play *Osorio:* "To worship NATURE in the hill and valley, / Not knowing what they love."[20]

But at the same time that he was publicly clearing him of the charges of pantheistic nature worship, in private correspondence Coleridge, disturbed by the dependency of the Wordsworthian soul on place and by a God immanent rather than transcendent, was identifying "the great Poet of our age" with the very "contagion" (a topos of high church Anglican polemics) to which he refers in *Aids to Reflection.* "I will not conceal from *you,*" he tells one of the most intimate of his later confidants, "that this inferred dependency of the human soul on accidents of birth-place and abode, together with the vague, misty, rather than mystic, confusion of God with the world, and the accompanying nature-worship, of which the asserted dependence forms a part, is the trait of Wordsworth's poetic works that I most dislike as unhealthful, and denounce as contagious."[21]

20. He alters his original phrase, "he loves," to "they love," to include all those estranged from the personal Father (*AR* 404). Wordsworth read *Osorio* with great care—and consequence: the phrase from "Tintern Abbey" later Wordsworth was most defensive about was his description of himself at the time as, like Coleridge and his Ferdinand, "a *worshipper* of nature" (151).

21. On the "contagion" and "infection" of atheism in eighteenth-century polemics, see Roger Lund, "Infectious Wit: Metaphor, Atheism, and the Plague in Eighteenth-Century London." The recipient of this letter, a young businessman who became a disciple of Coleridge's after attending his lectures in 1816, later became a friend with whom Coleridge shared many confidences and confessions. See Thomas Allsop, *Letters, Conversations and Recollections of S. T. Coleridge,* 1:107.

Thus spake the Anglican theologian. But where *does* one come down in terms of theological labeling? The distinction made by a friend of Emerson has the virtue, and the vice, of simplicity: "Pantheism is said to sink man and nature in God, Materialism to sink God and man in nature, and Transcendentalism to sink God and nature in man."[22] Depending on context, Wordsworth might be placed in any one of these categories, with the poet of the "Prospectus" closest to Transcendentalism. That is convenient, since Emerson's introduction to *Nature,* even more than his conclusion, is unmistakably indebted to the "Prospectus," a poem that anticipates early Coleridge's variation on apocalyptic marriage imagery ("Man . . . wedded to this goodly universe / In love and holy passion"), yet a work so religiously daring that even Blake was exasperated by what he took to be Wordsworthian arrogance and heathenism. On this question, Emerson is with Wordsworth—who was willing, amazingly enough, to make this audacious early work public as late as 1814—rather than with Blake. Interestingly enough, though, in the very same essay in which he praises Wordsworth's "Prospectus," Emerson also praises that astonishing "ocular" passage in Blake about seeing not with but "thro" the "corporeal Eye" (*EPP* 303)—enthusiastically if belatedly recognizing (as I have earlier suggested) a remarkable anticipation of his own image of the transparent eyeball, that ocular epiphany indebted to the moment in "Tintern Abbey" when Wordsworth feels empowered to "*see* into the life of things."

At his most "Orphic"—at moments in the essay "The Poet," or in the bardic voice of the "Orphic Poet" that supplies the rhapsodic peroration of *Nature*—Emerson is Coleridgean, Wordsworthian, and, with important reservations, also rather "Blakean." Considering Emerson's mythmaking, especially the internalized Fall and Redemption that concludes *Nature,* along with his gnomic, aphoristic wisdom and uncanny sense of humor, it is strange to think that, until quite late in his life, he knew nothing of Blake, a writer remarkable for precisely these qualities. But then there is that aphoristic and joyfully astringent mythmaker Nietzsche. That great liberator informs the free spirits projected in his prophetic imagination that once it is realized that we "no longer have any need" for an external God, "the whole drama of Fall and Redemption will be played out to the end in you yourself." Sibylline Nietzsche never read Blake at all, though, Nietzschean atheism aside, they certainly seem, as Yeats brilliantly and fruitfully realized, kindred spirits: "Nietzsche," said Yeats, "completes Blake and has the same roots." But perhaps much of what Yeats saw as Blakean in Nietzsche was really *Emersonian.* I am referring not only to the most daring playing out, in Nietzsche, of the doctrine of immanence, of what

22. Cyrus A. Bartol, *Radical Problems,* 283.

Wordsworth (apparently forgetting its Miltonic source in the hubris of fallen Man) also called "divinity within," but even to the demonstrable fact that much of Zarathustra may be found in that professor of Joyous Science, that Orphic Poet, Emerson—if not an atheist, at least an "infidel."[23]

Analogous to Blake and, subsequently, a direct influence on Nietzsche and Wallace Stevens, *Nature*'s introduction and final three chapters constitute a seminal document of American Romanticism. And where Emerson is at his most Orphic and visionary he resembles, along with Blake and Nietzsche, Wordsworth, whose ambition to write "immortal verse / Thoughtfully fitted to the Orphean lyre" (*P* 1:233–34) Coleridge deemed to have been fulfilled when he first heard his friend read the whole of *The Prelude,* an epic he instantly pronounced, in his poem "To William Wordsworth," "an Orphic song indeed," a "song divine of high and passionate thoughts / To their own music chaunted!" (45–47)—lines quoted, incidentally, by Emerson in an 1835 journal as evidence that "once in a while we meet with poetry which is also music" (*JMN* 5:74).[24]

Among other things, the introduction to *Nature* is Emerson's version of Wordsworth's "Prospectus," which, conceptually and rhetorically, strikingly anticipates the book's famous opening paragraph. Emerson's first biographer, Oliver Wendell Holmes—implying ideational analogy rather than the direct verbal influence that seems palpable—notes that we find "the same thought in the Preface to *The Excursion* that we find in the

23. Nietzsche, *Daybreak,* § 79; Yeats, *Letters of Yeats,* 379. Though Adam and Eve "feel / Divinity within them," this feeling overwhelms them, not when they are in the prelapsarian state of grace, but as the initial consequence of their fall—at the "completing of the mortal sin / Original" (*PL* 9:1003–13).

24. The lines of *The Prelude* echoed by Coleridge themselves involve a double Miltonic echo. As in the reference in *The Excursion* to "wisdom married to immortal verse" (*E* 7:536), Wordsworth's "immortal verse / Thoughtfully fitted to the Orphean lyre" echoes Milton's "soft Lydian airs, / Married to immortal verse," exceeding that of "Orpheus' self"—such "strains as would have won the ear / Of Pluto to have quite set free / His half-regained Eurydice" ("L'Allegro," 136–37, 145–50, *The Portable Milton,* 65). But both Wordsworth and Coleridge—and, later, Emerson, whose "Orphic Poet" dominates the finale of *Nature*—reverse Milton's more explicit rejection (in the exordium to book 3 of *Paradise Lost*) of the classical Muse who failed to save Orpheus and his wife. Shifting scenes from hell to heaven, Milton, in book 3 (15–19), looks back to his safe "flight / Through utter and through middle darkness borne," emphasizing how "With other notes than to the Orphean lyre / I sung of Chaos and eternal night." Instead of depending on the Muse who failed Orpheus (a failure dramatized in "Lycidas" and in the Nativity Ode), Milton has been "Taught by the heavenly Muse," already identified (*PL* 1:6) as Urania. In the "Prospectus" to *The Recluse,* Wordsworth will invoke "Urania," or a "greater Muse, if such / Descend to earth or dwell in highest heaven!" But in the opening book of *The Prelude,* with his focus even more on the earth, Wordsworth restores the Orphean lyre rejected by Milton—as Keats will later, in the "Ode to Psyche," restore to the pagan pantheon at least one goddess evicted in Milton's Nativity Ode.

Introduction to *Nature.*"[25] Emerson certainly *did* have the "Prospectus" in mind. Echoing Hazlitt on Coleridge and an age in which "we live in retrospect" and Webster on the nation's ancestral tombs, Emerson begins the famous introduction lamenting a "retrospective age" that "builds the sepulchres of the fathers." It is an age reduced to seeing "God and nature," not as foregoing generations did, "face to face," but "through *their* eyes," that is, mediated through the past. But why? he asks, now remembering Wordsworth, both of them anticipating Wallace Stevens.

> Why should not we also enjoy an original relation to the universe? Why should not we have a poetry and philosophy of insight and not of tradition, and a religion by revelation to us, and not the history of theirs? . . . Why should we grope among the dry bones of the past, or put the living generation into masquerade out of its faded wardrobe. The sun shines to-day also. . . . There are new lands, new men, new thoughts. Let us demand our own works and laws and worship. (*E&L* 7)

Even more audaciously than an echoing Emerson, who would call for us to discard the faded wardrobe of antiquated history and religion, Wordsworth dismisses both classical myth and Milton's Judeo-Christian Paradise. And he does so by asking the same resonant rhetorical questions and concluding that the momentous discovery we make will be simple and common, an entry into reality attended, as Emerson says in the final sentence of *Nature,* "with no more wonder than the blind man feels who is gradually restored to perfect sight" (*E&L* 49). Then comes the passage Holmes had in mind, several lines of which were actually quoted by Emerson himself in 1836, in praising not Wordsworth's poetry but the best of Coleridge's prose. "Beauty," says Wordsworth,

> a living Presence of the earth,
> Surpassing the most ideal Forms
> Which craft of delicate Spirits hath composed
> From earth's materials—waits upon my steps;

25. "No writer is more deeply imbued with Wordsworth than Emerson," wrote Holmes more than a century ago, "as we cannot fail to see in turning the pages of *Nature,* his first thoroughly characteristic Essay. There is the same thought in the Preface to *The Excursion* that we find in the Introduction to *Nature*" (*Ralph Waldo Emerson,* 91–92). The importance to Emerson of Wordsworth's "Prospectus," which he printed in full in *Parnassus* under the title "Outline," has recently been emphasized by Joel Porte and Saundra Morris, who also print it in full (without comment) in the section titled "Contexts" of "Transcendentalism" in the new Norton Critical Edition (*EPP* 575–77). Their four "Context" selections include, along with Madame de Staël's résumé of her *On Germany,* Sampson Reed on "Genius" and Henry Hedge's preamble, focusing on German philosophy, to his 1833 essay "Coleridge's Literary Character."

Pitches her tents before me as I move,
An hourly neighbor. *Paradise,* and groves
Elysian, Fortunate Fields—like those of *old*
Sought in the Atlantic Main—*why should they be*
A history only of departed things,
Or a mere fiction of what never was?
For the discerning intellect of Man,
When *wedded* to this goodly universe
In love and holy passion, shall find these
A *simple* produce of the *common day.*[26]

Here *common day* does not mean what it meant in the Platonic fifth stanza of the Intimations Ode, in which the splendor of eternity has faded into the "light of common day." Instead, *common* is honorific—as in the ode's opening stanza, when "The earth and every *common* sight" still seem "apparelled in celestial light." In these lines of the "Prospectus," however, emphasis is less on vestiges of eternal radiance than on temporal Beauty as "a living presence of the earth" pitching her tents "before me as I move, / An hourly neighbor." Remembering this passage, with its immediacy and personal engagement, Emerson will ask: "Why should we not have a poetry and philosophy of *insight* and *not of tradition,* and a religion by revelation to *us,* and not the *history of theirs*?" Of our dreams and visions, Wordsworth asks, "Why should they be a history only of departed things, / Or a mere fiction of what never was?" Borrowing from himself, Wordsworth would later insist—in famous lines Emerson knew since Coleridge had extracted the entire "Bliss was it in that dawn to be alive" passage from the French Revolutionary books of *The Prelude*—that he would exercise his skill,

Not in Utopia,—subterranean fields,—
Or some secreted island, Heaven knows where!
But in the very world, which is the world
Of all of us,—the place where, in the end,
We find our happiness, or not at all!
(*P* 11:140–44)[27]

26. Wordsworth, "Prospectus," 42–55 (*WP* 2:38; italics added). Emerson quotes lines 45–47 in his 1836 lecture "Modern Aspects of Letters" (*EL* 1:378–79; see also *EL* 2:273). For Holmes's comment, see *Ralph Waldo Emerson,* 91–92.

27. Coleridge had published the forty-line passage in *The Friend* (1:225–26). The immediate context of the lines—Wordsworth's enthusiastic response to the early stages of the French Revolution—may explain why Yeats singled them out as his example both of Wordsworth averting his eyes "from half of human fate" and proof of unwarranted political optimism. He may, however, have echoed the lines in "In Memory of Eva Gore Booth and Con Markiewicz," where one of the sisters "dreams I know not what, / Some vague Utopia."

He was recalling his own earlier, apolitical dismissal of dreams, myths, fables, and vague utopias, past or future, in the "Prospectus"—as does Emerson, both in the introduction to *Nature* and in "The American Scholar," in his embrace of the common, the familiar, the low. "Give me," he says, "insight into to-day, and you may have the antique and future worlds" (*E&L* 68–69). Like Wordsworth, who finds his paradise a "simple produce of the common day," Emerson is recalling Milton's Adam, who, having been instructed by the archangel Raphael to be "*lowly* wise," turns away from "things remote" to "know" instead that "That which before us lies in daily life / Is the prime wisdom" (*PL* 8:173, 191–94).

However exalted the heights they reach, Wordsworth and Emerson are "grounded" visionaries. Even when, in the "Prospectus," Wordsworth invokes the "prophetic Spirit," he also promises, echoing Milton there too, the "more *lowly* matter" of his own experiences. Thus, *The Prelude* offers the necessary autobiographical account of the building up of the mind and soul of the particular seer whose vision was to be imparted in the master project to be called *The Recluse*. Before that universalized vision could be conveyed, Wordsworth's personal bona fides had to be established. Thus, compelled to mix the high sublime and general with the lowly and particular, he will,

> with the thing
> Contemplated, describe the Mind and Man
> Contemplating; and who, and what he was—
> The transitory Being that beheld
> The Vision; when and where, and how he lived.
> (94–98)

Given this emphasis on the preliminary need to describe the particular individual, boy and man, who interacted in specific ways with the world of nature, it is not surprising that the "Prospectus" should resemble Emerson's introduction to *Nature,* and that book 1 of *The Prelude* should perform the same function as Emerson's opening chapter. In that chapter, Emerson will go on to vividly re-create—in a Wordsworthian recollection in tranquillity animated by all the wild ecstasies of the original, immediate experience—his own personal responses to the minute particulars of nature: what he observed, what he saw, in this or that season, on such and such a day, in a specific locale. The most famous instance, of course, is the transparent-eyeball passage. In short, the Emersonian epiphany, like the Wordsworthian spot of time, is, however it may evoke the transcendent, always rooted in the concrete reality of nature, its limited yet cherished point of origin. His book *Nature* succeeds or fails to the extent that the initial experiences recounted in the opening chapter move his readers, even (to use a relevant Whitmanian verb) "tally" with their own experiences.

The method is precisely that of Wordsworth, the opening book of whose *Prelude* re-creates, first his visceral, then his contemplative, responses as he lives through the changing seasons of the natural world. Those readers whom Wordsworth cannot engage, cannot "grab," with these opening scenes (the greatest of which, we noticed earlier, was a favorite of Emerson's) will probably not be moved by the rest of the work, the success and the effect of which greatly depend, just as in Emerson's *Nature,* on the impact of the great opening section. And what was true of *The Prelude* was true as well of *The Excursion.* Of the *Prelude*-paralleling lines in the opening book of *The Excursion,* the passage in which the "Wordsworthian" boyhood of the Wanderer is presented as a series of epiphanic moments experienced in the presence of Nature, Emerson declares (in his 1840 *Dial* essay "Thoughts on Modern Literature"): "Obviously for that passage the poem was written" (*EPP* 342).

The need to anchor prophetic sublimity in personal experience may help explain why, in the course of writing what was intended to be an autobiographical prolegomenon to the main work, Wordsworth discovered that he was in fact already writing much of the grand philosophic epic long urged upon him by Coleridge—a magnum opus never completed in the form intended.[28] At some point early on it must have dawned on Wordsworth that the "prophetic Spirit" invoked in the "Prospectus" was not all that different from—himself! To some extent, the union of the Wordsworthian or egotistical sublime with naturalistic humanism is traceable in the evolving drafts of the "Prospectus." In three manuscript versions, the "prophetic Spirit," instead of *inspiring* "the human soul of universal earth" and *possessing* "a" temple in the hearts of poets, seems identical with that soul and temple: "Come thou prophetic Spirit, *soul of Man*..."—a spirit and human soul that has "*Thy* metropolitan temple in the hearts / Of mighty Poets."[29] Given this equation of prophecy and human poetry, this divinity within, this fusion of man, soul, heart, and earth,

28. However, in a full-scale textual and biographical study (including close attention to the role of Coleridge), Kenneth R. Johnston argued in 1984 that, far from being a "great failure," *The Recluse* exists "not as an unrealized idea, but as a coherent though incomplete body of interrelated texts, comprising nearly twenty thousand lines of poetry susceptible of constructive reading" (*Wordsworth and "The Recluse,"* xi). This view of *The Recluse* as shaping Wordsworth's canon and motivating the whole of his subsequent writing agenda was extended in Alan Bewell's *Wordsworth and the Enlightenment: Nature and Society in the Experimental Poetry.*

29. For the "Prospectus" manuscripts, see the appendix to Abrams's *Natural Supernaturalism,* 470–79.

"Why" indeed "should" our dreams of paradise be *tuitional,* "A history only of departed things, / Or a mere fiction of what never was"—instead of being found *intuitively,* through our marriage with nature, hourly and immediately, as a simple produce of the common day?

❧ In the lines of the Shakespeare sonnet (107) Wordsworth is echoing, "the *prophetic soul* / Of the wide world" is depicted "dreaming on things to come." Among others, Wallace Stevens was to come, an appropriate poet with whom to end this chapter, and this section, since he is a disciple of both Wordsworth and Emerson, the author of a poem rhetorically and thematically indebted to the very texts we have been discussing.

Between them, Wordsworth and Emerson gave Stevens the precise formulation he would place in the consciousness of his woman in "Sunday Morning." As "the great modern poem of absenting oneself from church forever, of leaving religion for the pleasure of playing out to ourselves the origin and death of God,"[30] "Sunday Morning" is part of a literature that has found its starting point, as Hillis Miller and others have noted, in the Nietzschean death of God. But the poem is no less Wordsworthian and Emersonian than Nietzschean, especially in its celebration of the divinity within.[31] Refusing, like Emerson, to live in retrospect amid the "sepulchres" of the fathers, Stevens's woman chooses, instead of attendance at church, bright, quick things far from any faded wardrobe: "oranges in a sunny chair, / And the green freedom of a cockatoo," which mingle "to dissipate / The holy hush of ancient sacrifice," associated with "silent Palestine, / Dominion of the blood and sepulchre" (2–15). Structuring her position in the form of a series of rhetorical questions, the poet imagines her asking herself the very questions Wordsworth and Emerson had asked before her in their wilder, untamed versions of green freedom:

> Why should she give her bounty to the dead?
> What is divinity if it can come
> Only in silent shadows and in dreams?
> (16–18)

As part of the nature-embosomed vision of immanent "revelation" and new "worship" he passed on to Emerson and, eventually, to Stevens, Words-

30. Kazin, *God and the American Writer,* 18.

31. "Sunday Morning" (*Collected Poems,* 66–70) is, of course, in cadence and imagery, a Wordsworthian, Keatsian, Tennysonian poem. Perhaps its very plethora of antecedents, and his application to "Sunday Morning" of his theoretical paradigm, caused Bloom to omit Emerson as a precursor on this occasion. He discusses "Sunday Morning" in *Wallace Stevens,* 27–35.

worth sang his epithalamion in anticipation of that "great consummation" in which the human mind is "wedded" to the external world in love and holy passion. Then we will find the ideals we have projected in our fictive versions of paradise to be no more, and no less, than a "simple produce of the common day." "The sun shines to-day also," says Emerson in choosing an unmediated revelation rooted in our living interaction with nature and unburdened by the dead weight of historical religion. Stevens's woman seems even more immersed in a sunlit, earthly paradise:

> Shall she not find in comforts of the sun,
> In pungent fruit and bright, green wings, or else
> In any balm or beauty of *the earth*
> *Things* to be cherished like the *thought* of *heaven*
> *Divinity must live within herself.*
>
> (19–23)

As Stevens says elsewhere, "Poetry / Exceeding music must take the place / Of empty heaven and its hymns," for "the greatest poverty is not to live / In a physical world." We *must* live in this physical world, experiencing the very air "swarming," with the "metaphysical changes that occur, / Merely in living as and where we live."[32] We can trace the evolution, in "Sunday Morning," of an evermore natural and human form of worship, a mini-history of religion preeminently shaped by British High Romanticism and American Transcendentalism—at least the "realist" and immanent rather than the "idealist" and metaphysical aspect of Transcendentalism. In a rueful and realistic journal entry of March 1845, an amused, or at least amusing, Emerson prophesied that, "after this generation, mysticism should go out of fashion for a very long time." In his perceptiveness, Emerson may have anticipated the paradoxically "de-Transcendentalizing" current perspective stressed by those who, italicizing one long-suppressed "German" connection, have been presenting a notably Nietzschean, this-worldly Emerson.[33]

This is a perspective congenial to Stevens, who read Nietzsche in English and German and for whom heaven, conceived of as a realm metaphysical and remote, is necessarily emptied of significance if its principal tenant, God, is not "out" *there* but "in" *here,* within each of us. Having posited in the physical world palpable "*things* to be cherished like," and substituted for, the intangible, abstract "*thought* of heaven," Stevens's woman asserts

32. The poems quoted are, respectively, sec. 5 of "The Man with the Blue Guitar" and sec. 15 of "Esthetique du Mal" (Stevens, *Collected Poems,* 167, 325–26).

33. The term *de-Transcendentalizing* seems to have been coined by Buell. See Michael Lopez, "De-transcendentalizing Emerson," 77–139, and *Emerson and Power: Creative Antagonism in the Nineteenth Century.*

that "Divinity must live *within herself.*" As Stevens knew, Emerson had, in the Divinity School Address, rejected as the first impoverishing error of historical Christianity the concept of an external deity: "That is always best which gives me to myself. . . . Obey thyself. That which shows God in me fortifies me. That which shows God out of me, makes me a wart and a wen" (*E&L* 81). Stevens declares, in his prose "Adagia," that "God is in me or else is not at all (does not exist)." At such times he sounds like both Emerson and Nietzsche, and, in fact, it was in *The Gay Science,* a volume once prefaced by an epigraph from Emerson, that Nietzsche dreamed dreams of a Superman "once man ceases to *flow out* into a god."[34] Hence, divinity lives "within" us, as it does within the woman of "Sunday Morning."

In her third-person meditation, three rhetorical questions arise regarding the modern heirs of the earthly paradise legacy Stevens quarried from aspects of Nietzsche, Emerson before him, Wordsworth before *him,* and perhaps—and, as usual, at the head of the visionary procession—Milton's angel Raphael:

> Shall our blood fail? Or shall it come to be
> The blood of paradise? And shall the earth
> Be all of paradise that we shall know?
> (39–41)

These rhetorical questions evoke the question posed by Raphael in *Paradise Lost:*

> what if Earth
> Be but the shadow of Heaven, and things therein
> Each to the other like, more than on earth is thought?
> (*PL* 5:574–76)

In his thoughts about "Immortality," Emerson singles out these lines, lines he believed had "anticipated" Swedenborg's "leading thought," namely, the concept of a "future life" as a "continuing" of "earthly experience," an "intelligible heaven" in which "all nature will accompany us" (*W* 8:327). Stevens's female persona is "content" to equate paradise with the Wordsworthian green earth, not some utopian realm located "Heaven knows where," but—in the final lines of that *Prelude* extract (*P* 11:140–44) printed by Coleridge—"the very world, which is the world / Of all of us," the place "where, in the end, / We find our happiness or not at all" (*F* 1:226). In having her choose an earthly paradise, Stevens has her pass

34. Stevens, "Adagia," in *Opus Posthumous,* 172; Nietzsche, *The Gay Science,* § 285 (italics in original).

by—as Wordsworth does in the "Prospectus"—both terrifying monsters and visionary dreams:

> There is not any haunt of prophecy,
> Nor any old chimera of the grave,
> Neither the golden underground, nor isle
> Melodious, where spirits gat them home,
> Nor visionary South, nor cloudy palm
> Remote on heaven's hill, that has endured
> As April's green endures; or will endure
> Like her remembrance of June and evening, tipped
> By the consummation of the swallow's wings.
> (52–60)

But, less than fully persuaded by the all too aesthetic axiom that "Death is the mother of beauty," she "still feels," even in the "contentment" she claims, "The need of some imperishable bliss" (61–63). Here again are the apparently irrepressible immortal longings associated with traditional religion or the more heterodox Romantic and Transcendentalist intimations. But in the end, Stevens's musing woman seems to settle for that half of the Romantic-Transcendental polarity that remains, in keeping with the imperative of Nietzsche's Zarathustra, "faithful to the earth." It is a "pagan" yet essentially Wordsworthian and Emersonian "consummation," celebrating mind's marriage with nature; we may "live in an old chaos of the sun," unsponsored by any external deity (110–12), yet

> Deer walk upon our mountains, and the quail
> Whistle about us their spontaneous cries;
> Sweet berries ripen in the wilderness. . . .
> (114–16)

This is our condition, another Romantic consolation for loss and a finding of what will suffice—even though that image of the swallows' wings anticipates the *final* "consummation," when,

> in the isolation of the sky,
> At evening, casual flocks of pigeons make
> Ambiguous undulations as they sink,
> Downward, to darkness, on extended wings.
> (117–20)

Less heroically "Nietzschean" than Yeats's proud swan preparing, in "Nineteen Hundred and Nineteen," to "ride or play / Those winds that clamour of approaching night" (60–68), Stevens's death image could hardly be more gracefully tragic, an epitome of *amor fati.* And yet, and yet . . . for all their embrace of this green world, neither Wordsworth nor Emerson ever ceded it parity with the mind of man, the divinity within. And, perhaps, in the end, not even Wallace Stevens could be "content" with the earth, not because he thought (to employ his key terms) Reality was less to be valued than Imagination, but because he could not really eradicate *his* need for the imperishable. The Wordsworthian canon—his own poetry and the poetry and prose of those who followed in his, and Coleridge's, footsteps—is shot through with visionary gleams. And those gleams, colored but never obliterated by the pathos of mutability, remain, in some more than natural sense, "the light of all our day."

In this chapter as in those that precede it, I have tried to trace something of Emerson's Miltonic-Romantic heritage, not (as I said at the outset) so much to dramatically *alter* our contemporary image of Emerson as to *enrich* it and to reveal the ideational and even verbal genesis of some of his most audaciously "self-reliant" texts: borrowed and adapted texts that, nevertheless—in accordance with both the fusion of the individual with the Universal Mind and the paradox of originality—remain authentically "Emersonian." Having placed the opening of American Romanticism's seminal text, *Nature,* in its larger, international Romantic context, looking back to Coleridge and Wordsworth and ahead to Nietzsche and Stevens, this chapter has reached its own Stevensian "consummation." The next, and final, section of this study concentrates on the most personal aspect of Emersonian absorption within the Miltonic and Romantic visionary company: the impact of his "benefactors," Wordsworth above all, on Emerson's various responses to the deaths of those he loved.

Part IV

THE ART OF LOSING

Chapter 11

Emersonian "Optimism" and "The Stream of Tendency"

He is the youngest man I know. . . . At times he made me internally impatient with his inveterate and fatalistic optimism; he admits no facts that bear against his philosophy.

—CHARLES ELIOT NORTON to James Russell Lowell, describing Emerson on his seventieth birthday

Readers lulled by his confident tones have missed the precariousness by which he maintains his apparent equilibrium. We have mistaken equilibrium for equanimity.

—JOSEPH DOHERTY, "Emerson and the Loneliness of the Gods"

[Wordsworth] had sought for compensation, and found it, in the way in which he was now teaching me to find it.

—JOHN STUART MILL on the Intimations Ode

Rectitude is a perpetual victory, celebrated not by cries of joy, but by serenity, which is joy fixed or habitual.

—RALPH WALDO EMERSON, "Character"

The Intimations Ode, a numinous presence throughout this study, continues to shed its master light in these final chapters, on "The Art of Losing." Here the focus is specifically elegiac, on mourning and consolation in distress. In the great poem enshrining "intimations of immortality," the "radiance which was once so bright" is "now forever taken" from the poet's "sight," and, in the final stanza, the orange sky of evening that "died" away in the skating scene in book 1 of *The Prelude* (446) reappears in the form of "clouds" that, gathering "round / The setting sun" as at a deathbed, "take a sober colouring from an eye / That hath kept watch o'er man's mortality." Yet as a poem not merely about growing *old,* or even about growing *up,* the ode, as Helen Vendler has noted, finds its human and aesthetic consolation in the vision of a matured man and a master artist, able to convert suffering and the world of nature itself into poetic symbol.

Haunted as he was by Wordsworth's ode, it is all but inevitable that Emerson would be engaged in a related struggle—most fully developed if less than successfully resolved in "Threnody"—to find light in the lethal darkness, to regain what was "lost." Dealing with Emerson's supposed obliviousness to the pain and evil of the world and his mode of mourning the repeated early deaths of those he loved, I argue that his final affirmation is colored by Wordsworthian consolation, in the form either of "the light of all our day" or of Wordsworth's sober and muted assertion (in "Elegiac Stanzas") that it is "not without hope we suffer and we mourn." In that Wordsworthian light, Emerson's forms of mourning for his wife, brothers, and son—including the elegy for Waldo, "Threnody"—emerge as related and deeply felt exercises in the art of losing.

Because such a conclusion flies in the face of Emerson's reputation, this chapter engages, by way of preamble, the familiar issue of the absence in "serene" Emerson of a "tragic vision." Though plausible, that received portrait—the benignly smiling idealist complacently oblivious to evil and pain—is a caricature, based on at least partial misconception.[1] What has been understandably but inadequately described—reflecting that legendary

1. The following portrait of a famous American was presented in the October 10, 2002, issue of the *New York Review of Books.* The work of this "earnest, cheerful man" is "distinguished mostly by its sense of ease." His readers "enter a universe that seems to have no place for pain." An exponent of "tranquil gratitude," he seems less "troubled . . . than most of us are." For those not disposed to him, "his very serenity" may look "like complacency." He has "a great gift for seeing the best in things, a determined refusal to be troubled by too much complexity, [and] a winning ability . . . to offer a smiling reassurance." His "confidence" makes it "genuinely hard for him to understand those who don't share his sanguine view of things," his "determination not to look too closely at what's unsettling." But this "providential" and "resolute buoyancy can exact a cost." There "remains a reluctance to look at evil . . . It's always sunny and breezy in his world . . . and the boat is guaranteed always to return to harbor" (Pico Iyer, "Morning in America," 14). This sketch is of William F. Buckley Jr. That many readers would have guessed he was describing Emerson is a tribute to the power of received portraits. However much they exaggerate and distort, caricatures have their basis in fact, but, *in* fact, Iyer's portrait captures more of Buckley than it does of Emerson, however "Emersonian" it may sound.

Emersonian "optimism" impervious to evidence of evil—as a refusal to mourn actually takes the form, under the auspices of the inward or higher "light," of a reconciliation of such polar antagonisms as Fate and Freedom, defeat and victory, issuing in the conviction, even in the face of repeated personal and familial tragedy, that "hope" remains inextinguishable. The man who cries out in the wake of his boy's death, "I am *Defeated* all the time, yet to Victory am I born" (*JMN* 8:228), neither succumbs to Fate, *nor* refuses to mourn. Yet recent emphases by Emersonian scholars on "creative antagonism" rather than naive optimism, achieved "equilibrium" rather than complacent "equanimity," check and moderate rather than refute the received impression. When all is said and done, Emerson's stance remains (whether admirably, inexplicably, or maddeningly) serene. It seems only honest to set up, at the outset, what may be the single most substantial stumbling block to any argument that Emerson's was a darker and more complex vision than we tend to credit him with.

In his 1838 lecture series on human life, Emerson devoted talks to comedy and tragedy. Both were reprised in the *Dial,* "Tragedy" appearing as "The Tragic" in the April 1844 issue.[2] Like the tragedy lecture six years earlier, the essay "The Tragic" began with a now famous line borrowed from an 1827 letter to his aunt, "He has seen but half the universe who has never been shown the House of Pain." Emerson went on to refer to "vice, pain, disease, poverty, insecurity, disunion, fear, and death," only to conclude his opening paragraph by describing the items in this litany of horrors as "values" in any adequate "theory of life" (515). The "bitterest tragic element" in human life, he says in the process of making a crucial distinction, is "the belief in a brute Fate or Destiny," a terrifying concept to be "discriminated from the doctrine of Philosophical Necessity," a form of "Optimism" in which "the suffering individual finds *his* good consulted in the good of *all,* of which he is a *part*" (515–16; italics added). *This* form of optimism, which he endorsed throughout his life, derives in part from his absorption of Coleridge's concept of "each and all" (*F* 1:511) and faith in what Emerson elsewhere calls, repeatedly echoing Wordsworth, the beneficent "stream of tendency." In such a progressive vision, incorporating the long philosophic tradition in which "evil" is denied substantial "reality," even the worst apparent evil enhances "our strength."

> Frankly then it is necessary to say that all sorrow dwells in a low region. It is superficial; for the most part fantastic, or in the appearance and not in things. Tragedy is in the eye of the observer, and not in the heart of the sufferer. . . . The spirit is true to itself, and finds its own support in any condition, learns

2. For "Tragedy," see *EL* 1:104–10. My parenthetical page references are to "The Tragic," *Dial* 4 (April 1844): 515–21.

> to live in what is called calamity, as easily as in what is called felicity, as the frailest glass-bell will support a weight of a thousand pounds of water at the bottom of a river or sea, if filled with the same. (517–18)

Emulating the ancient Stoics (or the attitude expressed in the faces of Egyptian sculpture, "countenances expressive of complacency and repose," to which "the Greek genius added an ideal beauty, without disturbing the seals of serenity"), a man "should not commit his tranquillity to *things,* but should keep as much as possible the reins *in his own hands,* rarely giving way to extreme emotion of joy or grief." Thus, "human calamities" find their "particular reliefs . . . for the world will be in equilibrium, and hates all manner of exaggeration." Our tears will be dried by "the consoler, time," since "Nature will not sit still": "new hopes spring, new affections twine, and the broken is whole again" (518–19). The admitted "horrors of 'the middle passage'" provide a grotesquely unfeeling example of the supposed truth that "most suffering is only apparent" and apportioned to the capacity of the—in this case, "obtuse and barbarous"—sufferers (520). Finally, Emerson, after quoting a remark made by Napoléon, to which I will return, concludes by treating "the tragic" as both an aesthetic and an intellectual-spiritual phenomenon—a remarkable anticipation of Nietzsche, both in *The Birth of Tragedy* and in the major works of his maturity:

> The intellect is a consoler, which delights in detaching, or putting an interval between man and his fortune, and so converts the sufferer into a spectator, and his pain into poetry. . . . The torments of life become tuneful tragedy, solemn and soft with music, and garnished with rich dark pictures. But higher still than the activities of art, the intellect in its purity, and the moral sense in its purity, are not distinguished from each other, and both ravish us into a region whereinto these passionate clouds of sorrow cannot rise. (521)

Fine; but tragic joy seems more palatable, more authentically joyful, in Nietzsche's disciple, Yeats, and, certainly, in the *gaya scienza* and Dionysianism of Emerson's own disciple, Nietzsche himself.

As for that Napoleonic observation cited in the penultimate paragraph of "The Tragic," the remark Emerson quotes was made by the fallen emperor to one of his friends on Saint Helena: "Nature seems to have calculated that I should have great reverses to endure, for she has given me a temperament like a block of marble. Thunder cannot move it; the shaft merely glides along. The great events of my life have slipped over me without making any impression on my moral or physical nature" (521). Between the 1838 lecture "Tragedy" and the printing of "The Tragic" in the *Dial,* little Waldo died. In private letters and in the great essay "Experience," published in October 1844, Emerson would say, in perhaps the most disturbing and problematic passages he ever wrote, almost precisely this in describing his response to the death of his little boy.

Emerson's may be a case, especially after the death of Waldo, of what has been called a "demanding optimism," but it is optimism nonetheless. In his influential *Freedom and Fate* (1953), Stephen Whicher presents Waldo's death as the transformative event in Emerson's life and career, the point at which affirmation yielded to resignation, freedom to fate. Cogent corrective views begin with Newton Arvin's 1959 "The House of Pain" and continue in Gertrude Reif Hughes's *Emerson's Demanding Optimism* (1984), Christopher Lasch's *True and Only Heaven: Progress and Its Critics* (1991), and, in a more recent revisionist (and Nietzsche-influenced) interpretation, Michael Lopez's *Emerson and Power: Creative Antagonism in the Nineteenth Century* (1996). I participate in this tradition by placing Emersonian optimism in its experiential, Stoic, and Romantic contexts. No stranger to suffering, Emerson found his Freedom in Necessity, and much of his solace in the tempered affirmation ("Not without hope . . .") of Wordsworth. Thus, Emersonian optimism emerges as not the tragic joy of Nietzsche and Yeats, but at least a hard-won rather than facile affirmative vision of what Wordsworth's Wanderer calls "The mighty stream of tendency." From this elevated perspective, Emerson himself can seem either a naif or a cold fish. The Emersonian mask of serenity sometimes seems indistinguishable from the face beneath, and at times Emerson could *be,* not merely *seem,* unfeeling, aloof, indifferent to human suffering. For the most part, however, he recognizes "the tragic" and struggles, in his life and thought, to surmount it. He does so through the exercise of "character" and "power," and by reaffirming an assaulted but unconquerable belief in a divinity within, which he associates with Wordsworth's "fountain light of all our day."[3]

The caricature of Emerson as an unfeeling man whose theory of "optimism" so blinded him to a vision of evil as to render him incapable of experiencing pain and suffering may be corrected by examining, through a Romantic lens, his responses to the terrible sequence of deaths in his

3. Arvin's essay is reprinted in Milton Konvitz and Stephen Whicher, eds., *Emerson: A Collection of Critical Essays,* 46–59. Lasch's important observations are to be found in his subchapter titled "Emerson on Fate" (*True and Only Heaven,* 261–65) and the judicious pages on Emerson in his concluding "Bibliographical Essay" (546–51). As the other texts cited indicate, this question of Emerson and the tragic vision, related to the condescension with which he is often treated, has been the subject of fruitful recent reappraisal. "The Tragic," which appeared in the *Dial* in 1844 and was never reprinted by Emerson, may be found in *LL.*

family between 1831 and 1842. Wordsworth may have provided the threshold to a vision that would, "ideally," subsume and transcend an often harsh and unregenerate reality. But the experiential questions remain: What will be our response—philosophical, psychological, emotional, imaginative, "spiritual"—to our beautiful yet all too tragic scene, what Keats calls "this world of circumstances"? We know we suffer and mourn. But *is* it "not without hope"? And what form—in this world or another—does our possible consolation take?

Aware of the traditions and sources in which he was spiritually, intellectually, and emotionally steeped, one might expect an Emerson besieged by painful circumstances to turn primarily to his religion, or to the perennial philosophy of Plato and Plotinus, to the Stoicism of Seneca and Marcus Aurelius, to the Milton who offers, directly and through angelic dramatis personae, recompense for even the most grievous loss. He does, in fact, find consolation in lines spoken by the chorus in Milton's *Samson Agonistes,* but in his struggle to recover from the death of Charles in particular, a struggle that can be traced in his journal entries, Emerson resorts to Milton in order to articulate his grief rather than his recovery; for example, his lamentation that the wonderful qualities of Charles "will here be seen no more" echoes the death of Edward King and what "Shall now no more be seen" (43), in "Lycidas."

Above all, perhaps, one would expect Emerson to turn to his cherished Montaigne, that world-renowned counselor and practitioner of tranquillity of mind and a constructive calmness in affliction—especially since, like himself, Montaigne was no stranger to the House of Pain. Here was a man all of whose children but one (his only daughter, Leonora) had died in infancy—a "piercing" wound he endured, "if not without grief, at least without repining," and whose later years were shadowed by the prolonged and excruciating agony of kidney stones. Above all, he had endured a loss as transformative as the loss of Arthur Hallam (himself impressed by what he called "the felicity and brightness of Montaigne's genius") would later prove for Tennyson, or the early deaths in his own family for Emerson. The death of his great friend Etienne La Boétie was a tragedy the grief-stricken Montaigne never ceased to mourn but that nevertheless led to the writing of the *Essays*—rather as the death of Ellen changed Emerson's life and the death of his brother and closest friend, Charles, bore fruit in *Nature.* Persistently echoed in journal entries that constitute a bereft Emerson's elegy for Charles is the essay "Of Friendship," Montaigne's elegy for La Boétie. There is, one critic rightly observes, "a spooky link across more than two centuries" in the "close parallel between Emerson's loss of Charles and Montaigne's loss of La Boétie." The parallel extends to the posthumous papers left behind by the lost friends. "Like Emerson, Montaigne was forced to confront something about himself in the manuscripts his friend left him. And what those papers showed Montaigne changed him and his writing."[4]

The unexpectedly dark and hopeless papers left behind by Charles both shocked and challenged Emerson, who sought renewed hope, strength, and the "exhilaration" to go on "working" in very different kinds of writings—those not only of Montaigne, but of Wordsworth. Though no book was more important to him than Montaigne's *Essays,* written in words that, cut into, "would bleed; they are vascular and alive" (*E&L* 700, 701), Emerson also found consolation and assuagement of sorrow in that genius of "hope" William Wordsworth. It is hardly surprising that Emerson, struggling to sustain hope in the face of repeated tragedy, should turn to what, in one of his favorite Wordsworth poems, the "Prospectus" to *The Recluse,* the poet himself tells us will be his principal theme. He will sing, says Wordsworth,

> Of Truth, of Grandeur, Beauty, Love, and Hope—
> And melancholy Fear subdued by Faith;
> Of blessed consolations in distress.
>
> (14–16)

Consolation in distress formed a notable portion of Wordsworth's value to innumerable British and American readers in the nineteenth and early twentieth century, who benefited in varying degrees from what Matthew Arnold commemorated as Wordsworth's "healing power."

In "Memorial Verses," written in the very month (April 1850) that the poet died, Arnold observes that, in an "iron time," Wordsworth had "loosed our hearts in tears," had "laid us as we lay at birth / On the cool flowery lap of earth" (43, 47–49).[5] But having alluded to the sixth stanza of the Intimations Ode (where "*Earth* fills her *lap* with pleasures of her own"), Arnold evokes the ninth stanza, with its "*shadowy* recollections" of a numinous life in eternity. For now, joining the "pale ghosts" of wise Goethe and fiery Byron, Wordsworth himself has descended into the "shadowy world." In the course of time, "others" may bring us what Goethe and Byron did, but "who, ah! who, will make us feel?"

> since dark days still bring to light
> Man's prudence and man's fiery might,

4. The Emerson-Montaigne parallel is discussed by John Michael, in the chapter titled "Death and Friendship: Charles and the 'Other Self,'" in *Emerson and Skepticism: The Cipher of the World,* 92, 98, 104. Hallam is quoted from the edition of Montaigne edited by Hazlitt, *Works of Montaigne,* 26. For the earlier quotation, about grief without repining (from book 1, chap. 40), see p. 142 of this edition.

5. Arnold, *The Poems of Matthew Arnold,* 226–29.

Time may restore us in his course
Goethe's sage mind and Byron's force;
But where will Europe's latter hour
Again find Wordsworth's healing power?
(58–63)

Addressing the river that flows near Grasmere churchyard, where Wordsworth had just been buried, Arnold concludes by recalling the healer's own saving intercourse with Nature:

Keep fresh the grass upon his grave
O Rotha, with thy living wave!
Sing him the best! for few or none
Hears thy voice right, now he is gone.
(71–74)

For more than two decades before he was "gone," and even after his death, the great physician's "healing power" was drawn upon by Emerson, who went so far as to say, during his recovery from the death of Charles, that it constituted Wordsworth's "total value" (*JMN* 5:160). And what Emerson took from Wordsworth he handed on, unaware, to his most formidable reader, Nietzsche, who, during the major crisis in his own life, survived and creatively *re*vived by drawing upon Emerson in roughly the way Emerson had drawn upon Wordsworth. In both cases, *healing* power took the form of renewed *creative* power.

To Wordsworth's healing "power" there are many testimonials, a sampling of them available in the subchapter titled "Wordsworth as Evangelist" in M. H. Abrams's *Natural Supernaturalism.*[6] Among the many beneficiaries mentioned by Abrams was William James, whose reading of *The Excursion* was instrumental in his pivotal, if temporary, recovery from

6. Abrams, *Natural Supernaturalism,* 134–40. Abrams briefly discusses a number of American readers, including William Cullen Bryant (who told Richard Henry Dana in the 1820s of the heart-rejuvenating experience of reading *Lyrical Ballads*) and William Hale White (for whom Wordsworth "re-created" divinity: "God was brought down from that heaven of the books, and dwelt on the downs . . . and in every cloud-shadow which wandered across the valley"). After citing the classic passage from the "Crisis" chapter of John Stuart Mill's *Autobiography* (discussed below), William Hale White's semifictional *Autobiography of Mark Rutherford,* and the 1954 autobiography of Bede Griffiths, *The Golden String,* Abrams concludes, synoptically: "All process, Romantic thinkers believed, moves forward and also rounds back. Wordsworth's absorption of the personal God into a sacramental nature in communion with an apotheosized faculty of mind, which had resolved his own crisis and assisted other men to resolve theirs, and which had converted Mill from Benthamism and . . . White from Augustinianism, now helped put Bede Griffiths on the way back to the prototype of the mind's religious colloquy with nature" (139–40).

psychological crisis in the spring of 1873. But although James has a special relationship to Emerson, Abrams does not mention the troubled Sage of Concord. This seems odd since Emerson was even more indebted—over a longer period of time and with greater apparent success than James—to Wordsworth as his "benefactor," a source of Stoic fortitude and grief-transcending "hope."

Depending on our own beliefs and life experiences, these Wordsworth-inspired recoveries from crisis will seem dubious or persuasive, contemptible or noble—either outmoded indulgences in comforting illusion or vague but undeniable intimations of some ground of "hope" sanctioning the immortal longings in us. However shadowed by modern skeptical doubt or even ridicule, those longings, or "intimations"—whether the impulse is ontological or biological in origin—seem to be imperishable. That they remain ineffable is confirmed by Wordsworth's Great Ode itself, according to Emerson our "best modern essay" on the mystery of "immortality" (*W* 8:346). Whatever they are—"be they what they may," as Wordsworth says in the ode (151), candidly acknowledging his ignorance of ultimate mystery—these intimations, these *recollections* of a lost light, are eventually shadowed but not obliterated by mortality and pain. Indeed, the experience of human suffering is indispensable to any counterbalancing concept of "hope" and "power," as well as to any matured vision of the spirit as imperishable. Toward the conclusion of his ode-echoing elegy for his son ("Threnody," lines 286–87), Emerson evokes "Apples of Eden," but apples "ripe" only because they have been watered "with tears of ancient sorrow" (*EPP* 461–62). Since the bittersweet fruit of hard-earned affirmation arises from the pathos of mutability, neither these Emersonian "tears" nor Wordsworthian "Thoughts that do often lie *too deep for tears*" (Intimations Ode, 204) can be dismissed as a naively falsifying and cheery optimism impervious to evil and pain. Besides, however deficient Emerson's tragic vision, and *whatever* he "believed," it was no normative concept of "immortality."

At once skeptical and optimistic, Emerson acknowledges "two absorbing facts,—*I and the Abyss.*" But he often seems unwilling to peer too deeply into that abyss.[7] The same accusation has been leveled against Wordsworth. Even Arnold, a great admirer, claims that Wordsworth achieved his "sweet calm" only by averting his eyes "from half of human fate," a charge echoed by Yeats when he accuses Wordsworth of avoiding "obstacles" to his optimism by "blotting out one half of life." Emerson seems to ally

7. Emerson said in a note of September 1866, "For every seeing soul there are two absorbing facts,—*I and the Abyss.*" On the "abyss" and Emersonian optimism, see AnnLouise Keating, "Renaming the Dark: Emerson's Optimism and the Abyss."

himself with Wordsworth, explicitly accepting that charge as applied to himself in his ringing imperatives: "Speak the affirmative; emphasize your choice by utter ignoring of all that you reject," an optimism-dictated neglect of inconvenient facts that tested the patience even of his friend Norton.[8]

At the risk of trivializing, I offer a small example of what may constitute such repressive affirmation. The least known of Emerson's favorite Wordsworth poems, "Fidelity" (*WP* 1:646–48), can be taken in more than one way. A shepherd, unexpectedly encountering a dog in a remote region, shortly thereafter discovers on the ground nearby "a human skeleton." It is that of the dog's master, a man the shepherd had seen passing through some "three months" earlier, not long before the "ill-fated Traveler" had fallen to his death from the "perilous rocks" above. The dog, whose fidelity deserves the poet's "lasting monument of words," had hovered in this "savage place" all that time, watching "about the spot, / Or by his master's side." The poem evokes an eerie mountain solitude, but it was surely Wordsworth's spiritual conclusion—lines praised by Coleridge (*BL* 2:120)—that endeared "Fidelity" to Emerson enough for him to include it among Wordsworth's best (*JMN* 5:335):

> How nourished here through such long time
> He knows, who gave that love sublime;
> And gave that strength of feeling, great
> Above all human estimate!
>
> (62–65)

However reluctantly, one can, glancing again at those skeletal remains, conjure up a less mysterious, and anything but divine, explanation of the dog's "nourished" survival. But that unappealing scenario seems not to have occurred either to Wordsworth or Emerson—unless, as charged, they deliberately chose not to entertain the grisly thought, stressing idealist affirmation by means of what Emerson advocates as "utter ignoring of all that you reject."

Understandably more attracted to "love sublime" than to the dark side (including the necessity of caloric intake), most of us will nevertheless prefer the pluralism of William James. "The first thing to bear in mind," he says in *The Varieties of Religious Experience*, ". . . is that nothing can be more stupid than to bar out phenomena from our notice, merely because we are incapable of taking any part in them ourselves." He is almost cer-

8. See first epigraph to this chapter (Norton and Emerson shared the latter's seventieth birthday aboard a ship). See also Emerson, "The Preacher" (in *Lectures and Biographical Sketches*, 1883); Arnold, "Stanzas in Memory of the Author of 'Obermann'" (lines 53–54, *Poems of Arnold*, 132); and Yeats, "If I Were Four-and-Twenty," in *Explorations*, 275–76.

tainly thinking of Emerson—whose eyes, William's brother Henry would later claim, were "thickly bandaged to the evil and sin of the world." William James revered Emerson for his vision of the commonest individual as the potential conduit of "the great Cosmic Intellect," that "invisible divine" with which his "life was one long conversation." Yet Emerson, though not "an optimist of the sentimental type," seemed to James—as he did to Hawthorne and Melville, T. S. Eliot and Robert Penn Warren—a man deficient in comprehending the pain and suffering that plays so large a part in the reality of most people. William James felt, as "a distinct lack" in Emerson, "too little understanding of the morbid side of life."[9]

Despite such utterances, by others and, on occasion, by himself, and despite his severely tested but always reaffirmed "hope," Emerson was no foolish Pangloss. The long history of this image of Emerson as a "cheery, childlike soul, impervious to the evidence of evil," received something of a classical imprimatur in the 1911 essay I am citing, George Santayana's beautifully written, widely read, very influential, and rather unsubstantiated essay "The Genteel Tradition in American Philosophy." That image—of an open, admirable, yet thoughtless idealist—was qualified yet essentially reaffirmed in James Truslow Adams's 1930 essay "Emerson Re-read," in which we are told that Emerson, with his "fatally easy philosophy" and "shallow optimism," makes "life too easy by his insistence on intuition and spontaneity." Seizing on Emerson's remark in "Self-Reliance" about "the nonchalance of boys who are sure of a dinner" (*E&L* 261), Adams asks rhetorically: "Can any words better express the American attitude toward the universe, and, in spite of his spirituality and the somewhat faded fresco of his mysticism, does Emerson himself really give us anything deeper?" William James was fully aware of Emerson's limitations, yet his preparation for his lecture on the occasion of the 1903 centennial—"reading the whole of him over again"—"has made me feel his real greatness as I never did before." The effect of Adams's rereading of (some) Emerson in 1930 was quite different.[10]

Between Santayana and Adams there was the T. S. Eliot of the Sweeney quatrains, three exercises in the sardonic in *Poems* (1920). Vulgar Sweeney

9. *Varieties of Religious Experience* is cited from W. James, *Writings, 1902–1910,* 105. Also cited are *The Letters of William James,* 2:197; and James's "Address at the Centenary of Ralph Waldo Emerson, May 25, 1903," in *Writings, 1902–1910,* 1121, 1125. H. James's remark occurs in *Partial Portraits* (1888), 31, reprinted in James's *Literary Criticism.*

10. Santayana, "Genteel Tradition"; Adams, "Emerson Re-read," 188–91. An older Adams, Henry, in the opening pages of his *Education of Henry Adams,* dismissed Emerson as a "naif."

("Apeneck" in "Sweeney among the Nightingales") is also the representative of animalistic, spirit-denying flesh in "Mr. Eliot's Sunday Morning Service." In that poem's final stanza, while a Prufrockian "Mr. Eliot" goes to church, "Sweeney shifts from ham to ham / Stirring the water in his bath" (29–30), a split between the hyperconscious, inhibited intellectual and the sensualist of base but immediate gratification dualistically embodying Eliotic "dissociation of sensibility." But what has all *this* to do with the perception of the almost disembodied Emerson as a shallow idealist impervious to evil? Eliot had told us in the first (though the last written) of the Sweeney poems in the 1920 volume.

Its very title, "Sweeney Erect," may be a phallic pun on Emerson's insistence, in "Self-Reliance," on the "sovereignty" and "majesty" of "the erect position." Like "Self-Reliance," the poem is preceded by an epigraph from Beaumont and Fletcher (the epilogue to *Honest Man's Fortune* in Emerson's case, a passage from act 2, scene 2 of *The Maid's Tragedy* in Eliot's). In the poem itself Eliot cites Emerson by name, alluding to another famous formulation from "Self-Reliance" ("an institution is the lengthened shadow of one man" [*E&L* 267]), an axiom he fuses with the related statement in the immediately preceding essay, "History": "If the whole of history is one man, it is all to be explained from private experience" (*E&L* 237). Having risen (another "erect position") from bed, with "Gesture of orang-outang," Sweeney, "Broadbottomed, pink from nape to base," with "suds around his face," addresses the mirror "full length to shave." We are informed (in parentheses) that

> The lengthened shadow of a man
>   Is history, said Emerson
> Who had not seen the silhouette
>   Of Sweeney straddled in the sun.
>   (25–28)[11]

Of the ideas of his former Harvard professor George Santayana Eliot had a rather low opinion, an estimate reciprocated by the good professor

11. Eliot, *Complete Poems and Plays,* 35, 34, 25–26. Lines 33–38 of "Sweeney Erect"—in which the "ladies of the corridor" observe that hysteria "Might easily be misunderstood"—also echo Emerson's ironic dismissal of consistency in the 1841 edition of "Self-Reliance": "Ah, then, exclaim the aged ladies, you shall be sure to be misunderstood" (the ladies are dropped in the 1847 edition; *E&L* 265). The "relationship" between Eliot's poem and Emerson's "Self-Reliance" and "History" has been discussed by Charles Peake, "'Sweeney Erect' and the Emersonian Hero"; the sharp differences between Eliot and Emerson are noted in Robert G. Cook, "Emerson's 'Self-Reliance,' Sweeney, and Prufrock." Interestingly, the conclusion of "Sweeney among the Nightingales"—in which the birds' "liquid siftings" stain Agamemnon's "stiff, dishonored shroud"—recalls John Greenleaf Whittier's Emerson-echoing attack (in his poem "Ichabod") on Daniel Webster's "dim, / Dishonoured brow."

when it came to Eliot's own ideas. But they could agree to some extent on Emerson, whom Santayana admired even as he condescended to him, but who was for Eliot simply *not* (as he thought Hawthorne *was*) "a real observer of the moral life." Emerson seemed to Eliot the salient representative of the socially progressive, blandly optimistic Unitarian tradition he had inherited and that in some ways marked him but that he nevertheless despised and abandoned even before he got to Harvard.[12] Thus, in "Sweeney Erect," in line with the benign but distorted image presented by Santayana in the "Genteel Tradition" essay, we are offered an Emerson of childlike innocence, a naive idealist unaware of the all too real: the ugliness and evil he "had not seen," either because he was blind to it or because he refused to see it. In "Self-Reliance," Emerson's version of Carlyle's theory of history as the biography of great men stresses their "lengthened shadow," but Emerson's sunnily idealistic vision could not accommodate, Eliot insists, the image of simian Sweeney, this vulgarized Caliban shadowed in a glass.

If the blandly or blindly "optimistic" Emerson can be criticized for a failure to foresee the silhouette of the bestial Sweeney, he is also vulnerable to charges of inadequacy in the face of the truly dehumanized imago mirrored in a glass far more darkly. However much Emersonian history may be "biography," or the working out of what was latently enfolded in the first man, he had no foreknowledge of the history that was the lengthened shadow of a man named Hitler, the subject of more than one hundred biographies. Perhaps he *should* have anticipated such a possibility since ideas have consequences and there are troubling connections between Hitler and German idealist philosophy, the same philosophy that came to Emerson through the conduits of Coleridge and Carlyle. I have already noted that Hitler, attracted to Fichte's equation of the *Ich* with a

12. For his contrast of Hawthorne and Emerson, see Eliot's "American Literature." Eliot's grandfather—Unitarian minister, missionary, educator, and philanthropist William Greenleaf Eliot—was admired by Emerson, who met him in St. Louis (the center of American Hegelianism) and dubbed him "the Saint of the West." Though his grandson, born the year W. G. Eliot died, abandoned the family faith early, the old patriarch's role as leader, educator, and Emersonian rather than Yeatsian "smiling public man" remained to shape Eliot's own ethic. This case of public and private history as "the lengthened shadow" of a man, seems a Puritan-Victorian shadow compounding a caricatured Emerson and Matthew Arnold. We remember that while Eliot's "Cousin Nancy" (in the 1915 poem of that title) strode, rode, smoked, and danced, "Upon the glazen shelves kept watch / Matthew and Waldo, guardians of the faith, / The army of unalterable law" (*Complete Poems and Plays,* 17–18). At Harvard, Eliot's image of Emerson was shaped in part by his reading of Dante and by his favorite teacher, Irving Babbitt, whose estimate oscillated between praise (when Emerson seemed Buddhistic) and denigration (when he seemed Rousseauistic and Romantic). See Robert Bloom, "Irving Babbitt's Emerson."

"Divine-Me," was convinced that "If I live my life according to my God-given insights, then I cannot go wrong, and even if I do, I know I have acted in good faith"—a conviction remarkably like Emerson's insistence in "Self-Reliance" that "no law can be sacred" to him but that of his own nature and the integrity of his own mind, that he must "live wholly from within," and that, while his "impulses" seem to him to come not "from below," but "from above," even if "I am the Devil's child, I will live then from the Devil" (*E&L* 261–62). Given his equation of infinitude with the individual, and the categorical imperative of self-reliance and self-trust, Emerson, who has been blamed for so much by so many critics of unrestrained individualism, might even be blamed for that "devil's miracle man," the messianic psychopath whose will to power transformed the most culturally sophisticated nation on earth into the most barbaric and, together with that all too willing new Germany, produced worldwide carnage and a genocide so ferocious that it shattered our naively optimistic theories of progress and "disfigured the image of humanity itself."[13]

In fact, as we have seen, he *has* been blamed for Hitler. Emerson's apparent liberation of the unrestrained self could lead a man as intelligent as Cleanth Brooks to claim that "Emerson led to Hitler." But if Hitler, who subordinated the individual to the state, cannot fairly be laid at Emerson's doorpost—even when the liberated and liberating writings on that doorpost were reinscribed by an enchanted Nietzsche—a related question remains. What is there in Emerson, or, better, "Emersonianism," that would be answerable to a phenomenon such as the Holocaust? Responding to the manuscript version of Hyatt Waggoner's Emerson chapter in his Emerson-centered study of American poets, a friend objects with a series of questions:

> The question I must ask as a Jew living after Auschwitz is: What about the experience of extreme suffering, extreme cruelty, extreme dehumanization? Is God present also then and there? What would RWE say? Or why did he not say anything at all? Why did he choose essentially to ignore the theological implications inherent in the depths of awful experience, terrible and terrifying experience? After reading Elie Wiesel's *Night,* for instance, I find Emerson almost totally unsatisfactory in this regard—to the point where he has almost nothing to say to me whatsoever in precisely that area where he wants so much to be heard, and where you personally seem to find him at his greatest. Nothing in Emerson's poetry or prose reconciles me to this aspect of Emersonianism.[14]

13. Walter Reich, "The Devil's Miracle Man," 8–9.

14. Waggoner, *American Poets from the Puritans to the Present,* 94, 664. His Emerson chapter, "*Sursum Corda:* The Poet as Friend and Aid," alludes to Emerson's poem "Sursum Corda" and to Matthew Arnold, for whom Emerson was "a friend and guider" of those "who would live in the spirit." But Waggoner makes no reference to

If that *totally* and final *Nothing* are too sweeping, the earlier "*almost* nothing" seems fair enough. One looks largely in vain for any sustained confrontation of the depths of awful experience in the quintessential, or at least most familiar, Emerson. In the Divinity School Address, perhaps echoing *The Christian Doctrine,* where Milton claims that "every act is in itself good; it is only its irregularity, or deviation from the line of right, which properly speaking is evil," Emerson pronounces goodness and benevolence "positive" and "real," whereas "Evil is merely privative, not absolute" (*E&L* 77). Even in the great essay "Experience" itself, insisting that "the universe wears our color. . . . As I am, so I see," Emerson says of sin: the "intellect names it shade, absence of light, and no essence. The conscience must feel it as an essence, essential evil. This it is not; it has an objective existence, but no subjective." Citing the inner "spiritual law," Emerson distances himself from "the despair which prejudges the law by a paltry empiricism," choosing instead—and in the process echoing the Intimations Ode—to "entertain a hope and an insight which becomes the light of our life" (*E&L* 489, 492).

Whatever its sanction in an impressive tradition embracing Plato and Plotinus, Augustine and Milton, this doctrine strikes most of us as itself illusory and unreal, all the more so when, in that grim catalog of horrors, the essay "Fate," and in the peroration of his deepest study of skepticism, the essay on Montaigne, Emerson acknowledges Evil only to make it a means in a progressive or providential theory of irrepressible Good. "Through the years and the centuries," he insists in the Montaigne essay, "through evil agents, through toys and atoms, a great and beneficent tendency irresistibly streams" (*E&L* 709). Quoting this passage in 1959, but not noticing its Wordsworthian source, Newton Arvin professes astonishment: "'Irresistibly,' did you say? . . . To the ears of contemporary men there is a mockery of unreality in such language that makes the language of the Arabian Nights seem to ring with the strong accents of realism. In the fearful light of what has happened in history since Emerson said these things—not to speak of what happened before—can one be merely indignant if some thoughtful men have long since settled it that Emerson is not for them?"[15]

---

the author of the books to which *Arnold* would seem to be alluding (and to which Emerson was so indebted): Coleridge's *Friend* and *Aids to Reflection.* This may be attributable to Waggoner's focus on Emerson's *poetry,* though even he describes, as the central figure and "catalyst" in the American poetic tradition (xii) not the (not quite "legitimate") poet but the prose poet, the Emerson of the earlier writings.

15. Arvin, "The House of Pain: Emerson and the Tragic Sense," 49. Arvin goes on, of course, to attend to the darker aspects of Emerson's vision, even if it is a finally affirmative vision.

In responding to his obviously "thoughtful" friend's charges of inadequacy in the Emersonian response to human suffering, Waggoner admits that "I can think of no answer I would like to make to this objection," other than to say that we have "not yet, under proper conditions, tried Emerson's way," which means "listen[ing] for the Holy Spirit, as it speaks to us in history, in our personal history." Perhaps, but this defensive response, however "Emersonian," seems little more than a spiritual version of the "not-tried-yet-under-proper-conditions" apologia unreconstructed academic Marxists keep making faced with the abject failure of *their* peculiar historical "god."

Some of the American poets Emersonian Waggoner writes about are themselves, despite an often darker vision, Emersonians—though with reservations not unlike that of Waggoner's post-Holocaust Jewish friend. Even avowed anti-Emersonians cannot pass by without comment. "At every lunch that I happily shared with the poet-novelist Robert Penn Warren," Harold Bloom reported in 2004, "he would denounce Emerson as the Devil," blaming him for "the murderous John Brown and for most of what was destructive in American culture." Even this is to acknowledge the centrality of Emerson in that culture, and Warren's poetic tribute is no less backhanded. In "Homage to Emerson: On Night Flight to New York," Warren, setting Emersonian "hope" against the dark realities of experience, reduces Emerson's "optimistic" vision to a five-word axiom: "No sin, not even error." Seven years earlier, in the same year that Arvin's essay appeared, another major American poet who certainly knew about sin and error paid his homage in prose. The occasion was an auspicious one, Robert Frost's reception of the Emerson-Thoreau Medal before the American Academy of Arts and Sciences. Though he numbered Emerson among his "four greatest Americans" (the others were predictable: Washington, Jefferson, and Lincoln), Frost remarked that he had "friends it bothers when I am accused of being an Emersonian, that is, a cheerful Monist, for whom evil does not exist, or if it does, needn't last forever." Is a supposedly sounder "melancholy dualism" preferable? he asked rhetorically, affirming Emerson without quite denying the received charge of systematic and monistic idealism.[16]

16. Robert Frost, "On Emerson," 12. For Bloom on Warren, see *Where Shall Wisdom Be Found?* 191. Even in his "Homage" (first printed in the *New Yorker* in 1966), Warren retains much of an old, and Eliotic, argument. "After Emerson had done his work," he wrote in 1928, "any tragic possibilities inherent in [New England] culture were dissipated" ("Hawthorne, Anderson, and Frost," 400). For Perry Miller, Emersonian "optimism" is a dilution of Puritanism, "Edwardianism without original sin" ("From Edwards to Emerson"). Bloom applauds what Miller deplores: "Sin, error, time, history, a God external to the self . . . were precisely of no interest whatsoever" to Emerson (introduction to *Ralph Waldo Emerson,* 5).

Such a "denial" had come a century earlier from Bronson Alcott, in a little book given as a sixty-second birthday present to his mind-"emancipating" friend Emerson. Although "not a metaphysician," and "rightly discarding any claims to systematic thinking," Emerson was, said Alcott, "a poet in spirit, if not always in form," and—like Kant and Coleridge, for whom true "idealism" was also "the truest and most binding realism" (*BL* 12:261–62)—"the consistent idealist" yet "the realist none the less." Though Alcott's book was a rhapsodic eulogy ("honeypie" to the "weak stomach" of a man who disliked superlatives about himself), Emerson came to admire its "lyrical tone" and to acknowledge some of its accuracies.[17]

Rightly so, because Emerson *was* a thinker who increasingly leavened his "idealism" with realism, and he *was* too unsystematic, too volatile, to be anything but a "dualistic monist." The truth in these depictions of Emerson as a monistic optimist unengaged with the minute particulars and contingencies of the world is at best a half truth. Lawrence Buell, perhaps recalling the praise of Wordsworth's "sanity" by Coleridge and Emerson, recently remarked that "if you're looking for the courage to maintain sanity and resolution when the rest of society seems to have gone mad, Emerson may be your man." Overreacting to this sensible, and seemingly innocuous observation, John Updike, writing in the *New Yorker* in 2003, criticized as "excessively hedged" Buell's "linking [of] the sage's value to a presumed madness in society." Why? Because Emerson was "too much a realist," Updike thinks, "to dismiss the workings of a society as mad, even a society like his own, passionately riven antebellum America. He pitched his palace of the Ideal on the particularities and rationale of what existed. One of Buell's few wholehearted sentences exclaims, 'How many of the great essays end by propelling the reader out into the world!' Yes; Emerson wanted to encourage us, to make us fit for the world."[18]

Yet back in 1991, reprinting an earlier (1984) *New Yorker* piece, Updike, who has long harbored serious reservations about Emerson's grip on reality, could chastise the sage for having "scandalously excluded" from his work a whole "world of suffering." Neither naif nor stranger to suffering, Emerson kept it to himself, his stoic discipline buttressed by an affirmative

17. Alcott, *Emerson* (Cambridge, privately printed, 1865; reprinted in 1882 and again six years later, this time as *Ralph Waldo Emerson: Philosopher and Seer* [Boston: Cupples and Hurd, 1888]), 22, 31–32. (Emerson's comments about the book's "lyrical tone," and so on, were printed as a posthumous preface to this edition.) For other responses, including the "honeypie" remark, see *L* 5:406, 9:190 (including notes 82, 83).

18. Updike, "Big Dead White Male," 80. The Buell remark to which Updike initially responds appeared in the *Boston Globe,* which (Updike gleefully reports) reviewed Buell's magisterial book *Emerson* (2003) as "scholarly natterings."

vision in which evil is, not always easily, converted to good. It has been well said that whenever he "managed to wrestle his horrors back under control at those moments when they erupt into full consciousness, readers lulled by his confident tones have missed the precariousness by which he maintains his apparent equilibrium. We have mistaken equilibrium for equanimity."[19]

To be sure, Emerson, who divided men, as he told Oliver Wendell Holmes in March 1856, into "aspirants & desperants" (*L* 5:17–18), was temperamentally an aspirant, an "optimistic" position that can seem cloying and naive, even evasive in the face of real obstacles, obstacles of which, unlike the shadow of Sweeney and Hitler, he *had* knowledge. To visit for a moment the contemporary triplex of class-race-gender by taking a celebrated metaphor literally, it would have been difficult to obey Emerson's twice-repeated imperative, in the late essay "Civilization," to "Hitch your wagon to a star" (*W* 7:28, 30), if you happened not to *own* a wagon, or if the only one in the vicinity belonged to your white master, or to a husband who considered the wagon, along with *you,* his property. Emerson was not oblivious to such difficulties. For all his idealistic aspiration, he was aware, in his "skeptical" capacity, of the "yawning gulf . . . between the ambition of man and his power of performance," a gap between ideal and limited reality "which makes the tragedy of all souls" (*E&L* 708).

Characteristically, however, even this acknowledgment occurs in, and is absorbed by, an Emersonian serenity aligned with the Wordsworthian "stream of tendency." In the "recoil" portion of his essay on Montaigne, Emerson opens up some distance between himself and his admired mentor. There is "a final solution in which skepticism," even the "wise skepticism" of Montaigne—no "scoffer," but a natural theologian—"is lost." A "man of thought" who believes in the "supremacy" of "the moral sentiment" can "*behold with serenity*" that "yawning gulf . . . which makes the tragedy of all souls" (*E&L* 708). In a passage that parallels the function of "Providence" in the essay "Fate," Emerson says that

> things seem to tend downwards, to justify despondency, to promote rogues, to defeat the just; and, by knaves, as by martyrs, the just cause is carried forward. . . . the march of civilization is a train of felonies, yet, general ends are somehow answered. We see, now, events forced on, which seem to retard or retrograde the civility of ages. But the world-spirit is a good swimmer, and storms and waves cannot drown him . . . Through the years and the centuries, through evil agents, through toys and atoms, a great and beneficent tendency irresistibly streams. (*E&L* 709)

19. See Joseph F. Doherty, "Emerson and the Loneliness of the Gods." For Updike's discussion, see his essay "Emersonianism," 154.

That clinching phrase, the one cited by Newton Arvin, evokes Montaigne but alludes to Wordsworth's Wanderer, who tells us in the final book of *The Excursion* that, with the experience that comes with age, we can attain an eminence, a height above "the Plain below," where we may find conferred upon us

> Fresh power to commune with the invisible world,
> And hear *the mighty stream of tendency*
> Uttering, for *elevation of our thought,*
> A clear, sonorous voice, inaudible
> To the vast multitude.
>
> (*E* 9:81–92; italics added)

Well before he himself had attained the eminence of age, Emerson, only twenty-four at the time, recorded his approval of this privileged, "serene" perspective, that of a "poet represented as listening in pious silence 'To hear the mighty stream of Tendency'" (*JMN* 3:80). The phrase was later recruited, less in praise of piety than of creativity, in the essay "Art." The "need to create" must transcend the aesthetic because art's essential end is "nothing less than the creation of man and nature," its purpose "the awakening in the beholder the same sense of universal relation and power which the work evinced in the artist." Art's "highest effect is to make new artists," and the "real value of the Iliad, or the Transfiguration, is as signs of power; billows or ripples they are of the stream of tendency; tokens of the everlasting effort to produce" (*E&L* 437). Even in the essay "Fate," the "Universe" is described as "an ascending effort. The direction of the whole, and of the parts, is toward *benefit.*" Liberation of the individual is "the end and aim of this world. Every calamity is a spur and valuable hint; and where [the individual's] endeavors do not fully avail, they tell as *tendency*" (*E&L* 960; italics added).

Still, exasperating though it can be at times to those less certain of "the moral sentiment" and of the Wordsworthian stream of beneficent tendency, Emerson's affirmative vision is not to be contemptuously dismissed (as it so often is, despite recent correctives by Christopher Lasch and those who, like George Stack, David Mikics, and an increasing number of commentators, embrace rather than repress the Emerson-Nietzsche affiliation) as soft, sanguine, even saccharine sentimentality, or, alternatively and especially when it came to death, as evidence of a *too* serene composure, even of what he himself acknowledged some considered "unbecoming indifference." At that time, December 1831, Emerson, who considered "our [own] hearts" the principal agents of salvation or condemnation, claimed to have no fear of death (the fear of others, he said, derived from the "borrowed terrors" of vulgar opinion and "not from their own minds"). He was confident that God (and "my own mind" was "the divine revelation which I have from God") would never suffer his holy ones—as we are assured in Psalms and Acts—"to see corruption" (*JMN* 3:312–13).

❧ As this confidence wavered, his serenity reflected a hard-won embrace of Wordsworthian "hope," "recompense," and renewed power. In seizing on Wordsworth as the great poet of consolation in distress, of compensation and recovery, Emerson was, as usual, following in the footsteps of Coleridge. As he "listened with a heart forlorn" to Wordsworth's reading over several evenings of the whole of the 1805 version of "the poem for Coleridge," the epic we know as *The Prelude,* its humbled recipient, a man broken in spirit and physical health, drew (at least temporarily) revitalizing strength. The sudden recovery, in which he is stung into life, is compared to that of a drowning man saved from the sea or a child's abrupt awakening from sleep:

> The pulses of my being beat anew:
> And even as Life returns upon the drowned,
> Life's joy rekindling roused a throng of pains—
> Keen pangs of Love, awakening as a babe
> Turbulent, with an outcry in the heart.
> (62–66; *CPW* 1:407)

At the end of this January 1807 reading, Coleridge (and this is the final line of "To William Wordsworth") "found myself in prayer" (112). Though he would—in part by making the early Wordsworth retrospectively orthodox—always find consolation in his friend's greatest poetry, it was increasingly to prayer and philosophy that Coleridge would turn. With two other major nineteenth-century thinkers, the recovery from crisis took the opposite direction: from philosophy to the poetry of Wordsworth, at least until profound depression had been alleviated. In the case of John Stuart Mill, this recovery was, essentially, permanent; it would prove only temporary in the case of William James, who remained subject to lifelong depression, a condition that makes the sweetness of nature that endeared him to so many all the more admirable. As fellow beneficiaries of Wordsworth's healing power, Mill and James illuminate the relationship between Emerson and Wordsworth.

In the fifth chapter of his *Autobiography,* "A Crisis in My Mental Life: One Stage Onward," Mill describes the terrible apathy into which he fell at the age of twenty after years of utilitarian training by his Benthamite father. Writing in retrospect, that is, after having digested the major poems of Wordsworth and Coleridge, with which "I was not then acquainted," he epitomizes his anomie in those frightening (if slightly misquoted) lines of Coleridge's "Dejection: An Ode":

> A grief without a pang, void, dark and drear,
> A drowsy, stifled, unimpassioned grief,
> Which finds no natural outlet or relief
> In word, or sigh, or tear.
>
> (21–24)[20]

He also found "the dry heavy dejection of the melancholy winter of 1826–7" captured in other "lines of Coleridge, in whom alone of all writers I have found a true description of what I felt." He could not have known them in 1826–1827, because they were not published until the following year, but in "a later period of the same malady," the "two lines," from Coleridge's short poem "Work without Hope" (*CPW* 1:447), were "often in my thoughts": "Work without Hope draws nectar in a sieve, / And Hope without an object cannot live" (13–14).

In the process of recovering, Mill found support in the *Mémoires d'un père* of the otherwise mediocre Jean-François Marmontel, and in the prose of Carlyle, adopting a position resembling the theory of "anti-self-consciousness" he found described in two texts seminal for Emerson as well: the essay "Characteristics" and "the Everlasting Yea" chapter of *Sartor Resartus.* But it was the turning to Romantic poetry that was decisive, first that of Coleridge, then, even more emphatically, the poetry of Wordsworth. Here he found what he was "in quest of": the "very culture of the feelings" needed to dissolve a state of dejection he foresaw would not be alleviated even if all his reformist dreams for the betterment of humankind were to be realized:

> This state of my thoughts and feelings made the fact of my reading of Wordsworth for the first time (in the autumn of 1828), an important event in my life.... These poems [from the two-volume edition of 1815] addressed themselves powerfully to one of the strongest of my pleasurable susceptibilities, the love of rural objects and natural scenery.... What made Wordsworth's poems a medicine for my state of mind, was that they expressed,

20. Mill slightly misquotes the third of these lines; Coleridge has "no natural outlet, *no* relief" (*CPW* 1:364). References here and in the two paragraphs that follow are to the *Autobiography of John Stuart Mill,* 93–105. Elsewhere, in his essay "Coleridge," Mill examines the man as a political and religious thinker. He presents Coleridge and Jeremy Bentham as the most influential thinkers of the century, each the "completing counterpart" of the other.

> not mere outward beauty, but states of feeling, and of thought colored by feeling, under the excitement of beauty. . . . In them I seemed to draw from a source of inward joy, of sympathetic and imaginative pleasure.

At the end of the 1815 volume, Mill encountered "the famous *Ode*, falsely called Platonic, *Intimations of Immortality.*" He praised the poem's more than usual "sweetness of melody and rhythm" and registers a dual response to the two stanzas (the fifth and the ninth, "the so-called Platonic passages of grand imagery but bad philosophy") most cherished by the American Transcendentalists. What mattered to Mill above all was that "I found that he too had had similar experience to mine; that he also had felt that the first freshness of youthful enjoyment of life was not lasting; but that he had sought for compensation, and found it, in the way in which he was now teaching me to find it. The result was that I gradually, but completely, emerged from my habitual depression, and was never again subject to it."[21]

Though we associate the amiable William James with can-do pragmatism, his was a troubled soul. That makes him the apparent antithesis to "untroubled" Emerson; yet *both* men found much needed solace in the poetry of Wordsworth, especially *The Excursion.* James's dejection was exacerbated by his tormented worrying of the problem of evil: "Can one," knowledgeably and sincerely, "bring one's self so to sympathize with the total process of the universe as heartily to assent to the evil that seems inherent in its details?" He was also troubled by what he later depicted, in his introduction to his father's writings, as the irreconcilability of "religion," associated with a sense of "well-*being,*" and "morality," associated with "well-*doing.*" A person who feels passive and fatalistic, "sicklied o'er" (in James's allusion to *Hamlet*) with the sense of his own weakness,

> craves to be consoled in his very impotence, to feel that the Powers of the Universe recognize and secure him, all passive and failing as he is. Well, we are all *potentially* such sick men. The sanest and best of us are of one clay with lunatics and prison-inmates. And whenever we feel this, such a sense

21. Mill, *Autobiography of Mill,* 104–5. In an 1841 letter, Mill concludes a discussion of prose and poetry by celebrating Wordsworth. "Prose is the language of *business,* & therefore is the language to do good by in an age when men's minds are forcibly drawn to external effort. . . . True, this is only a part of the mission of mankind & the time will come again when its due rank will be assigned to Contemplation, & . . . love. . . . But that time is not yet, & the crowning glory of Wordsworth is that he has borne witness to it & kept alive its traditions in an age which but for him would have lost sight of it entirely & even poetical minds would with us have gone off into the heresy of the poetical critics of the present day in France who hold that poetry is above all & preeminently a *social* thing" (*The Earlier Letters of John Stuart Mill, 1812–1848,* 2:473–74).

> of the vanity of our voluntary career comes over us, that all our morality appears but a plaster hiding a sore it can never cure, and all our well-doing as the hollowest substitute for that well-*being* that our lives ought to be grounded in, but, alas! are not.[22]

Torn between the "Emersonian" polarities of Fate and Freedom, acquiescent passivity and active power, James envies those who can believe in a deity who could reconcile the radical discord between the "pluralism" of morality and the "monism" of religion. But, he movingly concedes in a letter of 1904, he cannot: "My personal position is simple. I have no living sense of commerce with a God. I envy those who have, for I know that the addition of such a sense would help me greatly." That last is an "understatement," as Louis Menand has said, for James knew that the pragmatism and pluralism he promoted "are not enough, that life confronts us with some situations that call for a different sort of response. . . . It is the poignancy of his life that he never found, for himself, that response." Instead, he "created a philosophy of hope expressly premised on the understanding that there is, finally, no *reason* for hope." What Menand says of James had been said, by Morse Peckham, of Nietzsche, that joyful surmounter of nihilism, who "solved" the nineteenth-century problem: "There is no ground to value; man joyfully creates it out of suffering and nothingness, simply in order to exist; from that nothingness flows an incomprehensible power which sounds the midnight bell and brings him into an existence which he, and he alone, unaided, and for no reason, earthly or transcendental, redeems." Less Romantic, and therefore more compromised by his own skepticism and lack of religious faith, James was, as Menand says, "too wise to believe that true melancholy can ever be overcome by a theory, and he was too honest to pretend to a spiritual satisfaction he was never able to feel."[23]

Philosophy was not the answer, James knew, but he also knew that it was all he had. He therefore drew comfort, the satisfaction of his craving "to be consoled," from the century's major *philosophic* poem of despondency and recovery, "Wordsworth's immortal *Excursion.*" Whatever we make of the significance of the morbid nightmare vision of the epileptic, experienced by James sometime between 1866 and 1872, there is little reason to doubt the accuracy of his father's account of his son's dramatic, if temporary, recovery in the spring of 1873 (coincidentally the year of

22. W. James, "Introduction to the Literary Remains of the Late Henry James" (1884), in *Essays in Religion and Morality,* ed. Burkhardt, 61–63.

23. James's letter (April 17, 1904) to James H. Leuba, is quoted in Ralph Barton Perry, *The Thought and Character of William James,* 2:350. See also Peckham, *Beyond the Tragic Vision,* 370–71; and Menand, "William James and the Case of the Epileptic Patient," 93.

Mill's death and the publication of his *Autobiography*). One afternoon in March of that year, William walked into the room where his father was sitting alone and remarked, with some astonishment, at the "difference... between me now and me last spring this time.... It is the difference between death and life." When his father asked what "specially in his opinion had promoted the change," William singled out the reading of Charles Renovier, particularly his phenomenalist vindication of the freedom of the will, and "Wordsworth, whom he has been feeding upon now for a good while."[24]

If, as the context suggests, the ingestive image was the son's rather than his father's, it would tend to confirm that he had indeed been "feeding upon" the poet who eats and drinks restorative nature, and who insists—in lines Wordsworthian "William" speaks to "Matthew"—"That we can *feed* this mind of ours / In a wise passiveness" ("Expostulation and Reply," 23–24; *WP* 1:356). In one of the great passages in the poem James pronounced "immortal," the Wanderer—a man accustomed to desires "that *feed* / On fruitage gathered from the tree of life"—describes a fire that *"feeds"* on and converts to hope all our mortal pains. And James's "well-doing" figures too since the Wanderer later tells us that "hope dies" unless nourished by the *"food"* of "meditated action" (*E* 4:1058–77, 1291–92, 9:20–22).

These very passages were of immense and demonstrable importance to Emerson as well. Wordsworth's insistence on the triumph of hope over despair, the theme of the fourth and ninth books of *The Excursion,* is nowhere more movingly presented than in the greatest of the Wanderer's symbolic passages. In Emerson's favorite book, the fourth, the Wanderer tells the Solitary that within us "a faculty abides," threatened by darkening interpositions that serve but to exalt the soul's "native brightness." His simile—lunar, celestial, spiritual, natural—impressed Coleridge, as well as both James and Emerson:

As the ample summer moon,
In the deep stillness of a summer even
Rising behind a thick and lofty grove,
Burns, like an unconsuming fire of light,
In the green trees; and, kindling on all sides
Their leafy umbrage, turns the dusky veil

24. Perry, *Thought and Character,* 1:337. The hideous vision of the "greenish-skinned" epileptic accompanying James's "horrible fear of [his] own existence" probably occurred between 1866 and 1872, a significant event that left James, as he reported three decades later (in one of the Edinburgh University Gifford Lectures later published as *Varieties of Religious Experience*), "sympathetic with the morbid feelings of others ever since." Emerson, in contrast, had "too little understanding of the morbid side of life" (quoted in Menand, "Epileptic Patient").

Into a substance glorious as her own,
Yea, with her own incorporated, by power
Capacious and serene. Like power abides
In man's celestial spirit; virtue thus
Sets forth and magnifies herself; thus feeds
A calm, a beautiful, and silent fire,
From the encumbrances of mortal life,
From error, disappointment—nay, from guilt;
And sometimes, so relenting justice wills,
From palpable oppressions of despair.
(*E* 4:1062–77)[25]

The "optimistic" argument may be the same as Milton's in *The Christian Doctrine;* the *poetry,* registering the very palpable oppressions of despair on which the triumphant fire feeds, makes all the difference. No more a stranger than was Milton to those oppressions, Emerson experienced his full share of pain and more than "apparent" evil. At the age of twenty-four, while in Florida recuperating from tuberculosis, and the eye disease of which it was the underlying cause, he wrote to his aunt, "He has seen but half the Universe who never has been shown the house of Pain. Pleasure and Peace are but indifferent teachers of what it is life to know." Here as elsewhere a precursor of his disciple Nietzsche, that prophet of self-overcoming and the will to power, Emerson struggled to triumph over his own physical weakness. From the harmonious, polarity-reconciling perspective to which he aspired, the mountaintop vision beyond tragedy, suffering and death could be seen as educating "values" to be incorporated in a larger affirming theory of life. If his stance is a glorious, self-preservative whistling in the dark, Emerson acknowledged the dark, most dramatically in "Fate," *and* refused to succumb to it, for there is that "other fact in the dual world" of polar impulses: "Power," which "attends and antagonizes Fate" (*E&L* 953).

However harshly circumstances dealt with him, he remained buoyed by the conviction he shared with Wordsworth and other affirmers in an underlying beneficent "tendency," by the belief that a moral law shone through this often problematic and cruel world and that "circumstances" could be *individually* triumphed over by what he called "power," which is a constant

25. Coleridge may be recalling these lines in his later description—a passage of *The Statesman's Manual* also influenced by Schelling—of the imagination as "that reconciling and mediatory power, which *incorporating the Reason in Images of the Sense,* and organizing (as it were) the *flux of the Senses* by the *permanence* and self-circling energies of the *Reason,* gives birth to a system of symbols, harmonious in themselves, and consubstantial with the truths, of which they are the *conductors*" (*LS* 29; italics added).

in his work, and "character," a term providing the title of no fewer than three Emerson essays. In the first of these, in *Essays: Second Series,* we are told that whereas "feeble souls," those drawn to the "negative pole," can do no more than "worship events" in the form of a connected "chain of circumstances," the person of "character" fearlessly and autonomously exercises "power" over external events. Like Wordsworth's "happy warrior," such a "hero sees that the event is ancillary: it must follow *him.*" No given order of events has the "power" to give him the satisfaction that

> the imagination attaches to it; the soul of goodness escapes from any set of circumstances, whilst prosperity belongs to a certain mind, and will introduce that power and victory which is its natural fruit, into any order of events. . . . If I quake, what matter it what I quake at? . . . If we are capable of fear we will readily find terrors. The covetousness or the malignity which saddens me, when I ascribe it to society, is my own. I am always environed by myself. On the other part, rectitude is a perpetual victory, celebrated not by cries of joy, but by serenity, which is joy fixed or habitual. (*E&L* 499–500)

Like Wordsworth, Emerson was secure in the belief that, amid the selfishness and cruelties encountered in the "dreary intercourse of daily life," no malignity shall "prevail against us" ("Tintern Abbey"), that, however often he was "defeated" by circumstances, "yet to Victory am I born" (*JMN* 8:228). Emerson was able, in William James's phrase, "to sympathize with the total process of the universe" because, for him as for the Wordsworth of "Expostulation and Reply," that total universe was a "mighty sum / Of things for ever speaking," and speaking in a morally intelligible way. Oscar Wilde once wittily remarked that Wordsworth found under stones the sermons he had already placed there, and that would seem to be true of Emerson as well, even when it came to the disruptions of death.

At its most troubling, his "optimistic" stance—the maintenance of "Emersonian" serenity in the face of every "chain of circumstances," no matter how apparently "malignant"—took the form of what has been understandably if inaccurately described as a resolute refusal to mourn, even when the dead included his father (who died when his son was seven and about whom that son is virtually silent); his beloved first wife, Ellen, only nineteen when she died in February 1831, in the sixteenth month of their marriage; his brother Edward who died three years later; and his closest brother, Charles, who died in 1836.[26] And then, unkindest cut of

26. The significant silence of Emerson regarding his father's death is the starting point for Barish's *Roots of Prophecy.* On Ellen's death, see *JMN* 3:226–27 (quoted below), the standard biographies, and Jerome Loving's "Emerson's Foreground," 48–49.

all: the sudden death, before he was six, of little Waldo, Emerson's "dear boy too precious & unique to be huddled aside into the waste & prodigality of things" (*L* 3:9–10).

Emerson was not deeply touched by the death of his father. But in all these other painful cases, having given himself up to intense if private mourning, he moved on, exercising that "character" that finally immunizes us from even the most horrific external events, and convinced that he had to focus on the living, not the dead, to preserve, concentrate, and expand his own vital powers rather than dissipate them in futile grief. Following Carlyle, who in turn was following Descartes and Fichte, Emerson distinguished between Me, or "the Soul," on the one hand, and, on the other, "all that is separate from us," philosophically, "the NOT ME," including nature, one's own body, and "all other men" (*E&L* 8). In the most "stern" of his applications of that distinction, the dead, even the most cherished, were, after the initial period of grief, to be understood as part of the NOT ME.

That, at least, was the idealist theory. Fortunately, Transcendentalist theory can take *two* forms. If we adopt the differing emphases in the penultimate and the final stanzas of the Intimations Ode, "the philosophic mind" (stanza 10) and "my heart of hearts" (stanza 11), we might characterize these two forms of Transcendentalism as a polarity between thought and emotion, head and heart, leaving us with either an intensification of the cleavage—mental, austere, dualistic—between the Me and the NOT ME *or* a still spiritual but circulatory and heart-centered vision that transcends the separation between the self and others, the individual creature and the whole of creation. As Emerson insists in "The Over-Soul": "Every friend . . . the great and tender heart in thee craveth, shall lock thee in his embrace. For the *heart in thee is the heart of all;* not a valve, not a wall, not an intersection is there anywhere in nature, but *one blood* rolls uninterruptedly an endless circulation through *all men,* as the water of the globe is *all one sea,* and, truly seen, its tide is *one*" (*E&L* 399; italics added).

This is the vision shared by Wordsworth and Coleridge—Coleridge's reciprocity between "each" and "all" (*F* 1:511), and what he calls (in the famous line later added to "The Eolian Harp") "The one Life within us and abroad" (26; *CPW* 1:101). Accordingly, Emerson's ideal Poet "apprises us not of his wealth, but of the commonwealth" (*E&L* 448). The art that results from such a vision is "not a private affair," but "an opening out," beyond our "personal sphere." And "precisely because" such a "visceral and experiential" art "expands our stock, it can be a source of inestimable value to those who hurt." I am quoting Arnold Weinstein, who frames the entire argument of a recent book on what literature teaches us about life by endorsing Emerson, in his opening and closing pages, on the circulatory "flow, or "arterial event," that connects "self and other, self and world."[27] The last words Emerson uttered on earth, forty years after the death of Waldo, were "praise" *and* "O, that beautiful boy!" Those deathbed words reveal the "hurt" hidden beneath his lifelong struggle to maintain equilibrium in the face both of suffering and of what, referring to the Me–NOT ME dichotomy, he himself admitted in the wake of that death was "the absence of any appearance of reconciliation between the theory & the practice of life" (*JMN* 9:65, a phrase, and an admission, repeated in *Representative Men* [*E&L* 705]). The ramifications—personal, philosophic, and literary—of the death in 1842 of little Waldo are addressed in my final chapter. Moving chronologically, however, I first take up the Wordsworthian aspects of Emerson's responses to the deaths of Ellen and Edward (Chapter 12) and then his pivotal response to the death of Charles (Chapter 13).

27. Weinstein, *A Scream Goes through the House: What Literature Teaches Us about Life*, xxv–xxvi, 8, 31, 395.

Chapter 12

Wordsworthian Hope

THE DEATHS OF ELLEN AND EDWARD

How often do hope and despair touch each other. Yet in a moment the one shall vanish; and to the other begin a career in the fullness of her joy.

—WILLIAM WORDSWORTH, *On the Convention of Cintra*

The gospel has no revelation
Of peace or hope until there is response
From the deep chambers of thy mind thereto.

—RALPH WALDO EMERSON, "Gnothi Seauton"

Our destiny, our nature, and our home
Is with infinitude, and only there;
With hope it is, hope that can never die,
Effort, and expectation, and desire,
And something evermore about to be.

—WILLIAM WORDSWORTH, *The Prelude*

In the days and nights (the "most eventful of my life," he told his aunt) of Ellen's final suffering, Emerson seemed to his brother Charles "a man over whom the waters have gone." As Emerson himself put it in one of his notebook lamentations:

The days pass over me,
And I am still the same;

The aroma of my life is gone
With the flower with which it came.[1]

He was sustained only by his young wife's selfless courage and religious faith. It would in fact seem to be even more *her* faith than his own that informs the conventional and pious Christian confidence that we find in both his immediate letter to his remarkable aunt and his long journal entry written five days later. "My angel is gone to heaven this morning," he wrote to his aunt Mary shortly after Ellen's death at nine o'clock on the morning of February 8, 1831. He was "alone in the world and strangely happy," relieved that her terrible tubercular ordeal had ended: "Her lungs shall no more be torn nor her head scalded by her blood nor her whole life suffer from the warfare between the force and delicacy of her soul and the weakness of her frame." "Say, dear aunt," he claimed and pleaded, "if I am not rich in her memory?" (*L* 1:318).

In the privacy of his journal, Emerson oscillated, registering grief, piety, faith, amendment, and questioning—ending in a recognition that this "first love" was unique and that, by implication, he would never again put himself in the position of having to endure an unrestorable loss, a loss so painful that it threatened to destroy him as well. "Five days are wasted since Ellen went to heaven to see, to know, to worship, to love, to intercede. God be merciful to me a sinner & repair this miserable debility in which her death has left my soul. . . . O willingly, my wife, I would lie down in your tomb." But he lacked the merits, purity, and single-heartedness of a woman who, in this journal and in the elegiac poems he wrote at this time, begins to resemble Dante's Beatrice; he therefore asks her to pray for him and hopes that they will be "united even now more & more . . . stay by me & lead me upward. Reunite us, o thou Father of our Spirits." But the paragraph that immediately follows is elegy without consolation, suffering and mourning with little or no hope:

> There is that which passes away & never returns. This miserable apathy, I know, may wear off, I almost fear when it will. Old duties will present themselves. . . . I shall go again among my friends with a tranquil countenance. Again I shall be amused, I shall stoop again to little hopes & little fears & forget the graveyard. But will the dead be restored to me? Will thy eye that was closed on Tuesday ever beam again in the fulness of love on me?[2] Shall

1. These unpublished lines are quoted from *CPT* 328–33 (330). The fragments are cited from *JMN.*

2. As always, Emerson is fixated on the eye; Ellen's figures prominently in his notebook elegies. "Does thy blue eye/ Ever look northward with desire[?]" he wonders; and again: "I miss thy radiant eye."

> I ever again be able to connect the face of outward nature, the mists of the morn, the star of eve, the flowers, & all poetry, with the heart & life of an enchanting friend. No. There is one birth & one baptism & one first love and the affections cannot keep their youth any more than men. (*JMN* 3: 226–27)

Emerson's emotional and spiritual agony, as well as the questioning of his own beliefs, testify to the intensity of his grief over the death of his young wife, and his longing to believe in personal immortality, both for Ellen and himself. I defer consideration of the thoughts gathered together in the late essay "Immortality," but much of Emerson's *feeling* on the subject can be gauged from this poignant notebook entry, and from the fragmentary poems written at the time—many of which reflect his immersion in Milton, Coleridge, and Wordsworth. For example, in one poem, written a week after Ellen's death, Emerson claims that to give up all belief in the capacity of human consciousness to survive death, though it would not turn him into an immoralist, would be self-destructive, involving the loss of the very Me. Were he to be convinced that he was "forgotten by the dead," and that "the dead is by herself forgot," while he would not "murder, steal, or fornicate, / Nor with ambition break the peace of towns," he would "bury" his "ambition," and surrender the "hope & action" of his "sovereign soul" in "miserable ruin. Not a hope / Should ever make a holiday for me." He "would not harm" his fellow man, but such a loss of hope would "*harm myself*" (*JMN* 3:228–29). The thought is similar to Coleridge's "Human Life: On the Denial of Immortality," a poem first published in *Sibylline Leaves.* There Coleridge too insisted on the pointlessness of human hopes and fears and joys if immortality were to be denied, rendering man a "vessel purposeless." If with death "we cease to be," if "total gloom" were thought to "Swallow up life's brief flash for ever," we would be no more than "summer gusts, of sudden birth and doom." Man's state would be "rootless" and "substanceless," our "being's being" mere "contradiction" (*CPW* 1:425–26).

Another of Emerson's poetic fragments opens with what sounds like an echo of Shelley's "Adonais." "Why fear to die," asks Emerson, when the "grave" has become "pleasant in my eye"? Like Shelley, Emerson may be recalling Wordsworth's Wanderer, a man capable of "rejoicing secretly / In the sublime attractions of the grave" (*E* 4:237–38). But the informing ideas behind this notebook poem—the absorption of the human in the divine, of the particular in a more inclusive whole, the reconstitution of hope, and recompense for what has been lost—reveal Emerson's deeper debt to Milton's great elegy, "Lycidas," in this case, I suspect, as "filtered" through Coleridge, writing about Wordsworth. Since that brings my three major figures together with their heir, Emerson, I will risk breaking this butterfly of an unpublished fragment on the wheel of allusion.

In a manuscript bereft of punctuation and scribbled in a barely legible hand offering mute testimony to his anguish over the death of his "dearest Ellen," Emerson hopes that they can "meet on / the midnight wing of dreams" and professes to know that "in the deep / Of new power & the realms of truth," her "affections do not sleep." But while he hopes that Ellen is still able to "love" him, she has been taken from this life. Thus, he asks himself, "Why should I live?" The future will simply "repeat the past," yet be unable to "give / Again the Vision beautiful[,] too beautiful to last." Yet death, he suddenly realizes with an exclamatory "O," might be a positive development:

> perhaps the welcome stroke
> That severs forever this fleshly yoke
> Shall restore the vision to the soul
> In the great Vision of the Whole.
> (*JMN* 3:230–31)

In this hope that his own death might restore to him Ellen, his lost "Vision beautiful," now reintegrated "In the great Vision of the Whole," Emerson seems to fuse "Lycidas," a poem he knew by heart, with "To William Wordsworth" (*CPW* 1:403–8), in which Coleridge, himself echoing Milton's great elegy, most fully engages the friend and poet who had by then (1807) outdistanced him. Milton evokes Saint Michael's Mount, "guarded" by the archangel, at the tip of Land's End in southeastern England, "Where *the great Vision* of the guarded mount / Looks" across the English Channel. But that gaze is quickly redirected by Milton: "Look *homeward, Angel*, now, and melt with ruth" ("Lycidas," 161–63). This is the same divided perspective (expansive vision countered by individual, domestic grief) we find in all elegy and certainly in Emerson's notebook attempts to come to terms with his wife's death. The lines quoted from Milton immediately precede the pivotal invocation to "Weep no more" (165), which initiates the majestic concluding assurance that, like the sinking and rising sun, Lycidas, having "sunk low," has finally "mounted high" (167–72).

Both of Milton's angelic visions, the expansive gaze and the redirected looking "homeward," appear in Coleridge's synopsis of *The Prelude*, the epic dedicated to him. Specifically, he recaptures the general "Hope" experienced by those who, like Wordsworth and himself in blissful youth, responded so ardently to the early days of the French Revolution. Then, reversing direction as swiftly as Milton, he turns to the subsequent disillusionment and its imaginative impact: "that dear Hope afflicted and struck down / So summoned *homeward*" (38–39). The borrowing of Milton's "homeward" is particularly apt, since the Romantics' movement toward internalization and repatriation was not only imaginative and political but, in Wordsworth's case, literal: in France in 1790–1791, he actually *had* been summoned "homeward" by events that would eventually lead to war between his native land and the country that then represented his heart's desire. Yet, reconstituted and housed in another visionary guarded mount, what Coleridge sublimely calls "the dread watch-tower of man's absolute self" (40), Hope remains able,

> With light unwaning on her eyes, to look
> Far on—herself a glory to behold,
> The *Angel of the vision!*
>
> (41–43)

That "Angel"—originally Milton's masculine archangel, Michael, but here the transformed and interiorized vision and female "Hope" of Wordsworth and Coleridge—becomes, in Emerson's variation, his Ellen, "my angel . . . gone to heaven," whom he hopes, in his version of the "large recompense" (184) of "Lycidas," to see again, "In the great Vision of the Whole." Thus, it is "not without hope" that Emerson mourns, a hope embedded, in this case, in his response to an ideational and verbal complex entangling Milton, Coleridge, and Wordsworth.

And there is yet another fusion. That the angel Hope is described by Coleridge as "herself a glory to behold" signals another of his many echoes of Adam's words to Eve on the arrival of the archangel Raphael in Eden:

> *behold*
> Eastward among those trees, what *glorious* shape
> Comes this way moving; seems another morn
> Risen on mid-noon.
>
> (*PL* 5:308–11)

As we have seen, that final phrase was also quoted by Wordsworth who, restored to the beloved sister from whom he had been separated for nine years, feels blest with a joy above all others, "that seemed another morn / Risen on mid-noon" (*P* 6:195–98). And, as Coleridge knew from the epic poem to which he was responding in "To William Wordsworth," it was Dorothy who had helped her brother, devastated by his disillusionment regarding the French Revolution, to attain a reconstituted form of hope. As Emerson says in "Circles," "Every end is a beginning; . . . there is always another dawn risen on mid-noon" (*E&L* 403).

Later in this notebook, in what he admits are mortal "Gropings in the dark," Emerson records his longing to believe that, though Ellen now walks "in heaven's day," she yet retains "a bond on earth," since the Universe cannot "blot" the true record of a "holy soul": "If the heart is raised by heavenly choirs / That which here made heaven is not lost." Emerson struggles to overcome loss by denying its ultimate reality, by uniting himself with that divinity beyond loss. In these fragmentary verses elegizing Ellen, however, it remains uncertain what form his "hope" takes. Is it Milton's spiritual "large recompense" or Wordsworth's echoing but secularized "abundant recompense" ("Tintern Abbey," 88)? And, in either case, "hope" can quickly change not only into a reconstituted or displaced form, but into its opposite: a hopeless vision beyond any compensatory consolation. This particular fragment ends by evoking Ellen's passing from human life and her sad knowledge that in the breast she loved, in the soul dear to her, "Dark hopeless visions roved / And a perpetual yew," so that "every day renews / The unrepaired regret" (*JMN* 3:233–34). At other times, like Laodamia, the titular figure in the Wordsworth poem he ranked second only to the Intimations Ode, Emerson seeks more than angelic consolation. In one fragment, after alluding to Isaiah and Corinthians in welcoming the day of salvation, he goes on to pray for a reunion as erotic as it is spiritual. God fills our souls with "mutual fires," so that "we should outlive [t]his firmament / And still relume these dear desires" (*JMN* 3: 234–35).[3]

3. As a handiwork of God (Emerson continues), Ellen had proven that "the innocent & affectionate thoughts / That harbor in the bosom of a child / Might live embodied in a riper form." The dead, he wrote in his journal, "do not return and sometimes we are negligent of their image. Not of yours Ellen—I know too well who is gone from me" (April 4; *JMN* 3:244). Three months later, in a more polished text dated "July 6, 1831," Emerson records how "lavish heaven"—having invested his wife with "all sweet perfections"—"hastes to take what it hath given." "As the delicate Snow / That latest fell the thieving wind first takes," so Ellen "must go, as spotless as those newfal'n flakes." But he repeats his earlier refrain ("Let me not fear to die"), and hopes to "live so well" that, with God and "thee dear heart," he yet "may dwell." This leads to a fully punctuated though unrhymed quatrain, a gnomic conclusion placing matters in final if less than fully persuaded or persuasive ocular perspective: "I write the things that are / Not what appears; / Of things as they are in the eye of God / Not in the eye of Man" (*JMN* 3:289–90). In distinguishing between human and divine, Becoming and Being, passing appearance and permanent reality, the struggling idealist still hopes that the particular "vision," Ellen, will be restored "In the great Vision of the Whole." Two weeks later he again addresses her directly: "When I think of you sweet Friend, wife, angel, Ellen on whom the spirit of knowledge & the spirit of hope were poured in equal fulness . . . I am sure we have not said everlasting farewells" (*JMN* 3:275).

"Gnothi Seauton" ["Know Thyself"], the free-verse meditation composed in the White Mountains in July 1831, also struggles to move through and beyond his painful individual loss.[4] As Emerson burns his way through his grief over Ellen's death, the poem becomes a hymn to the divinity within: "God dwells in thee.— / It is no metaphor or parable." Though we and the world know him not, this "shrouded" God "is the mighty Heart / From which life's varied pulses part," the "Infinite / Embosomed in a man." We are told that the "clouds that veil his light within" are the webs of sin God's glory struggles to shine through. Man is therefore to bear himself "up to the scale & compass of" his divine inner "guest," and to be "great" as beseem "The ambassador who bears / The royal presence where he goes." The human soul "is, I tell thee, God himself,"

> The selfsame One that rules the Whole
> Tho' he speaks thro' thee with a stifled voice
> And looks thro' thee shorn of his beams
> But if thou listen to his voice
> If thou obey the royal thought
> It will grow clearer to thine eye[;]
> The clouds will burst that veil him now
> And thou shalt see the Lord.
>
> (*JMN* 3:290–91)

Coleridge (*F* 2:509) provided Emerson's title, "Gnothi Seauton," though in untransliterated Greek, and these particular lines may recall Coleridge's "*clouds* that *veil*" God's "blaze" in a universe deemed "Symbolical, one mighty alphabet / For infant minds" (*The Destiny of Nations,* 17–20). Those lines were, as we have seen, often quoted or alluded to by Emerson. In fact, the year he first focused on them, 1831, had begun for Emerson with Ellen's death in February. Seeking, in the immediate aftermath of that tragedy, some assurance of personal immortality, for Ellen and eventually for himself, Emerson would have been open to Coleridge's lines about a cloud-veiled God of Light. But it was also his sustained reflection on Ellen's death that initiated Emerson's gradual abandonment of a belief in conventional immortality in favor of an eternal Now. In the 1833 shipboard journal he kept during his return from his first trip to Europe, Emerson, responding to apparent badgering by one or more scoffers among his fellow passengers, recorded the futility of seeking "mathematical certainty for moral truths." There is none to be found. "Yet they ask me whether I

4. Restricted to the journals (*JMN* 3:290–95), the poem was later published in the centennial edition (*W* 9:389–90).

know the soul immortal. No. But do I not know the Now to be eternal? Is it not a sufficient reply to the red and angry worldling, colouring as he affirms his unbelief, to say, Think on living, I have to do no more than you with that question of another life? I believe in this life. I believe it continues" (*JMN* 4:87).

As Emerson's "Gnothi Seauton" proceeds, the influence of Wordsworth becomes more apparent. His journals reveal that, at this time, seeking as he was some reassurance about the immortality of the soul, Emerson was rereading, along with Coleridge's *Friend,* some of his favorite Wordsworth poems: "Character of the Happy Warrior," "Tintern Abbey," "The Poet's Epitaph," "Laodamia," "Dion," the "Prospectus" to *The Recluse,* the "Ode to Duty," and—as always—the Intimations Ode.[5] Traces of the last three poems named are visible in the final movement of "Gnothi Seauton," from the opening lines of the "Ode to Duty," its inner law reflecting that "Stern Lawgiver," the "Voice of God"; through the crucial passage of the Intimations Ode, in which external material things are described as "Fallings from us, vanishings" (144); to the Wordsworthian location of Heaven and Hell within "the Mind of Man— / My haunt, and the main region of my song" ("Prospectus," lines 28–41).

> Thou art unto thyself a law
> And since the Soul of things is in thee
> Thou needest nothing out of thee.
> (Neither of moral nor material)
> The law, the gospel, & the Providence,
> Heaven, Hell, the Judgment, & the stores
> Immeasurable of Truth & Good
> All these thou must find
> Within thy single mind
> Or never find.
> Thou art the *law;*
> The gospel has no revelation
> Of peace or hope *until there is response*
> *From the deep chambers of thy mind thereto[.]*

The italicized final phrase seems to me Emerson's own "response" to a choral passage in *Samson Agonistes* (649–66), a passage commented on at

5. See *JMN* 3:305–7. Gilbert says Mill when she means Arnold, and offers no detail, but she exaggerates only slightly in saying that after Ellen's death "Emerson immersed himself so deeply in Wordsworth" that days of journal entries "deal solely with" him. As in the aftermath of his brother Charles's and his son Waldo's deaths, "Emerson turned to Wordsworth for what John Stuart Mill termed his 'healing power'" ("English Romantic Poets," 115).

length by Coleridge in *The Friend. In extremis,* Milton's Samson, "hopeless . . . , all remediless," thinks death the proper "close of all my miseries, and the balm" (649–51). At which point, the Chorus offers the sole remedy. The choral passage, which pivots on two words, *But* and the even more crucial *Unless,* was well known to Emerson, indeed, a probable source for his conflation of Within and Above:

> Many are the sayings of the wise
> In ancient and in modern books enrolled,
> Extolling patience as the truest fortitude;
> And to the bearing well of all calamities,
> All chances incident to man's frail life,
> Consolatories writ
> With studied argument, and much persuasion sought,
> Lenient of grief and anxious thought;
> *But with the afflicted in his pangs* their sound
> Little prevails, or rather seems a tune
> Harsh, and of dissonant mood from his complaint,
> *Unless* he feel *within*
> Some source of consolation from *above,*
> Secret refreshings that *repair* his strength,
> And fainting spirits *uphold.*
> (*Samson Agonistes,* 652–66; italics added)

Confronting the death of Ellen, and later, of Waldo, an agonized Emerson experienced "*un*repaired regret." *Samson Agonistes* offered help—in the case of "Threnody," the spiritual "repairs" of the natural decays he sought in writing the elegy for Waldo, as well as a source of those mysterious intuitions that, whatever their provenance, are felt "within" and that

> *Uphold* us, cherish, and have power to make
> Our noisy years seem moments in the being
> Of the eternal silence: truths that wake,
> To perish never.

These lines, from the ninth stanza of the Intimations Ode, verbally and thematically embrace the consolation and refreshings that, according to the Miltonic Chorus, "uphold" our fainting spirits. This choral guidance on the need for a transformation *within,* an upholding change of heart, or spirit, or soul incorporating a recuperative strength ultimately derived from *above,* was a favorite passage not only of Emerson but also of both of the two men he considered his best readers of Milton. Emerson never forgot the "diamond sharpness" of his brother Charles's "poetic recitation of *Samson Agonistes*" (*JMN* 5:107, 453), and he knew from his intensive reading of *The Friend* that Coleridge devoted several pages to this Chorus. In his essay on "Virtue and Knowledge," Coleridge quotes the crucial lines in the course of arguing that others cannot help in what are essentially internal, transformative crises: "Virtue would not be virtue could it be given by one fellow-creature to another." Coleridge leads into the Milton citation by observing that, faced with "human misery," the "question is not by what means each man is to alter his own character." To achieve that alteration, "all the means prescribed and all the aidances given by religion, may be necessary for him." Yet they may prove "vain, of themselves" (as he had recently said in the Dejection Ode, "We in *ourselves* rejoice," since one "may not hope from *outward forms* to win / The passion and the life, whose fountains are *within*"). He then quotes *Samson Agonistes* (652–53 and 663–66) as an illustration of the inefficacy of the sayings in books, "*unless*" one feels "*within* / Some source of consolation *from above*" (*F* 1: 100–106).

This doctrine is espoused by Wordsworth's Wanderer throughout *The Excursion,* especially in book 4. Interestingly, Emerson and Thoreau both quote a couplet of Seneca: "*Unless above himself* he can / *Erect* himself, how poor a thing is man." Emerson cites the couplet, in 1862, to illustrate how "puny" one is unless one becomes "a vehicle of ideas," and so "borrows their omnipotence"; Thoreau, three years earlier, in the course of his "Plea for Captain John Brown." In both cases, though Emerson misattributes the lines to Donne, and Thoreau cites no source at all, they are quoting the couplet in the Samuel Daniel translation of Seneca borrowed by Wordsworth for the climax of an important speech of the Wanderer (*E* 4: 295–331) on consolation, hope, and redemptive "spirit" from Emerson's favorite book of *The Excursion.*[6] In all these cases, the erecting, repairing, recuperative power is "within" yet deriving its self-transcending strength from "above." Emerson's solution was characteristically audacious: "Blessed is the day," he announces in a journal entry of 1834, "when the adventurous youth discovers that Within and Above are synonymous" (*JMN* 4:365).

6. Emerson quotes the couplet in his 1862 *Atlantic Monthly* essay, "American Civilization" (D. M. Robinson, *The Political Emerson,* 166). Seneca's pivotal *unless* was taken up not only by Milton, Wordsworth, Emerson, and Thoreau but, before all of them, by Henry Vaughan in his 1655 poem "The Waterfall." Though "Sublime truths" lodge in the streams formed by that cataract, those truths—especially that which, overcoming frail flesh's doubts, assures us "That what God takes" he will "restore"—are, in Vaughan's lovely allusion to Genesis 1:2, "Such as dull man can never find / *Unless* that Spirit move his mind / Which first upon thy face did move / And hatched all with his quickening love"; or, as Yeats would put it, internalizing the Spirit of God in "Sailing to Byzantium," an aged man is "but a paltry thing," a "tattered" scarecrow, "*Unless* soul clap its hands and sing, / And louder sing, for every tatter in its mortal dress."

To return to "Gnothi Seauton": Following a quatrain tracing a Plotinian or Miltonic epistrophe, the return of all things to the originating One ("There is nothing else but God"—"Where e'er I look / All things hasten back to him"), Emerson alludes to his poetic sources and poignantly acknowledges that he is not among the mighty bards—preeminently Milton and Wordsworth—who, themselves "immortal here below," are able with the "torch of genius" to pierce the "Secret" of God's "Seraphim who go / Singing an immortal strain." "I know the mighty bards," he says, employing Wordsworth's term for Milton (the "bard" who is his great predecessor in the "Prospectus") and Coleridge's for Wordsworth (the "great Bard" of "To William Wordsworth"). "I listen when they sing," says Emerson, when their torches pierce the clouds to reveal "the riches of the Universe." And even "if to me it is not given" to "bring one ingot thence / Of that unfading gold of heaven," he knows well that "royal mine" and the "sparkle of its ore." He is able to distinguish "Celestial truths from lies that shine," because he has read poetic explorers who in turn "teach us to explore" (*JMN* 3:294–95). Later cancelled, in what the editors tell us were "unusually heavy" strokes, are the heartbreaking words, "Enough[,] no more. Why can not I write verses"[?]

Given that cry from the heart, it is significant that Emerson should express in his notebooks for 1831 and 1832 real anger in rereading at this time poems by one of his two presiding bards, specifically the "Ode to Duty" and "Tintern Abbey." He is inwardly disturbed enough to claim that "I never read Wordsworth without chagrin." Despite his "great powers & ambition," Wordsworth repeatedly fails; if he is a genius, even angelic, he is a "genius that hath epilepsy, a deranged archangel." Perhaps emboldened by Coleridge's criticisms (in *Biographia Literaria*) of his friend's diction, Emerson charges: "The *Ode to Duty,* conceived and expressed in a certain high, severe style, does yet miss of greatness and of all effect by such falsities or falses as, 'And the most ancient heavens, thro thee are fresh and strong' [line 56], which is throwing dust in your eyes, because they have no more to do with duty than a dung-cart has" (*JMN* 4:63).

What is infuriating Emerson? Those "heavens" seem remote in space as well as time, not only "ancient" but also external to the divinity within, the voice of God inscribed in our own souls. Since, as Wordsworth himself pointed out in the prose commentary on the poem he contributed to Coleridge's *The Friend,* moral duty here implies "in its essence voluntary obedience" (*F* 1:405), what have these "ancient heavens"—inappropriately freshened and strengthened by God—to do with the present and with that duty which is voluntary and incised "*within thy single mind*"? In contemplating, as he said, "all modes of existence as subservient to one Spirit"

(*F* 2:384), Wordsworth, who concludes the ode by praying to become God's "Bondsman," may have seemed too submissive for the advocate of self-reliance.

Emerson is no less cutting, if far less accurate, in a comment on his next example, "Tintern Abbey." This time he is irritated that "that fine promising passage about 'the mountain winds being free to blow upon thee,' etc., flats out into *'me and my benedictions.'* If he had cut into his dictionary for words, he could hardly have got worse" (*JMN* 4:63). Actually, Wordsworth *did* "flat out," but by coming up with a "worse" word than *benedictions.* In the phrase Emerson is misremembering from "Tintern Abbey," Wordsworth directs Dorothy and his readers to "these my *exhortations*" (146). Quoting from memory, Emerson imports into "Tintern Abbey" Wordsworth's wonderful telescoping, in a dozen words of stanza 9 of the Intimations Ode, of past, present, and future, indeed, perpetuity: "The thought of our past years in me doth breed / Perpetual *benediction*" (135–36). Perhaps incapable of criticizing the ode, especially lines from his favorite stanza, Emerson may have transposed *benediction* to "Tintern Abbey." That he then criticizes the term suggests, though it is hardly consistent with his usual emphasis on self-reliance and the God within, that he finds Wordsworth's prayer for his sister in "Tintern Abbey" presumptuous, since he supplies his own "self-contained" blessing rather than invoking God's.[7]

In both of these outbursts, as their very vehemence would seem to confirm, the target of Emerson's scathing abuse is not Wordsworth's diction as such, but his religious vocabulary, whether the orthodox piety suggested by "most ancient heavens," or the spiritual presumptuousness of blessings bestowed by the poet rather than God, even if Wordsworth did not quite say "me and my *benedictions.*" Either way, at this particular time, he apparently found Wordsworth's religious certitude disturbing, disturbing enough to consciously or unconsciously distort "Tintern Abbey." Though we associate Emily Dickinson even more than Emerson with visceral disgust at hollow religious platitudes, perhaps at this stage of his mourning for Ellen, a crisis of faith that would contribute to his decision to give up

7. In "Emerson's Chagrin: Benediction and Exhortation in 'Nature' and 'Tintern Abbey,'" chap. 3 in *Emerson and Skepticism,* John Michael notes the intensity of Emerson's word ("an inwardly gnawing trouble") and sees significance ("Emerson's failure of memory is no trivial matter") in his mistaking *benedictions* for *exhortations.* Whereas an "exhortation depends upon its hearer," a "benediction does not. The power of a benediction is, as it were, self-contained; the blessing is delivered without needing the consent or even the consciousness of the one blessed," here, of course, the poet's sister (*Emerson and Skepticism,* 11, 77).

his pastorate, Emerson was particularly sensitive to such a vocabulary. As a bereaved husband longing for immortality (both for the young wife he had just lost and for himself, if he was to rejoin her), yet wavering in his belief, Emerson is, in effect, saying of such language: that's wormwood. That he sought comfort in Wordsworth's healing power remains significant, but in the aftermath of Ellen's death, and for some time afterward—indeed, until his revitalizing trip to England in 1833—there was little comfort to be found.

Nor would the ecstatic intensity of that "first love" ever really be replaced. Though he would marry again, in September 1835, there may be, in the form of a single adjective, Wordsworthian testimony supporting Emerson's premonition that his "first love" was indeed unique. With Ellen dead, the veiling "clouds" took, for Emerson, what Wordsworth had called in the Intimations Ode "a *sober* colouring from an eye / That hath kept watch o'er man's mortality" (197–99). In replacing his original "*awful* colouring" with the adjective *sober*, Wordsworth, already thinking of the "still, sad music of humanity" (91) in "Tintern Abbey," intended a functional echo of his use of *sober* in that earlier poem. There, reading his own "former pleasures in the shooting lights" of his sister's "wild eyes," he had anticipated, positively but with undisguised ambivalence, "after years," when "these wild ecstasies shall be matured / Into a *sober* pleasure" (118–19, 137–39). Significantly, when Emerson, in January 1835 became engaged to Lydia Jackson, he recorded in his journal feeling "very *sober* joy." While, in his letter of proposal, he was obeying his "highest impulses" in declaring to her his "feeling of deep and tender respect," and even repaired to Coleridge in saying that, on this occasion, he "rejoiced in my Reason as well as in my Understanding," his attachment to Lydia (soon to be transformed into "Lidian") did not approach the intensity of his love for "the Departed," Ellen, a fact of which his fiancée was quickly apprised. Emerson may have loved his second wife, but as we know from her troubled conversations with Margaret Fuller in the year of little Waldo's death, Lidian never felt that "intimacy" Emerson had shared with Ellen and, Lidian feared, with Margaret herself.[8]

8. Emerson's curious letter of proposal, at once impulsive and detached, remained an unpublished manuscript in the Houghton Library for almost a century and a half, until it was printed by Gay Wilson Allen (*Waldo Emerson,* 239–40). See also *L* 1:436. In one of their walks, Lidian talked "so freely" that Margaret felt justified in concluding that she was destined to remain distraught because she retained a "lurking hope" that Emerson would become capable of "an intimate union." Margaret's perhaps wise but somewhat chilly advice was for Lidian to simply "take him for what he is" (Joel Myerson, ed., "Margaret Fuller's 1842 Journal: At Concord with the Emersons," 331).

During the period that Emerson had begun walking every day to Ellen's tomb in the Roxbury Cemetery, news arrived of the death of his brother Edward, a young man whose "wondrous brilliancy" made Emerson's own promise "faint in comparison," according to a reminiscent Henry Hedge, but "whose immense expectation was doomed never to be fulfilled." Looking back in old age, Hedge declared that he had "never known a more brilliant youth." Edward was not merely "the first scholar in his class" (one class before Hedge at Harvard) but also "first by a long interval. His orations were epochs in college history." He was "looking to political life for his career but the overwrought brain gave out; he fell into conscious & irrecoverable ruin," his death hastened, Hedge thought, "by grief for his failed ambition."[9]

Edward, who had suffered a mental collapse in 1828, sailed, in failing health, to St. Croix and then to Puerto Rico, where he worked at the American consulate. Three years after Ellen's death, Edward, only twenty-nine, succumbed to a combination of mania and tuberculosis. Again, Emerson's response was entangled with the language of Coleridge and Wordsworth. When word of the death reached him from Puerto Rico, Emerson noted in his journal: "So falls one pile more of hope for this life. I see I am bereaved of a part of myself: 'Whatever fortunes wait my future life / The beautiful is vanished & returns not'" (*JMN* 4:325). The slightly misquoted lines are from what is by far the finest scene in Schiller's *Death of Wallenstein,* the second part of *The Piccolomini,* which Emerson read in Coleridge's translation. Emerson's response to the death of Edward is in fact strikingly close to that of Wallenstein to the death of the young Piccolomini. Wallenstein describes the noble youth as "fortunate," beyond "desire and fear," no longer subject "to the change and chance / Of the unsteady planets." Though he says he shall eventually "grieve down the blow," for "What does man not grieve down," Wallenstein adds:

> Yet I feel what I have lost
> In him. The bloom is vanished from my life
> . . . .
> Whatever fortunes wait upon my future toils,
> The beautiful is vanished—and returns not.
> (5.1.39–46, 57–68; *CPW* 2:795–96)

Nine days after he quoted those last two lines, and had almost given up "hope for this life," Emerson had reached the point where he could take some comfort, as had Wallenstein, in imagining the dead youth beyond

9. Hedge to James Elliot Cabot, September 14, 30, 1882, in Bosco and Myerson, *His Own Time,* 96, 98.

this world and its chaos: "Edward's fervid heart is . . . forever still, no more to suffer from the tumults of the Natural World." Those tumults, in large part political, were enough, says Emerson to almost make one lose all "hope" for the country. "Yet yet," he continues, "is 'Hope the paramount duty which Heaven lays / For its own honor on man's suffering heart' " (*JMN* 4:326). This time, he is quoting Wordsworth, not the "Ode to Duty," but an 1811 sonnet in which the poet reaffirms, in the shadow of the "throne of tyranny" and Napoleonic triumph, his own steadfast commitment to "virtuous Liberty" and to "hope" even in the "worst moment of these evil days" (*WP* 1:854–55).[10] The events to which Wordsworth was responding, in both poetry and prose, require a brief excursus if we are to fully appreciate the relevance of the historical moment to the present theme.

This specific historical context—the "evil days" of Napoleonic hegemony—produced a number of political variations on the Wordsworthian insistence that it is not without hope we suffer and we mourn. There was Wordsworth's major prose statement of his political position and his abiding principles, the pamphlet *On the Convention at Cintra,* and, in poetry, those "noble sonnets," as Emerson called them, eventually gathered together (in 1815) as *Poems Dedicated to National Independence and Liberty.* The 1811 sonnet just cited became the thirty-third in the series; the twelfth was quoted from by Emerson in "Spiritual Laws," to buttress his praise of "strong instincts" as more to be valued than sick intellectualism (*E&L* 306). As we have seen, that poem, honoring "the efforts of the Tyrolese," celebrated the alpine instinct of the Tyrolean rebels, who, in contrast to "sapient" but supine Germany, continued to resist Napoléon. Their leader, Andreas Hofer, courageously defended his homeland against occupying forces (Napoléon's Bavarian and Italian allies) even after the Austrians, crushed at the Battle of Wagram, had, in July 1809, withdrawn their help; even after, despite Hofer's decisive defeat of the Bavarians in August, Austria had again relinquished the Tyrol to Napoléon as part of the Truce of Znaim; even after, in accord with the terms dictated to the Austrians at the Treaty of Vienna, October 1809, Hofer had been abandoned to his enemies. Though this was a "worst moment" that must have tested even Wordsworth's commitment to undying "hope," it would seem to be at this juncture that he wrote his sonnet, composed sometime between late summer and early November 1809, and first published in Coleridge's *Friend* on November 16, 1809. It was in print, therefore, before the "worst" actually came. For Hofer, betrayed by one of his compatriots, was captured,

10. From the thirty-third sonnet in pt. 2 of Wordsworth's *Poems Dedicated to National Independence and Liberty.*

taken to Mantua, and—on February 10, 1810, on Napoléon's orders—executed, "murdered," according to an 1810 Wordsworth sonnet (*WP* 1: 837). Thus he joined Toussaint Louverture, that other nationalist hero betrayed to and executed by Napoléon. In Wordsworth's great sonnet on Toussaint, the dead hero is to "take comfort," both in the displaced "Powers that will work for thee" ("air, earth, and skies"), and in his "great allies," above all, "man's unconquerable mind" (*WP* 1:577).

All these sonnets paying tribute to independence struggles are related to Wordsworth's major production of 1809, his fifty thousand–word tract *On the Convention of Cintra.* For all its author's fury at expedience and betrayal, *On the Convention of Cintra* ends—as do most of his sonnets dedicated to these struggles—by reasserting Wordsworth's faith in ultimate victory and reaffirming inextinguishable "hope" and the potential of a revivified "joy" even in the depths of disaster. "But I began with hope; and hope has inwardly accompanied me to the end." The *Cintra* pamphlet's imagery of hope and regeneration suggests that the Spanish popular uprising of 1808 stirred in Wordsworth something of his old revolutionary ardor. That cause had been betrayed by the French themselves (the oppressed become oppressors in their turn), above all by Napoléon, described in the pamphlet as "that intoxicated Despot," who had appropriated the revolutionary lexicon: "'*I have created; I have regenerated.*'... [T]his is the language perpetually on his lips." But the true regenerative spirit was alive precisely where there was opposition to the despot, most recently in Spain, with its "new-born spirit of resistance, rising from the most sacred feelings of the human heart."[11]

And it is by the heart that, in the peroration of the text, "the life of Man is sustained." Wordsworth describes the heart as that "genial and vernal inmate of the breast," which—"by anticipations, apprehensions, and active remembrances; by elasticity under insult, and firm resistance to injury; by joy and love...—habitually expands itself, for [man's] elevation, in complacency toward his Creator." But the prerequisite of such "complacency," or spiritual tranquillity, is political and military action: specifically, the defeat of the French forces. "The French army was not broken?" Wordsworth asks archly, furious that the British generals in Spain had not destroyed the enemy. "Break it then—wither it—pursue it with unrelent-

11. Wordsworth, *Prose Works of Wordsworth,* 1:228, 319. According to the terms agreed to by the British in the Anglo-French convention signed at Cintra in August 1808, in return for a peaceful evacuation of Lisbon, Juno's army was to be transported (aboard British ships!) back to France, its soldiers, arms, and artillery intact and thus once again at Napoléon's command. Widely seen at the time as an ill-advised concession, this was, for Wordsworth, at once a cynical betrayal of patriots fighting for national independence against an international tyranny and a gift to the tyrant himself.

ing warfare—hunt it out of its holds." Of course, just the opposite had happened—months before even the *London Courier* excerpts (December 1808 and January 1809) from Wordsworth's tract had reached the public.

Still, this pamphleteer was *Wordsworth:* a visionary whose imagination penetrates the immediate to reveal invisible but deeper truths, *and* a champion of man's unconquerable mind. To quote famous lines (written in 1804, first published in 1845) from the crossing of the Simplon Pass in book 6 of *The Prelude:*

> Our destiny, our nature, and our home
> Is with infinitude, and only there;
> With hope it is, hope that can never die,
> Effort, and expectation, and desire,
> And something evermore about to be.
> (*P* 6:605–9)

Thus, in the Cintra pamphlet, he looks forward to what is "to be," envisaging—beyond the British cabinet's betrayal of the Spanish freedom-fighters, beyond the French imperium itself, now at its apogee—"a sublime movement of deliverance." Milton had, in *Areopagitica,* envisaged England as "a noble and puissant nation rouzing herself like a strong man after sleep, and shaking her invincible locks." Extending Milton's image of heroic resurrection to Britain's continental allies, Wordsworth cries out, "Let the human creature be rouzed; . . . let him rise and act . . . Regeneration is at hand."

It is the language—Miltonic, biblical, millennial—of Romantic revolution, of Blake's declaration-of-independence plate in *America,* where the apparent dead, "Reviving shake, inspiring move, breathing! Awakening!" now that "Empire is no more." Wordsworth, in effect, is choosing one empire over another, but in the circumstances we are, to cite the future imperatives of Shelley's Demogorgon, in act 4 of *Prometheus Unbound,*

> To defy Power which seems Omnipotent;
> To love, and bear; to hope, till Hope creates
> From its own wreck the thing it contemplates.
> (572–74)

However dejected he may have been in the "evil days" of 1809, Wordsworth, gazing across the Channel at a whole continent prostrate at the feet of the tyrant, still saw these national independence movements, temporarily crushed or betrayed though they might be, as what Shelley would call, in the great ode written at the same time as the apocalyptic final act of *Prometheus Unbound,* "wingéd seeds" lying, "Each like a corpse within its grave," until awakened by Italy's regenerating spring wind. (As Wordsworth himself would urge two decades later, in the first of his sonnets entitled "Leaving Italy": "awake, / Mother of Heroes, from thy death-like sleep!") In the *Cintra* pamphlet, the national independence movements of 1808–1809 were instruments of the divine will, part of a finally irrepressible supranational insurgency of a "mighty People" driven by Justice. Wordsworth imagines all Europe rising from defeat. Even Germany, despite its "corrupt princedoms" and "degenerate nobility," still has its "peasants, and its philosophers" ("strong instincts," as it were, united with "sapience"), and thus "will not lie quiet under the weight of injuries which has been heaped upon it."

> There is a sleep but no death among the mountains of Switzerland.... The stir of emancipation may again be felt at the mouths as well as at the sources of the Rhine. Poland perhaps will not be insensible; Kosciusko and his compeers may not have bled in vain... And for Spain herself, the territory is wide; let it be overrun: the torrent will weaken as the water spreads.... How often do hope and despair touch each other. Yet in a moment the one shall vanish; and to the other begin a career in the fullness of her joy.[12]

Thus, even in the darkest days, Wordsworth, in the peroration of his loyalist yet freedom-championing tract, goes beyond indignation to consolation in distress, precisely what Emerson most valued in him, in the Intimations Ode and elsewhere. From a despair "Heavy as frost, and deep almost as life!," Wordsworth can, "in a moment," and in the very next line of the ode, pivot to what he calls in the *Cintra* tract "the other": "O joy! That in our embers / Is something that doth live" (130–31). For Wordsworth, there seems always to be a mysterious and vital "something" to provide solace in despair: incipient victory in defeat, light in the darkness, a spark in the embers—as Shelley, despite having just lost his little boy, remembered in the final stanza of the "Ode to the West Wind." As Wordsworth's American disciple, Emerson, would memorably put it in the wake of the agonizing death of his own little boy, the son whose birth had consoled him in the wake of the death of his brother Charles: "I am *Defeated* all the time, yet to Victory am I born" (*JMN* 8:228). The Wordsworthian mixture of elegy and triumph, of suffering and the assertion of a divinity within, clarifies Emerson's otherwise mysterious adjectives, "Tyrtaean" and "Uranian," in a mid-1840s journal entry. Comparing Wordsworth and

12. Ibid., 1:341. *America* (pl. 6: 4, 15) is cited from *Poetry and Prose of Blake,* 52. For the passages from *Prometheus Unbound,* see Shelley, *Shelley's Poetry and Prose,* 210, 221.

Byron, and alluding to the Spartan war poet and elegist Tyrtaeus and to the Muse of both Milton and Wordsworth, Urania, Emerson asserts: "The office of poetry I supposed was Tyrtaean—consoling, indemnifying; and of the Uranian, deifying or imparadising. Yet Wordsworth was mindful of the office" (*JMN* 9:376).

Whatever the crisis at hand, whether it was personal grief or political despair that threatened the God within, Wordsworth, mindful of his dual office, provided the required consolation and "hope." Just as Nietzsche was to turn to Emerson during a profound emotional crisis, Emerson turns to Wordsworth for language to express and assuage "man's suffering heart" (*WP* 1:855), reinforcement of his own faith—deep yet at times desperate and half-disbelieving—that it is (as Wordsworth says in the tragically affirmative final line of the poem written in the aftermath of the loss of his own dearly loved brother) "Not without hope we suffer and we mourn" (*WP* 1:696). I will defer comment on that poem, "Elegiac Stanzas Suggested by a Picture of Peele Castle, in a Storm, Painted by Sir George Beaumont," in order to say a word about "Character of the Happy Warrior," a poem occasioned by news "of the Death of Lord Nelson," though, as Wordsworth told Isabella Fenwick, "many elements of the character here portrayed were found in my brother John" (*WP* 1:1014).

"Character of the Happy Warrior," written nine months after John, a ship's captain, drowned at sea on February 5, 1805, is frequently mentioned by Emerson as one of Wordsworth's finest poems (for example, *JMN* 5:335). That high ranking is reflected in his November 1831 journal remark on the poem: "Almost I can say Coleridge's compliment, *quem quoties lego, non verba mihi videor audire, sed tonitrua*" (whenever I read him, it seems to me that it is not words I hear, but thunder); and, writing to his brother Charles on January 19, 1832, Emerson refers to Wordsworth as "my thunderer" (*JMN* 3:306; *L* 1:344). Interestingly enough, Emerson is applying to the "Happy Warrior" Coleridge's praise (*F* 1:182) of the Wordsworthian pamphlet just discussed, *On the Convention of Cintra.* Though Emerson printed the entire text of the poem in the "Heroic" section of *Parnassus* (196–98), his admiration focused on its opening third, a passage cited by Coleridge, also profoundly moved by John's death, as the epigraph to his essay on Admiral Sir Alexander Ball (*F* 1:547). From the opening depiction of "the generous Spirit" engaged in "the tasks of real life," we move to the Happy Warrior's endurance of, and strengthening by, suffering; the conversion of evil into good, pain into self-knowledge; and, finally, his reliance upon the inner light and law of intuitive Reason. This kind of hero, whom we should all emulate, is he "Whose high endeavors are an inward light / That makes the path before him always bright" (1–7; *WP* 1:660). Perhaps following the Boethian imperative of Chaucer's Theseus in "The Knight's Tale"—"To maken vertu of necessitie"—the Happy Warrior,

> doomed to go in company with Pain,
> And Fear, and Bloodshed, miserable train!
> Turns his necessity to glorious gain;
> In face of these doth exercise a power
> Which is our human nature's highest dower;
> Controls them and subdues, transmutes, bereaves
> Of their bad influence, and their good receives.
> (12–18)

Emerson—who would, in "Fate," quote a pivotal passage of "The Knight's Tale" (*E&L* 944)—would see differences as well as similarities in these two texts. Instead of the cool, almost emotionless detachment pervading not only Theseus's keynote speech toward the end but the whole of the knight's tale itself, we have Wordsworthian compassion, intensified by the pain inflicted by the objective world, a heightened sensitivity ("more" is repeated six times) to the still, sad music of humanity. The Happy Warrior is "By objects, which might force the soul to abate / Her feeling, rendered more compassionate" (19–20);

> More skilful in self-knowledge, even more pure,
> As tempted more; more able to endure,
> As more exposed to suffering and distress;
> Thence, also, more alive to tenderness,
> —'Tis he whose law is reason; who depends
> Upon that law as on the best of friends.
> (23–28)

Wordsworth's characteristic transmutation of sorrow into strength, suffering into empathic tenderness, is even more personal in "Elegiac Stanzas" (*WP* 1:694–96), written shortly after John's drowning. After bidding "farewell" to the heart that imagines, blindly, that it "lives alone," and recognizing that "A deep distress hath humanized my Soul" (53, 36), Wordsworth concludes by welcoming "fortitude" and "patient cheer" in the face of even the worst sights: tragedies that are "to be borne!" for it is "Not without hope we suffer and we mourn" (57–60). Significantly, the best-known lines in this poem play a variation on the "celestial light" of the Intimations Ode, in effect restoring that Miltonic phrase to its original Miltonic meaning in book 3 of *Paradise Lost:* an *inner* light. Wordsworth speaks of

the gleam,
The light that never was, on sea or land,
The consecration, and the Poet's dream.
(14–16)

Emerson alludes to that more than natural light in "Beauty," the penultimate essay in *The Conduct of Life.* Discussing what it is we confer upon objects by means of what Coleridge, in "Dejection," calls the "beautiful and beauty-making power" of the joyous imagination (*CPW* 1:365), Emerson says: "There are no days in life so memorable as those which vibrated to some stroke of the imagination" (*E&L* 1111). Beauty may be transient, but we remain its lovers, "only transferring our interest to *interior* excellence," since even the loveliest things of the world do not actually become beautiful "until they speak to the imagination." Quoting the Neoplatonist Proclus, according to whom elusive, unpossessable beauty "swims on the light of forms," Emerson adds the typical Romantic emphasis on mind and the shaping power of imagination: "It is properly not in the form, but in the mind. . . . For the imagination and the senses cannot be gratified at the same time. Wordsworth rightly speaks of 'a light that never was on sea or land,' meaning that it was supplied by the observer" (*E&L* 1110). In emphasizing the subjective over the objective, the creative power of imagination over mere perception, Emerson is recalling but going beyond Wordsworth's celebration of

all that we behold
From this green earth; of all the mighty world
Of eye and ear,—both what they half create,
And what perceive.
("Tintern Abbey," lines 104–7)

He is also remembering, as John Stuart Mill may have in referring to Wordsworth's modification of "outward beauty" with "thought colored by feeling," Coleridge's citation of these same lines from "Elegiac Stanzas" in *Biographia Literaria.* This "light that never was, on sea or land," added "to all thoughts and to all objects," illustrates, says Coleridge, Wordsworth's "gift of IMAGINATION," the preeminent "power" by virtue of which he "stands nearest of all modern writers to Shakespeare and Milton" (*BL* 2:151).

Taken together, these memorable lines describing the "gleam," the "light that never was, on sea or land, / The consecration and the Poet's dream," embody the fusion of poetic imagination, the intuitive Reason, and the "inward light," the Intimations Ode's "light of all our day," that "master light of all our seeing." They also, in keeping with the poem's title, "Elegiac

Stanzas . . . ," complete a psychological and poetic trajectory in the progress of mourning. Devastating grief suffered intensely until met, first, with the blowing open of the isolated heart, then with Stoic "fortitude" and a more than Stoic bearing of tragedy with "patient cheer" based on a sorely tested but finally inextinguishable faith in the intuited "gleam"—the Wordsworthian "light of all our day"—that illumines even the darkest nights of the soul. In the humanizing pathos of the Great Ode's final stanza, that light is transmuted into the "sober colouring" conferred upon "The clouds that gather round the setting sun," clouds that "take" (Mill's "outward beauty" submitting to "thought colored by feeling") their somber glow "from an eye / That hath kept watch o'er man's mortality."

That eye is a "dread watch-tower" indeed, but not in any hopeless or solipsistic sense; even Coleridge did not intend *that* in referring to "the dread watch-tower of man's *absolute self*" (*CPW* 1:405). Instead, it is, again, part of the paradigm of compensation and reconstituted hope, a deeper seeing in which an adult—aware of suffering and human mutability and employing poetic language to explore the analogy between the human and natural worlds—is able to communicate to us the tears that are in things, even thoughts too deep for tears. This elegiac pattern ensures not only the mourner's human survival *but the renewal of imaginative creativity, a poetic "consecration."* In Emerson's case, it is this pattern we will see repeated, but far more strikingly, in the creative aftermath of Charles's death and in the period following the "worst moment" of Emerson's life: the death of his first son, Waldo.

It is *that* death in the family that has been seen, even more than the traumatic deaths of Ellen, Edward, and Charles, as *the* pivotal event of Emerson's life, the point at which, for many readers, Emerson himself dies, at least as an oracular High Romantic, to be replaced by the man who bows down to Fate, retaining his affirmative vision by actively "build[ing] altars" to Fate and by referring to it as "Beautiful Necessity" (*E&L* 967). That child's death and Emerson's various responses to it (in a letter written a week after the event, in the essay "Experience," and in his poetic elegy "Threnody") provide the material for my final chapter, where the death of the son and the father's response will be placed in the context of Emerson's relationship—intellectual, poetic, and personal—to Wordsworth's Intimations Ode. But I turn next to Emerson's response to the death of Charles, the third of his familial catastrophes—a response that is paradigmatically and demonstrably Wordsworthian.

Chapter 13

Mourning Becomes Morning

THE DEATH OF CHARLES

Unless I discover the alchemical trick of turning this—muck into gold, I am lost. Here I have the most beautiful chance to prove that for me "all experiences are useful, all days are holy and all people divine"!!!

—FRIEDRICH NIETZSCHE, quoting Emerson

❧

we live by hope
And by desire; we see by the glad light
And breathe the sweet air of futurity
And so we live, or else we have no life.

—William Wordsworth's WANDERER, *The Excursion*

❧

Those who have ministered to my highest needs . . . are to me what the Wanderer in the Excursion is to the poet. And Wordsworth's total value is of this kind. . . . Theirs is the true light of all our day. They are the argument for the spiritual world for their spirit is it.

—RALPH WALDO EMERSON, journal, May 9, 1836

I remarked earlier that Emerson's disciple, Nietzsche, was challenged and comforted by his mentor in roughly the same way that Emerson had drawn solace from his reading of Wordsworth. The particular Emersonian crisis focused on in this chapter is the death of Charles; the crisis Nietzsche had to face and overcome, indeed transmute, was his sense of betrayal by the brilliant and beautiful Lou Salomé. Nietzsche's emotional and creative triumph over despair was significantly aided by his reading of Emerson, just as Emerson's emergence from grief is partially attributable to the ministry of Wordsworth's Wanderer, the corrector of "Despondency" in books 4 and 9 of *The Excursion.* The fact that Emerson plays a role in both cases, as both receiver and giver of consolation in distress, suggests that juxtaposition may prove illuminating.

It is no exaggeration to describe Nietzsche's feeling of having been abandoned by Lou—the remarkable young woman he dreamed of making his soulmate, disciple, and possible lover—as the most devastating experience of his life. In a letter of December 1882 to Overbeck, his friend and fellow Emersonian enthusiast, Nietzsche poured out his soul about the shattering effect on him of what he felt was Lou's betrayal. "This last *morsel of life* was the hardest I have yet had to chew, and it is still possible that I may *choke* on it." His humiliation and torment took the form of an agon,

> a tension between opposing passions which I cannot cope with. This is to say, I am exerting every ounce of my self-mastery; but I have lived in solitude too long and fed too long off my "own fat," so that I am now being broken . . . on the wheel of my own passions. . . . Unless I discover the alchemical trick of turning this—muck into gold, I am lost. Here I have the most beautiful chance to prove that for me "all experiences are useful, all days are holy and all people divine"!!![1]

In this, the major crisis of his life, Nietzsche turns to Emerson, quoting him from his essay "History" (and this, in German, with "the saint" left out, was his original epigraph to *The Gay Science*): "To the poet, to the philosopher, to the saint, all things are friendly and sacred, all events profitable, all days holy, all men divine" (*E&L* 242). Though Nietzsche dropped the *saint,* he drew solace from Emerson's affirmative vision of the poet and philosopher who finds all things sacred, holy, divine, and even the most painful circumstances "profitable," a clear anticipation of the Nietzschean doctrine of purposeful suffering as the prerequisite to self-enhancement and creative achievement. Once again, the Emersonian "House of Pain" is an educational institution, a school whose hard lessons are ultimately valuable and power enhancing. Six months later, writing to Overbeck from the mountain heights of Sils Maria, Zarathustra country, Nietzsche described himself as "an incarnate wrestling match," but he anticipated a major "self-conquest."

This, in its most intimate manifestation, is that "self-overcoming" at the heart of Nietzsche's mature philosophy, the agonistic concept under-

1. Nietzsche, *Selected Letters,* 198–99. But Christopher Middleton does not cite the source of Nietzsche's climactic quotation. The Sils Maria letter quoted in the following paragraph may be found in this edition, 214–15.

lying his well-known axiom—profound enough to survive even the trivialization of T-shirt sloganeering: "Out of life's school of war: that which does not destroy me makes me stronger."[2] He anticipated, Nietzsche confided to Overbeck, an "absolute victory—that is, the transformation of experience into gold and use of the highest order." Here, as in his reference to the need, expressed in the earlier letter, to discover the "alchemical trick" of transmuting the "muck" of his personal suffering into immutable, imaginative "gold," Nietzsche may be recalling that in the "Beauty" chapter of *Nature* Emerson described "Art" as "nature passed through the *alembic* of man," man through whose mind and will beauty is wrought from nature. "All good is eternally reproductive. The beauty of nature reforms itself in the mind, and not for barren contemplation, but for new creation" (*E&L* 18–19).

Echoing Emerson, and anticipating Eliot's distinction, in "Tradition and the Individual Talent," between "the man who suffers and the mind that creates," Nietzsche, in his next comment in the letter to Overbeck, seals his victory, his transcendence of the personal in a transformative sublimation leading to "new creation." "That I should have thought and written this year my sunniest and serenest things, many miles above myself and my misery—this is really one of the most amazing and inexplicable things I know." The explanation, here as always, lies in Nietzsche's own spirit in triumphing over physical and emotional suffering and profound loneliness—that "solipsistic entrapment" and "loneliness of the gods" that has been applied to Emerson as well. But his solar serenity on this occasion is *less* "inexplicable" once we realize that the courage to go on, indeed the serene and sunny exaltation in which, having completed *The Gay Science,* he began *Zarathustra,* was conceived as a potentially "beautiful" response—"mak[ing] things beautiful" in accord with the doctrine of *amor fati*—to the tonic challenge presented by Emerson. That this self-overcoming and *gaya scienza* shared by Emerson and Nietzsche take many forms seems increasingly evident to anyone familiar with their lives and writing. It is therefore ironic that one of the earliest and best American students of Nietzsche, a New Hampshire man who also knew Emerson's work well, should write of Nietzsche that "he met his depression and triumphed over it," emerging as "one of the great affirmers of life. . . . But his joy is ever a warrior's joy—it is never the easy serenity, the unruffled optimism of Emerson." I am quoting W. M. Salter, who cites Emerson some twenty times in his book *Nietzsche the Thinker* without once indicating any awareness that that thinker read, was profoundly impressed by, and indeed

2. Nietzsche, *Twilight of the Idols,* "Maxims and Arrows," 8, in *The Portable Nietzsche,* 467.

based much of his heroic and joyous affirmation of life in the midst of suffering on the writings and personal example of this allegedly "unruffled optimist."[3]

The challenge was to *affirm* even in the midst of anguish, to find, as Emerson says in "Fate," that "Every calamity is a spur and valuable hint" (*E&L* 960). Just as Emerson had taken up Wordsworth's challenge (in "Character of the Happy Warrior") to "transmute" evil into good, "necessity to glorious gain," so Nietzsche—for whom "pain," as that formidable Muse Lou herself later astutely noted, "was always the origin of each new phase of development"—found in the creative alembic of Emerson a way to alchemically convert experiential muck into mental, imaginative, aesthetic gold. That golden smithy of Byzantium, Yeats, also affirmed the transmutation of heart into art in the midst of "life's school of war." As he put it in *Meditations in Time of Civil War:* "only an aching heart / Conceives a changeless work of art," in effect endorsing the notorious remark of *his* Lou Salomé, that elusive, heartbreaking, and inspiring Muse Maud Gonne: "O, Willy, you should thank me for not marrying you. You make such beautiful poetry out of what you call your unhappiness." Had that "proud woman not kindred of his soul" married him, or even understood him fully, Yeats wonders, "What would have shaken from the sieve?" He "might have thrown poor words away / And been content to live." That he says this *in a poem*—and one titled, significantly enough, "Words"—is yet another instance of alchemical transmutation, or, better, of what Freud called, following the Nietzsche he pretended not to have read, "sublimation."[4]

There is an uncanny parallel to Nietzsche's conversion of agony into ecstasy in Emerson's response to the crisis that preceded by six years the

3. Salter, *Nietzsche the Thinker,* 20. So fixed was the image of Emerson as the sunny optimist that it could not override Salter's many references to passages of Emerson's essays by way of analogy to Nietzsche, and, most surprisingly, there is no indication that Salter was aware that Nietzsche had actually *read* most of the very essays being cited. For the remark about "solipsistic entrapment" and divine "loneliness," see the earlier cited article by Doherty, "Emerson and the Loneliness of the Gods."

4. Yeats, "Words," "My Table," sec. 3 of Yeats's sequence *Meditations in Time of Civil War,* and "A Dialogue of Self and Soul," pt. 2 (*W. B. Yeats: The Poems,* 90, 202, 236). For Lou's response to Nietzsche, anticipating Maud's to Yeats, see her *Nietzsche,* newly edited and translated by Siegfried Mandel (originally published in 1894 as *Friedrich Nietzsche in seinen Werken*). Lou later became a valued confidante of Freud, who famously remarked that Nietzsche "had a more penetrating knowledge of himself than any man who ever lived or who was ever likely to live" (Jones, *The Life and Work of Sigmund Freud,* 2:344), and claimed to have stopped reading him because of the anxiety of influence, a claim persuasively challenged by Lorin Anderson, who notes, among other things, the indebtedness of *Civilization and Its Discontents* to the *Genealogy of Morals.*

death of his son: the death of his second and closest brother, Charles, just two years after Edward's death. Emerson and his even more intellectually accomplished brother had recently been reading Sophocles' *Antigone* and *Electra,* with Emerson—as Charles, the superior Greek scholar, told his fiancée, Elizabeth Hoar (April 3, 1836)—"quite enamoured of the severe beauty of the Greek tragic muse." To be thus enamored is to go some distance, at least aesthetically, toward Nietzschean *amor fati* and what Emerson himself would call, a decade and a half later in "Fate," submission to the essence of Greek tragedy, the will of Zeus in the form of "Beautiful Necessity" (*E&L* 967). A month after their reading of *Electra,* Charles, as though to put the beauty of tragedy to the test, was dead. Emerson wondered, as he turned from the grave with an enigmatic laugh, what there was left "worth living for." Two weeks later, though he could say, "night rests on all sides upon the facts of our being," he could also add: we "must own, our upper nature lies always in Day" (*L* 2:19, 20, 25).

That "upper nature," associated with the Wordsworthian "light of all our day," has to do with what Emerson calls "spiritual law." In "Experience," that great essay so closely related to the death of little Waldo, Emerson repairs (in a rather clumsy translation) to the locus classicus of that law:

> Since neither now nor yesterday began
> These thoughts, which have been ever, nor yet can
> A man be found who their first entrance knew.
> (*E&L* 473)

Emerson is quoting from one of the most famous speeches in Greek tragedy, from, in fact, *Antigone,* one of the two plays he had read in Greek with his brother shortly before Charles's death. Responding to Creon's charge that, in burying *her* brother, Polyneices, Antigone violated royal "laws," Antigone archly observes that she did not think that Creon's laws, those of a mere mortal even if he is a king,

> Could over-run the gods' unwritten and unfailing laws;
> Not now, nor yesterday's, they always live,
> And no one knows their origin in time.
> (*Antigone,* 455–57)

This is the earliest, and often cited, statement of the eternal, unwritten justice (*themis*): the inner, supreme, spiritual "law" to which Emerson repeatedly refers, with its ever living "truths that wake, / To perish never," their origins unknown in time and for that very reason imperishable. The truths of this unwritten and immutable law, divine and intuitive, are opposed to human, written legislation (*nomoi*), civil proclamations here today and gone tomorrow. As Emerson had said earlier in the paragraph,

"Underneath" the vicissitudes of Chance and life's "inharmonious and trivial particulars," there is a "musical perfection, the Ideal journeying with us, the heaven without rent or seam," in the form of a "spiritual law," revealed to us by the very "mode of our illumination" (*E&L* 472).

That "illumination" is allied with the assertion that "our upper nature lies always in Day," which is to be traced to Wordsworth's Intimations Ode: not the fading of celestial radiance "into the light of *common* day" (77), but that Plotinian "fountain light of all our day" (152)—the line of the ode to which Emerson most frequently alludes. Addressing the Child in the middle stanzas of the ode, Wordsworth speaks of "Thou, over whom thy Immortality / Broods like the Day" (119–20). Wordsworth is at once sublime, certain, and vague about the source of that fontal light; he gives thanks for

> those first affections,
> Those shadowy recollections,
> Which, be they what they may,
> Are yet the fountain light of all our day,
> Are yet a master light of all our seeing.
> (149–53)

It is in this luminous yet shadowy region, a region of mastery rather than servitude, that, says Emerson, "our upper nature lies," Experience's version of Wordsworth's "Heaven lies about us in our infancy" (66).

The central issue, as suggested by the title of Wordsworth's ode, had to do with our intimations of "immortality." But by 1836, Emerson was having increasing difficulty believing in either a personal divinity in the sense of a god external to the self, or in a conventional, religiously orthodox sense of immortality; he had *only* that Wordsworthian presence brooding over him "like the Day." Men can have no answers to their persistent but misguided questions about immortality and heaven, he writes in "The Over-Soul," mocking those who "dream that Jesus has left replies to precisely these interrogatories. Never a moment did that sublime spirit speak in their *patois*," never did he utter "a syllable concerning the duration of the soul" (*E&L* 393). Indeed, however "strange" it may seem to some, Jesus "never preaches the personal immortality" (*W* 8:348).

Emerson's thoughts on the subject are most fully presented in the text I have just cited, "Immortality," which appears as an essay in the late collection *Letters and Social Aims* (1876). Though Emerson allowed it to be printed, the essay was edited (as Glen M. Johnson has demonstrated) by Ellen Emerson and James Elliot Cabot from notes accumulated over many years, most of them gathered in a lecture first given in 1861, and often presented afterwards, in variously revised forms. Concurring with Johnson that the essay was "normalized" by Emerson's "handlers so as to make it several shades more theistic" than the 1861 lecture, Buell rightly concludes: "Even so, the published version dashes cold water on conventional theories of afterlife."[5] The essay includes, for example, Emerson's observation (first made in a journal entry of July 1855) that "the blazing evidence of immortality is our dissatisfaction with any other solution." But however "blazing," this "evidence" is proof of nothing beyond our dissatisfaction with other "solutions" to the mystery of what Shakespeare's Cleopatra calls the "immortal longings" in us.

Among the more appealing of such pseudoproofs is that stated by the superabundant Goethe, and quoted by Emerson in "Immortality": "To me the eternal existence of my soul is proved from my idea of activity. If I work incessantly till my death, Nature is bound to give me another form of existence, when the present can no longer sustain my spirit" (*W* 8: 342). And later in the essay, Emerson paraphrases Goethe, insisting that "a man's faculties" must be able to "fill a larger theatre and a longer term than Nature here allows him."[6] It must have pleased Emerson to find his own thoughts anticipated by an admired mentor. A year before he first read Goethe, struggling in the original German, Emerson, fitfully recuperating from tuberculosis at the time (May 1827), wrote to his aunt Mary that it has occurred to him that "we have a great many capacities which we lack time & occasion to improve." Should he, he wonders, be a novelist, a poet, a painter, or do these and other possibilities "play the coquette with my imagination & it may be I shall die at the last a forlorn bachelor jilted of them all." Yet these "seekings after," instead of being vain, may "point to a duration ample enough for the entire satisfaction of them all." Hinting at infinity, they suggest

> a just idea of the world to come[,] which has always been made repulsive to men's eyes from the inadequate representations of systems of religion which looked at it only in one aspect, and that, (I am forced to use a word in a limited sense it ought not to bear) a *religious* one. But regarding the future world not so much as the place of a final moral reward but as the *after state* of man . . . is assuredly more consistent with our most elevated & therefore

5. Johnson, having examined the roles of Ellen and Cabot in preparing this essay and others for *Letters and Social Aims* (*W* 8:321–52), concludes that, despite its collaborative nature, "Immortality" should "remain in the canon" and should be read closely along with the 1861 lecture on which it is primarily based "for evaluating Emerson's late thinking and habits of composition" ("Emerson's Essay 'Immortality': The Problem of Authorship"). See also Buell, *Emerson,* 176.

6. Emerson's quotation of Goethe in "Immortality" (from a letter of February 4, 1829, to Johan Peter Eckermann) is also cited by Van Cromphout, *Emerson's Modernity,* 125.

> truest notions of God[:] that the education of man should be carried on by furnishing space & excitement to the development of every faculty that can add accomplishment to the noble being. And though our poor tools of art[,] the colours, the pallet, the chisel, rhyme, & the pipes & strings of sound[,] must yield to finer & more efficient means, yet it would be unjust to the exhibitions of intended intellectual progress disclosed in our nature to doubt that scope w[oul]d be afforded to the compassing of the great ideal results, of wh[ich] these tools are now the poor inadequate instruments.

Our artistic instruments must yield in the "after state" to something "finer." In accord with Keats's "favourite speculation" (heaven as earthly existence in "a finer tone," a phrase borrowed from Wordsworth), Emerson ends *his* speculation by allying it with intuition and the numinous "visionary gleam" of the Intimations Ode: "But the muse is not yet propitious. I grieve to find myself clouding a gleam of truth with heaps of words" (*L* 1: 197–98).[7]

These gleams of the intuitive Reason do not pretend to be "rational" demonstrations. And by *scope* and *longer term* mature Emerson does *not* mean the sort of eternal life meant by most Christians. "Future state is an illusion for the ever-present state. It is not length of life but depth of life. It is not duration, but a taking of the soul out of time, as all high action of the mind does" (*W* 8:347). He made a similar point, if more optimistically, toward the end of his essay "Worship," in *The Conduct of Life:* "Of immortality, the soul when well employed is incurious. It *is* so well, that it is sure it *will be* well. . . . Immortality will come to such as are fit for it, and he who would be a great soul in *future,* must be a great soul *now*" (*E&L* 1075; italics added). Unable to base much on the "legend" of Christ's resurrection, Emerson posits, along with this intimation of immortality as an "ever-present state" in the here and now, his sense of—as a firmer "ground of hope"—"the infinity of the world; which infinity appears in every particle, the powers of all society, in every individual, and of all mind in every mind."

Like Wordsworth, who, despite his own residual skeptical "realism," still had no choice ("And I must think, do all I can, / That there was plea-

7. Keats's speculation that heaven might consist of earthly happiness but in "a finer tone" (*Letters of John Keats,* 1:184–86) echoes the Solitary's reference to "Music of finer tone" in book 2 of *The Excursion* (710). Writing precisely a century after Emerson's May 1827 letter, here is writer and cartoonist James Thurber: "I live in the hopes that the adventure of death is something equal to the adventure of life which is pretty colorful and interesting even if hard. It would seem strange to me if God made such a complicated world and such complicated people and then had no more to offer than blankness at the end." It is at once amusing and touching to note that Thurber was responding, in this letter to his brother Robert, to the death of Robert's beloved dog, Muggs.

sure there") but to believe in his own creed of a sentient, conscious, and spiritualized nature (*WP* 1:312), Emerson seems persuaded, "against all appearances," of the truth of this Transcendental faith in *some* form of "immortality," an ever present state in which the mind has intimations of eternity or infinity. "But whence came it? Who put it in the mind? It was not I, it was not you; it is elemental." It is also, for a reader of the Romantics, elementally Wordsworthian, mysterious yet certain—a "gleam" and "master-light." This "wonderful" idea, says Emerson, "belongs to thought and virtue, and whenever we have either, we see the beams of this light" (*W* 8:333).

This "*light*" of all our day, along with the "ground of *hope*," provide the crucial terms, for in assuming what is both mysterious and unprovable, Emerson is falling back on Wordsworth as his apostle of "hope" and his authority on the intuitive, rather than the cognitively demonstrable. As he said in all versions of "Immortality," beginning with the 1861 lecture, he would "abstain from writing or printing on the immortality of the soul" because he is bound to disappoint his readers' "hungry eyes" or fail to satisfy the "desire" of his "listeners." And, he adds,

> I shall be as much wronged by their hasty conclusions, as they feel themselves wronged by my omissions. I mean that I am a better believer, and all serious souls are better believers in the immortality, than we can give grounds for. The real evidence is too subtle, or is higher than we can write down in propositions, and therefore Wordsworth's "Ode" is the best modern essay on the subject. (*W* 8:345–46)

The "therefore" verges on the ironic since, as Emerson repeats in the very next sentence, "We cannot prove our faith by syllogisms," another variation on the familiar point that the "shadowy recollections" and "visionary gleams" of intuitive Reason cannot be categorized or proven ("be they what they may," as Wordsworth says in the Great Ode), even though they remain indisputable—proven, as it were, on the pulses. Wordsworth, and Emerson after him, anticipate the recent testimony of W. S. Merwin, who acknowledges that he is "not certain" as to how "the pain of learning what is lost / Is transformed into light at last."[8] Yet, as usual in Emerson, who refuses to dogmatize obscurity into a facile clarity, what matters is not doctrine but the mysterious, yet irresistible affirmative instinct. As he says in his crucial essay "Experience": "It is not *what* we believe concerning the immortality of the soul and the like, but the *universal impulse to believe,* that is the material circumstance and is the principal fact in the history of

8. From "Testimony," the keynote poem in Merwin's 1999 collection, *The River Sound,* 50.

the globe" (*E&L* 486; italics added). It is a matter, as Tennyson would put it in *In Memoriam,* of "Believing where we cannot prove," or, as it was famously phrased by William James, who found that he could not obey his own imperative: "the will to believe." Emerson was capable of correcting even what he took to be Wordsworth's position when it came to the indispensable Intimations Ode. Mistakenly expanding Wordsworth's comment (*WP* 1:979) about his employment of Platonic or Neoplatonic myth (making the "best use" he could of it "as a Poet") into authorial judgment on the revelations of the poem as a whole, Emerson, trusting the tale and not the teller, rose to the ode's defense: "Wordsworth wrote his ode on reminiscence, & when questioned afterwards, said, it was only poetry. He did not know it was the only truth" (*TN* 2:262).

Though, even in the days immediately following Charles's death, Emerson would echo the ode in asserting that "our upper nature lies always in Day," his own battered faith during this "gloomy epoch" offered little religious consolation in bereavement. In "Dirge," a heartbroken 1838 elegy for his two brothers, his "strong, star-bright companions," he envisioned, not heaven, but a sunset plain "full of ghosts" now "they are gone" (*CPT* 115). A more hopeful variation on that vision occurs in lines originally included in his long poem "May-Day," but subsequently extracted to form the conclusion of Emerson's still later poem "The Harp." "At eventide, / . . . listening" for "the syllable that Nature spoke" (but which, aside from the "wind-harp," has been "adequately utter[ed]" by none, not even "Wordsworth, Pan's recording voice"), the old poet suddenly finds himself in the visionary presence of the lost companions of his youth:

> O joy, for what recoveries rare!
> Renewed, I breathe Elysian air,
> See youth's glad mates in earliest bloom.
> (*CPT* 146, 226)

Once again Emerson is feebly but poignantly echoing the Intimations Ode. The recovery stanza (his favorite) opens with the same exclamation—

> O joy! That in our embers
> Is something that doth live,
> That Nature yet remembers
> What was so fugitive!

—and ends with a vision of immortal "children" sporting on the shore of eternity. In the lines that immediately follow in his own poem, Emerson concludes "The Harp" by expressing the hope of an eternal spring beyond the intruding grave:

Break not my dream, intrusive tomb!
Or teach thou, Spring! The grand recoil
Of life resurgent from the soil
Wherein was dropped the mortal spoil.
(*CPT* 226)

This chimes with another of the autumnal but affirmative Wordsworthian odes cherished by Emerson: the "Ode to Lycoris," which also concludes with a vernal intimation of immortality: "Still, as we draw nearer to life's dark goal, / Be hopeful Spring the favorite of the Soul!" (*WP* 2:354). For both Wordsworth and Emerson, the model for this "life resurgent" is, however intuitive and ineradicable, a tentative repetition in a finer tone of the season of perennial rebirth: "*hopeful Spring.*" But unlike Wordsworth, Emerson believed less in a normative conception of personal immortality than in "eternity," which he defined in 1838, in characteristic Emersonian style, as "the genius & creative principle of all eras *in my own mind*" (*JMN* 7:186; italics added), a phrase repeated in "History" (*E&L* 240).

Writing in 1837, Emerson looked back on the six years of religious inner struggle that had begun with the death of his wife, a death that almost destroyed him but, in the event, liberated him not only from anticipated domestic happiness but from conventional thinking. That disaster, which had triggered or at least accelerated his decision to leave the ministry, had been followed by the deaths of Edward and Charles. Now, an Emerson tested and tempered by the painful vicissitudes of life, posed a choice between opposites. That choice was later reworked in his essay "Intellect," in which form it may well have had a decisive influence on the life of Emily Dickinson and (demonstrably, though he would omit the opening "God offers . . .") on the life of Friedrich Nietzsche:

> God offers to every mind its choice between Truth and Repose. Take which you please,—you can never have both. Between these, as a pendulum, man oscillates. He in whom the love of repose predominates will accept the first creed, the first philosophy, the first political party he meets,—most likely his father's. He gets rest, commodity, and reputation. But he shuts the door to truth. He in whom the love of truth predominates will keep himself aloof from all moorings, and afloat. He will abstain from dogmatism, and recognize all the opposite negations, between which, as walls, his being is swung. He submits to the inconvenience of suspense and imperfect opinion, but he is a candidate for truth, as the other is not, and respects the highest law of his being.[9]

9. "Intellect" (*E&L* 425–26). For the earlier version, see *L* 2:256.

Despite the current surge of interest in the obvious but long-repressed Emerson-Nietzsche connection, no one seems to have noted the parallel passage, which occurs in a letter from the twenty-year-old Nietzsche to his sister, a crucial letter celebrating the difficulty and loneliness of the explorer—one of those dedicated and severe spirits, *philalethes,* friends of truth—striking out on new paths, even if they *were* paths blazed by Emerson:

> Is it decisive after all that we arrive at *that* view of God, world, and reconciliation which makes us feel most comfortable? Rather, is not the result of his inquiries something wholly indifferent to the true inquirer? Do we after all seek rest, peace, and pleasure in our inquiries? No, only truth—even if it be the most abhorrent and ugly. . . . Faith does not offer the least support for a proof of objective truth. Here the ways of men part: if you wish to strive for peace of soul and pleasure, then believe; if you wish to be a devotee of truth, then inquire.[10]

The passage echoed by Nietzsche was written in 1837. A year earlier, in the immediate wake of Charles's death, Emerson also seemed deprived of religious consolation, of the Repose that came with an unassailable belief in a spiritual and personal immortality. He tried at first to assuage his grief over Charles's death by constructing, with the dead man's fiancée, a secular immortality through shared memories. But it was during these conversations with Elizabeth that Emerson began to formulate a revised theory about ways to transcend death, to move beyond the tragic vision. Though more germane to Emerson's much debated response to the loss of little Waldo six years later, this new thinking—as a letter and several notebook entries show—began to evolve in the aftermath of Charles's death, and so should be mentioned here.

After three weeks of grieving, he concluded, "We are no longer permitted to think that the presence or absence of friends is material to our *highest* states of mind," that personal relationships pale in the light of the "absolute life" of our relationship to the divine. This perspective will emerge in *Nature,* in that highest state when Emerson, "uplifted into infinite space," becomes "a transparent eye-ball" and the "name of the nearest friend sounds then foreign and accidental: to be brothers, to be acquain-

10. Nietzsche, *The Portable Nietzsche,* 29–30. Unlike Walter Kaufmann, who sees connections but no affinity, and W. M. Salter, who sees affinity but no connections, George Stack, who sees *both,* also fails to draw attention to this striking parallel—even though he quotes (*Nietzsche and Emerson: An Elective Affinity,* 69n99) a portion of the passage from "Intellect." In an old essay of my own, "On Truth and Lie in Nietzsche" (*Salmagundi* [1975]), I quoted Nietzsche's letter, but was then unaware of the earlier passage in Emerson.

tances . . . is then a trifle and a disturbance" (*E&L* 10). This epiphany is Emerson's partial compensation for the loss of Charles. "Who can ever supply his place to me? None. . . . The eye is closed that was to see Nature for me, & give me leave to see" (*JMN* 5:152). Now Charles's metaphorical transmutation into an all-seeing but impersonal eyeball leaves Emerson at once exhilarated and isolated, friendship reduced to the foreign and accidental, even brotherhood a trifle. Similarly, "Experience," written in the aftermath of little Waldo's death, will proclaim the "inequality between every subject and every object," and the subsequent superficial nature of grief and love:

> The great and crescive self, rooted in absolute nature, supplants all relative existence, and ruins the mortal kingdom of friendship and love. . . . There will be the same gulf between every me and thee, as between the original and the picture . . . The soul is not twice-born, but the only begotten, . . . admitting no co-life. . . . We believe in ourselves as we do not believe in others. (*E&L* 487–88)

It all resembles those idealist, sense-transcending "High instincts" at the center of the pivotal ninth stanza of the Intimations Ode: those obstinate "questionings" of "sense and outward things, / Falling from us, vanishings." These are crucial, but nevertheless mysterious and unnerving "questionings" of that palpable, sensuous world, which, Wordsworth elsewhere tells us in a passage known to Emerson, is the world "Of all of us, the place where, in the end, / We find our happiness, or not at all" (*P* 11:142–44; cited by Coleridge, *F* 1:226). But if Wordsworth is abstract and austere in the ninth stanza, the crux of the ode, Emerson seems, in "Experience," positively cold, far removed from the spiritual and humane hope, expressed at the time of Ellen's death, that he might retrieve that lost "beautiful Vision" by entering *with her* into "the great Vision of the Whole" (*JMN* 3:230–31). In his new thinking, reflecting both a genuine idealist vision of transcendence (as in the epiphany of the transparent eyeball) and a need to numb himself to the pain of repeated loss, the human beings we love, the living and the dead, are said to have nothing to do with the "absolute life" of one's relationship with God, for in "that communion our dearest friends are strangers. There is no personeity in it" (*L* 2:21; *JMN* 5:150–61, 170).

But Emerson was not yet completely caught up in his own theory of a friend-estranging and personality-excluding communion with God. Thus, in another aspect of his collaboration with Elizabeth Hoar, he sought for the brilliant if hypersensitive Charles a literary immortality by trying to put the dead man's scholarly writings—that "drawer of papers" which formed Elizabeth's heritage—into shape for publication. He was no more successful than Montaigne had been in his similarly doomed attempt to adequately represent his friend La Boétie by posthumously publishing *his* papers. In fact, Emerson was shocked to discover from Charles's journals just how "melancholy, penitential, and self-accusing" his destructively ambitious and self-doubting brother had been; he found "little in a finished state and far too much of his dark, hopeless, self-pitying streak," the "creepings of an eclipsing temperament over his abiding light of character" (*JMN* 5:152). Emerson's own affinities, in precise contrast, were with a finally *un*eclipsed and abiding light, hope, and self-affirmation. Writing on March 19 after having read Charles's "noble but sad" letters to Elizabeth, letters containing "so little hope" that they "harrowed me," Emerson declared no book "so good to read as that which sets the reader into a working mood, makes him feel his strength. . . . Such are Plutarch, & Montaigne, & Wordsworth" (*JMN* 5:288–89). In the Intimations Ode, relief from suffering comes in the form of a "timely utterance," and "I again am strong"; no more "shall grief of mine the season wrong" (23–26). We can trace Emerson's recovery from the blow of Charles's death and his subsequent recovery of creative strength in a crucial journal entry—one revealingly centered not on Montaigne's "On Friendship," but on Wordsworth, this time quite explicitly, and predating by a week or more his dismissal of the presence or absence of friends as immaterial "to our highest state of mind."

Writing in mid-May 1836, after ten days of "helpless mourning," Emerson begins, tentatively, to recover. "I find myself slowly. . . . I remember states of mind that perhaps I had long lost before this grief, the native mountains whose tops reappear after we have traversed many a mile of weary region from our home. Them shall I ever revisit?" These "states of mind" are reflected in the conversation of friends who have "ministered to my highest needs," even that "intrepid doubter" Achille Murat, Napoléon's nephew, with whom Emerson had "talked incessantly" nine years earlier, during his return from his recuperative trip to Florida (*JMN* 3:77). The "elevating" discussions of such men, and these men themselves, "are to me," says Emerson, "what the Wanderer in the Excursion is to the poet. And Wordsworth's total value is of this kind. They are described in the lines at the end of Yarrow Revisited. Theirs is the true light of all our day. They are the argument for the spiritual world for their spirit is it" (*JMN* 5:160–61).

Given its profoundly personal context, and its cryptic yet specific allusions to major Wordsworthian texts, this passage is pivotal to my argument. I will return to the important reference to *The Excursion* and to the allusion to the Intimations Ode. As for the third Wordsworthian reference: Emerson is responding, not to the final lines of "Yarrow Revisited," that memorial of Wordsworth's 1831 visit to Sir Walter Scott, but to a passage printed "at the end" (in an Appendix) of Wordsworth's recently published volume, *Yarrow Revisited and Other Poems* (1835), "new poems of Wordsworth" he had taken up to read, says Emerson, "sure" that he would "find thoughts in harmony with the great frame of Nature, the placid aspect of the Universe. I may find dulness and flatness, but I shall not find meanness and error" (*JMN* 5:99). Emerson's language suggests that he is thinking simultaneously of *The Excursion,* in particular of his favorite book, "Despondency Corrected." In fact, the "lines at the end" of *Yarrow Revisited,* a passage Wordsworth had excerpted from the then unpublished *Prelude,* correspond to lines 220–78 in the book of *The Prelude* paralleling "Despondency Corrected," the book (12 in the 1805 version, 13 in 1850) titled "Imagination and Taste, How Impaired and Restored."

These lines put into poetry that section of the preface to the 1802 *Lyrical Ballads* in which Wordsworth, defending his choice of subject, celebrates "rustic life" as a condition in which "the essential passions of the heart find a better soil in which they can attain their maturity." We also learn to speak a plainer, "more emphatic language" since, in such a condition, "our elementary feelings coexist in a state of greater simplicity... and, lastly, because in that condition the passions of men are incorporated with the beautiful and permanent forms of nature" (*WP* 2:869–70). But he adds a crucial point of which Coleridge was perfectly aware but that, in his criticism of Wordsworth's linguistic "theory" in the *Biographia,* he seems occasionally to forget. In an indispensable addendum to "the real language of men" the poet must supply, says Wordsworth, "a certain colouring of imagination." There are linguistic questions worth raising, especially regarding the relation between poetic language and natural imagery.[11]

11. Influenced by the plain but impassioned and nature-based language of Wordsworth's rustics as passed through the alembic of imagination, Emerson tells us, in the "Language" chapter of *Nature,* that most writers fail to "clothe one thought in its natural garment," but that "wise men pierce this rotten diction and fasten words again to visible things" (*E&L* 22–23). He is echoing Wordsworth's condemnation, in the preface to *Lyrical Ballads,* of "poetic diction" in favor of the language of real men, peasants whose earthy language incorporates, and is closest to, elemental nature. Soon after he read the lines at the end of the *Yarrow Revisited* volume, Emerson began to energize his own language, infusing it with an indigenous version of Wordsworthian rusticity. In a lecture of November 1835, he fused Romantic philosophy with the earthy idiom of the American frontier, made vivid by "imagery... drawn from observation of natural processes." It is this (in a sentence Emerson incorporated in the "Language" chapter [*E&L* 22]) "that gives that piquancy to the conversation of a strong natured farmer or a backwoodsman which all men relish. It is the salt of those semisavages, men of strong understanding, who bring out of the woods into the tameness of refined

But the crucial point at present is the relevance of these lines, and the related philosophy of the Wanderer, to Emerson's search for consolation in the wake of Charles's death.

The Romantic correspondence between nature and the human mind, with preeminence vested in the latter, is at the heart of the passage of poetry Emerson singled out in the May 1836 journal entry. What particularly struck Emerson on this occasion was the fact that the Wordsworth passage fused the linguistic bond between nature and the mind with *the ethical, sorrow-converting function of that bond*—at least in the case of countrymen whose earthy language and rural self-reliance had alike developed in "Nature's presence." Summoning up "what then I saw" as a youth and "see daily now / Before me in my rural neighborhood," the poet states that he will "bend in reverence" to nature, "*and the power of human minds, / To men as they are men within themselves*" (*P* [1805], 12:220–25)—a formulation that must have registered with the future author of "Self-Reliance." Wordsworth goes on to praise "the very heart of man," a heart (and note the negative-affirmative constructions) "Not unexalted by religious hope" and "Not uninformed by books, good books though few," but essentially formed (and this accords with the main point Wordsworth made to Emerson during their 1833 interview)

> *In Nature's presence:* thence may I select
> *Sorrow that is not sorrow, but delight;*
> *And miserable love that is not pain*
> *To hear of, for the glory that redounds*
> Therefrom to *human kind and what we are.*
> (12:244–48; italics added)

circles a native way of seeing things, and there speak in metaphors." This is imported Romanticism, in the form of Wordsworth's invigorated language, flourishing in new and fertile American soil, native and even more untamed. As Buell notes: "Just as Wordsworth inverted the cultural authority of borderland and metropolis, so for Emerson the rustic postcolonial state that Europeans thought culturally impoverished seems a positive advantage" (*Emerson,* 111). The result is Emerson's own characteristic "style" at its most fluid and jocoserious, mingling dictions and crossing genres, tempering Transcendentalist afflatus with homely metaphors and, reciprocally, converting the low into the sublime. Having praised a popular comic series—Seba Smith's *Letters of Jack Downing*—for "the just natural imagery in which all the thoughts are expressed," Emerson went on in this lecture to define the "poet" as one who, through the power of imagination, "converts the solid globe, the land, the sea, the sun, the animals into symbols of thought" (*EL* 1:224). In the "Language" chapter, Emerson, stressing the "radical correspondence between visible things and human thoughts," insists that, in "its infancy," language was "all poetry," with "all spiritual facts . . . represented by natural imagery." But there is a reciprocity: "This immediate dependence of language upon nature, this conversion of an outward phenomenon into a type of somewhat in human life, never loses its power to affect us" (*E&L* 22).

He will, says Wordsworth, draw comfort from men whose hearts and minds, shaped in nature's presence and able to convert pain and misery into a higher delight, attain a humanity-glorifying form of tragic joy. Such men are "their own upholders, to themselves / Encouragement, and energy and will," and there are others, "Still higher," who are "framed for contemplation" rather than "words," which are "but under-agents in their souls." Theirs "is the language of heaven, the power, / The thought, the image, and the silent joy" (12:261–71). And "theirs," as Emerson says of such ministering men, "is the true light of all our day."

Though anything but wordless, one such man, as Emerson accurately noted, was the Wanderer, the "hero" of Wordsworth's *Excursion.* A stoic consoler in unmediated contact with Nature, a man who sees with the inward eye of true feeling, the Wanderer, who reminded Emerson of Bronson Alcott, is the composite character in whom Wordsworth concentrated, not all, but most of his own thoughts and feelings. He acknowledged, in remarks to Isabella Fenwick, that the Wanderer was an image of himself had his circumstances been different, living only "in Nature's presence," without the dubious benefits of "what is called a liberal education" (*WP* 2:952). Emerson was familiar with *The Excursion* as early as 1821, when he inscribed in his journal a synopsis of its nine books (*JMN* 1:271–72). He would have endorsed the following judgment: "Throughout this long poem, filled with the aspirations, struggles, and heartaches of humanity, Wordsworth tells us that even in the very midst of Mutability, loss and grief, there are, to the practiced eye, signs and symbols of eternal rest and peace. The Wanderer has the wisdom to perceive and the feelings to appreciate these symbols and has faith in what lies behind them."[12]

It is the Wanderer who, in the opening book, tells the moving rural story of Margaret. Though he feels her tragedy deeply and sheds tears in relating her story, the Wanderer is comforted by "natural wisdom" and by Margaret's faith—a faith he shares—"that consolation springs / From sources deeper far than deepest pain." Thus, he refuses to yield to the foolishness and impotence of "grief" (*E* 1:598, 600–602, 937–38). The Wanderer also tells the Author or Poet, a figure more susceptible to disabling grief, the story (in book 2) of the Solitary, the figure Emerson seems, at least primarily, to mean in referring to "the poet" in his journal entry. The Solitary, or Recluse, is a man who, like Emerson, had lost a young wife and, again like Emerson, had, though a minister, developed an "infidel contempt of holy writ," at least to the extent of becoming so skeptical of such doctrines as immortality that he "broke faith with them whom he had laid / In earth's dark chambers, with a Christian's hope!" (2:247–

12. Charles J. Smith, "The Contrarieties: Wordsworth's Dualistic Imagery," 1196–97.

49). This agnostic was so disillusioned by the second tragedy of his life—the failure of the French Revolution and with it the collapse of his "golden expectations" (2:217)—that he seems "dissevered from mankind" and hope (2:732).

He is not, not completely, as is clear from his act of humanity in helping to save the old turf gatherer stranded on the mountain during a storm, and the effect upon his mind of what amounts to the reward for that act: the moment on the mountain when, through an opening in the mist, he has the vision of a heavenly city (*E* 2:829–81). As we have seen, Emerson's comment on this passage is less faithful to Wordsworth's emphasis on mortality, suffering, and an act of human kindness than illustrative of Emerson's own "millennial" reluctance (in 1841, the date of the relevant journal entry) to engage in specific reformist acts, reduced to "little" gestures soon to be scattered like dreams by an outburst of "universal power" (*JMN* 8:51). In book 4, the Wanderer recurs to that experience when, "on a service bent / Of mere humanity," the Solitary climbed the mountain, and there was "suddenly revealed" to him "a marvelous and heavenly show." While the shepherds accompanying him on the rescue mission "heeded not, you lingered, you perceived, / And felt, deeply as living man could feel" (4:469–74). Since the Solitary *is,* for all his personal and political disillusionment and apparent misanthropy, a man of compassion, he remains, the Wanderer insists, eminently redeemable. Indeed, it is his task to correct the Solitary's "Despondency." That is the title of book 3, one reflecting Wordsworth's own state at the time. The Solitary's personal and political dejection was hardly alien to the Author, writing in 1812. Napoléon still ruled Europe and, as Emerson may have known, Wordsworth was describing that despondency in the aftermath of deaths in his own family: of his children, Catherine and Thomas, both of whom died in that one terrible year.

Parts of the opening book of *The Excursion* have always been admired, especially the account of the Wanderer's boyhood (a Wordsworthian seed time in Nature's presence, much cherished by Emerson) and his tale of Margaret and the Ruined Cottage. But it was book 4, "Despondency Corrected," that many readers (including Lamb, Keats, and Ruskin; Emerson, his aunt Mary, and his poet friend Jones Very) thought not only the best thing in *The Excursion,* but among the supreme achievements of Wordsworth's career. Indeed, it was his previous experience in reading book 4, and absorbing the philosophy and consolation offered by the Wanderer to the despondent Solitary, that made Emerson confident, when he picked up the latest volume of Wordsworth's poetry seeking consolation in the painful aftermath of Charles's death, that he would "find thoughts in harmony with the great frame of Nature, the placid aspect of the Universe"

(*JMN* 5:99). Anticipating Emersonian "optimism" and his precise dialectic of "conversion" in the essay "Compensation," the Wanderer describes, in Boethian / Miltonic terms, the operations of benign Providence, ever converting accidents "to good." The passage in which these lines occur epitomizes Wordsworth's own prose synopsis of the book's main "Argument": "A belief in a superintending Providence the only adequate support under affliction." According to the Wanderer, the sole support for the "calamities of mortal life" is

> an assured belief
> That the procession of our fate, howe'er
> Sad or disturbed, is ordered by a Being
> Of infinite benevolence and power;
> Whose everlasting purposes embrace
> All accidents, converting them to good.
> —The darts of anguish *fix* not where the seat
> Of suffering hath been thoroughly fortified
> By acquiescence in the Will supreme
> For time and for eternity; by faith,
> Faith absolute in God, including hope.
> (*E* 4:10–22)[13]

I earlier noted Emerson's repeated citation of the Wanderer's lines about the difficulty of maintaining "Heights which the soul is competent to gain" (4:138–39); the passage about the "curious child" listening to a seashell imparting tidings of invisible things, of ebb, flow, enduring power, "And central peace subsisting at the heart / Of endless agitation" (4:1133–47); and the Wanderer's attack (4:941–94) on coldly analytical scientists and philosophers who, probing and prying, view "all objects unremittingly / In disconnexion dead and spiritless": those naturalists, Emerson agrees (allying Coleridge with Wordsworth), who "freeze their subject under the wintry light of the understanding" (*E&L* 47). In the present context, had we world enough and time, I would revisit book 4 in detail (focusing on that long opening speech that struck such a chord with Unitarian readers in the United States, then on scattered remarks in the middle of the book, and, finally, on his resonant peroration) in order to fully demonstrate what

13. Joel Pace, who has studied the relation of Wordsworth's poetry to social reform in nineteenth-century America, notes that lines 10–93, excerpted under a title borrowed from Wordsworth's own prose "Argument," appeared in a cheaply priced 1846 anthology, thus providing popular reinforcement of the conviction of many conservative Unitarians that the working poor were to rely on Providence rather than reform. See his 2001 online article in the Romantic Circles Praxis Series: http// www.rc.umd.edu/praxis/.

it was in the speeches of the Wanderer that so moved Emerson when he read "Despondency Corrected," what "hope" it was that made him conclude that the "total value" of Wordsworth could be epitomized in "what the Wanderer in *The Excursion* is" both to the Solitary and to the narrator, "the Poet" himself. Instead, I will merely quote the climactic description of the Wanderer from the conclusion of book 4 and move on to book 9, the conclusion of *The Excursion* itself.

Though far too heterodox a believer in the God within to be in accord with every aspect of the Wanderer's religiosity, Emerson, through allusion and influence, in effect records his agreement with the Wordsworthian "Author," in the coda to book 4, that the words uttered by the Wanderer shall not pass away "Dispersed, like music that the wind takes up / By snatches, and lets fall, to be forgotten." They "sank into me," Emerson could say as well, the Wanderer's words forming the "bounteous gift / Of one whom time and nature had made wise" (1287–88):

> one accustomed to desires that feed
> On fruitage gathered from the tree of life;
> To *hopes* on knowledge and experience built;
> Of one in whom persuasion and belief
> Had ripened into faith, and faith become
> A *passionate intuition;* whence the Soul,
> Though bound to earth by ties of pity and love,
> *From all injurious servitude was free.*
> (1291–98; italics added)

In his famous review of *The Excursion,* Hazlitt devotes virtually all his attention to the first four books. Indeed, most contemporary readers of *The Excursion,* if they were impressed by the poem at all, were impressed by books 1 through 4, and by the finale (book 9). Many tended to skip over the middle books, starting with 5, which introduces the Pastor and from which point the Wanderer's residual pantheism is increasingly absorbed by his Christian theism. To judge from his comments on and allusions to *The Excursion,* Emerson, though he made an outline of the whole poem, seems to have followed that reading pattern. In addition to the Wanderer's evocation in "Despondency Corrected" of imaginative and moral means of transforming despair, Emerson seems also to have in mind in his allusion to the Wanderer's role in *The Excursion* the ninth and final book, titled "Discourse of the Wanderer, and an Evening Visit to the Lake."

That final book, written under the hopeful sign of an impending defeat of Napoléon, opens by outlining a "Tintern Abbey"–like version of the great Chain of Being. In one of the crucial passages in all of Wordsworth, lines echoed by Emerson in his essays "The Over-Soul" and "Immortality," as well as in lines 183–88 and 238–46 of "Threnody," the Wanderer asserts that "To every Form of being is assigned" an "*active* Principle" (1–3), a hopeful spirit that

> subsists
> In all things, in all natures; in the stars
> Of azure heaven, the unenduring clouds,
> In flower and tree, in every pebbly stone
> That paves the brooks, the stationary rocks,
> The moving waters, and the invisible air.
> Whate'er exists hath properties that spread
> Beyond itself, communicating good,
> A simple blessing, or with evil mixed;
> Spirit that knows no insulated spot,
> No chasm, no solitude; from link to link
> It circulates, the Soul of all the worlds.
> (9:4–15)

In "Immortality," Emerson posits "the infinity of the world" as "a firmer ground of hope" than conventional notions of immortality, an "infinity" that "appears in every particle, the powers of all society, in every individual and of all mind in every mind" (*W* 8:333). Having insisted that here is an "*active* Principle" that moves through every particle of existence, down to "every pebbly stone," the Wanderer also, in the lines that immediately follow, places climactic emphasis on the human mind:

> This is the freedom of the universe;
> Unfolded still the more, more visible,
> The more we know; and yet is reverenced least,
> And least respected in the human Mind,
> Its most apparent home.
> (9:16–20)

The paradox anticipates Transcendentalism in its sublimely "contradictory" telescoping of the individual and the universal, the Within and the Above. Precisely *how* this *universal* and "*active* Principle" is also compatible with *individual* freedom, and *how* the very place where it is least reverenced—the human mind—is also its "most apparent home": on these points, the voluble Wanderer is silent.[14] What he *does* tell his listeners, echoing his own earlier metaphor of the "fire of light" that "feeds" on and

14. See David Q. Smith, "The Wanderer's Silence," 163–67.

transforms even the most "palpable oppressions of despair" (*E* 4:1058–77), is that

> The *food* of *hope*
> Is meditated action; robbed of this
> Her sole support, she languishes and dies.
> We perish also; for *we live by hope*
> And by desire; we see by *the glad light*
> And breathe the sweet air of futurity
> And so we live, or else we have no life.
> (9:20–26; italics added)

Quite aside from historical recovery from revolutionary and post-revolutionary despondency, the signs of such hope, says the Wanderer, are ubiquitous. One such affirmative perspective—as we saw in Chapters 6 and 11—is conveyed in the Wanderer's metaphor of advancing age not as a decline, but an ascent, a "final EMINENCE" from which we look down upon the "VALE of years" (9:49–52). Thus "placed by age" upon a solitary height above "the Plain below," we may find conferred upon us power to commune with the invisible world, "And hear the mighty stream of tendency" uttering, "for elevation of our thought, / A clear sonorous voice" (9:81–92). In his twenties, Emerson endorsed this attitude, that of a "poet represented as listening in pious silence 'To hear the mighty stream of Tendency'" (*JMN* 3:80), and in later life he frequently alluded to the passage in advocating an elevated, enlarged, more affirmative perspective.

This elevated mountain perspective is reified in the grand sunset viewed by the Wanderer and the "thoughtful few" (9:658), including the Pastor and the Solitary, in the scene toward the conclusion of book 9. As in book 2, and in *The Prelude,* the climax of which is the ascent of Mount Snowdon, *The Excursion* comes to its end with a view from a mountain landscape—this time, however, not of a posttempest vision (*E* 2:830–81) or of the moon suddenly revealing itself to a solitary Wordsworth above the clouds on Snowdon (*P* 14:38–62), but of the sunset seen from a grassy hillside among "scattered groves, / And mountains bare" (9:505–6), a more "Emersonian" version of the sublime. The rays of light, "suddenly diverging from the orb / Retired behind the mountain-tops," shot up into the blue firmament in fiery radiance, the clouds "giving back" the bright hues they had "imbibed," and continued "to receive" (9:592–606).

Here, though the natural reciprocity of giving and receiving is retained, the beauty of the spectacle receives an orthodox Christian imprimatur. These very mountains, the Pastor exclaims, were once, "before the Name, Jehovah, was a sound / Within the circuit of this sea-girt isle," the scene of human sacrifice to the "terrible Idols" of the Celtic gods. Nothing of those rituals—ancient, barbarous and mysterious—survive, aside from a "few rude monuments of mountain-stone" (9:679–711). And "so wide [is] the difference" between dark savagery and the "bright" prospect offered Christian "worshippers" that, in the shared spectacle of this mountain sunset, a version of the natural Paradise envisaged in the "Prospectus" *seems* actualized:

> a willing mind
> Might almost think, at this affecting hour,
> That paradise, the lost abode of man,
> Was raised again, and to a happy few,
> In its original beauty, here restored.
> (9:712–19)

Emerson is as likely to be recalling the conclusion of *The Excursion* as were William James after him and, contemporaneously, his friend Carlyle, in the conclusion of his own great work of crisis and recovery. In the "Circumspective" chapter of the third and final book of *Sartor Resartus,* the supposed British biographer and editor of Teufelsdröckh summons a "Happy few! little band of Friends," to join him in the "highest work of Palingenesia," its redemptive purpose nothing less than the "Newbirth of Society." That "Happy few," though echoing the great battlefield harangue of Shakespeare's warrior king in *Henry V,* is more functionally derived from those "happy few," the "sons of the morning," in book 4, and, especially, the "happy few," the "little band," at the redemptive finale of *The Excursion* (*E* 4:230–32, 9:718, 729).[15]

Caught in his usual pull between Solitude and Society, Emerson is closer to the hopeful but elegiac Wordsworth than to the energetically apostolic Carlyle. If he *is* recalling the conclusion of book 9, Emerson would surely detect Wordsworth's self-echoing there of the Intimations Ode. The "little band" descends and makes its way in the boat across the lake in falling darkness, no trace remaining of "those *celestial splendours*" now "*too faint almost for sight*" (9:760, 763; italics added). The Solitary's parting words, he having bestowed on each "A farewell salutation; and the like / Receiving," seem casual: "'Another sun,'" he says, "'shall shine upon us, ere we part; / Another sun, and peradventure more'" (9:771–81). The Recluse (to call the Solitary by the name to be given to the Wordsworthian *magnum opus*) has not quite become the Philanthropist (the title of an earlier related and abortive project), but he has been gradually converted from a recluse isolated and despairing to one engaged in amity and social responsibility. Even at its most morbid and misanthropic, the Solitary's conversation

15. Carlyle, *Sartor Resartus,* 197, 198.

had, the Wanderer notes, "caught at every turn / The colours of the sun" (4:1125–26). Reciprocal salutation and anticipation of "another" and yet another shared "sun," coming from *that* "wounded spirit, / Dejected," indicates the degree of "renovation," "healing," and participation in "delightful hopes" (9:771–73, 793) that has been achieved by the end of *The Excursion.*

Appropriately, Wordsworth gives the Solitary words—including that repeated, hopeful "another . . ."—that seem to echo, along with the unforgettable description of Milton's comforting angel as "*another* morn / Risen on mid-noon" (*PL* 5:310–11), the ode's hard-earned victory: "*Another* race hath been, and *other* palms are won" (200). Six years after the death of his brother Charles, pitting the latent power of the divinity within him against, yet in concert with, the impersonal Fate that had just taken from him his precious boy, Waldo, Emerson ends one of his most justly famous journal entries: "I am *Defeated* all the time, yet to Victory am I born" (*JMN* 8:228). It has all the magnificent audacity of Milton's Samson or of Nietzsche's Beethoven. Blind and chained, taunted and threatened by the braggart Philistine giant, Harapha ("I thought / Gyves and the mill had tamed thee!"), Milton's defiant hero remains unconquered: "My heels are fettered, but my fist is free." With those nine words, pivoting on "but," with precisely four words given to each side of the polarity, Samson may be said to dramatize the whole, finally triumphant, argument of Emerson's essay "Fate," exemplifying how "necessity comports with liberty" (*E&L* 944). Out-Samsoning Samson, Beethoven is said to have died shaking his fist at God himself. In his biographer's phrase, one equally applicable to Nietzsche, that great admirer of Beethoven *and* of Emerson, "All of Beethoven's defeats were, ultimately, turned into victories."[16]

Though that is, of course, a far cry from the acquiescence in the divine Will espoused by the Wanderer, what binds all these Romantic strugglers together is their awareness, however affirmative their vision, that life involves loss, misery, pain, and ultimately death. There would be no *need* to seek so ardently for despair-transforming "hope" if there were not ample cause to despair in the first place. Even "optimism" arises from an *agon.* "He has seen but half the Universe who never has been shown the *house of Pain,*" Emerson confided to his aunt while recuperating from tuberculosis in 1827. "Pleasure and peace are but indifferent teachers of what it is life to know." In his opening words in "Despondency Corrected," the Wanderer tells the Solitary that he is to find in faith and hope the "one adequate

16. Solomon, *Beethoven,* 124. In *Samson Agonistes,* the humiliated Harapha retires; in the Chorus's witheringly sarcastic phrase, "His giantship is gone somewhat crestfallen" (lines 1092–93, 1235, 1244).

support / For the *calamities of mortal life*" (4:10–24), and for the more "Nietzschean" Emerson of "Fate," "Every *calamity* is a *spur* and valuable hint" (*E&L* 960). Freedom is always under challenge from oppressive forces, from the faculties of "sense" that would dominate imagination and darken the light of all our day, to the distinct yet related loss of "hope" in the state Wordsworth calls Despondency and Coleridge Dejection. What we require, says the Wanderer, is a faith that, once it becomes a "passionate intuition," liberates us "From all injurious servitude" (*E* 4:1296–98). Among the worse forms of human servitude is despair, the "Despondency" the Wanderer seeks to "correct." He may not, even by book 9, have succeeded completely. But the Solitary has come a long way—and that, too, is a victory.

Certainly, as his 1836 journal entry confirms, Emerson found solace, even, hyperbolically enough, Wordsworth's "total value," in the consolation offered by the Wanderer in *The Excursion.* When a grief-stricken Emerson, devastated by the death of Charles, hoped against hope to "revisit" his own "native mountains that reappear" after we have traversed many a weary mile from our "home," he thought of the Wanderer and his various doctrines—pantheistic, Stoic, Christian—of all-encompassing hope, at length in book 4 and, concisely, at the beginning of book 9. But his mountain imagery strongly suggests a recollection as well of the mountain sunset toward the end of this final book of *The Excursion.* Comforted and "elevated" by the talk of friends, by intellectual and emotional companionship with Wordsworthian men able to convert "sorrow" into "delight," the "palpable oppressions of despair" into the "*active* Principle" of hope announced by that Stoical yet enraptured visionary, the Wanderer, the grieving Emerson saw his own native mountaintops begin to reappear, to feel again that influx of hope, power, and "glad light" that is, in the familiar line he paraphrases from the Great Ode, "the true light of all our day": a spirituality incarnate in, and indistinguishable from, such self-upholding men, "their spirit" *being,* as Emerson insists, "the spiritual world" itself (*JMN* 5:160–61).

Chapter 14

Wordsworth's Ode, Waldo, and "Threnody"

The art of losing isn't hard to master,
So many things seem filled with the intent
To be lost that their loss is no disaster.
. . . .
Even losing you (the joking voice, a gesture
I love) I shan't have lied. It's evident
The art of losing's not too hard to master
though it may look like (Write it!) like disaster.

—ELIZABETH BISHOP, "One Art"

For this losing is true dying;
This is lordly man's down-lying,
This his slow but sure reclining,
Star by star his world resigning.

—RALPH WALDO EMERSON, "Threnody"

The single most devastating event of Emerson's life was the sudden death of his son, aged five, of scarlet fever. In this painful case, Emerson's "art of losing" takes its most acutely paradoxical form. His intense mourning for little Waldo is seemingly contradicted by the famous refusal, or inability, to mourn: "I chiefly grieve that I cannot grieve" (*L* 3:7–10). In other letters written in the immediate aftermath of the tragedy, the distraught father claimed that the loss of his beloved child, terrible as it was, was "dreamlike" and "superficial," a tearing away that left intact the surviving parent—in his quintessential, immaterial, "Emersonian" Self. Publicly, in the essay "Experience," the loss is compared to that of an "estate," no more.

Worse follows: the almost inhumanly clinical dismissal epitomized in the notorious and shocking statement that the loss of his boy "falls off from me, and leaves no scar. It was caducous" (*E&L* 473).

Though we hardly expect, in such a context, so technical a term (zoological, botanical, and legal) as *caducous,* its root meaning—a "falling off" or "falling from"—suggests that, in this case as in so many others, at least partial resolution of the dilemma is to be found in the ninth stanza of the Intimations Ode, where Wordsworth praises, as "most worthy to be blest," those

obstinate questionings
Of sense and outward things,
Fallings from us, vanishings....

This idealist dismissal of material, external things as nonessential, mere "Fallings from" our inmost being, clarifies the etymology of *caducous.*[1] In addition, though it is of course a lesser poem, Emerson's long-delayed elegy for Waldo, "Threnody," takes much from the Great Ode in its *full* trajectory: an elegiac poem of loss and compensation, and a Romantic fusion of thought and feeling, spirit and nature.

1. Usually (as with *cotyledons* and *agaric,* related technical terms employed by Emerson in, respectively, the poem "Merlin" and the essay "The Poet"), *caducous* describes a floral or organic rather than a strictly human phenomenon. The falling off of connected but separable parts occurs either prematurely or (when they have served their purpose), "naturally," as in the case of leaves or a placenta. The legal meaning brings in the sense of chance, or what "befalls" us. The word's Latin root, *caducus,* was applied in Roman civil law to testamentary gifts that, for some reason, have lapsed, a potential wind*fall,* so to speak, that somehow "falls away from" the donee. Such lapsed gifts, then and now, become subject to escheat, a forfeiture that—upon the occurrence of some default or chance event—reverts to the state, or, in the case of Emerson's forfeited child, to the One from whom he came. The idea of "chance" is immediately germane since the Latin root of that word as well as of *caducous,* is the verb *cadere,* "to fall," or *cadentia,* the "way in which things fall out." This fall or falling out is sometimes fortuitous, sometimes disastrous (a "*mis*chance"), in any case unpredictable, inexplicable—indeed, a "be*falling*" from "above" that, as Jacques Derrida remarks at the end of a long etymological passage on "chance," takes us by surprise and so "thwarts our expectation and disappoints our *anticipation.*" "As you know," he explains knowingly, "the words 'chance' and 'case' descend, as it were, according to the same Latin filiation, from *cadere,* which—to indicate the sense of the fall—still resounds in 'cadence,' 'fall' (*choir*), to 'fall due' (*échoir*), 'expiry date' (*échéance*), as well as 'accident' and 'incident.' But, apart from this linguistic family, the same case may be made for *Zufall* or *Zufallingheit,* which in German means 'chance,' for *zufallen* (to fall due, *zufaallig,* the accidental, fortuitous, contingent, occasional)—and the word 'occasion' belongs to the same Latin descent. A *Fall* is a case; *Einfall,* an idea that comes to mind in an apparently unforeseeable manner. Now, I would say that the unforeseeable is precisely the case, involving as it does that which falls and is not seen in advance. Is not what befalls us or descends upon us, as it comes from above, like destiny or thunder, taking our faces and hands by surprise—is this not exactly what thwarts our expectations and disappoints our *anticipation*?" ("My Chances/Mes Chances," *Taking Chances: Derrida, Psychoanalysis, and Literature,* 5).

Haunted by the ode from the time he first read it in his early twenties till the end of his life, Emerson was particularly drawn to the so-called Platonic or Neoplatonic stanzas—at first to the fifth stanza, then and forever to the ninth, where mere "fallings" from us are contrasted to that imperishable "light of all our day" that sheds its glow as well over the final stanzas, where philosophic idealism is replaced by a tragic yet affirmative humanism. Whatever his reservations about some of Wordsworth's poetry, they did not, as we have seen, extend to the ode, which Emerson described in 1856 as "the high-water mark which the intellect has reached in this age. A new step has been taken, new means have been employed. No courage has surpassed that, & a way made through the void by this finer Columbus" (*JMN* 14:98). He ends chapter 17 of *English Traits* by borrowing from this journal entry, concluding by saying of Wordsworth, whatever his political and poetic shortcomings, "Let us say of him that, alone in his time he treated the human mind well, and with an absolute trust. His adherence to his poetic creed rested on real inspiration. The Ode on Immortality is the high-water mark which the intellect has reached in this age. New means were employed, and new realms added to the empire of the muse, by his courage" (*E&L* 928). Writing in August 1865, in a passage later incorporated in the essay on "Immortality," Emerson acknowledges, as Kant had in *The Critique of Pure Reason,* that one cannot give purely rational "grounds" for belief in whatever it is we mean by the "immortality" of the soul. "The real evidence," he says, "is too subtle, or is higher, than we can write down in propositions, & therefore Wordsworth's Ode is the best modern Essay on the subject" (*W* 8:345–46).

Despite the high praise, there is something troubling about these responses to the poem that more than any other single Romantic lyric haunted, enraptured, and teased the Transcendentalists out of thought as did eternity itself. I would make two points in regard to these 1856 and 1865 comments.

First, Emerson's shift from his earlier emphasis on Wordsworth's "intellect" to his brilliant handling of a subject too subtle or too high for rational argument is of a piece with spiritual Boston's typical response to Wordsworth as great precisely because he was intuitive and feeling rather than disciplined and rational in the lower, or discursive, sense. For example, Richard Henry Dana Jr.—who, like his onetime mentor Emerson, had been introduced to Wordsworth's work while still a Harvard student—reports that he spent "nearly a whole day" reading and rereading the poem, becoming "infatuated with its spirit."[2] By "spirit," he, like Emer-

2. Dana, *Journal of Richard Henry Dana, Jr.,* 1:36. See also David Simpson, "Wordsworth in America."

son, in the conclusion of *Nature* and elsewhere, means intuitive Reason, the visionary gleam. Of course, the Emersonian shift, emphasizing Wordsworth's more than rational ability to express the ineffable, to some extent parallels the movement in the final stanzas of the ode itself: from the stress on "thought" and "the philosophic mind" in stanza 10 to the balancing emphasis on feeling and "my heart of hearts" in the final stanza. Too often missed is the subtlety of Wordsworth's *fusion* of thought and feeling, head and heart. "Thanks to the human heart by which we live," Wordsworth concludes the ode, "To me the meanest flower that blows can give / *Thoughts* that do often lie *too deep for tears.*" In rightly praising the "felt" greatness of the ode, the Transcendentalists tended to undervalue the complexity of Wordsworthian "thought." Emerson, emphasizing both thought and feeling, would seem to be an exception.

But, and this is my second point, there is something *aesthetically* troubling about the terms Emerson employs in judging Wordsworth's more than rational achievement as primarily, if paradoxically, one of "intellect," a judgment reinforced by his later comment on the poem as the "best modern *Essay*" on its "*subject.*" These remarks can be briefly placed in the context of Emerson's overall response to Wordsworth, exemplified by his quite similar observations on *The Prelude.*

Given the sheer bulk of both poems, we have to take with a generous helping of salt the report of a young acquaintance of Emerson's later years, C. J. Woodbury, that Emerson knew "by heart" much of *The Excursion* and "could quote almost the entirety of the book-length" *Prelude.*[3] It is true that he read and admired much of *The Excursion,* knew passages from *The Prelude* published in excerpts over the years, and did purchase two copies of the poem (one for himself, one for his aunt) after its posthumous publication in 1850. Long before that, Emerson would have been aware of the existence of this long poem from his reading of the prose preface to *The Excursion* and the "Prospectus," or poetic "plan of the Recluse," both of which place the long poem dedicated to Coleridge in canonical context. And, of course, we know from his own account of his 1833 visit that he raised the subject of the unpublished epic with Wordsworth himself, telling the poet "how much the few printed extracts had quickened the desire to possess" the whole work (*E&L* 777). Here is Emerson's verdict on the finally published *Prelude,* recorded in his journal for February 27, 1858: the long, and long-awaited, poem is "not quite solid enough in its texture" (*JMN* 14:202). To be sure, an epic is not a lyric, but, whatever its tedious stretches and flatlands, most serious readers have not found *The Prelude,* especially in its numerous "great" parts, lacking in

3. Woodbury, *Talks with Emerson,* 45–46.

"texture." But Emerson's comment would tally with his frequent complaint that Wordsworth's "thought"—even if, for a poet, it was "the highest thought in England in his time" (*JMN* 16:137)—did not always achieve adequate poetic expression, that the ideas were not transmuted into music (a judgment that applies only too well to some of his *own* strangely syncopated poetry). Emerson finds *The Prelude* not quite a poem but "rather a poetical pamphlet, though proceeding from a new and genuine experience" (*JMN* 14:202). That last point would place *The Prelude* high on the Emersonian scale, as does the qualifying remark that the poem is "like Milton's *Areopagitica.*" The *Areopagitica,* Emerson's favorite tract, was an example of that elevated Miltonic prose in which, as he said in his essay on Milton, "sometimes the Muse soars highest." Even so, and despite explicitly conceding that *The Prelude* is a "*poetical* pamphlet," Emerson speaks of Wordsworth's epic poem just as he speaks, at least in print, about the Intimations Ode, that "best Essay" on its subject.

This is eerily anticipatory of Helen Vendler's great corrective reading of Lionel Trilling's celebrated essay on the ode. Faulting Trilling for his almost exclusively moral emphasis on Wordsworth's ability to convey psychological experience, she asserts: "Adequacy to the complexity of experience is certainly one—but only one—of the criteria by which we judge great literature. It is disquieting how indistinguishable the Ode becomes, in Trilling's description, from an essay of Emerson or a lecture by Arnold." The problem is not with an Emerson essay or Arnold lecture, but with Trilling's failure to attend sufficiently to the purely aesthetic dimension of what is, after all, a great *poem.* Vendler is troubled by what she sees as his misconstrual of the ode's structural development, a misreading based on his failure to attend to, and work through, the labyrinthine density of its internal verbal echoing, its homeopathic "curing" of its own polarities. If the poem's dilemmas have not been totally resolved, the lacunae left by Trilling's essay have been admirably filled by Vendler's characteristically brilliant close reading.[4] Emerson's complaint about *The Prelude* was that it "was not quite solid enough in its texture." But perhaps the fault was with Emerson there, as it was with Trilling on the ode.

❧ The crucial ninth stanza of the Intimations Ode has already been discussed at some length. Here, I would like to focus for a few moments on the sixth stanza, paired with the famous fifth, and then on the final

4. First published in 1979 in *Salmagundi,* "Lionel Trilling and Wordsworth's Immortality Ode" is reprinted in Vendler's collection *The Music of What Happens: Poems, Poets, Critics,* 93–114; quote on 95.

stanza of the ode, specifically on the implications of the humble, thought-evoking flower, and on the significance, for a mature perceiver, of those "clouds that gather round the setting sun." Both images are relevant to "Threnody," as is Emerson's intriguing alteration of the opening line of stanza 6.

In that brief but memorable coda to the Neoplatonic fifth stanza, a "homely" nurturing Earth does

all she can
To make her Foster-child, her Inmate Man,
Forget the glories he hath known,
And that imperial palace whence he came.
(82–85)

While she seems a benign consoler, viewed sub specie aeternitatis "homely" Earth plays a more problematic role, trying to induce amnesia, to make man forget his true "home" in eternity and his genuine rather than *foster* parent, God. That Earth's foster child is an "Inmate" reminds us that, as the previous stanza asserts, the temporal world is a "prison-house" (67). To be sure, that prison is something of a country club since, as we are told in this stanza's opening line, "Earth fills her lap with pleasures of her own" (78). Wordsworth's ambivalence in these stanzas is reflected in two texts of Emerson. In the "Idealism" chapter of *Nature,* balancing the thrust of his own essential idealism, he insists that he has "no hostility to nature," but, instead, "a child's love," and so wishes to "speak her fair. I do not wish to fling stones at my beautiful mother, nor soil my gentle nest. I only wish to indicate the true position of nature in regard to man" (*E&L* 38). This is what Wordsworth does in stanza 6, depicting our foster mother in such a way as to indicate that true position. Man's immortal longings transcend those of Earth, who has "yearnings," but only "in her own natural kind" (79).

In his most spiritual mode, Emerson was unwilling, as we saw in Chapter 10, to simply concede that "Earth fills her lap with pleasures of her own." Echoing and altering the line, he deliberately replaced *pleasures* with *splendours,* denying Earth the latter ("*not* her own"), in order to assert that such splendors are in the eye of the human beholder, once "the mind is ripened." That ripeness attained, we go beyond mere perception to active, creative Wordsworthian coloring of natural phenomena. Then "we behold" nature's beauty and value, "and the time when we saw them not is like a dream. Not in nature but in man is all the beauty and worth he sees. The world is very empty, and is indebted to this gilding, exalting soul for all its pride. 'Earth fills her lap with splendours *not her own*'" (*E&L* 313). Such splendors depend upon, in fact are conferred by, man; without ripened human vision, the beauty and value of nature, whatever their ultimately divine provenance, "are like the stars whose light has not yet reached us" (*E&L* 313). Even in loading the dice against nature as presented by Wordsworth in stanza 6 of the ode, Emerson borrows from a later stanza—replacing Earth's natural pleasures with that "*splendour* in the grass" resulting from the celestial "radiance which was once so bright" (179, 176) but is now, according to stanza 10, irreversibly lost. Emerson may also have been aware of a passage in what became *The Prelude,* where "objects," transformed by "light divine" and the "visionary power" of poetry, are "recognized / In flashes and *with glory not their own*" (*P* 5:601–5). Wordsworth, who insists in the final stanza of the ode that the sunset takes its "colouring" from the eye of the human perceiver, would agree that the "splendours" he referred to in stanza 10 were, unlike the "pleasures" of stanza 6, not nature's "own" but conferred upon her by the gilding, exalting soul of the human perceiver and creator, a seer still attended by a vestige of the "light divine," the *original* "vision splendid."

In this passage in "Spiritual Laws," with its repeated "all" ("*all* the beauty and worth he sees, . . . *all* its pride"), Emerson goes beyond Wordsworth (who grants Nature her limited role) to Coleridge at his most subjective, asserting (in "Dejection") that "*in our life alone* does Nature live" (*CPW* 1:365). Such absolute idealism "empties" Nature not only of "splendours" and "glories" not her own but also of the "pleasures" with which Wordsworth fills Earth's lap. That they are pleasures shadowed by the implicit pains of earthly life explains why Margaret Fuller also echoed this stanza in criticizing Emerson in her otherwise favorable review of *Essays: Second Series.* Conceding the "great gifts" he had given the world, she still thought her idealist and erect friend, whose "only aim is the discernment and interpretation of the spiritual law by which we live," had "raised himself too early to the perpendicular and did not lie along the ground long enough to hear the secret whispers of our parent life. We could wish he might be thrown by conflicts on the lap of mother earth, to see if he would not rise again with added powers" (*EPP* 605). Emerson read this review, and his longing (in "Experience," the second essay in the volume she was reviewing) for a more painful "friction" and "contact" with hard-edged reality suggests that he anticipated and agreed with Fuller's assessment—in particular in his longing to truly *feel* in terms of genuine "contact" the pain of Waldo's death, a "disaster" that had "at last no rough rasping friction, but the most slippery sliding surfaces" (*E&L* 472, 473). He was anticipating—along with the Ludwig Wittgenstein of *Philosophical Investigations,* who wished to get off the linguistic "slippery ice where there is no friction," back to "the rough ground"—the Robert Frost of "To Earthward," for whom the "hurt" of leaning too hard on one hand

is not enough;
I long for weight and strength
To feel the earth as rough
To all my length.[5]

Wordsworthian transcendence, unlike Emersonian Transcendentalism at its idealist extreme, is always rooted in this Antaeus-like contact with the earth, *especially* in its least grandiose manifestations. What made Wordsworth "the most original poet now living," says Hazlitt in *The Spirit of the Age,* was his novel appreciation of nature, especially the "trivial" and "familiar." And it was more than a matter of perspective; as Hazlitt concludes: "No one has shown the same *imagination* in raising trifles into importance." The rooting of our most profound experiences in simple, humble things is distinctively Wordsworthian, says Walter Pater, the "peculiar genius" of a poet able "to open out the soul of apparently little or familiar things."[6] What we now take for granted was once a focus for denunciation of Wordsworth—by, among many others, a youthful Emerson. Writing to his aunt in June 1826, the young Stoic poses a rhetorical question that also hints at his later husbanding of his own resources: "Is it not much more conformable to that golden middle line in which all that is good and wise in life lies, to let what Heaven made small and casual remain the objects of a notice small and casual, and husband our admiration for images of grandeur in matter or in mind?" (*L* 7:148–49).

A critic writing anonymously in the *London Quarterly Review* in October 1815 complained that "when we are called upon to feel *emotions which lie too deep for tears with respect to the meanest flower that blows,* to *cry for nothing*. . . over every ordinary object and every commonplace occurrence . . . , all communion of feeling between the poet and those who know no more of poetry than their own experience and an acquaintance with the best models will bestow, is necessarily broken off."[7] Though *early* Emerson endorsed this complaint, its inaccuracy and wrongheadedness are obvious when we look again at those final lines of the ode, lines in which the Wordsworthian interaction between thought and objects, between heart and head, may be said to culminate:

5. Wittgenstein, *Philosophic Investigations,* 40c:1:107; Frost, *Poetry of Frost,* 227. Wittgenstein can sound Wordsworthian, as here, in rejecting the earlier *Tractatus,* whose "crystalline purity of logic" had, he came to feel, treated language in a way too abstracted from the details of common life. To get a grip on the actual problems of philosophy, we have to return our attention to "the subjects of everyday life" (sec. 106). "What *we* do is to bring words back from their metaphysical to their everyday use" (sec. 116).

6. Hazlitt, *Complete Works,* 11:88; Pater, "Wordsworth," 48.

7. For the comments of the anonymous critic (perhaps William Gifford), see "Wordsworth's *White Doe,*" 208; italics in original.

Thanks to the human heart by which we live,
Thanks to its tenderness, its joys, and fears,
To me the meanest flower that blows can give
Thoughts that do often lie too deep for tears.
(201–4)

What could be more Wordsworthian than *this* transaction between Within and Without, between feeling and thinking, mediated by nature in the form of a wild flower as one of the poet's representative "objects of all thought" ("Tintern Abbey," 101)? There is also a connection with Coleridge, whose "*Quantum sumus, scimus*" Emerson associated with Goethe's assertion that "every object, rightly seen unlocks a new faculty of the Soul." He ends the "Language" chapter of *Nature* with his own gloss: "That which was unconscious truth, becomes, when interpreted and defined in an object, a part of the domain of knowledge" (*E&L* 25). There was not only cognitive but also emotional and aesthetic significance in this initial concentration on a natural object. Once *contemplated,* such an object as this Wordsworthian flower radiates out into human, even cosmic significance, its "momentary eminency," depending on the "depth of the artist's insight," reaching "out to infinitude," as Emerson insists in his essay "Art" (*E&L* 433).[8]

It is both inevitable and important that Wordsworth would choose the "meanest" flower, or the "humblest flower," as he puts it in a late manuscript revision never incorporated in the text (left out, I would suggest, because he judged that "hum*bl*est" would have alliterated too strongly with "f*l*ower" and "*bl*ows," while he seems to have liked the fluid assonance of *fears, meanest, deep, tears*). Here, writ small, is the marriage of mind and

8. Blake began his "Auguries of Innocence" with a grammatical infinitive in which the infinite itself is inherent in the most minute particulars: "To see a World in a Grain of Sand / And a Heaven in a Wild Flower / Hold Infinity in the palm of your hand / And Eternity in an Hour" (*Poetry and Prose of Blake,* 481). The "flower in the crannied wall" that, understood "all in all," could tell Tennyson "what God and man is," may have its origin in Blake's "Wild Flower," or in that humble, "meanest flower" blossoming at the end the ode that could give a feeling and contemplative person "Thoughts that do often lie too deep for tears." Emerson claims in "Art" that its virtue lies in sequestering and concentrating on "one object," a "single form." Certain minds, those of artists, orators, social leaders, "give an all-excluding fullness to the object, the thought, the word, they alight upon, and to make that for the time the deputy of the world." The "power to fix the momentary eminency of an object, . . . depends on the depth of the artist's insight" into the contemplated object. "For every object has its roots in central nature, and may of course be so exhibited to us as to represent the world. . . . Presently we pass to some other object, which rounds itself into a whole, as did the first. . . . From this succession of excellent objects learn we at last the immensity of the world, the opulence of human nature which can run out to infinitude in any direction" (*E&L* 433).

nature Wordsworth projected in the "Prospectus," a "great consummation" in which "The discerning intellect of Man," when "wedded to this goodly universe, / In love and holy passion," shall find all the paradise it needs a "simple produce of the common day" (52–58). The *Quarterly* reviewer perversely had a weeping Wordsworth breaking off "communion of feeling" between himself and his readers at the very moment he was most profoundly connecting with them, at least with the more perceptive readers in Emerson's circle. As his aunt Mary said, in this same year, 1815, "At times a humble flower creates thoughts too deep for tears to use the high language of W," "W" being "the sublime Wordsworth," whose "Prospectus" she had also read.[9]

This emphasis on the mean, the simple, the humble, the common, the insignificant *made* significant by "thought," surely provided a hint for the agenda of the great American poet Emerson was calling for. "Thought makes everything fit for use," he says in "The Poet," an essay in which he insists that the "power of poetry" can "raise" what is "low," that "small and mean things serve as well as great symbols" (*E&L* 454; recognizing, as Wordsworth did, the biblical precedent, his immediate reference was to the poetry of the Hebrew Scriptures). Calling for "self-trust" in "The American Scholar," Emerson describes intuitive Reason as "deeper than can be fathomed—darker than can be enlightened," but this apparently counter-Enlightenment evocation of the bottomless and mysterious sublime is instantly balanced by his famous, and manifestly Wordsworthian, emphasis on the ordinary: "I ask not for the great, the remote, the romantic; . . . I embrace the common, I sit at the feet of the familiar, the low" (*E&L* 68–69). Even his sublime Orphic Poet tells us, in the climactic chapter of *Nature,* that redemption requires the fusion of "mind" and "affection," and "the wisdom to see the miraculous in the common" (*E&L* 47).

This is precisely what Wordsworth preached in the various prefaces to *Lyrical Ballads,* and practiced in much of his best poetry: the choice of objects, incidents, and situations from "common life," endeavoring to rouse men from their "torpor" by making "interesting," with the charm of novelty, those everyday things whose "lustre," as Coleridge said, had been "dimmed by the film of familiarity." More than a century ago, Émile Legouis rightly insisted, as Hazlitt and Pater had, that "the peculiar province of Wordsworth is that of the *common.* Wherever selection was possible he held it his duty to borrow nothing from those elements of the world which

9. Cole, *Mary Moody Emerson,* 151–52. That humble flower, and the "thought" it can bring, "thanks to the human heart," is a quintessentially Wordsworthian interaction. Such conversions registered with Emerson, who was struck, as we have seen, by Wordsworth's "true description" of stopping on skates, "so simple a fact that no common man would have trusted himself to detach as a thought" (*JMN* 5:454).

are marvelous or unusual."[10] By "Imagination," Wordsworth observes in a note to "The Thorn," "I mean the faculty which produces impressive effects out of simple elements" (*WP* 1:949)—a point repeated in the final book of *The Prelude,* where we are told, of the truly creative minds possessing imaginative "power," they "build up greatest things / From least suggestions" (*P* 14:101–2).

Emerson is in the tradition of what Hazlitt calls the "levelling" Muse of Wordsworth, when he insists, in *Nature,* on a poetic egalitarianism of the things of this world. The "distinctions" we make between "high and low, honest and base, disappear when nature is used as a symbol." Thus, we find miracle not only in the exalted manifestations of nature but in the most "common" as well, as at the conclusion both of *Nature* and of the Intimations Ode. As we saw in Chapter 7, Emerson even anticipates Joyce, another discoverer of miracle in the commonplace. "The aroused intellect," when it confronts "facts, dull, strange, despised things," discovers that "a fact is an Epiphany of God" (*JMN* 7:29). That the blossoming of a simple flower "can give / Thoughts that do often lie *too deep for tears*" hints as well at a variant of the response to loss for which Wordsworth and, even more, Emerson have often been criticized: a refusal to mourn. Despite legions of careless readers, the ode does *not* end with Wordsworth crying. Yet there is in the ode a profound and plangent awareness of a lost and irretrievable light—

> What though the radiance which was once so bright
> Be now for ever taken from my sight,
>   Though nothing can bring back the hour
> Of splendour in the grass, of glory in the flower
> (176–79)

—and of the somber coloring imparted to things by the seer conscious of mutability. Both moments are presented in the Virgilian music of "Sunt lacrimae rerum et mentem mortalia tangunt" (*Aeneid* 1:462), the "tears" inherent in "things," since "mortality touches the heart." That second moment occurs in the middle of the final stanza of the ode:

> The Clouds that gather round the setting sun
> Do *take* a sober colouring *from an eye*
> That hath kept *watch* o'er *man's mortality.*
> (197–99)

This is not the eye of the child of stanza 8, that "Seer blest," but the humanized and elegiac eye of an adult aware of suffering and death. The

10. Legouis, *The Early Life of William Wordsworth,* 446.

coloring it imparts to the gathering clouds at sunset replaces the celestial "radiance," which, though "once so bright," is "now forever taken from my sight." It was his "principal object," Wordsworth says in the preface to the second edition of *Lyrical Ballads,* to choose incidents from "common life," presented in the "language really used by men, and, at the same time, to throw over them *a certain colouring of the imagination.*" Thus, "ordinary things" would be "presented to the mind" so as to reveal "the primary laws of our nature." Accordingly, there is at the end of the ode a renewed and deepened bond between man and man, head and heart, and, above all, between man and nature—the latter a mature marital reciprocity in which both partners give and receive. Though *"nothing* can *bring back* the hour / Of splendour in the grass, of *glory in the flower,*" we were told in the tenth stanza that the formerly yoking "years" do "*bring* the philosophic mind." In the final stanza, thanks to the (universal) "*human heart* by which we live," to *"me* [the first-person singular, but transformed by the intervening sense of solidarity with all humankind] the meanest flower that blows can *give / Thoughts*" often too deep for tears. The clouds, replacing the radiance "*taken*" from the maturing poet's sight, "*take*" from the human perceiver a "sober colouring" that was, in the original version of the poem, a more sublime but less elegiac "*awful* colouring."

This deeply moving transformation of the observed scene is the result of a mature and mutable human perceiver whose "eye" is also creative. His adult experiences of suffering and death imaginatively confer on the sunset a glory—somber, human, elegiac—that is in muted but unmistakable contrast not only to the earlier example of the pathetic fallacy, in which the personified Moon looked round her "with delight" when the heavens were bare (stanza 2), but also to the bare heavens that would be perceived by an inexperienced child. "Nature always," as Emerson tells us, "wears the color of the spirit" (*E&L* 11), and again, in "Experience," and again recalling the "colouring" from both the preface to *Lyrical Ballads* and the final stanza of the ode, "inevitably does the universe wear our color, and every object falls successively into the subject itself. . . . As I am, so I see" (*E&L* 489). As the speaker channeling the female sensibility in Stevens's "Sunday Morning" says of the fruits and trees and rivers of a perfect paradise that mimics, but with "no change of death," our beautiful but perishing earth: "Alas, that they should wear our colors there" (76–84). For *our* colors are those of—precisely—"Experience." An Innocent, once we are past the ode's intermediate myth of the Child as a philosophic seer, would look at the evening sky as a *merely* natural phenomenon, its sunset clouds necessarily *not* wearing the sober color imparted by the eye of one aware of mortality. Such an inexperienced perceiver would be oblivious to the paradoxically "soothing thoughts that spring / Out of human suffering" (184–85), a listener unattuned to what the auditory rather than visual Wordsworth of "Tintern Abbey" calls "the still, sad music of humanity" (91).

Would the Transcendentalists have been as impressed and enraptured with Wordsworth's ode if they had perceived it as being, perhaps, more about mortality than immortality? Some of them *did.* As the late Christopher Lasch noted, for many of its American readers in the nineteenth century, the ode "conveyed the death of a childhood more vividly than it conveyed the consolations available to a mature and 'philosophic mind.'"[11] Emerson, who thought the ode a triumph of "intellect" in its grappling with the question of immortality, would seem to be in the other camp, though in fact his reading of the poem—replicated in his elegy for Waldo—acknowledges the thoughtful consolation without forgetting the elegy for childhood delight, a delight so rapturous that its loss continues to resist, almost successfully, the powerful assertion of recompense. In *Society and Solitude* (1870), Emerson would refer to Wordsworth as writing "of the delights of the boy in nature." He then quotes what are perhaps the poem's most famous elegiac lines, unconsciously mingling Shakespeare's most poignant lamentation with Wordsworth's "Though nothing can bring back . . ." Emerson's misquotation—"*For never will come back* the hour / Of splendor in the grass, of glory in the flower"—crosses memories of his own dead child with, I suspect, Lear's heartbreaking cry over the dead body of Cordelia: "Thou'lt *come no more, / Never, never, never, never, never*" (5.3.308–9).

Having quoted, or misquoted, these lines of the ode, Emerson adds: "But I have just seen a man, well knowing what he spoke of, who told me that the verse was not true for him; that his eyes opened as he grew older, and that every spring was more beautiful to him than the last" (*W* 7:299). The man was Thomas Treadwell Stone, a preacher and contributor to the *Dial,* who had told Emerson that "he did not find Wordsworth's Ode true for him," since he grew "more impressionable as he grew older," remarks Emerson quoted twice in his journals (*JMN* 14:228, 15:11). Unlike Stone, Emerson knew that, despite the splendor forever taken from his sight, Wordsworth's *final* emphasis was on the intensification of his response to nature "as he grew older." Few readers understood better, or more desperately needed, Wordsworth's healing doctrines of consolation and compensation for loss. But Emerson, again unlike Stone, knew and felt precisely what Wordsworth meant by lost and irretrievable radiance.

11. Lasch, *True and Only Heaven,* 90–91. Many in the nineteenth century chose to "idolize Wordsworth as the poet of 'rapture now forever flown,'" says Lasch, apparently deriving at least part of that judgment from Philip Davis, whom he cites on the ode (90–91n).

Even before he had suffered the loss of so many he loved, Emerson experienced the ode as essentially elegiac. At the age of twenty-three, he followed the ode in lamenting, in an unpublished sonnet, the loss of "the blessed light that once my woes beguiled." And the sonnet, which concludes with this echo of the opening stanzas of the ode, plays an even whinier variation on the final stanza's imagery of clouds, sun, and "eye." In Emerson's case, "Cloud after cloud my firmament deforms / While the sweet Eye of Heaven" pours rich rivers of Promethean "purple gleams" on everyone but him, a version of Wordsworth's "To me alone there came a thought of grief" (ode, 23).[12] Yet long before he praised its author as a "finer Columbus," navigating new and uncharted waters of mind, heart, and spirit, Emerson had probably plumbed the depths of the ode, especially following the death of Waldo. Though he never ventured in print or in his journals upon a close reading, what he *did* have to say explicitly makes it clear that he realized that the poem was less about "growing *old,*" as many have thought, than about "growing *up,*" as Lionel Trilling rightly insisted. And his own emphases elsewhere, especially in the "Language" chapter of *Nature,* assure me that he understood that, ultimately, the greatest poem of its length in English (excepting "Lycidas") was not *just* about "growing up," but, as Helen Vendler insisted in responding to Trilling's famous essay, about growing up to be a *Poet.*

A poet, as no one would have to tell Emerson, was a master of language, a maker of metaphors that draw their enduring power from the relationship—perceived, created, felt, and thought through—between nature and ourselves, with the human perceiver and metaphor maker the dominant partner. We "speak in continual metaphors of the morn, the noon, the evening of life . . . because the whole of nature is a metaphor or image of the human Mind," said Emerson in his 1833 lecture "The Uses of Natural History." He repeated that crucial analogy in the "Language" chapter of *Nature,* insisting that "words are signs of natural facts," and particular natural facts "symbols of particular spiritual facts." Though, as we have seen, Emerson defensively barred from *Nature* his repeated citation of those lines in which Coleridge deemed "all that meets the bodily sense" to be "Symbolical, one mighty alphabet," decipherable by human "minds" (*CPW* 1:132), Emerson continues to insist that it is "not words only that are emblematic; it is things which are emblematic. Every natural fact is a symbol of some spiritual fact. Every appearance in nature corresponds to some state of the mind" (*E&L* 20). Given that correspondence, outward phenomena cannot but affect us in our heart of hearts: "The motion of

12. The entry in which the sonnet appears (*JMN* 3:36) includes lines transcribed from stanza 5 of the ode.

the earth round its axis, and round the sun, makes the day, and the year. These are certain amounts of brute light and force. But is there no intent of an analogy between man's life and the seasons? And do the seasons gain no grandeur or pathos from that analogy?" (*E&L* 21–22).

The answer—implicit in the rhetorical questions themselves—is that, of course, they *do,* as is made poignantly clear in the diurnal grandeur and pathos of mutability that account for the coloring of the clouds that gather round the setting sun in the final stanza of the ode. Ask not for whom those elegiac clouds gather, for whom that sun sets; they gather, it sets, for *thee.* That analogous "intent" of which Emerson speaks is, of course, not inherent in nature; it is authorial intention. But is the author God or man, deity transcendent or immanent? Whatever else they may have in mind, both Wordsworth and Emerson, seeing *through* what Blake calls an "imaginative eye," remain intensely aware as well of the "perishing mortal eye." Emerson's "intent of an analogy" is above all the conscious intent of the human *poet.* He or she is the maker who finds the "words," derived in the first place, or "immediately," from a natural world ultimately symbolic of the spiritual, and so becomes a creative spirit possessing the power to convey and convert—in a reciprocal pattern—one world to the other. And, as Emerson says a paragraph later in the "Language" chapter: "This immediate dependence of language upon nature, this conversion of an outward phenomenon into a type of somewhat in human life, never loses its power to affect us" (*E&L* 22). Nowhere in all of English literature is that truth better demonstrated—more movingly, thoughtfully, and metaphorically *converted*—than in the final stanzas of Wordsworth's Great Ode.

These final stanzas also bring to fruition another conversion: of evil turned to good, loss to gain, a pattern of abundant recompense particularly prominent in Milton, Wordsworth, and Emerson. The Miltonic archetype is that of a painful but ultimately happy fall leading to a redeemed state; one Eden lost, another gained, "a paradise within thee, happier far," according to the promise of that "seer blest," the archangel Michael. In this tradition, Wordsworth, though acknowledging "the sorrows of the earth," insists that, "centring all in love," his life, "in the end," is "all gratulant" (*P* 13:185–91, 383–85). So—"*Thanks* to the human heart by which we live, / *Thanks* to its tenderness, its joys, and fears" (201–2)—is the ode. If we are to dismiss that gratulant position as cheery optimism blind to the vision of evil and the full experience of painful loss, we have to include Nietzsche and such post-Nietzscheans as Yeats and Wallace Stevens, along with others whose final *Yes* stems, admittedly, from an asserted and self-redemptive divinity within.

It is hard to know *precisely* where in this tradition we are to locate Emerson, suspended between his mentor Wordsworth and his disciple Nietzsche. But if we consider the alternating relation between mind and nature, between joyous union (or reunion) and painful, even devastating, alienation, and, in either case, the final pathos of the *human* significance of the rising and setting sun, and the beautiful but brief blossoming of a flower—if, in short, we consider the Romantic "marriage" of mind and nature, the analogy, for example, between man's life and the dying day and turning seasons, the final stanzas of the Intimations Ode, the single poem that meant most to Emerson and his circle, emerge as at once elegy and epithalamion. Thus, what Emerson thought the century's most courageous voyage—an "essay" perhaps not "on" but *into* the mystery of *immortality*—simultaneously and paradoxically inscribes itself in the memory as perhaps our most poignant testimony to *mortality,* including, however rhetorically or even experientially persuasive we may find the compensations given us, that which Nietzsche describes as *Unwiederbringlichen:* all those things that are irretrievable, including the visionary gleam and splendor, the loss of a radiance that was "once so bright."

No matter how heartbreakingly beautiful the lines in which Wordsworth registers that loss, to end by emphasizing the experiential loss, no matter how profound, rather than the hard-earned consolation of imaginative gain would be to violate the cognitive and emotional trajectory of the ode. At the same time, to stress the power and beauty of the lost radiance, even if it *is* compensated for, is to remain faithful to Wordsworth's career as a whole, at least his career as a *Poet.* The Intimations Ode comes, after all, at the very end of the two-volume 1807 edition of Wordsworth's poems, the edition that marks the end, as well, of his "Great Decade." What lay in the future was not, to quote the "Ode to Duty," the "genial sense of youth," personified as "Glad Hearts," but the "unerring light" of Duty. And when, "through confidence misplaced," such glad hearts "fail," it is Duty that is invoked to provide "thy firm support, according to their need" (12, 13, 16, 24). For all its undoubted moral weight, the language reveals this Duty (even in the ode addressed to it) as *both* the submissive longing (on the part of a man whom "unchartered freedom tires") for "a repose that ever is the same" (37–39) *and* a second-best compensation for failing powers whose loss is deeply felt. In effect, the poem pits stoic piety against the visionary powers of Romantic inspiration. The challenge facing Duty, like that facing memory and maturity in the Intimations Ode, is what to make of a diminished thing.

A religiously orthodox variant on that division between elegy for what was lost and gratitude for the vestigial recollections that provided the fire seeds of recovery, and hence the motive for gratitude, occurs in a poem Wordsworth wrote a decade after the great decade of his creativity had ended, "when"—to quote lines from "Adonais" in which Shelley, elegizing Keats, clearly referred to later Wordsworth—"the spirit's self [had] ceased to burn," leaving only "sparkless ashes" ("Adonais," 359–60). In the final ode-haunted stanza of "Composed upon an Evening of Extraordinary Splendour and Beauty" (1817), Wordsworth moves from poignant questioning to pious gratitude for at least this momentarily restored glimpse of the radiance that was once so bright. He had referred earlier in the poem to the "gleam" and "radiance" (19, 27) of this particular evening, concluding that such "magnificence" is not "wholly" that of the evening; rather, "From worlds not quickened by the sun / A portion of the gift is won" (37–38). Reminded of the "celestial" gifts "wont to stream" before his eye "in the morn / Of blissful infancy" (61–64), he replicates the pattern of sudden emotional shifts enacted in stanzas 3, 4, and 10 of the Intimations Ode and sadly fulfills his earlier premonition: "I see by glimpses now; when age comes on / May scarcely see at all" (*P* 12:281–82):

> "This glimpse of glory, why renewed?"
> Nay, rather speak with gratitude;
> For, if a vestige of those gleams
> Survived, 'twas only in my dreams.
> (65–68; *WP* 2:358–59)

The poem concludes with a prayer, modulating into a deeply affecting if self-accusatory and futile lamentation over lost light, then to a recovery in which he is born again. Finally, the moment of "visionary splendour" fades, as night and death approach (79–80). By this time in Wordsworth's life, the bond between Nature and the creative-perceptive Mind of Man, the threatened but enduring marriage that had produced his greatest poetry, had been put asunder, ironically enough, by a sincere but aesthetically crippling commitment to a normative theism lacking the poetic power of his more ambiguously numinous formulations. In a still later poem, "Not in the Lucid Intervals of Life," we are told (and the exclamation point amounts to a rebuke of his own earlier nature worship) that "By *grace divine, / Not otherwise,* O Nature! we are thine" (16–17). In 1835, this poem became the fourth in the *Evening Voluntaries,* a sequence that incorporated (as the ninth poem) "Composed upon an Evening of Extraordinary Splendour and Beauty," which had also concluded with a pious assertion. Were he (69–72) to "swerve" from the invoked "Dread Power!" or divine "THEE,"

> Oh, let Thy grace remind me of the light
> Full early lost, and fruitlessly deplored;
> Which, at this moment, on my waking sight
> Appears to shine, by miracle restored:

My soul, though yet confined to earth,
Rejoices in a second birth!
—'Tis past, the visionary splendour fades;
And night approaches with her shades.
(73–80)

As in the case of the Intimations Ode, especially in the tenth stanza's shift from the acknowledgment that nothing can bring back the splendor in the grass, the glory in the flower, to the insistence that we will not mourn that loss, individual readers will have to judge (and judgment may vacillate from reading to reading) how much relative weight to apportion to the pathos and poignancy of the question ("This glimpse of glory, why renewed?") and how much to the swift denial ("Nay, rather speak with gratitude"): an abrupt about-face that amounts to a more pious version of the ode's stoic assertion, at once more desperate *and, psychologically and poetically, far more persuasive,* that "We will grieve not, rather find / Strength in what remains behind . . ." (180–81).

This same tension between grief and consolation, loss and recovery, also plays out in Emerson's elegy for Waldo. I agree with Bruce Ronda and Mark Edmundson, who have described "Threnody" as Emerson's attempt to overcome grief by falling back upon, or at least asserting his own version of, Wordsworth's intimations of immortality.[13] And, I would add, where Wordsworth is we can also expect to find Milton, in this case, the Milton not only of "Lycidas" but also of *Samson Agonistes* and *Paradise Lost.*[14]

13. Ronda, "Literary Grieving and the Death of Waldo"; Edmundson, "Emerson and the Work of Melancholia" (included, revised, in his *Towards Reading Freud*). "Threnody" has not been well attended. David Porter devotes a chapter of his *Emerson and Literary Change* to an informed but unrelenting assault on the poem as lacking precisely the qualities that make Whitman's "When Lilacs Last in the Dooryard Bloom'd" a great elegy. I am closer to his judgment than to the excessive estimate of Gay Wilson Allen, echoed by Richardson, that "Threnody" is one of the "great elegies in the English language" (Allen, *Waldo Emerson: A Biography,* 397; Richardson, *Mind on Fire,* 359). Julie Ellison distinguishes between the tough prose of "Experience" and the lyric sentimentality of "Threnody" ("Tears for Emerson: *Essays, Second Series,*" 156–58). Though Robert Browning told Carolyn Sturgis he admired "Threnody," along with "Dirge" and "The Snow-Storm" (*L* 8:534–35), the rest is largely silence—a silence particularly revealing in the case of Harold Bloom. Waggoner praises the elegy, but discusses it in none of his three books on American and Emersonian poetry. One early commentator faults it on grounds precisely the opposite of Dr. Johnson's notorious attack on the artificiality of "Lycidas." According to W. R. Cairns, writing around 1911, "The 'Threnody' shows too intense personal sorrow to compete with smoother and more academic elegies" (*A History of American Literature,* 136).

14. Describing "Threnody" as neither pastoral elegy nor Christian consolation but an original attempt at resolution, Emerson wrote in old age: "When Lycidas has been

Emerson was desperate for consolation. Despite his notorious claim that he could not grieve, he was, in fact, devastated by the death of his son. His austere recording of the event in his journal the morning after—"28 January 1842. Yesterday night at 15 minutes after eight my little Waldo ended his life" (*JMN* 8:163)—was quickly elaborated on. On this same day following the death of "my wonderful little boy," in whom "daily & nightly blessedness was lodged," Emerson laments that "all his wonderful beauty could not save him," that "everything wakes this morning but my darling boy"—a shocking betrayal by indifferent Nature that Emerson will dwell on in the first part of "Threnody," especially in lines 105–25. On that morning when everything but little Waldo awakened, Bronson Alcott sent his nine-year-old daughter, Louisa May, to inquire about the condition of "little Waldo, then lying very ill." She never forgot what she saw and heard when Emerson entered the room. "His father came to me, so worn with watching and changed by sorrow that I was startled and could only stammer out my message. 'Child, he is dead' was the answer. . . . That was my first glimpse of a great grief," she recalled in commemorating Emerson's own death, forty years later, adding the telling observation that the "anguish that made a familiar face so tragic . . . gave those few words more pathos than the sweet lamentation of the Threnody." Similarly, the brother of Elizabeth Hoar—who had grieved with his sister when her fiancé, Emerson's brother Charles, died in 1836—said that he "was never more impressed with a human expression of agony than by that of Emerson leading the way into the room where little Waldo lay dead."[15]

Emerson's essay "The Poet"—a wonderful celebration of imaginative energy and renovative fire—may be read in part as his attempt, in the cold, dark months that followed the death of Waldo, to warm himself back into life. Though he will go on in the second half of this essay to describe the passage, or "ascension," of the soul "into higher forms," Emerson ends the first half of the essay with this proto-Darwinian meditation, in which "a certain poet" (and *this* "Orphic poet" is clearly Emerson himself) attributes Coleridge's word *Genius* to the process of recovery and new growth: "Genius is the activity which repairs the decays of things," whether they are "wholly or partly of a material and finite kind."

---

written, you shall not write an elegy on that key, unless you can do better than that. And so in each style of images or fables, after a best has been shown, you must come up to that, or pass it, or else abstain from writing" (*JMN* 15:109).

15. Alcott, "Reminiscences of Ralph Waldo Emerson," in *Youth's Companion* 55 (May 25, 1882), 213–14; reprinted in Bosco and Myerson, *His Own Time,* 89–90. For the reaction of Rockwood Hoar Jr., see Rusk, *Life of Emerson,* 294.

> Nature, through all her kingdoms, insures herself. Nobody cares for planting the poor fungus: so she shakes down from the gills of one agaric countless spores, any one of which, being preserved, transmits new billions of spores to-morrow or next day. The new agaric of this hour has a chance which the old one had not. The atom of seed is thrown into a new place, not subject to the accidents which destroyed its parent two rods off. She makes a man; and having brought him to ripe age, she will no longer run the risk of losing this wonder at a blow, but she detaches from him a new self, that the kind may be safe from accidents to which the individual is exposed. (*E&L* 475)

In the case of Waldo, the analogy between the natural and human "kingdoms" breaks down. There, Nature did *not* "insure herself" in the usual way. Instead of the parent being destroyed while the "new agaric" or seed survives accidents and is itself "brought . . . to ripe age," the *progenitor* survives while the exposed offspring, this "wondrous" and "beautiful" boy, suffers the cruelest of accidents, death in early childhood, with both Emerson and Nature "losing this wonder at a blow." But the repairing process is only "*partly* of a material and finite kind," for Emerson's little boy lost is found again, in "Threnody," the elegy his father wrote for him. That poem, long delayed by an emotional turmoil resistant to elegy's generic demand for consolation, struggled to achieve that "which repairs the decays of things"—a recuperative agency attributed to "Genius" in the paragraph just quoted.

In his notebook, Emerson gives the immediate credit to a story he read, and eventually published in the *Dial,* a rather preposterous allegory he and Lidian felt had valued Waldo's "precious ashes" and had given "a green leaf and a breath of music" to their "darling of Nature," bringing him, personally, said Emerson, the "native gold" of "consolation" (*L* 3:55, 74). In his journal entry on the story's author, Charles King Newcomb, and his bizarre "Dolon," Emerson records: "Let it be to his praise that when I carried his manuscript story to the woods, and read it in the armchair of the upturned root of a pine tree, I felt for the first time since Waldo's death some efficient faith again in the repairs of the universe, some independency of natural relations whilst spiritual affinities can be so perfect and compensating" (*JMN* 8:178–79).[16]

16. Newcomb, an acquaintance of Margaret Fuller, was a Loyola admirer to whom Emerson attributed "a Religious intellect." Aware of the connection between Waldo and "Dolon"—in which a robed figure ritually sacrifices a hypersensitive young boy—Emerson was moved enough to promise to publish the story, which he did, after some success in clarifying its garbled syntax. That it is still the weakest thing in the July 1842 *Dial,* the number with which Emerson took up the editorship relinquished

Having resolved the Wordsworthian choice between books *or* Nature by reading *in* Nature, Emerson also found in Newcomb's mawkish "Dolon" a Wordsworthian "timely utterance" bringing sufficient balm to his grief to at least initiate *poetic* utterance. He was inspired, and inspiration is always the Emersonian motive for reading, to write three lines that became part of "Threnody." The third line—"The deep Heart answered, 'Weepest thou?' "—was destined to become the pivot from the "threnody" proper, the dirge or unrelieved expression of grief, into the movement of consolation and recovery, culminating in the vision of Waldo as, in the elegy's final line, "Lost in God, in Godhead found!" ("Threnody," 186, 289).

Although the climactic line of "Threnody" is less than persuasive, this is at least to *attempt* to accomplish the "repairs" of "the decays," even the "repairs of the universe," through the power of Poetry. And poetry is, in fact, the subject of the *second* half of the pivotal paragraph of this essay, an essay that is, after all, titled "The Poet." Emerson starts again with a simile heroic in more than the rhetorical sense. He raises the analogy from the level of the material and finite to that of intellectual and imaginative spirit, from the temporal to the eternal "kingdom."

> So when the soul of the poet has come to ripeness of thought, she [Nature] detaches and sends away from it its poems or songs,—a fearless, sleepless, deathless progeny, which is not exposed to the accidents of the weary kingdom of time: a fearless, vivacious offspring, clad with wings (such was the virtue of the soul out of which they came), which carry them fast and far, and infix them irrecoverably into the hearts of men. These wings are the beauty of the poet's soul. The songs, thus flying immortal from their mortal parent, are pursued by clamorous flights of censures, which swarm in far greater numbers, and threaten to devour them; but these last are not winged. At the end of a very short leap they fall plump down, and rot, having received from the souls out of which they came no beautiful wings. But the melodies of the poet ascend, and leap, and pierce into the deeps of infinite time. (*E&L* 457–58)

Emerson's imagery echoes Shelley's "Adonais," in which the soul of Adonais-Keats—having "outsoared" the censurious calumny of "carrion kites that scream below"—attains its apotheosis and, "like a star, / Beacons from the abode where the Eternal are" (335, 352–55, 494–95). Though he thought himself but a "hoarse singer," Emerson was determined to attempt a sustained elegy of his own, a commemoration on extended wings,

---

by Fuller, indicates just how much personal meaning the story had for him—as grieving father rather than as literary critic or editor.

flying immortal above both mortal son and mortal parent. In accord with his own emotional need and temperament, as well as the demands of genre, he had determined from the outset that the elegy for Waldo would eventually turn toward consolation and compensation. But that turn, projected aesthetically and intellectually, would take four years to accommodate emotionally and existentially. The essay "Experience" had presented us with the idealist's denial of mourning, the loss of his son reduced to the loss of a "beautiful estate,—no more. I cannot get it nearer to me." Such a loss of property, however inconvenient, "would leave me as it found me,—neither better nor worse. So it is with this calamity: it does not touch me: some thing which I fancied was a part of me, which could not be torn away without tearing me . . . falls off from me and leaves no scar. It was caducous." The state of the Indian in Robert Southey's 1810 epic *The Curse of Kehama,* cut off from all feeling, is, adds Emerson, "a type of us all. The dearest events are summer-rain, and we the Para coats that shed every drop. Nothing is left us now but death. We look to that with a grim satisfaction, saying, there at least is reality that will not dodge us. I take this evanescence and lubricity of all objects, which lets them slip through our fingers then when we clutch hardest, to be the most unhandsome part of our condition" (*E&L* 473).

However conflicted he is, this is Emerson not only at his most idealist but also at his most notoriously cold, aloof, and impersonal—clinical in his severance of the quintessential Me from the caducous NOT ME, and as seemingly marmoreal as the fallen Napoléon he had quoted in "The Tragic," his temperament like a block of immovable marble, the "great events of my life hav[ing] slipped over me without making any impression on my moral or physical nature." This is a far cry from the paternal and domestic grieving that afflicted Emerson the man, a bereavement that dominates the first 175 lines of "Threnody." At the poem's nadir, the lost son—the impalpable "some thing" he merely (using Coleridge's lesser term) "*fancied* was a part of me"—is revealed as, in painful reality, "the largest part of me" (161), a beloved child whose loss prostrates a grieving father who preached "erect" self-reliance:

> For this losing is true dying;
> This is lordly man's down-lying,
> This his sure but slow reclining,
> Star by star his world resigning
> (162–65)

Beyond the loss of his boy, and one's own grimly anticipated death (that final "reality," one direct and essential rather than accidental and oblique), there had to be *something* resembling Miltonic-Wordsworthian recompense. Be it what it may, he would try to find it in the final hundred or so lines of "Threnody."

Emerson's images of poems as "deathless progeny," imaginative projections "flying immortal from their mortal parent," transcending "this weary kingdom of time," are clearly relevant to his attempt to immortalize his son in poetry. And when, in this same paragraph of "The Poet," he depicts "Genius" as the activity that "repairs the decays of things," he is equating such "repairs" with the guidance the Chorus urges upon a despairing Samson, who must "feel," within, "Some source of consolation from above, / Secret refreshings that *repair* his strength" (*Samson Agonistes,* 663–65). Those "repairs" are akin to the "large recompense" of "Lycidas" (184), and the "abundant recompense" of an echoing Wordsworth in "Tintern Abbey" (88), as well as to the turn in the Intimations Ode signaled by the exclamation, "O joy! that in our embers / Is something that doth live" (130–31). That compensation had to be emotional, intellectual, and spiritual. He had tried, in letters like that to Caroline Sturgis, to dismiss his agony, but Lidian knew that the gesture was, as she said, largely "in theory"; for all his idealist philosophy and personal inhibition, he, like she, was heartbroken.[17] Despite the remarks about grieving that he could not grieve, Emerson had not, in the months following the boy's death, reached the state where he could entertain "thoughts that do often lie *too deep for tears.*" In March 1842, he wrote his Transcendentalist friend the artist Sarah Clarke: "I have no skill, no illumination," no "nearness to the power which has bereaved me of the most beautiful of the children of men. I apprehend nothing of that fact but its bitterness. . . . It is nothing to me but the gloomiest sensible experience[,] to which I have no key, and no consolation, nothing but oblivion and diversion" (*L* 7:494). As he publicly acknowledges in "Experience," this is suffering without recompense, for it has brought no wisdom: "I grieve that grief can teach me nothing, nor carry me one step into real nature" (*E&L* 473).

In January 1844, Margaret Fuller wrote, requesting a copy of the long-delayed elegy, "even if it is not finished." The letter reveals her own inconsolable grief over the boy's death, a deep mourning compounded by her sense of Emerson's increasing withdrawal: "[T]o me this season can never pass without opening anew the deep wound. I do not find myself at all consoled for the loss of that beautiful form which seemed to me the realization of hope more than any other. I miss him when I go to your home, I miss him when I think of you there; you seem to me lonely as if he filled to you a place which no other ever could in any degree."

17. Lidian Emerson, *The Selected Letters of Lidian Jackson Emerson,* 87, 100.

She might have been reading the first part of the unfinished elegy she was requesting. She continues, insisting that "there was no fancy, no exaggeration in the feelings he excited. His beauty was real, was substantial." Having just read a note that Waldo had once brought her when she was visiting the Emersons, she claims to "see him just as he looked that day, a messenger of good tidings, an angel."[18] It seems only a step to her later claim to have seen the dead child, in a visionary dream, as a literal angel. In his response, Emerson explained why he had not yet been able to produce the elegy's intended movement into consolation. It had to do with the abyss between agonizing experience and theory, even his own Miltonic-Wordsworthian theory of compensation and the conversion of despair into hope. Synopsizing in his journal his response to Fuller, he wrote, "The astonishment of life is the absence of any appearance of reconciliation between the theory & the practice of life" (*JMN* 9:65). In the language of Wordsworth's ode, "the radiance which was once so bright" still seemed to Emerson "forever taken from my sight," and he was not yet ready to reconcile the irreconcilable by finding comfort in "the soothing thoughts that spring / Out of human suffering," thoughts of "the philosophic mind." Least of all, if it implied a conventional, doctrinal belief in the immortality of the soul, could he find comfort in that "faith that looks through death" (Intimations Ode, 176–87).

That failure to find comfort is salient in the elegy itself. With more than two-thirds of the poem written, the three lines inspired by his reading of "Dolon" had still not found their way into the elegy. The third of these lines—"The deep Heart answered, 'Weepest thou?' "—had not yet become, despite the precedent of Milton's "weep no more" in "Lycidas" (165), the pivot from loss to recovery. Even after the "deep Heart" speaks, for many lines the elegist dwells on memories of the once-living boy, now lost.

By all accounts a beautiful and wonderfully precocious child, little Waldo is further transfigured by the love of a father and the memory of a writer haunted by Wordsworth's ode. The child becomes a messenger sent to the elegist (not by any external God, but in some way by the deep Heart itself), and what was sent was not tuitional but intuitional, not "tutors," but the "joyful eye" of a miraculous child. Like that "Seer blest" or "Eye among the blind," the Wordsworthian Child of the seventh and eighth stanzas of the ode whose outer appearance (that of a pigmy) belies the immensity of the soul within, Emerson's small child contains greatness. The features of Waldo have their correspondence in nature, and, going

18. Fuller, *The Letters of Margaret Fuller,* 3:175–76.

beyond Wordsworth, Emerson, the radical who (in the Divinity School Address) equated each and all of us, potentially, with Jesus, virtually identifies his child with the Christ child. The deep Heart speaks:

"I came to thee as to a friend;
Dearest, to thee I did not send
Tutors, but a joyful eye,
Innocence that matched the sky,
Lovely locks, a form of wonder,
Laughter rich as woodland thunder,
That thou might'st entertain apart
The richest flowering of all art:
And, as the great all-loving Day
Through smallest chambers takes its way,
That thou might'st break thy daily bread
With prophet, savior, and head;
That thou might'st cherish for thine own
The riches of sweet Mary's Son,
Boy-Rabbi, Israel's paragon."
(209–23)

Little Waldo becomes the incarnate God at his most accessible and cherishable, and the eucharist at once a domestic version of the daily bread of the Lord's Supper and the simple produce of the common day, miracle in the ordinary. As Emerson would later say in the course of that earlier-cited passage from "Character" in which he quotes from the ninth stanza of the Intimations Ode, "Jesus affirms the divinity in him and us—not thrusts himself between it and us," thus pointing to "the presence of the Eternal" in each perishing individual. Even if Herod *had* killed the infant Jesus, Christianity would not have been extinguished since "God sends his messages, if not by one, then quite as well by another." Thus, "one noble person dwarfs a whole nation of underlings." One such noble person affirming the divinity within was Emerson's child, whose exterior semblance, belying his soul's immensity, is a small chamber that contains, and is illuminated by, "the great all-loving Day"—again, Wordsworth's "fountain light of all our day," that "master light of all our seeing" to which the child's "joyful eye" is aligned in the proper axis of vision. And in "Character," Emerson quotes the very next lines from the ninth stanza, in which Wordsworth's "High instincts" become the light of all our day, "Uphold us," and have the "power" to make "our noisy years" seem no more than "moments in the being / Of the eternal Silence." Such are the "truths that wake, / To perish never" (*W* 10:94–97).

Given all this, how naive must the mourning father be to think or hope that the residence of *such* a child could be long restricted to our temporal world, let alone that he could remain as a "guest" in a particular household in Concord? To think so would be not only to arrest the very dynamism, volatility, and fluxional nature of the round world repeatedly celebrated by that father but, even more important, to forget that the truth, simultaneously deep and higher, is—however speculative and inexplicable to discursive reason or the restricted understanding—an intuitive divining of the Spirit, and that, to this divinity within, "frail Nature" and even Death are subservient as to their lord and master. In "Gnothi Seauton," written in the wake of Ellen's death, the "guest" was "The Infinite / Embosomed in a man," a man who, bearing that "royal presence," had to bear *himself* "Up to the scale & compass of thy guest" (*JMN* 3:290). In "Threnody," the deep Heart reserves the word *guest* to the bereaved father's divinity-bearing son:

> "thoughtest thou such guest
> Would in thy hall take up his rest?
> Would rushing life forget her laws,
> Fate's glowing revolution pause?
> High omens ask diviner guess;
> Not to be conned to tediousness.
> And know my higher gifts unbind
> The zone that girds the incarnate mind.
> When the scanty shores are full
> With Thought's perilous, whirling pool;
> When frail Nature can no more,
> Then the Spirit strikes the hour;
> My servant Death, with solving rite,
> Pours finite into infinite."
>
> (224–37)

Like Wordsworth's mysterious "High instincts," these "High omens," resistant to tedious inquiry, reveal themselves only to the "diviner guess" of the intuitive Reason. Idealists, we were told in *Nature,* "might all say of matter, what Michael Angelo said of external beauty, 'It is the frail and weary weed, in which God dresses the soul which he has called into time'" (*E&L* 38, quoting sonnet 51). Having reasserted that sovereignty of Spirit over "frail Nature," including the unbinding power of "higher gifts" superior to the limited "incarnate mind," the deep Heart poses yet another rhetorical question. Will the mourner—especially *this* mourner, the celebrant of protean change, polarities, and ever generating circles—be so foolish as to try to arrest the circuitous journey of "overflowing Love" (192), the dynamic flux and reflux of Coleridge's many-seeming "one Life within us and abroad"? All things are part of an emanative pouring and overflow, a wild yet fated process that can be fixed or frozen only at the cost of entropy and extinction. The apparently Many are One, *not* None.

> "Wilt thou freeze love's tidal flow,
> Whose streams through nature circling go?
> Nail the wild star to its track
> On the half-climbed zodiac?
> Blood is blood which circulates,
> Life is life which generates,
> And many-seeming life is one,
> Wilt thou transfix and make it none?"
> (238–46)

"There are no fixtures in nature," Emerson tells us in "Circles." "The universe is fluid and volatile." And later in the same essay, the relationship between movement and stability, the Wordsworthian "central peace, subsisting at the heart / Of endless agitation," is clarified: "Whilst the eternal generation of circles proceeds, the eternal generator abides," at least as "some principle of fixture or stability in the soul" in contrast to the "incessant movement and progression" in which "all things" partake as they "renew, generate, and spring" (*E&L* 403, 412). This polarity is at the heart of David Porter's severe but largely judicious criticism of "Threnody." He argues that, for all its "explicit promoting of a world where life and love 'radiate' and 'generate' in a cosmic moral recirculation system [242–44], the poem itself finally imposes its own rigid deliverance figure." Though I will be disagreeing in a moment with the ultimate example he offers, he is surely right that too much of the elegy sacrifices the particularity and contingency of life to Emerson's preordained "deliverance schema," a schema oriented, I would add, to that "principle of fixity or stability in the soul."[19]

At this point in the poem, however, this powerful flow cannot be stopped, nor can it be delimited to even its most beloved and precious particular incarnation. For Love's "onward force" is "too starkly pent / In figure, bone, and lineament" (247–48). "Onward and onward!," cries a Carlylean Emerson in "Experience," in his paean to those "liberated moments" when we affirm the "mighty Ideal" that "journeys . . . before us" (*E&L* 486). Sounding increasingly like the stern God of the book of Job, the deep Heart asks rhetorically: "'Wilt thou, uncalled, interrogate, / Talker! The unreplying Fate?'" Each and All being synonymous, the "genius of the whole" is "Ascendant in the private soul," which cannot be beckoned

19. Porter, *Emerson and Literary Change*, 34.

"when to go and come." Just as we are embosomed in Nature for just a season, so the soul has its seasonal residence. The body is "fair," but less beautiful than that intuitive "expansive reason," which is a higher gift, its temporary embodiment mere portent and "sign," even if that building is a masterpiece:

> "Fair the soul's recess and shrine,
> Magic-built to last a season;
> Masterpiece of love benign;
> Fairer that expansive reason
> Whose omen 't is, and sign.
> Wilt thou not ope thy heart to know
> What rainbows teach, and sunsets show?"
> (255–61)

Significantly, the last two lines provide the opening of the ten-line excerpt from "Threnody" employed by Emerson in 1861 as epigraph to his lecture on "Immortality" (*W* 8:321). In keeping with that text's celebration of the Intimations Ode as our "best" exploration of the mystery of immortality, the teaching and showing here in "Threnody" regarding immortality is Wordsworthian. The omens and signs intimating both mortality and immortality echo the Intimations Ode and "Tintern Abbey." As a "sign," the "rainbow in the sky" (the subject of the lyric Wordsworth employed as epigraph to the ode) is both biblical covenant and emblem of change, since "The rainbow comes and goes" (Intimations Ode, stanza 2). The sunset, too, is both permanent and transient, a reminder of that mysterious Presence, "whose *dwelling* is the light of *setting* suns" ("Tintern Abbey"), as well as of that "setting sun" whose circumscribing clouds take a sober coloring from "an eye / That hath kept watch o'er man's mortality."

But transience can be reconciled with permanence discursively, more assertively but less persuasively than by means of Wordsworthian poetic images. There is, according to "Threnody," a "verdict" that "accumulates / From lengthening scroll of human fates," and it tallies with both the "Voice of earth to earth returned" and with "prayers of saints that inly burned." That reciprocal voice and those inner prayers alike declare that "*What is excellent / As God lives, is permanent.*" If "*Hearts are dust, hearts' loves remain; / Heart's love will meet thee again*" (262–69; italics in original). In a bow to theological decorum, we are to "Revere the Maker; fetch thine eye / Up to his style, and manners of the sky" (270–71). This "Maker," however, is no distant sky god, but a fecundating Lord of Nature, his heaven not the "imperial palace" of stanza 5 of the Intimations Ode, but the meadows, groves, and common flower of its concluding stanza:

"Not of adamant and gold
Built he heaven stark and cold;
No, but a nest of bending reeds,
Flowering grass and scented weeds;
Or like a traveller's fleeing tent,
Or bow above the tempest bent."
(272–77)

It is at this crucial—and Wordsworthian—point that I take issue with Porter, who here pushes his otherwise just criticism of Emerson's inorganic rigidity in "Threnody" to an extreme. To be sure, "Threnody" is a poor thing next to the great elegy to which Porter unfavorably compares it: Whitman's "When Lilacs Last in the Dooryard Bloom'd." But when he says of these lines that here "Emerson's rigid deliverance figure" terminates in an image in which "God the Maker" (whom he rightly terms "one of Emerson's analogues for the poet") "erects the symbolic monumental building," thus converting his son's death into "mental matter," he seems to have simply disregarded the "Not" and "No" at the beginnings of lines 272 and 274. In doing so, he ignores the fact that "Threnody" has its own version of lilacs blooming.

Emerson's heaven may be "built," but it is "*Not* of adamant and gold," "*Not* like a temple rich with pomp and gold"—also rejected by Wordsworth, in a passage of *The Prelude* (*P* [1805], 12:228) printed in 1835 and read by Emerson. "No," for the affirmative Emersonian heaven presented here is natural rather than an artifice of eternity, immediate rather than remote—tangible, visible, scented. Mother Earth's "gentle nest," so tenderly if unexpectedly referred to in the "Idealism" chapter of *Nature,* returns here as "a nest of bending reeds." This is particularly affecting, coming in this, the final movement of the elegy, and in this particular context—its soft, nurturing warmth contrasting with the conception of a remote heaven, adamant, stark, and cold. The tenderness with which Emerson presents, as a gentle heaven appropriate to his child, that ordinary nest formed by bent reeds recalls Wordsworth's "Earth," who "fills her lap with pleasures of her own," and, even more, the presentation of the humble "flower" blossoming at the end of the ode. Like that flower, the nest of bending reeds can evoke thoughts that lie too deep for tears.

The conclusion of "Threnody" is reminiscent not only of Wordsworth but also of Carlyle's supreme affirmation in *Sartor Resartus,* the remarkable book introduced to the United States by Emerson. Having passed through the Hell—the "Hades" or "Gehenna"—of his "Everlasting No," Carlyle's Teufelsdröckh finally utters his "Everlasting Yea." It takes the form of a "Divine moment, when over the tempest-tossed Soul, as once over the wild-weltering Chaos, it is spoken: Let there be Light!" In this "miraculous and God-announcing" replication of Genesis and of Milton's Creation of Light in book 7 of *Paradise Lost,* the "mad primeval Discord is hushed," deep foundations are "built beneath" a "skyey vault with its everlasting luminaries above. . . ." Instead of "a dark wasteful chaos, we have a blooming, fertile, heaven-encompassed World." And since "it is with Man's Soul as it was with Nature," a soul now triumphant, Carlyle can—through all his layered masks of protagonist and editor—say to himself, and to us: "Be no longer a chaos, but a World, or even a Worldkin. Produce! Produce!"[20] Carlyle had been a friend to whom Emerson confided his despair in letters grieving the loss of his son, that "morning star" he had dreamed of sending to childless Carlyle as his representative. It would not be strange if the peroration of the elegy recording and supposedly recovering from that loss, in particular the transformation wrought by Emerson's swift and all-restoring Lord, reflected Carlyle's own imperative to be "up and be doing"[21] as well as his "Divine moment," the conversion of darkness into light, of wasteful wilderness into blossoming fertility, of tempest-tossed chaos into a productive and coherent world:

"Silent rushes the swift Lord
Through ruined systems still restored,
Broadsowing, bleak and void to bless,
Plants with worlds the wilderness;
Waters with tears of ancient sorrow
Apples of Eden ripe to-morrow.
House and tenant go to ground,
Lost in God, in Godhead found!"
(282–89)

Emerson's fructifying imagery suggests, like Carlyle's, something other than a completely transcendent resolution. It suggests, in fact, the usual Romantic analogy between natural, human, and divine. Emerson's ideas "are not fixed upon any Reality that is beyond or behind or in any way apart," says John Dewey, anticipating the recent emphasis on an anti-Transcendentalist Emerson. Instead, "they are versions of the Here and Now."[22] "The secret of heaven is kept from age to age," contends Emerson in one of his few forays into the mystery of immortality, this time his essay on Swedenborg in *Representative Men.* Dismissing the literal aspects

20. Carlyle, *Sartor Resartus,* 146.

21. The "rainbow" bent above the "tempest" at the end of "Threnody" is "built / Not of spent deeds but of doing" (281). "Up and be doing," cries Carlyle in his review of Elliott's *Corn-Law Rhymes.* "Do one thing" and "a new light will rise to thee on the doing of all things whatsoever" (*Critical and Miscellaneous Essays,* 3:143).

22. Dewey, "Ralph Waldo Emerson" (1903), 28.

of the Swedish mystic's celestial visions, Emerson says, "No imprudent, nor sociable angel ever dropt an early syllable to answer the longings of saints, the fears of mortals." It is "certain," however, that any humanly answerable heaven must "tally with what is best in nature."

> It must not be inferior in tone to the already known works of the artist who sculptures the globes of the firmament, and writes the moral law. It must be fresher than rainbows, stabler than mountains, agreeing with flowers, with tides, and the rising and setting of autumnal stars. Melodious poets shall be hoarse as street ballads, when once the penetrating key-note of nature and spirit is sounded,—the earth-beat, sea-beat, heart-beat, which makes the tune to which the sun rolls, and the globule of blood, and the sap of trees. (*E&L* 686–87)

That corresponding "earth-beat, sea-beat, heart-beat" (like the breeze that "beats" against the poet's cheek at the outset of *The Prelude,* evoking a "correspondent breeze" within) is the final fruit of those Wordsworthian intertwinings (in the preamble to the skating scene) of enduring natural objects with human imagination and the "passions that build up our human soul," until "we recognize / A grandeur in the beatings of the heart" (*P* 1:409–14). For those whose soul, heart, and body are interwined with nature, heaven, be it what it may, "must *not* be," in terms of the earth, "inferior in tone"; indeed, it must be in what Wordsworth and Keats beautifully call "a *finer tone.*" The full context of Keats's echo of the Wordsworthian Solitary's "Music of finer tone" (*E* 2:710) reminds us that the Wordsworthian or Keatsian (or Emersonian or Stevensian) green earth can itself be what Carlyle calls a "heaven-encompassed World." Keats's "favorite" speculation—in a letter of November 22, 1817, to his religiously orthodox friend Benjamin Bailey—seems as relevant as Carlyle to the concluding, supposedly "Transcendentalist," lines of "Threnody." Projecting his intuitive-imaginative "Vision" as a "Shadow of reality to come," Keats speculates that "we shall enjoy ourselves here after by having what we call happiness on Earth repeated in a finer tone and so repeated."[23]

23. Keats, *Letters of John Keats,* 1:184–86. In its full context, the speculation joins rather than separates what Keats calls "Thoughts" and "Sensations" in a way that accords with intuitive Reason. The term *sensations,* derived from Hazlitt and often misunderstood, is not a Keatsian endorsement of crude sensual excitation, but a provisional rejection of "consequitive reasoning": that discursive, hyperrational "hunger . . . after Truth" that Keats, recalling Wordsworth's strictures against the ever "seeking" analytical intellect, attributes in the letter to his bookish friend. In place of such discursive reasoning, Keats calls for intuitive "Imagination," informed by, but not limited to, sense perception ("sensations"). Thus, Keats's notorious exclamation in the letter, "O for a Life of Sensations rather than of Thoughts!" can be translated, as H. W. Garrod suggested years ago: "O for the pure gospel of the *Lyrical Ballads*" (*Keats,* 32–33). Keats,

Fellow passengers on the ship taking him back to the United States in September 1833 annoyed Emerson by asking "whether I know the soul immortal." No, he answered in his journal, but he did know "the Now to be eternal," and thought it "sufficient reply" to say, "Think on living, I have to do no more than you with that question of another life. I believe in this life. I believe it continues" (*JMN* 4:87). In "Immortality," Emerson, like Keats, found his precedent for such speculation in *Paradise Lost,* in a question posed by Raphael, a question that he, like Keats and Emily Dickinson, appears to take in a more than rhetorical sense. Emerson came to Milton's necessary angel this time by way of that Swedenborg who "described an intelligible heaven," a "continuing" of "our earthly experience [in] the future existence. All nature will accompany us there." Emerson continues: "Milton anticipated the leading thought of Swedenborg, when he wrote . . . 'What if Earth / Be but the Shadow of Heaven, and things therein / Each to the other like more than on earth is thought?'" (*W* 8:327; quoting *PL* 5:574–76).[24]

Although this is not quite "Milton" speaking, his epic narrator at this point, the angel Raphael, *is* close to the author. Raphael's "what if," perhaps rhetorical, is certainly intriguing—raising at least the possibility of Earth as a *fore*shadowing of Heaven, seized on by such descendants of Adam as Keats (for whom earthly happiness was the "Shadow of reality to come"), Emerson, and Emily Dickinson, all of whom suggest that heaven will be a continuation, and substantiation, of its shadow: earthly experience. He will, Raphael says, explain the mysterious events of celestial warfare

---

however, going beyond that gospel, also looks back, as Wordsworth did, to Milton. He presents his speculation to Bailey by, first, alluding to Milton, going on to fuse the emphasis in poems like "Expostulation and Reply" and "The Tables Turned" (sensations endorsed over busy and bookish intellection) with Wordsworth's rather different emphasis, in the final line of the penultimate stanza of the Intimations Ode. Although he is not yet ready to fuse sensation and thought, Keats knows, even this early, that he is one "to whom it is necessary that years should bring the philosophic mind." He compares the human imagination, including his projection of an earthlike heaven, to "Adam's dream." That "he awoke and found it true" is meant to remind Bailey that, in *Paradise Lost,* Adam's "internal sight" was realized, beautifully embodied in Eve (*PL* 8: 452–90). The Keatsian heaven is thus at once tangible and the projection of a delicate spirit. It is "human life" in an "empyreal reflection" and "spiritual repetition"—in short, earthly happiness, but "in a finer tone" and as a "Shadow of reality to come."

24. In context, Raphael is explaining to Adam the revolt of the disloyal angels: the war that educated the angels even as the human race, in the form of Adam, is now being educated by one of those angels. In delineating "what surmounts the reach / Of human sense," Raphael repairs, as would any good Platonist, to analogy: the phenomenal world is to the spiritual world as shadow is to substance.

By likening spiritual to corporeal forms,
As may express them best, *though what if Earth*
Be but the shadow of Heaven, and things therein
Each to other like, more than on earth is thought?
(*PL* 5:573–76; italics added)

Apparently reversing Raphael's "therein," Emily Dickinson explains, "'Herein is love.'" And she goes on in this 1852 letter to her friend Susan Gilbert to echo Raphael's question: "But *that* was Heaven—*this* is but Earth, Earth so *like* to heaven that I would hesitate should the true one call away."[25] Even Coleridge can come close: "As a step to break the abruptness of an immediate heaven," the "Hereafter," though there would be no memory of our death, "must be a human life" (*CN* 2:2584). Except for Swedenborg's, all of these Raphaelesque speculations are subject to change. But the conclusion of "Threnody" is in their spirit: Heaven as Earth in a finer tone, Earth the shadow of Heaven.

The dirge movement of "Threnody" (lines 1–175) had ended with the grieving father "too much bereft"; with "truth and nature's costly lie" exposed; the world "dishonored" because "not ripe yet to sustain" the genius of this *wunderkind* born out of phase; the trusted prophecy "broken"; the "richest fortune sourly crossed," because the boy meant to redeem "the times to come" was dead: "Born for the future, to the future lost!" (140–41, 169–75). Now, presumably "in order," as Coleridge says, "to lose and find all self in GOD" (*BL* 1:283), the lost is still "lost," yet, paradoxically, "in Godhead found."

Waldo as a "child of paradise" (166) lost and found recalls Miltonic Paradise itself, Lost and Regained. Like Wordsworth in the ode, Emerson, at the end of "Threnody," echoes the final book of *Paradise Lost.* Leaving Eden, their punishment for having eaten the "*fruit*" of the forbidden tree, Adam and Eve drop "some natural tears" (*PL* 12:645), yet have their consolation. They have been assured by Milton's "seer blest," the archangel Michael, that the painful loss of Eden will yet prove a happy fall given the promised *final "fruits"*—"joy and eternal bliss" through the redemptive sacrifice of Christ—and the replacement of that lost Eden by "A paradise within thee, happier far" (*PL* 12:551–53, 586–87). Earlier in "Threnody," the world was "not ripe yet" for the coming of Emerson's own Christlike son; now, at the poem's conclusion, the unripe is projectively matured, but only by looking before and after: "Apples of Eden ripe to-morrow" because

25. Dickinson, *The Letters of Emily Dickinson,* 1:195; italics in original. The editors do not catch the echo.

watered with "tears of ancient sorrow." Even the bleakest, most barren "void" has been planted and blessed, yielding Edenic apples: no longer the forbidden and fatal fruit of the original Fall, but the ripened bounty of a projected and promised end, a paradisal compensation that tries to make the death of the boy a *felix culpa.*

It cannot be other than a willed fruition, the defeated and "down-lying" father resurrected as the sovereign, erect man, seasoned by suffering and ripened by the tears of sorrow, but still "Emersonian," still, however temporarily diminished, master of nature by virtue of the divinity within. In "The American Scholar" address, delivered when little Waldo was ten months old to the day, Emerson describes the duties of Man Thinking. We must not, he says, be "cowed" or "trustless." It is a "mischievous notion that we are come too late into nature; that the world was finished a long time ago." The "world was plastic and fluid in the hands of God," and it always will be to us, to the extent that "we bring to it" as much as we can of God's creative "attributes." In proportion as a man

> has anything in him divine, the firmament flows before him and takes his signet and form. Not he is great who can alter matter, but he who can alter my state of mind. They are the kings of the world who give the color of their present thought to all nature and all art, and persuade men by the cheerful serenity of their carrying the matter, that this thing which they do, is the apple which the ages have desired to pluck, now at last ripe, and inviting nations to the harvest. (*E&L* 65)

By the time he had reached the end of "Threnody," Emerson, still embodying, however painfully earned, a "cheerful serenity," had brought that harvest in. Watered with tears, the harvested fruit in "Threnody," as in Keats's *Lear* sonnet, is necessarily bittersweet, the "costly price" of its resolution not much less than everything—so "severe" an affliction that Emerson was sure that he could not "in a lifetime incur another such loss." There may be resolution. But "Death" is the ambiguous servant who provides the "solving rite" that "Pours finite into infinite." Still, if hearts become dust, "heart's loves remain," and Emerson's "Heart's love will meet thee"—his lost boy—"again." For when "house and tenant," body and spirit, "go to ground," it is somehow possible to be "Lost in God, in Godhead found!"—a Coleridgean and Transcendentalist truth intuited as a "diviner guess," be it what it may. What is certain is that it is not to be "conned to tediousness" ("Threnody," 229). When it *is,* it seems far too neat a chiasmus, six words less than persuasive in their formulaic, "balance-sheet" truncation. In fact, "Lost in God, in Godhead found" curiously resembles—along with Pope's epigrammatically facile theodicy in which "partial Evil" becomes "universal Good"—Milton's "So he dies, / But soon revives": the archangel Michael's surprisingly flip, almost perfunctory reference to the death and resurrection of the crucified Christ. Even though these two half lines (*PL* 12:419–20) are followed by assurance of the redemptive consequences of Christ's sacrifice (a truth Milton would feel little need to belabor), they still seem, especially given that this is the final book of an enormous epic, shockingly brief, in fact a crucial reversal also truncated—as in the final line of "Threnody"—to a mere six words.[26]

Nevertheless, in "Threnody"—as in Wordsworth's revision of *Paradise Lost* in the "Prospectus" to *The Recluse* and in the coda stanzas of the Intimations Ode—we are to seek essential meaning in the human mind and heart rather than in theology—whether abstract ("Godhead") or even incarnate (the death and resurrection of the historical Christ). On the psychological rather than theological level, one might say that, having gotten down to the emotional bedrock of the truly inner and anguished man, Emerson can listen to the "deep Heart" and its lesson of regeneration, the planting of the "void," darkness yielding to the light of all our day. Emerson once referred to a "tocsin just now struck," at once death knell and marriage bell, announcing the apocalypse of the mind (*L* 1:170). Yeats, at his most eloquently Paterian in *Per Amica Silentia Lunae,* would later say: "I shall find the dark grow luminous, the void fruitful, when I understand that I have nothing, that the ringers in the tower have appointed for the hymen of the soul a passing bell."[27] But before the darkness in "Threnody" could grow luminous, the void fruitful, it was necessary for Emerson to first empty himself out as grieving father. "I am nothing, I see all," he had said of the epiphany of the transparent eyeball—another moment of cosmic unity, though rhapsodic where the conclusion of "Threnody" is muted, having taken a "sober coloring" from the adult eye of an elegist who had certainly kept watch over man's mortality.

Bruce Ronda is surely correct in noting that, whatever the elements of "Threnody" that place it in the elegiac tradition of "Lycidas" and "Adonais," the "real poem" behind Emerson's elegy is the Intimations Ode:

26. Dr. Johnson is not alone in being put off by the facile resolution in which Pope, seduced by his own couplets and penchant for antithesis, pronounces "All Discord Harmony, not understood, / All partial Evil, universal Good" (*Essay on Man,* 1: 291–92). David Porter, though he refers to neither Pope nor Milton, notes that the deep Heart's "account ends exceedingly neatly," a lost-and-found "balance-sheet entry," with the poem assuming "the speaker's acquiescence." In Whitman "life is spontaneous and open to diversion"; in Emerson it is "impatiently converted into mental accounts. So much as his syntax excludes, that is the measure by which the contingent world is diminished." The "binary diction and syntax . . . and the paradoxes that expose the good concealed in the bad intersect with distilled purity in the concluding consolatory paradox" (*Emerson and Literary Change,* 44, 33, 40).

27. Yeats, *Mythologies,* 332.

> To put it hyperbolically, "Threnody" is the recognition of Emerson's failure to rewrite Wordsworth's poem. In the Intimations Ode there is genuine expression of joy in the intuitive and knowledgeable child, and sincere regret at its passing. But the consolation for that loss is just as genuine, . . . and finally the tone of the poem is not regretful, but sober, calm, quietly joyful. Before the death of Waldo and the writing of "Threnody" no such movement from loss of splendor to consolation would have been possible for Emerson. He would not have allowed for such an effect of memory, and would have insisted that the intuitive insight and immediacy of the child be carried wholesale into adult life.[28]

I find this accurate, not at all hyperbolic. Emerson surely failed to rewrite the Intimations Ode. Wordsworth's final stanzas—from the richly textured eighth, through the numinous mysteries of the ninth, to the brilliant cognitive and emotional revision of pastoral in the tenth and eleventh—are among the glories of English literature. On the other hand—admirable as many passages are, and necessary as the whole section is to the poem and to Emerson's own attempted movement from loss to consolation—the hundred or so lines of "recovery" in "Threnody" are too often abstract, clichéd, and persuasive only to the already Transcendentally persuaded. Nevertheless, there is, as I have already emphasized, a saving grace in Emerson's final naturalizing of supernaturalism.

The final adumbrations of a recovered Eden watered with tears reflects the fact that Emerson (as Ronda also rightly observes), working through his grief at Waldo's death, came to much the same conclusion as Wordsworth regarding the inevitability of "adult encounters with loss, grief, limitation and failure." But only (and here I deviate from Ronda's Whicherian argument) if we fall back on the received impression of Emerson as, prior to Waldo's death, a simplistically cheerful optimist, allegedly unaware of or unwilling to face the reality of evil, can we see that death as producing a *complete* reversal in Emerson's life and thought, the image, presented by Whicher above all, of a High Romantic broken by tragedy and henceforth submitting to the inexorable laws of Fate as "Beautiful Necessity." For Ronda, the second movement of "Threnody," whatever its forced quality, is "an absolutely necessary conclusion to the poem and a necessary turn in Emerson's thought," a turn, he insists along with Whicher, "away from the assertion of the power of the creative god-like self, toward an acceptance of the self's limitations in a world it has not made," and away from the former connection "between nature and the child-like self," a connection now "broken."[29]

28. Ronda, "Literary Grieving," 103.
29. Ibid., 104–5.

As in the Intimations Ode, where the child as "Seer blest" and "Eye among the blind" is replaced by the experienced adult whose "eye" has "kept watch o'er man's mortality," Emerson has indeed moved beyond any simple bond between nature and "the child-like self." But surely a version of that connection, in a finer tone, is reestablished, again as it is in the Intimations Ode, by reintroducing "Nature" at the end of "Threnody." And since "power," especially that of the "god-like self," is never *permanently* relinquished by Emerson, it even seems to me uncertain, to put things hyperbolically myself, just *who*—God, or Emerson himself—is to be *primarily* identified with the final lines' "swift Lord." That Lord's functions—broad sowing, planting, blessing, watering now-ripened Edenic apples with tears—seem at least as paternal as theistic. In short, I remain uncertain, even at the end of "Threnody," whether, in imagining the finite Waldo poured into the Infinite as a portion of the divine Spirit, we are to think of any traditional God or Godhead totally distinct from Emerson himself: father, and thus also a broad-sowing Lord, one whose human, all too human, tears water the gentle nest and ripened apples prepared for little Waldo in, if not an ontological eternity, *some* intimation of immortality. The one place we *know* that nest is prepared is *in the poem* we have just read, the work of Emerson not only as father but as creator, conferring upon his lost boy at least literary immortality. The long-labored-upon "Threnody" was now completed, the elegy for Waldo at last "flying immortal," however flawed, from a "mortal parent" who, however temporarily defeated and blast-beruffled, still believed in the divinity within, the godlike self.

We may end, as Emerson ended "Threnody," on a mysterious yet affirmative note—in some ways, a specifically Wordsworthian note, one anticipated both by James Marsh and by Emerson's brilliant but seldom hopeful brother Charles. Marsh, as we saw, concludes the "Preliminary Essay" to his edition of *Aids to Reflection* by praising Coleridge for his "productive ideas" and "living words," ideas and words he equates—there as in the peroration of his inaugural address as president of the University of Vermont—with Wordsworth's "truths that wake, / To perish never."[30] In 1837, a year after the death of his closest brother, Emerson, who had cited these lines himself in his January 1837 lecture "Religion" (*EL* 2:85), copied into his journal a letter Charles had written to his fiancée, Elizabeth Hoar, on February 10, 1835, some fifteen months before his death. The journal entry, quoting Charles, begins where Marsh had ended: "'Truths

30. The perorations—concluding with those "truths that wake / To perish never"—of both Marsh's "Preliminary Essay" and his presidential address, are discussed in Chapter 2.

that wake—to perish never.' This is sublime comfort to us that the distinct perception of a high truth, its warm welcome in the Soul[,] is a new seed of action & happiness sown in us that will germinate & send forth branches through all our future being" (*JMN* 6:264).

Charles's fusion of Spirit and natural sowing, germination, and growth anticipates the Lord of "Threnody," broad sowing, planting, fructifying. Given Emerson's marriage of spirit, mind, and nature, a nuptial in which he had been preceded by the British and German Romantics, especially Coleridge and Wordsworth, it seems appropriate that the fecund vision at the climax of the elegy for his son should be proleptically associated by Charles—Emerson's beloved brother, his spirit incarnate in Waldo—with the Great Ode's truths that wake, to perish never. Charles's death was the tragedy that was to be compensated for by the birth of Waldo, who, five months after that death, was "baptized in the self-same robe in which twenty-seven years ago my brother Charles was baptized" (*JMN* 5:324), only to join his uncle in death within six years. It was an identification sealed in the other world, at least according to Margaret Fuller, whose mourning for this "child of my heart," was long and intense. In a dream she had after the boy's death, the angelic Waldo appeared to her and announced that his name in eternity was—Charles.[31]

Though Emerson himself might not have endorsed its otherworldly details, that visionary dream is another form of imperishable truth, the truth of a miraculous child Lost and Found. Was he still lamenting that loss, or anticipating reunion ("Heart's love will meet thee again"), when, forty years after the devastating loss of his child and on the verge of his own death, Emerson cried out, in his last words on earth: "O, that beautiful boy!" At a climactic moment (part 3, canto 7) in *Notes toward a Supreme Fiction,* Wallace Stevens cries out, "It is possible, possible, possible. It must / Be possible" that we can attain "power" and "bliss," that "Out of nothing," we can, "desperate in our need," come upon a truth, which is yet

> The fiction of an absolute—Angel,
> Be silent in your luminous cloud and hear
> The luminous melody of proper sound.

Appropriately, Stevens here echoes both Wordsworth's likening of inspired poets to "angels stopped upon the wing by sound / Of harmony from Heaven's remotest spheres" (*P* 14:98–99) and Coleridge's "fair luminous cloud" and "sweet sounds," which emanate from the joyous "soul itself" in stanza 4 of "Dejection: An Ode."

31. Fuller, *Letters of Fuller,* 3:114.

The no less mysteriously ambiguous yet indestructible truths, those "truths that wake, / To perish never," to which Charles Emerson referred in his February 1835 note, are to be found not only in the ninth stanza of the Intimations Ode. As a skeptically affirmative basis, "be they what they may," for believing that "it is possible" to find consolation in despair, that it *is* "Not without hope we suffer and we mourn," they are to be found in much of the rest of Wordsworth's poetry and throughout the prose and poetry of Coleridge. They are to be found as well throughout the work and thought of their principal American heir, the most receptive and creative of those transatlantic "minds" Coleridge "excited into activity, and supplied with the germs of their after-growth!" (*BL* 1:220). But Emerson—who thought that "great men exist that there may be greater men," so that "the germs of love and benefit may be multiplied" (*E&L* 632)—could not have known, when he copied this letter of his dead brother, that within a few years he would again have painful reason to reevoke those waking and imperishable truths that are "the light of all our day," as well as to poetically revivify what an uncharacteristically "Emersonian" Charles had called "a new seed of action & happiness sown in us that will germinate & send forth branches through all our future being."

Despite this language of organic process with its multiplication and germination, resolution of the Romantic dialectic between mind and nature still requires a power that partakes in and reconciles the two. This "synthetic and magical power" Coleridge calls the Imagination, the intuitive Reason at its most creative, its most "poetic" (*BL* 2:14). The assertion and ultimate reconciliation of the "polarities" that dominate the thought and work of a notably Coleridgean Emerson are to be found primarily in his prose, his true poetry. In coping with the deaths of Ellen and of little Waldo, Emerson tried to express and assuage his feelings in poetry. The notebook poems for Ellen are at best fragmentary. In "Threnody," he chose to struggle with and try to reconcile the *most* painful challenge ever presented to his idealist theory by actual experience. Explaining to Margaret Fuller his inability at the time to make progress on the elegy, he acknowledged that the "astonishment of life is the absence of any appearance of reconciliation between the theory & the practice of life," a truth he thought important enough to repeat in *Representative Men* (*E&L* 705). Although his attempt to reconcile the two in an epigrammatic couplet may not succeed (the naturalizing of heaven is both more touching and more persuasive), we do not have to limit ourselves to "Threnody" in order to register Emerson's various responses to the death of his "beautiful boy." The assertion, made in the aftermath of that death, that, however often defeated, he is born to victory, confirms both a tragic vision and courage rather than complacency. In the case of the death of little Waldo, as in those other painful cases (the premature deaths of Ellen, Edward, and Charles), the Emersonian "art of losing" takes the form, rooted in a Romantic context, that it is—in the Wordsworthian equilibrium of "Elegiac Stanzas"—"Not without hope we suffer and we mourn."

Appendix

"LAODAMIA" AND "DION"

Emerson coupled "Laodamia" (*WP* 2:302–7) with the Intimations Ode as Wordsworth's "best" poem on at least two occasions: in an 1868 notebook entry (*JMN* 16:129) and, six years later, in his preface to his anthology of favorites, *Parnassus.* Even before its major revision in 1827, "Laodamia" was a poem at once passionate and restrained; after 1827, it was both more severe and more "Romantic" in its treatment of nature *and* more faithful to its classical sources.[1] Putting duty and the heroic code above all, Protesilaus knowingly chose to sacrifice earthly happiness with his new bride. He goes to war and becomes the first to fall at Troy—in some versions at the hands of great Hector himself. As reward for sacrifice and prayers to Jove, Laodamia is granted her wish to see her dead husband, under strict limitations regarding both time and contact. Though "unsubstantial Form eludes her grasp," the impassioned young widow of Wordsworth's poem longs for "one nuptial kiss" (27, 63). But "Jove frowned in heaven" (65), and the dead man himself reminds her that he is not flesh, but spirit:

> Nor should the change be mourned, even if the joys
> Of sense were able to return as fast
> And surely as they vanish. Earth destroys
> Those raptures duly—Erebus disdains:
> Calm pleasures there abide—majestic pains.
> (68–72)

Continuing this ghostly version of the superiority, as in "Tintern Abbey," of "sober pleasures" to "wild ecstasies," Protesilaus instructs Laodamia to

1. From book 2 of the *Iliad* Wordsworth learned that at the onset of the Trojan War, the Greek commander Protesilaus left behind a mourning wife and "half-finished house" (2.695ff). Later writers furnished the young widow of the newlywed hero with her own touching legend. Wordsworth was probably familiar with the account in Catullus (68b.73–130), and we know that he encountered the shade of Laodamia in book 6 of the *Aeneid* and in Ovid's *Heroides* (13). He also gleaned details for the character of Protesilaus from Euripides' description of Iphigenia in *Iphigenia at Aulis,* a play in which Protesilaus himself figures briefly.

"control / Rebellious passion," in favor of a divinely approved moderation, a "fervent, not ungovernable, love" (73–77). He, too, speaks of love, but of "such love as Spirits feel," associated with a supernatural nature: "more pellucid streams, . . . a diviner air, / And fields invested with purpureal gleams" (97–106). Although *he* had the fortitude to give up the joys of life for a higher purpose, *she,* "though strong in love," is "all too weak / In reason, in self-government too slow" (139–40). The "invisible world" has "sympathized" with her plight and permitted this present visitation; henceforth, however, she must sublimate desire and await "Our blest reunion in the shades below" (142). After 1831, these lines would have had personal and poignant meaning for Emerson. Five days after the death of his young wife that February, an anguished, imploring, and despairing widower prayed that he and Ellen would be "united . . . Stay by me and lead me upward. Reunite us, O thou Father of our Spirits," only, a moment later, to cry out: "But will the dead be restored to me . . . in the fulness of love? . . . No" (*JMN* 3:226–27). Yet, recalling the "mutual fires" divinely instilled in them, he hopes, beyond this firmament, to "still relume these dear desires" (*JMN* 3:234). The luminous image suggests that although he once dismissed them as ludicrous, Swedenborg's incandescent images of an erotic afterlife may have retained some appeal for Emerson, as they certainly did for Yeats.

In contrast, the ascent urged by Wordsworth's Protesilaus is purely ascetic. In trying to "lead" Laodamia "upward," in urging upon her a "blest reunion" in the other world, her ghostly husband falls back upon familiar doctrine, including the thought of the angel Raphael in his description to Adam of the scale or ladder leading from and back to God—both in book 5 of *Paradise Lost* and in his distinction between passion and love in book 8:

> In loving thou dost well, in passion not,
> Wherein true love consists not; love refines
> The thoughts, and heart enlarges, hath his seat
> In reason, and is judicious, is the scale
> By which to heavenly love thou may'st ascend,
> Not sunk in carnal pleasure, for which cause
> Among the beasts no mate for thee was found.
> (*PL* 8:588–94)

Sounding like Milton's angel, Protesilaus instructs Laodamia that she is to "Learn, by a mortal yearning, to ascend," seeking a higher object: "Love was given, / Encouraged, sanctioned, chiefly for that end" (145–48). Laodamia is too ardent to be attracted to this lesson—whether Platonic, Plotinian, Christian, Spenserian, or Miltonic. Unable to assent to the doctrine of the ascent, she "would have clung" to him, however vainly. But "no mortal effort can detain" the ghost of Protesilaus as he swiftly reascends toward the "realms" beyond our "earthly day." He "through the portal takes his silent way, / And on the palace-floor a lifeless corse She lay" (154–57). Details of her death are deliberately left ambiguous by Wordsworth, who implies that she expires in a transport of grief.[2]

As Emerson first encountered it, as it appeared in the first and second editions of Wordsworth's poems, "Laodamia" ended:

Ah, judge her gently who so deeply loved!
Her, who, in reason's spite, yet without crime,
Was in a trance of passion thus removed;
Delivered from the galling yoke of time
And these frail elements—to gather flowers
Of blissful quiet 'mid unfading bowers.

This was the version singled out for especially high praise in a well-informed article that appeared in Boston in 1825. Wordsworth's four-volume *Poetical Works,* published in Boston the year before, was warmly received by the anonymous reviewer, who admired in particular "Tintern Abbey," *The Excursion,* and that "masterpiece of decorum" "Laodamia," which was described toward the end of this long review as a "short but conclusive specimen of what he can accomplish when emancipated from the tyranny of system," that is, from Wordsworth's longstanding theoretical (but only occasionally acted upon) commitment to the language and characters of ordinary and rustic life.[3]

Wordsworth himself rather immodestly ranked "Laodamia" with his great competitor's elegy "Lycidas." The classical decorum, Stoic austerity, elevated language, and—as Emerson said later— the impressive "design" of "Laodamia" combined to make it a major accomplishment in Emerson's estimation as well. But two years after the reviewer's encomium just quoted from the *Atlantic Magazine,* "Laodamia" underwent an alteration. In 1827, the heroine, hitherto "without crime," was described as "*not* without crime" and "was doomed to wander in a grosser clime." The poet explained this harsher judgment in an October 1831 letter to his nephew,

2. In his commentary on the *Iliad,* Eustathius conjectures suicide on her part because her husband, even after death, desired her and wanted her to join him in eternity. According to Hyginus (followed by Ovid, *Heroides,* 13), when Laodamia's father, Acastus, burned the image of the husband upon whom his daughter continued to dote, she flung herself into the flames (*Fabulae,* 103, 114; this is the popular name for Hyginus's second-century handbook of mythology, the *Genealogieae*). In his own notes to the poem, Wordsworth mentions Virgil, Euripides, and (for the "account of the long-lived trees") Pliny's *Natural History,* 16:44 (*WP* 2:971).

3. Review of Wordsworth's poems, 433.

John Wordsworth: "As first written the heroine was dismissed to happiness in Elysium. To what purpose then the mission of Protesilaus? He exhorts her to moderate her passion; the exhortation is fruitless, and no punishment follows."[4] Yet despite his flawless reasoning, Wordsworth sought his nephew's "opinion" regarding the altered ending.

He was not uncertain of his classical sources. A poem having to do with sexual passion was, however, new terrain for him. The middle-aged poet may even have been uncomfortably reminded of Annette Vallon's sexual passion for the young lover taken away from *her* by war in the early 1790s. "I cannot be happy without him. I desire him every day," Annette wrote to Dorothy Wordsworth after William had left France and returned to England. She often called to her aid, she told Dorothy, "that reason which too often is weak and powerless beside my feeling for him." But reason was unavailing; she remained "mastered by a feeling which causes all my unhappiness." The "influence of his dear love on my heart" is such that his "image follows me everywhere." That and "my mistake," becoming pregnant by Wordsworth, "throws me into extreme melancholy."[5] Whatever his vestigial guilt, or his mature disapproval of the candidly erotic Annette's ungovernable passion, or even his nephew's opinion, Wordsworth has often been criticized for the change in the conclusion of "Laodamia." Responding to the new note of severity, modern readers may be divided between admiration and dismay—as Yeats was once when Lionel Johnson casually observed, "If only those who deny the eternity of punishment could realize their unspeakable vulgarity."

In 1832, Wordsworth, in a note to the final version of the poem, remarked that "Virgil places the Shade of Laodomia in a mournful region, among unhappy Lovers." If he was being a bit defensive, he was also accurate: Aeneus encounters the shade of Laodamia in "the Fields of Mourning," with the ghosts of others who have died for love, including his own recent victim, Dido (*Aeneid* 6:440–48). In that year, 1832, the poem ended as it does in the final text of 1845. Elysium is mentioned as a heavenly pastoral for other, *happy* spirits, though this severity—since Virgilian "tears to mortal suffering are due"—is softened by a touching tree fable. In the version he chooses for his anthology *Parnassus* (162–65), Emerson omits this stanza, going directly from the earlier ending (the stanza beginning "Ah, judge her gentle") to the revised ending, beginning, "Yet tears to mortal suffering are due."

4. Wordsworth, *Letters: Later Years,* 2:582.

5. Quoted in Mary Moorman, *William Wordsworth: A Biography,* 1:181. Though I have no evidence to support my speculation that memories of Annette may have entered Wordsworth's thinking regarding "Laodamia," the analogy is intriguing.

Thus, all in vain exhorted and reproved,
She perished; and, as for a wilful crime,
By the just Gods whom no weak pity moved,
Was doomed to wear out her appointed time,
Apart from happy Ghosts, that gather flowers
Of blissful quiet 'mid unfading bowers.

—Yet tears to mortal suffering are due;
And mortal hopes defeated and o'erthrown
Are mourned by man, and not by man alone,
As fondly he believes.—Upon the side
Of Hellespont (such faith was entertained)
A knot of spiry trees for ages grew
From out the tomb of him for whom she died;
And ever, when such stature they had gained
That Ilium's walls were subject to their view,
The trees' tall summits withered at the sight;
A constant interchange of growth and blight!
(158–74)

What sympathy there is comes from human and natural mourners, not from the "just" gods of Stoic law unmoved by "weak pity" in the lines Emerson omitted in *Parnassus*. We *do* hear, though, of an "appointed time," a purgatorial rather than an infernal punishment. In an affectionate tribute, a classical anticipation of the Romantic correspondence between the natural and the human, Nature empathizes with the dead (as, at first, it had *not* in "Threnody," Emerson's elegy for Waldo) by being as appalled (withering at the sight of Troy) as Laodamia was by the war that took her husband from her. With this final image of long-lived yet ever-blighted trees, the poem ends greatly, with "feeling" nature ennobling if not alleviating human suffering.

Such consolation as is afforded by "Laodamia" in this its final version comes with this "incident," as Wordsworth called it in his remarks on the poem to Isabella Fenwick. Most revealing is his later claim that it was this mitigating image of the constantly growing and withering trees—encountered in Pliny's *Natural History*—that "first put the subject into my thoughts." He had written the poem, he added in his comment to Fenwick, with the hope of giving the legend "a loftier tone than, so far as I know, has been given to it by any of the Ancients who have treated of it. It cost me more trouble than almost anything of equal length I have ever written" (*WP* 2:970). Though at first, according to Crabb Robinson, Wordsworth did not hold the poem in "much esteem," his struggles with its composition were rewarded. Originally included among the "Poems Founded on the Affections," it was shifted in the third (1827) edition, to a "loftier" category: "Poems of the Imagination." Arguably Wordsworth's last major poem, "Laodamia" deserves the "upgrading," and the esteem in which it was held by Emerson, by Walter Savage Landor, and—gradually—by Wordsworth himself.[6]

❧ Whereas "Laodamia" fuses a variety of classical sources, "Dion" (*WP* 2:344–45) draws on one: that Emersonian favorite, Plutarch. Predictably, Wordsworth, whose own source was North's 1579 translation of *Parallel Lives,* devotes less attention to Plutarch's external events than to the inner workings of Dion's "lofty" mind. In the form in which Emerson would have first encountered it, "Dion" began with a nineteen-line passage focused on a swan, a passage later deleted as deflecting from rather than adumbrating the subject. The final version of the poem falls into six parts. In the first, the "virtues" of Plato's pupil, "princely Dion," are described—in an image praised by Charles Lamb—as illuminated by the Master's teaching:

> the lunar beam
> Of Plato's genius, from its lofty sphere,
> Fell round him in the grove of Academe.
> (8–10)

As Wordsworth knew, Dion was first impressed by Plato when the philosopher visited Syracuse in 389. Following his unsuccessful attempt to transform the Syracusan ruler, Dionysius II, into a Platonic philosopher king, Dion was forced into exile, taking up residence in Athens for almost a third of a century, during which time he closely associated himself with Plato's Academy. Armed with Platonic wisdom, not to mention "five-thousand warriors" (pt. 2), Dion returns to Syracuse as "the great Deliverer" (compare book 9 of *The Prelude*), a demigod in the estimation of the people to whom he "brought their precious liberty again."[7]

6. In one of the longest exchanges in *Imaginary Conversations* (1824–1829), a work Emerson knew, Landor (whose idylls and "Hellenics" provided models for the author of "Laodamia") has his "Robert Southey" recite the whole of the 1815–1820 version of "Laodamia" as an example of Wordsworth's treatment of "a subject as an ancient poet of equal vigour would have treated it." His interlocutor, the great classical scholar Richard Porson, after acknowledging Southey's "animated recital of this classic poem," begins "to think more highly" of both Southey *and* Wordsworth.

7. In *The Prelude,* Wordsworth awards Dion a place of honor as a precursor of that noble spirit and sympathizer with the Revolution Michel Beaupuy, the aristocratic French officer with whom he had long conversations in France and who had such a personal and political impact on Wordsworth. Tragically, Beaupuy was killed in action before he could fulfill the redemptive role Wordsworth projected for him. Thinking of his conversations with Beaupuy, and describing the "hope" and "desire" of embodying

But an anticipatory elegiac note is struck in part 3, the section excerpted by Emerson for *Parnassus* (475–76). The hills and groves of Attica are thrice invoked to "mourn," lamenting what became of a man who gradually "to divinity aspired" and "overleaped the eternal bars" by trying to undemocratically impose idealism in Syracuse (42–45, 53). In the course of that attempt, he "stained the robes of civil power with blood, / Unjustly shed, though for the public good" (56–57), an allusion to Dion's murder of his former, and eventually more popular, lieutenant, Heracleides. That assassination initiated an increasingly authoritarian regime, though Dion never repudiated his Platonic principles. Dion is subsequently filled with doubts and second thoughts—too little too late. His cogitations sink as low, as "through the abysses of a joyless heart, / The heaviest plummet of despair can go" (61–62). In this dejection, suddenly lifting his eyes, he

> Saw, at a long drawn gallery's bound,
> A Shape of more than mortal size
> And hideous aspect, stalking round and round.
> A woman's garb the Phantom wore,
> And fiercely swept the marble floor.
> (66–70)

Dion tries (pts. 4 and 5) to dismiss this "sullen Spectre," this uninvited and "inexplicable Guest." But unsummoned "shapes" will not depart "when earthly voices call" (78, 81, 90–91). The fierce and hideous shape—Fate in the image of his own conscience—is the projection of Dion's inner guilt: "The spots that to my soul adhere." Once opened, the "visionary eye" maintains "that look / Which no philosophy can brook" (92–101). The sixth and final section registers Wordsworth's version of the dual verdict of historical tradition, which has been at once generous to Dion on the basis of his idealist principles and judgmental of his actions, alternately bloody and irresolute, in postliberation Syracuse. Worse yet in the estimation of Wordsworth, who doubtless had such French revolutionaries as Robespierre in mind, *others* have built their "hopes" on the "ruins" of the "glorious name" of Dion, pursuing him through the "portal of one moment's guilt" (102–4).

Dion himself became a victim of the sword, murdered in 354 at the instigation of Calippus, his follower and (a final irony) fellow Platonist. For

---

one's ideals "in action," to give hope "outwardly a shape, / And that of benediction to the world," Wordsworth says, "Such conversation, under Attic shades / Did Dion hold with Plato; ripened thus / For a Deliverer's glorious task." He describes Dion and his followers setting sail for Syracuse as an instance of "philosophic war, / Led by Philosophers" (*P* 9:401–17).

Wordsworth, this was an instance of "matchless perfidy" and "monstrous crime." But although "That horror-striking blade," which is "Drawn in defiance of the Gods, hath laid / The noble Syracusan low in dust," causing the marble city to weep and—a "Laodamia" touch—the surrounding forests to sigh, the appointed Victim himself now rests in "calm peace," having "fallen in magnanimity" (107–13).[8] That magnanimous spirit was, in lines admired by both Emerson and his brother Charles (*JMN* 6:272), too "capacious" to require that "Destiny" should change her course, too "just" to "his own native greatness to desire / That wretched boon, days lengthened by mistrust" (114–17). Thus, the "hopeless troubles," political and psychological, "that involved / The soul of Dion" were "instantly dissolved" (117–19):

> Released from life and cares of princely state,
> He left this moral grafted on his Fate;
> "Him only pleasure leads, and peace attends,
> Him, only him, the shield of Jove defends,
> Whose means are fair and spotless as his ends."
> (120–24)

This "spotless" moral had earlier been applied by Wordsworth to that bloodstained "Incorruptible" Robespierre, and even to Britain's greatest naval hero, Lord Nelson, his "public life stained with one great crime," the crushing of the patriotic Neapolitan revolt. A quarter century later he applied it to those in the British government who employed corrupt means to achieve their end in passing the 1832 Reform Bill. He claimed on the latter occasion that he himself would not have "violated a principle of justice." Means were—Wordsworth said at the height of his indignation about the tactics used to get the bill through—"in the concerns of this life, more important than ends . . . and the best test of an end is the purity of the means."[9] He was still perturbed by these events when Emerson visited him in 1833.

Emerson, who always set moral principles above political compromise, would insist on the same ideals of purity and justice in his turning away from Daniel Webster. His political disillusionment, reflected as early as his

8. Wordsworth may be echoing Plato's poem for Dion, in which, though "tears" are shed for Hecuba and the women of Ilion, still more are shed for Dion, for whom (in Dudley Fitts's translation) "our hopes were great, and great the triumph, / Cancelled alike by the gods at the point of glory. / Now you lie in your own land, now all men honor you— / But I loved you, O Dion!" (brought to my attention by Ann Haggerty).

9. Wordsworth, *Letters: Later Years,* 2:596, 591. For Wordsworth's criticism of Nelson, in a letter of February 11, 1806, see *Letters: Middle Years,* 1:7.

1846 Ode to Channing, culminated in condemnation after Webster's pivotal speech of March 7, 1850, in support of a package of bills—notably including the Fugitive Slave Bill. He had betrayed justice and himself by endorsing, however consistent and profoundly well intentioned the end, *means* that Emerson along with most of New England found despicable. "All the drops of his blood have eyes that look downward," said Emerson (*W* 11:203–4), who went on to vehemently oppose the Fugitive Slave Law, a "filthy enactment" he declared "I will not obey." Four years after the Civil War that Webster had compromised to avert, Emerson read the whole of "Dion" to a Boston audience.[10]

Finally, Emerson's placing of "Laodamia" and "Dion" near the pinnacle of Wordsworth's achievement points up their similarities. Both scrupulously revised poems were, in moral terms, austerely, even solemnly, principled—a morality at once Platonic and Stoic. Both Laodamia and Dion end tragically, she because, in the intensity of her grief, she cannot subordinate her sensual passion to the "higher" rational and spiritual standard demanded of her; he because, in seeking idealist ends, he violates his own principles by employing bloody means. Yet each of these tragedies is marked by pathos and dignity. On both poetic and ethical grounds, these two poems appealed enormously to an Emerson who was, as his brother Charles said, "quite enamoured of the severe beauty of the Greek tragic muse." In addition, for Emerson as for Wordsworth, "Dion" had *political,* "Laodamia" *personal,* resonance beyond their classical subjects. Indeed, the former had *both* a personal and a political moral for Emerson. Juxtaposing the two aspects of Wordsworth's Syracusan in categorical imperative, he reminded himself in 1839: "I must not bait my hook to draw men to me. I must angle with myself & use no lower means. Be Dion to Dion" (*JMN* 7:255). If "Laodamia" and "Dion" are less than popular, even, in the case of the latter, barely known to most modern readers, that may be more a comment on the audience than on the artistry of the two poems, poems not only "moral" but at once marmoreal and moving. Certainly, Emerson held them in high esteem ranking them second only to Wordsworth's Great Ode itself, which he considered the age's supreme exploration of the mysteries of mortality and immortality, of tragic, irretrievable loss and stoic compensation.

10. Though Webster's means were hardly "spotless," were even odious, they *did* prevent for ten years the fratricidal war it was his, and Henry Clay's, intention to prevent. During that breathing space in which the Union held together, the North grew immensely in industrial power and produced, at the end of the decade, a president capable of leading the national government to victory in war—a civil war Wordsworth had prophesied with rather too much relish but Daniel Webster had long struggled to prevent and never lived to see.

Bibliography

Abrams, M. H. *The Correspondent Breeze: Essays on English Romanticism.* New York: W. W. Norton, 1984.

———. *Natural Supernaturalism: Tradition and Revolution in Romantic Literature.* New York: W. W. Norton, 1971.

Abrams, M. H., et al., eds. *The Major Authors.* Vol. B of *The Norton Anthology of English Literature.* 7th ed. New York and London: W. W. Norton, 2001.

Ackroyd, Peter. *T. S. Eliot: A Life.* New York: Simon and Schuster, 1984.

Adams, James Truslow. "Emerson Re-read." In *The Recognition of Ralph Waldo Emerson,* edited by Milton Konvitz, 182–93. Ann Arbor: University of Michigan Press, 1972.

Aikin, Conrad. "An Anatomy of Melancholy." In *Twentieth-Century Interpretations: A Collection of Critical Essays on "The Waste Land,"* edited by Jay Martin, 52–58. Englewood Cliffs, NJ: Prentice-Hall, 1968.

Alcott, Bronson. *Emerson.* 1865. Reprint, Boston: Cupples and Hurd, 1888.

———. *The Journals of Bronson Alcott.* Edited by Odell Shepard. 2 vols. Boston: Little, Brown, 1938.

———. "Orphic Sayings." *Dial* (July 1840): 85–98.

———. "Wordsworth." *Boston Quarterly Review* (April 1839): 137–68.

Alcott, Louisa May. "Reminiscences of Ralph Waldo Emerson." In *Emerson in His Own Time,* edited by Ronald A. Bosco and Joel Myerson, 89–94. Iowa City: University of Iowa Press, 2003.

Alexander, J. W., Albert Dod, and Charles Hodge. "Transcendentalism of the Germans and of Cousin and Its Influence on Opinion in This Country." *Biblical Repertory and Princeton Review* (January 1839). Extracted in *The Transcendentalists: An Anthology,* edited by Perry Miller, 231–40. Cambridge, MA: Harvard University Press, 1950.

Allen, Gay Wilson. *Waldo Emerson: A Biography.* New York: Viking Press, 1981.

Allsop, Thomas. *Letters, Conversations, and Recollections of S. T. Coleridge.* 2 vols. London, 1836.

Anderson, Lorin. "Freud, Nietzsche." *Salmagundi* 47–48 (1980): 3–29.

Archibald, Douglas. *Yeats.* Syracuse, NY: Syracuse University Press, 1983.

Arnold, Matthew. *Discourses in America.* London: Macmillan, 1885.

———. *The Poems of Matthew Arnold.* Edited by Kenneth Allott. London: Longmans, 1965.

———. "Wordsworth." In *Matthew Arnold: Selected Prose,* edited by P. J. Keating. London: Penguin, 1970.

Arvin, Newton. "The House of Pain: Emerson and the Tragic Sense." In *Emerson: A Collection of Critical Essays,* edited by Milton Konvitz and Stephen Whicher, 46–59. Englewood Cliffs, NJ: Prentice-Hall, 1962.

Baker, Carlos. *Emerson among the Eccentrics: A Group Portrait.* New York: Penguin, 1995.

Baker, Nicholson. *Double Fold: Libraries and the Assault on Paper.* New York: Random House, 2001.

Barish, Evelyn. *Emerson: The Roots of Prophecy.* Princeton, NJ: Princeton University Press, 1989.

Barth, J. Robert, S.J. *Romanticism and Transcendence: Wordsworth, Coleridge, and the Religious Imagination.* Columbia: University of Missouri Press, 2003.

Bartol, Cyrus A. *Radical Problems.* Boston, 1877.

Bate, Jonathan. *Romantic Ecology: Wordsworth and the Environmental Tradition.* London and New York: Routledge, 1991.

Baumgarten, Eduard. *Das Vorbild Emerson im Werke und Leben Nietzsches.* Heidelberg, Germany: Carl Winter, 1957.

———. "Mitteilungen und Bemerkungen . . ." [Report and Observations Concerning the Influence of Emerson on Nietzsche]. *Jahrbuch für Amerikastudien* 1 (1956): 93–152.

Beer, John. Introduction to *The Rime of the Ancient Mariner,* by Samuel Taylor Coleridge. London: Cassell, 2001.

Behler, Ernst, ed. *Philosophy of German Idealism.* New York: Continuum, 1987.

Bercovitch, Sacvan, ed. *The Prose Writing, 1820–1865.* Vol. 2 of *The Cambridge History of American Literature.* Cambridge: Cambridge University Press, 1995.

———, ed. *Typology and Early American Literature.* Amherst: University of Massachusetts Press, 1971.

Berkowitz, Peter. *Nietzsche: The Ethics of an Immoralist.* Cambridge, MA: Harvard University Press, 1995.

Bewell, Alan. *Wordsworth and the Enlightenment: Nature and Society in the Experimental Poetry.* New Haven, CT: Yale University Press, 1988.

Blake, William. *The Poetry and Prose of William Blake.* Edited by David Erdman with commentary by Harold Bloom. Berkeley and Los Angeles: University of California Press, 1965.

Bloom, Harold. *Agon: Towards a Theory of Revisionism.* New York: Oxford University Press, 1982.

———. *The American Religion: The Emergence of the Post-Christian Nation.* New York: Simon and Schuster, 1992.

———. *The Anxiety of Influence: A Theory of Poetry.* New York: Oxford University Press, 1973.

———. "Bacchus and Merlin: The Dialectic of Romantic Poetry." In *The Ringers in the Tower,* edited by Harold Bloom. Chicago: University of Chicago Press, 1971.

———. *Genius: A Mosaic of One Hundred Exemplary Creative Minds.* New York: Warner Books, 2002.

———. Introduction to *Ralph Waldo Emerson: Modern Critical Views,* edited by Harold Bloom. New York: Chelsea House, 1985.

———. *A Map of Misreading.* New York: Oxford University Press, 1975.

———. *Modern Critical Views: William Hazlitt.* New York; New Haven, CT; and Philadelphia: Chelsea House, 1986.

———. "Mr. America." *New York Review of Books,* November 22, 1984.

———. *Poetry and Repression: Revisionism from Blake to Stevens.* New Haven, CT: Yale University Press, 1976.

———. *Wallace Stevens: The Poems of Our Climate.* Ithaca, NY: Cornell University Press, 1977.

———. *The Western Canon: The Books and School of the Ages.* New York: Harcourt, Brace, 1994.

———. *Where Shall Wisdom Be Found?* New York: Riverhead Penguin, 2004.

Bloom, Robert. "Irving Babbitt's Emerson." *New England Quarterly* (1957): 448–73.

Bosco, Ronald A., and Joel Myerson, eds. *Emerson in His Own Time.* Iowa City: University of Iowa Press, 2003.

Boudreau, Gordon. *The Roots of Walden and the Tree of Life.* Nashville, TN: Vanderbilt University Press, 1990.

Brantley, Richard E. *Coordinates of Anglo-American Romanticism: Wesley, Edwards, Carlyle and Emerson.* Gainesville: University Press of Florida, 1993.

Brinkley, Roberta Florence. *Coleridge on the Seventeenth Century.* Durham: Duke University Press, 1955.

Bromwich, David. *A Choice of Inheritance: Self and Community from Edmund Burke to Robert Frost.* Cambridge, MA: Harvard University Press, 1989.

———. *Hazlitt: The Mind of a Critic.* Oxford: Oxford University Press, 1983.

Broughton, Leslie Nathan, ed. *Wordsworth and Reed: The Poet's Correspondence with His American Editor, 1836–50.* Ithaca, NY: Cornell University Press, 1933.

Brown, Bertram Wyatt. *Yankee Saints and Southern Sinners.* Baton Rouge: Louisiana State University Press, 1985.

Brown, Lee Rust. *The Emerson Museum: Practical Romanticism and the Pursuit of the Whole.* Cambridge, MA: Harvard University Press, 1997.

Browning, Robert. *The Poems and Plays of Robert Browning.* New York: Modern Library, 1934.

Brownson, Orestes. *Orestes Brownson: Selected Essays.* Edited by Russell Kirk. Chicago: Regnery, Gateway, 1955.

Buckham, John Wright. "James Marsh and Coleridge." *Bibliotheca Sacra* 61 (1904): 305–17.

Buell, Lawrence. *Emerson.* Cambridge, MA: Harvard University Press, Belknap Press, 2003.

———, ed. *Ralph Waldo Emerson: A Collection of Critical Essays.* Englewood Cliffs, NJ: Prentice-Hall, 1993.

———. "Thoreau and the Natural Environment." In *The Cambridge Companion to Henry David Thoreau,* edited by Joel Myerson, 171–93. Cambridge: Cambridge University Press, 1995.

Burke, Kenneth. "I, Eye, Ay: Thoughts on the Machinery of Transcendence." In *Transcendentalism and Its Legacy,* edited by Myron Simon and Thornton H. Parsons, 3–24. Ann Arbor: University of Michigan Press, 1966.

Burkholder, Robert E. "Emerson, Kneeland, and the Divinity School Address." *American Literature* 58 (1986): 1–14.

Byron, Lord. *Don Juan and Other Satirical Poems.* Edited by Louis J. Bredvold. New York: Odyssey Press, 1935.

Cady, Edwin, and L. J. Budd, eds. *On Emerson: The Best from American Literature.* Durham, NC: Duke University Press, 1988.

Cairns, W. B. *A History of American Literature.* New York: Oxford University Press, 1912.

Calverton, V. F. *The Liberation of American Literature.* New York: Scribner's, 1932.

Carafiol, Peter. *Transcendent Reason: James Marsh and the Forms of Romantic Thought.* Gainesville: University Press of Florida, 1982.

Carlson, Eric, ed. *Emerson's Literary Criticism.* Lincoln: University of Nebraska Press, 1995.

Carlyle, Thomas. *The Collected Letters of Thomas and Jane Welsh Carlyle.* Edited by Charles Richard Sanders, Kenneth J. Fielding, and Clyde de L. Ryals. 24 vols. to date. Durham, NC: Duke University Press, 1970–1995.

———. *The Correspondence of Emerson and Carlyle.* Edited by Joseph Slater. New York: Columbia University Press, 1964.

———. *Critical and Miscellaneous Essays.* 4 vols. In *Carlyle's Works: Centennial Memorial Edition.* 26 vols. Boston: Dana and Estes, n.d.

———. *The Life of John Sterling.* 1851. Reprint, London: Chapman and Hall, 1897.

———. *On Heroes, Hero Worship, and the Heroic in History.* London: Chapman and Hall, 1901.

———. *Sartor Resartus.* Edited by Roger L. Tarr. Text established by Mark Engel and Roger L. Tarr. Berkeley and Los Angeles: University of California Press, 2000.

———. *Two Notebooks of Thomas Carlyle: From 23rd March 1822 to 16th May 1832.* Edited by Charles Eliot Norton. New York: Grolier Club, 1898.

———. *Wilhelm Meister's Apprenticeship and Travels.* 2 vols. In *The Works of Thomas Carlyle,* edited by H. D. Traill. 30 vols. Centenary Edition. London: Chapman and Hall, 1896–1899.

Casson, Lionel. *Libraries in the Ancient World.* New Haven, CT: Yale University Press, 2001.

Cavell, Stanley. *Cities of Words: Pedagogical Letters on a Register of the Moral Life.* Cambridge, MA: Harvard University Press, Belknap Press, 2004.

———. *Conditions Handsome and Unhandsome: The Constitution of Emersonian Perfectionism.* Chicago: University of Chicago Press, 1990.

———. "Emerson's Aversive Thinking." In *Romantic Revolutions: Criticism and Theory,* edited by Kenneth R. Johnston, Gilbert Chaitin, Karen Hanson, and Herbert Marks, 219–49. Bloomington: Indiana University Press, 1990.

———. *In Quest of the Ordinary.* Chicago: University of Chicago Press, 1988.

Chai, Leon. *The Romantic Foundations of the American Renaissance.* Ithaca, NY: Cornell University Press, 1987.

Chandler, James K. *Wordsworth's Second Nature: A Study of the Poetry and Politics.* Chicago: University of Chicago Press, 1984.

Channing, William Ellery. *Memoirs of William Ellery Channing.* 2 vols. London: George Routledge, 1850.

Cohen, M. R. *Reason and Nature: An Essay on the Meaning of Scientific Method.* 1931. Reprint, New York: Harcourt, 1932.

Cole, Phyllis. *Mary Moody Emerson and the Origins of Transcendentalism: A Family History.* New York: Oxford University Press, 1998.

Coleridge, Samuel Taylor. *Anima Poetae.* From the unpublished notebooks edited by E. H. Coleridge. London, 1895.

———. *Biographia Literaria.* Edited by John Shawcross. Oxford: Oxford University Press, 1907.

———. *Lectures 1795: On Politics and Religion.* Edited by Louis Patton and Peter Mann. Vol. 1 of *CC,* 1971.

———. *Lectures 1808–1819: On Literature.* Edited by R. A. Foakes. Vol. 5 of *CC,* 1987.

———. *Marginalia.* Vol. 6. Edited by H. J. Jackson et al. Vol. 12 of *CC,* 2002.

———. *On the Constitution of the Church and State.* Edited by John Colmer. Vol. 10 of *CC,* 1976.

———. *The Watchman.* Edited by Louis Patton. Vol. 2 of *CC,* 1970.

Conway, Moncure Daniel. *Emerson at Home and Abroad.* Boston: James R. Osgood, 1882.

Cook, Robert G. "Emerson's 'Self-Reliance,' Sweeney, and Prufrock." *American Literature* 42 (1970): 221–26.

Cox, James. "R. W. Emerson: The Circles of the Eye." In *Emerson: Prophecy, Metamorphosis, and Influence,* edited by David Levin, 57–81. New York: Columbia University Press, 1975.

Crane, Hart. *The Complete Poems and Selected Letters and Prose of Hart Crane.* Edited by Brom Weber. Garden City, NY: Doubleday, 1957.

Crawford, Walter B., ed. *Reading Coleridge: Approaches and Applications.* Ithaca, NY: Cornell University Press, 1979.

Dameron, J. Lasley. "Emerson and *Fraser's* on Coleridge's *Aids to Reflection.*" *American Transcendental Quarterly* 57 (July 1985): 15–20.

Dana, Richard Henry, Jr. *Journal of Richard Henry Dana, Jr.* Edited by Robert F. Lucid. 3 vols. Cambridge, MA: Harvard University Press, 1968.

Darbishire, Helen, ed. *The Early Lives of Milton.* London: Constable, 1932.

Dedmond, Francis B. "Men of Concord Petition the Governor." *Concord Saunterer* 15 (1980): 1–6.

De Quincey, Thomas. *The Collected Writings of Thomas De Quincey.* Edited by David Masson. 14 vols. London: A. and C. Black, 1896–1897.

———. *Recollections of the Lakes and the Lake Poets.* Edited by David Wright. London: Penguin, 1970.

Derrida, Jacques. *Taking Chances: Derrida, Psychoanalysis, and Literature.* Edited by Joseph H. Smith and William Kerrigan. Baltimore, MD: Johns Hopkins University Press, 1984.

Dewey, John. "Ralph Waldo Emerson." In *Emerson: A Collection of Critical Essays,* edited by Milton Konvitz and Stephen Whicher, 24–30. Englewood Cliffs, NJ: Prentice-Hall, 1962.

Dickinson, Emily. *The Letters of Emily Dickinson.* Edited by Thomas H. Johnson. With the assistance of Theodora Ward. 3 vols. Cambridge, MA: Harvard University Press, Belknap Press, 1958.

Dickstein, Morris. *Keats and His Poetry.* Chicago: University of Chicago Press, 1971.

Doherty, Joseph F. "Emerson and the Loneliness of the Gods." *Texas Studies in Literature and Language* 19 (1974): 65–75.

Donoghue, Denis. *The American Classics: A Personal Essay.* New Haven, CT: Yale University Press, 2005.

———. "Emerson at First." In *Reading America: Essays on American Literature,* by Denis Donoghue. New York: Knopf, 1987.

Duffy, John J., ed. *Coleridge's American Disciples: The Selected Correspondence of James Marsh.* Amherst: University of Massachusetts Press, 1973.

Edmundson, Mark. *Towards Reading Freud: Self-Creation in Milton, Wordsworth, Emerson, and Sigmund Freud.* Princeton, NJ: Princeton University Press, 1990.

Eliot, T. S. "American Literature." *Atheneum* 4643 (April 25, 1919): 236–37.

———. *The Complete Poems and Plays, 1909–1950.* New York: Harcourt, Brace, and World, 1962.

Elliot, G. R. "On Emerson's 'Grace' and 'Self-Reliance.'" *New England Quarterly* (January 1929): 100–110.

Ellison, Julie. *Emerson's Romantic Style.* Princeton, NJ: Princeton University Press, 1984.

———. "Tears for Emerson: *Essays, Second Series.*" In *The Cambridge Companion to Ralph Waldo Emerson,* edited by Joel Porte and Saundra Morris, 140–61. Cambridge: Cambridge University Press, 1999.

Emerson, Lidian Jackson. *The Selected Letters of Lidian Jackson Emerson.* Edited by Delores Bird Carpenter. Columbia: University of Missouri Press, 1987.

Emerson, Mary Moody. *The Selected Letters of Mary Moody Emerson.* Edited by Nancy Craig Simmons. Athens: University of Georgia Press, 1993.

Emerson, Ralph Waldo. *Parnassus.* Boston: Houghton Mifflin, 1874.

Empson, William. *Seven Types of Ambiguity.* Hammondsworth, England: Penguin, 1961.

Erdman, David. Introduction to *Essays on His Times,* by Samuel Taylor Coleridge. Vol. 3 of *CC,* 1978.

Everest, Kelvin. *Coleridge's Secret Ministry: The Context of the Conversation Poems.* New York: Barnes and Noble, 1979.

Foakes, R. A. "'Thriving Prisoners': Coleridge, Wordsworth, and the Child at School." *Studies in Romanticism* 28 (1989): 187–206.

Foucault, Michel. *Power/Knowledge: Selected Interviews and Other Writings, 1972–1977.* New York: Pantheon, 1980.

Freeman, Douglas Southall. *R. E. Lee.* 4 vols. New York: Scribner's, 1934–1935.

Friedl, Herwig. "Emerson and Nietzsche, 1862–1874." In *Religion and Philosophy in America,* edited by Peter Freese, 1:267–88. Essen, Germany: Die Blauie Eule, 1987.

Frost, Robert. “On Emerson.” In *Emerson: A Collection of Critical Essays,* edited by Milton Konvitz and Stephen Whicher, 12–17. Englewood Cliffs, NJ: Prentice-Hall, 1962.

———. *The Poetry of Robert Frost.* New York: Holt, Rinehart, and Winston, 1969.

———. *Selected Letters of Robert Frost.* Edited by Lawrance Thompson. New York: Holt, Rinehart, and Winston, 1964.

Frothingham, Octavius Brooks. *Transcendentalism in New England: A History.* New York: Putnam’s, 1876.

Frye, Northrop. *The Return of Eden: Five Essays on Milton’s Epics.* Toronto: University of Toronto Press, 1965.

Fuller, Margaret. *The Letters of Margaret Fuller.* Edited by Robert N. Hudspath. 6 vols. Ithaca, NY: Cornell University Press, 1983–1995.

———. *Margaret Fuller, American Romantic: A Selection from Her Writings and Correspondence.* Edited by Perry Miller. 1963. Reprint, Ithaca, NY: Cornell University Press, 1970.

———. *Memoirs of Margaret Fuller.* Edited by Ralph Waldo Emerson, W. H. Channing, and James Freeman Clarke. 2 vols. Boston: Phillips, Sampson, 1852.

Furman, Laura, and Elinore Standard. *Bookworms: Great Writers and Readers Celebrate Reading.* New York: Carroll and Graff, 1997.

Garrod, H. W. *Keats.* Oxford: Oxford University Press, 1926.

Garvey, T. Gregory, ed. *The Emerson Dilemma: Essays on Emerson and Social Reform.* Athens: University of Georgia Press, 2001.

Giamatti, A. Bartlett. *The University and the Public Interest.* New York: Atheneum, 1981.

Gibbs, Nancy. “Free the Children.” *Time,* July 14, 2003, 80.

Gilbert, Armida Jennings. “Emerson and the English Romantic Poets.” PhD diss., University of South Carolina, 1989.

Goethe, Johann Wolfgang von. *Gedenkausgabe der Werke, Briefe und Gesprache.* Edited by Ernst Beutler. 19 vols. Zurich: Artemis Verlag, 1948–1971.

Gonnaud, Maurice. *An Uneasy Solitude: Individual and Society in the Work of Ralph Waldo Emerson.* Translated by Lawrence Rosenwald. 1964 (in French). Reprint, Princeton, NJ: Princeton University Press, 1987.

Gougeon, Len. “The Anti-slavery Background of Emerson’s ‘Ode Inscribed to W. H. Channing.’ ” In *Studies in the American Renaissance, 1984,* edited by Joel Myerson, 63–77. Charlottesville: University Press of Virginia, 1984.

———. “Emerson, Poetry, and Reform.” *Modern Language Studies* 19:2 (1989): 38–49.

———. “Emerson and the Campaign of 1851.” *Historical Journal of Massachusetts* 16 (1988): 20–33.

———. *Virtue's Hero: Emerson, Anti-slavery, and Reform.* Athens: University of Georgia Press, 1990.

Gougeon, Len, and Joel Myerson, eds. *Emerson's Antislavery Writings.* New Haven, CT: Yale University Press, 1995.

Gravil, Richard. *Romantic Dialogues: Anglo-American Continuities, 1776–1862.* New York: St. Martin's Press, 2000.

Gravil, Richard, and Molly Lefebure, eds. *The Coleridge Connection.* Basingstoke, England: Macmillan, 1990.

Greene, Melissa Fay. "Sandlot Summer." *New York Times Magazine,* November 28, 2004.

Hanford, James Holly. *A Milton Handbook.* 4th ed. New York: Appleton-Century-Crofts, 1946.

Harding, Anthony John. *Coleridge and the Inspired Word.* Kingston, Canada: McGill-Queens University Press, 1985.

———. "Coleridge and Transcendentalism." In *The Coleridge Connection,* edited by Richard Gravil and Molly Lefebure, 233–53. Basingstoke, England: Macmillan, 1990.

———. "James Marsh as Editor." In *Reading Coleridge: Approaches and Applications,* edited by Walter B. Crawford, 223–51. Ithaca, NY: Cornell University Press, 1979.

Harris, Kenneth Marc. *Carlyle and Emerson: Their Long Debate.* Cambridge, MA: Harvard University Press, 1978.

Havens, R. D. *The Mind of a Poet.* Baltimore, MD: Johns Hopkins University Press, 1941.

Hazlitt, William. *The Complete Works of William Hazlitt.* Edited by P. P. Howe. 21 vols. London: Dent, 1930–1934.

Heaney, Seamus. *Preoccupations: Selected Prose, 1968–1978.* New York: Farrar, Straus, and Giroux, 1980.

Hedge, Frederic Henry. "Coleridge's Literary Character." *Christian Examiner* 14 (March 1833): 108–29.

———. "Emmanuel Swedenborg." *New Jerusalem Magazine* 5 (July 1832): 437.

Heffer, Simon. *Moral Desperado: A Life of Thomas Carlyle.* London: Phoenix, 1996.

Heidegger, Martin. *Nietzsche.* Edited by D. F. Krell. 4 vols. San Francisco: Harper and Row, 1979–1982.

Heller, Erich. *The Disinherited Mind: Essays in Modern German Literature and Thought.* Rev. ed. New York: Harcourt Brace Jovanovich, 1975.

Herbert, George. *The Poems of George Herbert.* Edited by Helen Gardner. London: Oxford University Press, 1961.

Hickey, Alison. *Impure Conceits: Rhetoric and Ideology in Wordsworth's "Excursion."* Stanford, CA: Stanford University Press, 1997.

Hodder, Alan D. *Emerson's Rhetoric of Revelation: Nature, the Reader, and the Apocalypse Within.* University Park: Pennsylvania State University Press, 1989.

Holmes, Oliver Wendell. *Ralph Waldo Emerson.* Boston: Houghton Mifflin, 1884.

Horwitz, Howard. "The Standard Oil Trust as Emersonian Hero." *Raritan* 6 (1987): 97–119.

Hubbard, Stanley. *Nietzsche und Emerson.* Basel, Switzerland: Recht and Gesselschaft, 1958.

Hughes, Gertrude Reif. *Emerson's Demanding Optimism.* Baton Rouge: Louisiana State University Press, 1984.

Hume, David. *Enquiry Concerning Human Understanding.* Introduction by Thom Chittom. New York: Barnes and Noble, 2004.

Huxley, Aldous. "Wordsworth in the Tropics." In *Do What You Will: Essays,* by Aldous Huxley, 113–29. London: Chatto and Windus, 1931.

Iyer, Pico. "Morning in America." *New York Review of Books,* October 10, 2002.

Jacobi, F. H. "Open Letter to Fichte." Translated by Diana I. Behler. In *Philosophy of German Idealism,* edited by Ernst Behler, 119–41. New York: Continuum, 1987.

James, Henry. *Partial Portraits.* In *Literary Criticism,* edited by Leon Edel. New York: Library of America, 1984.

James, William. *Essays in Religion and Morality.* Edited by Frederick H. Burkhardt, Fredson Bowers, and Ignas K. Skrupskellis. Cambridge, MA: Harvard University Press, 1982.

———. *The Letters of William James.* Edited by Henry James. Boston: Little, Brown, 1926.

———. *William James: Writings, 1902–1910.* New York: Library of America, 1987.

Jasper, David, ed. *The Interpretation of Belief: Coleridge, Schleirmacher and Romanticism.* Basingstoke, England: Macmillan, 1986.

Jehlen, Myra. *American Incarnation.* Cambridge, MA: Harvard University Press, 1986.

Johnson, Glen M. "Emerson's Essay 'Immortality': The Problem of Authorship." *American Literature* 56 (1984): 313–30.

Johnston, Kenneth R. *Wordsworth and "The Recluse."* New Haven, CT: Yale University Press, 1984.

Jones, Ernest. *The Life and Work of Sigmund Freud.* 2 vols. New York: Basic Books, 1953–1957.

Joyce, James. *Selected Letters of James Joyce.* Edited by Richard Ellmann. 1957. Reprint, New York: Viking Press, 1966.

———. *Stephen Hero.* Edited by John J. Slocum and Herbert Cahoon. 1944. Reprint, New York: New Directions, 1963.

Jung, C. G. "Letters to Freud (1910, 1912)." In *The Freud/Jung Letters,* edited by W. McQuire. Freud letters translated by R. Mannheim. Jung letters translated by R. F. C. Hull. Princeton, NJ: Princeton University Press, 1974.

Kant, Immanuel. *Critique of Pure Reason.* Translated and edited by Paul Guyer and Allen W. Wood. Cambridge: Cambridge University Press, 1998.

———. *On History.* Edited by Lewis White Beck. Translated by Lewis White Beck, Robert E. Anchor, and Emil L. Fackenheim. Indianapolis, IN: Bobbs-Merrill, 1963.

Kateb, George. *Emerson and Self-Reliance.* Modernity and Political Thought, no. 8. Thousand Oaks, CA: Sage Publications, 1995.

Kaufmann, Walter. *Nietzsche: Philosopher, Psychologist, Antichrist.* 4th ed. Princeton, NJ: Princeton University Press, 1974.

Kazin, Alfred. *God and the American Writer.* New York: Vintage, 1997.

Keane, Patrick J. *Coleridge's Submerged Politics.* Columbia: University of Missouri Press, 1994.

———. *Yeats's Interactions with Tradition.* Columbia: University of Missouri Press, 1987.

Keating, AnnLouise. "Renaming the Dark: Emerson's Optimism and the Abyss." *American Transcendental Quarterly* 4 (1991): 305–25.

Keats, John. *Letters of John Keats.* Edited by Hyder E. Rollins. 2 vols. Cambridge, MA: Harvard University Press, 1958.

———. *The Poems of John Keats.* Edited by Jack Stillinger. Cambridge, MA: Harvard University Press, Belknap Press, 1978.

Kermode, Frank. "Changing Epochs." In *What's Happened to the Humanities,* edited by Alvin Kernan, 162–78. Princeton, NJ: Princeton University Press, 1997.

———. *Pieces of My Mind: Essays and Criticism, 1958–2002.* New York: Farrar, Straus, and Giroux, 2003.

Kern, Alexander. "Coleridge and American Romanticism: The Transcendentalists and Poe." In *New Approaches to Coleridge: Biographical and Critical Essays,* edited by Donald Sultana, 113–36. London: Barnes and Noble, 1981.

Knights, Ben. *The Idea of Clerisy in the Nineteenth Century.* Cambridge: Cambridge University Press, 1978.

Knox, Bernard. "Tablets to Books." *New Republic* (May 14, 2001): 41–45.

Konvitz, Milton. *The Recognition of Ralph Waldo Emerson.* Ann Arbor: University of Michigan Press, 1972.

Konvitz, Milton, and Stephen Whicher, eds. *Emerson: A Collection of Critical Essays.* Englewood Cliffs, NJ: Prentice-Hall, 1962.

Lamb, Charles. Review of *The Excursion,* by William Wordsworth. In *Lamb as Critic,* edited by Roy Park. London, 1980. Originally published in *Quarterly Review* (October 1814).

Landor, Walter Savage. *Imaginary Conversations.* London, 1824–1829.

Langbaum, Robert. *The Word from Below: Essays on Modern Literature and Culture.* Madison: University of Wisconsin Press, 1987.

Lasch, Christopher. *The True and Only Heaven: Progress and Its Critics.* New York: W. W. Norton, 1991.

Lathrop, Rose Hawthorne. *Memories of Hawthorne.* Boston: Houghton Mifflin, 1897.

Lawrence, D. H. "Emerson." In *The Recognition of Ralph Waldo Emerson,* edited by Milton Konvitz, 168–69. Ann Arbor: University of Michigan Press, 1972.

Legouis, Émile. *The Early Life of William Wordsworth.* Edited by Nicholas Roe. 1896 (in French). Reprint, London: Libris, 1988.

Levin, David, ed. *Emerson: Prophecy, Metamorphosis, and Influence.* New York: Columbia University Press, 1975.

Liu, Alan. *Wordsworth: The Sense of History.* Stanford, CA: Stanford University Press, 1989.

Lopez, Michael. "De-transcendentalizing Emerson." *ESQ: A Journal of the American Renaissance* 34 (1988): 77–139.

———, ed. *Emerson/Nietzsche.* Pullman: Washington State University Press, 1998.

———. *Emerson and Power: Creative Antagonism in the Nineteenth Century.* De Kalb: Northern Illinois University Press, 1996.

Lovejoy, Arthur. *Essays in the History of Ideas.* Baltimore, MD: Johns Hopkins University Press, 1948.

Loving, Jerome. "Emerson's Foreground." In *Emerson Centenary Essays,* edited by Joel Myerson, 41–64. Carbondale: Southern Illinois University Press, 1982.

Lowell, James Russell. *A Fable for Critics.* New York: George P. Putnam, 1848.

———. *My Study Windows.* Boston: James R. Osgood, 1871.

Lund, Roger. "Infectious Wit: Metaphor, Atheism, and the Plague in Eighteenth-Century London." *Literature and Medicine* 22 (2003): 45–64.

Marovitz, Sanford. "Emerson's Shakespeare: From Scorn to Apotheosis." In *Emerson Centenary Essays,* edited by Joel Myerson, 122–55. Carbondale: Southern Illinois University Press, 1982.

Marsh, James. "Preliminary Essay." In *Aids to Reflection,* by Samuel Taylor Coleridge, 489–529. Edited by John Beer. Vol. 9 of *CC,* 1993.

Matthiessen, F. O. *American Renaissance.* 1941. Reprint, London: Oxford University Press, 1966.

———, ed. *The Oxford Book of American Verse.* New York: Oxford University Press, 1950.

McFarland, Thomas. *Coleridge and the Pantheist Tradition.* Oxford: Clarendon Press, 1969.

———. "A Complex Dialogue: Coleridge's Doctrine of Polarity and Its European Contexts." In *Reading Coleridge: Approaches and Applications,* edited by Walter B. Crawford, 56–99. Ithaca, NY: Cornell University Press, 1979.

———. *Originality and Imagination.* Baltimore, MD: Johns Hopkins University Press, 1985.

McQuade, Donald, et al. *The Harper Single Volume American Literature.* New York: Longman, 1999.

McQuire, W., ed. *The Freud/Jung Letters.* Freud letters translated by R. Mannheim. Jung letters translated by R. F. C. Hull. Princeton, NJ: Princeton University Press, 1974.

Melville, Herman. *Moby-Dick; or, The Whale.* Berkeley and Los Angeles: University of California Press, Arion Press, 1979.

Menand, Louis. "William James and the Case of the Epileptic Patient." *New York Review of Books,* December 17, 1998.

Merwin, W. S. *The River Sound.* New York: Knopf, 1999.

Michael, John. *Emerson and Skepticism: The Cipher of the World.* Baltimore, MD: Johns Hopkins University Press, 1988.

Mikics, David. *The Romance of Individualism in Emerson and Nietzsche.* Athens: Ohio University Press, 2003.

Mill, John Stuart. *Autobiography of John Stuart Mill.* Edited by John Jacob Coss. New York, 1924.

———. *The Earlier Letters of John Stuart Mill, 1812–1848.* Edited by Francis E. Mikeka. 2 vols. Toronto: Toronto University Press, 1963.

Miller, Perry. "From Edwards to Emerson." In *Errand into the Wilderness,* by Perry Miller, 184–203. Cambridge, MA: Harvard University Press, 1956.

———. "New England's Transcendentalism: Native or Imported?" In *Emerson's Prose and Poetry,* edited by Joel Porte and Saundra Morris, 668–79. New York and London: W. W. Norton, 2001.

———. "Thoreau in the Context of International Romanticism." *New England Quarterly* 24 (1961): 147–59.

———, ed. *The Transcendentalists: An Anthology.* Cambridge, MA: Harvard University Press, 1950.

Milton, John. *The Portable Milton.* Edited by Douglas Bush. New York: Viking Press, 1949.

———. *The Prose of John Milton.* Edited by J. Max Patrick. New York: New York University Press, 1968.

Mitchell, Charles E. *Individualism and Its Discontents: Appropriations of Emerson, 1880–1950.* Amherst: University of Massachusetts Press, 1997.

Montaigne, Michel de. *The Works of Michel de Montaigne.* Edited by William Hazlitt. Philadelphia: Lippincott, n.d.

Moorman, Mary. *William Wordsworth: A Biography.* 2 vols. London: Oxford University Press, 1957.

Morison, Samuel Eliot. *The Oxford History of the American People.* New York: Oxford University Press, 1965.

Mumford, Lewis. *The Golden Day: A Study in American Literature and Culture.* 1926. Reprint, Westport, CT: Greenwood Press, 1983.

Myerson, Joel, ed. *Emerson Centenary Essays.* Carbondale: Southern Illinois University Press, 1982.

———, ed. *A Historical Guide to Ralph Waldo Emerson.* New York: Oxford University Press, 2000.

———. "Margaret Fuller's 1842 Journal: At Concord with the Emersons." *Harvard Library Bulletin* 21 (1973): 320–40.

———, ed. *Studies in the American Renaissance, 1984.* Charlottesville: University Press of Virginia, 1984.

Neussendorfer, Margaret. "Elizabeth Palmer Peabody to William Wordsworth: Eight Letters, 1825–1845." In *Studies in the American Renaissance, 1984,* edited by Joel Myerson, 181–211. Charlottesville: University Press of Virginia, 1984.

Newcomb, Charles King. "Dolon." *Dial* (July 1842): 112–22.

Nietzsche, Friedrich. *Basic Writings of Nietzsche.* Translated and edited by Walter Kaufmann. New York: Modern Library, 1968.

———. *Daybreak.* Translated by R. J. Hollingdale. Cambridge: Cambridge University Press, 1982.

———. *Ecce Homo.* Translated by Walter Kaufmann. New York: Vintage, 1967.

———. *Friedrich Nietzsche: Werke in drei Bänden.* Edited by Karl Schechta. 3 vols. Munich: Carl Hanser Verlag, 1954–1956.

———. *The Gay Science.* Translated by Walter Kaufmann. New York: Vintage, 1974.

———. *Gesammelte Werke: Musarionausgabe.* 23 vols. Munich: Musarion Verlag, 1920–1929.

———. *The Portable Nietzsche.* Edited and translated by Walter Kaufmann. New York: Viking Press, 1968.

———. *Selected Letters of Friedrich Nietzsche.* Edited and translated by Christopher Middleton. Chicago: University of Chicago Press, 1969.

———. *Untimely Meditations.* Translated by R. J. Hollingdale. New York: Cambridge University Press, 1983.

———. *The Will to Power.* Translated by Walter Kaufmann and R. J. Hollingdale. New York: Random House, 1967.

O'Keefe, Richard. *Mythic Archetypes in Ralph Waldo Emerson: A Blakean Reading.* Kent, OH: Kent State University Press, 1995.

Osgood, Samuel. "Emerson's *Nature.*" *Western Messenger* 2 (1837): 385–93.

Ovid. *The Metamorphoses of Ovid.* Translated by Allen Mandelbaum. New York: Harcourt, Brace, 1993.

Pace, Joel. "Wordsworth in America: Publication, Reception, and Literary Influence, 1802–1850." PhD diss., Oxford University, 1999.

Packer, Barbara. *Emerson's Fall: A New Interpretation of the Major Essays.* New York: Continuum, 1982.

———. "The Transcendentalists." In *The Prose Writing, 1820–1865,* edited by Sacvan Bercovitch, 331–604. Vol. 2 of *The Cambridge History of American Literature.* Cambridge: Cambridge University Press, 1995.

Pagels, Elaine. *Beyond Belief: The Gospel of Thomas.* New York: Random House, 2003.

Parker, Theodore. *Theodore Parker's Experience as a Minister.* Letter to his church, published posthumously as a pamphlet, 1859.

Pater, Walter. "Wordsworth." In *Appreciations,* by Walter Pater, 37–63. 1889. Reprint, New York: Macmillan, 1906.

Paul, Sherman. *Emerson's Angle of Vision.* Cambridge, MA: Harvard University Press, 1952.

———. *Hart's Bridge.* Urbana: University of Illinois Press, 1972.

Peabody, Elizabeth Palmer. "*Nature*—a Prose Poem." Review of *Nature,* by Ralph Waldo Emerson. In *Emerson's Prose and Poetry,* edited by Joel Porte and Saundra Morris, 590–97. New York and London: W. W. Norton, 2001.

———. *Reminiscences of William Ellery Channing.* Boston: Roberts Brothers, 1880.

Peake, Charles. "'Sweeney Erect' and the Emersonian Hero." *Neuphilologische Mittelungen* 44 (1960): 54–61.

Pease, Donald E. *Visionary Compacts: American Renaissance Writings in Cultural Context.* Madison: University of Wisconsin Press, 1987.

Peckham, Morse. *Beyond the Tragic Vision: The Quest for Identity in the Nineteenth Century.* New York: George Braziller, 1962.

Perry, Bliss. *Emerson Today.* Princeton, NJ: Princeton University Press, 1931.

———, ed. *The Heart of Emerson's Journals.* Boston: Houghton Mifflin, 1926.

Perry, Ralph Barton. *The Thought and Character of William James.* 2 vols. Boston: Little, Brown, 1935.

Plotinus. *The Six Enneads.* Translated by Stephen MacKenna and B. S. Page. Chicago: University of Chicago Press, 1952.

Porte, Joel. *Emerson and Thoreau: Transcendentalists in Conflict.* Middletown, CT: Wesleyan University Press, 1966.

———. "Introduction: Representing America—the Emerson Legacy." In *The Cambridge Companion to Ralph Waldo Emerson,* edited by Joel Porte and Saundra Morris, 1–12. Cambridge: Cambridge University Press, 1999.

Porte, Joel, and Saundra Morris, eds. *The Cambridge Companion to Ralph Waldo Emerson.* Cambridge: Cambridge University Press, 1999.

Porter, Carolyn. *Seeing and Being: The Plight of the Participant Observer in Emerson, James, and Faulkner.* Middletown, CT: Wesleyan University Press, 1981.

Porter, David. *Emerson and Literary Change.* Cambridge, MA: Harvard University Press, 1978.

Quindlen, Anna. "Doing Nothing Is Something." *Newsweek,* May 13, 2002, 76.

Quint, David. *Origin and Originality in Renaissance Literature: Versions of the Source.* New Haven, CT: Yale University Press, 1983.

Rawls, John. *A Theory of Justice.* Cambridge, MA: Harvard University Press, 1973.

Raysor, T. R., ed. *Coleridge's Shakespeare Criticism.* 2 vols. Cambridge, MA: Harvard University Press, 1930.

Reich, Walter. "The Devil's Miracle Man." *New York Times Book Review,* January 30, 1999.

Reichert, Victor. "The Faith of Robert Frost." In vol. 1 of *Frost: Centennial Essays,* edited by Jac Tharpe, 415–26. Jackson: University of Mississippi Press, 1973.

Review of Wordsworth's *Poems. Atlantic Magazine* 2 (1825): 334–48.

Reynolds, David S. *Beneath the American Renaissance: The Subversive Imagination in the Age of Emerson and Melville.* Cambridge, MA: Harvard University Press, 1988.

———. *John Brown, Abolitionist.* New York: Alfred A. Knopf, 2005.

Richardson, Robert D., Jr. *Emerson: The Mind on Fire, a Biography.* Berkeley and Los Angeles: University of California Press, 1995.

Ripley, George. *Discourse on the Philosophy of Religion: Addressed to Doubters Who Wish to Believe.* Boston: James Munroe, 1836.

———. *"The Highest Form of Infidelity" Examined.* Boston: James Munroe, 1840.

Robinson, David M. "The Legacy of Channery: Culture as a Religious Category in New England Thought." *Harvard Theological Review* 74 (1981): 221–39.

———. "Poetry, Personality, and the Divinity School Address." *Harvard Theological Review* 82 (1989): 185–99.

———, ed. *The Political Emerson: Essential Writings on Politics and Social Reform.* Boston: Beacon Press, 2004.

Robinson, Henry Crabb. *Blake, Wordsworth, Coleridge, Lamb, Etc.* Edited by Edith J. Morley. Manchester, England, 1922.

———. *Henry Crabb Robinson on Books and Their Writers.* Edited by Edith J. Morley. 3 vols. London, 1938.

Ronda, Bruce. "Literary Grieving and the Death of Waldo." *Centennial Review* 23 (1978): 91–104.

Ronsley, Joseph. "Yeats's Lecture Notes for 'Friends of My Youth.'" In *Yeats and the Theatre,* edited by Robert O'Driscoll and Lorna Reynolds, 60–81. Toronto: Macmillan of Canada; Niagara Falls, NY: Maclean-Hunter Press, 1975.

Rorty, Richard. *Philosophy and Social Hope.* London: Penguin, 1999.

Rosenblatt, Louise. *Literature as Exploration.* Edited by Wayne Booth. 5th ed. New York: PMLA, 1995.

Rossi, William. "Emerson, Nature, and Natural Science." In *A Historical Guide to Ralph Waldo Emerson,* edited by Joel Myerson, 101–50. New York: Oxford University Press, 2000.

Rowe, John Carlos, ed. *Ralph Waldo Emerson and Margaret Fuller.* Boston: Houghton Mifflin, 2003.

Rusk, Ralph L. *The Life of Ralph Waldo Emerson.* New York: Charles Scribner's Sons, 1949.

Ruskin, John. *Modern Painters.* Vol. 3 of *The Complete Works of John Ruskin,* edited by E. T. Cook and Alexander Wedderburn. 39 vols. London, 1903–1912.

Ryback, Timothy W. "Hitler's Forgotten Library: The Man, His Books, and His Search for God." *Atlantic Monthly* (May 2003): 76–90.

Sacks, Kenneth S. *Understanding Emerson: "The American Scholar" and His Struggle for Self-Reliance.* Princeton, NJ: Princeton University Press, 2003.

Salomé, Lou [Andreas]. *Looking Back: Memoirs.* Translated by Breon Mitchell. New York: Marlowe, 1995.

———. *Nietzsche.* Translated by Siegfried Mandel. Urbana: University of Illinois Press, 2002.

Salter, W. M. *Nietzsche the Thinker: A Study.* New York: Henry Holt, 1917.

Sanders, Charles Richard. *Carlyle's Friendships and Other Studies.* Durham, NC: Duke University Press, 1977.

———. *Coleridge and the Broad Church Movement.* Durham, NC: Duke University Press, 1941.

Santayana, George. "The Genteel Tradition in American Philosophy." In *The Genteel Tradition: Nine Essays by George Santayana,* edited by Douglas L. Wilson, 37–64. Cambridge, MA: Harvard University Press, 1967.

Scharnhorst, Gary. "Longfellow and Emerson's Divinity School 'Address': An Unpublished Letter." *American Notes and Queries* 21 (1982): 44–45.

Schelling, F. W. J. von. *Naturphilosophie.* In *Samtliche Werke,* edited by K. F. A. Schelling. 14 vols. Stuttgart and Augsburg, Germany: J. G. Cotta, 1806.

———. *System des transcendentalen Idealismus.* In *Samtliche Werke,* edited by K. F. A. Schelling. 14 vols. Stuttgart and Augsburg, Germany: J. G. Cotta, 1800.

Schulz, Max. "Coleridge Agonistes." *Journal of English and German Philology* 61 (1962): 268–77.

Sealts, Morton M., Jr. *Emerson on the Scholar.* Columbia: University of Missouri Press, 1992.

Sealts, Morton M., Jr., and Alfred R. Ferguson, eds. *Emerson's Nature: Origin, Growth, Meaning.* 2d ed. Carbondale: Southern Illinois University Press, 1979.

Shelley, Percy Bysshe. *Shelley's Poetry and Prose.* Edited by Donald H. Reiman and Sharon B. Powers. New York: W. W. Norton, 1977.

Shulevitz, Judith. Review of *Genius: A Mosaic of One Hundred Exemplary Creative Minds,* by Harold Bloom. *New York Times Book Review,* October 27, 2002.

Simpson, David. "Wordsworth in America." In *The Age of William Wordsworth: Critical Essays on the Romantic Tradition,* edited by Kenneth R. Johnston and Gene W. Ruoff, 276–90. New Brunswick, NJ: Rutgers University Press, 1987.

Smith, Charles J. "The Contrarieties: Wordsworth's Dualistic Imagery." *PMLA* 69 (1954): 1196–97.

Smith, David Q. "The Wanderer's Silence: A Strange Reticence in Book IX of *The Excursion.*" *Wordsworth Circle* 9 (1978): 163–67.

Solomon, Maynard. *Beethoven.* New York: Schirmer Books, 1977.

Stack, George. *Nietzsche and Emerson: An Elective Affinity.* Athens: University of Georgia Press, 1992.

Star, Alexander. "The Paper Pusher." *New Republic* (May 28, 2001): 38–41.

Stevens, Wallace. *Collected Poems.* New York: Knopf, 1965.

———. *Opus Posthumous.* New York: Knopf, 1957.

Sultana, Donald, ed. *New Approaches to Coleridge: Biographical and Critical Essays.* London: Barnes and Noble, 1981.

Synge, John Millington. *The Playboy of the Western World.* In *Modern Irish Drama: A Norton Critical Edition,* edited by John M. Harrington. New York and London: W. W. Norton, 1991.

Thompson, E. P. *The Romantics: England in a Revolutionary Age.* New York: New Press, 1997.

Thompson, Frank T. "Emerson's Indebtedness to Coleridge." *Studies in Philology* 23 (1926): 55–76.

———. "Emerson's Theory and Practice of Poetry." *PMLA* 43 (1928): 1170–84.

Thompson, Lawrance, and R. H. Winnick. *Robert Frost: The Later Years, 1838–1963.* New York: Holt Rinehart Winston, 1976.

Thoreau, Henry David. *The Correspondence of Henry David Thoreau.* Edited by Carl Bode and Walter Harding. New York: New York University Press, 1958.

———. *Journals.* Edited by John C. Broderick et al. 8 vols. Princeton, NJ: Princeton University Press, 1981–2000.

———. *Walden: An Annotated Edition.* Foreword and notes by Walter Harding. Boston: Houghton Mifflin, 1995.

———. *The Writings of Henry David Thoreau.* Walden ed. 20 vols. Boston: Houghton Mifflin, 1906.

Trowbridge, J. T. *My Own Story.* Boston: Houghton Mifflin, 1903.

Updike, John. "Big Dead White Male." *New Yorker,* August 4, 2003.

———. "Emersonianism." In *Odd Jobs: Essays and Criticism,* by John Updike. New York: Knopf, 1991.

Valéry, Paul. *Collected Works.* Edited by Jackson Matthews. 15 vols. Princeton, NJ: Princeton University Press, 1956.

Van Cromphout, Gustaaf. *Emerson and Ethics.* Columbia: University of Missouri Press, 1999.

———. *Emerson's Modernity and the Example of Goethe.* Columbia: University of Missouri Press, 1990.

Vendler, Helen. "Lionel Trilling and the Immortality Ode." In *The Music of What Happens: Poems, Poets, Critics,* by Helen Vendler, 93–114. Cambridge, MA: Harvard University Press, 1994.

———. *Soul Says: On Recent Poetry.* Cambridge, MA: Harvard University Press, Belknap Press, 1995.

Waggoner, Hyatt. *American Poets from the Puritans to the Present.* 1968. Reprint, New York: Delta, 1970.

———. *American Visionary Poetry.* Baton Rouge: Louisiana State University Press, 1982.

———. *Emerson as Poet.* Princeton, NJ: Princeton University Press, 1974.

Warren, Robert Penn. "Hawthorne, Anderson, and Frost." *New Republic* 54 (May 16, 1928): 399–401.

———. *Selected Poems.* Baton Rouge: Louisiana State University Press, 2001.

Watts, Alaric Alfred. *Alaric Watts: A Narrative of His Life* [by his son]. 2 vols. London, 1884.

Webster, Daniel. *The Works of Daniel Webster.* 5 vols. Boston: Little, Brown, 1851.

Weinstein, Arnold. *A Scream Goes through the House: What Literature Teaches Us about Life.* New York: Random House, 2003.

Weisbuch, Robert. *Atlantic Double-Cross: American Literature and British Influence in the Age of Emerson.* Chicago: University of Chicago Press, 1986.

———. "Post-colonial Emerson and the Erasure of Europe." In *The Cambridge Companion to Ralph Waldo Emerson,* edited by Joel Porte and Saundra Morris, 192–217. Cambridge: Cambridge University Press, 1999.

West, Cornell. *The American Evasion of Philosophy: A Genealogy of Pragmatism.* Madison: University of Wisconsin Press, 1989.

Whicher, Stephen E. *Freedom and Fate: An Inner Life of Ralph Waldo Emerson.* Philadelphia: University of Pennsylvania Press, 1953.

———, ed. *Selections from Ralph Waldo Emerson: An Organic Anthology.* Boston: Houghton Mifflin, 1957.

Whitman, Walt. *Leaves of Grass.* Edited by Sculley Bradley and Harold W. Blodgett. New York: W. W. Norton, 1973.

Widdowson, H. G. *Stylistics and the Teaching of Literature.* London: Longman, 1975.

Widmer, Edward L. *Young America: The Flowering of Democracy in New York City.* New York: Oxford University Press, 1998.

Wilde, Oscar. *De Profundis.* Edited by Rupert Hart-Davis. Woodstock, NY: Overlook Press, 1998.

Williams, William Carlos. *Paterson (1946–58).* Edited by Christopher MacGowan. New York: New Directions, 1992.

———. *Selected Essays.* New York: New Directions, 1969.

Winters, Yvor. *In Defense of Reason.* Athens: Ohio University Press, Swallow Press, 1987.

Wittgenstein, Ludwig. *Philosophical Investigations.* Translated by G. E. M. Anscombe. London: Blackwell, 2003.

Wood, Barry. "The Growth of the Soul: Coleridge's Dialectical Method and the Strategy of Emerson's *Nature.*" In *Emerson's Nature: Origin, Growth, Meaning,* edited by Morton M. Sealts Jr. and Alfred R. Ferguson, 194–208. 2d ed. Carbondale: Southern Illinois University Press, 1979.

Woodbury, Charles. *Talks with Ralph Waldo Emerson.* London: Kegan Paul, 1880.

Woolf, Virginia. *A Room of One's Own.* In *The Major Authors,* edited by M. H. Abrams et al., 2153–214. Vol. B of *The Norton Anthology of English Literature.* 7th ed. New York and London: W. W. Norton, 2001.

Wordsworth, Christopher. *Memoirs of William Wordsworth.* 2 vols. Boston: Ticknor, Reed, and Fields, 1851.

Wordsworth, William. *The Letters of William and Dorothy Wordsworth: The Later Years.* Edited by Alan G. Hill. 2d ed. 5 vols. Oxford: Clarendon Press, 1967.

———. *The Letters of William and Dorothy Wordsworth: The Middle Years.* Part 1 (1806–1811) edited by Mary Moorman. Part 2 (1812–1820) edited by Mary Moorman and Alan G. Hill. Oxford: Clarendon Press, 1969–1970.

———. *The Prose Works of William Wordsworth.* Edited by W. J. B. Owen and Jane Smyser. 3 vols. Oxford: Clarendon Press, 1974.

"Wordsworth's *White Doe.*" *Quarterly Review* 14 (1815).

Yeats, W. B. *Autobiographies.* London: Macmillan, 1955.

———. *A Descriptive Catalog of W. B. Yeats's Library.* Edited by Edward O'Shea. New York: Garland, 1985.

———. *Essays and Introductions.* London: Macmillan, 1961.

———. *Explorations.* New York: Macmillan, 1963.

———. *The Letters of W. B. Yeats.* Edited by Allan Wade. London: Rupert Hart-Davis, 1954.

———. *Memoirs: Autobiography—First Draft.* Edited by Denis Donoghue. London: Macmillan, 1972.

———. *Mythologies.* London: Macmillan, 1959.

———. *Uncollected Prose by W. B. Yeats.* Vol. 2. Edited by John P. Frayne and Colton Johnson. New York: Columbia University Press, 1976.

———. *A Vision.* New York: Macmillan, 1937.

———. *W. B. Yeats: The Poems; A New Edition.* Edited by Richard J. Finneran. New York: Macmillan, 1983.

———. *W. B. Yeats and T. Sturge Moore: Their Correspondence, 1901–1937.* Edited by Ursula Bridge. New York: Oxford University Press, 1963.

Yoder, Ralph A. *Emerson and the Orphic Poet in America.* Berkeley and Los Angeles: University of California Press, 1978.

Young, Edward. *Conjectures on Original Composition.* London: A. Miller and R. and J. Dodsley, 1759.

———. *Night Thoughts.* Edited by Stephen Cornford. Cambridge: Cambridge University Press, 1989.

Index